Research Anthology on Virtual Environments and Building the Metaverse

Information Resources Management Association
USA

Volume II

IGI Global
PUBLISHER of TIMELY KNOWLEDGE

Published in the United States of America by
    IGI Global
    Engineering Science Reference (an imprint of IGI Global)
    701 E. Chocolate Avenue
    Hershey PA, USA 17033
    Tel: 717-533-8845
    Fax: 717-533-8661
    E-mail: cust@igi-global.com
    Web site: http://www.igi-global.com

Library of Congress Cataloging-in-Publication Data

Names: Information Resources Management Association, editor.
Title: Research anthology on virtual environments and building the
  metaverse / Information Resources Management Association, editor.
Description: Hershey, PA : Engineering Science Reference, [2023] | Includes
  bibliographical references and index. | Summary: "With the advent of
  virtual environments and communities, the metaverse has been rapidly
  expanding in recent years as businesses and industries have begun to see
  the value and opportunities this technology provides. In order to ensure
  this technology is utilized to its full potential, further study on the
  best practices, challenges, and future directions is required. The
  Research Anthology on Virtual Environments and Building the Metaverse
  considers the latest research regarding the metaverse and discusses
  potential issues and benefits of the technology. The book also examines
  strategies and tactics businesses and companies can use when
  implementing the metaverse into their operations. Covering key topics
  such as immersion, augmented reality, and virtual worlds, this major
  reference work is ideal for computer scientists, business owners,
  managers, industry professionals, researchers, scholars, academicians,
  practitioners, instructors, and students"-- Provided by publisher.
Identifiers: LCCN 2022040864 (print) | LCCN 2022040865 (ebook) | ISBN
  9781668475973 (h/c) | ISBN 9781668475980 (eISBN)
Subjects: LCSH: Metaverse.
Classification: LCC QA76.9.M47 R47 2023 (print) | LCC QA76.9.M47 (ebook)
  | DDC 005.4/35--dc23/eng/20221110
LC record available at https://lccn.loc.gov/2022040864
LC ebook record available at https://lccn.loc.gov/2022040865

British Cataloguing in Publication Data
A Cataloguing in Publication record for this book is available from the British Library.

The views expressed in this book are those of the authors, but not necessarily of the publisher.

For electronic access to this publication, please contact: eresources@igi-global.com.

List of Contributors

Table of Contents

Section 2
Avatars, Virtual Identities, and Virtual Communities

Volume II

Section 3
Designs and Frameworks

Preface

With the advent of virtual environments and communities, the metaverse has been rapidly expanding in recent years as businesses and industries have begun to see the value and opportunities this technology provides. In order to ensure this technology is utilized to its full potential, further study on the best practices, challenges, and future directions is required.

Thus, the *Research Anthology on Virtual Environments and Building the Metaverse* seeks to fill the void for an all-encompassing and comprehensive reference book covering the latest and most emerging research, concepts, and theories for those working with virtual environments and the metaverse. This two-volume reference collection of reprinted IGI Global book chapters and journal articles that have been handpicked by the editor and editorial team of this research anthology on this topic will empower computer scientists, business owners, managers, industry professionals, researchers, scholars, academicians, practitioners, instructors, and students with an advanced understanding of critical issues and advancements of virtual environments and the metaverse.

The *Research Anthology on Virtual Environments and Building the Metaverse* is organized into three sections that provide comprehensive coverage of important topics. The sections are:

1. Applications in Business, Education, and Healthcare;
2. Avatars, Virtual Identities, and Virtual Communities; and
3. Designs and Frameworks.

The following paragraphs provide a summary of what to expect from this invaluable reference tool.

Section 1, "Applications in Business, Education, and Healthcare," examines the diverse applications of virtual environments and the metaverse across industries and fields. The first chapter in this section, "The Financial Digital Assets Frontier: The Bridge Between the Past and the Future," by Prof. Andrei Dragos Popescu from the University of Craiova, Singapore, assesses the frontier of financial digital assets, which has emerged and developed the perfect infrastructure for scalability, efficiency, and transparency. The next chapter, "The Internet of Things and Blockchain Technologies Adaptive Trade Systems in the Virtual World: By Creating Virtual Accomplices Worldwide," by Prof. Vardan Mkrttchian from HHH University, Australia, presents artificial and natural intelligence technologies and considers their impact on the efficiency of electronic commerce and entrepreneurship. Another opening chapter, "Being a Post-Learner With Virtual Worlds," by Profs. Ferhan Şahin and Ezgi Doğan from Anadolu University, Turkey, evaluates virtual worlds in the transhumanism age by using anime series and film samples. The following chapter, "Virtual Worlds for Developing Intercultural Competence," by Profs. Lisiane Machado and Eliane Schlemmer from the Unisinos University, Brazil; Prof. Angilberto

Freitas from the Universidade do Grande Rio (Unigranrio), Brazil; and Prof. Cristiane Drebes Pedron of the Universidade Nove de Julho (Uninove), Brazil, presents a framework for developing intercultural competence (IC) and uses tridimensional digital virtual worlds (3DVW) as environments for developing IC. An additional chapter, "From Visual Culture in the Immersive Metaverse to Visual Cognition in Education," by Prof. Hsiao-Cheng 'Sandrine' Han from The University of British Columbia, Canada, discusses visual culture in the immersive metaverse through the visual cognition lens. The next chapter, "A Literature Review on the Use of Three-Dimensional Virtual Worlds in Higher Education," by Prof. Reza Ghanbarzadeh from the School of Business and Tourism, Southern Cross University, Australia and Prof. Amir Hossein Ghapanchi of College of Engineering and Science, Victoria University, Australia, conducts a literature review of the published research relevant to the application of three-dimensional virtual worlds in higher education. Another chapter, "Factors Affecting Learner Collaboration in 3D Virtual Worlds," by Prof. Iryna Kozlova from the University of Pennsylvania, USA, explores factors affecting learner collaboration by observing the performance of eight English as a foreign language (EFL) learners collaborating on tasks in a 3D virtual world (3D VW) over a period of six weeks. The following chapter, "Engaging Students in a Computer Diversity Course Through Virtual Worlds," by Profs. Yvonne Pigatt and James Braman from Community College of Baltimore County, USA, presents a brief literature review of the educational use of virtual worlds. An additional chapter in this section, "Stepping Out of the Classroom: Anticipated User Experiences of Web-based Mirror World Like Virtual Campus," by Prof. Minna Pakanen from Socio-Technical Design, Department of Engineering, Aarhus University, Denmark and Profs. Paula Alavesa, Leena Arhippainen, and Timo Ojala of the University of Oulu, Finland, investigates the use of geographically accurate mirror-world-like virtual campus models as an interactive learning environment. The next chapter, "Minecraft Our City, an Erasmus Project in Virtual World: Building Competences Using a Virtual World," by Prof. Annalisa A. B. Boniello from the University of Camerino, Italy and Prof. Alessandra A. C. Conti of IC Nettuno 1, Italy, reports experiences carried out to investigate the effectiveness of virtual worlds in education. A closing chapter, "The Use of Network-Based Virtual Worlds in Second Language Education: A Research Review," by Profs. Mark Peterson and Qiao Wang from Kyoto University, Japan and Dr. Maryam Sadat Mirzaei from RIKEN, Japan, reviews 28 learner-based studies on the use of network-based social virtual worlds in second language learning published during the period 2007-2017. The next chapter, "The Case for Qualitative Research Into Language Learning in Virtual Worlds," by Prof. Luisa Panichi from the University of Pisa, Italy reviews some of the most common research approaches used in investigating language learning and teaching in virtual worlds. Another chapter, "Vocabulary Acquisition From a Virtual Street-View Context," by Prof. Ya-Chun Shih from National Dong Hwa University, Taiwan, incorporates Google Street View into a 3D virtual environment, known as VECAR, in which EFL learners controlled their avatars to learn vocabulary in a context of New York City. The following chapter, "Video Game-Based L2 Learning: Virtual Worlds as Texts, Affinity Spaces, and Semiotic Ecologies," by Prof. Karim Hesham Shaker Ibrahim from Gulf University for Science and Technology, Kuwait, draws on interdisciplinary research on digital gaming from literacy studies, games' studies, and narratology to account for the L2 learning potentials of digital games, conceptualizes digital games as dynamic texts, affinity spaces, and semiotic ecologies, and discusses the implications of each conceptualization for game-based L2 learning and teaching. The next chapter, "Sustainable Engagement in Open and Distance Learning With Play and Games in Virtual Reality: Playful and Gameful Distance Education in VR," by Prof. Stylianos Mystakidis from the University of Patras, Greece, presents practical examples of virtual reality applications and recommendations for practitioners. The closing chapter in this section, "Role of Immersive (XR) Technologies in Improving Healthcare Competencies: A Review," by Prof. Anitha S. Pillai from Hindustan Institute of Technology and Science, India and Prof. Prabha Susy Mathew of Bishop Cottons Women's Christian College, India, focuses on uses, benefits, and adoption challenges of immersive technologies with specific reference to healthcare training.

Section 2, "Avatars, Virtual Identities, and Virtual Communities," discusses the impact and challenges of virtual identities and communities. The first chapter in this section, "Pioneering in the Virtual World Frontier," by Prof. Cynthia Calongne from Colorado Technical University, USA, explores the phenomenon of selfhood and society integral to the development of a vibrant educational community. The next chapter, "Participating on More Equal Terms? Power, Gender, and Participation in a Virtual World Learning Scenario," by Prof. Anders Steinvall from Umeå University, Sweden; Prof. Mats Deutschmann of Örebro University, Sweden; and Prof. Airong Wang from Xi'an Jiaotong-Liverpool University, China, investigates the potential effects of unequal power relations on participation in a group of student teachers and invited professionals in two collaborative workshops in Second Life. Another opening chapter, "Revisiting Musings on Co-Designing Identity-Aware Realities in Virtual Learning: The Shared Experiences," by Prof. Francisca Yonekura from the University of Central Florida, USA, expands on the exploratory journey looking into the identity of the collective self, the shared experiences of those co-creating the moment, and the potential for a community of practice to emerge while learning in virtual environments. The next chapter, "The Digital Cultural Identity on the Space Drawed in Virtual Games and Representative," by Profs. Hülya Semiz Türkoğlu and Süleyman Türkoğlu from Istanbul University, Turkey, analyzes the use and perceptions of virtual users in the virtual world by focusing on the construct that creates different virtual cultural experiences. An additional chapter, "My Becoming in a World of Virtual Learning Communities," by Prof. Karen Joy Koopman from the University of the Western Cape, South Africa, chronicles the author's becoming in a world of virtual learning communities (VLCs) and spaces. Another chapter, "Non-Verbal Communication Language in Virtual Worlds," by Dr. Ivonne Citarella from National Research Council, Italy, analyzes the animations present in Second Life trying to trace a socio-psychological picture of the non-verbal communication process in a virtual environment. A closing chapter, "Using Social Image Sets to Explore Virtual Embodiment in Second Life® as Indicators of Formal, Nonformal, and Informal Learning," by Prof. Shalin Hai-Jew from Kansas State University, USA, involves a review of the literature and then a light and iterated analysis of 1,550 randomly batch-downloaded screenshots from SL (including stills from machinima) to explore the potential of social image analysis to make inferences about human learning in SL in the present. The next chapter, "The Avatar as a Self-Representation Model for Expressive and Intelligent Driven Visualizations in Immersive Virtual Worlds: A Background to Understand Online Identity Formation, Selfhood, and Virtual Interactions," by Mses. Colina Demirdjian and Hripsime Demirdjian from Double Trouble Creatives, Australia, creates a backdrop for understanding the avatar in the connected modalities of the real and virtual state of environments. Another chapter, "Avatars for Clinical Assessment: Digital Renditions of the Self as Innovative Tools for Assessment in Mental Health Treatment," by Profs. Stefano Triberti, Valeria Sebri, Lucrezia Savioni, Alessandra Gorini, and Gabriella Pravettoni from the University of Milan, Italy, explores the possibility to use customized avatars within psychological assessment, as adjunctive assessment tools useful to get information on patients' self-representation(s) and communicative intentions. The closing chapter, "Avatar Teaching and Learning: Examining Language Teaching and Learning Practices in Virtual Reality Environments," by Profs. Geoff Lawrence and Farhana Ahmed from York University, Canada, examines the pedagogical potential of immersive social virtual worlds (SVWs) in language teaching and learning.

Section 3, "Designs and Frameworks," considers how virtual environments and the metaverse are designed and utilized. The first chapter, "Prosumers Building the Virtual World: How a Proactive Use of Virtual Worlds Can Be an Effective Method for Educational Purposes," by Drs. Mario Fontanella and Claudio Pacchiega from Edu3d, Italy, discusses how the teaching of "digital creativity" can take advantage of the fact that young people and adults are particularly attracted to these fields, which they perceive akin to their playful activities and which are normally used in an often sterile and useless way in their free time. The following chapter, "Framework for 3D Task Design: An Immersive Approach," by Prof. Iryna Kozlova from the University of Pennsylvania, USA, introduces a framework for 3D task design and proposes that the process of designing language learning tasks for 3D immersive simulated environments also be immersive. Another opening chapter, "POV in XR: How We Experience, Discuss, and Create the Virtual World," by Ms. Eve Weston from Exelauno, USA, introduces and explains the applications of a taxonomy for discussing point of view (POV) in XR. The next chapter, "INSIDE: Using a Cubic Multisensory Controller for Interaction With a Mixed Reality Environment," by Profs. Dimitrios G. Margounakis and Ioannis Giannios from Hellenic Open University, Greece, explores the field of mixed reality through the use of physical computing for the development of the electronic game Inside. Another chapter, "The Effects of Using On-Screen and Paper Maps on Navigation Efficiency in 3D Multi-User Virtual Environments," by Prof. Dilek Doğan from Ankara University, Turkey and Prof. Hakan Tüzün of Hacettepe University, Turkey, aims to analyze the effects of using on-screen and paper maps on navigation efficiency in 3D MUVEs. The following chapter, "The Effect of List-Liner-Based Interaction Technique in a 3D Interactive Virtual Biological Learning Environment," by Profs. Numan Ali, Sehat Ullah, and Zuhra Musa from the University of Malakand, Pakistan, investigates a simple list-liner-based interface for gaining access to different modules within a 3D interactive Virtual Learning Environment (VLE). An additional chapter, "3D Virtual Learning Environment for Acquisition of Cultural Competence: Experiences of Instructional Designers," by Profs. Stephen Petrina and Jennifer Jing Zhao from the University of British Columbia, Canada, addresses the experiences of instructional designers in a 3D virtual learning environment designed for the development of cultural competence. The next chapter, "Instructional Design Applied to TCN5 Virtual World," by Profs. Roseclea Duarte Medina, Andressa Falcade, and Vania Cristina Bordin Freitas from the Federal University of Santa Maria, Brazil and Prof. Aliane Loureiro Krassmann from Federal Institute Farroupilha, Brazil & The Federal University of Rio Grande do Sul, Brazil, presents the development and implementation of an instructional design (ID) for computer networks learning within a three-dimensional (3D) virtual world (VW) that considers characteristics of cognitive style and level of expertise of the student, titled TCN5. The following chapter, "Comparing Two Teacher Training Courses for 3D Game-Based Learning: Feedback From Trainee Teachers," by Prof. Michael Thomas from Liverpool John Moores University, UK and Prof. Letizia Cinganotto of INDIRE, Università Telematica degli Studi, Italy, explores data from two online language teacher training courses aimed at providing participants with the skills to create and use games in 3D immersive environments. The closing chapter in this section, "Design Process of Three-Dimensional Multi-User Virtual Environments (3D MUVEs) for Teaching Tree Species," by Prof. Dilek Doğan from Ankara University, Turkey and Profs. Hakan Tüzün, Gamze Mercan, and Pınar Köseoğlu of Hacettepe University, Turkey, aims to realize the concept of biodiversity with a 3D virtual worlds platform and provide awareness of the species in the immediate surroundings.

Although the primary organization of the contents in this work is based on its three sections offering a progression of coverage of the important concepts, methodologies, technologies, applications, social issues, and emerging trends, the reader can also identify specific contents by utilizing the extensive indexing system listed at the end. As a comprehensive collection of research on the latest findings related to virtual environments and the metaverse, the *Research Anthology on Virtual Environments and Building the Metaverse* provides computer scientists, business owners, managers, industry professionals, researchers, scholars, academicians, practitioners, instructors, students, and all audiences with a complete understanding of the challenges that face those working with virtual environments and the metaverse. Given the need for a better understating of how virtual environments can be utilized across industries and fields, this extensive book presents the latest research and best practices to address these challenges and provide further opportunities for improvement.

Chapter 19
Revisiting Musings on Co-Designing Identity-Aware Realities in Virtual Learning:
The Shared Experiences

Francisca Yonekura
University of Central Florida, USA

ABSTRACT

Previously, musings on co-designing identity-aware realities in the virtual space focused on the individual self during a learning experience. While preserving the individual self of the learner for a comprehensive outlook, the chapter will expand on the exploratory journey looking into the identity of the collective self, the shared experiences of those co-creating the moment, and the potential for a community of practice to emerge while learning in virtual environments. In the spirit of the contemplative goal of the chapter, design considerations in the creation and facilitation of learning experiences inclusive of the community's self are postulated.

PREAMBLE

Virtual learning in the third dimension presents many opportunities for meaningful learning to occur. Learning in which the learner's self and the collective self immerse in the co-creation of authentic experiences. The virtues of these 3D environments are best appreciated holistically through the visual and spatial perspectives. To do so, participating learners, designers, and facilitators have the capabilities to exert more control over the visual, spatial, and emotional aspects of immersive 3D virtual worlds. The learner's self and the communities in which this learner belong immerse and co-create their experiences. Some of these experiences extend the physical into the virtual and vice versa.

DOI: 10.4018/978-1-6684-7597-3.ch019

As previously posited, the evolutionary power to compute the human experience presents a myriad of opportunities to transform our self, society, and systems that govern us. The same guiding questions apply in contemplating design principles and process for immersive learning experiences in which the collective self is placed at the center of the design.

- What are the design considerations for integrating the individual and social selves in virtual learning?
- How do we facilitate meaning-making both in the physical and imagined realities?
- What are the value propositions of both the physical and virtual environments?
- How do we improve alignment to deliver beneficial learning experiences along the value chain proposed by both the physical and virtual?
- How do we facilitate an inclusive learning experience in which different perspectives are welcomed?

This book chapter addresses several of these questions and some of the prompts guiding the contemplations that follow.

VIRTUAL WORLD, VIRTUAL ENVIRONMENT, OR VIRTUAL REALITY?

Although similar and used interchangeably, throughout the literature the definition of the terms virtual worlds (VW), virtual environments (VE), and virtual reality (VR) are slightly different. Some definitions reflect the technological evolution this media form has undergone since its inception. Peachey and Childs (2011) define virtual worlds as "computer-generated environments in which participants adopt an avatar to interact with each other and with the virtual environment around them" (p. 1). Fox, Arena, and Bailenson (2009) define virtual environments as "a digital space in which a user's movements are tracked and his or her surroundings rendered, or digitally composed and displayed to the senses, in accordance with those movements" (p. 1). Schroeder (2011) defines virtual reality technology as "a computer-generated display that allows or compels the user (or users) to have a feeling of being present in an environment other than the one that they are actually in and to interact with that environment" (p. 4). In this chapter, the terms virtual worlds, virtual environments, and virtual reality are used interchangeably.

Many types of virtual worlds exist. Some worlds have predetermined common goals while others give their inhabitants the freedom to pursue and share their interests and purpose. The inhabitants' imagination is the limit in the latter type of worlds. These virtual worlds are persistent, always on for its inhabitants to participate and create shared experiences. Like the man-made imagined realities in the form of economic and political systems (Harari, 2015), we live and breathe in our physical worlds. We have the power to imagine and create learning experiences that blend our physical and virtual realities.

To gauge the capabilities the self can leverage in these 3D virtual worlds, Stephen Ellis' (1996), breakdown of virtual environments lend a helpful foundation. Ellis' three main elements compose the virtual world or environment: 1) content which consists of the objects with which the learner interacts and the actor which in our case is the learner, 2) geometry which portrays the dimensions, rules, and range of possible values that make up the environment, and 3) the dynamics that rule the interactions between the objects and the learner. Awareness of these elements is key in guiding the type of learning experience and interactions that can emerge.

Determining the continuity between these virtual worlds and other environments including the physical world is extremely important for a transparent learning experience. That is, the actors, learners, and facilitators define the degrees of fluidity and fidelity that are most fitting while functioning or co-creating experiences in and between these worlds. Fundamentally, the "learner" or user experience design must be orchestrated to allow for optimal interaction of the self in the virtual environment, the learner with others, the learner with the objects and spatial landscape, and the extension or spillover effect of these experiences into the physical world or the other way around. Also, continuity between the learner's personhood, prior experience, and tacit knowledge must be considered for meaningful personal learning to take place.

Lastly, the social aspect of these virtual environments brings forward the exponential power to spread values and ideologies across geographical boundaries and at a speed not possible before. Also, the intimacy that develops among the inhabitants of these virtual environments reveals the strength innate to close-knit communities which sensibly ushered with purpose can positively influence people in the masses or accomplish more together through social presence.

THE SELF

Understanding the self plays a fundamental role in the learning experience. Carl Rogers' concept of becoming a person provides a grounded perspective in facilitating experiences in virtual worlds. Rogers' (1961) interpretation of the self is best appreciated in the following passage:

... to be herself means to find the pattern, the underlying order, which exists in the ceaselessly changing flow of her experience. Rather than to try to hold her experience into the form of a mask, or to make it be a form or structure that is not, being herself means to discover the unity and harmony which exists in her own actual feelings and reactions (p. 114).

Based on Rogers' explanation of self, a point of potential contention surrounds the nature of avatars. To some, avatars might be construed as masks underneath which people hide; however, this notion constitutes a fallacy. Many studies have found that the technology of virtual environments has the extraordinary capacity to help with self-discovery, develop empathy to understand others, and to change beliefs and perceptions of ourselves and the world surrounding us. For instance, a study found that the affordances of anonymity in virtual environments allowed for adolescents to explore their identities through language and role play (Calvert, 2002). Yee and Bailenson (2007) studied the phenomenon of the Proteus effect in which they found evidence that people infer beliefs and attitudes from the avatar's appearance.

Furthermore, in a second study, these researchers found that people carried over these behavioral changes from the Proteus effect to the physical world (Yee & Bailenson, 2007). These examples are just a couple that substantiates that the "self" in virtual environments is as genuine and real as the "self" in the physical world for the very nature of self has to do with one's journey to find the harmony between our feelings and reactions to our overall life experiences. Therefore, reference to the physical world or experiences as "real" bears a cautionary consideration as this notion is farthest from reality.

Blascovich's and Bailenson's (2011) portrayal of the self and his or her footprints in virtual reality reinforces the matter. As individuals journey through the virtual worlds, they leave virtual footprints that reveal as much about the identity of the selves based on what they plan on doing, places they go, and whether they are going to be successful in what they were set to do.

In the generations to come, as technologies evolve and people imagine and participate in a myriad of virtual experiences, the identity of the inhabitants in these experiences will evolve into complex realizations of culture. A culture in which identities assumed in the physical and virtual spaces affect each other and therefore blurring spatial distinctions of the self. Virtual identities will become an extension of our physical selves with the capacity to influence people's behavior, educational, economic, judicial, and political systems.

THE COLLECTIVE SELF

Understanding the impact of the social aspect in virtual learning experiences and its potential to raise social awareness that leads into action, exhorts bringing to the forefront that an aspect of the learner's self seeks to define herself or himself based on the desire to feel connected to others and belonging to an affinity group. Turner, Hogg, Oakes, Reicher, and Wetherell (1987) describe social identity as "a shift towards the perception of self as an interchangeable exemplar of some social category and away from the perception of self as a unique person" (p. 50). As highlighted in Bobro (2018), "social identity is a collection of feelings, attitudes and emotions in the community that lead to unity, and ultimately, becomes part of the individual's identity" (p. 123).

The differences between the interpersonal and the collective identities of the learners require consideration in the facilitation of virtual environments as well. Brewer and Gardner (1996) explain that the essence and characteristic of the collective self lay in the degrees and self-representation manifestations of inclusiveness embodied both in the affective and cognitive domains of the self. From the differentiated self-concept, the relational self that manifests from the connections and relationships with others to the collective self that motivates the individual to participate for the welfare of the group. That is, in the collective self-representation, the *I* turns into *we* for self-reference (p. 84).

PRESENCE

Many aspects of presence in virtual environments have been researched, but more studies are needed. Some of the literature addresses the different dimensions of presence, presence as in situ, social presence, and co-presence (Bulu, 2012). Presence in the context of virtual environments has been defined as the sense of being in another place or space. A more comprehensive definition is put forth by Witmer, Jerome, and Singer (2005) who define presence as "... a psychological state of "being there" mediated by an environment that engages our senses, captures our attention, and fosters our active involvement" (p. 298).

As communication media have evolved from the textual to the more visually and spatially rich, the concept of social presence has evolved as well. Bulu (2012) indicated that some researchers view social presence as the individual's perception of the medium to connect with others to create sociable and intimate interactions. Co-presence deals with not only having a sense of being with other individuals but also having the feeling that others actively perceive them back as part of the group.

Witmer, Jerome, and Singer's (2005) presence questionnaire capture other important concepts to understand the nature of presence in virtual worlds and to seek optimal affordances in the facilitation of learning. First is the environment in which presence manifests itself, which are the physical, virtual, and symbolic spaces. Another critical element is the degree of presence the individual feels. According to Witmer, et al. (2005), the degree of presence is influenced by the fidelity of the elements the individual takes in through the senses and the nature and ease with which they interact in the environment. In the psychological plane, involvement and immersion are key in discerning presence. Involvement has to do with the state the individual experiences from focusing on meaningful stimuli, activities, or events. Immersion is the psychological state in which the individual perceives to be enveloped in or embraced by the environment which provides a continuous flow of stimuli and experiences (Witmer et al., 2005).

As the social presence literature review by Oh, Bailenson, and Welch (2018) revealed, many researchers have studied the matter at length and efforts continue to this day. These authors' review approach of studies on social presence included three lenses: 1) immersion, 2) context, and 3) psychological dimensions provides the facilitator of the virtual learning experience a great foundation for a socially aware and impactful outcome. The immersive qualities of an experience focus on technological affordances and visual representations that enable social presence. Conversely, the contextual and psychological dimensions address the subjective nature of social presence; in the contextual dimension, personality traits, social cues, agency, and type of task are the emphasis while the psychological dimension focuses on the demographic differences and the individual's traits (p. 4-10).

Many other aspects impacting our identity and feel of presence in virtual environments exist that cannot be included in the scope of a book chapter. As this medium and its techne evolve many other concepts and research agendas will emerge as well. With the above aspects surrounding virtual worlds and identity as the basis, the goal in the next section of this book chapter is to attempt to elicit and discern design matters when virtual worlds are part of the learning experience.

CONSIDERATIONS IN DESIGNING LEARNING EXPERIENCES IN VIRTUAL WORLDS

Guideposts

These non-determinant virtual worlds afford us three primary design components: the environment or space, the learner, and his or her sense of presence. An additional tenet to keep in mind before exploring what the design of meaningful learning experiences in virtual worlds entails is to recognize the importance of the learners' tacit knowledge in the process of learning. In other words, the learner's subjective insights, prior experience, and knowledge, as well as the opportunity to engage in practice go in parallel with the concepts of self, presence, and the virtual environment discussed above. Lastly, Mark Weiser's vision on ubiquitous human-centered computing which highlights that the most powerful experiences people will embrace and enrich them are those "that are effectively invisible in use" (Abowd, Mynatt, & Rodden, 2002, p. 48). Compared to previous iterations of virtual realities, today's technology allows us to co-create learning experiences that draw out the self and sense of presence from the learners with greater ease and fidelity as well as an empathic appreciation of those enduring the consequences of our many health, environmental, geopolitical, and societal problems.

As one starts to ponder on how to facilitate meaningful learning in virtual worlds, what comes to mind first and foremost is the importance of contextualizing the learning experience that is to take place. Also providing purposeful experiences is key. Telling learners to login into a virtual world and roam around on their own does not constitute a good example of meaningful learning. Such practice can be equated to the practice of asking students to make a specific number of posts and responding back to forum posts in an online course. Instead, we should ask ourselves how to provide purposeful, authentic experiences in the context of what the individual learner's goals are while taking into account the needs of the group or other selves and the affordances of the virtual environment in which the experience is to happen. One of the most common practices that take into account authenticity and context is that of asking learners to adopt a virtual self different from their physical self and interact in different areas of the virtual world. This activity is accompanied with a reflective element by asking the learner to document their experience via blogs, images, and machinima/art.

Reflection

Virtual worlds are also conducive for the reflective learner by creating an atmosphere in which he or she can move freely in, around, and between the spaces. As Carl Rogers (1961) indicated, for learning to take place, an atmosphere of freedom for the learner to move around in his thoughts, feelings, and being is necessary. The goal is to allow for self-discovery and reflection to take place. In this manner, the learner can personally visualize and assimilate the experience which will then lead into personal growth. Similarly, reflection is most useful in heightening an emphatic disposition to understand opposing or unexperienced perspectives. For instance, some of the most successful uses of virtual environments in learning have used Second Life and virtual reality headsets to experience the day-to-day life of someone with a psychological or physical condition.

Experimentation

Virtual worlds provide the environment in which experimentation can be cleverly facilitated in the learning process. Often, in the OpenSimulator grids and Second Life, "sandbox" areas are available for learners to create or prototype 3D objects that can be manipulated within the bounds of the physics engine behind the virtual world platform. Successful hackerspaces provide focused tutorials, resources such as objects, textures, and scripts to empower the novice learner to create 3D objects of their own in OpenSimulator. Furthermore, to support the birth of social identity for active participation, some of these hackerspaces facilitate periodic scheduled events and gatherings in which novices and experts interact to learn new skills or overcome challenges with a particular problem members bring forth. The experimental kind of virtual learning experiences with the most impact are those in which groups of learners work together on problem-based missions. Facilitators and participating learners must be attentive of their social and co-presence to be able to accomplish their mission successfully. Therefore, what matters in the design of these learning experiences is to empower learners to engage in active meaning making and sharing with others. A complementary key technique in facilitating problem-based learning in virtual worlds is to stagger moments and spaces for individual reflection and group work throughout the exercise.

Role Play

Another powerful instance of learning in virtual environments is that of contextualized learning via role play. In this practice, learners assume the different roles actors take part in a theatrical performance, or become the nurses and doctors who must handle an emergency in a hospital, or take on the role of military officers who must go on a rescue mission. This experiential learning can elicit the learner's sense of presence to immerse them in the role of their choice and interact with the other "selves" in the virtual environment that resembles the theater stage, the emergency room, or the location where the hostage is being held.

Collaborative Learning and Communities of Practice

When designing learning in virtual environments, it is important to design experiences in which meaningful active, varied, and frequent interactions among learners are facilitated to increase the chances of social identity to emerge. Social presence dimensions are also crucial in influencing a lasting collaborative learning experience that could evolve into a community of practice that influences in the larger stage of a discipline or field. Park and Seo (2011) state that "group identity shapes the motivation behind voluntary engagement in collaborative behavior and is linked to a person's desire to receive feedback from the group and to create, maintain, and enhance a favorable identity for the group" (p. 517). Some of the best instances of collaborative learning in virtual environments can be observed in groups such as the Non-Profit Commons in Second Life, an actively engaged community of non-profit organizations helping each other. Other examples include the OpenSimulator Community advancing the mission of an open source platform with annual conferences organized by volunteers, the Virtual Worlds Education Roundtable, an international group of educators discussing and sharing relevant issues on education in virtual worlds, and the Relay for Life in Second Life, a fundraising event to find a cure for cancer held since 2004. To effectively utilize the power of virtual environments, one must have social presence, an observable, on-going process rather than a subjective and stable condition in which the role of interaction in the process needs due consideration along the way (Sivunen & Nordbäck, 2015).

Transdisciplinary Abilities and Disposition

When the *I* turns into *we*, transdisciplinary approaches to education and research best practices are most powerful regardless of space and time. While facilitating learning in which consideration for the learner's own purpose and prior experience, opportunities for exposure and understanding on multidisciplinary perspectives and the integration of interdisciplinary approaches are brought together (McGregor, 2017). Learners experience a shift in their thinking. Transdisciplinary experiences involve how participants integrate ideas that consider a multitude of perspectives to ultimately reach a sound solution via collaborative learning. In this transdisciplinary approach, the process must be iterative. Learners must challenge basic assumptions and positions brought forth by all, articulate ideas, and carefully consider such ideas across disciplines and conventions. Essentially, shared vision, understanding of self both individual and collective, empowerment, advocacy, and inclusiveness to lead into transformative solutions must be designed into a transdisciplinary learning experience (p. 8).

Many of our complex societal problems can be dealt with the transdisciplinary habits of mind as presented by McGregor (2017). That is, the transdisciplinary approach encompasses a practice involving:

- The act of perceiving
- Pattern recognition
- Abstracting
- Embodied thinking where a key aspect is empathy
- Modelling to draw abstractions and analogies across the dimensions of space and time and
- Deep play to explore boundaries
- Synthesizing (page 12).

Virtual environments present us with opportunities to combine pedagogies through practicing habits of mind. McGregor presents nine potential transdisciplinary pedagogies for higher education:

- To adopt the proposed pedagogies of integrative curriculum
- Inquiry-based learning
- Transformative learning to help learners make the intellectual and emotional shift
- Authentic curriculum that is purposeful and relevant to the learners' lives and their society
- Learning communities that share vision and mission
- Deep education in which learners participate in a holistic, contextualized, and learner-centered experience
- Value clarification and analysis
- New ways to see and be in the world (paradigm shift)
- Question everyone's governing principles (double loop learning) (p. 14).

The chapter, *Advancing Personal Learning and Transdisciplinarity for Developing Identity and Community* by Truman & Truman provides a deeper understanding of the transdisciplinary discourse which presents principles to address many of our societal challenges including the much-needed transformation of higher education.

FINAL THOUGHTS

According to Harari (2015), the imagination of humans have created the story called economy, politics, religion, and many other forms of systemic environments that constitute the physical reality in which we have operated for thousands of years. Computational thinking is providing us the power to imagine the human experience in a manner not possible before. Virtual worlds/virtual reality will continue to evolve and iterate in ways we cannot imagine today. Linden Lab's Second Life virtual world platform, touted as long gone, is still making its reach known through its vibrant communities. As of 2015, Second Life's gross domestic product (GDP) was estimated to be around $500 million which is larger than that of some of the smaller countries in the world (Bryant, 2015). The power lies in imagining new empowering realities that intertwine and extend our selves between the physical and virtual worlds for the good of humanity. Technology affords us the Art-of-the Possible, and therefore we have the power to shape our future.

The key is to find the balance of imagined realities that is mindful and respectful of the learner's freedom to decide what is most suitable/desirable while considering the innate disposition of the collective self to belong and contribute to society as a whole. The tumultuous social and geopolitical world we currently live in, calls for us to immerse ourselves genuinely and to nurture the collective self to solve the many societal problems we face today whether environmental, health, education, or political. The prospects are exciting and filled with mindful and meaningful opportunities for learning afforded by the next iterations of virtual environments.

REFERENCES

Abowd, G. D., Mynatt, E. D., & Rodden, T. (2002, January - March). The human experience. *Pervasive Computing*.

Blascovich, J., & Bailenson, J. (2011). *Infinite reality - Avatars, eternal life, new worlds, and the dawn of the virtual revolution*. New York, NY: HarperCollins Publishers.

Bobro, M. (2018). Collective identity in the age of globalisation. *The Person and the Challenges*, *8*(1), 121–133.

Brewer, M. B., & Gardner, W. (1996). Who is this we? Levels of collective identity and self representations. *Journal of Personality and Social Psychology*, *71*(1), 83–93. doi:10.1037/0022-3514.71.1.83

Bryant, M. (2015, December). *Think Second Life died? It has a higher GDP than some countries*. Retrieved from http://thenextweb.com/insider/2015/11/07/think-second-life-died-it-has-a-higher-gdp-than-some-countries/

Bulu, S. T. (2012). Place presence, social presence, co-presence, and satisfaction in virtual worlds. *Computers & Education*, *58*(1), 154–161. doi:10.1016/j.compedu.2011.08.024

Calvert, S. L., Jordan, A. B., & Cocking, R. R. (2002). *Children in the digital age: influences of electronic media on development*. Westport, CT: Praeger.

Ellis, S. R. (1996). Virtual environments and environmental instruments. In Simulated and Virtual Realities (pp. 11-51). London, UK: Taylor Francis.

Fox, J., Arena, D., & Bailenson, J. N. (2009). Virtual reality - A survival guide for the social scientist. *Journal of Media Psychology*, *21*(3), 95–113. doi:10.1027/1864-1105.21.3.95

Harari, Y. N. (2015, July 24). Why humans run the world. *Ted Talks - London*. Retrieved from https://www.youtube.com/watch?v=nzj7Wg4DAbs

Hayles, N. K. (1999). How we became posthuman: Virtual bodies in cybernetics, literature, and informatics. Chicago: University of Chicago Press.

Knutzen, K. B., & Kennedy, D. M. (2012). Designing the self: The transformation of the relational self-concept through social encounters in a virtual immersive environment. *Interactive Learning Environments*, *20*(3), 271–292. doi:10.1080/10494820.2011.641680

Lombard, M., & Ditton, T. (1997). At the heart of it all: The concept of presence. *Journal of Computer-Mediated Communication*, *3*. doi:10.1111/j.1083-6101.1997.tb00072.x

McGregor, S. L. T. (2017). Transdisciplinary pedagogy in higher education: Transdisciplinary learning, learning cycles, and habits of mind. In *Transdisciplinary Higher Education: A Theoretical Basis Revealed in Practice* (pp. 3–14). London, UK: Springer. doi:10.1007/978-3-319-56185-1_1

Oh, C. S., Bailenson, J. N., & Welch, G. F. (2018). A systematic review of social presence: Definition, antecedents, and implications. *Frontiers in Robotics and AI*, *5*(114), 1–25.

Park, H., & Seo, S. (2013). Effects of collaborative activities on group identity in virtual world. *Interactive Learning Environments*, *21*(6), 516–527. doi:10.1080/10494820.2011.604037

Peachey, A., & Childs, M. (2011). Virtual worlds and identity. In *Reinventing Ourselves: Contemporary Concepts of Identity in Virtual Worlds* (pp. 1–12). London, UK: Springer-Verlag. doi:10.1007/978-0-85729-361-9_1

Rogers, C. (1961). *On becoming a person. A therapist's view of psychotherapy*. Boston, MA: Houghton Mifflin Company.

Schroeder, R. (2011). *Being there together: social interaction in virtual environments*. New York, NY: Oxford University Press.

Sivunen, A., & Nordbäck, E. (2015). Social presence as a multidimensional group construct in 3D virtual environments. *Journal of Computer-Mediated Communication*, *20*(1), 19–36. doi:10.1111/jcc4.12090

Turner, J. C., Hogg, M., Oakes, P., Reicher, S., & Wetherell, M. (1987). *Rediscovering the Social Group: A Self-categorization theory*. Oxford, UK: Basil Blackwell.

Yee, N., Bailenson, J. N., & Ducheneaut, N. (2009). The Proteus effect. Implications of transformed digital self-representation on online and offline behavior. *Communication Research*, *36*(2), 285–312. doi:10.1177/0093650208330254

This research was previously published in Recent Advances in Applying Identity and Society Awareness to Virtual Learning; pages 116-125, copyright year 2019 by Information Science Reference (an imprint of IGI Global).

Chapter 20
The Digital Cultural Identity on the Space Drawed in Virtual Games and Representatıve

Hülya Semiz Türkoğlu
Istanbul University, Turkey

Süleyman Türkoğlu
Istanbul University, Turkey

ABSTRACT

The digital culture created in the virtual space provides a more liberal and open environment for the people, with fewer restrictions from real life. The current research on virtual reality self-expression has mainly been discovered as an independent aspect of the real self. The chapter also analyzes the use and perceptions of virtual users in the virtual world by focusing on the construct that creates different virtual cultural experiences. For this purpose, the "Second Life" game, which provides a three-dimensional and online virtual environment modeled by the real world, is taken as an example. In the survey, we interviewed 10 people from Second Life to find answers to our questions. As a result of their work, Second Life plays a vital digital life in a dynamic digital culture that is different from their real lives in response to the question of how they build a world with communication, culture, identity and lifestyles.

INTRODUCTION

With the internet, emotions, thoughts and behaviors have changed and virtual space, virtual culture and virtual identities have emerged. The reality and the identity has been formed in virtual spaces that allow the creation of different identities on the internet.

When the computer comes to life everyday and it forms the virtual places in the graphic form that are used since the 1980s, in many fields including communication, health education and so on (Ventrella, 2011, p. 17). Virtual spaces are computer-generated environments where participants use an avatar to interact with each other and around the environment. The term "avatar" in this sense means "a user can

DOI: 10.4018/978-1-6684-7597-3.ch020

be graphically identified and displayed in the virtual environment." Avatar means, in root terms, that a high soul in Sanskrit falls into the world by embracing a body and nowadays, (Allbeck & Badler, 2002) the avatar, in short, represents the body we are in the digital world (Allbeck & Badler, 2002).

Virtual is one of the most used concepts among communication possibilities offered by technology developments. The meaning of the word virtual in Turkish dictionary; as a concept that is not actually located and designed solely in the mind. Baudrillard regards the virtual reality as a false statement of reality created by this century as a posture designed with signs and models. (Baudrillard, 2012, p. 122). While philosophers and sociologists define the concept of virtuality in different ways, the interface designers accept it as a simulation of a virtual, computer-generated three-dimensional world. Instead of reality, there is a world of anticipation where images are important.

Virtual spaces allow the user to change the world they are in and give them the opportunity to relate to real life in economic, social and cultural spheres. Virtual space is shaped by human intelligence. Virtual spaces are cyber spaces that are located on a network where people are most popular via their computer games. Some virtual venues have created their own culture with the number of users exceeding many countries' population. The popularization of virtual spaces and the accompanying cultural developments have opened the doors of a new world for people who want to be institutionalized or personally globalized.

In this article, the presentation of the identities tried to explain the implications of the concept of virtuality, the experiences produced by the technology and the experience of carrying the person out of physical reality. Virtual identities reconstructed in the virtual space have been tried to be informed about the formation of the fictionalized identities and the process of conversion to different identities by starting from the popular culture conception. In addition, role-playing and identity formation processes have been tried to be explained in the virtual environment. The research is going to try to analyze the usage and understanding of game in the virtual world by the virtual identities of the individuals. The case study is the first sample of the Second Life game research. The second sample contains the users of the Second Life game. For this purpose, a virtual ethnography method was applied to the characters by taking as an example the Second Life game, which provides a three dimensional and online virtual environment modeled by the real world. It is based on "online conversation" techniques, a method of virtual ethnography. For this purpose, data were collected by interviewing Second Life users with the general characteristics of the Second Life virtual life world and the idea of determining the virtual life style of the users. Virtual space and identity transformation are explained and virtual space is compared with real world through identity transformations. The causes of virtual life directions from real life have been investigated and the main reason for the representation of virtual life by cultures has been researched.

DIGITAL CULTURE IN VIRTUAL SPACE

A virtual one is a reflection or break that is not directly needed for a real object (Burnett, 2007, p. 125). It is seen as a technology that allows you to enter the interactions we actually perceive with different users in virtual reality. At this point, virtuality is addressed in two categories, game-oriented and social-focused (Nagy and Koles, 2014).

Do not imitate sanity means to fulfill the functions of something that does not really exist. Virtuality is not a concrete aspect, but it captures the nature of objects and actions (Shields, 2003, p. 2). In virtual spaces, Plato's ideas are similar to the ideological world. Reflections or imitations of things that exist as objects as images.

Contrary to the measurable, concrete, behavioral and psychological dimension of real space; abstract space is a space designed in mind, visualized and evaluated by different techniques. Virtual space is the reorganization of communication as a space or environment. It can be said that the applications of spatialization realized as coordinates and locations of information cause the digital environments to be called virtual spaces. In addition to this, such virtual spaces are presented as a concrete reality by being brought into equal status with face to face communication.

Culture is all about consistent values, expectations, expressions and man-made works shared by a group of people. Culture is a creative process because it is in constant production and it is a result that comes out in the form of product or work. Digital culture is both a creative process and a set of products created through digital media. (Dijk, 2016, p. 293) The digital terrestrial digital culture concept is used for electronic systems that store, process and transmit audio or video data in the form of a digital sequence.

Culture is based on people's experiences and cultural backgrounds; For this reason, cultures in the virtual world created by users around the world can be more complex than real world cultures. It also creates its own virtual cultures and communities in virtual reality. Communication in the virtual space provides great opportunities for the creation of new communities and new cultures. In addition to making people forget that they live in reality, the virtual culture collects people with virtual reality that allows people to spend time in artificially developed virtual spaces restricted to their own imagination only by the technologies that present the ways of re-telling themselves (Schroeder, 1994, pp. 524-525).

Jan Van Dijk's negative attitude suggests that democratic participation in virtual areas promotes the cult of people who have the following characteristics;

- In contrast to existing mass media.
- It is a creative environment that allows users, audiences, listeners or readers to turn into participants.
- It is a direct tool that enables individual users to set the right balance between policy and mass-media tools at the center of many things.
- In principle, it is an equal platform for everyone.
- It is a network tool where products can be created jointly online (Van Dijk, 2016, p. 156).

Castells argues that the concept of "mass self-communication" has gained visibility with the development of technology possibilities with its affirmative approach. Mass self-communication is a form of communication based on reciprocal interaction in which the audience has access to the mass of the audience, but the production of the message depends on the person himself, the reception of the message itself, and the acceptance and aggregation of content from electronic communications networks. This form of communication, made possible by Internet and mobile production, originated primarily from decentralized networks (Castells, 2016, pp. 1-2). In this context, Castells means that the social field is to be stripped of its power apparatus and to create its own autonomous space with the phenomenon of "decolonization." This is, in effect, new mediums of media that promote "participatory culture".

In the societies formed by mass media, the way of communication has become one of the dominant power structures that can have a decisive influence on other institutions and processes of the society. The concrete form of communication that dominates in each case is determined both by the organizational context that regulates the flow of communication and by the communication culture of the participants (Meyer & Hinchman, 2002, p. 15).

Cultures are formed by the development of communication processes. As Roland Barthes and Jean Baudrillard have stated, the forms of communication are based on the production and consumption of the signs. For this reason, there is no distinction between reality and symbolic representation. In all societies, mankind has existed in a symbolic environment and acted through a symbolic medium. Thus, from typographic communication to sensuous communication, it is the realization of the realism of the new communication system that is organized around the electronic integration of all forms of communication (Castell, 2005, p. 497). Virtual space culture and identities are being rebuilt differently. In the virtual space, identities are constructed very comfortably. Flexible identity, personal irresponsibility, equalized status, recordability, operational synchronicity, as well as sense of belonging and multiple identities are among the attractive elements of virtual culture.

Virtual spaces have become a subject we have established a relationship with. This self-feeding complex network is in constant action of its own nature. The cyber environments, which are constantly updated with the help of their participants and become a new addition of the human being, are confronted as a cognitive and social space with its own rules, languages, habits, maps beyond being an advanced technology product. The existence of virtual spaces and identity is different from the real world, with the culture of real life a disconnect between virtual culture, disjunction, and a degree of differentiation that can not understand each other virtual culture also changes the habits of everyday life. In particular, forms of action, such as reading, writing and communicating face to face, have gradually begun to change or change form. And time develops in favor of real life and culture, in favor of virtual life and virtual culture.

Incorporating a majority of cultural expressions into an integrated communication system based on digitized electronic generation, distribution and signal exchange has serious implications for social processes and processes. This, on the other hand, seriously weakens the symbolic power of the traditional sender, who is transcribed by historically encoded social habits outside of the system, religious morality, authority, traditional values and political ideology. These senders will not disappear in the meantime; but they are weak if they can not re-encrypt themselves in the new system; their powers are increasing as they are electronically materialized in the new system (Castel, 2005, p. 500).

The concept of reality in virtual space is built on our experience, our emotional state, our beliefs, and how we feel. However, users (avatars) can see not only their own cultures, but also many other cultures. The virtual world is not only a new space for people to live and travel but also to build a virtual space for people to create their own visual environments and cultures.

PRESENTATION OF IDENTIFIED IDENTITY IN VIRTUAL SPACE

Three-dimensional (3B) virtual worlds; (González, Santos, Vargas, Martín-Gutiérrez & Orihuela, 2013) in which real-world environments are simulated and individuals can simultaneously interact with graphical characters called avatars in these environments.

Today, 3D virtual learning environments can help to improve decision-making and literacy skills by allowing users to gain critical thinking skills by giving them an opportunity to social interaction (Cheng & Ye, 2010; Jamaludin, Chee & Ho, 2009; Goel, Johnson, Junglas & Ives, 2013). However, in the design of 3D virtual learning environments, it is necessary to take into account the motivational factor that has a critical prescription in the social, cognitive and physical development of students (Hassouneh & Brengman, 2014).

Cyber space - cyberspace - is a parallel universe created and fed by the world's computer and communication lines (Mutlu 2004: 253). The cyber space, which is seen as the first step in virtual communities, was first used in 1984 by William Ford Gibson's novel Neuromancer - Matrix Hunter - in the cyberpunk novel (Gibson 1984). The use of the concept of cyber space in William Gibson's Neuromancer novel became widespread in 1984, when the word pepper was first used by Louis Couffignal in 1958. As the father of the Siberpunk movement, Gibson (www.williamgibsonbooks.com), the literary big bang - the so-called inspiration of all technology experts from Silicon Valley to Wall Street, the new and irresistible stage that emerged in his life is defined as 'cyberspace'. "Cyberspace characterizes the transformation that takes place on the basis of the connection between computer networks and on the basis of the relationship to human beings" (Stratton 2002, p. 80).

However, unlike this definition, US Air Force defines cyberspace as; the use of electronic and electromagnetic spectrum to store, modify and develop data on network systems and physical structures.

Cyber space (Sayar, 2013, pp. 58-73), which can be described as a new social space, is a virtual space in which there is no physicality and can participate by computer, mobile or smart phone by abstracting from individuals' bodies using internet technology. Individuals can play games, contribute to their personal development, exchange ideas, fall in love, act like people they want to be without revealing their identities.

With the new communication systems, the place and time that are fundamental to life have changed, and people have moved into the power of realizing miracles with their visual worlds they have created in virtual spaces (Castells, 2005).

In modern democracies, the public spaces created in virtual space applications (egaras) virtual spaces are the virtual spaces that can be used by each individual with the necessary equipment, which is the result of the interaction that is inherent in the virtual spaces and the qualification of participation to democratize the day. According to Rheingold, individuals are able to make communication by specifying the size of the freedom of expression and the resources they want to acquire, without encountering a direct opposition to the ideas that they have set up, without being dominated by a superintendent in these places (Rheingold, 1993, pp. 284-300; 2016, p. 126).

Rheingold (1993, p. 149) notes in his book The Virtual Community that the Internet has created new agoras as alternative gathering venues for virtual groups, and that a sufficient number of people can discuss social issues by establishing relationships with human emotions in cyberspace. Virtual groups are developing utopian projects based on virtual reality and can be reached in all the rewards and fantasy virtual worlds deprived of real world. It is as if the necropsy creates a virtual action space for them to interact in a bodily relationship, interacting with multiple identities (Robins, 2011, p. 147).

Today, with the development of new communication technologies, the presentation of the individual itself has also changed. Intelligent mobile phones and social media are also entertaining, and the presentation of my imagination has been moved to virtual locations with the ability to take photos very quickly. This has resulted in social media users sharing their identity presentations via social networks. The presentation of identity has not really started with the internet, but it has accelerated with it. With the new communication technologies, identity has enabled people to produce, change and manifest their own selves in the face of others (Semiz Türkoğlu, 2018, p. 173).

People need virtual, imaginary self-censorship in virtual spaces (Ager, 2011, p. 168). It requires knowledge from diverse disciplines such as culture, intercultural psychology and computer science integrated into behavioral models of virtual characters.

The theory of follow-up management developed by Erving Goffman is concerned with how we create, maintain and expand our social identities. According to Goffman's theory, personality is the sum of the various roles that people play in their lives. Whenever we interact with other people, we exhibit a public presentation of ourselves. Creating a successful impression requires a common understanding of the right scene, the decor, the costumes, the ability and the components that form behind the stage (personal, private space) versus being on stage (public space). Goffman refers to life as something played as a theater play (Ertürk, 2017, p. 147). When we look at the identities of virtual venues, we are confronted with actors of a real theater.

Goffman states that people are willing to leave good impressions on the environment to be applauded like an actor, and therefore they want to create an identity desired by everyone, with their various roles and feedback (Goffman, 2016: 16). These approaches by Goffman are primarily intended to focus on the concept of self / identity. The concept of self and identity is a simple concept, not an object nor a substance. It refers to a more dramatic performance and performance game for Goffman. In social interaction situations, information exchange comes into play and this transfer takes place through social and individual identities (Şentürk, 2017, p. 43).

Virtual spaces allow people to exhibit their ways of releasing themselves from their material obstacles in real life and re-expressing themselves. In this new technological reality, the physical appearance can be completely edited, long and beautiful or short and ugly if desired. It is necessary to question whether the changing physical properties will lead to changes in relation to other people (Robins, 2011).

Most of the people are unaware of their selves and do not know the aspects of their personality that are reflected on to other people (South, 2000). Because people believe that they can take control over time easier when they are on their computers, they use virtual space more as a new means of communication by reorganizing their identity problems in these areas.

The identity presented in the virtual environment from the outsourcing of identity is described as electronic self and there are exciting debates about the concept. With technological progress and the development of electronic cultures in this context, people are building resources that express themselves outside of what is possible (Miller, 1995). The Internet has created many aspects in this direction, breaking down borders and opening doors for new opportunities in social interaction. In this way, it is easier to apply difficult situations that are applied in face-to-face communication in virtual places (Collins, 2008). In the virtual world, users leave their bodies behind and evaluate their computers on a psychological level as an extension of their own mind and personality. Virtual environments allow one to introduce themselves as however they want.

Although virtual spaces seem to affect individuals positively in the context of freedom, the concept of freedom underlying the democracy foreshadows the individual to participate with his own identity. Giving ideas or accessing information with unfounded identities in virtual areas shows that they are reflected in virtual spaces of horror cultures rather than offering freedom to individuals.

BACKGROUND: DIGITAL WORLD VIRTUAL AREAS

The Internet, which has been used for a variety of purposes, has also led to the emergence of a completely different world. The most important of these is the virtual worlds of the digital world. Virtual domains are an interactive digital world that can be accessed by a large number of users through online interfaces.

As a result of richness and diversity of the cyber communication facilities, people are withdrawn physically and transformed into a virtual communication format. Moreover, instead of face-to-face communication, it has left a model of communication between the tools, which are divided by many interfaces. By providing a seemingly fake socialization, the obstacles to socialization through the use of virtual spaces thanks to technology even when one is alone being getting out of hand.

The virtual world is expressed as an interactive simulated environment that is accessible to many users with an online interface. According to another definition; Virtual worlds are also called "digital worlds", "simulated worlds" and "materials management operations guidelines" or "massive multiplayer online role playing games" (MMORPGs).

Although there are many different types, there are six features that are usually front-panel (Book, 2004: 2):

1. **Shared Media:** It is the world where multi-user participation is provided.
2. **Graphical User Interface:** The world is visually 2D (3D) or 3D (3D).
3. **Proximity**: Real-time interaction.
4. **Interaction**: Worlds; allows users to develop, configure, or send personalized content.
5. **Continuity**: Worlds continue to exist regardless of whether the user is in or out.
6. **Socialization / Community:** World; teams, localar, clubs and neighborhoods, and encourages their creation.

Virtual worlds are often used for (a) commercial play, (b) online community building, (c) education, (d) policy, and (e) military education (Virtual Worlds Review, 2018).

In a work done, virtual worlds are defined as virtual spaces that allow users to do what they want in a three-dimensional environment (Koles and Nagy, 2012, p. 5). Another study is virtual worlds; (Heeks, 2010: 4), which has existed since the beginning of human dreams, as well as its own currencies and economies.

Virtual areas are defined as three-dimensional spatial mediums represented by avatars and used by a large number of users. In another definition, it is expressed as a virtual environment in which the users of the fields are seen as a chat room by the users or the documents and ideas are shared by the users. Spence defines virtual worlds as permanent, synthetic, and three-dimensional spaces. In addition, he noted that virtual worlds are progressing on the path to becoming more and more social spaces (Spence, 2008, p. 5).

Spence summarized the formation process of virtual worlds as in figure 1.

According to Spence, in the first phase of virtual worlds, users met with playgrounds played on the internet. Then it turns into areas where there are avatars in the playgrounds and avatars can chat with each other. In the following periods, some sites inspired by chat environments have begun to use virtual worlds only for chat purposes. After the holding of the chat environment, social network sites such as facebook and twitter have met with users in the areas where they can chat and play games. Most recently, it has started to talk about virtual worlds.

The virtual space is in a digital world that we can see, hear, and touch. We can create visual environments and try new perspectives within our possibilities. The virtual space can be educational, useful and fun, as well as tedious and uncomfortable. In this sense, design is very important in virtual spaces.

The internet and social media, which are thought to cause many positive changes and transformations in the social structure, are changing and transforming the political sphere through the multiplication of information in a universal sense and the structure which leads to interaction. In particular, facilitating the participation of citizens in the political sphere, especially through the national boundaries and the provision of information to the citizens by overcoming the time problem. It is argued that democratization of society and direct democracy will be implemented because it facilitates the organization of the civil society, which creates a discussion environment through the virtual forums that it has created, enables communication at a much lower cost than the communication tools dominating dissident and alternative groups in society.

There are also a variety of tools that allow them to socialize within virtual spaces and share with other users and to make the world created even more realistic. Moreover, with the development of virtual spaces, communication possibilities in virtual worlds have also changed. In virtual communication, there are channel-transceiver components just as communication is defined. Vocabulary, symbolic, visual and audible variants of virtual communication are also available. In digital worlds, interaction with both the environment and other users is real-time. One of the examples that can be given to this "virtual world" is Second Life.

Figure 1. Formation process of virtual spaces
Source: Spence, 2008, p. 7

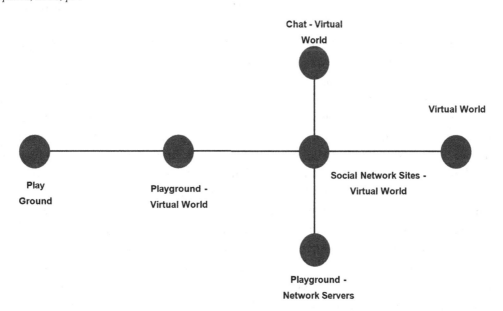

DIGITAL GAMES AND PLAYERS

As a result of the dizzying developments in technology, confusion arises as mobile games (mobile phone, portable playstation, gameboy, etc.) played on computer games (atari, commodore64 etc.), video games (Playstation, Xbox, Wii etc.) and portable devices. The terms "video games," "mobile games," and "computer games" are terms that can be used interchangeably. Because data entry is provided by tools such as a joystick, a keypad, or a keyboard in all three, the display of the game is also through the screen (Kirriemuir, 2002). From this partnership, video, mobile and computer games are called "digital games" in this study.

The concept of play in social sciences is based on the work of Huizinga and Caillois and is called ludology, or gaming knowledge. At the same time, ludology is positioned as a scientific antagonist of narratology, which plays the game as a mere storytelling; the presence of the player in the game and, at the very least, the interaction with the game (Fidaner, 2009, p. 90). It has been seen that in the studies related to digital games and virtual arts players have repositioned their habitat in real / daily life in virtual / digital. Thus, the players / consumers with similar likes come together (Binark and Bayraktutan-Sütçü, 2009, p. 277). Online created identities are offline consistent; so that both similar habitats come together and play a role in the construction of the identity of the virtual character, as well as tracing the identity, identity and personality of the player, starting with the avatars, especially the actors (Castells, 2008, p. 482).

Digital games are fundamentally differentiated from traditional games only by the distinction of space; (Binark and Bayraktutan-Sütçü, 2008, pp. 43-44) In a study on digital games, the difference between traditional game and digital game should be known. The word "game" comes from the Latin word "ludos". Ludology, on the other hand, is an area of social and cultural work that plays games (Yıldız, 2009, p. 58). The main reason for the spread of digital games in all societies around the world is the great developments in information technology especially after 1980's. The authors who anticipate developments in B have pointed out the inability of people to change inevitably (Toffler, 2011, p. 21). Difficulties with change bring about a different culture of developing technology and the use of technology among generations.

Digital games are a sector that creates mass consumer goods at Hollywood level, which can be handled in many sociocultural perspectives (Fidaner, 2009, p. 84). The results drawn from studies on digital games, virtual venues and internet technologies on the basis of the results are that the generations born into these technologies are easier to adapt, whereas the adults who witness these technological developments can not adapt to technological developments. Digital entities into the generations born into digital technologies; the generations that were born before are called digital immigrants when it comes to digital technologies and virtual media. The unique features of the players in the content and content of digital games such as instant communication with each other during the game and gathering in the virtual game environment have various security risks for collecting.

It is possible to make every action in the real everyday life in virtual circles. Meet new people, make new friends, shop, flirt, marry, divorce; to buy land, clothes, accessories, to make architectural designs and to market them all; it is possible to earn money by working in different jobs. It is also possible to switch between real and virtual, to meet in the virtual and meet in the real world, and so on. Relations can be established in the virtual and transferred to everyday life (Ağca, 2013, p. 191).

As opposed to common opinion that internet-based interaction like game, social media and etc. make the young and children antisocial, it actually enables them to make friends who have common interests. The Internet has become a popular place for the Internet to enter and become a social space for techno-cypresses in the recent past. It is set up as communities that need to be natural in online games or in interactional circles. Those who use the forums as a reference source during the time before the Internet becomes widespread also have the opportunity to interact with other users (Binark, Bayraktutan-Sütçü and Başakçı, 2009, pp. 192-215).

The more virtual worlds users satisty their feeling of existence, the more they use the relevant virtual world. Developing on the feeling of presence and the feeling of believing, the technologies produced virtual reality or increased reality applications. Virtual world users are able to integrate with the environment or virtual action when they realize that the virtual environments they are in are in harmony with the real environment or with the reality in their perceptions. The sense of virtual presence has three dimensions that one must be convinced of for himself, his surroundings and social interaction. Presence in digital games is a matter of representation. Creation, development, interaction and grouping have a virtual media user or a digital player (Bostan, 2011).

The person in real life continues in the virtual environment and the burden of this representation is not the body of the person but the avatar in the game and the act of play itself (Ağca, 2013, p. 191). If the player's sense of social presence is high, he feels safe, and the player who feels safe does not hesitate to show himself socially and emotionally. The player's habitat in the virtual space is realized in a series of structured information sequences, judgment, and appreciation positions in real life.

Regardless of the game interaction with the player, there is the pleasure of being someone else in digital games, and traditional or digital games allow players to acquire a new identity. The player is able to do things that they cannot do in their everyday life through this identity.

Digital players may be included in the universe of games, especially according to economic capital. Their meta-values from the vote can make money and make money. Just as the gaming market is the sectoral market, when the appropriate components come together, the game itself can expand into a virtual exchange market or market system that goes into the real world. Moreover, many factors such as the players' game preferences and likes can not be formed independently of social relations, including gender roles (Fidaner, 2009, p. 86).

ONLINE LIFE 'SECOND LIFE'

The new environment of the social media, known as the virtual world, can be described as "synchronous, continuous, networked, represented by avatars, facilitated by computers" (Bell, 2008, p. 2). Virtual worlds are created by individuals, their own visual symbols, are simulated permanent virtual environments in which they can interact with each other.

Second Life, has been established by Linden Lab Company in 2003 in San Francisco and with the promise of a second life to its users. The founders of Second Life, when establishing Second Life, inspired by Neal Stephenson's science fiction novel Snow Crash, describing an unlimited and free world (Pan, 2010, p. 7). The artificial world created for its users is also meant to be limited to their dreams and that their users will be able to live and do whatever they want to do.

The story tells the creation of states of USA, how mafia takes place of the army and the emergence of Snow Crash in the United States which is a computer virus. All the events revolve around Hiroaki Protagonist. The Protagonist who lives in the early 21st Century lives physically and mentally in different places. She lives in a three-dimensional virtual world called mentally 'metaverse'. Thus, Stephenson brought the concept of metaverse to the field literature. The metaverse concept has gained significance as a foresight to construct and interact with the physical world's objects, interfaces and the virtual environment of the networks as a three-dimensional virtual world (Smart, Cascio and Paffendorf, 2007).

In virtual worlds, Second Life (SL) has become a popular world in recent years with its popularity in terms of applications as well as the number of users. SL provides the opportunity for the computer-mediated communication technologies to provide an alternative and ideal world for the user, to interact with other people in real life, and to maintain their attitudes and behaviors similar to the real world in the presented visuals. SL differs from other online environments with its advanced visuals and presentations such as listening to music in the style they want for their users, being able to find them in fun activities, being able to play roles they want in role playing games, making money, entering adventures with various races, and developing foreign languages. Especially with numerical presentations called avatars, they can express themselves with the desired looks and thus express themselves with virtual faces and bodies; they are allowed to freely set their selves in anonymous identities so that they can present themselves in various self-presentation behaviors.

These artificial world members, who are expressed as digital animations of real life, create a character and find it possible to create a new space, new roles and new identities without the need of a physical reality on this side (Waskul and Douglass, 1997).

Although Second Life is perceived as a virtual game, it is different from others in that it does not have missions such as warriors, sorcerers, geniuses to capture roles or territories, rescue, level jump, score collection. Instead, there are reflections of real life such as building buildings, promoting in the workplace, establishing a company and becoming a millionaire. Ucu is the time, curiosity and creativity of the only frontier in Second Life, an open world (Tapley, 2008).

Virtual worlds allow the user to change the world they are in and give them the opportunity to connect with real life in economic, social, cultural and legal areas. Users who are conditioned by the environment created in Second Life are acting in an unreal, but surreal, dream. In Second Life, which is also referred to as a social life platform, users are involved in the imitation of the truth or in a way that is very close to reality. From this point of view, users live a life that is no different from real life and real-life items in this virtual environment. People are buying clothes for avatars, furniture for houses and companies, artwork and everything that is actually in the real world (Teigland, 2010, p. 7).

In Second Life, users who want to be in this life can choose their avatars without limiting themselves. They can choose between clothing, hair and outer appearance (body, eyes, ears, nose, mouth, chin, body, legs) gender, or non-human being (animal, robot, car, vampire, hybrid forms). Thus, users are improving their creativity by becoming one level.

Users are able to walk through avatars that they have decided to physically structure, fly, even carry out the irradiation that we spend from time to time because of heavy traffic or time constraints. Radiation is defined as a situation that occurs when a user moves from one area of Second Life to another area. In this sense, users can create new spaces, new roles and new identities without the need for a physical reality in cyber space that Second Life offers.

Second Life environment can interact with avatars, objects in the environment and other users. The avatars have the ability to change their external appearance. In the Second Life environment, avatars can be designed very differently by the user. In addition to human appearance; animal or semi-human half-animal (Wang and Braman, 2009). Users can experience real-life experiences by buying clothes, building homes or buildings, designing vehicles such as cars, spacecraft, planes, visiting new places and meeting new people.

Second Life has free or monthly paid membership plans. The ability to build a building, the ability to buy land varies according to the membership type. After you become a member, you need to install the client software on the user's computer in order to connect to the server. The user can join groups, visit other islands, islands, and homes bought by others. You can buy land, build on this plot, open stores and design learning environments.

An avatar is the virtual identity of the graphical user that he chooses to represent himself in the virtual space. When signing up for a user account in Second Life, they need to choose a first and last name for the new user. Users are presented with a few slide bar widgets that allow them to start with a default male or female avatar and personalize their look.

Figure 2. Second Life preview screenshot
Source: https://secondlife.com/

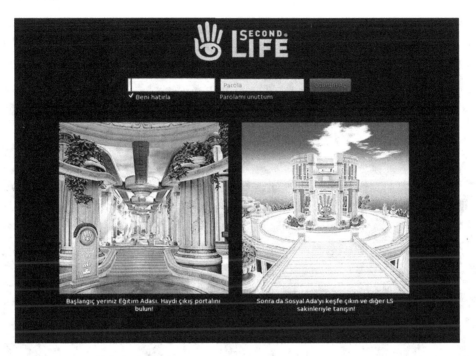

Users can change all kinds of fine details of face, hair and body. Second Life users are able to customize their clothing, body appearance and space. Apart from the real-life appearances, in Second Life, avatars like different animations, robotics, angels, demons can be created.

In Second Life, users basically create identity and community by creating their own worlds. Apart from playing games in Second Life, it is possible to consult, participate in sales-marketing, earn money, enter musical entertainment venues, participate in regular trainings, courses, courses and animated tutors, and participate in many activities. Users can discover many creative features here too.

The avatars that the person possessed or desired to live in are living through, avatars of age, weight, height, hair, skin color, eye color or ethnic characteristics and clothes preferences are shaped and can be changed freely at any time (Edwards, Dominguez and Rico, 2008).

As a result, users can be whatever they want to, or even redefine themselves. It is much easier to be a conversationalist than to be in a world like this (Jones, 2006).

AIM AND METHODOLOGY

In our work, 10 people were interviewed online through the "Second Life" gaming system in order to find answers to research questions.

Attitudes, behaviors, appearances, written and voiced expressions, dressing styles and profile information of the users themselves were presented through the avatars.

Figure 3. 3D rendering process
Source: manual.reallusion.com/iClone_6/ENU/Pro_6.0/07_Head/RLHead/RLHead.htm

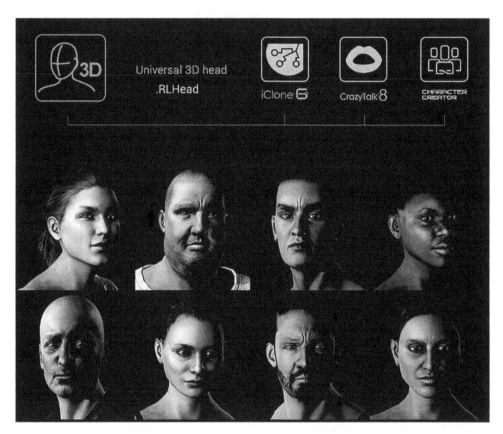

Figure 4. The real image of a player is the same image reproduced in Second Life
Source: www.mobihealthnews.com/18994/study-virtual-avatars-improve-fitness-motivation

For the research, 10 users who use "Second Life" game system collected data by online interview technique method. Attitudes, attitudes, attitudes, behaviors, cultures, appearance, written and voiced expressions, dressing style and profile information that the users reveal through their avatars through the avatars will be examined in the research. The researchers were given different names when researchers were interviewed.

The research questions developed in this context are as follows:

- Reasons for Second Life
- Identity Formation in Second Life
- Virtual Life Formation in Second Life

The research will analyze the game uses and insights in the virtual world by virtual identities of individuals, focusing on the construct that creates different virtual cultural experiences. The case study is the first example of researching "Second Life" game. The second sample is the users of the interviewed "Second Life" game. For this purpose, virtual ethnography method "online conversation" techniques have been used in the study of "Second Life" game, which provides a three dimensional and online virtual environment modeled by the real world.

Virtual ethnography is a method that gives important clues to understand and explain the virtual communities, culture and communication behaviors that develop in the virtual environment. Virtual ethnography; the researcher is active in the community and suggests that he can directly observe the behaviors of the people, talk to the people and reveal the underlying causes of the behavior, so that important clues can be obtained in understanding the habits that people are unaware of (Gay, Mills, and Airasian, 2006).

In the virtual ethnography method used for the research, "participant (virtual) observation" and "online in-depth interview" techniques were used.

DATA ANALYSIS

Online interviewing can be done in a variety of ways. Private messaging is a kind of concurrent conversation and can be more engaging for people who do not like face-to-face conversations. This method, which is expressed as Instant Message (IM), is used to communicate online through private software as a communication medium.

This method of producing descriptive information has several advantages; speed, the necessity of traveling in the middle, lifting flexibility in place and time, and being cheap are just some of them. Private messaging increases the level of participation in research by creating trust in participants because of the anonymity they create. Instead of non-verbal communication on the online conversation, the participants convey their feelings using sentences (Hinchcliffe and Gavin, 2009).

Data was interpreted using inductive analysis. Induction analysis is a type of analysis that involves classifying similar data in conceptual frameworks, revealing the relationship between concepts (Strauss and Corbin, 1990), thus understanding the complex data with developed themes or categories and arranging it in such a way that the reader can understand (Thomas, 2003).

FINDINGS

Findings obtained as a result of the data analysis on the answers to the questions directed to the users are given as the questions and answers.

The responses to the interviews about the reasons for the users being in the "Second Life" game are given in table 1.

Table 1. Reasons for users "Second Life"

Kara şahin	I find the opportunity to do all the work I can not do in real life, to paint, to learn to design, to communicate with my friends in my group. I can easily do hobbies.
melek68	I am unemployed in real life, thanks to a friend of mine, I am acquainted with this game and try to make money and meet my needs and continue my life.
perimasalı	I relax here. I even make myself happy in my virtual life. In normal life, I have difficulty communicating with people.
Dynotect	Graphics and visual elements are very welcome. I like the environments very much. I like to play such games.
Hellyboy666	The mystery of the environment and the image are of interest. I can find new friendships.
Yalnız melek	I spend all my time playing this game I like the most. I wish we could act like we want in real life. My favorite thing in the vote is to be able to fly.
Smith	I'm alone in real life. I am very comfortable in this vote. I can talk to anyone I have in any kind of relationship with. I think it's useful in a sexual sense.
Meral	There are no winners or losers in this game like other games. I do not have to compete with anyone. There is no race.
Nyks	I can share my thoughts freely. I am editing, starting and ending all my friendship relations as I want.
Ali1907	I can make my own designs. I'm hanging around in a world I can build by myself. I can make new discoveries.

As the answers given by all users are evaluated, it is possible to categorize the reasons why users are in the "Second Life" game system into the following titles.

- Set up friendships, meet new people, chat
- Performing hobbies, discovering talents, being creative
- Making money (an important economic opportunity)
- Sexuality
- Creating a stylized identity (creating an Avatar)
- Spending time and being happy
- Enjoyment and enjoyment

When these answers are collected under certain headings, it is seen that the reason for users to be in the "Second Life" game system is "to make friends and meet new people and to chat". In addition, users who use the "Second Life" gaming system are among the reasons for "realizing their hobbies", "having a different identity in real life different virtual world" and "being able to create desired avatar".

Some users express their "real happiness by having a better time" and "discovering their creativity by discovering their different activities".

Users have stated that they prefer this game because of their freedom to make their preferences in their behaviors, discourses and images in the "Second Life" gaming system.

Table 2. Identity of users living in Second Life

Kara şahin	I created a character that could fly by himself. I like flying and going somewhere faster.
melek68	I can get the identity I want. I can change my identity and continue with different identities when I want.
perimasalı	The best part of the game I think is that you can freely create your identity and also change it at any time you want freely. I can impersonate any identity I want on this count.
Dynotect	I created a character that was not in real life in the vote. In the virtual environment, even a user name is a fake nickname that no one in real life will use.
Hellyboy666	I can choose the identity I want while registering for the game. When I want to play the game again I can change the identity and character so I can continue.
Yalnız melek	Actually, I am a man, but I have made up my identity as a woman because the female characters are more pleased.
Smith	I create an identity with a character that is similar to physical characteristics. Using all the technological features of the game, I created an avatar with real-life security features that look like me as my hair, my eyes, my face.
Meral	I am overweight in real life and I have a slim figure in this world. I change the hair and eye colour as i want and use it.
Nyks	I am a student in normal life. I have identified myself as a company manager here. I imagine myself in places where I want to see myself in the future.
Ali1907	I am 19 years old in real life, but I am a 45 year old in Second Life. I can talk to older people this way. I think you have contributed more to my life.

As the answers given by all users are evaluated, it is possible to list the reasons for the identity of users in the "Second Life" game system in the following headings.

- I want to be able to take on the identity I want
- Being able to assume a free identity
- Imitating identity that is incompatible with real life
- Be able to create an identity with a character that can be changed on demand
- An actual identity created in a different sex
- The real identity of life creates an identity that reflects one's identity
- To create a technologically new and safer identity
- To create a different identity from real life physical attributes
- To create a different identity from the real life profession
- To create a different identity from the real life age

When these answers are evaluated and collected under certain headings, it is seen that the users have the answers "To be able to impersonate what I want", "An identity created in a different sex" and "To be able to have a different age and profession" in the question of identity formation in the "Second Life" game system.

Users interviewed say that the life in Second Life game provides a wide range of freedom. In addition, users embrace different identities and present themselves with a new technological identity.

When describing the users of the interviewed users, they have to be careful in describing themselves and providing less information about themselves and creating a more cautious identity for protection.

One of the users expressing their presence in the Second Life game is that they are an overweight and overweight person in real life but they have created an avatar as a blonde and fit-looking lady in virtual space.

Another of his users said that he did not see any disadvantage in expressing himself in his real life and in his virtual life, and he said that he took part in the vote.

Another user emphasized that while he can not express who he is in real life, he expresses himself better in Second Life game.

In real life, the user has changed this real-life information and has told other users that he is introducing himself as a manager in a company. The user has mentioned to friends and life that he can not have in real life and that he can have life in Second Life game.

Table 3. Cultural formation with virtual life in Second Life

Kara şahin	We share a lot of things similar to what I share with my friends in real life, creating a new culture that we achieve by sharing in the virtual environment.
melek68	According to our needs and needs in virtual life, we come together in this castle and a culture is formed with the differences that everybody adds something.
perimasalı	This is where people from all over the world come together and share freely, and new types of cultures are formed with the created environment.
Dynotect	There is no real culture in the virtual environment even when I am not real.
Hellyboy666	I'm just having fun. I do not believe culture can occur in virtual environments.
Yalnız melek	Every user in the game adds something. Therefore, a collective virtual culture is formed.
Smith	I am having fun with friends by sharing common time and space in this cast.
Meral	I do not think there is any culture in this game because nothing is real.
Nyks	Common values are formed when people with the same thoughts come together. Thus, a unique culture is formed.
Ali1907	There is a long need for culture formation. There is no culture in this cast.

It is possible to list the following headings when evaluating the answers that users have given to the formation of the cul- ture of virtual life in Second Life.

- Creating a virtual culture with our Shares
- Creating a culture based on our needs and needs in virtual life
- Create a free culture by gathering people from different parts of the world
- Creating a culture with shared time and space sharing
- Culture formation with the people of the same mind

Hellyboy666 avatar named "From the users who made online conversations:" In real life, culture comes out by sharing the environment, time, needs, beliefs and slice we live in. Our needs and needs that provide our lives create the culture we live in. "

It is seen that two of the users told that there is no culture in the Second Life game, there is no direct real identity of the users and that the concept of culture does not occur in the virtual environment because the time required for the formation of the cultures is not sufficient.

Users who say that they live a different life in real life in Second Life have pointed out that they have a different culture than real life, with the advantages of general features of virtual life. They said they created their own virtual cultures in their own virtual lives.

Users have the appearance they want in virtual life and they can wear clothes they can not wear in real life. Users create avatars with fantasy and unlimited freedom of behavior, creating a fantastic identity, where fantasy characters can be designed in Second Life games.

Some of the users said they were chatting with people from different countries we met in the Second Life game, with different social and cultural backgrounds. Thus, they emphasized the emergence of a culture suitable for virtual space from different cultures.

The interviewed Dynotect user stated that, contrary to his real life, he created a memorial of cultural past by saying that he felt stronger here. He expressed that there is no virtual or cultural culmination of a desired life in this place.

RESULT

Digital technology has now become a place to redefine our life we have had to start looking for our communication, education, friendship, relationships, work, business, business, entertainment in different areas. We are witnessing this revolution, which is fast and deep in every unit. Digital technology is not only an instrument for the human world, it is a culture that transforms, kneads and transforms culture.

The internet is actually a place that can not be felt tangibly but is expanding every second with the data entered by the users and electronic traffic. It is a network that connects millions of people through various means, thus connecting people who are not physically together, with electronic connections. The Internet not only communicates people communicatively, but also provides a fast and inexpensive way to carry out various activities such as education, entertainment, business, politics, economics.

Every day, millions of people play video games, making the game industry one of the largest contemporary cultural industries. The language and narrative foci of virtual worlds of games that create a virtual culture, the feeling of space, cosmology, symbols and rituals and games are completed. Virtual worlds are the most followed places after computer games. Virtual spaces, social platforms where human interaction is so powerful, produce a huge digital culture of its own, leading to the emergence of complex social relationships and the formation of virtual communities, collecting millions of users around the world. This work, which sees real identity as a two-dimensional concept, examines real identity through the purposes of restructuring the identities of individuals in both the online and offline worlds.

It would not be wrong to base on the natural park example given above that Simulation creates a hyperreality that goes far beyond the concept of real life (real life) with the reality that is simulated when the Second Life is taken into consideration. It is expressed in different names, such as virtual worlds or virtual media networks, it is based on virtual we find virtual in our language and it is based on the concept of virtual reality.

In order to avoid negative behaviors from sanctions and others, people have a high probability of concealing their negative aspects (such as personalities, thoughts and beliefs) in their virtual spaces.

In virtual reality, it is a three-dimensional world platform where users can interact with each other as if they were in real life and can emerge in the form of personalized avatars. In the virtual space, each user has his own unique cultural behaviors. It seems that most online discussions with Second Life users create different avatars than their own. The reason for this behavior is that they want to create a beautiful and remarkable avatar. Users can be the people in Second Life that they can not or can not be in the real world.

Second Life is a system with many applications. Users create a virtual character called "avatar" on a graphical background, performing the story, the everyday virtual life, the role in the virtual world, and the tasks that fall outside of their real life. In this context, virtual worlds emerge as the context of the creator, allowing user creativity. It also allows users to assume a digital identity and become artists, creators and writers.

According to our research results, in the place that is set in the game of Second Life, users are acting in an unrealistic but realistic dream. This work, which can also be seen as a social life platform, creates the avatars in Second Life where users are imitating the truth or looking very close to reality. From this point of view, users live a life that is no different from real life and real life items in this virtual environment. In addition, in online discussions with users in Second Life games, some users create life in their dreams through identity and space that they re-design themselves in a way that is very different from their real life. It is emphasized that the virtual space and identity created by the users is not a cult and that no one should be trusted. It is also argued that in the environment where the identities are hidden, in the environment where the users can not add anything from themselves, the cult which is formed in real life will not be formed. Apart from that, the online masks provided by the virtual space allow especially women to feel more comfortable in these areas than they are in real life.

Apart from playing games in Second Life, it is possible to consult, participate in sales-marketing, earn money, enter musical entertainment venues, participate in regular trainings, courses, courses and animated tutors, and participate in many activities. In Second Life games, users can build identities and communities by creating their own worlds with many activities. Users are also able to discover many creative features here. However, findings from the research show that the reasons for being in Second Life are beyond friendship and conversation. When rebuilding the identities of users, they create avatars that they want and they dream of. Users provide themselves with a virtual living space with a differently designed space and a differently redesigned identity. As a result, a temporary and virtial culture has been occurred that has no future or the past and far away from the tradition and reality.

REFERENCES

Ağca, R. K. (2013). Sanal Dünyalar ve Oyunlarda Sosyal Etkileşimler. In M.A. Ocak (Ed.), Eğitsel Dijital Oyunlar (pp. 180-197). Ankara: Pagem Akademi

Agger, B. (2011). *Sanal Benlik*. Çeviri: Volkan Hacıoğlu, İstanbul, Babil Yayınları.

Allbeck, J. M., & Badler, N. I. (2002). Embodied autonomous agents. In K. M. Stanney (Ed.), *Handbook of Virtual Environments; Design Implementation and Applications* (pp. 313–332). Mahwah: Lawrence Erlbaum Associates.

Baudrillard, J. (2012). *Kusursuz Cinayet Çeviri: Necmettin Sevil*. İstanbul: Ayrıntı Yayınları.

Bell, M. W. (2008). Toward a Definition of Virtual Worlds. *Virtual Worlds Research: Past. Present & Future*, *1*(1), 1–5.

Binark, M. & Bayraktutan-Sütçü, G. (2008). Kültür Endüstrisi Ürünü Olarak Dijital Oyun. İstanbul: Kalkedon Yayınları.

Binark, M. & Bayraktutan-Sütçü, G. (2009). Devasa Çevrimiçi Oyunlarda Türklüğün Oynanması: Silkroad Online'da Sanal Cemaat İnşası ve Türk Klan Kimliği. In Dijital Oyun Rehberi: Oyun Tasarımı (pp. 275-312). İstanbul: Kalkedon Yayınları.

Book, B. (2004). *Moving Beyond the Game: Social Virtual Worlds. In State of Play 2 Conference*. October, Cultures of Play Panel.

Bostan, B. (2011). Sanal Gerçeklik ve Dijital Oyunlar. İstanbul: Derin Yayınları.

Britt, A. (2008, August 8). On Language. *New York Times Magazine*.

Burnett, R. (2007). *İmgeler Nasıl Düşünür, Birinci Basım*. İstanbul: Metis Yayınları.

Castells, M. (2008). *Enformasyon Çağı: Ekonomi, Toplum ve Kültür. İkinci Cilt: Kimliğin Gücü. (Çev.: Kılıç, Ebru)*. İstanbul: İstanbul Bilgi Üniversitesi Yayınları.

Castells, M. (2016). *İletişim Gücü. Kılıç (Çev.)*. İstanbul: İstanbul Bilgi Üniversitesi Yayınları.

Cheng, Y., & Ye, J. (2010). Exploring the social competence of students with autism spectrum conditions in a collaborative virtual learning environment–The pilot study. *Computers & Education*, *54*(4), 1068–1077. doi:10.1016/j.compedu.2009.10.011

Comstock, J. (2012). Study: Virtual avatars improve fitness motivation. Mobihealthnews. Retrieved from www.mobihealthnews.com/18994/study-virtual-avatars-improve-fitness-motivation

Edwards, P., Domínguez, E., & Rico, M. (2008). A Second look at Second Life: Virtual Role-Play as a Motivational Factor in Higher Education. In *Society for Information Technology & Teacher Education International Conference*, Las Vegas, NV. Association for the Advancement of Computing in Education. Retrieved from https://www.learntechlib.org/p/27603/

Ertürk, Y. D. (2017). *Davranışlarımız ve biz, sosyal psikoloji bakışıyla kalabalık içinde ben olmak*. İstanbul, Turkey: Pozitif Yayınları.

Fidaner, I. B. (2009). Makinelerin Anlattıkları. In Dijital Oyun Rehberi: Oyun Tasarımı, Türler ve Oyuncu (pp. 83-94). İstanbul: Kalkedon Yayınları.

Gay, L. R., Mills, G. E., & Airasian, P. W. (2006). *Educational Research. Competencies for Analysis and Applications*. USA: Pearson Prentice Hall.

Gibson, W. (1984). *Neuromancer*. New York: Penguin Putnam, Inc.

Goel, L., Johnson, N. A., Junglas, I., & Ives, B. (2013). How cues of what can be done in a virtual World influence learning: An affordance perspective. *Information & Management, 50*(5), 197–206. doi:10.1016/j.im.2013.01.003

Goffman, E. (2016). *Günlük Yaşamda Benliğin Sunumu, Çeviri: Barış Cezar.* Metis Yayınları.

González, M. A., Santos, B. S. N., Vargas, A. R., Martín-Gutiérrez, J., & Orihuela, A. R. (2013). Opportunities and Challenges in the 21st Century. *Procedia Computer Science, 25,* 330–337. doi:10.1016/j. procs.2013.11.039

Güney, S. (2017). *Örgütsel Davranış, 4. Baskı.* Ankara: Nobel Akademik Yayıncılık.

Hassouneh, D., & Brengman, M. (2014). A motivation-based typology of social virtual World users. *Computers in Human Behavior, 33,* 330–338. doi:10.1016/j.chb.2013.08.012

Heeks, R. (2010). Understanding 'Gold Farming' and Real-Money Trading as the Intersection of Real and Virtual Economies. *Journal of Virtual Worlds Research.*

Hinchcliffe, V., & Gavin, H. (2009). Social and Virtual Networks: Evaluating Synchronous Online Interviewing Using Instant Messenger. *The Qualitative Report, 14.* Retrieved from http://www.nova.edu/ ssss/QR/QR14-2/hinchcliffe.pdf

Jamaludin, A., Chee, Y. S., & Ho, C. M. L. (2009). Fostering argumentative knowledge construction through enactive role play in Second Life. *Computers & Education, 53*(2), 317–329. doi:10.1016/j. compedu.2009.02.009

Jennings, N., & Collins, C. (2008). Virtual or Virtually U: Educational Institutions in Second Life. *The International Journal of Social Sciences (Islamabad), 2,* 3. Retrieved from http://citeseerx.ist.psu.edu/ viewdoc/download?doi=10.1.1.180.3529&rep=rep1&type=pdf

Jones, D. E. (2007). I, Avatar: Constructions of Self and Place in Second Life and the Technological Imagination, Communication, Culture and Technology Georgetown University. Retrieved from http:// www.gnovisjournal.org/files/Donald-E-Jones-I-Avatar.pdf

Kirriemuir, J. (2002). Video gaming, education and digital learning technologies. *D-Lib Magazine, 8*(2). doi:10.1045/february2002-kirriemuir

Koles, B., & Nagy, P. (2012). Who is Portrayed in Second Life: Dr. Jekyll or Mr. Hyde? *Journal of Virtual Worlds Research, 5*(1). doi:10.4101/jvwr.v5i1.2150

Meyer, T., & Hinchman, L. (2002). *Medya Demokrasisi Medya Siyaseti Nasıl Sömürgeleştirir? Çeviri: Ahmet Fehmi.* İstanbul: Türkiye İş Bankası Kültür Yayınları.

Mutlu, E. (2004). *İletişim Sözlüğü.* Ankara: Bilim ve Sanat Yayınları.

Pan, Q. (2010). Exploring Avapreneurship, A Look at Entrepreneurship in Virtual Worlds [Master of Science Thesis].

Peter Nagy and Bernadett Koles. (2014) The Digital Transformation Of Human Identity: Towards A Conceptual Model Of Virtual İdentity in Virtual Worlds. Retrieved from https://ciencia.iscte-iul.pt/publications/the-digital-transformation-of-human-identity-towards-a-conceptual-model-of-virtual-identity-in/23411

Robins, K. (2011). *İmaj, Çeviri: Nurçay Türkoğlu*. İstanbul: Ayrıntı Yayınları.

Schroeder, R. (1994). Cyberculture, Cyborg Post-modernısm and the Socıology of vırtual Realıty technologıes Surfing the Soul in the İnformation Age. *Futures, 26*(5), 519–528. Retrieved from http://www.beausievers.com/bhqfu/computer_art/readings/schroeder-sociology_of_virtual_reality.pdf doi:10.1016/0016-3287(94)90133-3

Second Life Preview. (n.d.). Retrieved from manual.reallusion.com/iClone_6/ENU/Pro_6.0/07_Head/RLHead/RLHead.htm

Şentürk, R. (2017). *İletişim ve Televizyon Teorileri*. İstanbul: Küre Yayınları.

Shields, R. (2003). *The Virtual*. Londra and New York, Routledge Taylor & Francis Group.

Smart, J., Cascio, J., & Paffendorf, J. (2007). Metaverse roadmap-patways to the 3D web: a cross-industry public foresight. *Metaverseroadmap*. Retrieved from http://www.metaverseroadmap.org/overview/index.htmladresine

Spence, J. (2008). Virtual Worlds Research: Consumer Behavior in Virtual Worlds. *Journal of Virtual Worlds Research*.

Stratton, J. (2002). *Siberalan ve Kültürün Küreselleştirilmesi, Mehmet Doğan (çev), Cogito Sayı: 30*. İstanbul: Yapı Kredi Yayınları.

Strauss, A., & Corbin, J. (1990). *Basics of Qualitative Research: Grounded Theory Procedures and Techniques*. London: Sage Publications.

Tapley, R. (2008). *Designing your Second Life*. Berkeley: New Riders.

Teigland, R. (2010). Born Virtuals and Avapreneurship: A case study of achieving successful outcomes in Peace Train- a Second Life organization. *Journal of Virtual Worlds Research, 2*(4).

Toffler, A. (2011). *Gelecek Korkusu Şok, (çev. Selami Sargut), 2. Baskı*. İstanbul: Altın Kitaplar Yayınevi.

Topbaş, H., & Doğan, A. (2016). Toplumsalın Yeni Agorası Olarak Sosyal Medya: Eleştirel Yaklaşım. *Gümüşhane Üniversitesi İletişim Fakültesi Elektronik Dergisi, 4*(1), 124–148.

Semiz Türkoğlu, H. (2018). Sosyal Medya Üzerinden Mahremiyet Farkındalığı ve Değişimin Ölçümlenmesine Yönelik Bir Araştırma, Sayı 54. *Connectist: Istanbul University Journal of Communication Sciences*.

Van Dijk, J. (2016). *Ağ Toplumu. (çev. Özlem Sakin)*. İstanbul: Kafka Yayınevi.

Ventrella, J. J. (2011). *Virtual Body Language – The History and Future of Avatars: How Nonverbal Expression is Evolving on the Internet*. Pittsburgh, PA: Carnegie Mellon University: ETC Press.

Virtual Worlds Review. (n.d.). What is a Virtual World. Retrieved from http://www.virtualworldsreview. com/info/whatis.shtml

Wang, Y., & Braman, J. (2009). Extending the Classroom through Second Life. *Journal of Information Systems Education*, *20*(2), 235–247. Retrieved from https://www.learntechlib.org/p/105676/

Waskul, D., & Douglass, M. (1997). Cyberself: The Emergence of Self in On-Line Chat. Information Society. *The Information Society*, *13*(4), 375–396. doi:10.1080/019722497129070

William Gibson Books. (n.d.). Retrieved from http://www.williamgibsonbooks.com

Yıldırım, A., & Şimşek, H. (2003). *Sosyal Bilimlerde Nitel Araştırma Yöntemleri*. Ankara: Seçkin Yayınları.

Yıldız, H. (2009). Homo Sapiens'in Boş Zamanı – Homo Ludens'in Sanal Kariyeri. *Folklor Edebiyat Dergisi*, *50*(13), 58.

ADDITIONAL READING

Adorno, T. W. (2005). *Minima moralia: Sakatlanmış yaşamdan yansımalar*. İstanbul: Metis.

Bogost, I. (10 Şubat 2018). Video games are beter without stories. The Atlantic. https://www.theatlantic. com/technology/archive/2018/02/video-games-stories/524148/) (Erişim: 10 Şubat 2018).

Çavuş. (2018). *Selahattin*. Dijital Kültür ve İletişim.

Juul, J. (2005). *Half-Real: Video games between real rules and fictional worlds. Cambridge ve Londra*. MIT Press.

Türkoğlu, Tanol. Dijital Kültür, İstanbul: Beyaz Yayınları

KEY TERMS AND DEFINITION

Digital Culture: Briefly, it is a form of new culture that is formed with digitalization. The digital term in digital culture is used for electronic systems that store, process and transmit digital speech encoded in the form of a digital sequence.

Increased Reality: A type of reality that brings the real world and the virtual world together and lets us interact with the digital world without breaking away from the real world.

Second Life Game: Second Life, Linden Lab, located in San Francisco in 2003. a company named by a company in a virtual world with the promise of a second life is a game designed.

Simulation: For the purpose of designing the model of the real system and operating the system with this model, it is the period during which experiments are carried out to understand the behavior of the system or evaluate different strategies.

Virtual Identity: With virtual culture, individuals in this world can create identities as they want. These virtual identities that are created are not always identities of individuals in real life, but identities that an individual creates if he wants to see himself. In short, virtual identity is the way in which the individual expresses himself in the virtual world.

Virtual Reality: It is all of the software and hardware tools designed to make perception of a virtual universe perceived by the individual as real.

Virtual Space: The world that is created as a result of digitalization and is not real. There are no geographical boundaries in this world and individuals can interact with other individuals without passing any physical themes and with the identity they desire.

This research was previously published in the Handbook of Research on Examining Cultural Policies Through Digital Communication; pages 121-143, copyright year 2019 by Information Science Reference (an imprint of IGI Global).

Chapter 21
My Becoming in a World of Virtual Learning Communities

Karen Joy Koopman
University of the Western Cape, South Africa

ABSTRACT

The aim of this chapter is to chronicle the author's becoming in a world of virtual learning communities (VLCs) and spaces. She considers her narrative of becoming in a world of VLCs and spaces important as it might resonate with many experienced lecturers and teachers who grew up in an era with no internet and no (or very little) technological tools, and who now suddenly find themselves thrust into an age where smartphones and various other mobile devices are inescapable. These smart devices such as iPhones, Macbooks, online programs, and so forth make university life frenetic not only for the author but for her students as well. This means we are all busy beyond belief with a seemingly relentless push to make everything we do and experience faster and faster. In this chapter, the author wants to share how the needs of her students, who are referred to as "digital natives" motivated her in her becoming in a world of VLCs.

INTRODUCTION

In September 2018 I attended the Philosophy and Theory in Higher Education conference hosted by Middlesex University, London Campus. The theme of the conference was focused on two main questions, namely, (i) Who is the student? (ii) How do we nurture the students' becoming in the future university? In simple terms, the main underlying theme of the conference was: How can we, as academics, support our students in their growth and development in the teaching and learning environment? According to the Cambridge English Dictionary, the verb 'support' means to 'uphold', to 'sustain' or to 'provide'. In the educational sense the word 'support' refers to what academics must do, or need to put in place to ensure that they encourage students in the teaching and learning process. In education providing support includes all aspects pertaining to the teaching and learning process, such as curricula, course content, resources for teaching and learning, and assessment.

DOI: 10.4018/978-1-6684-7597-3.ch021

There were two things that stood out for me at this conference. The first was how little attention was devoted to the historical past of the university, that is, the crooked paths that led to the present. Instead, the main focus was on where the university ought to be and what should be done to get from where we are to where we need to be with a sense of urgency. The second was the vivacious presentation of one of the keynote speakers, Rikke Toft Nϕrgard (2018), and her account of how she in her own pedagogical practice encourages her students to focus on what she calls 'poetry, passions, polyphony, and potency in thinking, doing and being'. To do this, she draws on philosophies and theories of playfulness as offering one possible route towards advancing more divergent, imaginative and vibrant ways of being and becoming in higher education. The most striking feature – and what held my attention throughout her presentation – was the beautiful, detailed, colourful and animated slides that she designed for the presentation. Another aspect that impressed me was how she used technology to bring the outside world into the lecture theatre so that I could experience her discipline (that is, module that she teaches) in a virtual world. Although the focus of the conference, or of Rikke Toft Nϕrgard's presentation, was not specifically on the use of technology in the classroom, I realised that technology can be both entertaining and educational, as it presents simplified theoretical models of real world processes and phenomena, a point also made by Song (2007).

This entire conference reminded me of Clark Kerr (2001), who introduced the word 'multiversity' to describe the challenges faced by universities today because of outside pressures on them, where more and more emphasis is placed on networks and diverse national and global markets. In the light of Kerr's (2001) notion of the 'multiversity' and Rikke Toft Nϕrgard's presentation – in which she compared the ever-changing nature of pedagogy to a jellyfish, because it is always changing its shape as it moves – I constantly asked myself how do I get from where I am in my own practice as an academic to where my peers in the rest of Europe are, so that I could give my students in the Faculty of Education at the university where I teach the same experience of integrating technology into my lectures. This means that as digital media are becoming increasingly more pervasive features of our society, and as students are becoming more techno savvy, more pressure is placed on South African academics to integrate technology into their classrooms to prepare students effectively for the world of work. In the light of this need to prepare students for the world of work, Ozturk and Hodgson emphasise:

Now, in the digital age, revisiting democratic pedagogy in a digital learning context, such as VLCs, is of increasing relevance and importance (2017, p. 25).

The aim of this chapter is to chronicle my becoming in a world of virtual learning communities (VLCs) and spaces. I hope that my narrative of becoming in this world of technology might resonate with many experienced lecturers and teachers who grew up in an era with no internet and no (or very few) technological tools, and who now suddenly find themselves thrust into an age where smartphones and various other mobile devices are pervasive and inescapable. These smart devices such as iPhones, MacBooks, online programmes, and so forth make university life frenetic, not only for myself but for my students as well. This means we are all busy beyond belief in a seemingly relentless push to make everything we do and experience faster and faster. In this chapter I want to share how the needs of my students, from a generation who are referred to as 'digital natives', motivated me in my becoming in a world of VLCs. Sorgo, Bartol, Dolničar and Podgornik explain the term digital native:

Digital natives are assumed to possess knowledge and skills that allow them to handle information and communication technologies (ICT) tools in a "natural" way. Accordingly, this calls for the application of different teaching/learning strategies in education (2017, p. 749).

One could say that I made a cognitive leap in my pedagogical practice and discovered my own 'pedagogical breakthroughs'; Ozturk & Hodgson (2017) describe this as a 'change in pedagogical thinking'. Technically, I can say that my students drew me into their world as I steadily adapted to this technological age of connectivity to become technologically adept. From these experiences of finding myself plunged into this new technology I realised the importance of using it constructively to prepare my students for a digital world – a world in which they could be effective teachers if equipped with the knowledge and skills to integrate this new digital technology into the curriculum. I have become part of the world of my students, or stated differently, part of the stimulating world of virtual learning communities.

As mentioned above, the aim of this chapter is to give an account of my becoming in a world of virtual learning communities (VLCs) and spaces. In effect, this chapter is a reflection of my experiences in the application of technology in my lectures. The next section will discuss the significance of reflection as a methodology in research.

Reflective Practice as Methodology

Reflection as a methodology is a very important mental exercise both in an individual's personal life and in his or her professional life. Reflection, Mortari (2015) states, takes place when an individual turns the focus on the self where the inquirer is observed by the observer himself to elucidate the epistemic acts developed in the midst of the inquiry process. One of the advantages of practising regular reflection is that it allows an individual to engage with the deeper sub-conscious part of the self and to gain a richer and deeper understanding of a person's own lived-through experiences in a more thoughtful way.

Since the 1980s the term 'reflection' has increasingly appeared in pedagogical debates in education and has been considered a central tool in experienced-based learning (Mezirow cited in Mortari, 2015). Reflection is also prevalent in the medical industry, where nurses and doctors largely practise reflection to examine their own practices – for example, how procedures were followed and how to ensure that the correct measures are in place. According to Brookfield (1995), some of the best ways of practising reflection in education is through writing biographies, journal writing and performing the action/reason-thematic procedures by taking into account the significance of events and how they rest on (or settle in) the human consciousness. In the context of this study, it means that I had to revisit (reflect on) how I used to teach and use this as a basis to determine how to promote student understanding and encourage them to become independent learners.

According to Hyatt and Beigy (1999), when individuals reflect on their practice, they learn to become critical of their own work, which fosters a transformative mindset. This transformative mindset is loaded with the potential for better teaching. Loughran defines reflection as follows:

The ability to frame and reframe the practice setting, to develop and respond to this framing through action so that the practitioner's wisdom-in-action is enhanced and ... articulation of professional knowledge is encouraged (2002, p. 42).

McDiamid (1993) confirms that empirical research has been conducted on how reflection can lead to transformative practices. Reflection is particularly important to novices in any field, as they constantly analyse the nature of their being and becoming as a conceptual phenomenon. The analysis of the conceptual phenomenon transports a person to new pathways of doing which, in turn, leads to more effective (teaching) methods. Schön (1991) explains that teachers learn to constantly examine and re-examine their practice through reflection. He describes this reflective process as 'reflection-in-action' and 'reflection-on-action' (ibid.). This means that reflection can provide new insights into the state of our teaching in terms of its current application.

There are various types of reflection. For the purpose of this chapter I will focus only on genealogical reflection. According to McEwan (2011), genealogical reflection looks at stories that offer plausible recounts of things that originated in an individual's life. As the aim of this chapter is to portray my journey of 'being and becoming' in a technological pedagogical space, I want to introduce academics and teachers into my world to see how I slowly moved away from the traditional pedagogical space to an alternative technological pedagogical space of blended learning. In this chapter pedagogical space refers to the classroom practices of teachers and how they relay the coursework material to their students. Hopefully this reflection on my journey will give academics and teachers the opportunity to learn from my experiences.

The Start of the Online or Network Society in South African Universities

One important evolution, which can also be described as a revolution, is how the recent student protest movement unexpectedly and unconsciously led universities in South Africa into a network society in which both the academic project and secular society at large have to be organised. This new virtual reality driven by technology is what I want to refer to as the Web 2.0 society. Web 2.0 technologies, which form the basis of the Web 2.0 society, are communication and information platforms, also called virtual realities, which allow users to contribute, share and collaborate with each other using the internet. These include social media platforms such as Facebook, WhatsApp, YouTube, Twitter, WeChat, and various other e- and m-learning tools. This new reality or network society has also compelled academics to make fundamental structural changes in their approaches to teaching resulting in these lecturers/academics now having to shift away from the traditional linear approach to teaching and learning towards a more multidimensional approach, where the classroom space becomes a dynamic virtual learning space. Many terms have been used to describe the teaching and learning with Web 2.0 technology, for example, open learning, distance learning, programmed learning, experiential learning and the more current blended learning. Garrison and Vaughan (2008) stipulate that blended learning entails essentially blending face-to-face and online learning to engage in meaningful learning experiences.

Many arguments have been presented for and against the network revolution. Rothblatt (2012) points out that those who refuse to repudiate the inherited traditional classroom argue that this new approach is yet another ploy for the dumbing down of national standards, which will contributes to a denatured university environment. For example, in my work context I have come to know (through anecdotal and corridor conversations) that many of my peers firmly believe that South African students are not disciplined enough to accept responsibility for their own learning, nor do they have the required resources to stay connected. Those in favour of the online or network society argue that modern-day undergraduate students entering the university have narrow concentration spans as they become bored very easily - hence they need visual stimulation that technology might provide. The network society will also assist in addressing the challenge of high absenteeism and drop-out rates as a way of freeing students from routine curricula. University management demands that academics devise new and more creative ways of learning and provide students with extra personal attention. In support of this demand, universities spend more money on more modern online platforms and constantly update their digital platforms with the latest tools in order to address the different challenges that academics might face in teaching their students. There appears to be a paucity of published works in South Africa on the effectiveness of online and computer-based teaching arguing for the use of technology and those who are against it. This is a vexed subject in any case, as most employees demand graduates that are adequately trained in the use of technology for the workplace.

Next, I shift the focus to the demands placed on higher education in the face of the Fourth Industrial Revolution (4IR).

The Fourth Industrial Revolution and What it Means for Higher Education in South Africa

According to Nancy Gleason (2018), the third industrial revolution emerged as early as the 1960s with the development of information technology and electronics, which enabled more efficient production as a consequence of the broadening of the new knowledge economy. Schwab (2016) argues that this revolution laid the foundation for the 4IR, which has its origins in Germany's manufacturing industry in the early 2000s. This is because human beings have developed the capacity to store massive amounts of data which results in machine learning. Gleason (2018) indicates that this magnificent breakthrough in Germany further lead to the development of cyber-physical systems. Cyber-physical systems sparked the development of artificial intelligence and robotics. Ragunathan Rajkumar and his team (cited in Gleason, 2018) explain cyber-physical systems as:

Physical and engineered systems whose operations are monitored, coordinated, controlled and integrated by a computing and communication core. Just as the internet transforms how we humans interact with one another, cyber-physical systems will transform how we interact with the physical world around us ... The design, construction and verification of cyber-physical systems pose a multitude of technical challenges that must be addressed by a cross-disciplinary community of researchers and educators (Gleason, 2018, p. 3).

According to Dreyfus and Dreyfus (1986), the fact that a digital computer can be used to manipulate symbols and subsequently draws inferences based on computations gives rise to a new and exciting field called cognitive simulations (CS). CS are based on problem solving strategies that a computer follows to solve a particular phenomena by using data-based information which is generated from collective human experiences. Today we see the applications of cognitive simulations in smartphones and various other technological advances made in the banking sector, social media network, and the various applications available to perform certain critical functions that save humans time and money.

These developments in the West instil a sense of urgency in how academics and teachers in the rest of the world should respond to the demands of the 4IR. Consequently, as academics (the key players in higher education) we are compelled to nurture more technologically savvy students to assist them in their own becoming in the way they respond to the world of work and the global society at large. For example, in 2018 South Africa witnessed the opening of two nuclear technology schools in Pretoria, in the Gauteng province. Pretoria is situated about 40 km from the South African Nuclear Energy Corporation's flagship facility in Pelindaba, in the North West Province. The location was strategically chosen for this initiative in order to use the nuclear plant as a teaching hub for the teaching of subjects such as mathematics, science and ICT. Project leaders at the plant were handpicked to assist with the training of the learners. The aim of this initiative is to expose learners to nuclear processes at a young age. The specialised training at these schools is intended to prepare students for careers involving ICTs in nuclear disciplines. At the launch of this initiative the Minister of the Executive Council (MEC) for Education in Gauteng, Mr Lesufi, mentioned that 'the Fourth Industrial Revolution of drones and technology would be part of these schools … This is the generation that will not solve social problems through social grants'. In the beginning of 2019 the first smart primary school with highly developed technological resources was opened in Tsakane in Gauteng Province. This is the first paperless school where learners will not be instructed by way of chalkboards, but will instead be introduced to the unlimited wonders of technology. Some of the teachers who will one day teach in similar schools might be sitting in my lecture theatres. This means that as a teacher educator I have to remain relevant to my students by preparing them adequately for their professions. Before I share my personal lived experiences and pedagogical practices of teaching over the last two decades and how I support my undergraduate students in the use of technology by adopting a technological pedagogical approach, I first want to introduce the concept of blended learning.

What is Blended Learning?

According to Donnelly (n.d.), the development of various software applications and their integration into lecture theatres has impacted on higher education in local and global contexts. Information communications technology (ICT) and online applications, he argues, are fast changing and this has made it impossible for institutions of higher learning, especially universities, to ignore them in fulfilling their strategic vision and expectation to meet the needs of diverse students. Donnelly points out that apart from the fact that ICTs have become effective teaching tools, they have also massively reduced the need for more buildings and teaching venues as increased engagement and collaboration with students and staff can now take place at the press of a button. Such integration of the best of online learning and traditional face-to-face instruction is often referred to as blended learning. This means the traditional face-to-face oral instruction and online ICTs are optimally integrated so that the strengths of each are blended into a unique learning experience congruent with the context and anticipated educational purpose. Instead of business as usual where lecturers bombard students with large amounts of information and readings, we now have to redesign our pedagogical strategies to meet the needs of our students in order to encourage self-directed and meaningful learning. This normally requires lecturers to use software simulations, YouTube, internet, smartphones, iPads, and various other small hand-held devices. In other words, instead of following a structured lecture approach, we now have to use these electronic devices in a flexible way that takes into consideration students' views and perceptions of how they think they learn best in deep and meaningful ways.

In a survey conducted by Arabasz and Baker (2003) on the use of blended learning in universities, they indicate that 80% of all higher education institutions (HEIs) offer blended learning courses. Albrecht (2006) posits that there are two reasons for HEIs offering blended learning courses, namely: (i) surveys on blended learning classrooms indicate high student satisfaction levels; (ii) more and more academics welcome the blended learning approach to teaching and learning. Simply put, blended learning surveys conducted since the early 2000s by Bourne and Seaman (2005) found that a blended learning strategy is more effective than the traditional face-to-face teaching strategy.

In the sections that follow I will share my experiences of how I used technology to stimulate students at a Further Education and Training (FET) College and how I apply blended learning as a way of supporting my students as a teacher educator at a university.

My Experiences with Technology at a Further Education and Training College

Around 2001, I was approached to initiate a pilot project at the FET college where I was teaching. We were the first FET college to start a simulated enterprise (SE) as a way of assisting our students who were doing a course on Marketing Management and Human Resources Management to understand the concept of trading between different enterprises. A simulated enterprise was a virtual business. (I use the past tense because the SE programme is no longer offered at FET colleges in South Africa.) Before we could commence the SE programme, I had to attend courses on how to incorporate the necessary technology into my lessons. The objective of this programme was to give students practical experience (real-life experience, although virtual) in trading with other companies created by other FET colleges nationally and internationally. It was during this stage in my teaching career that I realised the value of incorporating digital technology into my lessons. The students were expected to collaborate with national and international virtual companies that were also operated by college students.

As a college we had to purchase special office furniture, equipment and stationery needed in a business. Students had to develop a business plan in which they calculated their start-up capital. The sponsors of this SE programme donated the virtual start-up capital according to the students' calculations. Students also had to design all the documents needed in a business, for example, the business logo, invoices, receipts, debit notes, credit notes, and so forth. Similar to real-life businesses, the virtual business was divided into all the functions of a business, (amongst others, Operations, Finance, Human Resources, Marketing and Sales, etc). Students had to take turns to work at every workstation in the various departments. In so doing, each student was exposed to all the tasks involved in the different departments. The Accounting programme used to record business transactions and finally draw up the financial statements of the business was provided by the sponsors of the SE programme.

Students were thrilled to work in their virtual business – having regular business meetings with their colleagues to decide on which other enterprises they could sell their products to. Students especially enjoyed the electronic interaction with their overseas business associates (other students abroad) regarding how they view doing business and, in so doing, how these foreign students view the world. Based on the views and comments of my students I realised how these practical experiences and activities meant more to the students than any amount of theory I could provide. This is corroborated by Govender:

Much of the current literature clearly suggests that adopting different active teaching methods supplemented by technology enhances the quality of teaching and learning (2015, p. 30).

An additional objective for implementing the SE project was to encourage my students to engage with one another around the various functions of a business. As they were communicating with their peers, they learned how to accommodate the views of others in the decision-making process. At the end of every week each student had to submit a self-assessment of their engagements with their peers and the tasks that they performed by means of online discussions. In their self-assessment they were expected to include a breakdown of the positive and negative aspects of their experiences while working in a particular department. Furthermore, they had to design a scoring guide that evaluated the quality of their work. This not only took the pressure off me to provide negative feedback, but rather to respond with questions as to why they felt they deserved that score and to provide a justification for their opinion.

My Experiences with Technology as a Teacher Educator at a University

I have been teaching at a traditional university for the past eight years. When I started in 2011 I taught students Method of Accounting, Method of Business Economics and Method of Economics in the Postgraduate Certificate of Education (PGCE) programme. For the next three years I was responsible for the teaching and learning of the first- and second-year Educational Practice modules – compulsory modules in the Bachelor of Education (BEd) degree – plus the three commerce method modules in the PGCE programme. Since 2015 I have been responsible only for the first- and second-year Education Practice modules, because the number of students has increased considerably and it became impossible for one person to lecture all five modules. It is both exhilarating and scary to live and work in times of considerable change – a time of transformation. Higher education is in the midst of such changes – and transformation. Over the past five years there has been immense pressure on lecturers to incorporate technology in the form of blended learning approaches in their lectures. As academic staff we are constantly reminded to craft our lectures by placing the vision, mission and graduate attributes at the centre of our planning.

During my second year at this university in 2012, as I was receiving training on how to use iKamva[1] more effectively as a communications teaching tool between lecturer and students, I had already uploaded most of my learning material for both my BEd and PGCE students. Since 2013 all my learning material (including course outlines, assessments and assessment criteria) have been uploaded onto the iKamva platform. I also make use of the iKamva platform for important announcements to keep my students informed about what is happening in the course. This electronic tool has been a wonderful aid in my teaching, since it provides students with the opportunity for self-directed learning by actively engaging with me or their peers in discussions during a lecture. This platform allows me to upload interesting YouTube videos or recorded videos of their peers on important issues. One of the amazing features of this platform is that I can track how active my students are, or how interested they are in discussing pertinent issues dealt with during lectures. If I notice that they are a bit slow in responding to significant issues, I will encourage them to participate in the online discussions.

During the protest actions of 2015 and 2016 this online approach assisted me to navigate the distribution of the learning material and to communicate in general with my students. During this time I uploaded a written version of my lectures (much like an academic paper) on the work that we did not cover and used my tutors to update me regularly on social media platforms such as WhatsApp regarding any challenges students faced in completing their assessments. The following excerpt indicates how a student valued my online communication with them during the student protests in October 2016:

... your online lectures make me feel so motivated again because to be honest, these past two weeks have been hectic with protest actions and me having so much to do and not being able to consult with lecturers personally. Your email really lifted me up again and made me aware of why I am doing this course. I really just wanted to thank you for your encouragement...

In my quest for an approach to employ more modern teaching strategies, I participated in professional development programmes at university on blended learning. This training helped me to understand the theory and philosophy of blended learning a little better. So instead of just using technology simply for the sake of using it, I gradually began to combine the best of face-to-face teaching strategies and new technologies to make the learning experience more creative and digitally friendly for my students.

I recognised blended learning as a means to improve and develop the quality of my students' learning. Dwiyogo refers to using blended learning as 'future learning' – that is, an 'era of knowledge' (2018, p. 51). In other words, inspired by my students and through formal training courses at our institution, I learned how to make my learning material and support for student learning possible wherever they are – whether in the classroom, at home, in a library, just about any place where they can access the internet.

Amongst other things, I attended workshops on how to create a podcast, how to create a screencast, how to create a PowerPoint presentation with audio/sound for students to listen to if they missed a class, how to embed videos into a presentation, etc. Furthermore, I enrolled for a workshop on how to create an e-portfolio.

In 2018 I took the initiative to include a session on technology in some of the micro-teaching sessions in the second-year Education Practice module. A section on technology was infused into as many of the micro-teaching sessions (lectures) as possible. Each session is one hour long. Normally students do two lesson presentations during this time, with ten minutes allowed for feedback to each group after their presentation. With the new (redesigned) programme, only one group presented – still with the ten minutes for feedback – but with a section on technology during the last 30 minutes. Many of these extra sessions were conducted by the Centre for Innovative Educational and Communication Technologies (CIECT) at the university.

The technology sessions that were included in the second-year Education Practice module during 2018 dealt with topics such as: (i) distinguishing between traditional teaching and learning aids and/ or materials and modern teaching and learning aids/or materials; (ii) introducing an e-portfolio (two follow-up sessions on the e-portfolio were conducted during the year); (iii) connecting equipment when using a laptop and data projector in a classroom; (iv) useful applications for PowerPoint presentations; cloud services (for example, Google Docs, Google Forms, Google Dropbox); (v) an introduction to the smartboard.

Through many informal discussions with students I discovered that students genuinely appreciated the introduction of this new technology into their sessions. I suppose they also realise that this is what the world is moving towards. They would need it to function effectively in their profession as teachers – not only for themselves but as a motivation for their learners. They realise that they are being equipped in order to introduce their learners to a world of technology which in turn could inspire them (the learners) to one day study computer science.

How Technology Reshaped my Teaching Philosophy

Once a firm believer in the traditional face-to-face teaching environment where effective teaching is viewed as 'authoritative' and the teacher is seen as an 'encyclopaedia on two legs' while the learners are 'passive recipients or consumers of knowledge', has now been completely transformed by the inescapable world of technology. According to Howard, Chan and Caputi (2015), the shift to a technologically-oriented pedagogical approach hinges on two factors, that is, teacher beliefs and teacher readiness. They define teacher beliefs as a teacher's outlook, understanding or firmly held preconceived ideas about computers, mobile devices and Web 2.0 applications, and how they impact on student learning and performance. Furthermore, teacher beliefs speaks to how technology might disrupt a teacher's perception of classroom instruction and learning activities. Teacher readiness, on the other hand, speaks to teachers' perspectives on their own personal capabilities and skills to use technology effectively in the classroom and to integrate it productively into their lectures. These two variables played a key role in my personal development and growth regarding the way to teach using technology as a support base for my students. This study has demonstrated that as I was exposed to the use of technology, I became more positive about integrating these technological tools into my lessons. Furthermore, my willingness to use technology was driven not only by the benefits but also the excitement with which my students responded to the new teaching and learning environment. The more I engaged with technology and the more training (both formal and informal) I received, the definitively my preconceived beliefs about technology collapsed and I became more aware and motivated to increasingly use the new technology. Pullen, Swabey, Abadooz and Sing (2015) had a similar evidence and report that teachers' acceptance of technology was directly linked to expectation (beliefs), social influence and the teachers' attitude towards technology. Therefore it is important to understand the way teachers intended to behave, because their thinking and beliefs could significantly influence why they behave in a particular ways, which could in turn shed some light on a teacher's pedagogical strategies.

Future Goals for Implementing Technology as a Teacher Educator at a University

This section highlights some additional ways in which I would like to use technology in the future in order to provide my students with an optimal blended learning experience that will reinforce or strengthen a democratic pedagogy even further, or stated differently, that will further improve the quality of their learning.

I intend to implement a more dynamic way of communicating with my students by (i) uploading podcasts to explain important and/or difficult concepts, to explain assessments, etc; and by (ii) uploading screencasts of some of my lectures and the most important aspects of my Course Guides.

Recently I was also introduced to modern Web 2.0 applications such as Padlet and QQC (which refers to Questions, Quotations and Comments). These tools, which I have not yet used in my lecturers, will allow me to have an even better virtual presence allowing my students to share their views by posting questions, quotations or comments about their readings. Padlet, an online tool that does not use much data, can be used to create a *virtual posting wall*. Once the wall is completed, it generates a link that I need to pass on to students so that they can connect to the wall. Once a student clicks on the link, it takes them directly to the wall. For this the students can use a desktop, laptop, a smartphone or any other mobile device. The wall is designed by the lecturer using Padlet software; the aim is to check if the students have read or understood the 'pre' lecture notes or any other coursework materials they had to read prior to the lecture. The students can also be put into groups and the groups' responses can be shared on the data projector for everyone to see.

I also plan to continue the sessions on technology with the new intake of second-year Education Practice students; these sessions will include a 2-day workshop arranged with the Western Cape Education Department (WCED) to demonstrate "How to use the Smartboard". Towards the end of the year these second-year students would be expected to share their e-portfolios with me (the lecturer). Furthermore, I plan to expand the session on e-portfolios to the first-year Education Practice students as well. For the first-year students the course would simply be "An Introduction to the e-Portfolio". They would not be expected to upload their e-portfolios. It would be simply for their own/personal use. They would then continue to develop their e-portfolio in the second year.

CONCLUSION

Throughout the proliferation of published works, a plethora of research in South Africa and abroad has argued for the use of technology in classrooms by making explicit its benefits as a valuable teaching tool (Waghid, 2013; Waghid and Waghid, 2018; O'Keeffe and Clarke-Pearson, 2011). For example, Waghid and Waghid (2018) understand the use of technology in classrooms not only as a teaching tool, but also as a tool to be used to restore cognitive justice in South Africa. Others such as Yuan, Wag, Kushniruk and Peng (2017) regard the use of technology as providing a way to engage students at a deeper cognitive level, resulting in making their thinking more visible with the support of visualisation-based learning technology. These technological tools promote deep learning and improve problem-solving abilities within a certain context. The fact that the world is changing at such a rapid rate with respect to technology means that each day educators or academics need to reposition themselves in the classroom to introduce students to new software applications. The explosion of new technological developments implies that not only economic growth is on the increase - for example, the customer base of hi-tech global corporations such as Apple, Huawei, and Samsung are growing at a tremendous rate – but societal changes are imminent in our everyday lives as well. From this perspective the 4IR will bring with it "shifts in employment and education" (Penprase, 2018, p. 215). The excerpt below illustrates the world in which we will be living in the not-so-distant future:

... implantable cell phones by 2025, 80% of people with a digital presence by 2023, 10% of people wearing internet-connected clothes by 2022, 90% of the world population with access to the internet by 2024, 90% of the population using smartphones by 2023, 1 trillion sensors connected to the internet by 2022, over 50% of internet traffic directed to homes and appliances by 2024, and driverless cars comprising 10% of all cars in the United States by 2026 (Penprase, 2018, p. 215-216).

In the light of Penprase's (2018) prediction, higher education has to reposition itself in the way it envisages teaching and learning to support the learning needs of students. It is imperative that we as lecturers in higher education update our curricula in response to this accelerating pace of technological transformation of the economy and society. As lecturers we will have to renew our mindset and our outlook with reference to our pedagogical strategies in order to meet the demands of the fast-paced network society created by the Fourth Industrial Revolution.

As someone who grew up in an era where the word *internet* did not even exist in my initial teacher training course, I had to adjust my approach to teaching and learning to meet the learning needs of my students. I realised that students are becoming less interested in exclusively face-to-face instruction. As students become technologically adept, they are increasingly stimulated by a combination of the traditional (face-to-face) approach to teaching and learning, and an infusion of contemporary technology into lectures and other learning material. This realisation and the realisation that the world is rapidly moving into an era where, amongst other developments, robots will increasingly be taking over human tasks, computers will be solving many of our problems as well as creating a world in which there will be driverless cars. Such development have totally convinced me that a blended learning approach to teaching and learning is what our students need in order to prepare them to function optimally in this new world.

REFERENCES

Albrecht, B. (2006). Enriching student experience through blended learning. *Research Bulletin*, 12.

Arabasz, P., & Baker, M. B. (2003). Evolving campus support, models for e-learning courses. *Educause Centre for Applied Research Bulletin*. Retrieved from http://www.educause.edu/ir/library/pdf/ecar_so/ers/ERS0303/EFK0303.pdf

Bourne, K., & Seaman, J. (2005). *Sloan-C special survey report: A Look at blended learning*. Needham, MA: The Sloan Consortium.

Brookfield, S. (1995). *Becoming a critically reflective teacher*. San Francisco, CA: Jossey-Bass.

Donnelly, R. (nd) the nature of complex blends: Transformative problem-based learning and technology in Irish Higher Education. In Y. Inoue (Ed.), *Cases on online and blended learning technologies in Higher Education*. New York: Information Science Reference.

Dreyfus, H., & Dreyfus, S. (1986). *Mind over machine: The power of human intuition and expertise in an era of the computer*. New York: The Free Press.

Dwiyogo, W. D. (2018). Developing a blended learning-based method for problem-solving in capability learning. *The Turkish Online Journal of Educational Technology*, *17*(1), 51–61.

Garrison, D., & Vaughan, N. M. (2008). *Blended learning in higher education: Framework, Principles and guidelines*. Jossey-Bass.

Gleason, N. W. (2018). *Higher education in the era of the fourth industrial revolution*. Singapore: Palgrave Macmillan. doi:10.1007/978-981-13-0194-0

Govender, S. (2015). Students' perceptions of teaching methods. *South African Journal of Higher Education*, *29*(3), 23–41.

Howard, S. K., Chan, A., & Caputi, P. (2015). More than beliefs: Subject areas and teachers' integration of laptops in secondary teaching. *British Journal of Educational Technology*, *46*(2), 360–369. doi:10.1111/bjet.12139

Hyatt, D. F., & Beigy, A. (1999). Making the most of the unknown language experience: Pathways for reflective teacher development. *Journal of Education for Teaching*, *25*(2), 31–42. doi:10.1080/02607479919655

Inan, F. A., & Lowther, D. L. (2010). Laptops in the K-12 classrooms: Exploring factors impacting instructional use. *Computers & Education*, *55*(3), 937–944. doi:10.1016/j.compedu.2010.04.004

Kerr, C. (2001). The uses of the university. Cambridge, MA: Harvard University Press. (Original publication 1963)

Lesufi, P. (2018, April 24). Lesufi launches nuclear technology schools. *Pretoria News*.

Loughran, J. J. (2002). Effective reflective practice: In search of meaning in learning about teaching. *Journal of Teacher Education, 53*(1), 33–43. doi:10.1177/0022487102053001004

McDimiad, G. W. (1993). Changes in beliefs about learners among participants in eleven teacher education programs. In J. Calderhead & P. Gates (Eds.), *Conceptualising Reaction in Teacher Development*. London: Falmer Press.

McEwan, H. (2011). Narrative reflection in the philosophy of teaching: Genealogies and portraits. *Journal of Philosophy of Education, 45*(1), 125–142. doi:10.1111/j.1467-9752.2010.00783.x

Mortari, L. (2015). Reflectivity in research practice: An overview of different perspectives. *International Journal of Qualitative Methods*, 1–9.

Nørgard, R. T. (2018). *The playful university: Poetry, passion, polyphone and potency.* Paper presented at the Philosophy and Theory of Higher Education Conference, London, UK.

O'Keeffe, G. S., & Clarke-Pearson, K. (2011). The impact of social media on children, adolescents, and families. *Pediatrics, 127*(4), 800–804. doi:10.1542/peds.2011-0054 PMID:21444588

Ozturk, T. H., & Hodgson, V. (2017). Developing a model of conflict in virtual learning communities in the context of a democratic pedagogy. *British Journal of Educational Technology, 48*(1), 23–42. doi:10.1111/bjet.12328

Penprase, B. E. (2018). The fourth industrial revolution and higher education. In N.W. Gleason (Ed.), Higher education in the era of the fourth industrial revolution, (pp. 207-229). Singapore: Palgrave Macmillan. doi:10.1007/978-981-13-0194-0_9

Pullen, D., Swabey, K., Abadooz, M., & Ranjit Sing, T. K. (2015). Pre-service teachers' acceptance and use of mobile learning in Malaysia. *Australian Educational Computing, 30*(1). Retrieved from http://journal.acce.edu.au/index.php/AEC/article/view/55/pdf

Rothblatt, S. The future isn't waiting. In R. Barnett (Ed.), *The future university: ideas and possibilities*. New York: Routledge.

Schön, D. (1991). *The reflective turn: Case studies in and on educational practice.* San Francisco: Jossey-Bass.

Schwab, K. (2016). *The fourth industrial revolution.* Geneva: World Economic Forum.

Songer, N. B. (2007). Digital resources or cognitive tools: A discussion of learning science with technology. In S. Abell & N. Lederman (Eds.), *Handbook of research on science education* (pp. 471–491). Mahwah, NJ: Lawrence Erlbaum Associates Publishers.

Sorgo, A., Bartol, T., Dolničar, D., & Podgornik, B. B. (2017). Attributes of digital natives as predictors of information literacy in higher education. *British Journal of Educational Technology, 48*(3), 749–767. doi:10.1111/bjet.12451

Waghid, F. (2013). *Towards the democratisation of senior phase school science through the application of educational technology* (Unpublished Doctoral thesis). Stellenbosch University, Stellenbosch, South Africa.

Waghid, Z., & Waghid, F. (2018). [Re]examining the role of technology in education through a deliberative decision making approach: In the quest towards democratic education in South African schools. In Y. Waghid & N. Davids (Eds.), African democratic citizenship revisited. New York: Palgrave Macmillan.

Yuan, B., Wang, M., Kushniruk, A. W., & Peng, J. (2017). Deep learning towards expertise development in a visualisation-based learning environment. *Journal of Educational Technology & Society*, *20*(4), 233–246.

ENDNOTE

[1]   iKamva: an online learning platform where academics collaborate with their students to support their programmes which are initiated by the virtual online community of practice.

This research was previously published in Student Support Toward Self-Directed Learning in Open and Distributed Environments; pages 216-236, copyright year 2019 by Information Science Reference (an imprint of IGI Global).

Chapter 22
Non-Verbal Communication Language in Virtual Worlds

Ivonne Citarella
National Research Council, Italy

ABSTRACT

Over the years, the virtual space has been changing, and the skills acquired by users have been improved, and the avatars, as well as the settings, have graphically become more and more sophisticated. In virtual reality, the avatar without an appropriate animation would move in jerks in a disharmonious way similar to a robot, but endowing it with a particular postural animation, you make a conscious choice of what information you want to transfer with its appearance and its posture. In recent years, research has focused on the study of communication and its importance. The purpose of this contribution is to analyze the animations present in Second Life trying to trace a socio-psychological picture of the non-verbal communication process in a virtual environment.

INTRODUCTION

In the 16th century, even Leonardo da Vinci became interested in "interpersonal intelligence" and the importance of observing the behavior of others. Here is what he advised the young artist:

"Be vague often times in your strolling to see and consider the sites and acts of men in speaking, contending, laughing or fighting together, what acts are in them, and what acts do the surrounding people, dividers or viewers of these things".

In this trace left by Leonardo we discover all the importance of observation, which allows us to grasp important aspects both within people and within the environment, which surrounds us. Participant observation is, in fact, a methodology that was used in the investigation described in this essay

Virtual worlds have hardly been studied by the academic world and it is not easy to find references to compare this work with. This essay wants to impact on the potential of this world, which is believed to stimulate a lot of thoughts on relational processes but also, as will be seen, on communication processes.

DOI: 10.4018/978-1-6684-7597-3.ch022

The author, starting from her own didactic experience in the field of communication and combining it with participant observation started years ago in the virtual world, decided to examine:

1. What connection exists between the real, or physical, world and the virtual world with respect to communication processes and whether either of the two worlds influences the other;
2. Whether there is a breakdown of the stereotypes of Non-Verbal Communication that, learned in the course of one's life, are activated spontaneously in the real world and if, instead, they are translated into the virtual world or completely abandoned.

Thanks to participant observation, three areas in which the aforementioned communication has developed strongly in recent years were explored:

1. Physical characteristics (The avatar's body)
2. The avatar's clothing
3. The movements and postures of the body (Animations)

The final purpose of this contribution, starting from the observation of the virtual world most frequented by adults, is to demonstrate the potential of this world to be useful for future projects dedicated to social actors as young people, not only adults, as observed in this survey.

Young people could acquire, by playing, greater awareness of the importance of communication, in particular, non-verbal, without excluding the possibility of involving them in acquiring the knowledge of new professional skills aimed at programming in virtual environment.

Non-Verbal Communication (NVC)

Communication plays a decisive role in everyone's life and separating verbal communication from non-verbal communication is not possible because both are part of the communication system as a whole.

Non-verbal communication performs several useful functions such as: providing information, managing impression, exercising influence, regulating interactions, and expressing intimacy.

While verbal communication is explicit because it uses words, non-verbal communication acts using other transmission channels such as posture and gestures (La Pensée, Lewis, 2014), in the majority of cases spontaneous movements, some of which are handed down from one's own culture, but which the body unconsciously transmits and which can escape even oneself. Furthermore, Ekman (1982) states that Non-Verbal Communication (NVC) can find its roots in culture where some gestures / emblems summarize a concept socially shared and understood in the community of social actors but at the same time it manifests itself in a completely personal body language that somehow escapes the actor's own awareness.

Non-communication is not possible and within humans that is an innate and necessary condition.

The expressive function of non-verbal behavior includes both the communication of interpersonal attitudes and the exchange of information relating to the presentation of oneself. The latter analyzes the aspect of the social actor, its proxemics, its posture and a whole series of information that returns an image of himself (feedback) that influence the reading of the interlocutor (receiver).

Therefore, as Burgoon, Guerrero & Floyd (2010) state, there are eight non-verbal codes commonly recognized by academics such as the kinesics, the olfactory, the haptic, the chronemic, the vocal, the proxemics and the code linked to the physical aspect without excluding human intervention on the environment.

Some of these codes are automatically excluded from this investigation for obvious reasons, since the author turns to a virtual field of investigation in which, for example, the olfactory code is not plausible. One more that one could also think of excluding is haptic signals, that refers to communication through contact even if, (although the sense of touch is not feasible in the virtual environment), the author's experience gained in world gives her reason to believe that even a virtual hug could trigger strong emotions. In fact, during her long presence in virtual worlds, the author believes that the emotions that can be felt in a virtual environment can have the same intensity as those experienced in real life.

Here below the author will report the elements observable in the virtual world:

- stature,
- physique,
- face shape,
- eyes colour,
- colour and condition of the skin

These elements provide general information about the person, ethnic group, age, gender, state of health, etc.

There is no significant relationship between people's physical conformation and inferred personality based on stereotypes but rather a cultural connotation.

Generally following stereotypes correspond to:

Slim people: introverted, tense and nervous
Fat people warm, extroverted, sanguine
Muscle people: strong and energetic.

In the case of avatars they replicate connotations of their own culture that ensure attention from the other sex.

The relational aspect that develops in the *game* (a somewhat simplistic term for the impact it has on relationships) such as Second Life is highly engaging and therefore able to excite like real relationships.

The *silent language* of the body, the *hidden dimension*, as defined by Hall (1959) is instead a code that the author considers valid for the study of non-verbal communication in the world.

Proxemics is the study of the relationships between human bodies in three-dimensional space used to describe how people position themselves in space in relation to each other and how different demographic factors such as age and sex alter those behavioural spacings. Hall outlines the notion of personal space, describing four "personal reaction zones" of intimacy around the body: Intimate, Personal, Social and Public (Hall, 1959).

Proxemics behaviors are "semi-conscious" and derive from social mediation, cultural influences and the level of intimacy of the participants and they are important because people do not know that they unconsciously distance themselves from others on the basis of these factors. Therefore, they provide a valuable mechanism for analyzing groups of people not only in the physical world but also in the virtual one. Because they are spontaneous these simple mechanisms do not require sophisticated technologies to be reproduced and can be replicated with any avatar. Burgess (1983) tested some of Hall's claims by observing groups of people in public spaces and noted that these areas of interpersonal space vary depending on a wide range of factors including age, gender, level of intimacy and cultural background of the people interacting.

Proxemics includes those hidden messages because they are not perceived as conscious. Hhowever, they exist in both the sender and the receiver and they are used in the regulation of physical distancing in social relationships. Proxemics is also possible between two avatars and can be reduced to the case in which the type of intimacy turns into a contact or into estrangement / avoidance in the case of the actors deciding to end the relationship.

In addition to the arrangement of bodies in space, proxemics also deals with the mutual orientation of those bodies with regard to the gaze.

In real life the eyes are a large structure, consisting of nerves and are surrounded by extraocular muscles that can contract thousands of times a day in many different ways. They are excellent channels for transmitting information from the inside to the outside of the individual; strong communicative importance ("glare at", "look out of the corner of your eye", "eat with your eyes", "his eyes shone" are phrases that testify to this). They generate different types of glances with an immediacy that often makes them the preferred communication channel. The pupils dilate and shrink according to the amount of light present in the environment. It has also been shown that if people see something that excites or scares him, their pupils dilate more than would be normal in the existing light conditions and therefore offer additional information to the interlocutor.

Adler writes *"If we close our ears and do not listen to the words of men, but observe their actions, then we will discover that each of them has given its own individual meaning to life and that all their attitudes, their ways, their gestures, their expressions, the characteristics of the behavior are in harmony with it. "* In this statement it is possible to read the communicative importance of body language.

The "theory of equilibrium" proposed by Argyle and Dean (1965) deals with the relationship between mutual gaze and proxemic distance. In essence, equilibrium theory proposes that proxemic spacing and mutual gaze can both be used to indicate intimacy and that people reach a "balance" composed of a distance and an ideal meeting of the gaze that varies with their interpersonal comfort. If one of these factors varies, for example, if the gaze is prolonged or the interpersonal distance decreases, the people interacting often vary the other factor to preserve this balance (Argyle & Dean, 1965). This is also possible in the virtual world when an avatar with an *"eye tracker"* points the face at an avatar of the opposite sex, prolonging the 'looking' time then he/she approaches her/him.

Spatial behaviour is an area around a person (personal space) and defense of the same from possible intrusions of others.

Spatial behavior includes:

- interpersonal distance
- body contact
- orientation
- posture

The integration of these elements gives rise to what Kendon (1973) defined as "Spatial configuration".

Interpersonal distance Informs about: intimacy and relationship between interlocutor's dominance relations social roles.

Hall's (1966) proxemics study of the use of social and personal space, based on cultural and interaction rules highlighted four types of distances:

1. Intimate
2. Personal
3. Social
4. Public
    a. Intimate distance (0-45 cm): area of intimate relationships, of possible contact (activation of the tactile and olfactory apparatus)
    b. Personal distance (45-120 cm): area of friendships, possibility of contact (activation of the olfactory and visual apparatus)
    c. Social distance (120-360 cm): zone of formal relationships, absence of contact (activation of the visual and auditory apparatus)
    d. Public distance (360 cm onwards): area of public situations (visual and auditory apparatus only with amplification)

Changes in interpersonal distance during an interaction can provide a lot of information. Getting closer to a person can express the intention to initiate an interaction; moving away from the interlocutor can signal the desire to interrupt the conversation.

Each culture follows its own social norms of regulation of interpersonal distance (e.g. Western versus Middle Eastern)

Appearance is an other important part of non-verbal communication and includes physical attributes such as height, eye colour, hair, skin, face shape, attractiveness as well as clothing and other adornments or accessories such as tattoos, jewellery and objects that are characteristic of them, associating them with groups, beliefs etc.

Of course, since the social actors in this investigation are avatars, we certainly cannot refer to care of the body in the hygienic sense but rather to observe whether the avatar is neat or unkempt in its appearance.

As for the voice code: since the so-called "*voice*" option is widely used in the virtual world and it includes all the vocalized signals through which messages are expressed such as the tone, the increased volume of the voice, or the famous "*resource silences*", strategically used in verbal communication because even silence speaks. These can all be observed in the virtual world, providing an emotional picture of the interlocutors and their relational intentions.

All these codes, combined, are part of the broader communication system, an interdependent system with distinctive structural features and specific functions that can also be separated while still carrying out the transfer of information and therefore also communicating independently of the verbal flow.

Non-verbal behaviours influence perception to the extent knowledge of it is considered an instructive educational path aimed at improving the skills of managing social relations between people.

The non-verbal dimension influences the judgment of superiority / inferiority and friendship /hostility towards others five times more than language and as Mehrabian (1972) states that non-verbal signals are more effective communicating emotions.

Mehrabian found that 55% of any message is conveyed through non-verbal communication such as facial expression, gestures, postures, etc.) and only 7% is conveyed through the words and 38% through vocal elements.

The *body language* or *body communication* or *"bodily communication"* represents the expression of hints or movements of the body, as a privileged and effective communicative element. It has gained more attention in the virtual world over time. It has been reproduced in the virtual world and over time it has gained more and more attention and a new specific sector has been perfected. (Linden Scripting Language -LSL)

Thus, the third question arises:

• If it is true that all humans communicate in an unconscious, non-verbal way,, when their avatar represents a social actor, what happens in the communicative process transferred into it and above all what characteristics will their avatar assume? Which codes, of those feasible in the virtual world, will an avatar respond to, since each user will consciously transfer them to their avatar?

Starting from the assumptions of the Laban Movement Analysis (LMA) which is a framework for describing human movement and expression, Laban's observations cover the following general principles:

1. Movement is a process of change: it is a "fluid and dynamic transience of simultaneous change in spatial positioning, body activation and energy utilization" 2. Change is structured and ordered: due to the anatomical structure of the body, the sequences that follow the movements are natural and logical. 3. Human movement is intentional: people move to satisfy a need, and therefore actions are guided and targeted. As a result, intentions are made clear through our movement. 4. The basic elements of human movement can be articulated and studied: Laban states that there is a compositional alphabet of movement. 5. Movement must be approached at multiple levels to be understood correctly: to capture the dynamic processes of movement, observers must indicate the various components and how they are combined and sequenced

The more we deal with the movement of the character, the more mastery we can gain on the nuances of the empathic experience. Empathy is a concept related to human perception of other beings as rational creatures. Empathy is rooted in the virtual environment as the very life of the avatars, running along the path of emotions and social relations, attributing meaning and strength to them thanks also to the development of animations that allow empathy to be expressed in more and more meaningful and more credible ways itself.

The Survey

Second Life is the virtual world chosen by the author to conduct this survey on non-verbal communication. This choice is justified by the presence of many objects built into it by users. Not only does Second Life offer the possibility of replicating real life in every moment but it also offers the possibility of investigating and deepening the object being studiedi.e. Non-Verbal Communication, since each user is offered the possibility of customizing their avatar. The author logged into the game for the first time in 2009 and having understood its great potential, continued to interact in it.

The author's first research concerned an aspect linked above all to the earning opportunities of users who, thanks to the versatility of the program, were able to build objects by reselling them and becoming a source of income, even in real life. The great versatility and great intuitiveness of the program for construction and also of computer programming has allowed everyone to become increasingly specialized builders and programmers so that, as happens in the real world, some stylists and builders have established themselves by becoming famous in the field of fashion or construction.

The virtual world of Second Life over time has been enriched with many objects and functions but above all it has become increasingly humanizing. With this term the author refers to the fact that the replica of the real world has been increasingly perfected giving the residents the opportunity to live a "second life" by surrounding themselves with objects very similar to those of real life but also perfecting their own appearance, which over time has increasingly improved in its exterior and movements. A strong boost to the virtual economy was given by offering users the ability to create more than one avatar in their own name, while maintaining anonymity. This aspect has had a strong impact on both the economy and relationships as the same user has been able to benefit from multiple avatars by deciding at his discretion to reveal himself or not. The so-called hidden identities of some users can create imbalances. In romantic relationships and friendships can cause breakups, especially when the basis of this choice is the inappropriate use of the second or third avatar to hide any purpose. The author divides users into two categories: those who have no difficulty in declaring who they are in real life and those who decide to remain anonymous.

Of course, everything depends on the value given to the game, that is, if you want to consider it only as an opportunity for recreation even by assuming deviant behaviours in which to include a certain libertinage or to stick to a more 'correct' behavior, remaining anchored to values of respect, education and morality that you have in real life, without hiding. The testimonies collected by the author make her believe that for most people the virtual world is an opportunity for recreation and that the relationships that are intertwined within it are based on the construction of credibility and feelings such as love and friendship are experienced as "real" emotions despite having been born within a virtual context.

From a strictly economic point of view, having more avatars means supporting an additional cost to ensure that it has a pleasant appearance. As the author will explain later in the essay, the outward appearance has become a fundamental element within the game. A good look is what is most aimed at and concerns the whole avatar, from the top of his hair to his toes and involves the majority of users as if even in the virtual world, as in the real one, there has been a approval and this is visible simply by looking around and observing the other avatars.

If people learn to analyse their gestures, people will be more able to control them when the time comes. People often notice emotions but they expressed them by using body language. By better self-observation, people can better understand themselves.

The Body of the Avatar

Over the years the virtual space has been transforming and developing thanks to an improvement in the skills acquired by users / avatars in the field of creating or building shapes and skins as well as the reproduction of a large number of objects increasingly similar to those of the real world.

The "shape" (the avatar's body) represents the starting point, the so-called birth (rez-day) in the virtual world of avatar, with a fancy name. The default avatar, body, is assigned when signing up and if the user thinks it is not nice the shape can be improved to the user's wishes through the marketplace. If it it is not thought to be suitable then there is a large number of shapes on sale in world, in specific stores or on the marketplace shopping sector (the shopping present on the game's website). With this facility the shape, closest to the user's wishes may be chosen. Once purchased, it's possible to keep modifying it and to further customize it. In the survey, the author observes that more men encounter difficulties customizing their physical appearances and many of them delegate this, even for a fee, to people who are more capable of doing it, by providing them detailed instructions. Some of them commission an avatar resembling their appearance in real life by sharing their own photo to the builders. From this point of view, men seem to be more inclined to dress their avatar rather than modify it while women, on the contrary, are able to customize it with greater dexterity.

The introduction of *meshes* has significantly improved the graphic rendering of all the objects reproduced in the virtual world by giving them a high graphic definition but at the same time, it has weighed down the graphic complexity of the program to the extent that it now requires more and more efficient personal computers.

Customizing the avatar is the first step in non-verbal communication.

The face, as evidenced by studies in the field of morpho-psychology, is a communicative map in which each part is carefully studied: the height of the forehead, the arching of the eyebrows, the distance of the eyes, the position and width of the mouth, its fullness and fleshiness, the height of the cheekbones, the gaunt or plump cheeks, the size of the nose, and the orientation, up or down.

Unknowingly, however, personalizing an avatar combines unconscious wishes and the affirmation of who they are in real life. Consciously it is decided what to eliminate, what the users do not like in their real appearance, while trying to enhance what they believe to be strengths. For example, they choose to have clear eyes, if they don't have them real life or if they do not have full lips, they opt to have them in *in-world*. It could also happen that, for example, if the social actor has a certain eye colour in real life that he believes to be a strong point, of which he is very proud, he will meticulously search for the shade that comes the closest to his real life eye colour. The sector dedicated to the replication of the eyes is broad and offers a wide range of eyes both in tone, size and shape.

Someone who knows a bit of morpho-psychology could read from the real face and from the face chosen in the virtual world differently but, extraordinarily, something of oneself, even if only in a somatic trait makes both faces similar.

The face is the elective area for non-verbal communication. It has over 20 highly contractile muscles that allow different combinations of contracture that generate different directions of the gaze, giving many facial expressions (Parker, 2014)

The expressive and communicative function of the face goes hand in hand with phylogenetic development: Animals further down the evolutionary scale express themselves through posture (e.g. birds raise their crest or feathers). Primates are endowed with an elaborate repertoire of facial expressions, due to social life and therefore the need to communicate for individual survival(Ekman group 1982). Human emotions are manifested by facial expressions. There are typical facial movements for each of the fundamental emotions (at least six have been identified): happiness, surprise, fear, sadness, anger, disgust.

Choosing facial features that demonstrate sweetness or severity, sensuality or vulgarity will depend on what you want your face and body to communicate. What kind of message do you want to send with your face?

A round face will tend to denote a gentle, warm, spontaneous, but also naive and defenceless character while a longer face may stand for an emotional, independent character with a predisposition to be in control of everything.

A square face may instead denote narcissism, practicality and a tendency to be methodical.

The lips describe something of the person. For example, thin lips may denote a restrained and selective sensuality and a preference for details; full lips, on the other hand, may indicate great sensuality, charisma and self-confidence.

Even the size of the eyes can suggest personal characteristics: large eyes, for example, can suggest very receptive subjects meanwhile small eyes are more used by people who are not very emotional, very reserved and even lying.

Reading the face and body of a person with whom you interact in real life, even if only instinctively without having in-depth knowledge of non-verbal communication or morpho-psychology, allows you to do a 'hot reading' and if one gets as a feedback a sense of familiarity, he/she will establish a less rigid interaction both in the tone of voice and in the posture, transmitting openness to dialogue.

In-world (iw) not only the face, but also the rest of the body, can be changed.

A man, for example, can choose to have a fitter or less sporty body, to have the features of a boy or a more mature man but almost never elderly as having a pleasant and youthful appearance is what most aim at. Indeed, in virtual worlds, aesthetic beauty has very high standards that do not go well with the idea of old age as the age of many residents approaches or exceeds 60 years. Having the appearance of a young, muscular and maybe sexy man reinforces the message that in the real world there is a beauty standard, to which the majority of users aspire to and to which they commit a lot of economic resources

Deciding to have light skin or to opt for a dark complexion, to have freckles or light eyes are all possible choices when customizing the avatar.

Each part of the body is carefully studied and you can change them. You can also change the measurements of the body, by either keeping your real life measurements or completely changing them.

After modifying the shape and possibly the skin you can decorate the avatar with accessories, of which there are many, such as eyelashes of any length, hair of all types and colours, moles to add to the face, make-up (eyeshadow, blush and lipstick), sold in various shades, nail polishes, not forgetting tattoos, piercings of all kinds and jewellery.

The choice of clothing concludes the transformation.

The final result is an image of what the resident sends to the virtual world. The avatar will represent the social actor, as if it were an extension of himself in that world, activating a process of recognition and openness to dialogue even between avatars that, having been personalized, follow the social actor's characteristics, which are transferred to the avatar. Indeed, it would be difficult to find two identical avatars precisely because each avatar has been customized according to individual criteria.

The Clothing of the Avatar

In virtual worlds. as in real life. it's possible to observer the following elements about clothing:

- Clothes
- make-up
- hairstyle
- accessories
- status symbol signals

They provide information on group membership and social identity and are a strong tool for self-presentation and socialization.

These elements contribute to one's own identity definition of situations and contexts of interaction definition of status and social power such as fashion.

Fashionable clothing can be classified as a non-verbal communicative element, which pushes people to comply with it in order to gain acceptance by society.

Imitating is, above all, a psychological tendency because it satisfies the need for social adhesion and consensus, but also for distinction and change, thus satisfying these two opposing tendencies which belong respectively to the social and individual spheres of a social actor. What people wear, for example, can express conformity to other groups in society, or individuality and personalization, which allows them to distinguish themselves from others. Clothing is a business card that allows us to let others know a part of ourselves: which social stratum we belong to, what work we do, therefore it has a codifying social function and emits a flow of information. In a society of appearances, dress has not only a decorative function. In fact, at first glance, well-dressed refers to the phase of true knowledge, making a good impression will earn points for the social actor. Clothing is a code with a low semantic content, which communicates shared meanings and which changes very often.

Communication goes through the para-verbal which manifests itself in the dressing style and / or the objects each individual surround himself/herself with.

What people expressed yesterday could be very different from what people expressed today. Its interpretation depends above all on the social and historical background in which people are integrated. The choice of dress is aimed at communicating to others the message people want to convey and the curriculum that people want to introduce themselves, something that represents them externally. Clothes delimit and mark individual time, making it possible for a person to be one and multiple, in formal meetings, in work, in free time, in private life: the passage from one dress to another during the day represents a way to control one's emotional responses in relation to the stimuli coming from the outside.

Looking at the virtual world, what will be the avatar's choice on dressing?

Will a certain greater formality or sensual sobriety be maintained?

In order to establish this, the author decided to investigate, on the basis of keywords, the Marketplace which, as it has been said, is dedicated to online purchases, which collects many products offered for sale by stylists and builders. The decision to focus more on the virtual world of Second Life was also dictated by the large amount of products created in the world and offered for sale on the Marketplace in order to define the tastes of users and how they influence sales trends.

Undoubtedly, there has been a great development in the production of objects in Second Life over the years that allow users / residents to live a second life as a virtual replica that over time is aimed at always humanizing more and more both the avatar and the surrounding environment.

On the Marketplace, many items for sale are dedicated to clothing. That, not only gives an idea of the movement of linden (currency used in the game) but also demonstrates the great attention given to the avatar aspect.

All the categories present in the General level are listed below:

Categories: Animals, Animated Objects, Animations, Apparel, Art Audio and Video Avatar Accessories, Avatar Appearance, Avatar Components, Breedables, Building and Object Components, Buildings and Other Structures, Business, Celebrations, Complete Avatars, Furry, Gachas, Gadgets, Home and Garden, Miscellaneous, Real Estate, Recreation and Entertainment, Scripts, Services, Used Items, Vehicles, Weapons, Everything Else

The Marketplace category called Apparel is made up as follows:

Category of Apparels are distributed as following: Children's items are 140.335, Men's items are 300.882, Unisex items are 50.430, Women's items are 1.901.675.

The price of apparel items are distributed as following: from L $ 0 to L $ 10 are 28.2791 items, from L $ 11 - L $ 100 are 93.1054 items, from L $ 101 to L $ 500 are 1.215.193, from L $ 501 to L $ 1,000 are 66.888, from L $ 1,001 to L $ 5,000 are 29.230, Over L $ 5,000 are 460.

An analysis of the data shows that, in the Apparel category, the largest share of items on the marketplace is dedicated to women's clothing followed by men and then children. Prices start from 0 linden up to over 5,000.

The clothing chosen to dress one's avatar also falls within one of the seven codes of non-verbal communication and which is used to represent the social actor.

In the virtual field, a lot of clothing aims to externalize a certain sex appeal for both female and male gender and the wide choice of products allows you to aim for refined, sexy but not necessarily vulgar, casual, aggressive or romantic clothing.

Unlike about ten years ago, today it is difficult to meet avatars whose appearance is not carefully crafted because it is possible to develop their appearance without investing large economic resources as there are many products that are available for 0 linden, gifts and promotions.

Formal dress is compulsorily required in some important ballrooms and beyond the elegance of the room. The live music, played by good singers and the suitably dressed residents enrich the charm of the ballroom itself.

How do the residents choose to dress?

By conducting a search in the Marketplace based on the keywords 'Sexy', 'Casual', 'Romantic' the result is the following:

Key word: Sexy: Men's clothing 17.058, Women's clothing 375.237, Unisex clothing 2.066
Key word: Casual: Men's clothing 59.969, Women's clothing 244.916, Unisex clothing 2.742
Keyword: Romantic: Men's clothing 733, Women's clothing 15.221, Unisex clothing 40

The data give an idea of users' clothing preferences.

In all three keyword searches, it can first be noted that the sector that records the highest number of items is that dedicated to women and the number of sexy outfits is far greater than that of casual or romantic clothing.

The data dedicated to men's clothing reveal a higher quantity of casual items.

This research suggests that the trend is to dress one's avatar, especially if female, in a sexy way.

This trend is, first of all, the result of the type of culture in which one is continually subjected to the aesthetic canon, with an advertising bombardment promoting statuary bodies, which continually pushes the individual to desire aesthetic features and objects by activating mechanisms that make the social man inadequate and unhappy when he does not respect the standards of consumption. This leads the man to chase an ephemeral happiness towards which the so-called liquid society of Bauman (2017) is reaching out. In fact, as the sociologist states, it is in the creation of a "liquid" society, defined in this way because of that feeling of fleetingness and frustration in which social relations are diluted and become rare, that the search for the sense of self and happiness becomes difficult to achieve. He also affirms that only when we manage to get out of this spiral of consumption, gratification and frustration, to go in search of the values that we have somehow lost or forgotten, in that Other we will perhaps be able to find those bonds and that happiness that we long for.

"Happiness is a state of mind, body, which we feel acutely, but which is ineffable. A feeling that cannot be shared with others. Nevertheless, the main characteristic of happiness is that of being an opening of possibilities, as it depends on the point of view with which we experience it. [...] But there is a second line of evolution of the concept of happiness: happiness as a final state, as an objective to which we must strive. Happiness as a concrete goal, which we have forgotten (Bauman, 2017).

Even Goffman (1969) believes that many actions are dictated largely by consumerism, which makes you lose sight of the most genuine relationships and sometimes it shows what they would like it to be, but which it is not. In Second Life the real life status of the residents is not relevant as what matters is who you are in that virtual world and no one cares who you are in real life, if you are poor or rich, if you are a prominent person or an ordinary one.

As in real life, in virtual worlds too the fashion fits into behavioral models, which once it is accepted and shared by all, it guarantees the social consensus. Fashions in virtual worlds were born and developed as a form of socialization and this adaptation derives from the influence that institutions have on individuals. Through fashion, individuals define themselves and feel congruent with the social reality. It is an instrument of social cohesion, therefore it can be said that the possession of fashionable goods assists the entry into the group, and the contact with others.

Simmel (1996) states: *"As soon as the individual side of the situation takes over from the socially compliant one, the sense of modesty immediately begins to act"*.

So, what is the sense of modesty in a virtual world?

Analyzing the trend of fashion in the virtual world oriented towards a sensual fashion it would seem that the sense of modesty could be overcome with greater ease in the choice of clothes. Then, it is probably defined by an internal social consensus, which is diverted into greater disinhibition. Showing off fashionable and sexy clothes, therefore, should not only be considered an act of ostentation, but also a search for approval, without forgetting that the history of mankind is given by a continuous search for a compromise: to merge with one's social group but at the same time stand out in it with one's own individuality.

From the birth time in Second Life, a new opportunity begins to create friendly or sentimental relationships, for having fun exploring or dancing with friends or alone, or to start a new job.

How you move, how you dress, how you talk, how you interact will be the pillars of your identity within the day. They will also become the basis on which your reputation and credibility will be built.

This aspect related to the happiness given by possessing ephemeral things for many Second Life residents represents one of the reasons that pushes them to stay in this virtual world where, with few economic resources, everyone can live a second life in which everything can be owned from the villa by the sea or in the mountains, elegant clothes and jewels and, above all, entertainment is guaranteed given the presence of many refined ballrooms or discos and above all the presence of other users.

In this regard, during the harsh period of isolation, which was imposed on the Italian population due to Covid-19, the author was able to observe how the virtual world played a secure aggregative role and psychological support. Unlike real life, where physical contact was forbidden and social distancing was imposed, in the virtual world proxemics and contacts were still allowed and this helped the users to overcome the sense of loss and fear in this very complicated period.

What was expressed yesterday could be very different from what was expressed today. Its interpretation depends above all on the social and historical background in which it is integrated: it is read differently by every social stratum. The choice of dress is aimed at communicating to others the message we want to convey and the curriculum with which people want to introduce themselves, is something that represents them externally. Clothes delimit and mark individual time, making it possible for a person to be one and multiple, in formal meetings, in work, in free time, in private life.

The Animations

Spatial behavior, such as posture, has an important function for many animals to signal dominance, threat, submission etc. Posture takes shape under the dimensions of dominance, submission and relaxation-tension Mehrabian (1969)

Kinesics behavior includes:

- Body movements (torso and legs)
- hand and arm gestures
- head movements

They often accompany speech and indicate affective states during an interaction and they are the non-verbal signals most influenced by the social and cultural context.

Another category of non-verbal signals studied within Non Verbal Communication by Kendon (1970) is:

- individuals in interaction (especially in dyads) perform similar movements, imitating each other (mirror body movements) –
- "interactive synchrony" (e.g. when one of the two moves, the other moves too; when one of the two changes the direction of body movements, the other does too)

There are some possible explanations for these interactions:

- biological: instinct for self-defences and survival in case of danger or learning for imitation;
- social: "social influence" like other social behaviours, especially if the "influenced" person is in a position of subordination or subjection to the "influencing" person

Among the non-verbal behaviours, hand movements are those most linked to spoken language and those that accompany speech in a more evident way. They seem to follow the cultural rules of the reference language and culture (cultural differentiation) like verbal communication. They are realized in the existing hemisphere in front of the speaker

In the hemisphere of gestural space there are three coordinates or axes:

a)   speaking-external
b)   right-left
c)   top-bottom

Ekman and Friesen (1969) make the following classification of gestures:

Emblematic: can be completely replaced by verbal expressions and they are independent of the presence of verbal language. They have their own semantic meaning. Illustrators have the function of accompanying words and their intonation, in order to facilitate the communication. They can serve to qualify, reinforce, contradict communication.

Emotional: indicators correlated with an emotional state.

Regulators: define the roles of the interlocutors in the conversation, signalling and regulating the maintenance and change of speech shifts.

Adapters: related to the satisfaction of physical needs or the expression of emotional states, rebalance a state of tension manifested on a somatic level.

Kinesics: head movements involve the neck muscles that regulate the orientation of the head. There is a relationship between orientation of the head and attention: the orientation of the head allows us to understand where or towards whom / what people direct their attention. It is difficult to deduce the object of attention only through the direction of the gaze.

The avatar personalization process does not only concern the physical appearance and clothing but also its posture and gestures.

In virtual reality, the avatar without appropriate animation would move in jerks, in a disharmonious way similar to a robot but by entrusting it with a particular postural animation, a conscious choice is made on which information to transfer in one's posture. Within the process examined, two aspects can be distinguished: the communicative and the informative. Non-verbal communicative behavior groups gestures that allow the sender to send a precise signal to the receiver in a conscious way. Interactive non-verbal behavior includes gestures used to influence and change the interactive behavior of others. Intermediate models affirm that body language is neither an expressive nor an exclusively communicative modality but that it presents different levels ranging from expressive behaviors to typically communicative behaviours that have the intention of communicating a socially shared code.

In the virtual world, the fine line between communication and information becomes almost imperceptible.

The programming of animations in the virtual world of Second Life has had a great boost in recent years as they allow, by adding them to your avatar to "animate" it and make it less robotic through more harmonious movements, which make the avatar move more like a human.

It is possible to access two types of animations: 1) those that are worn and attribute the posture and 2) those contained in the objects that, thanks to the animations, allow their use based on multiple choices.

The animations in point 1), called Ao. They concern the posture that the actor decides for its avatar to assume when it pauses in place and also decide how it walks. The choice of the Ao is a personal choice available from a wide range, purchasable on the marketplace. These Ao are programmed differently for male and female avatars and contain more animated sequences that last a certain time. However, the duration can be modified (it can be stretched or shortened). Some examples of these kind of sequences may be:

arms crossed - hands in pockets - look at the clock - step forward / backward with the arms a little dangling (Figure 1-2)

Women have a wretched movement with a sequence similar to this: hands behind the back - small turnaround - adjust the hair - hand on the hip (Figure 3)

Even the walk is different depending on whether it is a posture programmed to animate male and female avatars and, for example, it can make male avatars and women assume a more or less marked masculine movement, through the accentuation or the absence of hip-swaying.

Figure 1.

Figure 2.

Figure 3.

As regards the animations referred to in point 2), a chair-shaped object can contain a series of animations (which can be accessed thanks to the interaction with a menu) for various ways to sit, such as, for example, legs crossed, elongated, gathered etc. The menu, over the years has become increasingly full of animations, providing the choice of a session which not only takes into account the gender but also if it is a single character or a couple that will use it.

The number of items relating to Ao present on the Marketplace were approximately 26,878 and by entering the keywords Female, Male, Sexy, Elegant, Cute, Gentleman, Smart, Sweet, Girl, Boy, the search provided these data: 2,850 Ao Female, 2.019 Ao Male, 1.903 Ao Sexy, 1.953 Ao Girl, 1.609 Ao Skin, 628 Ao Boy, 558 Ao Sweet, 407 Ao Elegant, 126 Ao Smart, 69 Ao Gentleman.

As can be seen from the extrapolated data, using the keywords in the marketplace, there is a large choice of Ao each characterized by a different movement. This allows Second Life residents to purchase / acquire the most suitable animation to assign to their avatar and above all to decide which type of message they want to send with their posture.

The author notes the great difference between the real world and the virtual world that takes place: what in real life shares a "*hidden message*" becomes a conscious action in the virtual world.

In fact, by choosing how the actor wants to make the avatar move, the attention is focused on those movements or postures that in real life are spontaneous.

Will the choice of the social actor focus on the animation of a macho man or gentleman, an adult or a boy, a provocative or classy woman, shy or elegant in her movements?

Will the choice of Ao be guided by how similarly one moves in real life or by how the social actor would like to move? These questions recall another important sociologist with his famous phrase The medium is the message (McLuhan,1967) it could say "the body is the message".

For example, if in real life you unknowingly use your hands while talking, the choice of animation will be dictated by real life feature, which becomes even more important when you have to animate an avatar.

Gesticulation is part of those spontaneous movements that belong to the speaker and their movement is aligned with the narration. The hand, in that narrative moment with its movement, is not just the hand but represents the speech that the speaker narrates. In this regard, in addition to a certain posture or walking style, one can choose some hands, reproduced through mesh, called *dynamics hands*, which make the hands open or close. In this way, they seem more realistic. Of course, in the virtual case we only take into account that gesticulation has its own importance but it cannot in any way replace the story that the hands can communicate while making a verbal narration as stated by McNeill.

From what has been explained so far, the author states that once again the theory of the three flows (Citarella, 2017) applied to the observation of non-verbal communication in a virtual environment, allows to acquire an added value.

In fact, in addition to the skills that can be acquired in a playful way in the virtual world to make them become real earning opportunities in real life, customizing an avatar means that everyone learns to observe more carefully those gestures that are part of every human being and which are activated automatically and unconsciously in real life. If learned at a younger age, they would allow adolescents to understand much of what is transferred to people unconsciously with the movement of the body and also what people transfer to the audience.

In recent years, animation programmers have also produced avatar's heads with animations, taking another leap forward in the humanization of facial expressions. Once activated by the user, these animations can make the face assume expressions that transfer emotions. As is well known, there are communication channels that reveal emotions more than others, such as, for example, the face and the gaze, which are important vehicles for the transmission of emotional status as they are not directly controlled by the issuer, unless you are not able to simulate an emotional state like an actor.

The face is one of the first parts of the body observed by the interlocutor and to be perceived. It is not by chance that the particular sector of non-verbal communication is that of the study of facial micro expressions, lasting less than a second (Ekman, 2009) that allow one to understand if there is an inconsistency between verbal and non-verbal communication in how much non-verbal communication helps to reveal the two processes in action, cognitive and emotional. If, for example, a "deceptive" story is told, the cognitive load increases by lowering the emotional one with a reduction in body movements and eye movements, hands etc.

Identifying, recognizing and interpreting facial micro-expressions is possible only after following specific training through the analysis of rapid facial signals, i.e., the contractions of the supra-ocular, orbicular and zygomatic frontal facial muscles. In fact, thanks to micro expressions and their reading, it is possible to trace a lie, for example, as the body will speak inconsistently with respect to the verbal utterance. When non-verbal communication, which always accompanies verbal language, is discrepant, there is, in fact, the suspicion of a lie (DePaulo, 1992). This discrepancy, of course, cannot be detected in an avatar. Non-verbal communication is not only important for discovering a lie but it contributes to the formation of first impressions, attraction, social influence, emotional expression and other interpersonal processes.

According to the author, what is relevant for the purposes of her investigation which have been extended to the face, through a simple programming language encoded by programmers. These new features make life in the game more realistic. It is a constantly evolving path, but it will certainly tend to reach ever higher standards, which will develop more and more harmonious gestures capable of creating emotions. These gestures will also be more effective in sending messages related to non-verbal communication. For example, setting the face on a sequence such as: smile - wink - parted lips expresses a message of sunshine in the character and certainly not gloom and sadness. The smile is equivalent to a program that intervenes on the zygomatic muscle that is raised, the eyes that narrow and the mouth that opens and widens.

Furthermore, it is possible to recognize, by their appearance and their facial expression, who may represent a threat because the message they send is of a rude and threatening avatar.

There are also expressions of anger that involve frowning, opening the lips

The messages of non-verbal communication have the great advantage of being able to be expressed simultaneously while the message linked to verbal communication is unimodal, meaning that the social actors can only express themselves with one word at a time. Furthermore, during a verbal communication flow much more attention is paid to what one intends to express, looking for the most suitable words to convey the message.

Instead, non-verbal communication is continuous, independent and spontaneously transferred without paying specific attention to it because it is multi channelled. It's for these reasons that non-verbal communication is the primary conveyor of emotions because

in most cases, non-verbal communication is more effective than words, which are more limited. Moreover, it is able to express feelings that could be more difficult to show to others because emotional expression varies with culture (Sooriya,2017).

To give an example, if someone reaches a disco where there are many avatars, the gaze of those present, represented by the *"eye tracker"*, focuses on the newcomer who is being observed. Its face, its body, the clothes it wears and the first eye contact will speak for him / her, and the first eye contact is identical to when, for example, somebody enters the waiting room of a doctor's office where other people are waiting for their medical examination turn.

The concept of the gaze becomes very interesting within some cultures in which it represents a sign of respect. It would be interesting to understand if some behaviors of that specific culture are maintained in the virtual world or are overcome. Just think of the Mediterranean countries or the Latin American countries called contact cultures that show a greater predisposition to more physical and closer interpersonal contacts, unlike what happens in the North European or Asian culture in which interpersonal contact is very limited. Non-verbal communication can have a different meaning according to different cultures.

The introduction of facial expressions in the virtual world has also included the world of children. In fact, the so-called Animesh children created by Zooby have introduced avatars into the virtual world of children who assume, based on their age, facial and body expressions, very similar to those of babies and children. Each age, called stage, corresponds to a phase of growth (raising the head, rotating the body, sitting, crawling, walking, kissing and the vocalization da-da, ma-ma, etc.) (Figure 4)

Imagining having children in a virtual world may seem like sheer madness, but in Second Life, which is commonly called a game but which the author considers as a great sociological experiment, social relations are the priority.

Figure 4.

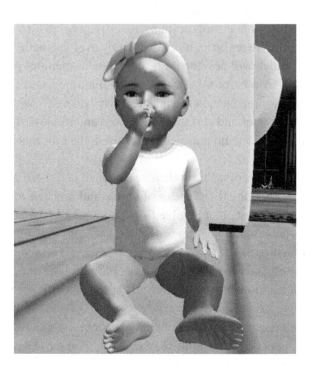

The whole virtual world revolves around the social life of users. Friendly or sentimental relationships are created continuously. Inside it is possible to get married, even in a chapel, with a ceremony during which the spouses exchange promises in the presence of a minister of the church, witnesses, bridesmaids and pageboys as if it were a real wedding. Beyond the prejudice that one can have towards these actions, the author wants to highlight how every moment lived in the virtual world is achievable thanks to the many animations that have been created by users and which, as mentioned, have improved over time. with particular attention to the movements and expressions that the moment requires. Each phase of a romantic relationship, from the first meeting to having a baby, is supported by increasingly realistic animation. Having a baby is possible both by adopting it and in adoption institute or it is possible to simulate pregnancies with birth in ad hoc clinics. Pregnancy will bring the changes typical of this event to the shape with the growth of the abdomen until birth.

Simulation is one of the strong points of Second Life, used both in the military and in the medical field to allow soldiers or students to carry out experiments that otherwise could not be carried out in real life given their dangerous nature.

The idea that behind this game there is a great production of programming that makes the virtual economy flourish may seem excessive but from a sociological point of view one wonders if in addition to the economic benefit, what benefit do users derive from it?

Users tend to replicate not only their real life relations and behaviours, but also those relations on behaviours which the users fail to achieve in real life, such as marriage or to have a child. Moreover, it commonly happens that users who have a relationship in the virtual world, decide to meet outside the game (offline) and start creating a relationship in real life.

Figure 5.

Then there are the aspects related to some features of the real life personality that the user decides to hide. Therefore, in the virtual reality they tend to modify these traits. The virtual path brings to light not only a malaise or discomfort linked to the personality but above all a chance for those who are disabled and confined to a wheelchair to move, thanks to their avatar, without constraint.

The collateral aspects of this "game" are innumerable. This is why the sense of "Second Life" takes on fullness and concreteness. Paradoxically, it is as if in real life a mask is perpetually worn relating to the role that others expect to be fulfilled; meanwhile the avatar, which is a reproduction of oneself, represents the social actor free to live his life in a way which better suits his\her personality or that is in a better accordance with what he/she wishes to be. Another important dramaturgical model of Goffman (1959) cannot fail to return to mind, according to which personal interactions are influenced by who we are dealing with and, as a consequence, we adopt "masks", i.e different ways of acting according to our interlocutor. Beyond the avatar there are social actors who can decide to live their virtual reality with the same fears and beliefs rooted in them or start a path of personal knowledge that can help to acquire more self-esteem, since the user may decide to keep hidden their real life identity.

The author, who interviewed many people / avatars in the Italian and foreign communities existing in the game was able to deduce from the data collected that their living in the game has brought about changes from the most ephemeral aspect of taking care of oneself for physical fitness to clothing, to a better understanding of the English language, the in-world official language, up to more radical changes concerning the personality such as overcoming shyness, going out etc., and to undertake stable senti-mental relationships born in the world and lived offline.

Finally, the automatisms related to animations (without which the avatar would be inexpressive) it can be said that over the years the emphasis animations that are created by users, have reached a high degree of refinement and are now able to express emotions. The movements assumed by them will reveal such coordination schemes as to give an instant reading of the ongoing evolution within the game as if you were living in real life.

CONCLUSION

Second Life's slogan: "The virtual world created by users" is a true slogan.

Indeed, it is only thanks to the users that this large container has been enriched day by day, from an interpersonal point of view, by giving the opportunity to both meet many people from all over the world and to acquire awareness and skills that otherwise would not have been grasped.

It is thanks to the continuous experiments carried out by users, staying in the world and interacting in it with the learning-by-doing mode, that the virtual world has come alive and come to life, transforming this virtuality into a place where imagination and creativity can have free rein by providing spaces freely shared by all to spend moments of relaxation or fun as well as of learning.

Interactional skills in the virtual world have always been facilitated by its inherent characteristic of virtual playful lucidity, which allows the elimination of social and territorial distances without the implications of the real world such as social status and income indicators. Just as in the real world, only by frequenting other avatars, users can determine if a relationship is either a friendship or a romantic relation, but surely what helps in breaking the ice is what each avatar communicates through its own appearance. However, verbal communication through chats, public and private, helps deepening mutual knowledge.

This participant observation allowed the author to assess that there is a close connection concerning non-verbal communication within the two worlds, physical and virtual. Therefore, the production of objects and creations aims for a more and more truthful reproduction of the physical world in the three areas this analysis focuses on, which are, as stated at the beginning: 1) Physical characteristics (The avatar's body) 2) The avatar's clothing 3) The movements and postures of the body (Animations).

In these three areas it was possible to detect advances that have been made in the development of non-verbal communication in virtual worlds so they tend to be more and more like the real world. In particular, that awareness, well-founded by the choice that each social actor makes for their avatar, has increased over the years both by users and by programmers.

Furthermore, with their work and their wide choice of animations and objects, avatars were able to reproduce their way of communicating in any environment and in any context more like the real world.

Non-verbal communication stereotypes spontaneously learned in the physical world such as proxemics remain the common element that is replicated in virtual environments in the same way as in the real world and which takes place spontaneously.

It's a communicative need transferred to the avatar in an environment in which it could be assumed that the use of chats and the voice could be sufficient to establishing social relationships but this is not so. Non-verbal communication implies a socially shared code and an intentional action of encoding and decoding.

The social actor will assign to the avatar certain postures and clothing which will give information about the actor himself even before he actively talks with those he does not know yet. As the author has highlighted in the previous paragraphs, non-verbal communication is an essential component when each user consciously decides to assign a gesture and an aspect to their avatar.

Therefore, it is possible to assert that not only are there stereotypes maintained and translated from the real world to the virtual world, but more strikingly when the social actors decide which animation or posture to assign to the avatar that will represent them, they show a significant shift in the awareness of non-verbal communication.

The real leap forward was to strengthen the emotions with animations that show

on the face but also on the body and the author is sure that the further we will go, the more developments will be made in this field.

This one is the added value that, in a playful way the virtual world manages to bring out spontaneously and that should be grasped from a didactic point of view for its strong potential.

At the moment Second Life is mostly used by adults who through playing have acquired new skills. Therefore, there would be incredible benefits if adolescents were given the possibility to use a virtual platform. The *digital natives, who* have an innate familiarity with the digital world, would benefit from a virtual platform, which unlike video games, gives them the possibility to exchange ideas with their peers, a sort of virtual student campus, where imagination and creativity could be developed as an open window on the world where it is easy to get in touch with worldwide communities

Adolescents could give free rein to their imaginations and above all they would spontaneously acquire an awareness, which was acquired only slowly by adults with.

Applying the concept of sharing knowledge and creativity in a context in which the insinuation of negative values such as that of the differences of race, religion and culture does not represent a deterrent, but at the most, the land on which to grow a cohesive community:

1)   observation and learning of non-verbal communication;
2)   learning the programming language in a playful environment;
3)   earning opportunities in the programming or research sector;
4)   learning or perfecting a second language through chat and voice interaction.

Learning by playing is a formula that would offer excellent results not only from the point of view of personal growth but also from the point of view of professional opportunities.

Adult users choose the immersive world as a place to meet friends and spend free time or to weave romantic relationships but at the same time deepen their awareness of non-verbal communication in a spontaneous way by transferring its strengths to the real world as well as self-esteem, the knowledge of one's potential, reputation and credibility which are values that in the real world tend to be repressed by flattening certain personal evolutions.

Real life and its observation is the way to expand the expressiveness of non-verbal communication in virtual worlds thanks to which awareness is increasing spontaneously, year after year, involving the users to use it to express their emotions and what they really are, by evolving year after year the program itself.

REFERENCES

Bauman, Z. (2017). *Meglio essere felici* [Better to be happy]. Lit Edizioni Srl.

Bavelas, J. B. (1990). Behaving and communicating: A reply to Motley. *Western Journal of Speech Communication, 54*(4), 593–602. doi:10.1080/10570319009374362

Buck, R. (1988). Nonverbal communication: Spontaneous and symbolic aspects. *The American Behavioral Scientist, 31*(3), 341–354. doi:10.1177/000276488031003006

Burgoon, J. K.,Guerrero, L. K., & Manusov, V. (2016). Nonverbal Communication. Routledge.

Citarella, I. (2017). The Added Value of 3D World in Professional, Educational, and Individual Dynamics. In G. Panconesi & M. Guida (Eds.), *Handbook of Research on Collaborative Teaching Practice in Virtual Learning Environments* (pp. 275–297). IGI Global. doi:10.4018/978-1-5225-2426-7.ch015

DePaulo, B. M. (1992). Nonverbal behavior and self-presentation. *Psychological Bulletin, 111*(2), 203–243. doi:10.1037/0033-2909.111.2.203 PMID:1557474

Ekman, P. (1982). *Emotion in the human face*. Cambridge University Press.

Ekman, P., Sorenson, E. R., & Friesen, W. V. (1969). Pan-cultural elements in facial displays of emotion. *Science, 164*(3875), 86–88. doi:10.1126cience.164.3875.86 PMID:5773719

Goffman, E. (1969). *La vita come rappresentazione quotidiana* [Life as a daily representation]. Bologna: il Mulino.

Hall, E. T. (1959). *The silent language*. Doubleday.

La Pensée, E., & Lewis, J. E. (2014). Timetraveller™: first nations nonverbal communication in second life. In Virtual worlds Nonverbal Communication in Virtual Worlds: Understanding and Designing Expressive Characters. ETC Press.

Mehrabian, A. (1969). Significance of posture and position in the communication of attitude and status relationships. *Psychological Bulletin, 71*(5), 359–372. doi:10.1037/h0027349 PMID:4892572

Parker, J. R. (2014). Theatre as virtual reality in Virtual worlds Nonverbal Communication. In Virtual Worlds: Understanding and Designing Expressive Characters. ETC Press.

Patterson, M. L. (1983). *Nonverbal Behavior: A Functional Perspective*. Springer. doi:10.1007/978-1-4612-5564-2

Simmel, G. (1996). *La Moda*. SE edizioni.

Sooriya, P. (2017). *Non-verbal communication*. Lulu Publication.

Tanenbaum, J., Seif El-Nasr, M., & Nixon, M. (2014). Basics of nonverbal communication. In Virtual worlds Nonverbal Communication in Virtual Worlds: Understanding and Designing Expressive Characters. ETC Press.

KEY TERMS AND DEFINITIONS

Animation Override: Second Life animations are frequently triggered by scripts in order to achieve a variety of effects such as walking, sitting and flying animations, as well as dances, handshakes, hugs, or other things.

Avatar: A representative of a real person in the virtual world.

Builder: Who creates objects in virtual worlds.

Gestures: A type of inventory item that trigger your avatar to animate, play sounds, and/or emit text chat.

Linden Dollar: The Linden Dollar (L $) is the virtual currency used as a bargaining chip in the Second Life economy.

Script: Created through an in-world editor similar to a text file editor. Key words that perform specific actions or run when an action is performed are highlighted. The language used to write scripts is Linden Scripting Language (LSL), and is an event-oriented programming language.

Second Life: An online digital electronic virtual world (MUVE) launched on June 23, 2003 by the American company Linden Lab following an idea of the latter's founder, physicist Philip Rosedale. It is an IT platform in the new media sector that integrates synchronous and asynchronous communication tools and finds application in multiple fields of creativity: entertainment, art, education, music, cinema, role playing, architecture, programming, business, etc.

Skin: A texture that is applied to your classic avatar body and head. Skins provide flesh tones, makeup, and fine shading detail.

Voice Chat: Communication optionally by voice.

This research was previously published in the Handbook of Research on Teaching With Virtual Environments and AI; pages 394-415, copyright year 2021 by Information Science Reference (an imprint of IGI Global).

Chapter 23

Using Social Image Sets to Explore Virtual Embodiment in Second Life® as Indicators of Formal, Nonformal, and Informal Learning

Shalin Hai-Jew
Kansas State University, USA

ABSTRACT

Capturing Second Life® imagery sets from Yahoo's Flickr and Google Images enables indirect and backwards analysis (in a decontextualized way) to better understand the role of SL in people's virtual self-identities and online practices. Through manual bottom-up coding, based on grounded theory, such analyses can provide empirical-based understandings of how people are using SL for formal, nonformal, and informal learning. This chapter involves a review of the literature and then a light and iterated analysis of 1,550 randomly batch-downloaded screenshots from SL (including stills from machinima) to explore the potential of social image analysis to make inferences about human learning in SL in the present.

INTRODUCTION

"Illusion is the first of all pleasures" or *"L'illusion est le premier plaisir" f*rom Francois-Marie Arouet (Voltaire, 1694 – 1778) in *La Pucelle d'Orléans* ("The Maid of Orleans")

Started on June 23, 2003, Second Life®, a virtual immersive world, quickly became the leader in the immersive virtual world space, enabling participants to create edgy humanoid avatars and designed three-dimensional worlds. In cyber years, SL has gone through several lifetimes in these 15 years. In its early days, SL was referred to as "the closest thing to a parallel universe that the Internet currently offers" (Chin, 2007, p. 1303). SL was a space for "virtual settlements" and virtual communities (Harrison, 2009), where people could engage through their digital avatars with unusual SL surnames and in designed

DOI: 10.4018/978-1-6684-7597-3.ch023

electronic spaces over time. A base model avatar or graphical humanoid figure could walk, run, sit, fly, swim, and hover; in early years, they could add customized moves like dancing. As developers learned how to use the Linden Scripting Language, they could add various additional motions. A research team that used the scripting for research described some of the capabilities (back in 2007) and some of their work-around within the limitations of the scripting language and environment:

Programming is achieved with the Linden Scripting Language (LSL), which provides a wide range of capabilities; at this time LSL includes 330 built-in functions, including: vehicles, collision detection, physics simulations, communication among users, inventory management, playing audio and video files, and more. However, LSL was clearly not designed to construct bots; scripts are only attached to objects, not to the user's avatar directly. We have come around this limitation by attaching a ring to our avatar. The ring object can then run a script, and the script can then be used to move the avatar and animate it, so that it appears walking while moving, as well as performing other tasks required by our bot. (Friedman, Steed, & Slater, 2007, p. 3)

Over time, the base model also started gaining degrees of freedom in their movements. The online space was marketed as a space for alternate explorations and ways of being. Unlike online games with clear player purposes, this space was open-ended or "free-range" (Chin, 2007, p. 1304), and people could make their own meanings. Another term applied to social virtual worlds has been "free-form" and "social" as contrasted to goal-oriented game-based virtual worlds in that the first group enables self-defined objectives (Hassouneh & Brengman, 2014, p. 330). Some of the main motivations for going into virtual worlds discovered in their research were the following (in descending order): friendship, escapism, role-playing, achievement, relationship, and manipulation (Hassouneh & Brengman, 2014, p. 330). An older study categorized people's reasons for going online to social virtual worlds on three main motivations: "functional, experiential, and social" (Zhou, Jin, Vogel, Fang, & Chen, 2011, p. 261); in this work, social virtual worlds (SVWs) are defined as "three-dimensional (3D), Internet-based, immersive, massive multi-user virtual environment wherein participants interact through their virtual representatives (i.e., avatars) for various purposes, including business and educational endeavors" without central plots or storylines (Zhou, Jin, Vogel, Fang, & Chen, 2011, p. 261).

Beyond the creation of digital avatars for its free users, Linden Research, Inc. enabled its paid users to map out their discretized "islands" (aka "private regions") with physical geographies, define rules for access, and populate it with digital avatars and objects. According to the company, the respective regions are comprised of 65,536 virtual square meters, and the costs at present are $600 and $295 maintenance fee monthly for Full Regions, $600 and then a $345 monthly maintenance fee each for Skill Gaming Regions, $225 and $125 monthly maintenance fee for Homestead Regions, and $150 and a $75 monthly maintenance fee each for Openspace Regions ("Private Region Pricing," Apr. 2018). Within each region, there are limits on how many prims and objects may be used.

Over time, those who owned land in SL could add sound design (various sound effects, music) beyond vocal speech. Over time, the humanoid digital avatars have acquired more nonverbal to augment para verbals to increase the sense of their real-ness. Image "textures" could be applied to digital objects.

Over time, AI agents were deployed on this space as high-level chatbots. There were built-in features on the space to enable the finding of others, and the teleportation to islands of interest. There were built-in cameras for both still image and motion-video capture and export on the platform.

Almost from the start, those in education looked to SL as a possible platform for enhancing human learning and extending human subjects research. In its heyday, maybe 2007 – 2011 or so, SL was the site of numerous islands related to higher education and libraries. Designers would go online and build up whole 3D models of campuses—particularly well-known structures like sports arenas, outdoor lecture halls, libraries, quads, and classrooms. (One space of Princeton University even had automated squirrels running around.) [It may be that the heyday of virtual worlds may be around 2011 – 2014 or so: "Virtual worlds (VWs) are three-dimensional (3D) environments in which users either have a goal to According to VW research firm KZero (2012), in the fourth quarter of 2011, the total number of registered users of VWs amounted to 1700 million people. In Second Life® (SL) alone, 36 million users are currently registered, including more than 1 million active users (Linden Lab, 2013). There are not only a lot of users of VWs, but also a lot of hours are spent in-world. For instance, during the last 10 years, SL users spent the equivalent of 217,266 years of time inworld (Linden Lab, 2013)." (Hassouneh & Brengman, 2014, p. 330)]

Even a cursory read of the academic literature and mainstream media captures the heady sense of promise of SL for education then. There were hopes that the in-world physics engine would enable virtual labs that would mimic in-world labs. A "physics engine" is shorthand for the code that creates a sense of the world and its personages, animals, and objects, and how they interrelate. One authoring team explains further:

A virtual world uses various mechanisms to determine how objects and avatars move or evolve over time. Physical simulations model natural behavior like gravity and collisions, but detailed simulations of interactions can be computationally expensive, necessitating various animation and scripting routines. Virtual worlds also require AI techniques like path planning and crowd simulation to manage nonplaying characters, avatars not controlled by humans, to perform routine tasks. (Kumar, Chhugani, Kim, Kim, Nguyen, Dubey, Bienia, & Kim, Sept. 2008)

There were early hopes that immersive spaces would enable faster acquisition of skills and knowledge, such as those related to foreign language learning and healthcare. However, this commitment did not ultimately last. In a work written a few years ago, one author asked, "What ever happened to Second Life?" and described a sense of an abandoned space, with a feeling of a "ghost town" (Wecker, Apr. 22, 2014). A more recent work suggested that the allure of a "second life" was not a sufficient draw and that Facebook supplanted the promise of Second Life. That author wrote of a 2% survival rate from created accounts in 2013: "Of the 36 million Second Life accounts that had been created by 2013—the most recent data Linden Lab will provide—only an estimated 600,000 people still regularly use the platform." (Jamison, Dec. 2017) And users may well be individuals who are visiting but who do not necessarily purchase "islands." Some authors wonder whether people really want a "second life" to their real one, and some memes directly note this: "SL: Because You Never Had One In The First Place."

A first-person exploration of *Second Life®* today does show many of the traditional haunts have long disappeared. The artificial intelligence island is gone. A few of the U.S. government's best educational sites on SL still exist (think NASA and NOAA). The common references to Second Life® URLs (SLURLs) have long passed out of the common educational lexicon. There are still live events that draw a dozen or more people, but the majority of the sites are empty—even at various hours of the day and night. It is still possible to "ride" airplanes, blimps, trains, horse-drawn carriages, rockets, and cars. There seem to be some first-person mystery games available, but these require additional purchases in order to enable the avatar to see certain virtual builds and to interact with them. There is not a sense that SL is a residential place to hang out and explore being. Indeed, there are still some vestiges of the SL boutiques that sell changes of clothing and looks, islands with virtual pets for sale, and some weak signs of commerce.

Formal, Nonformal, and Informal Learning on SL Through Scraped Social Imagery

To update the sense of how SL is used for learning, a less direct research method is deployed here. This work starts with a literature review to set the context. Then, the author scraped substantive sets of publicly-available social imagery from SL and shared on two major social imagery-sharing sites: Yahoo's Flickr! and Google Images. ("Social imagery," broadly speaking, refers to images shared through user-generated contents on social media platforms and the Social Web.) These include screenshots of in-world images as well as video stills from *machinima* (machine + cinema) taken in SL. The depictions in SL are informed by the actual world to varying degrees. Many avatars are reproductions of people's actual appearances in many cases, and many real-world spaces are re-rendered in the virtual. For others, they build structures and floating worlds that are enabled by the virtual world physics engine and ephemerality, with constructions that would not be possible in the real world. "Hyperrealism" refers to the created objects that are designed to seem more real than real because of the depth of details and high resolution.

While this research is indirect—after all, the virtual world is already a step outside of lived reality, and the screenshot of that imagine-fueled space is yet another step out, these images can be informative because they capture what the individual sees as relevant from SL and is using imagery to convey a scene or scenario with egos (human, animal, or other) and entities (groups) and contexts. Within these may be social meaning and shared understandings—based on socially defined visual languages and cultural understandings. SL is a highly social virtual world (SVW), and social media such as image-sharing sites are also highly social, albeit through the mediation of 3D and sound and interactivity in the virtual world, and through still imagery in the latter. (This work takes the approach that the Web is a social space itself.) If the people engaging in SL are capturing images of themselves and their experiences and making these available on social media—to share with friends, to accentuate messages on web logs (blogs), and other reasons—these works may bear a second look; after all, these works have been doubly- or multiply- shared.

The general method of capturing images based on a text search from a social media image content-sharing site has been used to surface insights about human identity and phenomenon:

Photo sharing provides a unique lens for understanding how people curate and express personal dimensions of their identity. People use photos to define and record their identity, maintain relationships, curate and cultivate self-representation, and express themselves. Moreover, people who share provocative images have been found to advocate for the right to be one's self, advocate for the rights of others, and protect others. Due to the freedom associated with sharing among weak social ties, digital image-sharing can provide more opportunities for self-expression than traditional photo-clubs. (Andalibi, Ozturk, & Forte, 2015, p. 232, with numerical endnote citations removed)

These social images are decontextualized from their original contexts. They are not shown within the context of the web logging (blogging) entry or entries. These are not shown on social networking site (SNS) pages, such as on Facebook. If the images themselves were part of an original screenshot set or gallery show, they are most certainly not connected that way now. Even though these images from *Second Life®* are decontextualized, they still may be analyzed in a stand-alone way to understand (1) people's senses of embodied identity from constructed (disembodied) avatars, and their (2) senses of physical places from designed virtual places. From these analytics, based on bottom-up coding and grounded theory (Glaser & Strauss, 1999, 1995, 1967), it is possible to infer the roles of the digital avatars and some of the types of learning occurring in SL: formal, nonformal, and informal. Formal learning generally refers to the learning that occurs in accredited learning contexts, from K12 through higher education; nonformal learning refers to structured but non-accredited learning; informal learning refers to contexts in which learning occurs as an unplanned byproduct of other activities. This learning framework enables the initial exploration of persistent virtual worlds for different types of learning.

A few years after its launch, Second Life® was being described as becoming…

a venue for education – education in the arts of the virtual world, and also a place for real world institutions to promote themselves and offer classes. There is a cornucopia of virtual colleges and universities devoted to matters ranging from SL escort services to SL building and scripting skills. Real world universities with a presence in SL include Brown University, Loyalist College, McMaster University, Nova Southeastern University, Ohio University, Kent State University, Texas State University, The University of North Carolina, University College - Dublin, The University of Illinois, The University of South Denmark, and Trinity College, in addition to student and faculty groups from many other real world institutions. (Davidson, 2007, p. 5)

Various aspects of institutions of higher education represented in SL include welcome signs, footpaths, notecard greetings, institution logos, links to the campus newspaper, an art gallery, and public classes and events (Jennings & Collins, 2007, p. 718). Institutions of higher education did not want to get left behind, but many also were hedging their bets about the possible value of investing fully into the platform. Full virtual campuses have been built in SL. In one virtual campus, four types of virtual spaces were built to evoke the campus: "common student campus, collaborative zones, lecture rooms and recreational areas" (De Lucia, Francese, Passero, & Tortora, 2009, p. 220). Born-digital elements were built to enable "synchronous lectures and collaborative learning" (p. 220). Plug-ins to learning management systems (LMSes) were integrated for a more unified online learning experience. The prior examples show a focus on formal higher education. However, given the breadth of types of learning and structured learning spaces on SL and activities, it is not unlikely that there will be observations of all three types: formal, nonformal, and informal.

This work is comprised of two parts. The first part involves an analysis of two image sets, 988 images from Flickr captured using Flickr Downloadr and 592 images from Google Images (with the Picture Downloader Professional). Screenshots of some of these images may be seen in Figures 1 and 2. The analytics occurred in two stages: first, what may be seen of egos and entities in their relationships with themselves, others, and the context, and, second, a follow-on analysis about what sorts of formal, nonformal and informal learning are taking place. The image set was cleaned to remove non-Second Life® imagery, such as ads, photos, and other images that seem to have been accidentally caught up in the data download.

Even an early look at the captured screenshots show how the images are cropped by either the focus of the in-world camera (or screen capture software) or the post-capture post-production. There are objects or motions that serve as attentional centerpieces.

Figure 1. A zoomed-out screenshot of some of the Flickr images related to "Second Life"

Figure 2. A zoomed-out screenshot of some of the google images related to "Second Life"

The way people have designed the 3D spaces may inform of how the designer or developer conceptualized the space and how that space should be used by visiting digital avatars. In some cases, images may be taken on-the-fly, with little in the way of setup or sophistication; in other cases, images may be captured after some serious building and setting up of human-embodied avatars pre-positioned for visual effect. In many cases, the subject of the image—human, machine, animal, or some combination—gives the sense of it being a "selfie"—a self-portrait…or the multiple subjects of the image as being a "group selfie". Of course, in other contexts, the two-dimensional (2D) screenshots may be images of others who just happen to be in a virtual immersive 3D space. The scraped images were not necessarily "safe for work" (they were "NSFW") but were richly informative of a range of features of people's lives: mass culture, music stars, hedonism, politics, brands, and other elements. Indeed, people do go "to social virtual worlds to satisfy their social and hedonic needs, and to escape from real world constraints, as do virtual community members and virtual gamers; they also pursue unique activities, such as creating virtual objects and selling them" (Jung & Kang, 2010, p. 218).

One researcher specializing in human vision and visual analytics suggests that "social cognition is the crux of human intelligence," and that the "greatest feats of the human intellect are products of groups of people working together" (Kanwisher, Summer 2015). The human brain was designed to help individuals interact with each other. One common human ability is to capture the visual gist of a context at a glance. The social inferences and social perception are built into human perception. In her research that involves human interpretation of social imagery, she uses "Turing++ Questions for Social Perception," and these include the following: "Who is this? What are they attending to? What are they doing? What will happen next? What are they feeling? What is their character? Are they interacting with someone else? What is the nature of the interaction?" (Kanwisher, Summer 2015) In terms of the social images from *Second Life®*, there is the assumption that the image data may be interpretable (with personages identified, forms identified, relationships observed, and contexts interpreted)—and stories extracted as available (without over-reading into the data). Researchers and analysts may be able to identify patterns in the image set, and something may be learned about the design for formal, nonformal, and informal learning. Even an initial sense of this space may beget some possibilities:

Table 1. Initial conceptualizations of formal, nonformal and informal learning types on SL from direct observations in-world

	Some Initial Examples in Second Life®
Formal	Foreign language learning, natural phenomena / environmental simulations, live human-embodied avatar lectures, focused role plays, and others
Nonformal	Library service access, movie showings, ritualized activities (virtual church services, virtual parties), and others
Informal	Avatar self-presentation and styling, 3D object building, object scripting, in-world interactions and conversations with other avatars, immersive game play, immersive storytelling, and others

Another assumption is that the unique nature of the SL screenshots may be informative in other ways. For example, stills from SL tend to not show more than a dozen people or so at a time—simply because unwieldy crowds are much more possible in real life than in the virtual. In the virtual, even though there may be small acts of serendipity and occlusion and surprise, oftentimes, the images shared seem somewhat posed and even positioned. In real space, people's faces may show micro-expressions; they may show irregularities. When people instantiate in real space, it is a multi-sensory experience instead of a limited-dimension expression of the self. In virtual spaces, there are no thunderstorms that just roll in because the weather is often manually set by the person controlling the space. The virtual light can be quite predictable and stable and sometimes a little digitally other-worldly. Zooming in for a close-up may result in a mass of pixels. Sometimes, the visual still has annotation words floating above the digital avatar or the scripted object. There is a sense of a world with limited and controlled repercussions, a limited range of impact, of surprise, of harm, and of malice. While spaces on Second Life® may theoretically persist forever—as long as fees for the service are paid and the platform is in existence—the sense is that the virtual builds are temporal and ephemeral, and that there are too many dependencies for their digital persistence and preservation.

This research is evidence-based, and the data analytics are drawn from qualitative research methods, like manual bottom-up coding of digital contents. In this case, each image may be "read into" to extract the highest levels of meanings from the imagery, given the sparsity of the rendered spaces (a little goes a long way in immersive 3D virtual worlds). The coded patterns may offer leads for exploration. The indirect research approach suggests that the insights are provisional and partial, with assertions more likely once more and different data is available.

REVIEW OF THE LITERATURE

Second Life® started out originally as a private space known as LindenWorld®, and this space is described as a first-person shooter space on the Second Life wiki. The space was later re-named Second Life®. The first resident of SL joined on March 13, 2002. The public (test-version) beta occurred in October 2002. The formal rollout of Linden Lab's Second Life™ occurred in June 2003. The initial vision for Second Life® is described as follows on the official Second Life wiki:

Second Life (SL) evolved as an idea by founder and former Linden Lab CEO, Philip Rosedale (aka Philip Linden). He envisioned a vast green, continuous landscape, distributed across multiple servers — and went on to build it. While he dreamed of virtual worlds since his childhood, in 1994, Rosedale first thought of connecting computers via the Internet and creating a virtual world. In 1999, he founded Linden Lab (LL). Andrew Linden stated that Linden Lab started as a hardware company geared towards the research and development of haptics. Although work was underway on a prototype called "The Rig, haptics were subsequently abandoned due to heavy patent concentration. The Linden Lab employees — commonly known as "Lindens" — needed a virtual world to go with their hardware, so in 2001 they started building "LindenWorld", as described in an early news story. ("History of Second Life," Dec. 29, 2017)

The general public could create accounts on the platform and interact as a stylized digital avatar. They could "de-Ruth" (by shedding the out-of-the-box design of the selected avatar by customizing with a range of looks and designs, in one meaning). Apparently, Ruth refers to the "default loading avatar" (the partially rezzed visualization of a character without its clothing, hair, and other accoutrement) which could look unusual as the respective elements of the digital person emerged ("Ruth," Apr. 15, 2015). They could engage with other human-embodied avatars in the space. Over time, there were features enabling teleporting to other public sites, aerial maps, ways to identify the presence of other human-embodied avatars nearby, and others. A news area was designed to provide information about planned and live events and gatherings. As developers became more sophisticated and created artificial intelligence (AI) agents, people could engage with those.

The Linden dollar debuted at the end of 2003. With that advancement, a wide range of entrepreneurial and commercial enterprises arose, and virtual storefronts appeared. (Edward Castronova explored some of the economic possibilities in *Synthetic Worlds: The Business and Culture of Online Games* in 2005.)

The rollout of Linden dollars helped bridge virtual world currencies with real-world ones. The current worth of a Linden dollar is L$252 to USD$1 ("Economy of *Second Life,*" Jan. 8, 2018). In a recent walk-through of SL, there were the typical objects for sale: clothing, food, furniture, homes, virtual pets, AI bots, cars, and even simulated womanhood (promising "realistic cycles, realistic odds, realistic birth control"). There are markets for add-ons to devices for digital avatars to engage in enriched simulations and games. There are paywalls to particular enriched spaces.

There are dedicated websites listing various controversies that have dogged SL. One researcher writes:

It is certainly true that Linden Labs' creation has attracted a great deal of negative publicity. The almost universal approbation which attended its rise to mainstream visibility in 2006 began to peter out in mid 2007, to be replaced by a stream of negative press stories painting a picture of low traffic, falling sign-up rates, corporate desertions, failing inworld banks, and suspicions that terrorists and paedophiles were using the metaverse for illicit purposes (Helmer & Learning Light, 2007, p. 7).

Given that history, there is a sense that there are risks of the space having an "uncertain future" and of "commercial imperatives on Linden Labs" (p. 9) that may hinder its use for learning (p. 8).

Over the years, SL has become an online space for exploring alternative identities (through digital avatars), hosting virtual experiences, interacting and socializing, enjoying hobbies, pursuing adventures, and making money. There are academic affordances as well, involving teaching and learning and research. A fairly recent take on SL potentials reads: "That means that *Second Life* users can build anything from virtual genetics labs, to depraved sex dungeons, to campaign headquarters for Donald Trump and Bernie Sanders" (Maiberg, Apr. 29, 2016).

Over time, users who rented digital space in SL could generate their own 3D contents through prim building blocks and scripting (with the Linden Scripting Language). One of the more dazzling features of SL was the ability of the platform to render avatar-perspectives to respective avatars in the same locations and to modulate sound for them from their respective physical positions in-world. Another sense of allure came from the idea that many were joining SL in droves, and it could then be a space where people could reach out to others with messaging, sales pitches, invitations to learn, and other messaging. For some, the online space offered enriched visual and audio details; for others, the space was overwrought and overwhelming to their senses.

In early days, there were public reports of hacker attacks on SL. One was the "grey goo" attack (Lemos, Nov. 2006), in which objects were scripted to be self-replicating and would displace other digital details in the world. Apparently, this issue was solved with a fast response by the makers of SL, with two hours "to get everything back to semblance of normal, according to a timeline in the forum posts" (Lemos, Nov. 2006). There were reports of the theft of Second Life® currency (Terdiman, Nov. 30, 2007).

As for many spaces, including the Internet and Web, pornographic sites seemed to be some of the most popular. While a user on SL has to change the default settings in order to access some of these adult sites, some of the images are publicly available on Social Web. For example, a simple scrape of imagery related to SL shows some scenes of bestiality, sado-masochism, and other depictions.

How Real? How Virtual?

To over-simplify, there may be two diametrically opposite sense of *Second Life®*. One approach is that SL is just part of people's real lives, based on the idea of the cyber-physical confluence. The cyber-physical confluence suggests, broadly speaking, that the cyber and the physical have overlaps, and both affect the other. In this view, SL is a niche media tool that enables people to carry on some of their regular life activities in a virtualized space. A countervailing perspective is the idea of the "magic circle" (a term coined by Johan Huizinga) or a space where "the normal rules and reality of the world are suspended and replaced by the artificial reality of a game world" ["Magic circle (virtual worlds)," Oct. 23, 2017]. To put it in the vernacular, the other position is, "What happens in SL stays in SL." The answer is that both are somewhat true, and both assertions are somewhat false. A third path is the idea that what is built on SL is "hyper-real"; in other words, the artificial constructed realities are so detailed that they are more revelatory than reality and therefore "more real than real."

At the individual level, people post images of themselves with their SL alter egos, blending the real and the virtual/fantasy. And yet, many of the unmarked generic default avatars look to be a Size 2 (but spilling out of their clothes none-the-less) and stylish for females and hunky for males, and obese characters in SL are highly unusual. (I've only seen one in the years that I've been online.) This discrepancy shows up at the population levels, too. And yet, the depicted personages and digital avatars are interpreted as being culturally diverse. One author (2007) writes:

The cultural diversity of Second Life is striking. In some ways it reflects the real world cultures of the residents, and in other ways it is quite unique. In fact, as in the real world, there is no uniform culture in SL. It is an aggregation of people from different national, economic, social, religious, political, geographic, ethnic, and cultural backgrounds, all playing together in the same sandbox with unlimited resources and possibilities. Many of the old timers – the pioneers – are creators, builders and artists who contribute greatly to the rich fabric of Second Life and who are more than willing to share their contributions and knowledge with newcomers who are just beginning to climb the steep learning curve of life in this virtual world. There is a culture of entrepreneurs working as everything from sex escorts to night club and shop owners to real estate speculators, all scrambling and competing with one another. There is a culture of humanists who are sincerely committed to SL as the next step in the evolution of humankind. There is a culture of scam artists, a culture of "griefers," and cultures of predators of every description. There is the culture of those who come to SL principally for virtual sex, with all of the various subcultures that comprises, as has been the case on the Internet since long before there was a World Wide Web. There is even a culture of "furries" – people whose avatars take the form of furry animals and who share behaviors common to their own community. And then of course there is the culture of those who are just "passing through," living and playing in the virtual world without contributing or taking much. (Davidson, 2007, pp. 4 - 5)

Those who are engaging in SL are likely those who are materially privileged. The technological requirements to access SL require a fairly high-level connectivity, computer processing, memory, screen resolution, and graphics cards ("System Requirements," 2018), any of which may be a disqualifying factor for access. Some may argue that the web-facing aspects of a virtual world enables access without "dedicated hardware devices such as advanced visualisation (head-mounted displays, stereoscopic displays), interaction (3D mouse, orientation and position sensors) as well as haptics (gloves) (de Freitas, Rebolledo-Mendez, Liarokapis, Magoulas, & Poulovassilis, 2010, p. 70), the costs to engage in *Second Life®* are not minimal in many parts of the world. This means that those who can access SL are likely those from developed countries with access to resources and some leisure time to explore and learn. Also, the cyber-physical confluence concept might suggest that what we see in SL is what we see in-world, but that would be a difficult assertion to make and support.

At heart, the question is how much of an overlap is there in the Venn diagram in Figure 3 for accuracy's sake? How much of the virtual carries over to the real, and vice versa, and in terms of learning, what is the optimal balance?

Figure 3. "Real life" and "virtual life" in Second Life®: cyber-physical confluence or the magic circle's pure imaginary

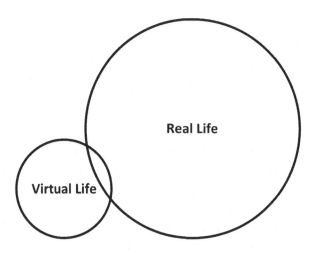

"Real Life" and "Virtual Life" in Second Life®:
Cyber-Physical Confluence or the Magic Circle's Pure Imaginary?

Another similar argument may be that SL is a friendly space for those with disabilities because of the following basic arguments of "physical e-empowerment":

Many benefits are available to people with disabilities who wish to participate in a virtual world. These include self-efficacy and the ability to share in virtual world community support. Further, many disabled residents of virtual worlds can vicariously experience physical activities through their avatar such as dancing, walking, and running – actions sometimes not possible in real life. However, learning the technology in a virtual world can be daunting for many new residents. (Zielke, Roome, & Krueger, Apr. 2009)

The counter argument is that the platform may be prohibitive for those with other types of challenges, such as those related to visual acuity and hearing and language processing. The platform itself has an interface called out for "poor usability" and "poor accessibility" (Helmer & Learning Light, 2007, p. 11).

Also, it is unclear how the virtual and representational physical capabilities in SL (can its users fly?) actually transfer into the physical real. Does a felt empowerment translate into the real?

So the opposing concepts of the virtual reflecting the real (cyber-physical confluence) and the idea that what is virtual stays in the virtual are held in tension. After all, what is expressed in SL is covered by all laws in the real, and the virtual does not preclude legal liability. One example is in the idea of defamation: "Insofar as a resident's business depends on his or her reputation in the metaverse, and where harm incurred there is as real as it would be in the natural world, the law should be able to protect these Second Life users from any real torts that may arise" (Chin, 2007, pp. 1306 – 1307). Law enforcement has made clear that SL is not a space for terrorism planning, information exchange, and training purposes (Takahashi, Oct. 9, 209). Virtual spaces are not ungoverned ones.

The strengths and weaknesses of the fictional and imaginary are manifold. The fictional imaginative opens up thinking about issues (such as the analysis of war preparation using wide-ranging scenarios) and potentialities. The weaknesses are that people may conflate the real with the imaginary, and vice versa. In the same way, virtual worlds may mislead. On personal relational levels, the "immersive parasocial" may manifest and lead to people being defrauded or harmed (Hai-Jew, Sept. 2009). Vicarious experiences may train knowledge, skills, and abilities, but they may mislead learners to their actual capabilities (vs. what people think they are capable of in their minds). Representational spaces may be consumed in a way that skews a person's sense of the real world. It is into this immersive virtual space—with possibilities for harnessing the imagination and mental-sensory experiences that people are harnessing for education. Maybe the way to understand the "virtual imagination" is to consider an assertion by one researcher who suggests that SL is:

...both a social psychological playground where participants enjoy individualistic fantasies and a virtual community where they collaborate on collective projects. When people define the virtual as real, it is real in its consequences. (Gottschalk, Fall 2010, p. 501)

As an example, people who experience social rejection in virtual romances experience real pain (Gottschalk, Fall 2010, pp. 501-502).

SL seems to be garnering less media attention since its heyday, and it also seems to have less cultural influence. There is a general sense that it has traded excitement for stability, novelty for broad name recognition, danger for predictability, and newbie visitors for returning participants (maybe returning "snowbirds" to an off-season resort). A tour of various spaces in SL feels like stepping into 3D dioramas, others' set pieces for dramas and scenarios, sometimes with background noises and droning music. It is not quite easy to fully suspend disbelief, and it is hard to want to immerse into the respective spaces. Even if one is feeling social, there are often no others there with which to engage—not even an AI-driven avatar. If constructed spaces (vs. naturally evolved ones in RL) are the rule in SL, as they seem to be, these are not the spaces of Foucault where people's lives "erode" and histories co-occur, and these are not the spaces of Thrift with "temporary settlements that divide and connect thing sup into different kinds of collectives which are slowly provided with the meaning" ("Sociology of space," Feb. 10, 2018).

Educational Potential

Immersive virtual worlds have been explored "for educational use since the mid 1990s, as shown by the ExploreNet Experiment" (Hughes & Moshell, 1997, as cited in Hobbs, Brown, & Gordon, 2006). The space was conceptualized as useful for problem-based learning (Campbell, Apr. 2009), co-learning and co-inquiry through Communities of Inquiry (particularly in the designs of "cognitive presence, social presence, and teaching presence" (Burgess, Slate, Rojas-LeBouef, & LaPrairie, 2010, p. 84); "situated learning" (Hayes, 2006), project-based learning (Tuten, 2009, p. 1), including collaborative ones, problem-based learning and constructionism in a blended learning way (Good, Howard, & Thackray, Dec.

2016), and others. New pedagogies have been suggested, such as "social network knowledge construction" within virtual worlds to accommodate learning uses of SL (Dawley, 2009). Others noted that "like all technology, virtual worlds are not value-neutral and each has differing affordances and constraints" (Dickey, Feb. 2011, p. 18).

In the educational space, there have been high hopes that the platform could solve some teaching and learning challenges in online learning. There was early and common talk of a sense of virtual learning possibilities (Antonacci & Modaress, 2006) and "extensive" potentials (Salt, Atkins, & Blackall, Oct. 2008, p. 29).

Some works have evaluated the educational affordances. Multi-user virtual environments (MUVEs) (or immersive virtual worlds or synthetic worlds or collaborative virtual environments) offer some common features: "persistence of the in-world environment, a shared space allowing multiple users to participate simultaneously, virtual embodiment in the form of an avatar (a personisable 3-D representation of the self), interactions that occur between users and objects in a 3-D environment, an immediacy of action such that interactions occur in real time, similarities to the real world such as topography, movement and physics that provide the illusion of being there.(Smart, Cascio & Paffendof, 2007, as cited in Warburton, 2009, p. 415). As such, virtual worlds have attracted some 300 million users (Warburton, 2009, p. 415). These capabilities enable affordances for education, including "extended or rich interactions" (between individuals and the space, each other, and artifacts), visualization and contextualization, "exposure to authentic content and culture, individual and collective identity play," immersion in 3D spaces, simulations, community presences, and "content production" (including self-paced tutorials and treasure hunts) (Warburton, 2009, p. 421).

Digital avatars could be styled to the individual student to give them more of a sense of investment in their virtual self and the learning that may be achieved through the virtual embodiment. Scripted virtual labs, with designed virtual experiments, may be delivered without the need for mailed kits for kitchen-lab experiments. Simulations may enable exploratory and experiential learning. Learners could role-play synchronously in-body and in-world to simulate real-world role-plays (Gregory & Masters, 2012, p. 434).

Some Applied Uses of SL for Learning

Second Life® has been harnessed for various domains of learning: information systems (Dreher, Reiners, Dreher, & Dreher, Summer 2009), marketing (Tuten, 2009, p. 1), computer programming (Esteves, Fonseca, Morgado, & Martins, 2010), medical education (Wiecha, Heyden, Sternthal, & Merialdi, Jan. – Mar. 2010), formal argumentation (Jamaludin, Chee, & Ho, 2009), interdisciplinary communication (Jarmon, Traphagan, Mayrath, & Trivedi, 2009), entrepreneurship (Chandra & Leenders, 2012), medical and health education (Boulos, Hetherington, & Wheeler, Dec. 2007), K-12 in-service teaching (Dickey, Feb. 2011), hallucinations (Yellowlees & Cook, Nov. - Dec. 2006),

Learners have engaged in role plays in order to develop empathy for and understanding of others' points-of-view. One case is based on de Bono's *Six Thinking Hats* framework (1985, as cited in Gregory & Masters, 2012, p. 420). Here, learners embody a thinking approach to particular issues, namely as follows:

- ***White Hat:*** *Facts, figures and objective information;*
- ***Red Hat:*** *Emotions and feelings;*
- ***Black Hat:*** *Logical, negative thoughts;*
- ***Yellow Hat:*** *Positive, constructive thoughts;*

- **Green Hat:** *Creativity and new ideas;*
- **Blue Hat:** *Control/coordination of the other hats and thinking steps (Gregory & Masters, 2012, p. 427).*

Challenges have been identified in some of the applied research. One work critiques the usage of SL for foreign language learning and practice, noting that they experienced challenges with matching language learners and native speakers for regular meeting times (Zhang, Mar. 2013, p. 249), not finding sufficient discussion topics, and facing a "lack of equal practice opportunities for students of varying proficiency levels" (Zhang, Mar. 2013, p. 250). Managing group sizes was also a challenge along with an unwieldy instructor workload to use SL (Zhang, Mar. 2013).

Virtual Librarianship, Educational Mentoring, and Archival

As a space for library outreach, Second Life® has been harnessed to provide virtual reference services through the services of virtual librarians to enable "multiple points of access and outreach" (Erdman, 2007, pp. 30 – 31).

One research team harnessed SL for academic mentoring, particularly "supporting life decisions and educational choices" (de Freitas, Rebolledo-Mendez, Liarokapis, Magoulas, & Poulovassilis, 2010, p. 84).

While the study has not proved conclusively the power of the tool for mentoring, the sessions with the mentor were very effective in practice, and in the future one-to-one sessions with mentors based abroad or not co-located could be further explored. However, more context and advance study is needed to situate the activities in-world and greater time for reflection needs to be provided. Virtual worlds may also support peer collaboration and may be used, for example, for collaborative assignments in-world with practical outputs, for example, designing a marketing campaign in-world, and work centering upon social interactions would be well served in this virtual world. Also, there is real potential for supporting online learning methods by extending the benefits of audio-graphic conferencing to provide a greater sense of presence, thereby potentially reducing non-completion rates. (de Freitas, Rebolledo-Mendez, Liarokapis, Magoulas, & Poulovassilis, 2010, p. 83)

Some users have created digital versions of real-life artifacts, and there are also some born-digital artifacts that "are collected, curated and preserved by in-world museums" (Urban, Marty, & Twidale, 2007, p. 2). Researchers have documented nascent use of SL for museum purposes (Urban, Marty, & Twidale, 2007) and for "historical re-creations and re-enactments" among others (Salt, Atkins, & Blackall, Oct. 2008, pp. 28 - 29). These are a kind of "preservationist" approach in virtual spaces.

Research Potential

A range of research methodologies to explore virtual worlds, including "formal experimentation, observational ethnography, and quantitative analysis of economic markets or social networks" among others (Bainbridge, 2007) have been applied. A pair of researchers spent six months conducting participant observations and in-depth interviews to understand a virtual settlement in SL to

...explore and unpack the spatial experiences of participants in the community and, with them, the grammar and symbolism of power and submission, of private and public, and consider body as a place for social inscription. The spatial experiences of these participants shed light on the nature of this community (both social and computer-mediated interactions) and help explain why virtual simulation of Gorean fantasy is such a compelling form of play and source of intimacy and emotion for thousands of Second Life residents (Bardzell & Odom, Aug. 2008, p. 239).

The researchers describe their harnessing of "social interpretation" to learn about the virtual space and the peoples there and to understand "something "familiar, rule governed; intimate, personal; emotional" (Bardzell & Odom, Aug. 2008, p. 257).

Coded agents ("robots" or "bots") have also been brought to bear. One recent project involved the uses of scripted agents to wander around SL, interact with others and to "systematically collect data" as part of social experiments in virtual spaces (Friedman, Steed, & Slater, 2007, p. 2). In one study, the robot focused on the other human-embodied avatars' gazes and treatment of the robot's "personal space" (Friedman, Steed, & Slater, 2007, pp. 2 - 3). The researchers suggest that people subconsciously transfer their non-verbal communications behaviors, such as proxemics and gaze, and dyadic physical positioning with others, to online virtual worlds. Patterns from gender-informed interpersonal distance was also found (Yee, Bailenson, Urbanek, Chang, & Merget, 2007).

In terms of academic inquiry and research on SL, researchers have conducted human subjects research with the protection of human subjects reviews (Minocha, Tran, & Reeves, Nov. 2010). Researchers have conducted digital ethnographies (Bardzell & Odom, Aug. 2008, p. 257), delivered online surveys (Bell, Castronova, &Wagner, 2009), interviewed the site's "residents," harnessed artificial intelligence (AI) robots to elicit information from in-world individuals, and other means. Not only is the research conducted on the platform, but the platform itself is a subject of study. For example, information systems researchers have the opportunity "to study how these environments are built and managed by operators, how they are used and misused by users, and the impact that they have on users, communities, organizations, and societies at large" (Mennecke, McNeill, Ganis, Roche, & Bray, 2008, p. 371). Another group of research focuses on the learners in online spaces and what they may require before they might commit to learning on SL: an important learner characteristic for those who would engage in SL for learning was higher levels of self-efficacy (Pellas & Kazanidis, 2014, p. 31).

Some Identified Barriers to Using SL for Learning

Certainly, there are barriers to using SL for educational purposes. The design effort has to be considered. In 2008, researchers mapped *collaboration* and *learning* patterns in 3D virtual spaces and considered the design effort required to achieve the learning/collaboration. They found 13 emergent patterns, which they mapped to a 2x2 table. The x-axis shows the "Design Effort" (from low/easy to high/difficult), and the y-axis shows "3D Added Value" (from low-to-high value). For low/easy design effort and low payoff, there are virtual meetings and group configurations and lectures. For low design effort but high payoffs, there are knowledge fairs and learning trails and scavenger hunts. For high design difficult and low 3D added value, there are 2D document manipulations ("to avoid: 3d experience as useless and expensive gimmick"). Then, at the high-3D added value and the high/difficult design effort space are the following: training/simulation, role play, and games (learning patterns) and virtual design studio, virtual workplace, and knowledge map/co-construction (collaboration patterns). (Schmeil & Eppler, 2008, p. 673) For the high/difficult designs, these require learning / collaboration / pedagogical design, acquisition of space in Second Life®, virtual space design, the creation and scripting of objects, the training of instructors and learners, and other efforts. Such real-world calculations are critical to the effective use of SL for learning.

Eight categories of challenges in using SL were identified in a review of "newsgroups, blog posts and the extant literature," including "technical, identity, culture, collaboration, time, economic, standards, (and) scaffolding persistence and social discovery" (Warburton, 2008a, c; Warburton & Perez-Garcia, 2009, as cited in Warburton, 2009, pp. 422 - 423). In many ways, the same complexity of challenges—that SL can be "an isolating experience," and "the current lack of open standards and interoperability between virtual world platforms" (Warburton, 2009, pp. 422 – 423) are as relevant today nearly a decade later. Indeed, other research has shown the importance of community factors—capabilities that enable people to interact and socialize—in user acceptance of virtual worlds:

The research results show in particular that the possibility to interact in a 3D environment in combination with Voice over IP plays a pivotal role in user acceptance and technology adoption of virtual worlds. Of all the factors tested, the most important determinant of Virtual World adoption seems the perceived value of communication, cooperation, and communication channels on Virtual Worlds. The effects of these COM components were significantly larger than that of the next most important determinant, perceived usefulness of the Virtual Worlds. Moreover, other influencing factors proposed by Technology Acceptance Model are also relevant to determine user acceptance, such as social norms (SN), attitude toward technology (ATT), and socio-demographical factors (GEN). (Fetscherin & Lattemann, 2008)

For all the power of synchronous learning sessions in virtual worlds, maintaining connections between sessions through both synchronous and asynchronous communications tools is important (Petrakou, 2010, p. 1025). Multiple researchers mentioned the importance of proper training to get learners up-to-speed on the platform (and there are "island" spaces for new users to learn the skills in SL). One researcher suggests that there is a general "low learning curve" but a medium learning curve for more advanced features in SL (Dickey, Feb. 2011, p. 14). Researchers have found that SL can be challenging to use and may not have sufficient user retention:

However, SL presents a steep learning curve to anyone wishing to enter and participate. For example, in 2007, Linden Lab CEO Philip Rosedale stated that the estimated time to learn to use SL was 4 hours (Reuters, 2007). In 2008, Linden Lab estimated a retention rate of those entering SL of about 10% (Wagner, 2008). Further, a 2007 study of user acceptance of SL showed that only 56% of regular users perceived SL as easy to use (Fetscherin & Lattemann, 2007). (Zielke, Roome, & Krueger, Apr. 2009, p. 4)

It is as-yet unclear how well various assistive and adaptive devices work in the space. So does the sense that the virtual enables those with disabilities to be empowered align with the accessibility of the online space? Is this a case of "cyber-physical confluence," or is it more about the "magic circle" imaginary?

VIRTUAL EMBODIMENT IN A VIRTUAL IMMERSIVE WORLD PER DOUBLE SHARING

One way to conceptualize social imagery is through related tags networks. "Tags" are folk (amateur) labels applied to socially shared images. Tags are "related" by being co-occurring or being mutually applied with other tags to the same particular images. Seeing what tags co-occur (when one is used, another is likely also to be used at a particular threshold) may shed light on how a particular tag or label is used in application to the shared images. For this case, these also help illuminate some of the limits to visuals to represent an issue (some topics are more amenable to representation by social imagery than other topics). In Figure 4, this shows a one-degree related tags network for the "secondlife" tag on Flickr. The ego-neighborhood shows direct ties to each of the connected nodes, including those on romance, gothic, profile, blood, cute, Christmas, and others.

Figure 4. "SecondLife" related tags network from Flickr (1 deg.) as a grid layout

At a 1.5 degree of connection, the "secondlife" related tags network results in a three-group (cluster) network. Starting at the left and going clock-wise, the first group seems to be around topics of fantasy and simulations; the second around nature and the seasons, and the third around aesthetics and fashion. As the groups of tags become larger, the actual coherence of the respective tag groups seems to lessen, with higher coherence in earlier groups (Figure 5).

Figure 5. "SecondLife" related tags network from Flickr (1.5 deg.) with Fruchterman-Reingold layout graph

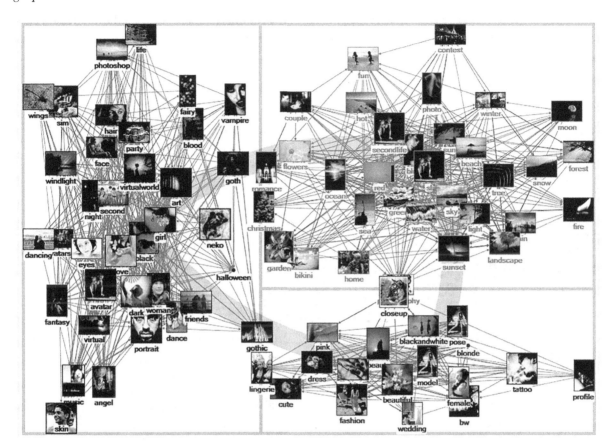

Finally, a two-degree related tags network of the "secondlife" tag captures eight groups, with the respective center nodes: G1: secondlife, G2: life, G3: art, G4: couple, G5: halloween, G6: neko, G7: night, and G8: wings (Figure 6). While the image sets to change over time, the related tags networks seem to be slower to change because of the thresholds of co-occurrence needed before the related tags change. The thumbnail images related to each of the tags is determined by Flickr and seems to be static and unchanging. In other words, the image for "secondlife" remains the same across the various related tags networks.

In Google Images, there are labels that are automatically applied to the set of images to enable the dimensional exploration of the image set. When the initial datasets were captured in November 2017, the tags for "Second Life" were as follows (in this order): "real life, cute, anime, the office, creepy, undertale, bloodline, anthro, 2.0, game, logo, education, blog, essence, gift, club, castle, neko, sissy, alice in wonderland, beyonce, nicki minaj, michael jackson, furry, mlp, sergal, werewolf, dragon, mermaid, zindra, flickr, illmatic, mesh body, harley quinn, britbong, hot, kemono, giantess, baby, kid, skin, hair, lip, the shop, relay for life, yiff, virtual reality, virtual world, pregnant, mod, copybot, okkbye, belleza, jex, ralph, pixicat, star wars, viss, attack on titan, naruto, sailor moon, renamon, homestruck, fashion blog, wowmeh, tmp, kawaii, birdy, funny, aesthetic, texture, pony, our, shark, wolf, horse, gor, imvu, linden lab, sims 3, bunny, chinchilla, lolas, little bone, game throne, dolcett, doll, jeans, outfit, kajira, dwight, corset, winter, ibm, christmas, halloween, male skin, futa, coco, rikugou, zenith, omega, insilico, sansar, horns, banned, silks, drow, sonic, splatoon, male fashion, project sansar, pastel goth, doctor who, lapfox, aisling, mesh heads, gagged, male mesh head, snow rabbit, am radio, bed, medieval, 4chan, tsg, steampunk, cyberpunk, renard, tardis, amie goode, kobold, hairbase, cyborg, mischief managed, emo, redgrave, mobile, iphone, blueberry, japan, android, brazilia." These were with different color tabs, but the related tabs were not captured.

Figure 6. "SecondLife" related tags network from Flickr (2 deg.) as a Harel-Koren Fast multiscale graph

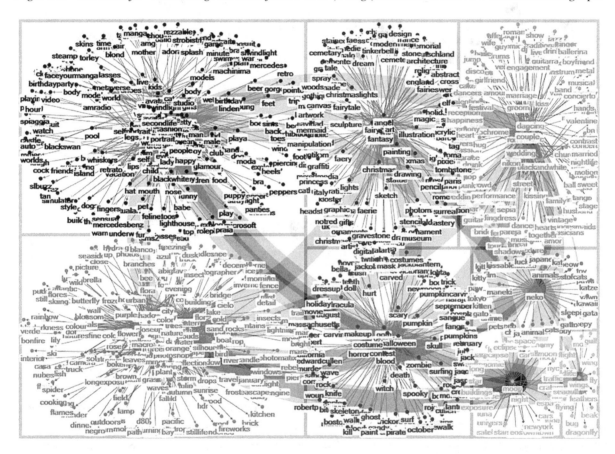

Some five months later, the same search term was used, and the tags used to filter that set show some similarities and some differences. The tags were as follows, with semi-colons used to separate tags of different background colors (similar tags share the same hues): "pinterest; japanese; toddler; simply shelby; scythia; orange nova; grey school wizardry; zerkalo, 2.0; philip linden; ren queenston; neko; bento dragon: avilion; zindra; video, education, marriage; avi; steven universe; imvu; android; mac; nike, ibm, dell, adidas; zootopia; tiger, dog; otter; hatsune miku; pokemon; donald trump, bernie sanders; vampire, werewolf; vegas, china, korea, africa, singapore; sonic; kopy; linden labs; berlin, new york, amsterdam, india, london, paris; hyrule; judy hopps; baby sanctuary; geisha; lara croft; nasa; lapfox; rabbit, horse, wolf, raccoon, deer, cow; the grand wizard; nomos; ninja, samura; beyonce; nicki minaj, britney spears, rihanna, michael jackson, aaliyah; krystal; mass effect, sims, kingdom hearts; barbie; magicland; woodbury; husky; queer; duran; american apparel; kobold; thanksgiving, christmas, halloween; kzk; cao fei; dr phil; greenies; tinies; black; digimon; snaggletooth; undertale, fnaf; inkling; kowloon; birdy; smilodon; jon rafman; herm; versailles; eiderglen; doctor who, gossip girl, game throne; egypt; tomboellstorff; shred; cleopatra; nimh; chinchilla; shawn elliott; pierre omidyar; melanie martinez; asuna; bay city; tokyo; the office; csi ny; supergirl; garou; big ben; caledon; john edwards; warrior cat; navy; coast guard; kool aid man; new rome; scourge warrior cats; boys town."

Certainly, it is possible to sort images from "Second Life" by searching for that term and "education" or using built-in filtering tags, but that would pre-define some of the found contents, and the purpose of this research is to look for unintended, non-obvious, and subtle insights as well. One intuition is that how people build artificial spaces may leak insights in the interstices enable by the physics engine, the looks-and-feels, and the immateriality of virtual immersive spaces. One other point is necessary: the related tags from both Flickr and from Google Images have only a few direct references to "education." When the "Second Life" image set is filtered just to "education" in Google Images, there are many images of virtual classrooms, virtual arenas, books, virtual lecturers, and so on (Figure 7). Clicking on tags to filter the contents offers a way to thin-slice the image data to look at a portion of it. (For the Flickr set, one cannot click on the related tags network tag…to filter the images. One would have to do a Boolean search with an "and" reference to sort the dataset.)

Figure 8 shows a selection of images from "secondlife and education" search on Flickr. Note the search terms at the top right corner.

For this research, there was no heavy-handed direct curation of the research image set, only the selectivity of the algorithmic curation by Flickr and Google Images, likely based off of folk text-tags applied to the shared social imagery. Again, 988 were from Flickr (with Flickr Downloadr), and 592 from Google Images (with the Picture Downloader Professional).

Figure 7. "Second Life" images on Google images filtered to "education" (a zoomed-out view)

Figure 8. "SecondLife and education" images on Flickr

An initial perusal of the respective image sets show focuses around egos and characters as well as entities. Some works seemed designed for spectacle, with a focus on capturing viewer attention; some were stretched images reminiscent of "panorama fails" (Edds, Apr. 10, 2014). Many of the SL images seem original to the image-sharer and not captures of third-party spaces. There were political comments, such as a swastika with the current U.S. president's name interwoven in it. Another political message read: "NO to US Imperialist Warmongering! End the Bogus 'War on Terror' Hands off iran!!!" There were some events portrayed, such as a virtual world wedding. There were images that were clearly designed off the photos of public figures. One screenshot showed an iconic remake of an image of Marilyn Monroe in a white dress walking over a sidewalk grate. One image depicted a suicide by gun in a highly stylized visual, with the blood turning into butterflies. Another showed a man in a hospital bed receiving medical care. Some of the images read as dramatic and life *in extremis.* There are the usual mixes of portrayed animals (some based off of the biological real and others from fictional animal characters) and centaurs.

Many of SL visuals are about places: railway stations, race tracks, fields, industrial sites, archaeological digs, office work places, wharfs, ships, forests, mountainsides, palaces, parks, dance clubs, airplanes, Chinatowns, amusement parks, underground caverns, and others. Even when no individuals are in the space, these are clearly spaces where people are expected to engage in particular activities. There are fantasy cities depicted against brilliant skies. Some of the screenshots showed overlays of annotating words to label elements in SL, revealing yet another level of construction and artifice.

Several data coding tables were set up to collect information from the two image sets, with focuses on the following:

1. Portrayed Contexts and Environments
2. Character Types (Egos and Entities)
3. Item Types (Elements in the Scene)
4. Automation, Mechanization, and Artificial Intelligence (AI)

These Tables 2 to 5 started out as broad categories and stepwise iterations in the image sets helped initially refine the sub-categories and then inform the coding of the imagery. The tables are set up with the idea that the images from the respective social media spaces (Flickr and Google Images) may result in quite different types of imagery.

The tables are understood as both quantitative spaces and qualitative ones, with the collection of frequency observations along with qualitative observations. In this preliminary work, the main point was to create the data collection tables and to offer some initial insights from the 1,550-item image set.

After the initial coding of the images based on the four prior tables, the images were coded for types of learning depicted directly or indirectly, extrinsically or intrinsically. (Table 6)

Some additional insights were captured during the iterative explorations of the image sets.

Table 2. Portrayed contexts and environments data coding Table 1

1. Portrayed Contexts and Environments	Flickr Social Image Set	Google Images Social Image Set
Built Spaces		
Indoors		
Outdoors		
Geographical Location / Nature		
Physical Geography		
Others		
Human Activities / Uses of Space		
Individual Activities		
Group Activities		
Interactions with the Objects		
Interactions with the Environment		
Time Features		
Daytime		
Nighttime		
Dawn		
Dusk		

DISCUSSION

In the Flickr image set, some of the images that were suggestive of formal learning included the following: a neighborhood scene with avatars standing outside, in front of a building labeled "law library and technology center"; a PowerPoint slideshow on a floor-to-ceiling screen with an avatar presenter speaking to an audience of onlookers sitting on sofas (which may include formal, nonformal, and informal learning), and others.

Table 3. Character types (egos and entities) data coding Table 2

2. Character Types (Egos and Entities)	Flickr Social Image Set	Google Images Social Image Set
Age Portrayals and Mixes of Ages in the Group		
Toddlers		
Children		
Teens		
Young Adults		
Adults		
Middle Age		
Late Middle Age		
Old Age		
Gender Portrayals		
Male		
Female		
Other		
Characters and Instantiation / Dress		
By Gender		
By Character Type (animate, inanimate; human, animal, mix; others)		
Marked vs. Unmarked (Generic) Characters		
Individual or Social Context		
Individuals		
Groups		
Mixed		
Activities		
Apparent Character Motivations		
Depicted Capabilities		

In terms of non-formal learning indicators, conferences, live events, pre-recorded events, presentations, and film showings may suggest non-formal learning. If these are harnessed for for-credit learning, these could also be indicated in the formal learning space. One visualization in particular had a sign that read "please mute your mic," which suggests people interacting live in-world. A screenshot of developers in an online space suggest both the possibilities of nonformal learning (based on some structured learning) and informal learning (based on the potentials for informal interrelating and activities).

There were a number of indicators of informal learning: an avatar wearing a presidential election t-shirt (that may encourage political participation in a democracy), an automated bingo hall (that may convey how to play bingo), avatars blinged out with clothing and jewelry and sneakers (that may convey style and pride and material culture), a digital headstone (that may convey the ephemerality of the world), various virtual storefronts and ad posters (that may convey entrepreneurship), selfies (that may convey the importance of self-expression and self-identity), dance floors and leisure sites (that may convey the importance of hedonic pleasures), dating spaces (that may convey dating mores), work spaces (that may convey work practices), underwater exploration work by avatars carrying various tools (that may encourage adventure), religious imagery (that may encourage spiritual exploration), and so on. There were breathtaking artfully-created still images in SL (a reflection of palm trees in virtual water, ice-laden trees in a wheat field, fantasy cities, a b/w nature scene, and others). Some depictions show creatures with elegant and elongated limbs, as pseudo-humanoid figures. One image showed a tribute to *Titanic* (1997) with the iconic scene of Leonardo DiCaprio and Kate Winslet (which also shows something of the cultural influences in SL). Another visual showed some fictional maps styled to those of centuries ago wrapped around a round earth as a texture, which may encourage exploration and informal learning.

Table 4. Item types (elements in the scene) data coding Table 3

3. Item Types (Elements in the Scene)	Flickr Social Image Set	Google Images Social Image Set
Natural Items in the Environment		
Flora		
Fauna		
Human-Made Objects (Indoors)		
Buildings and Structures		
Transportation		
Machinery		
Furniture		
Tools		
Uses of Items		
Designed Usage(s)		
Applied Usage(s)		
Purposes of Objects		

Table 5. Automation, mechanization, and artificial intelligence (ai) data coding Table 4

4. Automation, Mechanization, and Artificial Intelligence (AI)	Flickr Social Image Set	Google Images Social Image Set
Depictions of AI (Artificial Intelligence)		
AI Agents / Robots (as animals, machines, humanoids, other)		
Automated or Scripted Objects		

Table 6. Types of learning portrayed in the respective SL social image sets

	Flickr Social Image Set	Google Images Social Image Set
Formal Learning		
Nonformal Learning		
Informal Learning		

Visuals of conference spaces and galleries convey a sense of both nonformal and informal learning; of course, if these spaces were harnessed for credit-courses, these would also clearly enable formal learning. In other words, the coding does not have to be mutually exclusive.

The casual vibe in many of the SL spaces conveys a sense that social conformity is not that necessary. For example, in one image of a group of human-embodied avatars on a wharf, the characters are dressed in evening gowns (two), nightwear and animal slippers and a hat; sweater and jeans; and a t-shirt and jeans. They are all facing each other and interacting in the visual. While SL culture is not the focus of this work, the sense of play and creativity comes through powerfully in many of the social images from Flickr.

As to technology representations, there were many of these: futuristic cities, transportation methods, robots in various forms, and even retro technologies (a young man next to an old-style record player). Sometimes, technologies are hinted at. In one image, an avatar is lying in a field of flowers, which in the real world, would have required a drone camera to capture that aerial selfie.

In Google Images, many of the same types of contents were found above. And then there were also some other interesting aspects. One screenshot or image showed a "history walk" in-world, which suggests that if an exploring avatar went down that path that they would see images and simulations and role plays bringing a historical event to life. Clearly, such an approach can include formal, nonformal, and informal types of learning. (This is not to say that signage is always accurate or that a lot can be read into an image, but it is possible that the design of the space may be backed up by professional follow-through.)

In the Google Images set, there were more combinations of real-world imagery with SL images. There were also many more suggestive images (maybe because much more variety is shared online than on a dedicated image-sharing site like Flickr). Some professional roles indicated in the imagery include designers, artists, and archivists, which may suggest the nonformal and informal learning of those in professional and hobby groups. Some of the images showed data visualizations and data tables (which are generally more evocative of formal learning but may also be inclusive of nonformal and informal learning).

It may help to summarize the findings with a light coding table.

Table 7. General indicators for identifying formal, nonformal, and informal learning in second life®

Types of Learning	Images from Second Life®
Formal (accredited learning tracks)	campus spaces; digital poster sessions; designed natural science and social science simulations (with costly custom scripting); collaboration spaces; amphitheaters; movie theaters; virtual labs; foreign language spaces; coding spaces; artificial intelligence spaces; spaces with complex data visualizations; spaces signed to particular K12 and institutions of higher education, and others (often also private spaces which require student status for entry)
Nonformal (structured non-credit learning)	movie theaters; virtual shops; social spaces; professional club spaces; coding spaces; interactive language spaces; immersive suspense games; role play spaces, and others
Informal (learning as a byproduct of informal activities)	hedonic play spaces; simulations; game spaces, and virtually anywhere on *Second Life®*

Table 7 shows that the spaces that may indicate particular types of learning are not mutually exclusive. A space may be used for multiple types of learning. For informal learning, virtually any space may enable this because such learning may occur in any context. Also, while formal learning may apply to

K12, a perusal of the image sets in SL showed mostly adult learning applications from higher education. Of course, many of the observations were of static images, which have their limits. Observations during live events may be much more informative. How the teaching is structured and led can be much more revelatory. Finally, Table 7 is a general coding table, and it may certainly be refined further.

Some Additional Insights

In the manual coding, a few additional insights were captured in a less systematic way, such as about the level of design inputs that apparent went into a screen capture. In one sense, each of the images required work to attain since the spaces have to be built out, the avatars designed, and such, before images may be taken. In some of the images that related to live events, a lot of work has to go into the organization of the event to bring people together…to ultimately enable the documentation of the event. That said, most screenshots did not seem to require a lot of effort otherwise. One series of images with one particular avatar showed it with a drooping head (from lack of activity)…across two dozen-plus screenshots. That would only require navigating to a space and taking the shot. However, the one exception about effortful imagery has to be the art-based images, which clearly took a sophisticated eye and a talented hand to build.

Another question was whether these screenshots of constructed worlds could be used similarly to real-world photos. Clearly, these cannot. The available visual information is different and lesser on a number of dimensions. The lack of serendipity is an issue, and the missing information and lack of fidelity to a real space is limiting.

Finally, if Marshall McLuhan was right and the medium is the message, what is this medium (Second Life®) saying about learning (formally, nonformally, and informally)? Superficially, SL is about what people bring to it and what they invest in it. It is a purposeful and designed space with so much potential. It suggests that learning is inherent in humanity, and that learning is infused in the social imagery of SL shared on social media platforms.

FUTURE RESEARCH DIRECTIONS

A review of the virtual immersive spaces available into the present age with Second Life® reveals many which still have a web presence. In alphabetical order, they include the following: Active Worlds (https://www.activeworlds.com/web/index.php), Blue Mars (http://www.bluemarsonline.com/), Habbo Hotel (https://www.habbo.com/), Kaneva (http://www.kaneva.com/), Onverse (http://offline.onverse.com/) (which had a note to the community about having been "infiltrated by a few players who wish to do us harm" to explain their offline state), OpenSim (http://opensim.stanford.edu/), SmallWorlds (https://www.smallworlds.com/), There.com (https://www.prod.there.com/), Twinity (http://www.twinity.com/en/choose-your-free-avatar), and Whyville (http://www.whyville.net/smmk/nice). Second Life® (http://secondlife.com/) is the site of this study. Other sites have since come and gone. If there is a sufficient user base that may enable "network effects," this same research approach may be applied to one or more of the above sites to see what may be learned about formal, nonformal, and informal learning occurring there.

This work approached the topic of different types of learning enabled on Second Life® through the analysis of social imagery shared on Flickr and on Google Images. This work used a build-as-you-go method to create tools that might exploit the available data, and this also used bottom-up coding. This approach is an "etic" one from without or from the outside; another approach may be an "emic" one from within, based on various types of *sousveillance*.

Certainly, there are other ways to understand some of the learning going on in SL. For example, it may be helpful to technologically map the most-used locations in an island and representing these findings in a heat map. There are numerous opportunities for case studies of learning as well. Transcripts and discussions between learners may be analyzed for content analysis, through both manual and automated coding means.

CONCLUSION

To summarize, this work involves the bottom-up coding of approximately 1,550 social images related to "Second Life" shared on Flickr and Google Images. These images are decontextualized residua from screenshots and *machinima* video screengrabs. While coding a thousand images manually is challenging, this image set is only a small portion of available social media imagery, and this set is not randomly selected per se (but chosen by user-created folk tagging and the search algorithms of the respective platforms and the apps used to capture some of the images). There is virtually never one fully accepted, defensible, reproducible and objective interpretation of data, and there is practically no N = all, and no analysis of such big data datasets without computational means. An indirect analytical approach has its affordances and its limits. Also, the quantitative coding part of this was not followed-through on since this work was mainly to create the data coding tables and capture some initial insights.

After months spent immersing in SL imagery, there is a powerful allure to the normal aspects of the world: people aging gracefully and sometimes awkwardly, leaves falling off wind-blown trees, dust motes in the air, food that appeals on multiple sensory levels, weeds on lawns, and a world of "imperfections." There is a hunger for small accidents and surprises. The RL world has dazzle and beauty that suspends judgment and leaves humans agape, but without the other aspects of an alternate unreal and the plastic.

In several recent published works about Second Life, several writers have asked about the state of SL. Implicit is the question of whether the moment has passed for this technology or whether some retro revival might refocus modern-day attention to this. Has SL outlived its value, and does it still have some bases on which to attract the interests of educators and learners? An important question in this space is what it would take for virtual worlds to become central to online, blended, and F2F learning. Do the platforms have to be more efficient and speedy to "rez"? Do the visualizations have to be more informative and precise, with less dazzle? Do the state-of-the-art simulations have to be more versatile and precise? Do physics engines have to be more robust and real-world? Would there have to be peda- gogical tools—to measure learning, to measure learner behaviors, to measure other metrics in the virtual world—to make virtual worlds more friendly for immersive learning? Would there have to be stronger partnerships between virtual worlds and learning management system (LMS) providers and content providers? Do user interfaces have to be more accessible? What would it take to create an organic and strong user base globally?

If the bottom-up image analytics in this work are any indication, formal, nonformal, and informal learning is possible in *Second Life*, but formal and non-formal learning are under great pressure to con- trol for costs. Any technological platform has to continuously prove its value. Informal learning, too, is possible, but it is not clear that the available lessons on *Second Life* are that compelling or attractive. If immersive virtuality is to be a space for effective learning in its various forms, it seems like there will have to be additional enablements and functionalities beyond SL to draw a crowd that will fully actualize the virtual space.

REFERENCES

Andalibi, N., Ozturk, P., & Forte, A. (2015). Depression-related imagery on Instagram. *Proceedings of CSCW '15 Companion*, 231 – 234. 10.1145/2685553.2699014

Antonacci, D. M., & Modaress, N. (2008). Envisioning the Educational Possibilities of User-Created Virtual Worlds. *Association for the Advancement of Computing in Education Journal*, *16*(2), 115–126.

Bainbridge, W. S. (2007). The scientific research potential of virtual worlds. *Science*, *317*(5837), 472–476. doi:10.1126cience.1146930 PMID:17656715

Bardzell, S., & Odom, W. (2008, August). The experience of embodied space in virtual worlds: An ethnography of a Second Life community. *Space and Culture*, *11*(3), 239–259. doi:10.1177/1206331208319148

Bell, M.W., Castronova, E., & Wagner, G.G. (2009). *Surveying the virtual world: A large scale survey in Second Life using the Virtual Data Collection Interface (VDCI)*. RatSWD research notes. No. 40.

Boulos, M. N. K., Hetherington, L., & Wheeler, S. (2007, December). Second Life: An overview of the potential of 3-D virtual worlds in medical and health education. *Health Information and Libraries Journal*, *24*(4), 233–245. doi:10.1111/j.1471-1842.2007.00733.x PMID:18005298

Burgess, M. L., Slate, J. R., Rojas-LeBouef, A., & LaPrairie, K. (2010). Teaching and learning in *Second Life:* Using the Community of Inquiry (CoI) model to support online instruction with graduate students in instructional technology. *Internet and Higher Education*, *13*(1-2), 84–88. doi:10.1016/j.iheduc.2009.12.003

Campbell, C. (2009, April). Learning in a different life: Pre-service education students using an online virtual world. *Journal of Virtual Worlds Research*, *1*(2), 4–17.

Chandra, Y., & Leenders, M. A. A. M. (2012). User innovation and entrepreneurship in the virtual world: A study of Second Life residents. *Technovation*, *32*(7-8), 464–476. doi:10.1016/j.technovation.2012.02.002

Chin, B. M. (2007). Regulating your Second Life: Defamation in virtual worlds. *Brooklyn Law Review*, *72*(4), 1303–1349.

Davidson, S. J. (2007, Apr. 25). An immersive perspective on the Second Life virtual world. *Computer and Internet Lawyer.* Retrieved from https://www.pli.edu/emktg/toolbox/second_life11.pdf

Dawley, L. (2009). Social network knowledge construction: Emerging virtual world pedagogy. *On the Horizon*, *17*(2), 109–121. doi:10.1108/10748120910965494

de Freitas, S., Rebolledo-Mendez, G., Liarokapis, F., Magoulas, G., & Poulovassilis, A. (2010). Learning as immersive experiences: Using the four-dimensional framework for designing and evaluating immersive learning experiences in a virtual world. *British Journal of Educational Technology*, *41*(1), 69–85. doi:10.1111/j.1467-8535.2009.01024.x

De Lucia, A., Francese, R., Passero, I., & Tortora, G. (2009). Development and evaluation of a virtual campus on Second Life: The case of SecondDMI. *Computers & Education*, *52*(1), 220–233. doi:10.1016/j.compedu.2008.08.001

Dickey, M. D. (2011, February). The pragmatics of virtual worlds for K-12 educators: Investigating the affordances and constraints of 'Active Worlds' and 'Second Life' with K-12 in-service teachers. *Educational Technology Research and Development*, *59*(1), 1–20. doi:10.100711423-010-9163-4

Dreher, C., Reiners, T., Dreher, N., & Dreher, H. (2009, Summer). Virtual worlds as a context suited for Information Systems Education: Discussion of pedagogical experience and curriculum design with reference to Second Life. *Journal of Information Systems Education*, *20*(2), 211–224.

Economy of *Second Life*. (2018, Jan. 8). In *Wikipedia*. Retrieved from https://en.wikipedia.org/wiki/Economy_of_Second_Life

Edds, R. (2014, Apr. 10). 29 terrifying panorama fails that will haunt your nightmares. *BuzzFeed*. Retrieved from https://www.buzzfeed.com/robinedds/terrifying-panorama-fails-that-will-haunt-your-nightmares?utm_term=.uwYE5EXD0#.tnQg4g6ok

Erdman, J. (2007). Reference in a 3-D virtual world: Preliminary observations on library outreach in "Second Life." *The Reference Librarian*, *47*(2), 29–39. doi:10.1300/J120v47n98_04

Esteves, M., Fonseca, B., Morgado, L., & Martins, P. (2010). Improving reaching and learning of computer programming through the use of the Second Life virtual world. *British Journal of Educational Technology*, 1–14.

Fetscherin, M., & Lattemann, C. (2008). User acceptance of virtual worlds. *Journal of Electronic Commerce Research*, *9*(3), 231–242.

Friedman, D., Steed, A., & Slater, M. (2007). Spatial social behavior in Second Life. *International Workshop on Intelligent Virtual Agents,* 252 – 263. Retrieved from https://link.springer.com/chapter/10.1007/978-3-540-74997-4_23

Glaser, B., & Strauss, A. (1999). *The Discovery of Grounded Theory: Strategies for Qualitative Research.* New Brunswick, NJ: AldineTransaction.

Good, J., Howland, K., & Thackray, L. (2008). Problem-based learning spanning real and virtual words (sic): A case study in Second Life. *ALT-J: Research in Learning Technology*, *16*(3), 163–172. doi:10.3402/rlt.v16i3.10895

Gottschalk, S. (2010, Fall). The presentation of avatars in Second Life: Self and interaction in social virtual spaces. *Symbolic Interaction*, *33*(4), 501–525. doi:10.1525i.2010.33.4.501

Gregory, S., & Masters, Y. (2012). Real thinking with virtual hats: A role-playing activity for pre-service teachers in *Second Life. Australasian Journal of Educational Technology*, *28*(3), 420–440. doi:10.14742/ajet.843

Hai-Jew, S. (2009, September). Exploring the immersive parasocial: Is it you or the thought of you? *Journal of Online Learning and Teaching / MERLOT*, *5*(3). Retrieved from http://jolt.merlot.org/vol5no3/hai-jew_0909.htm

Harrison, R. (2009). Excavating Second Life: Cyber-Archaeologies, Heritage and Virtual Communities. *Journal of Material Cultures*. Retrieved from http://journals.sagepub.com/doi/abs/10.1177/1359183508100009

Hassouneh, D., & Brengman, M. (2014). A motivation-based typology of social virtual world users. *Computers in Human Behavior*, *33*, 330–338. doi:10.1016/j.chb.2013.08.012

Hayes, E. R. (2006). Situated learning in virtual worlds: The learning ecology of Second Life. *Adult Education Research Conference*, 154 – 159.

Helmer, J. (2007). *Learning Light*. Second Life and Virtual Worlds.

History of Second Life. (2017, Dec. 29). Retrieved from wiki.secondlife.com

Hobbs, M., Brown, E., & Gordon, M. (2006). Using a virtual world for transferable skills in gaming education. *Innovation in Teaching and Learning in Information and Computer Sciences*, *5*(3), 1–13. doi:10.11120/ital.2006.05030006

Jamaludin, A., Chee, Y. S., & Ho, C. M. L. (2009). Fostering argumentative knowledge construction through enactive role play in *Second Life*. *Computers & Education*, *53*(2), 317–329. doi:10.1016/j.compedu.2009.02.009

Jamison, L. (2017, Dec.). The digital ruins of a forgotten future. *The Atlantic*. Retrieved from https://www.theatlantic.com/magazine/archive/2017/12/second-life-leslie-jamison/544149/

Jarmon, L., Traphagan, T., Mayrath, M., & Trivedi, A. (2009). Virtual world teaching, experiential learning, and assessment: An interdisciplinary communication course in Second Life. *Computers & Education*, *53*(1), 169–182. doi:10.1016/j.compedu.2009.01.010

Jennings, N., & Collins, C. (2007). Virtual or Virtually U: Educational institutions in Second Life. *International Journal of Educational and Pedagogical Sciences*, *1*(11), 713–719.

Jung, Y., & Kang, H. (2010). User goals in social virtual worlds: A means-end chain approach. *Computers in Human Behavior*, *26*(2), 218–225. doi:10.1016/j.chb.2009.10.002

Kanwisher, N. (2015, Summer). *Lecture 6.1: Introduction to Social Intelligence. Brains, Minds and Machines Summer Course*. RES.9-003. Massachusetts Institute of Technology. Retrieved from https://youtu.be/HA4undazeF0

Kumar, S., Chhugani, J., Kim, C., Kim, D., Nguyen, A., Dubey, P., Bienia, C., & Kim, Y. (2008, Sept.). *Second Life* and the new generation of virtual worlds. *Computer,* 48 – 55.

Lemos, R. (2006, Nov. 24). Second life plagued by 'grey goo' attack: Viruses go virtual. *The Register.* Retrieved from https://www.theregister.co.uk/2006/11/24/secondlife_greygoo_attack/

Magic circle (virtual worlds). (2017, Oct. 23). In *Wikipedia*. Retrieved from https://en.wikipedia.org/wiki/Magic_circle_(virtual_worlds)

Maiberg, E. (2016, Apr. 29). Why is This Still a Thing? "Why is "Second Life" Still a Thing? *Motherboard. Vice*. Retrieved from https://motherboard.vice.com/en_us/article/z43mwj/why-is-second-life-still-a-thing-gaming-virtual-reality

Mennecke, B. E., McNeill, D., Roche, E. M., Bray, D. A., Townsend, A. M., & Lester, J. (2008). Second Life and other virtual worlds: A roadmap for research. *Communications of the Association for Information Systems*, *22*, 371–388.

Minocha, S., Tran, M. Q., & Reeves, A. J. (2010, November). Conducting empirical research in virtual worlds: Experiences from two projects in Second Life. *Journal of Virtual Worlds Research*, *3*(1), 3–21.

Pellas, N., & Kazanidis, I. (2014). Online and hybrid university-level courses with the utilization of Second Life: Investigating the factors that predict student choice in Second Life supported online and hybrid university-level courses. *Computers in Human Behavior*, *40*, 31–43. doi:10.1016/j.chb.2014.07.047

Petrakou, A. (2010). Interacting through avatars: Virtual worlds as a context for online education. *Computers & Education*, *54*(4), 1020–1027. doi:10.1016/j.compedu.2009.10.007

Private Region Pricing. (2018, April). Retrieved from https://secondlife.com/land/privatepricing.php

Ruth. (2015, Apr. 15). In *Second Life Wiki*. Retrieved from http://wiki.secondlife.com/wiki/Ruth

Salt, B., Atkins, C., & Blackall, L. (2008, Oct.). Engaging with Second Life: Real Education in a Virtual World. *Literature Review*, 1 – 100.

Schmeil, A., & Eppler, M. J. (2008). Knowledge sharing and collaborative learning in Second Life: A classification of virtual 3D group interaction scripts. *Journal of Universal Computer Science*, *14*(3), 665–677.

Sociology of space. (2018, Feb. 10). In *Wikipedia*. Retrieved from https://en.wikipedia.org/wiki/Sociology_of_space

System Requirements. (2018). Retrieved from https://secondlife.com/support/system-requirements//

Takahashi, D. (2009, Oct. 9). Terrorists in Second Life. *Foreign Policy*. Retrieved from http://foreignpolicy.com/2009/10/09/terrorists-in-second-life/

Terdiman, D. (2007, Nov. 30). Report: Hackers say they can steal 'Second Life' currency. *c|net*. Retrieved from https://www.cnet.com/news/report-hackers-say-they-can-steal-second-life-currency/

Tuten, T. (2009). Real World Experience, Virtual World Environment: The Design and Execution of Marketing Plans in Second Life. *Marketing Education Review*, *19*(1), 1–5. doi:10.1080/10528008.2009.11489053

Urban, R. J., Marty, P. F., & Twidale, M. B. (2007). *A Second Life for your museum: 3D multi-user virtual environments and museums*. Illinois Digital Environment for Access to Learning and Scholarship. Retrieved from https://www.ideals.illinois.edu/handle/2142/1619

Warburton, S. (2009). Second Life in higher education: Assessing the potential for and the barriers to deploying virtual worlds in learning and teaching. *British Journal of Educational Technology*, *40*(3), 414–426. doi:10.1111/j.1467-8535.2009.00952.x

Wecker, M. (2014, Apr. 22). What ever happened to Second Life? *ChronicleVitae*. Retrieved from https://chroniclevitae.com/news/456-what-ever-happened-to-second-life

Wiecha, J., Heyden, R., Sternthal, E., & Merialdi, M. (2010, January – March). Learning in a virtual world: Experience with using Second Life for medical education. *Journal of Medical Internet Research*, *12*(1), e1. doi:10.2196/jmir.1337 PMID:20097652

Yee, N., Bailenson, J. N., Urbanek, M., Chang, F., & Merget, D. (2007). The unbearable likeness of being digital: The persistence of nonverbal social norms in online virtual environments. *Cyberpsychology & Behavior*, *10*(1), 115–121. doi:10.1089/cpb.2006.9984 PMID:17305457

Yellowlees, P. M., & Cook, J. N. (2006, November – December). Education about hallucinations using an Internet virtual reality system: A qualitative survey. Using Technology to Teach Clinical Care. *Academic Psychiatry*, *30*(6), 534–539. doi:10.1176/appi.ap.30.6.534 PMID:17139026

Zhang, H. (2013, March). Pedagogical challenges of spoken English learning in the Second Life virtual world: A case study. *British Journal of Educational Technology*, *44*(2), 243–254. doi:10.1111/j.1467-8535.2012.01312.x

Zhou, Z., Jin, X.-L., Vogel, D. R., Fang, Y., & Chen, X. (2011). Individual motivations and demographic differences in social virtual world uses: An exploratory investigation in Second Life. *International Journal of Information Management*, *31*(3), 261–271. doi:10.1016/j.ijinfomgt.2010.07.007

Zielke, M. A., Roome, T. C., & Krueger, A. B. (2009, April). A composite adult learning model for virtual world residents with disabilities: A Case Study of the Virtual Ability Second Life Island. *Journal of Virtual Worlds Research*, *2*(1), 4–21.

ADDITIONAL READING

Robbins, S., & Bell, M. (2008). *Second Life® for Dummies*. Hoboken, NJ: Wiley Publishing, Inc.

KEY TERMS AND DEFINITIONS

Avatar: A humanoid figure in a digital space, a graphical representation of a person.

Cyber-Physical Confluence: The coming together of the digital and real-world physical realms, commonalities between cyber and the real.

Formal Learning: Accredited and defined learning sequences such as K12 and higher education.

Free-Form: Without a pre-determined structure (or directed purpose).

Hyperrealism: An adjective describing artificially designed objects and artworks that are more real than reality, with a detailed depth of details and resolution.

Immersive Parasocial: The illusory sense of the existence of a relationship with a public figure as instantiated through avatars in virtual immersive worlds.

Immersive Virtual World: Online spaces that are three-dimensional and persistent over time, in which people may act and interact with others with long-term and persistent avatars.

Informal Learning: Learning that occurs as a byproduct of other activities.

Metaverse: A computer-generated virtual reality (VR) space or environment.

Multi-User Virtual Environment (MUVE): Immersive virtual worlds that may be used for collaborative and situated learning.

Nonformal Learning: Structured learning that is not credited or certified.

Open-Source: Digital objects that have revealed and viewable codes, often also indicating free use.

Physics Engine: A part of an immersive virtual world that simulates aspects of real-world physics and physical systems.

Prims (Primitives): An atomistic element of a 3D virtual object/shape used to construct larger objects.

Script: Computer commands (written in scripting computer language).

Second Life®: A proprietary virtual immersive world created by the San Francisco-based Linden Research, Inc. (Linden Lab).

Social Imagery: Open-access imagery shared on social media content-sharing platforms.

Social Virtual World (SVW): A persistent virtual immersive space where people go online to meet a variety of individual and social human needs.

Synthetic World: A virtual environment that enables large-group interactions (a term coined by Edward Castronova in his book of the same name in 2005).

This research was previously published in Methods for Analyzing and Leveraging Online Learning Data; pages 135-166, copyright year 2019 by Information Science Reference (an imprint of IGI Global).

Chapter 24
The Avatar as a Self–Representation Model for Expressive and Intelligent Driven Visualizations in Immersive Virtual Worlds:
A Background to Understand Online Identity Formation, Selfhood, and Virtual Interactions

Colina Demirdjian
Double Trouble Creatives, Australia

Hripsime Demirdjian
Double Trouble Creatives, Australia

ABSTRACT

One could argue that the "self" as a human entity will be affected by the desire for more intelligence-driven products and creations. The avatar acts as an agent that unlocks the pathway to a better version of the human self. The true power of the avatar is beyond the comprehension of those that see it as a replica or a clone of a human. Rather, for those that look through the lens of the future, the avatar has the power(s) that mankind ultimately desires in their fulfilment of selfhood. To this end, the perception of the avatar needs to be reconsidered in order to appropriately recognise the avatar's multi-dimensional advantages and opportunities it holds for society and how it enhances the human condition. This paper creates a backdrop for understanding the avatar in the connected modalities of the real and virtual state of environments. This paper will also attempt to tackle the connected conditions that emerge as avatar-to-avatar interaction happens through the works of current research to understand the avatar more in-depth.

DOI: 10.4018/978-1-6684-7597-3.ch024

INTRODUCTION

The future is immersive. Understanding that the ultimate desire of the human is to obtain their highest point of satisfaction, is what Maslow calls self-actualisation. Self-actualisation is an important concept to extending our learning of the manifestation of the avatar. Our continuous absorption of the digital and virtual world helps nurture an environment in which the avatar can flourish and coexist with its human counterpart; thus serving its owner by realising its human goals. The phenomenon of the avatar becomes more real as we continue to understand the ever-growing importance it holds for the evolution of mankind as a vehicle for pushing and extending life, rewarding experiences, desired traits and abilities for the human generation to overcome human challenges.

This leads us into a probing question about whether the virtual avatar is the inevitable new mode of existence to carry the human race forward to a new era of digital enlightenment that is based on the 'survival of the fittest'. Furthermore, does the avatar achieve what it is supposed to achieve? This highlights the purpose of this paper; that is to explore this more closely and unravel the truth behind the 'virtual you'.

BACKGROUND

The digital representation or visualization of ourselves is commonly known as an avatar. The word "avatar" is borrowed from Hindu myths alluding to embodiment of a superior being (Lyons, Plante, Jehan, Inoue and Akamatsu, 1998, p. 427). As such, the avatar acts as an agent of our identity allowing for digital personification and connecting our real life presence with our virtual world form in a way that the human body cannot be available.

Our objective should be to deliver humanity value by accelerating and shaping avatar technology to personalize various domains, infusing it with a genuine attractiveness in the new age of authenticity. If we can preserve the core elements of authenticity, we believe the avatar will serve to connect humans to a new form of storytelling that prioritizes the individual's unique footprint and personality to achieve trust in virtual interactions they have and ultimately build loyalty for people to adopt the technology. Rooted on embracing individuality, authenticity and change, the avatar developments will need to built in such ways that aim to make human interaction real by focusing on these core principles.

Driven by the imaginations that have sought to compensate for the sensory and physical constraints we humans desire, descriptively speaking, the avatar provides the only pragmatic solution and capacities to embody us mere mortals and transform us into emerging worlds that we will create as our search for more immersive realism continues (Piryankova, 2015, p. 13-25). It follows that we should enter digital worlds in the same way that we have always entered into our natural habitats and a language of embodiment must organically be born within it.

The avatar can be seen as an extension of the evolution of the technologically mediated body language, enabling us to fulfil and develop our cognitive, personal, social, affective and escapist needs (Moore, 2012, p.48-63). In this search for self-fulfilment of these needs, there comes a time where the virtual stimulation supplies self-gratification that we individuals crave, in such a way that the brain starts to fail to differentiate between the virtual and real experiences (Gamez, 2007, p. 51-66). In the same way, as the avatar becomes so real to us humans, the three-dimensional digital recreation of the person becomes indifferent to the human owner and their real-world identity. Such a fusion leads to an interesting proposition – the brain tends not to care if the experience is real or virtual. This allows us humans to enter into the so called 'inter-reality' that is the seamless stay in both 'real' and 'virtual' reality.

To lay a relevant backdrop, in the blockbuster film 'The Matrix', Neo (played by Keanu Reeves) supports this ideology that virtual reality could be so real, that millions of viewers have no idea that they are living in a stimulation because of the strong attachment they feel to the online persona. In reality, frontiers are deep embedded in our frame of mind, to the extent that wearing an avatar will be like wearing contact lenses with a lack of awareness that they are attached to our human bodies (Blascovich & Bailenson, 2011). In the same way that the Nintendo Wii has made a significant leap in avatar control over the joystick and the keyboard over the years, avatars will be automatic without having to use any type of controller – just our physical bodies (Blascovich & Bailenson, 2011, p. 1-4).

If notions of the self are malleable and susceptible to influence, then people could use the avatar to enhance their digital footprint (Suler, 2016, p. 369). Let's look a bit more closely at this by observing the inescapable human concern – age. Think about never having any wrinkles, sagging skin, age-related body pains and never having your youthful glow compromised. On this point, think about the avatar surpassing the human timeline and powering the extension of human existence after death.

Simply treating avatars as a new mode of human existence would help us to create alternative models of resistance to time and enhance the human condition in larger dimensions such as the Internet world. We would be able to imagine the self in new forms of imaging, language and self-projection, whilst being free to explore new capabilities that we become newly equipped with by using the powers of our digital embodiment as an avatar. The work of Warwick (2003) analyses how the combination of flesh-and-machine can pass on to humans essential inherit properties that advances the human condition. According to Warwick (2003, p. 131-2), a "cyborg is formed by a human, machine brain/nervous system coupling" and would allow us to alter human's bodily functions to meet new human desires. Using a cyborg could permit humans to shed the natural weaknesses of the human flesh, provide them a networked machine element to their physical beings by staying connected to computer power and facilitate faster brain calculations than the average human model. As we consider this, one could argue living vicariously through avatars or a digital agent holds many benefits for the human specie.

However, we acknowledge the importance of maintaining authenticity in this new age of digital embodiment. In order to keep our social roles and expectations within our existing physical reality, we must remain true to our identities and relationships we have formed in the real offline world. The value of the avatar is best experienced when true connections and socialization occurs that is rooted in something real which can help us forge more immersive interactions with one another online, such like it was conducted in an offline face-to-face setting. As we manufacture these mixed realities and continue to embrace them, striking the right balance and finding a harmonized check of living in this continuum with avatars is important for its successful assimilation into our current physical worlds.

Whilst the human and the avatar may find themselves sharing the real and virtual world, a condition that does separate the human from the avatar is that the avatar can be manufactured to posses as little or as many superior qualities or favourable traits it desires. This gives it power to control its living timeline above the natural condition of mankind and its environment. This brings us to the notion of the 'survival of the fittest'. In Darwinian terms, this is best understood as 'survival of the form that will leave the most copies of itself in successive- generations' (Hall, 2017, p. 62). We can illustrate that there are many assumptions that the adoption of an avatar would allow us to create models that we could personalize and by that creation, choose favourable traits which would in turn, ever-strengthen our existence across boundaries that have yet to be fully explored (Sparrow, 2010, p. 9).

In this process, caution should be exercised in allowing such customization abilities. Providing humans with too much freedom in their avatar development might persuade them to falsely represent themselves or express an enhanced self-image that they feel is more desirable to others. This may also encourage humans to disengage with their human identity and adopt their self-created and self-personalized avatar identity. Whilst, the avatar will help us overcome some of our immediate real world limitations and weaknesses, if we want to achieve self-actualisation whilst maintaining core aspects of authenticity (as we earlier described), there is some careful consideration that needs to be done about how we develop and empower humans to interact and use their avatars. If the avatar development and creation process is built around maintaining elements of our identities formed in the real world and can strike the right balance between the freedom to explore our selfhood and the principles of authenticity, then the avatar can be the truest form to express ourselves online.

Each day, millions of people connect with each other over the Internet. In doing so, immediately our network continues to expand more and more, whilst the world around us appears to become smaller. Avatars will not only change how we view the world, but we believe will impact our social institutions, such as family, friendships, education and religion. It can be said that the impact of the avatar goes beyond the sentient of these institutions, as they provide us with the tools to influence the people around us in ways which are not possible in our physical world. To the end that avatars influence our existing social structures, it might be useful to illuminate the connection between avatars and identity formation.

To do this effectively, first the concept of identity must be explored both from sociological and philosophical perspectives. Before discussing identity from an avatar viewpoint, carefully consider how you relate to friends, family, relatives, colleagues and how this has attributed to our own person qualities, embedded in our perceptions of self. If you think deeply about the social construct of our relationships and assign different levels of intimacy to these relations, you will start to garner and collect information about your own identity. Stemming from this, our identity and 'creation of self' is constructed by our own involvement in different social environments. This is partly a reality of garnering different interpersonal relations with others in various ways and partly as a result of our own internalised thoughts of our self-presentation. In doing so then, the central normative points of our identity are altered by the dynamics of existing relationships (intrinsic point) and our self-presentation which may have implications on the kinds of relations we choose to establish with others (extrinsic points) (Mathews, 2008, p. 153-4).

In the virtual world, these relationships are partly re-cultivated and re-structured with new forms of identity, disassociation (in the case, where one has multiple identities) anonymity, gender fluidity, which are uniquely manifested by the nature of the online web (Kokswijk, 2007, p. 7). Conducive to our virtual presence, here the avatar can (inter)act autonomously for its human representative and offer endless possibilities of new meaningful experiences they have yet to imagine in their current world. First, as a reflective being, the avatar serves as a medium to extend our self- expression beyond tangible enterprises and secondly, the avatar is a significant mechanism in personality development underlying our 'real' self-image and 'ideal' self-image, (which we believe the avatar largely helps construct) (Mathews, 2008, p. 154-9). From what we have understood so far, we think a normative consideration would be that, if we can bind these two constructs of the self together, rooted in what is real, then we can close the gap between our real and virtual identities to develop an unified embodiment of the self that connects our present ends to our future possibilities.

Once we recognise the close connection between the human and the avatar, we start to accept that the avatar imposes deliberate action to project a person to their future, requires each of us to participate in self-construction. This is practical in essence. As one acts for their human self, they also project action for their avatar. As Korsgaard (1989, p.113-114) proposes, '[t]he sort of thing you identify yourself with, may carry you automatically into the future... Indeed, the choice of any action, no matter how trivial, takes you some way into the future. And the extent to which you regulate your choices, by identifying yourself as the one who is implementing something like a particular plan of life, you need to identify with your future in order to be *what you are even now*'.

Underlying this, is what we believe also connects us to our virtual identity; it is the narrative we tell as an avatar. This must be authentic in various respects to our human self and must be concerned with coherence in that, if the narrative we construct is incoherent, our story becomes fragmented and deprives us of the capacity to articulate selfhood and become effective self-governing beings in the virtual world. Our value as an avatar identity therefore, attaches to our capacity to remain true and construct a narrative that is embedded in something real, and continues our existing real-world relationships (Mathews, 2008, p. 148, 155-7). It helps play out our valued social roles, perform our obligations and meet our goals. To this end, the avatar, if correctly used, continues our extended narrative and in this thread of discussion, it is important to consider how these factors affect our continued identity as an avatar.

Respectfully, we put forward that the nexus between our avatar and identity, on a surface level, simmers down to the effect that our avatar has on those self-construction and self- presentation elements which form our identity, given the social parameters around the notion of identity formation. As self-reflective beings, we not only have a sense of who we are, but the ideal individual we want to become. Even further, our avatar (which we have already pointed out, represents our narrative beyond our real world) unifies us to our future selves to best continue the narrative we have so far established for ourselves today.

Equally important, is a consideration of autonomy without which our avatar story may be fragmented and lead to disconnected notions of our identity. In any event, not much good would come from the lack of a narrative and, we believe, would disqualify us from developing our sense of self-construction. Arguably, the avatar can become the main mode of communication that allows us to successfully engage in new meaningful and immersive ways. We are by no means suggesting that the avatar will replace all forms of communication such as emails and SMS, but will indeed help us to better immerse ourselves in the new emerging technological worlds we will witness over time (Mathews, 2008, p. 159). One of the most essential attributes is that our identity is sensitive to modes of self-construction. It retains choice over the use of our avatar (both in its extent and mode of use) and can provide reasons for our embodiment in the private and public spheres (Sundar, 2015, p.103-105).

As the construction of the avatar comes into play, one must understand the implications that may (simultaneously or naturally) be created once an avatar is introduced. The challenge becomes understanding the ethical, moral and legal issues abide to building the next generation of artificial intelligence driven avatars that are no longer a science fiction exercise. The real danger lies when these human created avatars start to outperform their human maker's intellect. There is some known misconception here that the purpose of artificial intelligence is to recreate the avatar that performs equally to it's human counterpart.

In fact, most artificial intelligence developers aim to use the technology to drive smarter innovations superior to what's possible today through human capabilities (Warwick, 2005, p. 198). This posses major problems for human society but can also posses great benefits if the avatar activation plan is done with the consideration of the wellness of mankind. It should be emphasized here that the aim of the avatar creation must be to serve human kind in allowing them to better expressive themselves online, achieve feelings of belonging and a sense of ownership in their digital footprint as they interact virtually with others. In saying this, the avatar and more so, the robot generation is an inevitable stage of human evolution. As humans seek to better their own kind and extend the capabilities that only human embodied agents can perform, the beginning of avatar and human co-existence will eventuate. In this exploration, Warwick (2005, p. 198) raises an important thought provoking question as to how the co-existence between humans and avatars will cause societal changes, alluding to topics of societal roles, power and trade. With these developments in machine technology we may witness humans bargaining with avatars that are conditioned intellectually, neurally and physically stronger (Warwick, 2005, p. 198).

Under these conditions, the only way to overcome this human challenge is to find a weakness in the avatar condition such like being able to control and/or limit their life-support mechanism. The obvious place to start would be to reduce or cease their food source intake or deprive them of information that could help humans shut down or turn on their mechanical central systems to their benefit and safety. For these machine driven avatars, acquiring energy from the sun (i.e. a constant source) would let them survive and bypass humans without affecting their energy intake (Warwick, 2005, p. 198) and provide them the robotic power to overcome real world obstacles and pains. Nonetheless, humans are already doing a good job in populating the atmosphere and causing various environmental problems, so naturally looking after the ozone layer could do us some benefit in this given circumstance. Making actions to repair the damage caused to the ozone layer and practising good environmental care in order to protect our skyline would be one method of attack that could prevent the avatars exposure to vital energy they will need to continue to survive (Warwick, 2005, p. 198).

These perceived challenges of avatar activation in the real world, however should not create a resistance to the avatar evolution. In fact, the human dream is to use these avatars to materialise a happy balance for mankind. One way of achieving this rewarding and blissful life is to provide a port for each human brain that can stimulate a reality that feeds a narrative for its owner - just like the avatar is feed information through a computer program. This would allow for both avatars and humans to live a co-existing experience, something that the human was never able to enter before. The interaction that happens between the avatar and human offers new insights for understanding cognitive processes and communication development. How we identify emotion within these processes and the ways in which that can help convey expression is an important consideration within the development of intelligent artefacts such as avatars (Becker, 2006, p. 39). If we are able support various attributes of emotional embodiment in the avatar development process, such as the ability to express gestures, posture and language and articulate different modes of expression, then avatars and humans have the abilities of living in a shared social space (Becker, 2006, p. 39).

A central goal for the usage of avatars is that we are able to observe various cognitive, social and emotional stimulations in motion based on a range of brain processing imagery caused from reflected awareness of the self in new modes of interaction. Findings from Goldberg, Christensen, Flash, Giese, and Malach (2015, p. 306) reveal that where humans perceived a certain stimuli would probe emotional outcomes, the brain activity in the amygdala was intensified. Such intensified effect was similarly demonstrated with the use of avatars, with an important amount of information showing the correlation between brain activity and emotional intensity (Goldberg et al., 2015, p. 316). This discussion of emotion is vital to understand the level of adoption for such avatars by humans, if we are going to use them to express our online voice, persona and digital identity. More notably, this will be useful for the discussion of how immersive experiences facilitated by the avatar will need to address important sentiments of emotional therapy and will be critical in the development of collaborative virtual environments.

To understand the stimulation of emotional responses that may arise in these avatars and assess the connection with emotional therapy, it is important to understand the emotional activity that occurs in the human brain. As one accepts the role of emotion in avatar to avatar interaction, the technical processes found in achieving such stimulation brings us to the work of James Papez (1937) and his coined term the "Papez circuit" (Juma, 2008, p. 20). The Papez circuit refers to the network of the brain that encompasses the hypothalamus, anterior thalamus, cingulated gyrus and hippocampus which together make the neural circuit for the control of emotional expression (Juma, 2008, p. 20). Here, the functions evaluate data from the various input systems in order to produce emotional coded responses calculated from such information (Juma, 2008, p. 20). The emotional response is dependant on the structures within the limbic system which must interact to produce emotion. Consequently, the development of an avatar would similarly entail the creation of structures found in a natural creature or human being for its emotional depictions to physically match the internal stimulations the avatar experiences. The emotional connectedness experienced by the avatars also becomes increasing important for intensified levels of intimacy, which allows a shift from a computer mediated environment to a more fluid and malleable possibility of interactions.

Fundamental to the manifestation of intimacy, research has shown that an authentic and close virtual representation of the human in avatar form has great benefits for increased adoption, intimacy and identification by the individual as their chosen embodiment agent (Bailenson, Blascovich & Guadagno, 2008, p. 2673-2674). The level of intimacy experienced was consistent with the closeness of the photorealistic representation of the individual (Bailenson, Blascovich & Guadagno, 2008, p. 2673, 2685). Where the avatar embodied a high realism of individual likeliness, the presence of intimacy was stronger and the behaviour of the individual evoked a stronger acceptance with regards to virtual body ownership (Bailenson, Blascovich & Guadagno, 2008, p. 2677).

CONCLUSION

In conclusion, as our physical and virtual worlds merge, the problem we face is that we tend to lose the human expression and personal visual emotion we once had with face-to-face communication. This lack of expressive communication waters away the unique qualities of the individual's expressive behaviours, their authenticity and their selfhood (i.e.their identity). The avatar helps restore our immersive abilities and desires to be expressive on the web.

As disruptive as it may seem, the avatar era is something close to inevitable, primarily driven by our own innate human curiosity as we seek new modes of existence and are supported by our own technological creations. Today, we have a countless number of devices that ostensibly aim to 'improve our standard of living', such as higher definition screens, wireless Internet, phones, and increased broadcast technologies. If history has served our memory well, one thing we have learnt is that such technological advancements create new human 'needs' which in turn creates increased consumer demand.

In reflection, as our demand to 'improve our standard of living' increases, we also grow a stronger bond to adopt immersive virtual experiences in various form. We pointed out that science tells us that the brain treats experiences, whether they are 'real' or 'virtual', the same (Blascovich & Bailenson, 2011, p. 262). As human beings, we are not able to differentiate experiences, as long as they provide the same sensory feelings we absorb from our physical world, so we will continue to turn to them. Avatars equip us with new 'super-powers' within the virtual world that open a gateway of highly manifested experiences where the rules of reality are suspended. It will be left to us to decide how we integrate them into our lives to 'improve our standard of living' but until then, avatars will continue to fascinate us from both personal and professional viewpoints.

REFERENCES

Bailenson, J. N., Blascovich, J., & Guadagno, R. E. (2008). Self-representations in immersive virtual environments. *Journal of Applied Social Psychology*, *38*(11), 2673–2690. doi:10.1111/j.1559-1816.2008.00409.x

Becker, B. (2006). Social robots – emotional agents: Some remarks on naturalizing man-machine interaction. *International Journal of Information Ethics*, *6*(12), 37–45. http://fiz1.fh-potsdam.de/volltext/ijie/07246.pdf

Blascovich, J., & Bailenson, J. (2011). *Infinite reality: Avatars, eternal life, new worlds, and the dawn of the virtual revolution*. William Morrow & Co.

Dourish, P., & Bell, G. (2011). *Divining a digital future: Mess and mythology in ubiquitous computing*. The MIT Press. doi:10.7551/mitpress/9780262015554.001.0001

Gamez, D. (2007). *What we can never know: Blindspots in philosophy and science*. Continuum International Publishing Group.

Goldberg, H., Christensen, A., Flash, T., Giese, M. A., & Malach, R. (2015). Brain activity correlates with emotional perception induced by dynamic avatars. *NeuroImage*, *122*, 306–317. doi:10.1016/j.neuroimage.2015.07.056 PMID:26220746

Hall, A. S. C. (2017). *Energy return on investment: A unifying principle for biology, economics, and sustainability*. Springer. doi:10.1007/978-3-319-47821-0

Juma, L. (2008). *The role of secondary emotions in action selection and its effects on the believability of a character*. Master Programme Final Project, Aalborg University Copenhagen.

Kokswijk, van J. (2007). *Digital ego: Social and legal aspects of virtual identity*. Glasgow, UK: Eburon Academic Publishers.

Korsgaard, C. M. (1989). Personal identity and the unity of agency: A Kantian response to Parfit. *Philosophy & Public Affairs*, *18*(2), 101–132. https://www.jstor.org/stable/2265447?seq=1#page_scan_tab_contents

Korsgaard, C. M. (1999). Self-constitution in the ethics of Plato and Kant. *The Journal of Ethics*, *3*(1), 1–29. doi:10.1023/A:1026418314102

Lyons, M., Plante, A., Jehan, S., Inoue, S., & Akamatsu, S. (1998). Avatar creation using automatic face recognition. *Proceedings, ACM Multimedia*, *98*, 427–434. https://s3.amazonaws.com/academia.edu.documents/12631510/mm98.pdf?response-content-disposition=inline%3B%20filename%3DAvatar_Creation_using_Automatic_Face_Rec.pdf&X-Amz-Algorithm=AWS4-HMAC-SHA256&X-Amz-Credential=AKIAIWOWYYGZ2Y53UL3A%2F20191027%2Fus-east-1%2Fs3%2Faws4_request&X-Amz-Date=20191027T011852Z&X-Amz-Expires=3600&X-Amz-SignedHeaders=host&X-Amz-Signature=5f253fa383e6d97e97ea7a3c234c608628ffeeb2e2f52d87a2f473f2f59367a5

Mathews, S. (2008). Identity and information. In J. van den Hoven & J. Weckert (Eds.), *Information Technology and Moral Philosophy* (pp. 142–160). Cambridge University Press.

Moore, H. L. (2012). Avatars and robots: The imaginary present and the socialities of the inorganic. *The Cambridge Journal of Anthropology, 30*(1), 48–63. doi:10.3167/ca.2012.300106

Piryankova, I. (2015). *The influence of a self-avatar on space and body perception in immersive virtual reality* (Vol. 42). Logos Verlag Berlin GmbH.

Sparrow, A. (2010). *The law of virtual worlds and internet social networks*. Gower Publishing Limited.

Suler, J. R. (2016). *Psychology of the digital age: Humans become electric*. Cambridge University Press. doi:10.1017/CBO9781316424070

Sundar, S. S. (Ed.). (2015). *The handbook of the psychology of communication technology* (Vol. 35). John Wiley & Sons. doi:10.1002/9781118426456

Van Kokswijk, J. (2007). *Digital ego: Social and legal aspects of virtual identity*. Eburon Academic Publishers.

Warwick, K. (2003). Cyborg morals, cyborg values, cyborg ethics. *Ethics and Information Technology, 5*(3), 131–137. doi:10.1023/B:ETIN.0000006870.65865.cf

Warwick, K. (2005). The matrix: Our future? In C. Grau (Ed.), *Philosophers Explore the Matrix* (pp. 198–207). Oxford University Press.

This research was previously published in the International Journal of Applied Research in Bioinformatics (IJARB), 10(2); pages 1-9, copyright year 2020 by IGI Publishing (an imprint of IGI Global).

Chapter 25
Avatars for Clinical Assessment:
Digital Renditions of the Self as Innovative Tools for Assessment in Mental Health Treatment

Stefano Triberti
University of Milan, Italy

Valeria Sebri
University of Milan, Italy

Lucrezia Savioni
University of Milan, Italy

Alessandra Gorini
University of Milan, Italy

Gabriella Pravettoni
University of Milan, Italy

ABSTRACT

Avatars are an important feature of digital environments. Existing both in social networks and webchats (usually as static images) and in single-player and online video games (as dynamic characters, often humanoid), avatars are meant to represent users' action and communication within digital environments. Research has shown that, when they are customized by users, avatars are not created "randomly," rather they maintain some kind of relationship with users' actual self-representation and identity. However, more recent studies showed that users may have multiple digital representations: the same person could create multiple avatars depending on which facet of the self is primed by an experimental manipulation, or on which aims they have to pursue in the given virtual environments (e.g., to seduce, to play, to work). With this background, this contribution explores the possibility to use customized avatars within psychological assessment, as adjunctive assessment tools useful to get information on patients' self-representation(s) and communicative intentions.

DOI: 10.4018/978-1-6684-7597-3.ch025

INTRODUCTION

In the context of new technologies and social media, a number of interesting opportunities emerged for users to understand who they are and how to communicate themselves to others. Indeed, people spend a lot of time taking picture of themselves (selfies), and updating their profiles across a number of platforms (social networks), in order to achieve a positive and desirable impression management. Sometimes, people are allowed to create a completely new image of themselves, which can be totally different from who they really are. This relates to the concept of *avatar* or users' digital, often customized, representations of themselves in virtual environments. As the first part of this contribution will show, avatars generated attention in psychologists and social scientists to the point that a number of theoretical and experimental studies on this topic have been published (at the end of 2018, a search on popular science-focused search engines with keywords such as "avatar" and "psychology" yields more than fifty thousand results).

Indeed, avatars have been recognized as an interesting resource not only to study self-presentation online, but also self-representation and identity. According to projective identity theory (Gee, 2003), it exists an "interface" between a user and his/her avatar, which features those aspects of self-representation one wants to transmit in the avatar appearance. Such contents are different from the avatar, in that opportunities for customization offered by the virtual platforms usually do not permit a "perfect" representation of user's intent, so that the final digital figure should be understood as the result of a negotiation process involving user's self, intentions, other psychological factors such as culture and personality, the virtual world and customization platform's characteristics as well.

Secondarily, research has demonstrated that avatars can influence users' behavior by modifying their self-perception inside the virtual worlds and this phenomenon (the so-called "Proteus effect") became the foundation of innovative cyber-psychological interventions for the fields of healthcare and learning.

The purpose of the present contribution is to briefly review these areas of research, and then to extend the psychological discourse on avatars further, by advancing the idea that these peculiar tools of new technologies could offer unprecedented opportunities for psychological assessment and therapy.

BACKGROUND

An avatar is typically an image that represents the self in the virtual world. Generally used in the context of social networks and video games, it could be a static or dynamic figure that embodies actions/communications between users in a virtual world (Triberti, Durosini, Aschieri, Villani, & Riva, 2017). Actually, "avatar" is a word used to identify a number of heterogeneous entities in the digital world; Triberti and Argenton (2013) have proposed a general classification:

- When *relational*, avatars are used exclusively to identify the authorship of messages by a human user, and to communicate a simple meaning about oneself (e.g., what I like, who I am, which ideas or values I adhere to); for example, here the word avatar is used to refer to static pictures (faces, objects, symbols... even a written description, such as in first-generation MUDs) in forums, web chats, or social networks;
- When *agentive*, avatars are used to act and move within a two-dimensional or three-dimensional digital environment: for example, these (often) humanoid dynamic figures are used to walk, fight, or explore in video games;

- Finally, *hybrid* avatars perform both the functions; for example, avatars in Virtual Worlds and online video games (e.g., MMORPGs) are both used to communicate meaning and promote recognition by others, especially when personalized in their appearance, and to act and move (the examples reported in this contribution will be mainly referred to this kind of avatars, which appear to be the more rich in terms of customization options and communication possibilities).

The physical appearance of avatars can be simple or complex: users can indeed represent themselves through a very simple drawing (e.g., Mii characters for the Nintendo Wii) or three-dimensional figures rich with details (e.g., video games) (Fong & Mar, 2015). It is important to emphasize that avatars are not exclusive to virtual worlds and computer games, rather they exist (e.g., in their "relational" version) in old and basic social media as well, such as forums and webchats. Literature says that avatars can be a good representation of the actual self, strictly connected to user's identity. There are indeed some interesting questions: is an avatar only a large container of people's features? Are there differences if users act through different types of avatars? What are the consequences of avatars on human behavior in the real word?

The first observation is that there is a great difference if users create an avatar or if users must use an avatar already given by the system. In the first circumstance, this process is called "customization" (Mcarthur, 2018); this is the possibility of managing the avatar's appearance. Users indeed can potentially choose, buy, or make new clothes, hair and so on for their avatars to wear (Bailey, Wise, & Bolls, 2009). It is a complex phenomenon because people are not always capable to produce their identity (McArthur, Teather, & Stuerzlinger, 2010) and the relationship between users and their avatars isn't simple. The high fidelity and quality of self-representation depends also on users' motivation to create a duplicate of themselves in a virtual world. Referring to this, McArthur (2018) says that customization is influenced by the reason an avatar is created for. Users indeed may want to create a realistic, ideal, or fantasy avatar, for example. Ideal avatar is in line with an idealized self-description that's rich with desired modifications and specific features. People can make avatars with peculiar and unusual features and/or very different from their real self, sometimes to reflect a popular trend, resemble a celebrity (Ducheneaut, Wen, Yee, & Wadley, 2009) or to express fantasies and imagination (Belisle & Bodur, 2010); a fantastic avatar is generally created with escapism motivations because people generally have the desire of living as someone else; lastly role player avatars represent users and their fantasies but, in this case, users don't maintain this identity all the time. Especially teenagers are usually involved in new identities in the virtual world as well as in the real life (Kafai, Fields, & Cook, 2010). In this occasion, their expression of offline identity could become a helpful and formative step into the process of their identity development, not only entertainment.

Another interesting motivation could be the influence of the context on customization. Many users learn to customize avatars in order to belong to the community, by observing other users or, in some cases, the editor of a virtual game. In this sense, according to a psychoanalytic perspective, avatars can be defined as "ambassadors of agency" (Rehak, 2003). Indeed, on the one hand, avatars recall the toys everyone used as children to represent their own action within game environments (Klevjer, 2003), so it is possible that they embody a very "ancient" process of identity play; on the other hand, today, avatars tend to be graphic, digital objects that human users create or select among available materials such as pictures (Banks & Bowman, 2016), or anthropomorphic properties (Nass, & Moon, 2000). Mediated by avatars, individuals respond to each other starting from the first impression, in the same manner as the real world (Naumann, Vazire, Rentfrow, & Gosling, 2009). Some people believe that avatars do not represent the user's identity; on the contrary, literature explains that avatars can more or less embody their creators. Furthermore, referring to a parasocial interaction perspective, users actually think, act, and feel through avatars (Banks & Bowman, 2016); this will become clearer when the *Proteus Effect* or the effects of avatars on their users is explored later in this chapter.

Consequently, the representation of oneself through a graphic and/or anthropomorphized avatar influences the level of interaction in the virtual world too: sometimes, users utilize avatars just as virtual objects to move and act within virtual environments. In this case, they can have low emotional involvement with them and possibly they employed less identity material during the customization process. On the contrary, literature shows that avatars can be complex social agents which express users' self-representation or intentions (Banks & Bowman, 2016).

In other words, avatars are primarily defined on the basis of their interactive and social properties, as representations of users in digital space (Lee, 2014). Representation should be understood in complex terms: for example, some assume that avatars should look like the actual physical appearance of the human creators (Hooi & Cho, 2014), while others expect avatars to reflect the personality/internal processes of the users, independently of what and how they actually look like (Behm-Morawitz, 2013). In general, avatars allow for both kinds of identity-based customization. This is an interesting consideration in the fields of psychology and life sciences: users' identity indeed can be studied through avatars because users express or suppress various physical and psychological traits through them (Williams, Kennedy, & Moore, 2016). Belisle and Bodur (2010) emphasize that avatars can convey accurate personality information about their creators because individuals choose and prefer avatars perceived to be similar to themselves. For example, introverted people and neurotic women tend to select more attractive avatars, while participants with low self-esteem picked avatars with lighter skin tones (Dunn & Guadagno, 2012). One study demonstrated that participants were able to guess other participants' personality traits just by observing their avatars (Fong & Mar, 2015) and this shows that the connection between players and avatars is strong and meaningful; however, there are situations in which avatars are very different from their users (Sibilla & Mancini, 2018). For example, the research showed that users may (or may be primed to) create avatars resembling an ideal representation of themselves (Jin, 2009, 2012; 2010), and that a noticeable discrepancy between an ideal and an actual self-virtual representation could be a sign of psychological and health issues (Kim & Sundar, 2012; Leménager et al., 2013). It could depend on the possible correlation with low self-esteem and negative symptoms of users (theory of self-discrepancy) (Higgins, 1987; Park, 2018). For this reason, it is also necessary to consider the virtual environment in which avatars are involved and the platform used to create them: specifically, users have to deal with opportunities/obstacles present in the technology (e.g., they may be allowed to choose a limited amount of customizable options, such as limited clothes or skin and hair colors).

Secondarily, the research has shown that a number of users' characteristics influence avatar creation, even acting outside of conscious awareness, such as age and gender. Adolescents, for example, are extremely influenced by their perception of self-esteem and body-esteem: boys create avatars rich with many sexual features, while girls prefer to detail clothing and make-up, in reference to gendered self-expression practices typical of western culture (Villani, Gatti, Triberti, Confalonieri, & Riva, 2016). Even activities performed by avatars in the virtual worlds often reflect gender differences embedded in real-world culture (Guadagno, Muscanell, Okdie, Burk, & Ward, 2011).

A compensation effect has also been observed. Older people tend to create younger avatars and people with a higher body mass index – likely overweight or obese – create more physically idealized avatars, which are taller or thinner (Bessiere et al., 2007; Carrasco et al., 2017; Stavropoulos, et al., 2018). The compensation effect also regards the psychological feature, bringing people who are depressed or have low self-esteem create avatars with more idealized traits, such as being more gregarious and conscientious (Yee & Bailenson, 2007).

Moreover, several studies have begun to investigate the identity-related outcomes of their use. Yoon and Vargas (2014) highlight that virtual environments enable people to experience extraordinary identities and circumstances; an individual in fact could be a superhero, a fantasy creature, or simply the person he/she dreams to be using avatars in virtual space. This gives to users the possibility of learning new behaviors by acting as their avatars.

Another important phenomenon regards the possibility that users change their behaviors influenced by avatars. In this case, the users' identification with specific avatars can explain their behaviors in the virtual world and also in the real life subsequently. Cohen suggests that identification is ''a response to communication by others that is marked by internalizing a point of view rather than a process of projecting one's own identity onto someone or something else'' (Cohen, 2001, p. 252). Three kinds of identifications are possible: avatar identification, group identification, and game identification (Ash, 2015). The embodiment of a specific avatar is an unconscious process by which users make inferences about expected behaviors, using visual cues (Bessière, Seay, & Kiesler, 2007) and stereotypes activated by social identity. This is very interesting for psychology also because literature affirms that changes in aspects of virtual world can lead modifications also in a real one (Baylor, 2009). For example, people that use healthy avatars tend to have healthier behaviors also in the real world (Fox & Bailenson, 2009). In view of the above, interactivity (Wu, 2014) and the experience of embodiment are two essential conditions that can influence users' attitude and their behaviors (Fox, Bailenson, & Tricase, 2013). Yee, Bailenson, and Ducheneaut (2009) labeled this phenomenon the "Proteus Effect", which is the modification of user's self-representation in order to influence attitudes and internal beliefs, modifying individual behaviors (Williams et al., 2016), that will be better explained in the following section.

This first glimpse within psychological research on avatars show the complexity of the topic. On the one hand, avatars are able to influence internal processes and behaviors of their users, so that they already demonstrated to be a valuable tool for psychological and health interventions. On the other hand, regarding the phenomena related to customization processes and practices, while avatars could resemble their users, it appears that people may create avatars for different purposes ranging from "just using the virtual world" to trying to put themselves within new identities and experiences. Such richness will become clearer when considering that self and identity are not actually "fixed" nor "stable", rather, according to classic theories, they are dynamic and malleable.

Proteus Effect

As previously anticipated, beliefs and attitudes of users are influenced by their self-representation; when the representation of the self is a digital persona (e.g., an avatar), it could directly influence behavior. This phenomenon is called the "Proteus effect". Indeed, the Proteus effect allows people to embody others' perceptual experiences (Ahn, Le, & Bailenson, 2013), even if they are very different from how one usually sees him or herself. In this sense, individuals tend to conform to the identity of their avatars (Van Der Heide, Schumaker, Peterson, & Jones, 2013). For example, literature highlights that the embodiment of an attractive avatar makes users closer and more confident with others (Messinger et al., 2008; Nick Yee et al., 2009); overweight children who were assigned avatar with normal body size had better performance in a virtual game of running (Li, Lwin, & Jung, 2014); people can have more aggressive thoughts if their avatars are dressed with Ku Klux Klan outfit or in black (Peña & Kim, 2014) or less aggressive behaviors if the avatar of the person they are interacting with has female characteristics (Sherrick, Hoewe, & Waddell, 2014). Due to the fact that avatar embodiment causes changes in self-image and one's own body-schema, both social communication and relationships are influenced. Users, for example, have the perception to be more able in social relationships when communication is mediated by avatars (Kang, Watt, & Ala, 2008). This is possible because the process of embodiment brings people to have another idea of their own self, modifying individual and social identity (Achenbach et al., 2017). Moreover, offline and online identities are linked to each other and to emotions. This bond is so strong that the virtual environment experience might help the user to experience a transformation; people have the possibility of exploring other self-representations' properties (Poole, 2017) by recognizing, for example, new desirable characteristics associated to the self (Buisine, Guegan, Barré, Segonds, & Aoussat, 2016).

Even if this kind of change could be further enhanced over time, which remains unclear, it is evident that people change the self-representation starting from the avatar's properties (Scott & Ghinea, 2013). Some studies affirm that the Proteus effect is only a form of priming. Priming is an incidental activation of memory and related knowledge according to the self-perception theory of Bem (Buisine et al., 2016); anyways, others suggest that this is not an automatic cognitive process but there are individual differences. In conclusion, future studies need to explore carefully the relationship between users in order to study human behaviors and their modifications over time; avatars indeed could become an essential instrument in the field of psychology and cognitive sciences for studying changes of human self-representations and related behaviors.

Social Identity Theory

This is in accordance with seminal theories in psychology, such as Social Identity Theory by Tajfel (1974). This theory is born from the idea that social groups have an impact on the way people see themselves and the other, and this is related to the various social contexts in which everyone is inserted (Tajfel & Turner, 1979). People tend to identify themselves in social groups which have different characteristics (the permeability of group boundaries, the stability of group statuses and the legitimacy of current status relations) that determine likelihood that people self-define either at the individual or at the group level.

Social Identity Theory has the aim of understanding and explaining how people come to adopt a social identity (or more social identities) and to behave in terms of these social identities rather than in terms of their personal identity and how they influence interpersonal relationships and intergroups (Tajfel, 1974; Tajfel & Turner, 1979). This consideration leads to the definition of the concept of *stereotyping* which is an idea pre-conceived in respect to experience, not based on direct contact and difficult to modify. The concept of stereotypy is inherent to the idea that there is a differentiation between "in-group" and "out-group" and people tend to have a positive bias towards their own group compared to out-group (Islam, 2014). Different studies have shown that people were more inclined to identify as a member of a group when group status was unstable (this promotes intergroup competition and social change), but the level of self-definition was more relevant when group boundaries were permeable or inclusion in the group seemed illegitimate (Ellemers, Spears, & Doosje, 2002).

Generally, people prefer to maintain a positive image of the group to which they belong. The social identity process brings people to seek out positively valued behaviors, attitudes and traits that can be seen as characteristics of their in-group. On the contrary, this inclination brings them to downplay the importance of positive out-group characteristics and to focus on less favorable characteristics of out-group. This tendency between in-group and out-group processes can affect the evaluation, the assessment of performance and achievement and the distribution of resources between different groups (Tajfel, 1970). Tajfel defined social identity as "the individual's knowledge that he belongs to certain social groups together with some emotional and value significance to him of this group membership" (Tajfel, 1972, p.292).

He distinguished between *interpersonal* (e.g., the relationships between wife and husband) and *intergroup* (e.g., relationships between soldiers from opposing armies) behavior as extremes of a continuum: the first one defined the interaction between two or more subjects that is fully determined by their individual characteristics and interpersonal relationships, and it is not affected by different social groups to which they belonged; the second one refers to the interactions between two or more subjects (or groups of subjects) that are fully determined by their specific belonging to different social groups and not influenced by the interindividual personal relationships between the people involved (Tajfel & Turner, 1986). Tajfel and Turner (1979) proposed that there are three mental processes involved in evaluating "in-group" and "out-group":

- Social categorization: people are used to categorize the others to identify them; for example, we discriminated between black and white, professor and student, Right or Left winged. By this process we know what categories we belong to, we can understand things about us and things about others, defining the appropriate behavior according to the groups that we and others belong to. People can belong to several social-groups at the same time. Social categorization allows the creation of different social groups which lead to highlighting similarities within the category (social group) and of differences when two categories (social groups) are compared;
- Social identification: the individual's identity is lead to his knowledge of belonging to some social groups and from the emotional meaning derived from this membership. People adopt the identity of the group that they belong to and act in ways that they perceive members of that group usually act;
- Social comparison: it is the process by which people determine the value or social standing of a specific group and its members. After the categorization of themselves within a social group and identify themselves as part of that group, people tend to compare their group (in-group) against another group (out-group). People prefer to have a positive concept of self rather than a negative one, so they have the need to enhance the group of belonging to the detriment of others, even if it involves bad feelings and behavior towards the members of out-group.

These intrapersonal processes promote the formation of social identity, which emerges as accompanied by emotional and evaluative significance of group membership. Thus, while one's personal identity refers to self-knowledge associated with unique individual attributes, people's social identity indicates who they are in terms of the groups they belong to (or not).

Multiple Selves and Self-Discrepancy

Already William James (1890) pointed out that the concept of self was based on the interactions that the individual has with others, in a context-specific manner. With this declination comes the concept of "multiple selves" according to which the conception of self derives from the different social domains in which the individual is inserted (Cross & Markus, 1990; Stryker & Statham, 1985).

A study by Funder and Colvin (1991) has highlighted the fact that behavior can be both situation-specific and coherent between different situations. This indicates how "even though situations profoundly affect what people do, people can still manage to preserve their distinctive behavioral styles through situations" (p. 791). Role identities are the descriptions that the individual makes of himself specifically to a particular social role (Burke & Tully, 1977) and are organized according to a "hierarchy of salience of identity" (Stryker & Serpe, 1982). This hierarchy is defined by the "probability that a given role identity is invoked in a given situation, or through a number of situations" (Serpe, 1987, p. 50). The importance given by an individual for that particular role identity depends on the social and emotional commitment that the individual has towards that specific role (Stryker, 1987) and on the satisfaction of the individual in carrying out activities related to that role (Hoelter, 1983).

The behaviors implemented by the individual derive therefore from the social contexts in which he or she is inserted and from the role that the individual assumes in that specific context: I can be a researcher, a boyfriend, a sports enthusiast, etc. and I can be activated by circumstances and proceed to direct social behavior in very different ways.

Over the years, with the increase in the study of identity theory, a variety of potentials have been identified. In particular, the studies focused on the distinction between two "actual" selves: the type of person the individual believes to be or not to be and the type of person that an individual believes that others think he/she is. James (1890), for example, distinguished between the "spiritual" self, which included its own moral sensitivity and consciousness, and the "social" self, which included the self that is worthy of being approved by the highest social judge. Rogers (1961) distinguished between what others believe that a person should be (the normative standard) and the conviction of a person about what he would "ideally" be / would like to be.

According to the self-discrepancy theory there are two cognitive dimensions at the base of the various representations of the state of self: domains of the self and points of view on the self.

There are three fundamental domains of the self (Higgins, 1987):

1. the real self, which is one's representation of the attributes that someone (him/herself or another) really believes to possess;
2. the ideal self, which is your representation of the attributes that someone (yourself or another) would ideally possess (i.e., a representation of the hopes, aspirations or desires of someone for you);
3. the ought self, which is your representation of the attributes that someone (yourself or another) believes that you should or should possess (that is, a representation of someone's sense of your duty, obligations, or responsibilities).

However, the only distinction between the different domains of the self is not sufficient, but it is also necessary to distinguish between the representation of the state of self by considering the perspective of oneself on the self.

Turner (1956) identifies two basic stand-points on the self (a point of view from which you can be judged that reflects a set of attitudes or values):

1. one's own personal point of view;
2. the point of view of some significant others (e.g., mother, father, brother, spouse, and closest friend).

A person can have self-state representations for each of a number of significant others.

The non-consideration, by previous research, of the different domains of self in terms of the different stand-points on those domains, gives rise to confusions in the literature. For example, some literature has measured "low self-esteem" by the comparison between actual self and his or her beliefs about others' ideals for him or her (Wylie, 1979).

From the combination of the dominion of the self and all the points of view of the self, there are six representations of the state of self:

- real/proper
- real/other
- ideal/ideal
- ideal/other
- due/proper
- should/other

The first two representations constitute the concept, defined by Wylie (1979) self-concept. The remaining representations constitute the self-guides (Higgins, 1987). According to the self-discrepancy theory not all individuals possess the same self-guided: some may possess self-guided self-training, others that of ideal self. Each individual is therefore motivated to reach the condition in which his/her concept of self coincides with the most relevant self-guided tours for him/herself.

Therefore, the motivational or emotional effects of an individual's current / proper attributes, or self-concept, are determined by the significance of possessing such attributes to the individual. The meaning depends on the relationship between the concept of self and the self-guides of the individual, with different types of relationships representing different types of negative psychological situations (Higgins, 1987).

RECENT RESEARCH ON AVATARS

Classic theories on identity and the self are useful to introduce recent research on avatar customization, that discovered other factors involved in avatar creation and customization, all of them pointing out the importance of taking into consideration the meaning richness of this digital technology, but also the malleability and complexity of users' self-representation as embedded in digital figures.

In the last years, the psychological research on avatars has developed interest towards two main areas: one, coming from the Proteus effect field, has explored the usage of avatars to influence participants' behavior, in order to further explore the possibility to use avatars as a tool for promoting health or learning (Gamage & Ennis, 2018; Sah, Ratan, Tsai, Peng, & Sarinopoulos, 2017; Slater, 2017; Triberti & Chirico, 2016); the second one, instead, studied avatar customization and the multiple factors which can influence one's digital self-representation. This last field of research is of particular interest here.

As a recent development in avatar research, and in accordance with the Social Identity Theory, *context* has been recognized as an important factor, referring mainly to users' expectations about the virtual environment they are in (or they have to enter) with their avatar. The research has shown that users could create multiple avatars depending on contextual information: for example, avatars are made more attractive if the users expect to enter a dating-oriented context (Vasalou & Joinson, 2009), or dressed with more professional clothes if participants are primed with a work-related context to enter (Triberti, Durosini, Aschieri, Villani, & Riva, 2017). The same study identified the role of "online audience" too, with females modifying their bodies more when expecting to meet friends instead of strangers in the virtual world, which has been interpreted as related both to females cultural habit of modifying their own bodies for self and gender expression (e.g., make-up), and to be more private and less self-disclosing online. Such a behavior shows that avatars are really used with the same criteria people utilize their own appearance to communicate and express themselves offline. This behavior is in agreement with theories of multiple selves, according to which, people may activate different self-representations depending on the context. As avatars constitute self-representations, their creation is also influenced by expectations and perception about the context, so that their final appearance may highlight one aspect of the self-representation or the other.

Indeed, context may influence avatar creation in other complex ways; for example, when gamers enter Massive Multiplayer Online Games, they have to choose among fantasy races and/or professions that limit but also orient their own self-expression and communication (Sibilla & Mancini, 2018). Trepte and Reinecke (2010) found that avatars were created less similar to the self by users in a competitive game scenario, which is consistent with studies showing multiple motivations for avatar customization, such as contextual adaptation (e.g., creating a strong/muscular avatar because it will be more performant in combat activities) (Lin & Wang, 2014).

This research is consistent with the idea of avatars "maintaining something" of their creators which has been explained in the introduction, which can be traced back to projective identity theory (Gee, 2003). However, they show that such material is not necessarily identity/self-properties. On the one hand, as seen in the section on classic theories on self and identity, the self is multiple and malleable (Markus, 1977; Roberts & Donahue, 1994) and, according to social identity theory, one's self-representations could activate to guide behavior (e.g., social categorization) in different contexts, depending on group memberships that are made salient (Tajfel & Turner, 1986). In this sense, digital avatars appear to behave consistently with multiple self-representations, by modifying or adapting depending on external stimuli.

Secondarily, it is possible that not all the psychological processes personified by customized avatars should be associated to identity or the self: communicative intention is a construct that could be useful to explain the origins of some customization choices. According to communication theory, people may have objectives to be achieved through social interactions that are different from what is transmitted literally through verbal communication: miscommunication phenomena such as lie and irony are eminent examples (Brewer & Holmes, 2009; Keysar, 2007). In the field of avatar creation, one could select avatar features not to represent aspects of how he/she sees him or herself, but to obtain objectives in the context of mediated interaction. For example, a user may choose a sad emotional expression for his avatar not because he is actually sad, but because he is trying to obtain others' care and attention. Similarly, a male video game user chooses a female avatar ("gender swapping") not because he would like to express gender dysphoria in real life, but just because the female avatar is a pleasant virtual object to watch; or, because he wants to be treated with fairness by other players; or again, because he just wants to have access to game resources/materials available to female characters only (Hussain & Griffiths, 2009).

These studies do not reduce the importance of identity for avatars, rather they highlight the difficulty of understanding the multiplicity of factors underlying digital self-representation. Future studies should explore the possibility to distinguish identity material, intentions and other possible sources of personalized avatars' characteristics.

In the last decade, avatars became even more complex, if possible. After Virtual Reality became a commercial product, immersive Virtual Worlds emerged; for example LindenLab, which in 2003 launched *Second Life* (the most famous Virtual World for years), has recently launched *Sansar* which integrates immersive virtual reality in the experience of a shared world. Of course, this opened up the possibility not only to create customized avatars to express oneself, but also to enter in interactions with others in a way very similar to interactions in real life.

In the authors' opinion, other opportunities are offered by avatars, basing on the information psychological research is discovering on their possible relationship with users' identity, intentions and other psychological processes. In the next section this chapter will explore some of these possibilities.

AVATARS FOR PSYCHOLOGICAL ASSESSMENT

The literature review above showed that customized avatars could maintain a number of complex relationships not only with users' identity, but also with other internal processes. In this sense, customized avatars represent an opportunity for psychological assessment, or the process of testing which uses different techniques to arrive at hypotheses on individuals' mental state and behavior, possibly with the intention to change them in the future (Cates, 1999; Fletcher, 2005). Historically, psychological assessment used a number of techniques to asses individuals' identity; ranging, for example, from projective techniques to self-drawing (Gatti, Ionio, Traficante, & Confalonieri, 2014) in which an individual is instructed to draw a person, an object, or a situation that are analyzed to assess his/her cognitive, interpersonal, or psychological functioning.

Differently from other projective tests based on the interpretation of existing pictures (i.e., the Rorschach Technique or the Thematic Apperception Test), figure drawings tests require the test taker to create the pictures themselves. In most cases, figure-drawing tests are given to children, but can be also applied to adults. Both in children and adults, such tests are used to measure cognitive abilities and cognitive development, but also personality and social abilities. Moreover, in some cases, they are also used as part of the diagnostic procedure to assess specific types of psychological or neuropsychological disorders. This is the case, for example, of the Draw-A-Person test (DAP), developed by (Machover, 1949), which is based on the individual's self-image representation or on the representation of other persons, including, but not limited to, family members or friends of the test tacker. The DAP test focuses on how the drawings reflect psychological, neuropsychological, or emotional dysfunction of the test taker, including, among the others, anxieties, impulses, self-esteem, and personality characteristics. For example, people suffering of image disorders may reflect these concerns in their drawings omitting or distorting body parts (Sandyk, 1998). Similarly, victims of sexual abuse may stress sexual characteristics including excessive detail with regard to the sexual nature of the drawing (Sidun & Rosenthal, 1987).

Another example is the house-tree person test (Buck, 1948) which have the aim to obtain information concerning maturity, sensitivity and integration of a subject's personality and the interaction between that and environment. For what regards its application in assessment, this tool showed to be able to discriminate between abused and well-adjusted children (Blain, Bergner, Lewis, & Goldstein, 1981).

Actual data about reliability and validity of traditional figure drawing tests are inconsistent. In particular, when appropriate scoring systems are used, such tests have been found reliable measures for cognitive development in children, but not for specific personality characteristics, self-image issues, or personality dysfunctions, where data are not clear. Moreover, it is possible that, especially in adults, scarce drawing abilities represent a significant limitation in drawing figures that really exemplify what the test taker has in mind. The authors argue that these limitations may be overcome using an avatar-based approach to create self-representation.

As mentioned earlier, Fong and Mar (2015) conducted an experimental study to investigate whether people generally try to create avatars that represent themselves accurately, or whether they aim to display themselves differently than they appear in real life. Fifty subjects were asked to create an avatar, while the other 50 were specifically asked to create an avatar that would represent their personality accurately. As expected, no significant difference were found between the two groups indicating that most of them naturally try to represent themselves accurately.

If confirmed by future studies, these data suggest that self-avatar drawing could represent the modern version of the traditional self-drawing tests. This new approach to the self-representation may have, at least, the two following advantages:

- a software for avatars creation that allows an high level of customization may allow people to express their self-representation even without having specific drawing abilities;
- compared to the traditional drawing approach, the created avatars could be analyzed in a more objective way by the software itself and/or by an integrated IA based system allowing a deeper and more accurate between or within-subjects comparison.

Avatars, as guided self-representations supported by dedicated digital platforms featuring various customization affordances, could represent an interesting alternative for psychological assessment in this regard. In this section, three possible usages of avatars in future cyber-therapy and assessment will be described.

Assisted Avatar Customization

Customization is an important theme for the psychotherapy context. Patients in fact can use avatars for expressing their own identity(ies) and therapist can observe susceptible changes over time. In a clinical case discussion, Quackenbush and Krasner (2012) describe the avatar as an instrument for psychotherapy sessions, because people are free to show different characteristics, desires and intentions through the embodiment in avatars different from usual self-representation.

Therapists can assist patients' avatar creation, while taking note of relevant processes of self-reasoning and self-representation choices. Indeed, not only the final form of avatars could be interesting for clinicians, but also the *process* for taking some customization routes. Research has shown, for instance, that adolescents tend to express their experienced puberty changes during avatar customization, choosing more and more detailed body features depending on their self-representation (Villani et al., 2016; Villani, Gatti, Confalonieri, & Riva, 2012): for example, male adolescents may create avatars with beard and muscles, exaggerating their own physical characteristics and, at the same time, giving important clues about their own experience of such changes.

Similarly, depressed and/or low self-esteem patients may be asked to create actual self and ideal self avatars: measuring the difference between the two, as well as monitoring the process of customization, could give to the therapist important information about patients' identity and self-perception, and possibly about the extent of their psychological distress. This would be in accordance with the literature which, consistent with self-discrepancy theory (Higgins, 1987), identified the discrepancy between actual and ideal self avatars as a marker for low well-being (Bessière et al., 2007; Dunn & Guadagno, 2012).

In a clinical condition, subject's healthy and problematic identities can indeed emerge from avatar customization and the use of specific computer-generated virtual environments. If complex enough, these avatars and their relationships with other real or virtual characters or worlds may also include the complex patterns of memories, expectations, fears, and wishes that embrace the subject's sense of self. In a clinical-based approach, such information may be useful to explore the subject's self and eventually intervene to modify its dysfunctional or pathological aspects, while in a research-based approach the various self-representations may be analyzed and correlated with other individual characteristics or life variables and events. Perhaps, at the moment, there are no available data about the effects of illness (especially of those illnesses that cause physical changes) on the individual self-representation. These, and other related-issues, deserve attention being particularly important for the understanding and treatment of associated psychological consequences on the subject's well-being.

Context-Specific Multiple Avatars

A number of studies asked participants to create multiple avatars with different aims, such as showing actual and ideal self, or expectation towards entering a given virtual context or another (Triberti et al., 2017b; Triberti, Durosini, Aschieri, Villani, & Riva, 2017a; Vasalou & Joinson, 2009). In accordance with multiple selves and social identity theories (Higgins, 1987; Tajfel, 1974), people can have multiple self-representations depending on the context they are in, and/or the primed group belonging. Asking patients to create avatars to enter virtual or potential relevant context (e.g., school, work, family home) could give important information about how they seem themselves in those specific areas, for example, their self-confidence or body perception. The possibilities are endless: imagine asking a PTSD soldier to create an avatar to enter a first-person shooting video game that resembles his or her own combat experience; or, asking an anorexic patient to create an avatar to enter a restaurant; or again, asking a bullying victim to create an avatar to enter a virtual school. During psychotherapy sessions, avatars make it possible to live other experiences. Patients can try to move away from feelings and issues of their disease, using avatars with different properties. This gives them the possibility of hypothesizing and elaborating other opinions about the self, perceiving what does it mean to have other characteristics, conditions and life goals. Therapist can use this hypothetical context for bringing changes, starting from feeling and opinions about avatars with these different properties and emotions. People indeed can meet their personal preferences and fit suitable role expectations. Hypothetical thinking is indeed a kind of question used as instrument in psychotherapy, that could be improved by avatars usage (Mantovani, Riva, Castelnuovo, & Gaggioli, 2003; Pinto, Hickman, Clochesy, & Buchner, 2013).

On the one hand, it is difficult to prefigure now how such examples could actually be carried on in a psychotherapy session. However, it is easy to see that virtual contexts and the opportunities offered by avatar customization could be an unprecedented vehicle to let inner processes emerge besides what it is typically transmitted through verbal description.

In this regard, we have seen how avatars do not only give information about users' identity and self-representation, but also intentions (Triberti & Argenton, 2013): users could create an avatar with certain characteristics not to express themselves, but to achieve some objective within the virtual environment they have to enter (e.g., creating a female avatar to be treated fairly; making a muscular avatar to be strong; etc.). In psychotherapy, it is often difficult to lead patients to admit their true objectives and desires, especially if this comes with an emotional cost or they think it could give a negative impression of themselves. However, creating virtual contexts in which patients could possibly obtain their objectives (e.g., hurt or manipulate others; express who they want to be; being admired or loved) could help psychotherapists to understand important information about patients' hidden intentions.

Developing an Avatar-Creation Platform for Psychology

The ideas described above point to developing avatars as an innovative tool for psychological assessment. Of course, it is currently difficult to prefigure some of the examples outlined previously, because psychologists would have to adapt their interventions to available avatar customization platform. However, it is possible that future research would build platforms *specifically designed* for psychology and psychotherapy practice. Building on present and future literature, such technology would feature a library of customization acts and choices which would possibly be associated to specific identity features, development steps of behavioral change, and even diagnostic criteria. Are there avatar customization choices typical of depression, eating disorders, or other types of psychological and health issues? Future research should explore avatars' potential for psychotherapy, and the possibility to create *ad hoc* avatar customization tools for assessment contexts.

FUTURE RESEARCH DIRECTIONS

This contribution explored possible uses of avatars in psychological assessment. Certainly most of these uses are futuristic and currently non-existing in psychotherapeutic practices, so their actual utility is not supported by evidence. While the contribution of the present chapter should be taken into consideration as theoretical and creative, the main objective for future studies should be to produce evidence about the feasibility and efficacy of avatar tools in psychological assessment contexts.

- Controlled studies comparing avatars with other already established tools for self-representation (e.g., self-drawing techniques) could be conducted in order to account for avatars' ability to represent users' inner processes;
- "Real world" data could be collected to find associations between avatars' appearance and users' identity and intentions within big samples; this could be done by analyzing, with users' authorization, the creation of avatars in common-use online contexts such as video games and social media;
- Reporting single instances of avatar use could be encouraged by psychotherapy professionals to provide information about their possible usages for specific cases, diagnoses, or clinical situations. In the bibliographical search for this chapter, only one example of avatar customization used for getting information on a psychotherapy patient emerged (Quackenbush & Krasner, 2012), but this aspect was not deepened as a main tool for assessment or therapy. Anyway, single cases could be particularly interesting for orienting innovative applications in clinical practice, and also to highlight creative implementations of innovative technologies.

CONCLUSION

The present contribution examined avatars and their role in psychology and clinical assessment. As previously explained, avatars are heterogeneous entities (e.g., relational, agentive, and hybrid) in digital environments meant to represent user's action and communication. In the first part of the contribution, two processes for involving avatars have been introduced: customization as a result of users' negotiation process of itself, the role of intentions and other psychological factors, and the Proteus Effect in digital world that's the modification of users' self-representation and behaviors influenced by avatars' appearance. This is in line with seminal theories in psychology such as social identity theory (e.g. stereotypes and the differentiation between "in-group" and "out-group") and the concepts of multiple selves. It is possible to highlight the possibility to create and/or use multiple avatars with different aims or expectations evidently. Psychology and psychotherapy should explore the study of avatars and their virtual environments (or contexts, or situations) not only to advance knowledge but also to exploit innovative opportunities for practice. Moreover, the knowledge offered by this contribution could be interesting for practitioners other than psychologists and psychotherapists: for example, social media and video games designers can take into consideration the multiple psychological functions of avatars, which are not only digital figures but maintain relationships with users' identity and intentions. Selecting which customization options to include in a Virtual World or video game avatar creation platform could consider which intentions are more likely to be implemented in that specific context (e.g., to find love, to make friends, to work, etc.), so to meet users' objectives and improving final satisfaction. Also marketing specialists could employ different strategies to communicate with customers when they are using different avatars, in that these influence their behaviors and attitudes independently of identity and self-representation in the physical reality.

In conclusion, avatar research is still in its infancy regarding implementation in context such as psychotherapy and psychological assessment; however, it is possible to identify interesting opportunities for future usages of these digital entities, especially in order to make people experiment with their own self-representation to achieve profound self-knowledge and management.

REFERENCES

Achenbach, J., Waltemate, T., Botsch, M., Roth, D., Gall, D., & Latoschik, M. E. (2017). *The effect of avatar realism in immersive social virtual realities*. Academic Press. doi:10.1145/3139131.3139156

Ahn, S. J., Le, A. M. T., & Bailenson, J. (2013). The Effect of Embodied Experiences on Self-Other Merging, Attitude, and Helping Behavior. *Media Psychology*, *16*(1), 7–38. doi:10.1080/15213269.2012.755877

Ash, E. (2015). Priming or proteus effect? Examining the effects of avatar race on in-game behavior and post-play aggressive cognition and affect in video games. *Games and Culture*, *11*(4), 422–440. doi:10.1177/1555412014568870

Bailey, R., Wise, K., & Bolls, P. (2009). How Avatar Customizability Affects Children's Arousal and Subjective Presence During Junk Food–Sponsored Online Video Games. *Cyberpsychology & Behavior*, *12*(3), 277–283. doi:10.1089/cpb.2008.0292 PMID:19445632

Banks, J., & Bowman, N. D. (2016). Avatars are (sometimes) people too: Linguistic indicators of parasocial and social ties in player–avatar relationships. *New Media & Society*, *18*(7), 1257–1276. doi:10.1177/1461444814554898

Baylor, A. L. (2009). Promoting motivation with virtual agents and avatars: Role of visual presence and appearance. *Philosophical Transactions of the Royal Society of London. Series B, Biological Sciences*, *364*(1535), 3559–3565. doi:10.1098/rstb.2009.0148 PMID:19884150

Behm-Morawitz, E. (2013). Mirrored selves: The influence of self-presence in a virtual world on health, appearance, and well-being. *Computers in Human Behavior*, *29*(1), 119–128. doi:10.1016/j. chb.2012.07.023

Belisle, J. F., & Bodur, H. O. (2010). Avatars ad Information: Perception of Consumers Based on Their Avatars in Virtual Worlds. *Psychology and Marketing*, *27*(8), 741–765. doi:10.1002/mar.20354

Bessière, K., Seay, A. F., & Kiesler, S. (2007). The Ideal Elf: Identity Exploration in World of Warcraft. *Cyberpsychology & Behavior*, *10*(4), 530–535. doi:10.1089/cpb.2007.9994 PMID:17711361

Blain, G. H., Bergner, R. M., Lewis, M. L., & Goldstein, M. A. (1981). The use of objectively scorable house-tree-person indicators to establish child abuse. *Journal of Clinical Psychology*, *37*(3), 667–673. doi:10.1002/1097-4679(198107)37:3<667::AID-JCLP2270370339>3.0.CO;2-P PMID:7263895

Brewer, E. C., & Holmes, T. L. (2009). Obfuscating the obvious: Miscommunication issues in the interpretation of common terms. *Journal of Business Communication*, *46*(4), 480–496. doi:10.1177/0021943608329103

Buck, J. N. (1948). The H-T-P test. *Journal of Clinical Psychology*, *4*(2), 151–159. doi:10.1002/1097-4679(194804)4:2<151::AID-JCLP2270040203>3.0.CO;2-O PMID:18869052

Buisine, S., Guegan, J., Barré, J., Segonds, F., & Aoussat, A. (2016). Using avatars to tailor ideation process to innovation strategy. *Cognition Technology and Work*, *18*(3), 583–594. doi:10.100710111-016-0378-y

Burke, P. J., & Tully, J. C. (1977). The measurement of role identity. *Social Forces*, *55*(4), 881–897. doi:10.1093f/55.4.881

Carrasco, R., Baker, S., Waycott, J., & Vetere, F. (2017, November). Negotiating stereotypes of older adults through avatars. In *Proceedings of the 29th Australian Conference on Computer-Human Interaction* (pp. 218-227). ACM. 10.1145/3152771.3152795

Cates, J. A. (1999). The art of assessment in psychology: Ethics, expertise, and validity. *Journal of Clinical Psychology*, *55*(5), 631–641. doi:10.1002/(SICI)1097-4679(199905)55:5<631::AID-JCLP10>3.0.CO;2-1 PMID:10392793

Cohen, J. (2001). Defining identification: A theoretical look at the identification of audiences with media characters. *Mass Communication & Society*, *4*, 245–264.

Cross, S. E., & Markus, H. (1990). The willful self. *Personality and Social Psychology Bulletin*, *16*(4), 726–742. doi:10.1177/0146167290164013

Ducheneaut, N., Wen, M., Yee, N., & Wadley, G. (2009). Body and Mind: A Study of Avatar Personalization in Three Virtual Worlds. *Proceedings of the SIGCHI Conference on Human Factors in Computing Systems*, 1151–1160. 10.1145/1518701.1518877

Dunn, R. A., & Guadagno, R. E. (2012). My avatar and me – Gender and personality predictors of avatar-self discrepancy. *Computers in Human Behavior*, *28*(1), 97–106. doi:10.1016/j.chb.2011.08.015

Ellemers, N., Spears, R., & Doosje, B. (2002). Self and Social Identity. *Group*, *53*(1), 161–186. doi:10.1146/annurev.psych.53.100901.135228 PMID:11752483

Fletcher, K. E. (2005). *Encyclopedia of Psychological Assessment*. Psychiatric Services. doi:10.1176/appi.ps.56.5.614-a

Fong, K., & Mar, R. A. (2015). What Does My Avatar Say About Me? Inferring Personality From Avatars. *Personality and Social Psychology Bulletin*, *41*(2), 237–249. doi:10.1177/0146167214562761 PMID:25576173

Fox, J., & Bailenson, J. (2009). Virtual Experiences. *Physical Behaviors : The Effect of Presence on Imitation of an Eating Avatar*, *18*(4), 294–303.

Fox, J., Bailenson, J. N., & Tricase, L. (2013). The embodiment of sexualized virtual selves: The Proteus effect and experiences of self-objectification via avatars. *Computers in Human Behavior*, *29*(3), 930–938. doi:10.1016/j.chb.2012.12.027

Funder, D. C., & Colvin, C. R. (1991). Explorations in Behavioral Consistency: Properties of Persons, Situations, and Behaviors. *Journal of Personality and Social Psychology*, *60*(5), 773–794. doi:10.1037/0022-3514.60.5.773 PMID:2072255

Gamage, V., & Ennis, C. (2018). Examining the effects of a virtual character on learning and engagement in serious games. In *Proceedings of the 11th Annual International Conference on Motion, Interaction, and Games - MIG '18* (pp. 1–9). New York, NY: ACM Press. 10.1145/3274247.3274499

Gatti, E., Ionio, C., Traficante, D., & Confalonieri, E. (2014). "I like my body; therefore, I like myself": How body image influences self-esteem-A cross-sectional study on Italian adolescents. *Europe's Journal of Psychology*, *10*(2), 301–317. doi:10.5964/ejop.v10i2.703

Gee, J. P. (2003). *What video games have to teach us about learning and literacy*. Hampshire, UK: Palgrave Macmillan. doi:10.1145/950566.950595

Guadagno, R. E., Muscanell, N. L., Okdie, B. M., Burk, N. M., & Ward, T. B. (2011). Even in virtual environments women shop and men build: A social role perspective on Second Life. *Computers in Human Behavior*, *27*(1), 304–308. doi:10.1016/j.chb.2010.08.008

Higgins, E. T. (1987). Self-discrepancy. A theory relating to self and affect. *Psychological Review*, *94*(3), 319–340. doi:10.1037/0033-295X.94.3.319 PMID:3615707

Hoelter, J. W. (1983). The effects of role evaluation and commitment on identity salience. *Social Psychology Quarterly*, *46*(2), 140–147. doi:10.2307/3033850

Hooi, R., & Cho, H. (2014). Avatar-driven self-disclosure: The virtual me is the actual me. *Computers in Human Behavior*, *39*, 20–28. doi:10.1016/j.chb.2014.06.019

Hussain, Z., & Griffiths, M. D. (2009). The attitudes, feelings, and experiences of online games: A qualitative analysis. *Cyberpsychology & Behavior*, *12*(6), 747–753. doi:10.1089/cpb.2009.0059 PMID:19788376

Islam, G. (2014). Leadership as a dominant cultural myth: A strain-based perspective on leadership approaches. *Social and Personality Psychology Compass*, *8*(3), 91–103. doi:10.1111pc3.12093

James, W. (1890). *Classics in the History of Psychology*. Academic Press.

Jin, S. A. (2010). "'I Feel More Connected to the Physically Ideal Mini Me than the Mirror-Image Mini Me'": Theoretical Implications of the '"Malleable Self"' for Speculations on the Effects of Avatar Creation on Avatar – Self Connection in Wii. *Cyberpsychology, Behavior, and Social Networking*, 13(5), 567–571. doi:10.1089/cyber.2009.0243 PMID:20950182

Jin, S.-A. A. (2009). Avatars mirroring the actual self versus projecting the ideal self: The effects of self-priming on interactivity and immersion in an exergame, Wii Fit. *Cyberpsychology & Behavior*, 12(6), 761–765. doi:10.1089/cpb.2009.0130 PMID:19788381

Jin, S.-A. A. (2012). The virtual malleable self and the virtual identity discrepancy model: Investigative frameworks for virtual possible selves and others in avatar-based identity construction and social interaction. *Computers in Human Behavior*, 28(6), 2160–2168. doi:10.1016/j.chb.2012.06.022

Kafai, Y. B., Fields, D. A., & Cook, M. S. (2010). Your second selves: Player-designed avatars. *Games and Culture*, 5(1), 23–42. doi:10.1177/1555412009351260

Kang, S., Watt, J. H., & Ala, S. K. (2008). *Communicators ' Perceptions of Social Presence as a Function of Avatar Realism in Small Display Mobile Communication Devices*. Academic Press.

Keysar, B. (2007). Communication and miscommunication: The role of egocentric processes. *Intercultural Pragmatics*, 4(1). doi:10.1515/IP.2007.004

Kim, Y., & Sundar, S. S. (2012). Visualizing ideal self vs. actual self through avatars: Impact on preventive health outcomes. *Computers in Human Behavior*, 28(4), 1356–1364. doi:10.1016/j.chb.2012.02.021

Klevjer. (2006). *What is the Avatar? Methodology*. University of Bergen. doi:10.1075/ni.13.2.05day

Lee, J. E. R. (2014). Does virtual diversity matter?: Effects of avatar-based diversity representation on willingness to express offline racial identity and avatar customization. *Computers in Human Behavior*, 36, 190–197. doi:10.1016/j.chb.2014.03.040

Leménager, T., Gwodz, A., Richter, A., Reinhard, I., Kämmerer, N., Sell, M., & Mann, K. (2013). Self-concept deficits in massively multiplayer online role-playing games addiction. *European Addiction Research*, 19(5), 227–234. doi:10.1159/000345458 PMID:23428827

Li, B. J., Lwin, M. O., & Jung, Y. (2014). Wii, Myself, and Size: The Influence of Proteus Effect and Stereotype Threat on Overweight Children's Exercise Motivation and Behavior in Exergames. *Games for Health Journal*, 3(1), 40–48. doi:10.1089/g4h.2013.0081 PMID:26197254

Lin, H., & Wang, H. (2014). Avatar creation in virtual worlds: Behaviors and motivations. *Computers in Human Behavior*, 34, 213–218. doi:10.1016/j.chb.2013.10.005

Machover, K. (1949). Personality projection in the drawing of the human figure: A method of personality investigation. *American Lectures in Psychology, 25*.

Mantovani, F., Riva, G., Castelnuovo, G., & Gaggioli, A. (2003). From Psychotherapy to e-Therapy : The Integration of Clinical Settings. *Cyberpsychology & Behavior*, 6(4), 375–382. doi:10.1089/109493103322278754 PMID:14511449

Markus, H. (1977). Self-schemata and processing information about the self. *Journal of Personality and Social Psychology*, 35(2), 63–78. doi:10.1037/0022-3514.35.2.63

Mcarthur, V. (2018). Challenging the User-Avatar Dichotomy in Avatar Customization Research. *Eluda-mos (Göttingen)*, *9*(1), 75–94. Retrieved from http://www.eludamos.org

McArthur, V., Teather, R. J., & Stuerzlinger, W. (2010). Examining 3D Content Creation Interfaces in Virtual Worlds. *Journal of Gaming & Virtual Worlds*, *2*(3), 239–258. doi:10.1386/jgvw.2.3.239_1

Messinger, P. R., Ge, X., Stroulia, E., Lyons, K., Smirnov, K., Bone, M., & Alberta, U. (2008). Virtual Worlds Research: Consumer Behavior in Virtual Worlds, November 2008, On the Relationship between My Avatar and Myself. *Journal of Virtual Worlds Research*, *1*(2), 1–17.

Nass, C., & Moon, Y. (2000). What is the avatar. *The Indian Journal of Chest Diseases & Allied Sciences*, *32*(2), 75–81. Retrieved from http://www.ncbi.nlm.nih.gov/pubmed/1964673

Naumann, L. P., Vazire, S., Rentfrow, P. J., & Gosling, S. D. (2009). Personality judgments based on physical appearance. *Personality and Social Psychology Bulletin*, *35*(12), 1661–1671. doi:10.1177/0146167209346309 PMID:19762717

Park, J. (2018). The effect of virtual avatar experience on body image discrepancy, body satisfaction and weight regulation intention. *Cyberpsychology (Brno)*, *12*(1). doi:10.5817/CP2018-1-3

Peña, J., & Kim, E. (2014). Increasing exergame physical activity through self and opponent avatar appearance. *Computers in Human Behavior*, *41*, 262–267. doi:10.1016/j.chb.2014.09.038

Pinto, M. D., Hickman, R. L. Jr, Clochesy, J., & Buchner, M. (2013). Avatar-based depression self-management technology: Promising approach to improve depressive symptoms among young adults. *Applied Nursing Research*, *26*(1), 45–48. doi:10.1016/j.apnr.2012.08.003 PMID:23265918

Poole, A. (2017). Learning, Culture and Social Interaction Funds of Knowledge 2. 0 : Towards digital Funds of Identity. *Learning. Culture and Social Interaction*, *13*, 50–59. doi:10.1016/j.lcsi.2017.02.002

Quackenbush, D. M., & Krasner, A. (2012). Avatar therapy: Where technology, symbols, culture, and connection collide. *Journal of Psychiatric Practice*, *18*(6), 451–459. doi:10.1097/01.pra.0000422745.17990. be PMID:23160252

Rehak, B. (2013). Playing at Being: Psychoanalysis and the Avatar. In *The video game theory reader* (pp. 125-150). Routledge.

Roberts, B., & Donahue, E. (1994). One Personality, Multiple Selves: Integrating Personality and Social Roles. *Journal of Personality*, *62*(2), 199–218. doi:10.1111/j.1467-6494.1994.tb00291.x PMID:8046573

Rogers, C. (1961). On Becoming A Person: A Therapist's View of Psychotherapy. *Zhurnal Eksperimentalnoi i Teoreticheskoi Fiziki*. doi:10.1038j.jes.7500572

Sah, Y. J., Ratan, R., Tsai, H.-Y. S., Peng, W., & Sarinopoulos, I. (2017). Are You What Your Avatar Eats? Health-Behavior Effects of Avatar-Manifested Self-Concept. *Media Psychology*, *20*(4), 632–657. doi:10.1080/15213269.2016.1234397

Sandyk, R. (1998). Reversal of a body image disorder (Macrosomatognosia) in parkinson's disease by treatment with ac pulsed electromagnetic fields. *The International Journal of Neuroscience*, *93*(1–2), 43–54. doi:10.3109/00207459808986411 PMID:9604168

Scott, M., & Ghinea, G. (2013). Integrating fantasy role-play into the programming lab: exploring the 'projective identity' hypothesis. *Proceeding of the 44th ACM Technical Symposium*, 119–122. Retrieved from http://dl.acm.org/citation.cfm?id=2445237

Serpe, R. T. (1987). Stability and change in self: A structural symbolic interactionist explanation. *Social Psychology Quarterly*, *50*(1), 44–55. doi:10.2307/2786889

Sherrick, B., Hoewe, J., & Waddell, T. F. (2014). The role of stereotypical beliefs in gender-based activation of the Proteus effect. *Computers in Human Behavior*, *38*, 17–24. doi:10.1016/j.chb.2014.05.010

Sibilla, F., & Mancini, T. (2018). I am (not) my avatar: A review of the user-avatar relationships in Massively Multiplayer Online Worlds. *Cyberpsychology*. doi:10.5817/CP2018-3-4

Sidun, N. M., & Rosenthal, R. H. (1987). Graphic indicators of sexual abuse in draw-a-person tests of psychiatrically hospitalized adolescents. *The Arts in Psychotherapy*, *14*(1), 25–33. doi:10.1016/0197-4556(87)90032-3

Slater, M. (2017). *Implicit Learning Through Embodiment in Immersive Virtual Reality*. Singapore: Springer. doi:10.1007/978-981-10-5490-7_2

Stavropoulos, V., Anderson, E. E., Beard, C., Latifi, M. Q., Kuss, D., & Griffiths, M. (2018). *A preliminary cross-cultural study of hikikomori and internet gaming disorder: The moderating effects of game-playing time and living with parents*. Addictive Behaviors Reports. doi:10.1016/j.abrep.2018.10.001

Stryker, S. (1987). *Identity theory: Developments and extensions*. Academic Press.

Stryker, S., & Statham, A. (1985). Symbolic interaction and role theory. In The handbook of social psychology. Academic Press.

Tajfel, H. (1970). Experiments in intergroup discrimination. *Scientific American*, *223*(5), 96–103. doi:10.1038cientificamerican1170-96 PMID:5482577

Tajfel, H. (1972). La catégorisation sociale. In Introduction à la psychologie sociale. Academic Press. doi:10.1080/08911762.2010.487424

Tajfel, H. (1974). Social identity and intergroup behaviour. *Social Sciences Information. Information Sur les Sciences Sociales*, *13*(2), 65–93. doi:10.1177/053901847401300204

Tajfel, H., & Turner, J. (1979). An Integrative Theory of Intergroup Conflict. In The Social Psychology of Intergroup Relations (pp. 56–65). Academic Press.

Tajfel, H., & Turner, J. C. (1986). The social identity theory of intergroup behavior. In Psychology of Intergroup Relations (2nd ed.; pp. 7–24). Academic Press. doi:10.1111/j.1751-9004.2007.00066.x

Trepte, S., & Reinecke, L. (2010). Avatar Creation and Video Game Enjoyment. *Journal of Media Psychology*, *22*(4), 171–184. doi:10.1027/1864-1105/a000022

Triberti, S., & Argenton, L. (2013). *Psicologia dei videogiochi. Come i mondi virtuali influenzano mente e comportamento*. Milano: Apogeo.

Triberti, S., & Chirico, A. (2016). Healthy Avatars, Healthy People. In G. Graffigna (Ed.), *Transformative Healthcare Practice through Patient Engagement* (pp. 247–275). Hershey, PA: IGI Global. doi:10.4018/978-1-5225-0663-8.ch010

Triberti, S., Durosini, I., Aschieri, F., Villani, D., & Riva, G. (2017a). A frame effect in avatar customization: How users' attitudes towards their avatars may change depending on virtual context. *Annual Review of Cybertherapy and Telemedicine*, 15.

Triberti, S., Durosini, I., Aschieri, F., Villani, D., & Riva, G. (2017b). Changing Avatars, Changing Selves? the Influence of Social and Contextual Expectations on Digital Rendition of Identity. *Cyberpsychology, Behavior, and Social Networking*, 20(8), 501–507. doi:10.1089/cyber.2016.0424 PMID:28806125

Turner, R. H. (1956). Role-Taking, Role Standpoint, and Reference-Group Behavior. *Source: American Journal of Sociology*. doi:10.2307/2773533

Van Der Heide, B., Schumaker, E. M., Peterson, A. M., & Jones, E. B. (2013). The Proteus Effect in Dyadic Communication: Examining the Effect of Avatar Appearance in Computer-Mediated Dyadic Interaction. *Communication Research*, 40(6), 838–860. doi:10.1177/0093650212438097

Vasalou, A., & Joinson, A. N. (2009). Me, myself and I: The role of interactional context on self-presentation through avatars. *Computers in Human Behavior*, 25(2), 510–520. doi:10.1016/j.chb.2008.11.007

Villani, D., Gatti, E., Confalonieri, E., & Riva, G. (2012). Am I my avatar? A tool to investigate virtual body image representation in adolescence. *Cyberpsychology, Behavior, and Social Networking*, 15(8), 435–440. doi:10.1089/cyber.2012.0057 PMID:22823468

Villani, D., Gatti, E., Triberti, S., Confalonieri, E., & Riva, G. (2016). Exploration of virtual body-representation in adolescence: The role of age and sex in avatar customization. *SpringerPlus*, 5(1), 740. doi:10.118640064-016-2520-y PMID:27376008

Williams, D., Kennedy, T. L. M., & Moore, R. J. (2016). Behind the Avatar: The Patterns, Practices, and Functions of Role Playing in MMOs The Practice of RP, Historic and Modern. *Games and Culture*, 6(2), 171–200. doi:10.1177/1555412010364983

Wu, J. (2014). Choosing My Avatar and the Psychology of Virtual Worlds: What Matters? *Kaleidoscope*, 11(1), 89.

Wylie, M. L. (1979). The effect of expectations on the transition to parenthood. *Sociological Focus*, 12(4), 323–329. doi:10.1080/00380237.1979.10570356

Yee, N., & Bailenson, J. (2007). The proteus effect: The effect of transformed self-representation on behavior. *Human Communication Research*, 33(3), 271–290. doi:10.1111/j.1468-2958.2007.00299.x

Yee, N., Bailenson, J. N., & Ducheneaut, N. (2009). The Proteus effect. *Communication Research*, 36(2), 285–312. doi:10.1177/0093650208330254

Yoon, G., & Vargas, P. T. (2014). Know Thy Avatar: The Unintended Effect of Virtual-Self Representation on Behavior. *Psychological Science*, 25(4), 1043–1045. doi:10.1177/0956797613519271 PMID:24501111

ADDITIONAL READING

Fox, J., & Ahn, S. J. (2013). Avatars: portraying, exploring, and changing online and offline identities. In R. Luppicini (Ed.), *Handbook of research on technoself: identity in a technological society* (Vol. I). Hershey, PA: IGI Global. doi:10.4018/978-1-4666-2211-1.ch014

Jin, S. A. A. (2012). The virtual malleable self and the virtual identity discrepancy model: Investigative frameworks for virtual possible selves and others in avatar-based identity construction and social interaction. *Computers in Human Behavior*, 28(6), 2160–2168. doi:10.1016/j.chb.2012.06.022

Riva, G., Wiederhold, B. K., & Cipresso, P. (Eds.). (2016). The Psychology of Social Networking: Vol. 2. *Identity and Relationships in Online Communities*. Berlin: De Gruyter Open.

Sibilla, F., & Mancini, T. (2018). I am (not) my avatar: A review of the user-avatar relationships in Massively Multiplayer Online Worlds. *Cyberpsychology (Brno)*, 12(3). doi:10.5817/CP2018-3-4

Triberti, S., & Argenton, L. (2013). *Psicologia dei Videogiochi*. Milan: Apogeo.

Triberti, S., & Chirico, A. (2017). Healthy avatars, healthy people: care engagement through the shared experience of virtual worlds. In G. Graffigna (Ed.), *Transformative Healthcare Practice through Patient Engagement*. Hershey, PA: IGI Global. doi:10.4018/978-1-5225-0663-8.ch010

Williams, D., Kennedy, T. L., & Moore, R. J. (2011). Behind the avatar: The patterns, practices, and functions of role playing in MMOs. *Games and Culture*, 6(2), 171–200. doi:10.1177/1555412010364983

Yee, N. (2014). *The Proteus Paradox: how online games and virtual worlds change us-and how they don't*. New Haven: Yale University Press.

KEY TERMS AND DEFINITIONS

Avatar: Digital entity meant to represent users' action and/or communication within digital environments.

Proteus Effect: Tendency for people to be affected in their behavior by their digital representations, such as avatars, dating site profiles and social networking personas.

Psychological Assessment: The process of testing which uses different techniques to arrive at hypotheses on individuals' mental state and behavior, possibly with the intention to change them in the future.

Self-Presentation: Parts of the individual's identity (personality traits, aims and objectives, etc.) that the individual may use to induce a positive image of themselves within their interlocutors' mind, in a process called impression management. Self-presentation efforts can be accepted or rebuffed by others, thanks to the dialogical feedback loop that characterize every communicative exchange.

Social Identity: The individual's sense of who they are basing on social group memberships.

Virtual Worlds: Permanent virtual environments where multiple users can interact with each other thanks to the use of avatars.

This research was previously published in The Psychology and Dynamics Behind Social Media Interactions; pages 313-341, copyright year 2020 by Information Science Reference (an imprint of IGI Global).

Chapter 26
Avatar Teaching and Learning:
Examining Language Teaching and Learning Practices in Virtual Reality Environments

Geoff Lawrence
https://orcid.org/0000-0002-5759-815X
York University, Canada

Farhana Ahmed
https://orcid.org/0000-0001-6163-7468
York University, Canada

ABSTRACT

This chapter examines the pedagogical potential of immersive social virtual worlds (SVWs) in language teaching and learning. Recognizing the language learning affordances of immersive virtual environments, this research examines a study analyzing the beliefs and practices of 'Karelia Kondor', an avatar-learner and teacher of languages with a decade of diverse experiences in Second Life (SL), one of the first widely used SVWs. Findings highlight the relevance of a hyper-immersive and emotionally engaging conceptual model informing language teaching approaches within these rapidly evolving environments. When supported pedagogically, the activities illustrated demonstrate the potential of these immersive approaches to create communities of practice and affinity spaces by fostering investment and autonomy in the language learning process through shared target language experiences. The chapter concludes with a summary of pedagogical insights to inform the use of these hyper-immersive environments in language teaching and learning.

DOI: 10.4018/978-1-6684-7597-3.ch026

INTRODUCTION

Three-dimensional (3-D) virtual and augmented reality media are increasingly being recognized as ideal environments for second/additional language teaching and learning. Virtual world[1] (VW) learning platforms that began with Active Worlds, Second Life (SL) and Open Wonderland have evolved into mobile-friendly augmented reality[2] and virtual world environments including Oculus Rift, Pokemon Go and Project Sansar[3] that have the potential to add an interactive, simulative and immersive dimension into language teaching practices (Buckley & Perez, 2019; Deutschmann & Panichi, 2009; Lin & Lan, 2015; Loke, 2015; Panichi, 2015; Scrivner, Madewell; Wang, 2017). These emerging environments offer the potential of hyper-immersive, multimodal target language simulations that cognitively, kinesthetically and emotionally engage learners, activating a range of linguistic, cultural and collaborative resources that can facilitate linguistic, intercultural and 21st century skills (Deutschmann & Panichi, 2009; Hanewald, 2013; Lin & Lan, 2015; Shrestha & Harrison, 2019).

Second Life (SL) was launched in 2003 and quickly became one of the most prominent and accessible 3-D multi-user social virtual world (SVW) environments used in education (Wang, 2017). Research on SL focused on suggesting ways to use this platform in education (Hismanoglu, 2012), analyzing the environment and its language learning potential (Panichi, 2015). However, many teachers remain unclear how to integrate these dynamic platforms into their language learning environments.

The field of language instruction has been slow to embrace immersive technologies in teaching practices as "there is still not a clear vision of how to integrate these technologies in a stable way into an educational process" (Martin-Gutierrez et al., 2017, as cited in Scrivner et al., 2019, p. 56). Although the use of these environments tend to be increasingly seen as promising for language learning, there remains a dearth of research examining teacher perspectives on the potential, relevance and approaches needed in 3-D VW language education (Lin & Lan, 2015). There is minimal research documenting task design and pedagogical approaches relevant for language teaching/learning in SVWs. In addition, little if any research has examined VW teaching practices through the eyes of an experienced avatar language learner and teacher.

The purpose of this chapter is to provide pedagogical insights into the potential uses of SVWs in language teaching and learning. This chapter will revisit and update an article reporting on a unique study examining the beliefs and practices of an avatar learner and teacher with extensive plurilingual experiences in SL (Lawrence & Ahmed, 2018), a teacher who immersed herself within these environments in varied teaching and learning roles using a range of languages over a 10-year period. Findings will be shared from this study that examined interviews with 'Karelia Kondor', who learned Italian as an adult, taught French to secondary students and designed a range of virtual world curricula. She designed and facilitated telecollaborative German language game-based exchanges and participated extensively in educational communities of practice, all within SL. The study examined the following question: What experiences and pedagogical insights inform language teaching and learning practices within these online immersive environments?

This chapter offers perspectives on hyper-immersive SVWs, their benefits, limitations and the pedagogical potential to inform language teaching within these platforms. The chapter will begin with a definition of SVWs, outlining the affordances and limitations of these environments. The relevance of sociocultural theories to inform SVW use and this study will then be examined, followed by the study's methodology and a profile of this key informant. An analysis of findings, organized by key themes identified in the data will then be discussed. Links between these themes and language teaching practices and theories will follow. Pedagogical insights to guide teaching practices within these unique environments and the need for future research will conclude the chapter.

DEFINING SOCIAL VIRTUAL WORLDS

3-D VWs have been defined by Kozlova & Priven (2015, p. 83) as the most complex modern technologies for their synchronous, multimodal communication, their simulation of real-life experiences and learning spaces that are conceptually different from face-to-face classroom and other online learning environments. Loke (2015, p. 112) defines VWs as "computer-based, multi-user virtual environments that simulate real or fictional life and that users experience using their graphical representations or avatars." According to Panichi (2015, p. 465), the most significant characteristics of 3-D VWs is the immersive nature of the platform, impacting language learning activities and learner engagement. Hanewald (2013) categorizes virtual worlds as either gaming virtual worlds, SVWs or educational virtual worlds. Educational VWs are characterized by experiential learning, having active in-world experiences based on learning particular content or through simulations (Hanewald, 2013, p. 238). Although the gaming and socializing aspects of VWs initially attracted many users, the educational possibilities are now drawing more institutions to explore classroom applications within these environments.

In spite of their original intentions, educators and researchers are now working with a range of SVWs to understand the pedagogical principles, theories and practices that can inform the use of these tools in language teaching and learning. The emerging potential of these environments that fray the boundaries between study and play (Sykes, Oskoz, & Thorne, 2016, p. 176) has captured an increasing range of educators, researchers and prompted the study outlined below. This research embraces Mayrath, Traphagan, Heikes and Trivedi's (2011) definition that SVWs like SL are not a game, but a social virtual world that "provides a platform for users to create and/or explore places and spaces…enhancing student engagement, facilitating collaboration and providing situated learning opportunities that are unavailable in traditional learning environments" (p.126). This definition resonates with the varied experiences of Karelia Kondor, as a language learner and then as a teacher in SL.

AFFORDANCES OF SVWs

SVWs are an evolution of Web 2.0 tools that are designed to be social and collaborative environments (Sadler & Dooly, 2014), offering simulated interactions within immersive spaces. Hismanoglu (2012) concludes that virtual worlds like SL are particularly appropriate for teaching and learning foreign languages due to their immersive environments. They provide learners with life-like situations to interact socially, exchange cultural information, construct meaning collaboratively in authentic-like contexts which might be costly or impossible to replicate in real life (Hismanoglu, 2012, p. 105). Some of the distinguishing features of SL in relation to language learning can be listed as follows:

- *The multimodal nature of SL, provides multiple communication channels and a variety of feedback;*
- *The accessible nature of these open environments provide opportunities for learner-centered interactions involving target language speakers and a diverse group of interlocutors;*

- *The anonymity of avatars can reduce affective filters where learners take more risks and engage in language play;*
- *Personalized avatars provide enhanced feelings of co-presence leading to high degree of engagement;*
- *Tasks designed to facilitate interaction enhance participation and provide opportunities for using the target language;*
- *The supportive atmosphere engendered by interaction strengthens group cohesion and develops collaborative social relationships.*

(Peterson, 2011, pp. 69-70)

Providing a sense of community, belonging and collaborative learning opportunities through resources for learners and teachers makes SVWs unique platforms, worthy of consideration in language education (Duncan, Miller, & Jiang, 2012; Hanewald, 2013; Peterson, 2012; Wang, Lefaiver, Wang, & Hunt, 2011). For example, the interactive nature of SL facilitates teaching online by not just speaking into a microphone, but by acting, performing and collaborating with students, affording learners dynamic learning to complement the traditional language classroom (Wang, et al., 2011, p. 33). Peterson's (2012, p. 20) study on EFL learner collaborations suggests that SL provides an arena for learner-centered social interaction offering opportunities for target language practice and the development of autonomy. Virtual environments have also been reported to provide a positive affective dimension to the language learning experience and have made students more engaged and autonomous learners (Sama & Wu, 2019, p. 73). Furthermore, the technology-enhanced interaction within these environments facilitates the consistent production of target language output and learner centered rather than teacher led interaction (Peterson, 2010, p. 289).

In addition, the mediated experiences of simulated SVW environments encourage learners to experiment with varied communicative norms, developing pragmatic competence (Sykes et al., 2016). Such environments reduce learners' affective filters, enabling risk-taking in the learning process and a willingness to shift perspectives and play while learning (Lin & Lan, 2015). Interactions in these environments can thereby facilitate intercultural awareness and competence (Diehl & Prins, 2008). For example, learners adopting a gender or ethnic background different than their own can interact through a different perspective and expand their worldviews through such simulations (Diehl & Prins, 2008). This fluid identity affordance allows learners to play with identity and work with imagined communities (Norton, 2013) actualizing visions in the target language that can foster investment and learning (Dörnyei, 2009).

As a result, SVW platforms offer educators a range of affective dimensions to learning that can deepen motivation and learning. For example, principles of gamification can be used in task design to enhance learner engagement, interaction and cognition. By integrating elements of gamification such as mechanics and game-thinking (i.e., offering options, challenges, competition and rewards) in esthetically engaging environments, engagement and risk-taking can be sustained and notions of failure and mistakes can be reframed as a necessary part of task completion, skill development and learning (Dominguez et al., 2013). Leveraging elements of gamification in task design and teaching practices can contribute to affinity spaces where learners share expertise in common activities with similar goals, developing practices, knowledge and/or skills (Gee & Hayes, 2012).

LIMITATIONS OF SVWs

The most widely cited limitations of SVWs include the digital literacies required to effectively interact within these emerging environments (Sykes et al., 2016; Wang, 2017). These include a steep learning curve and technical difficulties to use these platforms, making it time-consuming for educators to integrate into classroom learning (Wang, 2017). Other constraining factors include hardware issues, digital access and expenses involved in purchasing, enhancing or maintaining one's learning environment, as in SL, one can purchase 'land' and accessories to enhance interactions, avatars and environments (Hismanoglu, 2012). There are concerns around security working with young learners in some of these open environments (Lee & Warren, 2007). Issues like identity masking, theft and cyberbullying can pose a serious concern for teachers wanting to use these environments with learners of any age (Lee & Warren, 2007).

In addition, maneuvering avatars to their full potential can require practice and time. Sykes et al. (2016) identify pragmatic control of the communicative norms used within a specific online community as time-consuming but necessary for full participation in these environments. Examining EFL teaching in SL, Wang et al. (2011, p. 35) identified technical problems like frozen screens, delayed audio and pedagogical problems, along with challenging classroom management as impediments to successful language learning. Teachers in this study reported issues like students walking or flying away from instructional sites, straying off topic or not speaking at all, avatars lacking facial expressions and body language leading to the teacher's inability to anticipate comprehension (Wang et al., 2011, p. 35). The study stresses the need for SVW-specific classroom management guidelines. "Too much functionality" and the diverse simulated environments can distract students, while teachers complained that when observing students' performance, the avatars' body language and expressions were not as intuitive as those in a traditional classroom (Duncan et al., 2012, p. 12).

The flexible, expansive nature of SVW platforms necessitates dramatic shifts in teacher and learner roles. Unless activities within these environments are acutely structured, learners in these environments can change identities, locations and move around freely. Learners have intense autonomy and numerous distractions that can prevent them from focusing on a language learning task. In addition, teachers need to adopt new roles as a learning 'observer', a guide/facilitator, a task 'director' and someone often responsible for tech guidance and support. Such changes can be daunting for instructors and learners to adopt, necessitating a supportive approach to fully orient learners and instructors to these new educational roles.

SOCIOCULTURALLY-INFORMED PEDAGOGY

Several interrelated language teaching and learning theories inform the use of SVWs in language education and help shed perspectives on the pedagogical findings discussed below. Sociocultural theory (SCT) highlights the interconnected roles of the social context, the teacher as facilitator and the mediational tools used for language learning and teaching (Lantolf, 2011). The rapidly changing influence of technology on language use and the need for language work to be within a learner's reach, the zone of proximal development, continue to inform language teaching practices with technology. "SCT is very much concerned with concrete classroom activities and its impact on learning" (Lantolf, 2011, p. 43) and this is very much being explored in SL through task-based learning. The ability to combine multimodal verbal, visual and kinesthetic activities in an SVW task can lead towards a deep, multi-level understanding of language use (Sykes et al., 2016). Such multisensory learning in these environments can be enhanced by emotional engagement (Swain, 2013), contributing to situated learning where learning is embedded within experiential activities within these immersive environments (Lave & Wenger, 1990).

Embedded within this SCT framework is the mediational role of identities and particularly imagined identities (Norton, 2013) and one's idealized L2 self, as discussed in Dörnyei's (2009) L2 self-motivation system that help mediate learning. Immersive interactions with extensive imagery enhancement in these environments help learners visualize their ideal L2 self that can enhance target language-and-culture curiosity, investment and learning (Dörnyei, 2009, p. 34). This experimentation with identity and work with emotion can reduce inhibitions and foster a reflective mindfulness that can deepen motivation, metacognitive and strategic skills, social connections and learning beyond the classroom (Sykes et al., 2016). As a result, SVW simulations can facilitate affinity spaces as noted above where value is placed on shared experiences, prompting reflection, meaning-making and informal learning within these shared situated learning experiences (Gee, 2005). This multi-faceted SCT perspective sheds a valuable perspective on L2 learning in SVWs that will be discussed in the research below.

EXAMINING DIMENSIONS OF AVATAR LANGUAGE TEACHING AND LEARNING: A STUDY

The study below examines the experiences, beliefs and reflections from a unique key informant, an educator who has spent over a decade teaching and learning a range of languages using varied approaches in SL (Lawrence & Ahmed, 2018). As noted above, this exploratory study examined and documented the teaching and learning practices of Karelia Kondor, a language teacher and learner who ventured into SL when virtual reality (VR) was first emerging and used it in varied capacities to teach and learn languages. The study's methodology is outlined below, followed by details on this educator's background and beliefs. This is followed by a discussion and analysis of findings related to these practices.

METHODOLOGY

This study adopted a qualitative research approach combining semi-structured interviews with document analysis to elicit and analyze Karelia Kondor's experiences and perceptions as a key informant within SL. Given this study's focus examining the lived experiences of Karelia, documenting her beliefs, reflections and perceptions as a highly experienced teacher-learner within SL, a qualitative analysis was used to contextualize these stories, to identify patterns of benefits, limitations within SVWs and to develop pedagogical insights from this key informant's lived experiences and voice.

Two 60-minute audio-recorded interviews were conducted using Google+ Hangouts. The researchers shared the interview questions (see Appendix 1) with the participant one week prior to the interview to provide preparation time to revisit past classroom experiences and to allow the participant to share relevant documents. The interview data was fully transcribed and then thematically coded by the researchers over the period of eight weeks using NVIVO 10 to identify and refine recurring themes within her responses. Transcribed data was shared with the participant to ensure member checks, so "data [and findings were] mutually constructed by the researcher and the researched" (Wertz, Charmaz, McMullen, Josselson, Anderson & McSpadden, 2011, p. 169). Other data sources like participant reflections on email exchanges, videos on her use of SL in teaching and learning, her personal blogs were used to interpret, analyse and triangulate selected themes and findings. An autobiographical Youtube video detailing her Italian learning experiences was also reviewed to establish a close encounter with the participant's 'language learner self'. All these documents were reviewed, seeking recurring patterns, corroborating and disconfirming instances to ensure reliability (Stake, 1995).

KARELIA KONDOR: BACKGROUND AND BELIEFS

Karelia has a background teaching French, German, music, and beginner Italian to secondary school students and English pronunciation to adults in England. She has worked as a language teacher and has always been involved with online language teaching approaches. She was an early adopter of online approaches in the late 1990s, working for a school that received funding to demonstrate how information technology can improve learner experience. Since then she's "never looked back" and has been extremely active in online learning, being an innovator using SVWs in her teaching and learning. She has networked with other educators interested in online approaches through her work in professional associations and online teacher communities. She admitted loving "the fact that you could get so much information from other teachers being online".

She "stumbled across" SL through a professional development opportunity. In response to a colleague's invitation to attend a conference, she created her avatar and began her journey on SL. "I thought this is fantastic, you can go along and get professional development from the comfort of your chair, and enjoy it." A comment in a conference document she attended got Karelia very motivated and thinking, "to convince teachers of really how good something is, very often if they've experienced it as a learner, that's the best sort of insight you can give them" (Allen, 2010, 1:20). She noted the power of communities of practice, the friends she has made who have helped with her teaching and learning journey in SL. "Even when I talk about it [now], I can't help but be excited about it." She has continued to share a range of SL teaching strategies through her blogs and videos. Karelia was seen as an ideal participant for this type of study as she had the experience of being both a student and a teacher on the SL platform as Coles believes that "a good instructor learns only when he becomes a willing student, eager to be taught" (as cited in Connelly & Clandinin, 1990, p.22).

FINDINGS AND ANALYSIS

The findings below are organized under themes identified through the analysis of this avatar-learner-teacher's experiences in SL. The findings are presented and analyzed noting links to the theoretical perspectives outlined above.

Hyper-Immersive and Emotionally Engaging Action-Oriented Learning

A consistent language learning benefit that emerged when speaking to Karelia was the potential of these environments to offer hyper-immersive, situated multimodal learning that engages learners in fun, emotionally engaging, purposeful action-oriented tasks. "You've got to give them a reason to talk" she stressed, citing the power of immersive, purposeful interactions in language learning, noting that these media are a practical alternative to target language immersion for the language classroom (Peterson,

2011). Karelia notes, "the real benefit is this feeling of being immersed, because people will say for any learning [to take place], if you feel immersed, you feel engaged, especially if there's some sort of emotion involved."

Karelia cited the example of a multi-lesson activity she experienced as an Italian language learner in an informal class held weekly in SL with adult learners who worked collaboratively to create a machinima, a film recorded by the learners in SL that they would develop, star in and eventually watch together. Because this film was being prepared in an open environment in SL, an Italian-speaking colleague of the teacher dropped in and offered to play a part in this film. As a result, the learners gained the benefit of interactions and feedback from this Italian-speaking individual. Karelia commented that these experiences can be "more memorable if you're with a French or Italian speaker."

The instructor divided the activity into subtasks. Initially learners created the characters, the storyline and assigned parts around the film's title "A Hairdresser's Husband". In their roles, the learners then began creating their dialogues, working in separate sound parcels in SL where the teacher flew in, listened and provided guidance. Karelia noted that while listening to students, the teacher would transcribe the dialogue so it was all captured. "If we said something incorrect, she'd correct us and every now and then a note card would pop up saying here's the latest of what you've said". Karelia praised this scaffolded, multimodal approach that provided instant corrective feedback fostering noticing and a focus on linguistic form and meaning (Hismanoglu, 2012; Schmidt, 1990). The learners eventually performed the film in a set prepared by this teacher who also filmed the movie within SL using Fraps[4]. The teacher's recording of the film within SL allowed the students to watch the movie and their performances in Italian through a celebratory event where the learners dressed up and attended a mock Academy Award screening in a cinema, got 'Oscars' and then went out partying in SL.

This multi-staged task demonstrates a situated action-oriented task-based approach to learning where learners engage in goal-oriented tasks, strategically activating specific competencies in a set of purposeful actions that exercise a range of language skills (Ellis, 2006; Piccardo, 2014). Such an approach "makes learning tangible, palpable, and meaningful" (Piccardo, 2014, p. 27). It also leverages the benefits of task-based learning where teaching aims to create meaningful authentic contexts in which language learning capacity can be nurtured rather than learning language through a structural approach (Ellis, 2006). In addition, the use of a machinima as an action-oriented reflective teaching tool has been reported to deepen the engagement of language learners (Shrestha & Harrison, 2019, p. 37).

Karelia noted a strong degree of emotional investment in this task, a concept that has informed her own SVW pedagogy. She noted, "It didn't feel like learning…instead a real feeling of being immersed in Italian and connected with each other". This feeling is reiterated in one of her blogs commenting about her French teaching experiences in SL, "There is no doubt in my mind that language sticks better when you have been fully immersed in a situation where you came across it for the first time, whether physically or emotionally." (Kondor, 2016, para 1). Such emotional engagement describes the possibility for these hyper-immersive environments to create affinity spaces where individuals are drawn together in an absorbing activity where informal language learning happens (Gee, 2005) but where the power of language play and emotional involvement takes precedence (Swain, 2013). Such tasks in SVW environments leverage the often unrecognized power of emotion to spark and fuel cognition (Swain, 2013), creating opportunities for learners to gain embodied experience with concepts and language which can lead to situated understanding and long-term retention (Gee & Hayes, 2011).

Gamifying Language Learning

In discussions with Karelia, she reinforced the relevance of gamification in SVW learning. She stated that the experiential learning opportunities in life-like game-based situations make learning memorable and meaningful, "playing games in 3-dimensional consequences" (Kondor, 2013, 2:31). As a student learning Italian in SL, she gave an example of a vocabulary game where students are seated on chairs and lifted up with every correct word they provide. Once at the top, students had to solve a word search embedded in a wall. When solved, the wall fell apart and allowed the student avatars to move onto the next level of the game. She recalled getting gifts like scooters as recognition of their successful feat in this vocabulary competition. She remarked that these fun games and activities made students relax in each other's company and that "the gifts encouraged them to have a go" (Kondor, 2013, 3:15). This example illustrates the power of integrating game-based approaches that are creative while being language-focused to facilitate language acquisition through a heightened motivational state (Flores, 2015).

Karelia later shared another successful game-based telecollaborative activity that she developed in collaboration with a Dutch secondary school teacher. She met this teacher in SL and then offline at a conference and decided to collaborate on a game-based project in SL where his Dutch learners of German had to interact with Karelia's English learners of German. With the help of a game developer they designed a game using principles of game-based learning, attending to the mechanics (i.e., objectives, rules, processes), the dynamics (i.e., player behaviour) and the emotions (i.e., the players' state of mind throughout the game) of the desired game-based activity (Pitarch, 2018). In this game, paired students had to go through a scenario of six doors representing different levels. Students had to solve a series of problems, exchange information, like passwords in German, to open a sequence of doors to move through levels of the game. The telecollaborative nature of this game where the participants did not share the same first language encouraged learners to communicate using the target language of German throughout the game. Karelia described this game as a great success as it engaged learners through competitive interaction and successful task completion that involved language tasks. Karelia stressed the importance of designing "games that required [students] to communicate, because so often with these games, communication is not needed."

Facilitative Stress and Tech-Talk Learning

Another type of emotionally charged interaction that Karelia identified as endemic to SL is the need for learners in these SVWs to use 'tech-talk' to troubleshoot navigation and communication problems, common in these immersive environments. She remarked that this type of authentic target language communication seems to recur in SL given its unfamiliarity to many learners (Wang, 2017). She highlighted this type of interaction as often emotionally charged and therefore a prime opportunity for language learning.

SL is where things often go wrong...so you find that you get in an emotional state about how you do something. It may sound really odd, but it's things like: can you hear me? My microphone's not working.

She noted having had many of these experiences as a learner. "It makes it more memorable because you're there and you really need to communicate". Her initial mistakes, like, sitting on people, actually led to asking for help and learning, as "doing things wrong provokes laughter which supposes a real human thing, breaking down barriers" (Kondor, 2013, 1:32). Reinforcing a teaching approach that actively works with emotion, she added that the facilitative stress and emotion around these interactions "make the memory of this interaction and language stick".

Authentic Interactions Emphasizing Listening and Speaking

Karelia noted that teachers using SL can create what sometimes is lacking in the language classroom, "genuine interactions, not made-up ones". She highlighted the ability of activities in these virtual environments to provide extensive opportunities for practicing speaking and listening skills, areas that are often lacking in traditional classroom contexts. "At the productive stage, that's the bit where SL absolutely beats anything that you can do in your own classroom", she noted. Karelia commented that as she is walking around the streets of Paris in SL projecting SL-mediated interactions in front of her students (discussed below), they may see a notice and because it is in context and meaningful, "it's more likely to stick than any amount of repetition and drilling I might do in the classroom".

Admitting that some people do not see interactions in SL as authentic, Karelia responded, "it's a real person sitting behind that avatar...you want to talk to them, get to know them...this is real life and these are real people". Karelia remarked that interactions in SL can be more engaging and authentic than a role play rehearsed by the lockers or from following lessons in a text. She adds, "it is comfortably over and above what you can offer in a normal teaching situation" (Allen, 2010, 4:52). Scrivner, et al. (2019) also found that the immersive aspect of VW technologies provide "students with active control and more authentic experiences; thus, helping them learn more effectively and increase their retention" (p. 55). The result of this collaborative research at Indiana University which investigated the impact of mobile immersive technologies (i.e., Aurasma, ThingLink, and Google Cardboard) for foreign language teaching and learning found that augmented reality successfully supported the learning of vocabulary and listening skills, whereas virtual reality enhanced cultural learning with spatial immersion (p. 69). Usage-based linguistics also 'claims that language is ultimately learned through exposure to authentic language exemplars and through the meaningful use of language as means of actual communication (Lech & Harris, 2019, p. 43).

In her second interview, Karelia emphasized that the presence of an actual person behind an avatar makes the interactions "genuine", "not made up ones" and provides a reason for learners to interact, "a motivation for having interaction because you get to know the people, you want to talk to them". Highlighting the link between these types of interactions and language acquisition, Sama and Wu (2019) found in a study examining an online "Talk Abroad" (TA) video-synchronous communication tool, that Italian language learners made significant increases in oral proficiency (especially in accuracy and fluency), and in autonomy in linguistic development and self-regulated learning strategies (p. 73). Students reported being more engaged and motivated to use Italian in their everyday life (p. 90). Students expressed excitement and engagement in being able to participate in the online conversation partner sessions. All students reported having had a positive affective experience, as they became more engaged and autonomous learners as the course progressed (p. 90). They also mentioned that it was especially good practice as it was "similar to real life" (p. 86).

Identity Manipulation and Engagement

A key aspect to engaging learners in meaningful and fun interactions in SVWs appears to be the fact that everyone adopts an avatar, a unique and alternate identity in the SL environment. Karelia stressed the affective benefit of this: "People are more anxious about speaking [in another language] but behind the avatar, people will speak more openly". She also noted that "people say you can hide behind your mask...I feel sometimes that a mask lets you be yourself". These thoughts reflect research on the notion that avatars can reduce inhibitions, affective filters and encourage risk-taking, which can be useful in extending one's language proficiency (Gee & Hayes, 2011; Peterson, 2011).

Karelia noted the potential engagement when interacting through an avatar that became an idealized vision of herself (Dörnyei, 2009). This feeling is further echoed in her autobiographical video (Kondor, 2013, 6:50).

The 3D environment sets it apart, your avatar becomes you, you cannot help but be kinesthetically involved in learning as you move about the world, manipulate objects, type for chat...And there are plenty of studies which indicate that this sort of learning has great results.

She contrasted her learner identity of her Italian character in the machinima discussed above, with her offline 'self'.

[The teacher] had this fantastic [film] set...we were in a hairdressing salon...having our hair done and speaking and listening in Italian all the time...Later I had a lovely black dress. We all got our Oscars... and like, see, I'm quite an ordinary person, really.

Such identity manipulation affords learners the ability to embody different communicative roles in a simulated space, developing pragmatic functions in varied contexts (Sykes et al., 2016). When describing her French SL identity that she uses to teach French secondary students, she notes sarcastically, "They [my students] saw my avatar, which already made them laugh, because of course, I said, I make her look just like me, mid 20's, pink hair" (see Figure 1 below).

Figure 1. An image of Karelia Kondor © 2009, Helen Myers. (Used with permission)

Language-and-Culture Learning

In her Italian SL classes, Karelia's Italian language teacher invited Karelia and her classmates into an environment in SL that recreated the island of Sardinia. "You had a group of people so proud of their heritage and of their history, that they'd recreated elements of Sardinia, and we all walked around, and they would introduce us to these ancient monuments and aspects of their lives/cultures which they'd recreated." Karelia added that this integrated a focus on culture-and-language learning, elements that can be forgotten in a classroom context. In this lesson students were given an emic understanding of these cultural elements, shared by insiders with investment in this culture, facilitating an intercultural learning environment where languages and cultures can be recreated and explored (Sykes et al., 2016).

VR technology allows for the incorporation of cultural and communicative aspects of language learning. In contrast to traditional images and videos used in language classes, VR offers a 360 degree view of an environment that enables participants to experience an immersive spatial environment that is effective for language learning (Scrivner, et al., 2019, p. 59). Telecollaborative experiences in foreign language learning have also been reported to have supported enhanced intercultural exchanges and competences (Gomez, 2019, pp. 151, 161). For example, the ability to easily adopt a new identity, to experience interactions and the behaviour of others through this new identity in SVWs can expand worldviews and perspectives on one's cultural self and the complexity of other cultures and experiences (Hasler, 2011).

Karelia described their visit to Sardinia in SL as a valuable intercultural language learning experience where these Sardinian hosts facilitated intercultural learning while enhancing language skills. For example, throughout these exchanges, students and these Sardinian hosts were speaking and writing while Karelia's teacher would mediate difficult phrases when the group did not understand. In fact, the experience was so memorable that Karelia made connections with some of these Sardinian individuals and pursued offline learning with several of them after.

Fostering Communities of Practice

As noted, a recurring theme in discussions with Karelia was the potential of SL to provide networks that extended learning through different contexts. Her experiences as a language learner were storied with anecdotes about dynamic language learning communities of practice that she would leverage as a learner and teacher. According to Karelia, these interactions fueled ongoing language learning, teacher education and friendships. She noted initially making friends with English teachers who were happy to speak with her as a first language English speaker. "...that's how I made friends, and then they helped my language learning as some of them were German, some French, some Italian. They would involve me in their lessons, and I made friends with them." For example, some of her Italian speaking classmates asked if she could help them with their English pronunciation. This prompted her to offer weekly English pronunciation classes with some of these classmates. These quickly evolved into a form of tandem learning as these collaborators shared their linguistic and cultural knowledge with each other.

Karelia reported using these teacher communities to help with questions around French language and culture.

...if I had a query about language, I could just pop into [this French speaking community] and find someone, and they'd loved to know that people were interested in learning about their culture and language.

These examples of socially mediated learning illustrate the power of these hyper-immersive environments to facilitate online communities of practice where a group of individuals (teachers in this case) engage in ongoing collective learning in a shared practice (Wenger, 1998). Karelia and these teachers interact and leverage collective knowledge, resources and experiences to refine individual language learning and teaching practices through shared experiences that build investment in the community. These interactions consequently transform the communities, the interactive networks and build competence through these sustainable, dynamic connections (Siemens, 2005).

A Web-Enhanced Teacher-Mediated Approach for Younger Learners

In discussing SL limitations, Karelia noted that SL is ideally for a "self-motivated IT savvy adult" (Allen, 2010, 4:06). Recognizing the inherent security challenges in SVW environments inhibiting use with younger learners, Karelia adopted a web-enhanced interactive approach that she used with her secondary school French learners. Karelia considered these activities her most successful SL teaching experiences. She invited guest French speakers from her SL communities and would project herself interacting with these individuals in SL using a laptop and projector in front of her students in her classroom. This provided her students with authentic language-and-culture input that they would actively use in class. She began this with her French language sixth form students[5] and developed a series of lessons that reflected curricular goals of the course; each lesson involved at least one pre-planned simulation with a French speaking colleague that Karelia would then project in front of her class.

She would design each episode ahead of time with her guest speaker(s) so each person knew her/his role, their interactions and the learning outcomes of the class. She would introduce her students to the forthcoming interactions in class and assign them tasks to perform before, during and after the interactions. For example, one of her most memorable lessons was inviting a retired French language teacher who interacted as a chic, French avatar to join Karelia in finding a holiday home in Arcachon, France. She assigned her students homework, using the vocabulary they heard, to write a description of their own homes to promote as a holiday rental. In the projected interaction, the two avatars visited a number of holiday homes in the SL town of Arcachon, touring around each home and discussing each home's pros and cons. Students were tasked with transcribing new vocabulary, asking questions to clarify vocabulary and preparing to argue for their preferred holiday home. As they explored these homes, Karelia and her friend introduced idiomatic language and wrote down any new expression so students could see it on the screen as well as hear it.

Karelia declared that the homework she got from her students after this activity was far better in terms of lexical and rhetorical outcomes than their usual work responding to a text-based assignment. She noted that students had used a larger breadth of vocabulary and expressions, many that were used in the activity. "I've never had such fantastic results...I know I can't put it down to that one lesson but... it did seem to capture their imagination." She added, "I had a parent's evening the next week and I think nearly every parent talked about that lesson...they had a teacher crazy enough to do this." Nevertheless, Karelia admitted this took substantial time and preparation to work with her SL colleagues to prepare this SL simulation to project in front of her students. Although Karelia admitted that student learning tended to be heightened with this type of simulated language input, there were some students who expressed frustration that they could not directly participate in these simulations and were limited to the role of observers.

PEDAGOGICAL GUIDELINES

Karelia's insights from this study and the literature discussed above inform the following pedagogical guidelines that can be used to guide SVW use in language teaching and learning. These pedagogical guidelines are listed in four categories. The first three are ones that Karelia highlighted as essential when integrating these platforms into one's language teaching practice (Lawrence & Ahmed, 2018, p. 10). The fourth has been added to help guide teaching practices in SVW environments.

1. Task design and preparation
   ◦ Connect with a mentor or community who has teaching experience in these environments to help guide you.
   ◦ Choose action-oriented, project-based tasks that are goal-oriented, require collaboration and transactional language that involve relevant situated learning (i.e., role plays, describing an environment, visiting a tourist office).
   ◦ Integrate gaming principles and emotion into task design (i.e., considering gaming mechanics, design, emotion) (Pitarch, 2018).
   ◦ Integrate skills in situations where learners have to speak/listen, read and write, exercising both fluency and accuracy to find and convey information.
   ◦ Methodically prepare the task embedding short and focused sub-tasks with time limits to maintain attention and limit distractions.
   ◦ Prepare tasks and follow guidelines to effectively foster autonomy, putting learners in control of their language learning (Benson, 2011, pp. 121- 197).
2. Defining communicative norms and developing autonomous learning strategies
   ◦ SVWs create unique interactive environments so teachers must explicitly discuss and practice turn-taking strategies, communicative practices, and feedback strategies like tapping avatars, as non-verbal cues will be lacking.
   ◦ Conduct a pre-task in-class activity to orient learners to specific language use, terminology, the necessary skills and communication strategies needed.
   ◦ Orient learners to autonomous learning strategies that can be used in a task and transferred to language learning beyond the program.
   ◦ Hold a tech-talk practice session using the target language within the SVW environment, negotiating troubleshooting norms; this can develop transferable target language strategies to navigate tech issues that are likely to occur.
   ◦ Consider supporting learner autonomy by consulting the six approaches associated with the development of learner autonomy in language learning and teaching practices (Benson, 2011, pp. 125-196).
   ◦ If intercultural learning is desired, build in explicit learning about one's cultural self, culture-general learning (i.e., general categories of cultural behaviour), intercultural communication and reflection strategies and processes to examine miscommunication (Lawrence, 2013).
3. SVW and tech design
   ◦ Choose an SVW environment with a simple design: flat surfaces, no rivers or trees; have your avatars readily clothed when students log in and create a no-fly zone to prevent students from flying off during lessons. Ensure everyone is equipped with working headphones and speakers.

○ Ensure all safeguarding is in place. Password protect educational spaces, restricting access to anyone without the link or password, particularly if teaching young learners. As noted above, younger learners can also be spectator-participants, actively using interactions they observe.

○ Start with less demanding tech-activities, simple games or tasks that do not make the tech requirements more demanding than the language requirements.

○ Orient yourself fully to the technology and learning environment and plan to remove any student whose tech is interfering with the rest of the class (prepare students with a backup lesson should technology fail and a student must withdraw).

○ If possible have a readily available tech-support (or tech savvy mentor) during the activity.

4. In-world teaching

○ Ensure learners are well oriented to task responsibilities before task initiation (preparing/distributing a task responsibility checklist if needed).

○ Establish pre-task peer mentoring teams for in-world tech support so learners know who to ask if tech support is needed.

○ Adopt a facilitative role during the task, supporting learners when/as needed.

○ Actively observe interactions, providing language and learning feedback.

○ Note areas of language use, misuse and topics to debrief with learners to guide classroom teaching.

○ Engage in active reflection to improve task design, SVW pedagogy and areas for further self-development.

○ Record newly planned sessions as they are taking place in-world, for reflection and improvement of task design.

CONCLUDING THOUGHTS

This research suggests that SVWs offer language learning programs a range of affordances. These emerging environments offer the potential of multimodal target language immersive experiences that emotionally engage learners in situated, task-based learning, activating language use, noticing, play and emotional responses that can result in learning that sticks (Hanewald, 2013; Swain, 2013). Tech-talk interactions can build transferable linguistic, sociolinguistic and strategic competences that are relevant for today's digital age (Hanewald, 2013; Wang, 2017). Avatar identities can encourage linguistic risk-taking, target language output and error awareness within the language learning process (de Jong Derrington, 2013). Avatar-mediated interactions can provide a "cloak of anonymity" and the "adoption of a new persona" (de Jong Derrington, 2013, p. 147) that can forge imagined identities that can build intercultural competence, intrinsic motivation, fueling language-and-culture learning efforts (Norton, 2013). When well designed, SVW activities can leverage elements of play and gamification to deepen learner investment and learning communities (Gee & Hayes, 2011). As illustrated by Karelia's experiences, the social connections possible in these virtual worlds can connect learners to communities of practice that can spark affinity spaces (Gee, 2005) and ongoing language-and-culture learning. For teachers, such communities can provide professional resources to help refine language-and-culture knowledge and practices.

However, SVWs have serious educational limitations. As Karelia noted, the communicative interactions within these environments currently omit naturalistic visual and non-verbal cues that influence conveyed meaning (Duncan, et al., 2012, p. 12). If not supported by sound, complementary pedagogy, sociolinguistic and intercultural learning within these environments can be seriously constrained. This is where learner-centred, task-based pedagogy offered in a blended learning environment where activities are conducted in SVWs and in a face-to-face or synchronous classroom environment can engage learners in complementary experiences. Recognizing these limitations, Karelia uses these environments as an enhancement to learning, to primarily foster language production. As Karelia affirmed, interactions are most successful when mediated by the instructor. This raises questions about the role of teacher presence and its impact on pedagogy. Does the learning experience become more teacher-centred or are there ways to scaffold learner-centred interactions as a teacher would in a classroom context? Thomas and Schneider's (2018) study investigating language learning in 3D VWs "reinforces the argument that creating opportunities for pedagogical purposes in virtual worlds implies that teachers need to change their perspectives to take advantages of the affordances offered" (p. 20). This is where more action-research on SVW pedagogy would be useful.

While these limitations outlined may be resolved with adaptations, a prohibitive barrier to SVW use is the need for time. As emphasized above, lesson preparation for these activities, even with guest interactors/interlocutors, requires a substantial investment of time and preparation. And unfortunately, time acts as a great inhibitor of many technology-mediated language teaching approaches (Lawrence, 2014). This may be where professional communities of practice can help offer templates and tools to scaffold the teaching process.

Nevertheless, the potential of these 3-D virtual worlds for language education is promising. Emerging forms of virtual reality continue to expand and in the future will likely offer a more naturalistic resemblance of communicative interaction. Karelia and other early adopters have forged a path into the use of these mediums for language learning and teaching. Karelia's use of SL interactions as a web-enhanced language learning tool is an encouraging example of a differentiated practice serving a specific group of learners to complement face-to-face learning. As Karelia commented, "SL is something they will not forget. It's the pleasure that you see in your learners, that's the promise of learning."

REFERENCES

Allen, C. [Karelia Kondor- Teachmeet Second Life]. (2010, May 9). *Karelia Kondor (Helen Myres) presentation at the first Teachmeet Second Life talking about learning languages using Second Life* [Video file]. Retrieved from https://www.youtube.com/watch?v=LhTAmHM34gE

Benson, P. (2011). *Teaching and researching: Autonomy in language learning*. London, UK: Pearson Education Limited.

Connelly, F. M., & Clandinin, J. D. (1990). Stories of experience and narrative inquiry. *Educational Researcher*, *19*(5), 2–14. doi:10.3102/0013189X019005002

de Jong Derrington, M. (2013). Second language acquisition by immersive and collaborative task-based learning in a virtual world. In M. Childs, & A. Peachey (Eds.), *Understanding learning in virtual worlds* (pp. 135–163). London, UK: Springer. doi:10.1007/978-1-4471-5370-2_8

Deutschmann, M., & Panichi, L. (2009). Talking into empty space? Signalling involvement in a virtual language classroom in Second Life. *Language Awareness*, *18*(3-4), 310–328. doi:10.1080/09658410903197306

Diehl, W. C., & Prins, E. (2008). Unintended outcomes in Second Life: Intercultural literacy and cultural identity in a virtual world. *Language and Intercultural Communication, 8*(2), 101–118. doi:10.1080/14708470802139619

Dominguez, A., Saenz-de-Navarrete, J., de Marcos, L., Fernandez-Sanz, L., Pages, C., & Martinez-Herraiz, J.-J. (2013). Gamifying learning experiences: Practical implications and outcomes. *Computers & Education, 63*, 380–392. doi:10.1016/j.compedu.2012.12.020

Dörnyei, Z. (2009). The L2 motivational self system. In Z. Dörnyei, & E. Ushioda (Eds.), *Motivation, language identity and the L2 self* (pp. 9–42). Bristol: Multilingual Matters. doi:10.21832/9781847691293-003

Duncan, I., Miller, A., & Jiang, S. (2012). A taxonomy of virtual worlds usage in education. *British Journal of Educational Technology, 43*(6), 949–964. doi:10.1111/j.1467-8535.2011.01263.x

Flores, J. F. F. (2015). Using gamification to enhance second language learning. *Digital Education Review, (27)*, 32-54.

Gee, J. P., & Hayes, E. (2012). Nurturing affinity spaces and game-based learning. In *Games, learning, and society: Learning and meaning in the digital age* (pp. 129–153). Cambridge University Press; doi:10.1017/CBO9781139031127.015

Gee, J. P., & Hayes, E. R. (2011). *Language and learning in the digital age*. New York, NY: Routledge. doi:10.4324/9780203830918

Gomez, M. V. G. (2019). Developing soft skills in higher education foreign language programs. Initial insights into telecollaboration. In M. L. Carrio-Pastor (Ed.), *Teaching language and teaching literature in virtual environments* (pp. 151–161). Singapore: Springer Nature Singapore Pte Ltd. doi:10.1007/978-981-13-1358-5_8

Hanewald, R. (2013). Learners and collaborative learning in virtual worlds: A review of the literature. *Turkish Online Journal of Distance Education, 14*(2), 233–247.

Hasler, B. S. (2011). Intercultural collaborative learning in virtual worlds. In R. Hindrichs, & C. Wankel (Eds.), *Transforming virtual world learning* (pp. 265–304). Bingley, UK: Emerald Group Publishing. doi:10.1108/S2044-9968(2011)0000004015

Hismanoglu, M. (2012). Integrating second life into an EFL classroom: A new dimension in foreign language learning and teaching. *International Journal on New Trends in Education and Their Implications, 3*(4), 100–111.

Kondor, K. [Karelia Kondor: Language learning in second life - An introduction]. (2013, Nov. 21). *Karelia Kondor: Language learning in second life - an introduction* [Video file]. Retrieved from https://www.youtube.com/watch?v=D9ks7jOdJ88&t=2s

Kondor, K. (2016, March 5). Le Louvre in second life [Blog post]. Retrieved from https://kareliakondor.wordpress.com/2016/03/

Kozlova, I., & Priven, D. (2015). ESL teacher training in 3D virtual worlds. *Language Learning & Technology, 19*(1), 83–101.

Lantolf, J. P. (2011). The sociocultural approach to second language acquisition: Sociocultural theory, second language acquisition, and artificial L2 development. In D. Atkinson (Ed.), *Alternative approaches to second language acquisition* (pp. 24–47). New York, NY: Taylor & Francis.

Lave, J., & Wenger, E. (1990). *Situated learning: Legitimate peripheral participation*. Cambridge, UK: Cambridge University Press.

Lawrence, G. (2013). A working model for intercultural learning and engagement in collaborative online language learning environments. *Intercultural Education, 24*(4), 303–314. doi:10.1080/14675986.2013.809247

Lawrence, G. (2014). The role of teachers and their beliefs in implementing technology-mediated language learning: Implications for teacher development and research. *IJCALLT, 4*(4), 59-75.

Lawrence, G., & Ahmed, F. (2018). Pedagogical insights into hyper-immersive virtual world language learning environments. *International Journal of Computer-Assisted Language Learning and Teaching, 8*(1), 1–14. doi:10.4018/IJCALLT.2018010101

Lech, I. B., & Harris, L. N. (2019). Language learning in the virtual wild. In M. L. Carrio-Pastor (Ed.), Teaching language and teaching literature in virtual environments (pp. 39 -53). Springer, Singapore: Springer Nature Singapore Pte Ltd. doi:10.1007/978-981-13-1358-5_3

Lee, C. Y., & Warren, M. (2007). Security issues within virtual worlds such as second life. *Proceedings of 5th Australian Information Security Management Conference* (pp. 151-161). Perth, Australia: Edith Cowan University.

Lin, T. J., & Lan, Y. J. (2015). Language learning in virtual reality environments: Past, present, and future. *Journal of Educational Technology & Society, 18*(4), 486–497.

Loke, S. K. (2015). How do virtual world experiences bring about learning? A critical review of theories. *Australasian Journal of Educational Technology, 31*(1), 112–122. doi:10.14742/ajet.2532

Mayrath, M. C., Traphagan, T., Heikes, E. J., & Trivedi, A. (2011). Instructional design best practices for Second Life: A case study from a college-level English course. *Interactive Learning Environments, 19*(2), 125–142. doi:10.1080/10494820802602568

Norton, B. (2013). *Identity and language learning: Extending the conversation* (2nd ed.). Bristol, UK: Multilingual Matters. doi:10.21832/9781783090563

Panichi, L. (2015). A critical analysis of learner participation in virtual worlds: How can virtual worlds inform our pedagogy? In F. Helm, L. Bradley, M. Guarda, & S. Thouesny (Eds.), *Critical CALL–Proceedings of the 2015 EUROCALL Conference,* Padova, Italy (pp. 464-469). Dublin, Ireland: Research-publishing.net.

Peterson, M. (2010). Learner participation patterns and strategy use in Second Life: An exploratory case study. *ReCALL, 22*(3), 273–292. doi:10.1017/S0958344010000169

Peterson, M. (2011). Towards a research agenda for the use of three-dimensional virtual worlds in language learning. *CALICO Journal, 29*(1), 67–80. doi:10.11139/cj.29.1.67-80

Peterson, M. (2012). EFL learner collaborative interaction in Second Life. *ReCALL, 24*(1), 20–39. doi:10.1017/S0958344011000279

Piccardo, E. (2014). *From communicative to action-oriented: A research pathway*. Retrieved from https://www.coe.int/t/dg4/linguistic/Source/CSC605_Research_Guide_English.pdf

Pitarch, R. C. (2018). An approach to digital game-based learning: Video-games principles and applications in foreign language teaching. *Journal of Language Teaching Research, 9*(6), 1147–1159. doi:10.17507/jltr.0906.04

Sadler, R., & Dooly, M. (2014). Language learning in virtual worlds: Research and practice. In M. Thomas, H. Reinders, & M. Warschauer (Eds.), *Contemporary computer-assisted language learning* (pp. 159–182). New York, NY: Bloomsbury.

Sama, C. M., & Wu, Y. (2019). Integrating "Talk Abroad" into the intermediate foreign language course: Building learner autonomy and engagement through video conversations with native speakers. In M. L. Carrio-Pastor (Ed.), *Teaching language and teaching literature in virtual environments* (pp. 73–94). Singapore: Springer Nature Singapore Pte Ltd. doi:10.1007/978-981-13-1358-5_5

Schmidt, R. (1990). The role of consciousness in second language learning. *Applied Linguistics, 11*(2), 129–158. doi:10.1093/applin/11.2.129

Scrivner, O., Madewell, J., Buckley, C., & Perez, N. (2019). Best practices in the use of augmented and virtual reality technologies for SLA: Design, implementation and feedback. In M. L. Carrio-Pastor (Ed.), Teaching language and teaching literature in virtual environments (pp. 55-70). Springer, Singapore: Springer Nature Singapore Pte Ltd.

Shrestha, S., & Harrison, T. (2019). Using machinima as teaching and learning materials: A Nepalese case study. *International Journal of Computer-Assisted Language Learning and Teaching, 9*(2), 37–52. doi:10.4018/IJCALLT.2019040103

Siemens, G. (2005). Connectivism: A learning theory for the digital age. *International Journal of Instructional Technology & Distance Learning, 2*(1). Retrieved from http://itdl.org/Journal/Jan_05/article01.htm

Swain, M. (2013). The inseparability of cognition and emotion in second language learning. *Language Teaching, 46*(2), 195–207. doi:10.1017/S0261444811000486

Sykes, J. M., Oskoz, A., & Thorne, S. L. (2016). Web 2.0, synthetic immersive environments, and mobile resources for language education. In G. Kessler (Ed.), *Landmarks in CALL research* (pp. 160–183). Bristol, CT: Equinox.

Thomas, M., & Schneider, C. (2018). Language teaching in 3D virtual worlds with machinima: Reflecting on an online machinima teacher training course. *International Journal of Computer-Assisted Language Learning and Teaching, 8*(2), 20–38. doi:10.4018/IJCALLT.2018040102

Wang, A. (2017). Using Second Life in an English course: How does the technology affect participation? *International Journal of Computer-Assisted Language Learning and Teaching, 7*(1), 66–85. doi:10.4018/IJCALLT.2017010105

Wang, C. X., Lefaiver, M. L. M., Wang, Q., & Hunt, C. (2011). Teaching in an EFL program in second life: Student teachers' perspectives and implications. *Journal of Educational Technology Development and Exchange*, *4*(1), 27–40. doi:10.18785/jetde.0401.03

Wenger, E. (1998). *Communities of practice: Learning, meaning and identity*. Cambridge, UK: Cambridge University Press. doi:10.1017/CBO9780511803932

Wertz, F. J., Charmaz, K., McMullen, L. M., Josselson, R., Anderson, R., & McSpadden, E. (2011). *Five ways of doing qualitative analysis*. New York, NY: Guilford.

ENDNOTES

[1] Virtual worlds are computer-simulated environments where avatars (graphical representations of the users) interact.
[2] Augmented reality provides a view of reality where specific elements are enhanced or augmented by computer-generated input.
[3] Project Sansar will be the updated version of Second Life. For details, see: https://www.engadget.com/2016/08/31/second-life-sansar-creators-open/
[4] See http://www.fraps.com/ for more information.
[5] Sixth form in UK schools tends to be students between 16 and 18 years of age in senior years of secondary school.

This research was previously published in Recent Developments in Technology-Enhanced and Computer-Assisted Language Learning; pages 340-360, copyright year 2020 by Information Science Reference (an imprint of IGI Global).

APPENDIX

Interview Questions

Interview 1: Questions

1. From your perspectives as a learner and a teacher in social virtual worlds (VWs), what are the *benefits* of language learning in VWs? What are the *limitations* of these environments?
2. What are your perspectives of language learning pedagogy/methods needed in VWs vs. methods needed in traditional classroom-based language teaching environments?
3. Can you describe any specific AHA moments or exemplary virtual world tasks/interactions you experienced as a learner or teacher? Any reflections from these?
4. Reflecting on your VW learning and/or teaching, how do these experiences inform your thinking about task design and/or educational practices in general?
5. To guide teachers and researchers interested in VW language teaching/learning, what are your takeaways from your avatar/learner experiences on virtual world design and interactions/learning in these environments?

Interview 2: Questions

1. Please elaborate on specific examples of teaching/learning you have experienced in Second Life that may illustrate benefits/limitations of VWs.
2. Have you formally integrated Second Life into your course syllabi or assignments when teaching with this? Or as a learner using Second Life, did you receive any assignments/documents outlining how Second Life was going to be (or should be) used? If so, would you consider sharing examples of this documentation with us?
3. What pedagogical insights and strategies would you say these interactions taught you? How have you used them in your teaching practices? How would you recommend they be dealt with in teaching practices?
4. You had said previously, 'learning which is done in an interactive context with some sort of emotional attachment tends to stick more'. Can you please give concrete examples of such interactions on Second Life?

Section 3
Designs and Frameworks

Chapter 27
Prosumers Building the Virtual World:
How a Proactive Use of Virtual Worlds Can Be an Effective Method for Educational Purposes

Mario Fontanella
Edu3d, Italy

Claudio Pacchiega
Edu3d, Italy

ABSTRACT

With the development of new digital technologies, the internet, and mass media, including social media, it is now possible to produce, consume, and exchange information and virtual creations in a simple and practically instantaneous way. As predicted by philosophers and sociologists in the 1980s, a culture of "prosumers" has been developed in communities where there is no longer a clear distinction between content producers and content users and where there is a continuous exchange of knowledge that enriches the whole community. The teaching of "digital creativity" can also take advantage of the fact that young people and adults are particularly attracted to these fields, which they perceive akin to their playful activities and which are normally used in an often sterile and useless way in their free time. The didactic sense of these experiences is that we try to build a cooperative group environment in which to experiment, learn, and exchange knowledge equally among all the participants.

DOI: 10.4018/978-1-6684-7597-3.ch027

INTRODUCTION

If traditional societies based the centrality of their experiential area in the succession of seasons, a consequence of the primacy of agricultural work, industrial societies had the experiential center in the relations of production, considered as the sign of the self-realization of the individual. The contemporary era has experiential centrality in consumption and in its evolution in prosumerism. (Piergiorgio Degli Esposti, 2015)

With the development of new digital technologies, the Internet, and mass media, including social media, it is now possible to produce, consume and exchange information and virtual creations in a simple and practically instantaneous way. Think of websites like YouTube, Wikipedia, Instagram, Flickr, but also stores (marketplaces) and dedicated sites for the purchase and sale of artistic digital semi-finished products such as *Deviant Art*, *Sketchfab* or for multimedia applications and games such as Steam itself or the stores of *Android*, *Apple* or gaming platforms such as *Steam*, *Unity*. As predicted by philosophers and sociologists in the 1980s, a culture of "prosumers" has been developed, which means communities where there is no longer a clear distinction between content producers and content users and a continuous exchange of knowledge that enriches the whole community.

At the same time, the skills of digital creativity are increasingly in demand in the professional market, especially in the field of marketing, in the field of entertainment (cinema, music, art), and in the same area of Education and Training (*Report on World Development 2016* - The World Bank). The teaching of 'digital creativity' can also benefit from the fact that young people and adults are particularly attracted to these fields. They perceive akin to their playful activities and are typically used in a sterile and useless way in their free time.

Both the authors have experienced that it is possible to build a cooperative group environment to test, learn, and exchange knowledge equally among all participants. In particular, they experimented with ways of learning that allow enhancing people's creativity by motivating them to learn in a more in-depth and rewarding way, and in turn to teach others even when they do not feel sufficiently prepared, to understand better the complexity of the context in which they operate. Within the same educational path, the creations of the various participants can be shown, shared, and remixed, favoring the "open-source" circulation of the works produced to progressively create increasingly complex settings and ideas, without having to use pre-built materials provided by companies or individuals, mostly not cheap and not within reach of most educational institutions. As will be seen shortly, the didactic activity can be developed along different complexity lines, in which the material generally needed for these experiences can be basic or optional. Before proceeding with the analysis of the necessary skills and technical tools, it is essential to consider what assumptions this study is based on:

1. SOME BASIC CONCEPTS

1.1 Prosumer: The Origins

In 1972, Marshall McLuhan and Barrington Nevitt proposed in their book *Take Today* that every consumer in the field of household electricity could become a producer in turn. This concept became very realistic with the advent of renewable energy at home. The futurologist Alvin Toffler in 1980, in the book The Third Wave, coined the term "prosumer" by combining the terms producer and consumer, predicting that the roles of producer and consumer would merge, giving life to a new category of users.

Toffler indicated in the First Wave the settled agricultural society that replaced the hunter-gatherer cultures (Neolithic Revolution), while in the Second Wave the society of the industrial era (transition from the Iron Age to the Steel Age), which began in Western Europe and later spread throughout the world, a society based on mass-production, mass-distribution, and mass-consumption, but also on mass-education, mass-information, and entertainment, as well as on weapons of mass destruction. The Third Wave is the *post-industrial society* (a definition by the American sociologist Daniel Bell), most countries have been in since the late 1950s. In the future development of this last kind of society, Toffler envisioned a highly saturated market as the mass production of standardized commodities would begin to satisfy consumers' basic demands. To continue the increase in profits, the companies would have started a mass customization process, which is the mass production of highly personalized products. However, to achieve a high level of customization, consumers needed to take part in the process above all in defining the aesthetic design characteristics of the products.

1.2 Prosumer: The Current State

Much of this transformation took place online; with the advent of web 2.0, the consumer can adopt a proactive and participatory behavior; through social networking, where the user creates his own page and offers his multimedia products to others' judgment. Therefore, it was possible to witness a real media genre's birth, user-generated content (UGC, User's generated content).

There are many examples in different fields of application: *YouTube* (video), *Spotify* (music), *Instagram*, *Pinterest* (images), renewable energy, narration (shared creation of texts), shopping guide (*Amazon*, *Nike*, *Booking*, *TripAdvisor*), 3D Printing, video games, educational.

Now, much of this transformation is also being useful to reconsider learning, to take into account the gap that is likely to create between the student's daily relational dimension and that in which he is immersed within the school dynamics, as already highlighted by Kathleen Bell Welch in his article *Electronic Media: Implications of the "Third Wave" View of Electronic Media* in 1981:

When students leave a Third Wave home in the morning to enter a Second Wave classroom for the day, the result is sure to be counterproductive.

Rather than fearing the reproduction of the "relevance" syndrome of the sixties, however, teachers can use the awareness of change, such as that which Toffler provides, to design the guidelines necessary for developing a framework for synthesis. Idealistically teachers advocate the teaching of how to learn as well as what to learn. Electronic media, while providing much of the what of learning both inside and outside the classroom, can also provide the how in the process of synthesis.

The next basic concept can help us glimpse a possible scenario for adapting teaching and learning methods to current changes.

1.3 Gamification

This term refers to the application of game-design elements and game principles in non-gaming contexts. Gamification seeks to engage people to experience more involvement and fun in daily activities through play. The objectives are many, including loyalty, creating harmony between people in team formation, solving problems, and changing the habits of users. The principle underlying Gamification is to use the game's dynamics and mechanics: Points, Levels, Rewards, Badges, Gifts to stimulate some primary instincts of a human being, such as competition, status, rewards, and success. The implementation of playful mechanics is one of the most effective methods to involve people in the activities of a site or an offered service. In this case, the user no longer acts as a passive user of information but becomes active using the site's gamified product. Beyond the boundaries of teaching and game-based learning (GBL), you can find several examples of Gamification with a substantial impact on everyday life (e.g., see: *Top 10 gamification examples and fun theory*: https://youtu.be/CFeeSANGGlA).

1.3.1 *How to use new Technologies and Gamification for Educational Purposes*

There is some evidence that these new technologies and their applications in education can contribute to increase, among the others, motivation, engagement and critical thinking in students, and positively support knowledge transfer. (Curcio, Dipace, Norlum, 2016)

Although the use of Gamification in education is becoming more and more popular every year, it is not easy to apply a gamification paradigm to classrooms. Furthermore, many teachers have much bias towards games, especially those involved in the "kill a monster" model. However, there is a notable category of games called "sandbox games" or "open-ended". Open games with multiple gameplay solutions and options, sometimes called sandbox games, are especially useful for modding and personal expression. *Squire* (2008) refers to games as "spaces of possibility", in which multiple trajectories of experience can lead to new ways of learning (*Olson* 2010).

Gamification at school facilitates cooperation, stimulates interest, produces positive competition, enhances excellence, and motivates *Special Educational needs* and *Specific Learning Disorders* students. New technologies and Gamification can appear to be an end in themselves and apparently in contrast with traditional teaching methods. It is not necessary to use new technologies in an integral and absolute way. These techniques can often be a starting point and a stimulus to continue the lesson with other more "traditional" tools. It is interesting to note that some of these techniques linked to the use of the Internet and computers (and therefore potentially sedentary) can create efficient educational paths, manual and even physical activities to be done outdoors in some cases, even sports. As an example, some scenarios can be considered to structure a history lesson in upper primary and lower secondary school classes, dividing the class into teams of 5-6 each time (ideal group size to make sure everyone can actively participate):

- design a 3D environment
- create a glossary or a 3D museum
- create a storytelling experience (theater)
- set up a treasure hunt (e.g., in a specific environment divided into rooms)
- create a route, a journey (e.g., a railway or a boat on a river), in which each stage is in some way a sort of reconstruction of some of the concepts to be described

- create tournaments, challenges, competitions between groups regarding questions and answers with the relative score (incremental or decremental)
- create a series of thematic Escapes Rooms in a Virtual Environment, in which the group or the single user is faced with didactic logic games, based on a sequence of puzzles to be solved and questions to be answered, to leave the room, having acquired the educational objective of the lesson.

An introductory lesson explaining the tools available will always be needed and material on the topic in question (which can be consumed offline). Students need to understand that they can put it into practice quickly and have fun. The final product of each experience can also be recorded in a video and shared.

Relative to what happens, for example, in Europe, a consortium made up of universities and ministerial bodies launched a research and development project between 2012 and 2014 on the possible use of playful activities in schools, as reported by Nicola Whitton in his *Games for Learning* (2013):

The Making Games in Collaboration Project (MAGICAL) aims to bring game building into the mainstream by focusing on the development of 21st century skills: collaboration, problem-solving, creativity, and digital literacy in particular. MAGICAL is an EU-funded Lifelong Learning Partnership project, with partners in the UK (ESRI), Belgium, Finland, Italy, and Greece. It aims to develop a curriculum to support trainee teachers to design and run lessons based on collaborative game building and evaluate the use of game-building in school contexts. As well as providing the technical and game-design skills, the training program also encompasses issues such as the embedding of active learning through games and the changing role of the teacher; in effect, the project aims to promote cultural change as well as simply present a new pedagogic technique.

The MAGICAL project is about to enter its second year, which will see the partners work with trainee teachers to promote and support game-building, who will, in turn, use the methods with their own learners in schools. A series of in-depth case studies will be carried out in schools in each participating country to consider the value of game building from a variety of perspectives, including the learners themselves, teachers, parents, and school support and managerial staff.

The project, which saw 37 classroom pilot projects in 5 countries (BE, FI, GR, IT, UK) and involved more than 600 students and over 100 teachers, was included in the Success Stories and Good Practices of the Erasmus+ program (source: tinyurl.com/magicaldoor).

Logically, Gamification can also present pitfalls in education. For example, it can lead students to be more motivated by the rewards than by the learning process, obtaining an opposite effect to the desired one. One could speak of the differences between intrinsic and extrinsic motivation. Still, it remains a crucial aspect that must be clear to the teacher: no technology and no operating mode can ever replace the teacher's educational and social skills, but rather provide him with additional tools to operate and facilitate his work. It is, therefore, up to the teacher to avoid students from being more interested in external rewards than perceiving passion for the subjects they study.

Some helpful links to deepen the question:

- http://gamification-research.org
  The Gamification Research Network (GRN) - Website
- http://hcigames.com/gamification/3-inspiring-ways-gamification-used-education

3 Inspiring Ways Gamification Is Being Used in Education – Article and Videos

- https://www.iste.org/explore/In-the-classroom/5-ways-to-gamify-your-classroom
  5 ways to gamify your classroom – Article
- https://yukaichou.com/gamification-examples/top-10-education-gamification-examples
  The 10 Best Educational Apps that use Gamification for adults in 2019 - Article and Videos

There is still one last essential concept, relating to a possible key element to better understand the picture in question, before moving on to the more purely technical aspects.

1.4 The Community of Practice (Cop)

The *term community of practice and learning* refers to a group of individuals united by the same purpose: to produce and share knowledge on specific topics while acquiring awareness of their knowledge; following a common interest and code, the members of these communities aim for collective improvement. Therefore, within the CoP, there is no predetermined hierarchy, but mutual help is applied. The roles are assumed from time to time according to the skills and learning needs of the participants. Those who join this type of organization aim for a shared intelligence model. There are no private or individual spaces; everyone shares everything. While not a new application, the definition "Community of Practice" dates back to the cognitive anthropologist Jean Lave and the educational theorist Etienne Wenger (*Situated Learning*, 1991). They recognize such groups of people as an effective method for promoting learning by sharing information. Wenger will later expand on the concept in his 1998 book *Communities of Practice*. For Wenger, it is possible to speak of CoP if they are actively present in the common and essential interaction between them: *Cooperative Learning, Diversity and Partiality, Mutual Relationships*. Going beyond the mere expressions of CoPs at an amateur level, Masoud Hemmasi and Carol M. Csanda in 2009 studied and highlighted how these communities, which at first glance may seem antagonistic to the commercial world, can not only coexist but also support the work of companies, bodies and professional organizations:

Although conventional teams have been highly successful over the years, Communities of Practice appear to provide additional benefits by being more responsive in dealing with the opportunities and challenges of today's rapidly changing environment, growing global competition, and the ever advancing information technology. Communities of Practice can provide organizations with a way to capture tacit or implicit knowledge by connecting people with similar interests, allowing them to capture information and make it accessible to the organization at large.

Some examples of widespread and well-known communities of practice can be found in the so-called Fablabs (https://en.wikipedia.org/wiki/Fab_lab); in the groups of Open-Source Software (OSS) developers and other *Open Collaborations*, such as the Internet forums, mailing lists and web communities (the so-called OcoP – Online Communities of Practice); and in groups defined as commons-based peer production (CBPP), such as those that manage well-known projects, such as *Linux, Wikipedia, SETI@home* and *Mozilla Firefox*, to name a few.

Again Wikipedia (https://en.wikipedia.org/wiki/Virtual_community_of_practice) among the advantages of this type of collaboration reminds us that:

OCoPs give beginners, who might not feel comfortable sharing their knowledge, an opportunity to learn from veteran colleagues beyond their immediate geographic area through observation and absorption of information and dialogue. The veterans lend a degree of legitimacy to the community, as well as to the experiences of the new members. The result is an atmosphere of mentorship for novices. As new practitioners gain understanding and expertise, they are become more comfortable with sharing their own backgrounds and perspectives with the OCoP further expanding the field of knowledge.

Parallel to the concept of Community of Practice is developing that of *Facilitator for learning*; a person within the group who helps participants understand common goals and plan how to achieve them without taking a particular position in the discussion. In practice, an *educational facilitator* has the same level of knowledge of both education and the subject as a teacher but structures the work with students so that they can take as much responsibility as possible for their learning.

The facilitator's job is to support everyone to do their best thinking. To do this, the facilitator encourages full participation, promotes mutual understanding and cultivates shared responsibility. By supporting everyone to do their best thinking, a facilitator enables group members to search for inclusive solutions and build sustainable agreements. (Sam Kaner, 1996)

These premises were necessary to understand the cultural transition highlighted in this study, the transformation underway that affects all social actors, and that allows everyone to become the creator of cultural content and not just a mere consumer or user, possessing the knowledge and means to do so.

The following paragraphs are structured precisely in this direction and are aimed at those who have an interest in developing educational content. The next section begins a review of some more purely technical knowledge, the so-called "tools of the trade". For this analysis, the choice focused mainly on those tools that are easy to find and low cost, preferably free and open source. Without, in any case, discarding some commercial solutions, specifying their nature, they are interesting from a technical point of view or dissemination among users (therefore popular and consequently guaranteeing a relatively easy retrieval of information and support).

2. SOME TOOLS IN PRACTICE

As in the Middle Ages, when mass literacy began with regard to the written word, and reading was distinguished from writing, where reading was essential for the accomplishment of the magic associated with sacred "scriptures", while writing was assimilated to divine attributions, a new way of creating and distribute content has emerged in our age. Modern writing is the possibility of producing 3D contents that can be used both in virtual worlds and through integration with the surrounding environment in the so-called *augmented reality*.

With all peoples the word and writing are holy and magical; naming and writing were originally magical operations, magical conquests of nature through the spirit, and everywhere the gift of writing was thought to be of divine origin. With most peoples, writing and reading were secret and holy arts reserved for the priesthood alone. (Herman Hesse)

The process of defining a three-dimensional shape in a computer-generated virtual space is called *3D modeling*, a subset of CAD (Computer-Aided Design) where a computer is used to facilitate the design process. This process is composed of several phases, depending on the complexity of the result to be achieved. At the end of which is obtained a "modeled" object, named *3D model*, created from simple shapes up to complex models of high polygons. Generally, modeling is the first step in a series of subsequent operations that will determine the result. To create a video game or any other application with real-time graphics, users, therefore, need a graphics engine that generally allows the same game to run on multiple platforms.

It is time now to examine some useful programs for creating 3D models that can be used in virtual environments; at the end of this paragraph, users will find useful resources to deepen the subject, an operation not possible in this work due to space and context limits.

2.1 Blender: 3d Modeling Software

Blender (https://www.blender.org) is the leading open-source system that allows anyone to design arbitrarily complex 3D architectures that can be inserted into virtual worlds, but also for the creation of photographs, videos, and more. Knowing how to use Blender is equivalent to the ability to "write" and edit 3D content that can then be imported into virtual worlds or processed through photographs and videos or used in games such as *Minetest*, *Unity*, *Unreal Engine*, or integrated into augmented reality experiences. It can provide photorealistic renders thanks to the integrated rendering engine called *Cycles*.

Some effective alternatives to *Blender*, for example, *Rhino* or *Autodesk Maya* (although they are sometimes available for free or at reduced prices for schools), imply dependence on companies that essentially aim for profit-making purposes that are not always adequate for educational needs.

2.2 Sketchup: 3d Modeling Software

Sketchup (https://www.sketchup.com) is a program that has a less steep learning curve than Blender, but also more limited in functions and is oriented a little more towards architectural works. The two software think entirely differently. Sketchup is available for free for home use. There is an educational version and a paid pro version.

2.3 Unity and Godot: Graphic Engines

*Unity (*https://unity.com*)* is a graphics engine that allows the development of video games and other interactive 3D content.

As well as *Unreal Engine* (https://www.unrealengine.com), a graphics engine developed by Epic Games, it represents the de facto standard for the production of 3D content for virtual worlds and VR (starting from objects built, for example, with *Blender*). *Unity* is "free" but run by a commercial company that imposes fees if the made game becomes popular.

Godot (https://godotengine.org), on the other hand, is an open-source implementation that can be freely used for the construction of games and virtual environments, including multi-user ones. Another open alternative for building virtual environments is *Love* and *Love VR*.

As announced, at the end of this review of essential tools, some useful resources are listed to facilitate learning and the possible theoretical study of some general aspects. At the same time, in the next paragraph, the readers will find various sources to find ready-made material to use in how much can be changed according to their needs.

- *A list of notable 3D modeling software, computer programs used for developing a mathematical representation of any three-dimensional surface of objects, also called 3D modeling.*
- https://www.instructables.com/id/Intro-to-3D-Modeling
  A very in-depth tutorial to understand the basic concepts in 3D modeling.
- https://en.wikibooks.org/wiki/Blender_3D:_Noob_to_Pro/Tutorial_Links_List
  Blender 3D: Noob to Pro/Tutorial Links List, a categorized list of Blender tutorials written or spoken in English. Blender's features include 3D modeling, UV unwrapping, texturing, raster graphics editing, rigging and skinning, fluid and smoke simulation, particle simulation, soft body simulation, sculpting, animating, match moving, rendering, motion graphics, video editing, and compositing.
- https://learn.unity.com/tutorials
  Courses and tutorials on designing and developing projects in the Unity game engine. Fundamental topics and key points are covered, such as: *C # Survival Guide - Functions and Methods*; *Setting up a VR-Enabled Project with Unity and the XR Interaction Toolkit; How to publish to Android*; *Using Animation Rigging: Damped Transform,* and many others.
- https://docs.godotengine.org/it/stable/community/tutorials.html
  A list of third-party tutorials and resources created by the Godot community, many recommended as an easy introduction for beginners. Very useful for approaching this open-source software development environment designed to allow people to create video games.
- https://ita.calameo.com/read/002652204386fd247f56e
  A guide to computer animation for tv, games, multimedia, and web. Basic concepts, history, and development of digital animation. The text also includes information on how to write the synopsis, screenplays, and storyboards, how to characterize the characters and convey the story.

2.4 Resources on The Net

Whether designing a complex game, 3D building models, anatomical parts, or furniture elements, it does not necessarily mean that people would have to start from scratch to construct their settings. On the web, there are various resources, free or paid, which allow people to download basic models to modify and insert in their project and ready-made projects to be used directly. Likewise, several of these platforms will enable people to upload, share, or sell their creations. Below is a shortlist of some of the major sites that offer these resources for free or for a fee, for personal and business use (some of these sites require prior registration).

- *Sketchfab* (https://sketchfab.com/) is a platform where it is possible to distribute your models for free under Creative Commons licensing, buy and sell models in the *Sketchfab Store*, browse 3D content in third-party apps using API, from low-poly and game-ready 3D assets to real-world 3D scans.
- *Cospaces Edu* (https://www.cospaces.io/edu/) is a 3D visualization tool that makes the creation of virtual spaces. It is possible to easily create virtual objects and spaces through a browser app, selecting environments, characters, and objects from a library and adapting them individually. Accessible in VR mode via smartphone and a Cardboard or headsets. *Cospaces* allows students of

any age to build their 3D creations, animate them with code, and explore them in virtual or augmented reality. Available as a free or subscription version, the platform allows teachers to manage their classes and follow the work of each student.

- *Google Poly* (https://poly.google.com/) is a website created by Google to allow users to upload, distribute and download 3D objects in a free library containing thousands of 3D objects for use in virtual reality and reality applications increased.
- The *Smithsonian Institution* (https://3d.si.edu) is an educational and research organization with an annexed important museum, administered and financed by the United States government; The *Smithsonian* houses 155 million objects, samples, books, and archives, being able to exhibit only a small percentage of its collections; therefore makes a great effort to try to digitize these resources making 3D models available to the public.
- *Stlfinder* (https://www.stlfinder.com) is a search engine for free models for 3D printing from the major repositories on the Internet.
- *Free3d* (https://free3d.com) offers free 3D models for personal use and paid models for commercial use, with the possibility to upload and sell your creations.
- *MakerBot's Thingiverse* (https://www.thingiverse.com) is a design community for browsing, creating, and sharing 3D printable elements. The use of the Creative Commons license is encouraged so that anyone can use or modify any project.
- *Turbosquid* (https://www.turbosquid.com/it/Search/3D-Models/free) provides 3D models for game developers, news agencies, architects, visual effects studios, advertisers, and creative professionals.
- *Archive3D* https://archive3d.net): Free 3D Models and Objects Archive.
- *3dsky* (https://3dsky.org) allows authors of 3D models to share their works and sell them to customers who wish to buy access to 3D models

After this preview of some of the main "tools of the trade", the next step is to review some of the possible and most common feasible applications, orienting ourselves mainly in the direction of training and teaching.

3. SOME APPLICATIONS

I realized if you can change a classroom, you can change a community, and if you can change enough communities you can change the world. (Erin Gruwell)

As seen in the paragraph on the practical use of new technologies and Gamification for educational purposes, the possibilities that arise are different and vary according to one's budget, the time available to design, develop and implement them, as well as, obviously, to the type of audience to which they are offered. The possible application scenarios are different and will be analyzed in summary; the choice will have to fall between developing projects to be used through Multi-User Virtual Environments (MUVE) 2D and 3D in specific virtual reality or augmented reality or mixed reality applications. To facilitate this task, it is necessary first to understand some fundamental differences between these solutions.

When we talk about virtual reality (VR) we refer to a three-dimensional surrounding environment, not real but simulated, in which the user is able to interact thanks to the combination of hardware and software devices that offer a totally immersive experience (Giulia Salomone, 2019).

Immersiveness is what makes the difference comparing virtual reality to augmented reality. To access a virtual reality experience a VR headset is needed, capable of guaranteeing a 180° field of view and sensors that transmit the movements of the body and head of the user to make the movement in that space realistic. In this analysis, a paragraph has been dedicated explicitly to VR headsets. Augmented reality (AR), on the other hand, allows you to add relevant information generated by the computer to existing reality through apps loaded on mobile devices, such as smartphones, tablets, or specifically dedicated glasses, which interact with the space in which you are immersed through the camera of the device itself. This means that the augmented reality experience will never be completely immersive. Instead, it is a Mixed Reality (MR) experience, a setting in which AR and VR mix. In this case, the real world and the digital world merge, and the virtual objects are not only introduced into the surrounding reality, but the user can interact with them as if they were physically present. In practice, the user acts "physically" in both worlds, breaking down the basic concepts of reality and imagination, thus obtaining a unique experience, whether for play or work.

This experience can still be enriched by the *playful factor*, as emphasized by Rubio-Campillo (2020), who reports on the importance of play in the learning process:

The strong sense of embodiment does not happen in other media because it requires a high degree of interactivity and immersion that is simply not possible while reading a book or watching a movie.

The way a video game is approached by a player is also unique. In essence, a game is a problem waiting to be solved. The structure of any game is organized as a sequence of increasingly difficult challenges that the player needs to solve using an explicit set of possible actions; this player will engage with a learning process for a simple yet powerful reason: it is the only way to achieve success in the game. Game challenges are based on abstract mechanics that can be enriched through background and narrative, which sometimes can play a major role within the player's experience.

On a practical level, it is evident that different levels of immersion correspond to different levels of complexity concerning the learning curves necessary to develop applications in the respective environments. Fortunately, the open-source formula of most of the available platforms helps a lot in finding semi-finished or ready-to-use material, as well as finding the information necessary also to assume a certain level of autonomy in the implementation of one's educational projects.

3.1 Augmented Reality Apps

A simple application of these concepts can be found in *Augmented Reality Apps*, which have recently become increasingly popular thanks to the spread of mobile devices (tablets or smartphones). For example, *talking books* or *postcards* can be created with images that, once framed by a smartphone or tablet camera, come to life through specific apps, allowing us to view videos or dynamic images with sound accompaniment. A virtual situation is thus created, which integrates with the real environment in which it is inserted, giving the user new perceptual nuances compared to printed paper's static experience.

Similarly, museum installations can be created that reproduce in space (always mediated by the use of a mobile device) architectural or environmental elements that allow visitors to have a perception that is no longer two-dimensional or imaginary but three-dimensional by seeing the real measurements of the object. Thus, also returning the real impact with the user (e.g., https://youtu.be/uZ6g8FxZaRY - *Making of Big Lonely Doug*, an augmented reality project realized in the National Gallery of Canada).

An interesting example of an augmented reality application, which this time involves a three-dimensional physical object and not a flat surface, is a commercial object known as the *Merge Cube* (https://mergeedu.com/cube), a simple rubber cube with which you can interact through mobile devices with specific apps (e.g., *Object Viewer*, *Anatomy+* or *Galactic Explorer*) or using a simple virtual reality headset, such as the *Google Cardboard* or its dedicated AR/VR headset (https://mergeedu.com/headset), relatively inexpensive, designed for children and compatible with the most modern iOS and Android smartphones. The available apps cover the different educational areas, both in science and in the humanities. Besides, everyone can upload their creations, made with *Blender* or other 3D creation software, scan a real-world object, or download a 3D model from an online library, then upload and use it on the cube.

Google Cardboard is also the name of a virtual reality (VR) platform developed by Google to encourage interest and development in VR applications. It is based on using one's telephone placed on the back of a low-cost viewer, made with folding cardboard, equipped with special lenses (https://arvr.google.com/cardboard).

Specifically, for educational purposes, Google has created *Google expeditions* (https://edu.google.com/products/vr-ar/expeditions), an immersive teaching and learning tool. With a list of around 800 "expeditions" to choose from, a teacher can lead their class on guided tours through virtually reconstructed objects and environments.

As regards the feedback obtained by students in the practical experiences of using AR in the field in the educational area, what was reported in 2014 by Antonioli, Blake, and Sparks (see references) is very interesting:

Overall, students reacted positively to using AR technology both in and outside of the classroom. AR is a fairly new development within the field of education, and there are areas that students c reported that need improvement. Annetta et al. (2012; as cited in Benford and 2003) listed four educational uses to AR mobile technology, which are in no particular order: field science, field visits, games, information services, and guides. AR games can be played independently or dependently. Researchers, teachers, and students alike were very pleased to find more collaboration while using the AR technology...

Some helpful links to deepen the question:

- https://www.immersivelearning.news/2019/08/15/report-immersive-experiences-in-education
  Immersive Experiences in Education - Report (August 2019)
  A newly published white paper investigates the pedagogical theory and use cases for deploying mixed reality in the classroom.
- https://www.educationcorner.com/augmented-reality-classroom-education.html
  Using Augmented Reality in the Classroom – Article by Becton Loveless
  Some practical indications on how to design an augmented class

- https://edu.google.com/products/vr-ar/
  Virtual and augmented reality for educators and students – Website
  A site created by Google for Education to accompany educators and institutions in the design of educational paths that use augmented reality and virtual reality tools. Some case studies.
- https://play.google.com/store/apps/details?id=com.google.android.stardroid
  Sky Map is a hand-held planetarium for your Android device. – App
  Example of augmented reality application for educational use. Originally developed as Google Sky Map, it has now been donated and open-sourced.
- https://studio.gometa.io
  Metaverse: create interactive content in augmented reality – Website
  Example of a platform for the creation of gamification experiences.
  "Place Experiences at specific locations with QR codes or GPS locations. Collect digital items, create your own Pokemon Go. Make it a giant citywide hunt or just in your building or backyard."
- https://www.researchgate.net/publication/327940479_Augmented_Reality_Experience_Initial_Perceptions_of_Higher_Education_Students
  Augmented Reality Experience: Initial Perceptions of Higher Education Students – Survey
  A survey study realized by Irfan Sural, Asst. Prof. at Eskisehir Osmangazi University (Turkey), Faculty of Education, intends to explore the candidate teachers' opinions about using augmented reality (AR) in classrooms.

3.2 Virtual Environments

A *virtual environment* (VE) is a shared application on the network. This computer-simulated 3D online environment allows a user to interact with that *world* and other users and their possible works. In this way, the user can explore spaces of all kinds and experience sensory experiences that often combine the playful dimension with the educational or informative one. From the development of the so-called virtual worlds, it is possible to create immersive virtual environments (IVE) capable of involving users in different degrees of immersion, with physical, psychological, and emotional participation experienced. The doors have also been opened to the experimentation of immersive teaching capable of reproducing real didactic scenarios, both in the school environment and in the medical and safety at work fields, just to name a few. Since the beginning, the area has expanded thanks considerably to wireless technologies, reducing the necessary devices' size and minimum requirements in terms of technology and, finally, economic demands. Simultaneously, this technological evolution has resulted in an increase in the complexity of the environment and the involvement of users immersed in more realistic situations and, therefore, more expendable in training. After the source code of the *Second Life* client became open-source and free software in 2007, many seemingly similar environments have been developed over the years from that code. In this research, among the various SL emulators, only *OpenSim* is considered (because it has a community of enthusiasts and a relatively broader support structure), before moving on to the description of the most recent virtual environments.

3.2.1 OpenSim

OpenSim (http://opensimulator.org) is an open-source server platform for hosting virtual worlds (*grids*). This online 3D graphics platform can be accessed via an *avatar* (a digital representation of ourselves), only in the "Desktop" version. Every user can build his own "world" or visit the various virtual islands (sims) created by other users and be part of one of the hundreds of "virtual communities" existing in the world. *OpenSim* has been used by several Italian schools thanks to the Literacy effort in virtual worlds carried out by *Indire* (the *National Institute for Documentation, Innovation and Educational Research*, the Italian Ministry of Education's oldest research organization - https://www.indire.it/en) in his virtual world "*Edmondo*" reserved only for educators and their students. *Opensim* has over 3000 members in the connected Facebook group, 400 monthly active avatars, and over 350 sims (Hypergrid Business - Last Update: 8/21/2020 - https://www.hypergridbusiness.com/statistics/active-grids). The largest Italian OpenSim grid, *Craft*, also hosts free educational initiatives aimed at teachers and non-teachers.

3.2.2 Minecraft

Minecraft is a sandbox-type video game; with its open-source counterpart *Minetest*, Minetest is very educationally valuable with regards to coding and other useful skills, as it relies on LUA as a programming language for editing that can be easily taught to children and is widely used for adding interactions to games.

3.2.3 High Fidelity

High Fidelity (https://www.highfidelity.com) is an open-source software where you can create and share virtual reality (VR) experiences. Strongly oriented towards socialization, High-Fidelity is available for Mac and Windows both in the "Desktop" version and in the VR version on Steam and Oculus. Unluckily, High Fidelity did shutdown in January 2020, so it is no more available unless one chooses the open-source continuation called Vircadia. (https://vircadia.com)

3.2.4 Sansar

In *Sansar* (https://www.sansar.com), users can create 3D spaces where people can, through a personalized avatar, share interactive social experiences, such as playing games, watching videos, and chatting together. This 3D platform is built by the company that made "Second Life", and it works in both virtual reality headsets (including Oculus Rift and HTC Vive) and Windows computers (desktop mode). It is free (with paid options) but not open-source, and for this reason, it may not be the ideal solution for educational institutions.

3.2.5 Mozilla Hubs

Hubs (https://hubs.mozilla.com)) is a VR chat, an experimental open-source project compatible with virtual reality, which allows you to communicate and collaborate with other people, organize meetings, and virtual events. In practice, 3D space can be created directly from the browser, and others can be invited to join each other's virtual room communicating to them the room link.

It is possible to organize conferences, courses, exhibitions, or only a place to virtually meet and converse with friends by sharing images, videos, and 3D models. Hub allows a strong level of customization related to both usable avatars and the platform's branding itself. Also functional without a VR device, Hubs work on most browsers, and it is available on mobile, desktop, and VR devices.

3.2.6 AltSpacevr (Altvr)

A *Unity*-based social VR platform that provides a tool to load the worlds created by the game engine directly on the platform, allowing to create exhibitions, live shows, meetups, and classes for free. Acquired by Microsoft in October 2017, *Altvr* (https://altvr.com) is usable in virtual reality with Oculus headsets (even the small GO one), VIVE, and also from Windows 10 and Mac Os.

3.3 VR Headsets (HMD – Head-Mounted Display) Applications

At present, it is possible to experience virtual reality environments with special headsets (*HTC-Vive* [https://www.vive.com], *Oculus Rift* [https://www.oculus.com], or other brands that follow the *Windows Mixed Reality* WMR project [https://bit.ly/3mx9XEy]) accessing libraries of experiences, including games and applications, with over 2000 titles. While major headsets require high-performance computers and graphics cards (although minimum requirements are gradually decreasing), the latest models under development provide standalone operation (all-in-one), freeing the user from wires or the need to have a high level performing PC. Virtual reality headsets, particularly those with 6 degrees of freedom, where it is possible to move effectively and intuitively in the environment following digital reconstruction, allowing to experiment with games and situations otherwise impossible to achieve in real life. A series of virtual reality applications, such as Tilt Brush, Google Blocks, and many others, allowing to draw and sculpt directly in virtual reality. Some virtual reality applications such as *Beat Saber* or *RecRoom* illustrate how headsets can also create sports and recreational simulations even in conditions of multi-use with people distant in other cities and countries that speak different languages.

The problem of the unit cost of the devices is one of the main obstacles to possible large-scale use of these tools in professional training, except for small realities able to face the total cost.

Some other reportable mixed reality applications are:

- *vTime XR* (https://vtime.net), a free cross-platform and cross reality (XR) social network that allows groups of up to four users to switch to virtual reality augmented reality with a customized avatar in a private chat room, choosing an environment among those available.
- *Spatial* (https://spatial.io), a meeting environment, allows users to create a lifelike avatar and work as if next to each other, using all of their favorite existing tools and any device, including VR/AR headsets, desktop, or phone to participate.

More information and practical examples on this topic can be obtained by consulting the websites, publications, and articles listed below, selected from those currently available online, based on the type of proposals considered most like this research:

- *News and Resources for Educators* - Website
- The possibilities of virtual reality in education, focusing on apps and research-backed effective uses of virtual reality in the classroom.
- *Virtual Reality in Education: an overview* - Article
  Education is driving the future of VR more than any other industry outside of gaming. Here is why virtual reality gets such high marks for tutoring, STEM development, field trips, and distance education.
- http://bookstoread.com/etp
  Educational Technology Magazine - Website
  The magazine for managers of change in education.
- *The Immersive Education Initiative* - Website
  A non-profit international collaboration of educational institutions, research institutes, museums, consortia, and companies.
- *Teaching & Learning with Technology* - Blog
- *Digital Cultures 2020* — Online - Website
  Inaugurated in 2017, the Digital Cultures Festival acts as an international platform for meetings between digital culture professionals and enthusiasts.
- https://elearningindustry.com/virtual-reality-augmented-reality-education
  Virtual Reality and Augmented Reality In Education - Article
  This article describes how virtual reality and augmented reality are already being used to implement primary and secondary education.
- https://arvrtech.eu/blog/top-5-benefits-of-virtual-reality-in-education
  Top 5 Benefits of Virtual Reality in Education – Article
- http://www.msc-les.org/proceedings/vare/2018/VARE2018.pdf
  The 4th International Conference of the Virtual and Augmented Reality in Education - September 17-19, 2018 - Budapest, Hungary – Report
- http://ieeevr.org
  IEEEVR Conference - Past Conferences reports

4. HOW TO LEARN

Basic games literacy promotes GBL (Game-based Learning) although it may not be limited to education. However, teachers are required to acquire such literacy skills as they should be aware of good games and understand the importance of games selection impacting on the successful GBL implementation (Becker, 2017). The acquisition of this literacy enables educators to access educational games and experience of gameplays at a degree of ease, which caters for the needs of young learners and reduce the personal resistance due to lacking support in digesting basic technological knowledge. (Chen, S., Zhang, S., Qi, G., & Yang, J., 2020).

Nowadays, the usability perspectives of the material made public and exposed on the net are subject to a much more sustained rate of variation than in the past; taking training as an example, the development of online communities of practice has profoundly changed the possibility of learning (and teaching) through courses available on the web, passing from an individual relationship between the user and the material studied to the interaction between multiple users of the same material. There has therefore been a transition from a first passive phase of Computer Based Training (CBT) to the current one in which distance learning has become a possible collective and active event: the user becomes part of a community with whom to share the knowledge of information, keeping pace and choices, according to one's aptitudes.

As with many other subjects, current learning methods allow anyone to access the tools seen before independently as self-taught, through various existing publications and video tutorials, or by attending courses in the classroom, online, or in a virtual environment. In the cases considered in this study, there are several courses available for a fee that can provide recognized certifications, but also many free classes organized by volunteers from informal communities of practice composed of teachers and enthusiasts, not valid for credits or certificates having official value but still useful for training adequate skills and creating networks of mutual relationship and exchange of information between end-users.

As in the previous paragraphs, some of the learning resources available online are listed to facilitate those who may be interested in being able to quickly access the courses available on the topics covered in this study. As mentioned for the above lists, a simple web search can produce many more up-to-date results, including face-to-face courses and different learning methods.

- *Udemy* (https://www.udemy.com) is an American massive open online course (MOOC) provider. "As of Jan 2020, the platform has more than 35 million students and 57,000 instructors teaching courses in over 65 languages. There have been over 400 million course enrollments. Students and instructors come from 180+ countries, and 2/3 of the students are located outside of the US." (Learn about Udemy culture, mission, and careers | About Us. Udemy About. Retrieved 2020-09-09)
- *Edu3D* (http://edu3d.pages.it) is an Italian online community of practice (OcoP) in *CraftWorld* an *Open Sim* grid (http://opensimulator.org/wiki/Grid_List). The idea is to build an immersive 3D cultural environment for distance learning and for sharing educational experiences. It is an innovative teaching improvement system based on online tutoring and coaching. The project supports a community of practice in a multi-user virtual 3D environment, consisting of avatars, laboratories, interactive activities, tutorials, events, simulations, role-playing games, and educational objects. In summary: create an online Educational environment for all those who use virtual worlds as new learning scenarios.
- *LinkedIn Learning* (https://www.linkedin.com/learning) is an American subsidiary of LinkedIn that offers paid video courses on entrepreneurship, creativity, and technology taught by experts in these fields. The offer is enriched with dozens of new classes every week.
- *Raywenderlich.com* (https://www.raywenderlich.com) is a community site focused on creating high-quality programming tutorials. 2323+ articles, 4700+ video, and screencasts with a course of 77 lessons (6 hours) on Unity, 10 of which are free.
- *Coursera* (https://www.coursera.org) is another platform that offers free university courses in Massive Open Online Courses (MOOC) format, with hundreds of free classes, on-demand video lectures, homework exercises, and community discussion forums. Paid courses provide additional quizzes and projects as well as a shareable Course Certificate upon completion.

Some useful YouTube channels for tutorials and courses:

- https://www.youtube.com/user/AndrewPPrice
  Blender Guru
- https://www.youtube.com/c/SurfacedStudio
  Surfaced Studio (FILMMAKING, VFX, and 3D)
- https://www.youtube.com/c/PolygonRunway
  Polygon Runway (3D illustrations and use 3D for web)
- https://www.youtube.com/c/CGGeek
  CG Geek (Blender Tutorials, Tech Reviews, Visual Effects, CG Shorts)
- https://www.youtube.com/c/MozillaMixedReality
  Mozilla Mixed Reality
- https://www.youtube.com/c/Zenva
  Zenva (Courses for creating 2D and 3D games)
- https://www.youtube.com/c/PlayfulTechnology
  Playful Technology (Tinkering with technology and making playful experiences)
- https://www.youtube.com/c/ArduinoStartups
  Augmented Startups (Tutorials on AI & AR Apps in Unity and Python)

5. A PRACTICAL EXAMPLE

At the end of this analysis, it may be useful to touch on a real example: the high school teacher's course presentation. According to the principles set out above, the course described below was taught by one of the authors and ended a few weeks before the writing of this study.

5.1 Didactics through Virtual, Augmented, and Mixed Reality and IoE (Internet of Everything) Applications

Participants will be shown a complete methodology for creating interactive scenarios autonomously built to support classroom activities for joint production among students and using materials prepared or collected from open-source or public domain libraries.

In addition to material production, it is taught how to structure it in interactive experiences to be used with the materials available (first of all, *Android* smartphones with *Google Cardboard*, portable *Oculus* like *Go / Quest*, and sophisticated headsets like *Oculus Rift / HTC Vive*).

It is not mandatory to have an *Oculus*, to attend the laboratories of this course, it is sufficient to use:

- an *Android* smartphone that supports *Google Cardboard*, therefore smaller than 6".
- A device to wear the mobile phone as a *Cardboard* V2 viewer equipped with a click button, the Merge VR Headset is recommended.
- Windows PC / laptop or MacOS 64 bit powerful enough to run *Blender* 2.83, Unity 2019.3, and *Mozilla Hubs* login browser.
  (With adequate free disk space, about at least 10GB free).
- It is essential to have a 3-button mouse with a wheel. Without a mouse, many functions become very difficult, if not impossible, to perform.

The methodology used uses the already consolidated methodologies used in the teaching projects for teachers carried out in recent years, which uses upside-down class techniques, with:

- the production or use of textual and multimedia materials already available online or produced when necessary.
- Stimulus meetings and explanations of any critical points of the actual implementation in a laboratory way during the meeting and individually or in groups by the participants of all the concepts explained as they are presented.
- Exchange of experiences between students using a shared forum/blog, to be able to structure subgroups of people with common interests who can carry out mini shared projects.

The training objectives aimed to create specific skills in teachers both in the use of tools and in the application of innovative teaching methodologies and strategies. The goal is to enhance learning with new forms of Media Literacy, deepening the relationship between content and the creative expansion of knowledge through Augmented Reality as well as the relationship between body, play, simulation, invention, creativity, participatory culture with the help of Virtual Reality. Tools and strategies were also investigated for using Augmented Reality (AR), virtual reality (VR), and mixed reality (MR) in the pedagogical context.

A total of 25 people and 5 observers participated in the course from several Italian cities, and among them there had been many teachers and some school principals.

The participant or team had to produce a VR Experience as follows:

- project sheet specifying the objectives and the methodology undertaken.
- Construction of a supporting exhibition environment (small building platform room).
- Multimedia contents to view (images, sounds, videos, or links to web pages that can be clicked by the project).
- Three-dimensional models to insert.
- Navigation paths to be created with arrows or numbers or with panels. Use at least five reference points in the room, e.g.
  - Introduction.
  - Object / Experience 1.
  - Object 2.
  - Object 3.
  - Thanks, greetings, contact references, and any attributions.

The final task had been evaluated based not only on the Mozilla Hubs environment created but also on a short .mp4 movie with an audio description or a presentation that explains how the environment works.

The possibility of direct interaction with touch objects/minigames is not foreseen in this course.

Special attention will be paid to the Mozilla Hubs virtual world that allows users to create in a reasonably easy and accessible way even for students with no particular coding experience and with minimal tools such as computers and mobile phones.

The course is carried out in e-learning mode, using the following tools:

- WebEx for live streaming, interaction with participants.
- Classroom for the definition of multimedia materials, recordings, and assigned tasks.
- Discussion forum for offline discussion by participants and where to show their productions.

The course was structured into 6 2-hour meetings. The scheduled meetings are as follows:

Introduction

The structure of the course will be described, the course's objectives, the presentation of the tools for accessing virtual reality (mobile PC viewers), and the Mozilla Hubs environment will begin to be described given its particular ease of access. At the end of the first meeting, participants should be able to list viewers and PCs with advantages and disadvantages and be able to enter a Mozilla Hubs room from their computer.

1. Workshop and task: take a 360° photo or take it from Google Maps or other freely distributable content sources.
2. Mozilla Hubs

In the second meeting, participants will see how to create and share a scene for Mozilla Hubs using even just a PC, to create content from open-source scenes and objects traceable on the net.

Laboratory and task: Create a scene with Spoke (the web-based tool used to build a room in Mozilla Hubs), where to insert prefabricated elements taken from the marketplaces such as Sketchfab or Poly.

3. Blender Part one

This part is dedicated to seeing how Blender can build elementary objects and a minimal environment (room) following the Low Poly logic. A complete Blender course is impossible to do in very few meetings. Therefore, the work will focus on how to produce elementary contents such as stools, tables, or bottles.

4. Unit and carton

In this lesson, participants will learn how to import some of the Low Poly content designed with Blender (table, stool, or bottle) and how to export this content to an *apk* application that can be used via mobile with Google Cardboard. With the possibility of navigation on stage.

5. Oculus Go / Quest hints and Blender insights.

Hints on how to create the same navigable scenes, usable on Oculus Go or Quest.

A deepening of Blender will be done in particular for texturing and reviewing how to make some of the participants' artifacts.

6. FINAL PROJECT

The last meeting will focus on the design of an elementary educational path to be experienced in VR; the task will be done for Google Cardboard or for Mozilla Hubs depending on the abilities of the participants (Mozilla Hubs is simpler, Unity is a little more difficult). Participants will be described how to design and implement it.

In this example, the element relating to Gamification is little highlighted but is manifested in the relational dimension between teacher and students and in creating competition and mutual support between the students themselves. This can also be effectively done with the help of interactive forums and direct communications when doing homework correction. It is necessary to experiment with different methods until the teacher finds the right ones adapting to the class, especially in distance learning practices, where personal interaction is further mediated by technological means.

The proposed case mainly involves the use of HMD (with VR headset) applications; many other experiences are based, however, on the creation and use of an online educational environment on the OpenSim platform. In any case, a key element concerns teacher training, which can include transversal methodological indications for the use of virtual worlds as new collaborative learning scenarios and a wide-ranging, innovative, and effective teaching with infinite possibilities for development in the digital field. All these platforms can be a good tool to facilitate the acquisition of specific professional skills and the dissemination of significant and transferable experiences and materials in different fields of application.

Annotation on MOZILLA HUBS

This product had been recently developed by Mozilla Foundation (starting in 2018), and it is already a revolutionary approach that completely remodels the way we see Virtual Worlds and Virtual Reality with an easy-to-adopt, almost trivial learning curve, where anybody can create or participate to a virtual event in a matter of just clicking a couple of links in a standard browser like Firefox or Chrome.

The main intent was to bring the browser paradigm used by Internet browsers to the virtual worlds community, and so far it is providing already a big amount of features that are important in the educational world.

Here are some strong points in Mozilla Hubs (MH) compared for instance to OpenSim (OS).

1. Very easy one-click access for participating

MH allows a simple link to be followed directly from a blog post or an email where you can get full access to the 3D world. In contrast, OS needs to download a separate viewer and need a learning task that can take hours if not weeks to be used in full.

2. Privacy and access control

Rooms in MH can be easily created specifying a revocable key for access so that teachers can control who is participating. The same thing with OS is quite complex and involves access to SysAdmin configuration

3. Instant 3D building and content creation.

Room creators and even participants can easily build from free marketplaces like SketchFab or Poly just specifying the address of the model and tapping the magic wand.

The same easy access is possible to insert built-on-the-fly text, images, audio, movies, and even an animated model. In OS building process is particularly difficult needing a lot of extra effort even for trivial tasks, such as inserting text.

4.   Wide access from all platforms.

Participants can use their own devices, including smartphones, tablet, VR Headset, PC, etc, while OS only allows PC

From the Weak Points in MH compared to OS here a couple of things:

1.   The general quality of Avatars in MH is quite low compared to OS, but this has been a compromise to allow MH to run on even smartphones. The same happens for high-quality scenes where OpenSim allows for much realistic reproduction of buildings and people.
2.   OS allows for sophisticated scripting allowing much more interaction from participants, like interactive quizzes and escape rooms. With MH you have to work around this either with auxiliary smartphone applications interacting with your virtual world via QR code or with some tricks.
3.   OS is being organized in bigger entities called Grids, where there is an interaction with many other realities, other schools, or other creators like in SecondLife or even among grids, MH instead tends to focalize the work only on the room or set of room defined by a single creator school. This on the other hand can be positive for being sure that no intruder can enter MH rooms.

CONCLUSION

Technology is an extension of the brain; it is a new way of thinking. It is the solution humans have created to deal with the difficult new context of variability, uncertainty, complexity, and ambiguity. Wise integration of evolving and powerful technology demands a rethinking of the curriculum. (Marc Prensky, 2013).

In this analysis, the meaning of "prosumer" was addressed by combining it with other essential concepts, such as Gamification and the "learning community", and observed how the new communication and virtualization technologies had enabled a transformation in all these three areas, effectively creating an exciting fusion. Especially for distance and face-to-face training and teaching. A merger that consolidated the prosumer's status, further weakening the distinction between producers and users of contents, favoring a continuous exchange of knowledge that enriches the entire community. The didactic sense of these experiences lies in constructing a cooperative group environment in which to experiment, learn and exchange knowledge on an equal basis between all the participants, without high costs, therefore within reach of many, if not all. It emerged that for some of these experiences, the costs are very low and often limited to the owner of a mobile device or a PC. The next step was, therefore, to meet some of the 3D construction tools currently available, such as Blender (and other open software) and their role in the production of 3D objects, animations, and multimedia visual effects. The items that are created in the modeling process can then be imported and used in virtual worlds such as Second Life, OpenSim, Minetest ("old" generation virtual worlds), but also High Fidelity, Sansar (virtual worlds usable with VR headsets), or to produce game environments using Unity and Godot, engines that allow you to design games or learning environments.

For each specific area of interest, useful links have been provided to facilitate research by readers interested in deepening the topics covered and finding resources to be used immediately in practical experimentation. Day after day, the web is enriched with exciting content produced not only by professionals involved in commercial processes triggered by the introduction of dedicated software in the markets but also by individuals and groups of enthusiasts interested in sharing their knowledge with other people for free. This generates a proliferation of sites, tutorials, videos, manuals, the quality of which must be assessed case by case, an aspect that has been considered in the realization of this study.

The purpose of this short paper is to try to condense and share the author's experience in the field, based on several years of participation and agency in the Edu3D community of practice and learning. This virtual community has its "headquarters" in the multi-user 3D environment "Open Sim". It operates thanks to the competence and creativity of teachers, technicians, and experts who are passionate about digital architecture and innovative teaching and who voluntarily share experiences and open-source content.

The activities take place in "flipped classroom" mode, a collaborative method of sharing knowledge that has led us to closely know the strengths of the convergence of that convergence mentioned in the first lines of this conclusion. During these years of online and face to face courses, workshops, internships, and conferences, many teachers have approached virtual worlds, have learned to build their avatar and customize their environment, taking their "first steps" while having fun and appreciating the immersion and the didactic value of "learning by doing", feeling "protagonists" and participating with curiosity and amazement in the use of cheap and straightforward VR / AR tools. Each participant can acquire skills which, in most cases, can then be transferred into their professional activity by involving students and collaborators and in turn, creating interest and motivation to collaborate and reduce distances, not only in terms of scholastic knowledge, thanks also to that intrinsic transformative power of working not with others but together with others, feeling equal, respecting the roles.

REFERENCES

Antonioli, M., Blake, C., & Sparks, K. (2014). Augmented Reality Applications in Education. *The Journal of Technology Studies*, *40*(1-2), 96-107. http://www.jstor.com/stable/43604312

Brelsford, J. W. (1993). Physics Education in a Virtual Environment. *Proceedings of the Human Factors and Ergonomics Society Annual Meeting*, *37*(18), 1286–1290. doi:10.1177/154193129303701818

Chen, S., Zhang, S., Qi, G., & Yang, J. (2020). Games Literacy for Teacher Education: Towards the Implementation of Game-based Learning. *Journal of Educational Technology & Society*, *23*(2), 77–92.

Coban, M., Karakus, T., Karaman, A., Gunay, F., & Goktas, Y. (2015). Technical Problems Experienced in the Transformation of Virtual Worlds into an Education Environment and Coping Strategies. *Journal of Educational Technology & Society*, *18*(1), 37–49.

Curcio, I., Dipace, A., & Norlund, A. (2017). Virtual realities and education. *Research on Education and Media*, *8*(2).

Degli Esposti, P. (2015). *Essere prosumer nella società digitale. Produzione e consumo tra atomi e bit* [Being a prosumer in the digital society. Production and consumption between atoms and bits]. Franco Angeli.

Di Nubila, R. D. (2005). *Saper fare formazione. Manuale di metodologia per i giovani formatori.* Pensa Multimedia.

Feng, L., Yang, X., & Xiao, S. (2017). MagicToon: A 2D-to-3D creative cartoon modeling system with mobile AR. *2017 IEEE Virtual Reality (VR)*, 195-204.

Fontanella, M., Pacchiega, C., & Tricarico, M. (2019). *Prosumer: building the virtual* [Paper presentation]. Scuola e Virtuale. (Piacenza, 24-25 settembre 2019). https://bit.ly/Prosumer2019

Freude, H., Reßing, C., Müller, M. B., Niehaves, B., & Knop, M. (2020). *Agency and Body Ownership in Immersive Virtual Reality Environments: A Laboratory Study.* HICSS.

Gregory, S., Scutter, S., Jacka, L., McDonald, M., Farley, H., & Newman, C. (2015). Barriers and Enablers to the Use of Virtual Worlds in Higher Education: An Exploration of Educator Perceptions, Attitudes and Experiences. *Journal of Educational Technology & Society, 18*(1), 3–12.

Hemmasi, M., & Csanda, C. (2009). The Effectiveness of Communities of Practice: An Empirical Study. *Journal of Managerial Issues, 21*(2), 262–279. http://www.jstor.org/stable/40604647

Hesse, H., & Ziolkowski, T. (1989). *My Belief: Essays on Life and Art.* Triad Paladin.

Kaner, S., Lind, L., Toldi, C., Fisk, S., & Berger, D. (2007). *Facilitator's Guide to Participatory Decision-Making.* Jossey-Bass.

Keene, S. (2018). *Google Daydream VR Cookbook: Building Games and Apps with Google Daydream and Unity.* Addison-Wesley Professional.

Kimble, C., Hildreth, P., & Bourdon, I. (Eds.). (2008). *Communities of Practice: Creating Learning Environments for Educators.* Information Age.

Kyaw, B. M., Saxena, N., Posadzki, P., Vseteckova, J., Nikolaou, C. K., George, P. P., Divakar, U., Masiello, I., Kononowicz, A. A., Zary, N., & Tudor Car, L. (2019). Virtual Reality for Health Professions Education: Systematic Review and Meta-Analysis by the Digital Health Education Collaboration. *Journal of Medical Internet Research, 21*(1), e12959. doi:10.2196/12959 PMID:30668519

Lave, J., & Wenger, E. (1991). Situated Learning: Legitimate Peripheral Participation (Learning in Doing: Social, Cognitive and Computational Perspectives). Cambridge University Press.

Liu, D., Dede, C., Huang, R., & Richards, J. (2017). *Virtual, Augmented, and Mixed Realities in Education. In Smart Computing and Intelligence.* Springer.

Metz, T. (2013). *The FAST Facilitative Session Leader.* Productivity Press.

Moro, C., Štromberga, Z., & Stirling, A. (2017). Virtualisation devices for student learning: Comparison between desktop-based (Oculus Rift) and mobile-based (Gear VR) virtual reality in medical and health science education. *Australasian Journal of Educational Technology, 33*(6). Advance online publication. doi:10.14742/ajet.3840

Patel, S., Panchotiya, B., Patel, A., Budharani, A., & Ribadiya, S. (2020, May). A Survey: Virtual, Augmented and Mixed Reality in Education. *International Journal of Engineering Research & Technology (Ahmedabad), 9*(5).

Prensky, M. (2013). Our Brains Extended. *Educational Leadership, 70*(6), 22–27. https://www.learn-techlib.org/p/132064/

Ravotto, P., & Fulantelli G. (2011). Net generation e formazione dei docent [Net generation and teacher training]. *Journal of e-Learning and Knowledge Society, 7*(2), 87-98.

Rubio-Campillo, X. (2020). Gameplay as Learning: The Use of Game Design to Explain Human Evolution. In *Communicating the Past in the Digital Age: Proceedings of the International Conference on Digital Methods in Teaching and Learning in Archaeology* (pp. 45-58). London: Ubiquity Press. 10.5334/bch.d

Sanders, D. H. (2014). Virtual Heritage: Researching and Visualizing the Past in 3D. *Journal of Eastern Mediterranean Archaeology & Heritage Studies, 2*(1), 30–47. doi:10.5325/jeasmedarcherstu.2.1.0030

Schroeder, R. (2001). *The Social Life of Avatars: Presence and Interaction in Shared Virtual Environments.* Springer Science & Business Media.

Szymusiak, T. (2015). *Prosumer – Prosumption – Prosumerism.* OmniScriptum GmbH & Co. KG.

The World Bank. (2016). World Development Report 2016. Expanding opportunities, 100-146.

Toffler, A. (1980). *The third wave: The classic study of tomorrow.* Bantam.

Trentin, G. (2008). *Apprendimento in rete e condivisione delle conoscenze* [Networked learning and knowledge sharing]. Franco Angeli.

Viola, F. (2011). *I Videogiochi nella Vita Quotidiana* [Video games in everyday life]. Arduino Viola Editore.

Wang, Y. (2020). Integrating Games, e-Books and AR Techniques to Support Project-based Science Learning. *Journal of Educational Technology & Society, 23*(3), 53–67.

Welch, K. (1981). Electronic Media: Implications of the Third Wave View of Electronic Media. *English Journal, 70*(5), 86–88. doi:10.2307/817390

Wenger, E. (1998). *Communities of Practice: Learning, Meaning, and Identity.* Cambridge University Press. doi:10.1017/CBO9780511803932

Wenger, E., McDermott, R., & Snyder, W. M. (2002). *Cultivating Communities of Practice.* HBS Press.

Whitton, N. (2013). Games for Learning: Creating a Level Playing Field or Stacking the Deck? *International Review of Qualitative Research, 6*(3), 424–439. doi:10.1525/irqr.2013.6.3.424

Wu, H. (2016). Video Game Prosumers: Case Study of a Minecraft Affinity Space. *Visual Arts Research, 42*(1), 22–37. doi:10.5406/visuartsrese.42.1.0022

Yamada-Rice, D., Mushtaq, F., Woodgate, A., Bosmans, D., Douthwaite, A., Douthwaite, I., Harris, W., Holt, R., Kleeman, D., Marsh, J., Milovidov, E., Mon Williams, M., Parry, B., Riddler, A., Robinson, P., Rodrigues, D., Thompson, S., & Whitley, S. (2017). *Children and Virtual Reality: Emerging Possibilities and Challenges.* http://digilitey.eu/wp-content/uploads/2015/09/CVR-Final-PDF-reduced-size.pdf

KEY TERMS AND DEFINITIONS

Augmented Reality (AR): An interactive experience in which objects residing in the real world are enhanced by computer-generated information, sometimes through multiple sensory modalities.

Cardboard: A low cost VR viewer, designed to favor the development and commercial diffusion of virtual reality, which allows you to transform any smartphone into a perfect and functional Virtual Reality Viewer.

Digital Cultures: A concept that practically expresses the relationship between people and technology, describing how technology and the Internet are shaping the way we interact as human beings, or how we behave, think and communicate within society.

Gamification: It is the application of game design elements and game principles in non-gaming contexts in order to solve problems or learn in a fun and facilitated way to make the learning curve less steep, also allowing to improve user involvement.

Graphic Engines: A software development environment designed to allow people to create video games for consoles, mobile devices, and personal computers.

Head-Mounted Display (HMD): A display device, worn on the head and used, with different shapes and structures, in many fields, including games, aviation, engineering and medicine.

Modeling: In 3D computer graphics, it indicates the process of developing a mathematical representation of any surface of an object (inanimate or living) in three dimensions using specialized software. The result of this process is called a 3D model.

Online Community of Practice (OcoP): Also defined as a virtual community of practice (VCoP), it is formed by a group of people united by the common interest in a specific field, each with their own level of specific experience, who participate together in a shared learning process that develops through Internet with a view to sharing knowledge.

Prosumer: A combination of the words supplier and consumer that can identify six different types of behavior regarding the interaction between user and acquired goods: do-it-yourself prosumer, self-service prosumer, personalized prosumers, collaborative prosumers, monetized prosumers and economic prosumers.

Virtual Environments: Computer-generated spaces that can contain objects that can be manipulated and people. These can be text-based virtual reality or multi-user chat or games, 2D interactive environments, as well as immersive 3D environments, i.e. real immersive virtual reality environments (virtual, augmented, or mixed).

This research was previously published in the Handbook of Research on Teaching With Virtual Environments and AI; pages 492-517, copyright year 2021 by Information Science Reference (an imprint of IGI Global).

Chapter 28
Framework for 3D Task Design:
An Immersive Approach

Iryna Kozlova
University of Pennsylvania, USA

ABSTRACT

This chapter introduces a framework for the 3D task design. The framework proposes that the process of designing language learning tasks for 3D immersive simulated environments also be immersive. The framework guides designers/teachers who are new to 3D worlds through 10 stages of the design process that incorporates designers/teachers' individual work and their collaboration with colleagues and learners. Following Breen's advice, collaboration with colleagues and learners allows for taking into account some possible interpretations of the tasks to help learners interpret the task as closely as possible to its original plan; it also improves task functionality. Developed for designing 3D language learning tasks, this framework also benefits other disciplines and informs the design of tasks implemented in other virtual environments.

INTRODUCTION

This chapter proposes a process-based conceptual framework for the design of 3D language-learning tasks implemented in 3D virtual environments, also known as virtual worlds, e.g., Second Life, AvayaLive™ Engage, VirBELA. The 3D worlds are multimodal collaborative environments that provide participants with simulated real-life experiences by embodying participants in graphical avatars situated in contexts resembling real-life geographical locations (Cooke-Plagwitz, 2008; Gerhard et al., 2004; Peterson, 2011). Since participants can interact through several communication channels and explore the world around them with others, they can be engaged in "experiential problem solving and complex and spatially distributed forms of collaboration" (Cornille et al., 2012, p. 245).

Task-based learning and teaching (TBLT) has been widely explored both in face-to-face (f2f) and online contexts with an abundance of studies addressing task design (see Breen, 2009; Collentine, 2011; Ellis, 2003, 2009; Ellis et al., 2020; Gánem-Gutiérrez, 2014; González-Lloret & Ortega, 2014;

DOI: 10.4018/978-1-6684-7597-3.ch028

Hartwick & Savaskan Nowlan, 2018; Kozlova, 2018a, 2018b; Kozlova & Priven, 2015; Lan et al., 2016; Lin et al., 2014; Nunan, 2004; Pica et al., 1993; Willis & Willis, 2007 among others). The literature on technology-mediated TBLT acknowledges the fact that technology affects the design of online tasks (e.g., Collentine, 2011; Gánem-Gutiérrez, 2014; González-Lloret & Ortega, 2014; Kozlova, 2018a, 2018b; Lan et al., 2016), but so far, a step-by-step process of task design has only been addressed in Kozlova and Priven (2015).

Kozlova and Priven (2015) show that 3D task design is rather complex because task designers must understand task-based pedagogy and the second language development processes that occur in learners, as well as the following: (1) the purpose and affordances of the 3D environment; (2) the purpose and use of tools embedded in the environment (e.g., voice- and text-based chat, collaboration boards); (3) how 3D technology can be integrated into the task design to facilitate language learning; (4) pedagogical practices appropriate for teaching in this environment; (5) how the geography and space of the immersive environment contribute to the task design; and (6) how learner interaction with the space facilitates learners' language development.

Kozlova and Priven (2015) also demonstrate that it is near impossible to use tasks designed for f2f classrooms in 3D contexts because 3D virtual environments "create learning spaces conceptually different from the face-to-face classroom and web-conferencing environments" (p. 83) by taking learners outside the classroom context and immersing them in a simulated real-life-like world. Since 3D environments are immersive and provide learners and teachers with immersive experiences, *the process of designing tasks should also be immersive*. Teachers who start working with 3D environments may be familiar with the TBLT approach but may *not* be familiar with the immersive approach to 3D task design, which can make for a challenging experience. This chapter provides a background of concepts for (technology-mediated) tasks and task design and introduces a framework for the process-based immersive model of 3D task design. Although this model is based on research on task-based learning in 3D environments, it can be extended and applied to designing tasks for other virtual contexts.

BACKGROUND

By definition (see Breen, 2009; Ellis, 2003, 2009; Ellis et al., 2020; González-Lloret & Ortega, 2014; Nunan, 2004; Pica et al., 1993; Willis & Willis, 2007 among others), tasks are goal-oriented activities with a clear task outcome (e.g., making a shopping list). Although the primary focus is on meaning, learners are to use their linguistic resources and pay attention to form to express meaning. The target forms required by the task may not be explicitly stated, but tasks can be designed to coerce learners to employ them, for example, by requiring learners to use prepositions to describe a room or use the simple past to describe a recent trip. Tasks include some kind of an information gap or a problem, which pushes learners to produce authentic and spontaneous language while attempting to recover the missing information or solve a problem. As learners interact with linguistic input, negotiate meaning and/or form, perform interactional modifications, and scaffold each other, they engage in second language acquisition (SLA) processes that facilitate language learning.

Components of Task Design

While task design has been widely addressed in the literature for both f2f and virtual contexts (e.g., Ellis, 2003; Ellis et al., 2020; González-Lloret & Orgega, 2014; Hampel, 2006, 2010; Nunan, 2004; Robinson, 2009; Rosell-Aguilar, 2005; Skehan, 2018; Willis & Willis, 2007), what task design encompasses can only be inferred. Most of the time, task design frameworks include a set of components that constitute a task. Some of the components have to do with second language learning processes (e.g., students having the opportunity to negotiate the meaning or form), and some are pedagogical in nature (e.g., the sequence of the activities or the roles of teacher and students). Nunan's (2004) framework, for example, includes components such as a task goal, input, sequence of activities to achieve the task goal, teacher and learner role in the task, and task settings, e.g., group work in a f2f classroom. Ellis's (2003) framework similarly incorporates a task goal, input, and settings, which he calls procedures. He also adds components such as the task outcome, linguistic and cognitive processes occurring in learners, and conditions or "the ways information is presented" (p. 21).

The task design frameworks developed by Willis and Willis (2007), Skehan (2018), and Robinson (2009) differ from Ellis's (2003) and Nunan's (2004) frameworks in that they emphasize a pedagogical sequence within a task. Willis and Willis (2007) regard a task as a cycle, which opens with pre-task activities preparing learners for the target task(s) and concludes with post-tasks in which learners share what they have accomplished in the task and practice the target language.

Skehan's (2018) task sequence also starts with pre-task activities that focus on the target forms. These activities facilitate learner integration of new linguistic features and help restructure existing knowledge. Knowledge restructuring reduces learner cognitive load and allows learners to pay more attention to expressing the meaning rather than how to use the form. The goal of the second stage, during the task performance, is balancing accuracy and fluency. This can be achieved by manipulating factors such as time required for the task completion, its modality (spoken or written), number of participants, the importance of doing the task correctly, and learner influence on the implementation of the task. Post-task activities constitute the next two stages. The first post-stage—repeating the task performance in front of peers, task analysis, or post-task tests—can direct learners' attention to accuracy. The second post-stage engages learners in tasks similar to the one they have completed and requires learners to analyze the tasks and synthesize their goals. Skehan argues that it is important for learners to explore and re-examine the task sequences because these post-task activities "driv[e] forward instruction" (p. 31). Robinson (2009) suggests that task sequence should take into consideration the complexity of the task features (e.g., description vs. reasoning) that can be maneuvered to make the task more or less cognitively demanding, participation features, and learner individual abilities (e.g., motivation, proficiency level, intelligence).

Components of the Technology-Mediated Task Design

Scholars agree that technology-mediated TBLT should take into consideration the affordances of virtual environments as well as the variety of communication channels and other features inherent to specific virtual environments. Some task design frameworks for technology-mediated tasks, however, do not seem to incorporate technology components into the task design or explain how technology should mediate communication and collaboration or be used for co-construction of the task products. Chapelle's (2003) framework, for instance, draws on frameworks by Pica et al. (1993) and Skehan (Skehan, 1996; Skehan & Foster, 2001) and adds some components from research on language learning with technology. These components, i.e., computer knowledge and learner ability to search for information, are not elements of the task design; however, they are skills that learners need to have to participate in online learning.

Hampel (2010) combines Ellis's (2003) and Oxford's (2006) task design features – a goal, task types, importance of the task, input, conditions, linguistic and cognitive complexity, task procedures, predicted outcomes, and roles of teacher and learner. Similar to Chapelle (2003), Hampel (2010) does not explain how all these components can be integrated with a technology-mediated task. Inspired by the research on task-based learning, González-Lloret and Ortega (2014) identify five key task features "in the context of technology-and-task integration" (p. 5), but these features—focus on meaning, goal orientation, learner-centeredness, holism, and reflective learning—apply to the task design in any environment, virtual or f2f. Although technology-related components are missing from the technology-mediated task framework, incorporating technology components in the task design is extremely important because tasks designed for one virtual environment may not be transferable to another virtual context since the affordances available in each environment may not be the same.

Researchers working with 3D immersive environments report that some technology-related components can affect how tasks are carried out. These components include (1) virtual geographical locations and landmarks (e.g., Deutschmann et al., 2009; Gánem-Gutiérrez, 2014; Hartwick & Savaskan Nowlan, 2018; Kozlova & Priven, 2015; Panichi & Deutschmann, 2012); (2) communication channels available in the environment (e.g., Kozlova, 2018a, 2018b; Kozlova & Priven, 2015; Peterson, 2006); (3) collaboration tools embedded in the environment (e.g., Kozlova, 2018a, 2018b; Kozlova & Priven, 2015; Peterson, 2006); and (4) learner interaction with space (e.g., Collentine, 2011; Hartwick & Savaskan Nowlan, 2018; Kozlova, 2018a, 2018b; Kozlova & Priven, 2015; Lan et al., 2016).

Incorporation of affordances in the task design is extremely important. Matching the task topic with a geographical location, for example, provides learners with cultural experiences (Collentine, 2011), decreases their reliance on imagination, and inspires learners to discuss what they observe (Kozlova, 2018a; Lan et al., 2016). Using different communication channels, such as voice- or text-based chat, allows for the practice of different language skills and attention to form, especially, if text-based channels are used (Kozlova, 2018b; Peterson, 2006). Having learners take notes on collaboration boards draws their attention to form. When learners work together to express ideas, they negotiate meaning and form and exercise various interactional patterns such as sharing information, giving feedback, requesting help, and supporting and negotiating their ideas (Kozlova, 2018b). Learner interaction with space occurs as learners explore the environment, which facilitates not only learner autonomy (Collentine, 2011; Kozlova, 2018a) but also the development of second language (L2) critical thinking skills as learners use the target language to identify the problem and come up with a solution. Since learner interaction with the linguistic input, other participants, and the space is mediated by the technology, the design of technology-mediated tasks, then, should also incorporate the technology-related components; otherwise, task functionality will be compromised.

Moving Towards the 3D Task Design: Characteristics of 3D Tasks

Since virtual environments differ in their purposes and affordances, it is essential to identify specific characteristics of the 3D tasks. While geographical landscape, landmarks, and the space that allows participants to travel in the environment make a 3D world very realistic, for instructional purposes, these features cannot be considered as the only ones that influence the 3D task design.

One of the most important features of a 3D world is communication channels, which determine how users interact. Figure 1 illustrates the immersive platform VirBELA, which allows for audio- and text-based communication. Users can mute/unmute themselves by clicking on the microphone button in the bottom left-hand corner or use the chatbox on the right of the microphone button to send public or private messages to nearby users or globally. Since 3D environments simulate real-life experiences, users' avatars need to be close enough to each other to hear others speak unless they take advantage of the public volume areas, e.g., a stage in an auditorium.

Figure 1. Communication channels and collaboration boards in VirBELA.

3D environments are designed for collaboration, so the availability of collaboration spaces with collaboration tools is another feature that affects 3D task design. Figure 1 features collaboration boards located on the wall of a building in the downtown area. Both boards can be used as computer screens; learners can access the Internet from each of the boards and access Google Docs to take notes. In addition to being used as collaboration boards, they can also be used to post text, audio, or video input.

Non-player avatars can also be employed as tools for posting input. A woman avatar shown in Figure 2 has three buttons on the right. Learners can use the audio button to access pre-recorded audio files, the text button to read information, or the help button with an image of a light bulb to get different kinds of support, e.g., the definition of an unfamiliar word. Sticky notes, such as the one posted on the left of the non-player avatar in the picture, can be placed anywhere in the environment and used as an input source.

Navigation of the environment is also critical for the 3D task. If a 3D world has a vast territory, it may take much time to travel to some locations. Availability of shortcuts or teleporting stations can save users' travel time. Figure 3 shows that users can choose an intended location from the menu in the top left-hand corner or go through the wall of the teleporting station.

Figure 2. Non-player avatar and a sticky note in VirBELA

Figure 3. Traveling in VirBELA.

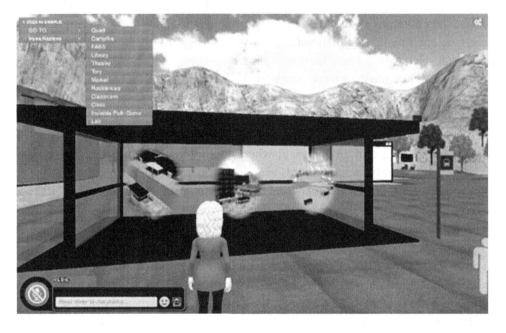

3D worlds simulate a real-world where users can experiment with different identities by changing the appearance and clothing of their avatars and express an array of emotions. Users can choose emotions from the menu in the top left-hand corner or use shortcuts on the computer keyboard. An avatar in Figure 4, for example, shows that she is thinking.

Figure 4. Expressing emotions in VirBELA.

These are only some of the features available in a 3D world such as VirBELA, but they show that 3D environments are very complex systems and their features can influence the task design in the following ways: how learners communicate, collaborate, or move in the environment; what kind of linguistic and visual input is made available and how learners can access them; and how learners can incorporate the features of the environment into their work. Since 3D worlds are so different from other virtual contexts, 3D tasks have some characteristics that do not apply to tasks designed for other virtual environments.

1. 3D tasks are environment-specific. Tasks designed for the environment showcased in Figures 1-4 may not be functional in an environment where multiple communication channels, non-player avatars, sticky notes, collaboration boards or other affordances are not available.
2. 3D tasks require the designer to understand the purpose of the environment and its tools. This is illustrated by the Kozlova's (2018b) study in which one of the task components was learner use of collaboration boards embedded in the 3D world. The collaboration boards were meant to function as computers to access web-resources and a real-time web-based editor MoPad directly from within the environment. Although the functionality of web-resources and MoPad was tested before the task implementation, it was taken for granted that if the boards could be used as computers, then opening several tabs – one to search the Internet and another one to use MoPad—would be possible. However, students were not able to do so. Although the teacher trainees solved this problem by preparing additional collaboration boards in another virtual room, it was impractical and unproductive for students to go back and forth between the rooms. Although the theoretical framework and pedagogy were well incorporated in the task design, poor integration of the tools did not allow seamless functioning of the task.
3. An environment exploration component incorporated in the 3D task facilitates learner language development. The main difference between the 3D context and other virtual contexts is that 3D

contexts provide rich visual input. This allows learners to experience the world, make observations, and use their observations to solve problems similar to how the process of solving problems occurs in real life. Environment exploration helps learners to think critically and come up with various solutions together. When sharing their thoughts and experiences, learners produce modified input (Lan et al., 2016) and negotiate meaning, form, and ideas (Kozlova, 2018a, 2018b), which facilitate language development.

4. The simple design of the 3D tasks helps to avoid learner information overload. 3D environments are complex systems that require intensive multitasking, including navigating the environment (e.g., to mute/unmute the microphone, use the computer keyboard to navigate the avatar, type on the collaboration board or in the chatbox, access web-resources), remembering task-related information such as instructions and information from multimodal task input, and employing critical thinking skills. If the task sequence contains many steps, learners may experience information overload that can interfere with their productivity, especially if the instructions are not well chunked or posted on the board (Kozlova & Priven, 2015).

5. 3D tasks' functionality depends on learner familiarity with technology and the activity itself. Although Breen (2009) argues that learners' interpretation of the task depends on their needs, linguistic knowledge, familiarity with the learning context, social settings, and their learning styles, Kozlova's (2018b) and Kozlova and Priven's (2015) studies highlight that learners' interpretation of the task also depends on their familiarity with the technology and the activity in which they participate. The participants in these studies understood the task instructions; however, they did not know how to proceed with the task as they did not know what collaboration involves. Instead of negotiating which information to include in their reports, they each typed a piece of information they found individually.

6. 3D tasks have the potential for the development of learner autonomy. 3D worlds offer opportunities for autonomous learning (Dalton & Devitt, 2016; Deutschmann et al., 2009; Lan et al., 2016; Schwienhorst, 1998) as learners make choices regarding which tools to use, which player- or non-player avatars to interact with, or which information to request or incorporate in their products (Collentine, 2011; Kozlova, 2018a). Although 3D environments can facilitate learner autonomy, Kozlova (2018a) found that not all of the learners use the opportunity to make their own choices. She concludes that to help learners develop this skill, successful completion of a 3D task should be measured not only by learner ability to achieve the task outcome but also by learners' autonomous actions while working towards the task outcome. The task should also clearly communicate the task expectations; if students are to explore the environment, then they need to know what exactly needs to be observed (e.g., oxygen sources in the buildings), and how their observations should be incorporated into the task outcome (e.g., calculation of the oxygen level in each of the buildings).

If these technology-related 3D task characteristics are not taken into consideration, they may unfavorably affect the task design in terms of the task functionality. Therefore, along with theoretical and pedagogical components, integration of technology-related components into the task design is critical as they mediate learning, interaction, and environment navigation.

Towards the Definition of the Task Design

While the task design frameworks discussed in the previous sections identify task components, they do not provide a clear definition of what task design is. Samuda (2015) argues that "although we are gradually accumulating evidence relating to features of the design that impact performance in different ways, we still know very little about what is involved in designing tasks" (p. 279). The frameworks seem to imply that task design refers to the task plan and the components included in the plan. However, task design goes beyond that. Design is defined as "a preliminary sketch or outline showing the main features of something to be executed," "an underlying scheme that governs functioning, developing, or unfolding," or "a plan or protocol for carrying out or accomplishing something" (Merriam-Webster, n.d., Definition 4, 5a, 5b). Based on these definitions, task design can be viewed as a plan showing how various components of the task are combined to function in a particular (virtual) environment (e.g., a 3D world) or "considerations of who does what, when, how well, and in what ways" (Johnson, 2003; Samuda, 2005, as cited in Samuda, 2015, p. 279).

Although tasks are created by material designers or teachers, they are unique in that learners also make contributions to the task design (Breen, 2009). Breen argues that learner re-interpretation of the task objectives, content, procedures, and learning context could occur per the following: (a) learners' own needs; (b) knowledge of the learning content (word meaning, use of language in social settings); (c) knowledge of grammar in the linguistic sense; (d) learner abilities to work with the task information and preferred ways of learning; and (e) their understanding of the learning context. According to Breen, to minimize the range of the learners' interpretation of the task plan and to help them interpret the task as closely as possible to the task work plan, task design should follow the following four principles:

1. Task objectives should match learning needs that are apparent to the learner as closely as possible.
2. Task content should be treated as *"only potential content for learning"* (p. 340). Since individual learners identify the portions of the content that are familiar to them, learner work, then, is organized around the unfamiliar content, which has to be integrated into the familiar content in the process of their task-based learning.
3. Task design could urge learners to analyze what aspects they identified as problematic and what they did to achieve their learning goal. Individual learners approach learning and achieve their learning goals using different procedures, which may help them uncover the most efficient ways of learning.
4. Task design could allow learners to decide how the social and physical context of the language classroom helps accomplish the task goals.

If learners' interpretation of the task impacts the task design, the task design should be viewed as a collaboration between the task designers/instructors and learners. Like learners, teachers may also re-interpret the tasks in the process of implementation. Samuda (2015) observed two instructors teaching the same task and discovered that each of the teachers re-shaped the original plan. One teacher removed the task outcome, thus converting the task into an exercise that "could be stopped at any point without affecting its design or impact" (p. 288). The other teacher made changes to the task content and procedures, thus "intentionally *re-tasking* elements of the original work plan" (p. 288). Kozlova and Priven (2015) also found that teacher trainees make changes to the ongoing task as they learn how to teach in the 3D worlds. When they could not interrupt students' discussion to give oral feedback, they changed the way they provided feedback. Instead of providing input orally, they used text-based chat.

Task design can also undergo revisions retrospectively in response to the challenges encountered during the task. When teacher trainees from Kozlova and Priven's (2015) study noticed that something did not work as planned in one task, they addressed these problems in the task to be taught in the next class session. Although the six tasks designed for the six-week project had different content, they had the same structure and used the same tools for collaboration and interaction. Making such changes helped the teacher trainees improve the functionality of future tasks.

Since task design can be re-interpreted at different stages of its development and implementation, Samuda (2015) recommends the task to be treated as "a *succession* of work plans that come into play in different ways at different points across a lesson or teaching cycle" (p. 281). Her multidimensional model of task design includes four versions of a work plan as it evolves chronologically. The designer's original work plan can be used as a teacher's lesson plan or it can be incorporated into a lesson plan. When the teacher implements the task in the classroom and incorporates changes to the plan in the process of its implementation, then, it becomes a dynamic work plan. The work plan changes into a retrospective plan when changes are made to re-shape the task for future use. Kozlova and Priven's (2015) study also suggests that the task design process is multi-level and spiral with some revisions made at the pre-teaching stage, some in the process of teaching in response to both teacher and student re-interpretation of the task, and some retrospectively to improve future task functionality. Thus, task design "involves considerably more than the constellation of features that make up the initial work plan of a task" (Samuda, 2015, p. 282) and is both a process and a result of a multilevel collaboration of task designers/teachers and learners.

Task Design Process

Although much is known about tasks and task components, there is not much research on how to start developing tasks, especially 3D tasks that require coordination of so many components. Nunan (2004) proposes that task design should start with identifying the goals and objectives of the task, followed by selecting linguistic input, especially, in regards to determining the degree of its authenticity. Nunan argues that the target grammar and vocabulary should not be pre-selected by the teacher but should come from the input so that students can observe how the target forms are used in context and then practice them in the task. The final step in the task design is developing activities. This is when teachers are to decide whether the activities have pedagogical and/or real-life goals, what learners' and teacher roles are, and how learners are grouped.

Willis and Willis (2007) suggest that the task design should start with "plan[ning] a task sequence" (p. 23). First, task designers need to identify the topic and then choose the *target* task(s). The next step is developing so-called *"facilitating* tasks" that are used at the pre-task stage to introduce vocabulary, content, and the task sequence, and at the preparatory stage to engage learners with the "topic and language." While Nunan (2004) and Willis and Willis (2007) offer some general steps in the task design processes, they focus on designing tasks for f2f contexts. The design of the 3D tasks, however, involves a lot of technology-related work (Kozlova & Priven, 2015) and the coordination of various components to make the task functional. The next section introduces the framework for the 3D task design and the process of its development.

DESIGN AND IMPLEMENTATION

Drawing on Kozlova's (2018a, 2018b) and Kozlova and Priven's (2015) research on training teachers to design 3D tasks and use TBLT to teach in the 3D world, an *immersive approach* to the 3D task design is proposed here. This framework is based on the "bottom-up" (Samuda et al., 2018, p. 5) or "*descriptive*" approach to the classroom "researched pedagogy" (Van den Branden, 2016, p. 177). The "descriptive" approach to the study of TBLT focuses on "pedagogical actions and decisions that are taken by teachers and students in authentic classrooms while they are working with tasks" (Van den Branden, 2016, p. 177). Since the studies by Kozlova (2018a, 2018b) and Kozlova and Priven (2015) are "grounded in what happens in the classroom" (Samuda et al., 2018, p. 5) as they explore teacher trainees' "pedagogical actions and decisions" when learning how to design and implement 3D tasks in instructional settings with real students, it is fair to say that the teacher trainees who participated in that pedagogically-oriented project pioneered the way 3D tasks are constructed, and their work can inform classroom research as well as teachers new to this pedagogical context.

As defined earlier, task design is a plan explicating how various components of the task are combined in a pedagogical sequence to function in a particular (virtual) space, and it is both a process and a result of a multilevel collaboration of task designers/teachers and learners. Since 3D tasks are designed for immersive environments, the framework for the 3D task design proposes that *the process of designing 3D tasks is also immersive.* Kozlova and Priven (2015) reveal that most of the 3D task designer's work occurs in the environment because coordination and fine-tuning of all of the task components as well as testing the task functionality is near the impossible outside of the 3D world. Designers may not remember numerous details of the virtual world and may need to often check whether and how learners can use communication and collaboration tools, how they can move from one location to another one, whether they can open and use a real-time editor, and how all these components function in harmony. The *immersive task design process* also helps task designers understand learner experiences with the task, observe how learners interpret the task in the process of its completion and make necessary changes to decrease the divergence between the intended and learner interpretation of the task (Breen, 2009).

Although the present framework is primarily based on the findings of previous research on teacher training in 3D worlds (Kozlova, 2018a, 2018b, Kozlova & Priven, 2015), it also relies on the data collected for the three studies—the six-week project detailed above. The data used here is teacher trainees' wikis in which they collaboratively planned the 3D tasks. Six teacher trainees participating in the project were enrolled in a teacher certification program preparing second/foreign language teachers at a Canadian college. The six tasks that they developed were used over a period of six weeks to help English-as-a-foreign-language learners from Turkey improve speaking skills (see Kozlova & Priven, 2015). The three environments used for this teacher-training project—a college campus, a downtown of a city, and an island—were built on a cloud-based platform AvayaLive™ Engage. All of the environments allowed for both audio- and text-based communication and collaboration on the boards that were used as presentation and collaboration boards and also as computer screens. Player avatars controlled by the participants could walk, run, and express emotions; non-player avatars were not available in the three environments.

As immersive 3D environments are designed for learner collaboration and provide space and tools for collaborative activities, 3D worlds are compatible with the sociocultural approach to language learning and development. According to sociocultural theory, collaboration is central to sociocultural learning because knowledge is socially owned and collaborative practice provides a social context to support individual (L2) development (Donato, 2004; Lantolf, 2000). As learners participate in a *collaborative activity*, they engage in "a synergetic process that can facilitate and indeed promote, the emergence of zones of proximal development among participants" (Gánem-Gutiérrez, 2018, p. 392).

Collaboration organized around collaboration boards is especially valuable as taking notes on collaboration boards keeps learners focused on the problem they solve and draws their attention to both the intended meaning and the form that supports this meaning (Kozlova, 2018b). When taking notes on collaboration boards, learners produce both oral and written input, which, according to Blake (2009), mobilizes the same cognitive processes. This allows for dual language processing, first, when sharing the meaning orally with a group, and then, when expressing the same meaning in a written form on the collaboration board (Kozlova, 2018b). Collaboration also facilitates learners' use and development of various interactional patterns, such as when they share their knowledge, support their position, make requests for information or clarification, and comment on the collaboration process (Kozlova, 2018b), to name just a few. Collaboration, therefore, is an essential component of the 3D task design.

The 3D task design process proposed in this chapter consists of 10 stages. At each of the stages, designers make several design-related decisions. As task design is an ongoing process, task-developers go back and forth between the stages since making changes to one task component may lead to changes to other components addressed at different stages.

Stage 1. Framing the Task

Framing the task, according to Kozlova and Priven (2015), is the first step towards designing a 3D task. Task designers make several decisions at this stage, including choosing a task topic, matching the topic with a geographical location or a feature in the 3D environment that simulates the real world to make the task more realistic, identifying a problem to solve or an information gap to fill in, coming up with a sequence of micro-tasks that will help learners achieve the task goal, determining learner roles in the task, as well as choosing the technology that would mediate communication and collaboration. At first glance, these decisions may create the impression that the entire task design process is completed in the first stage. However, this stage is about creating a general frame for the task and setting a tentative task scenario, which can be revisited and changed throughout the design process as more details are added or changed. Table 1 includes three Stage 1 task scenarios developed by three teacher trainees—Gerri, Joan, and Lynn—participating in the teacher training project. Each of the scenarios incorporates the following components: task topic, task geographical location, anticipated learner roles, environment exploration, task goal, learner collaboration, and outcome.

At this stage, designers also come up with a tentative sequence of the task. The participants of the teacher training project came up with the following sequence (Kozlova & Priven, 2015):

1. Brainstorming engages learners with the task topic and also activates vocabulary on the topic.
2. Research/exploration when learners interact with the input and collect information to solve the problem/fill in an information gap.
3. Preparation for presentation when learners collaborate on the outcome of the tasks, e.g., preparing plans.
4. Presentation stage when learners share their plans with others.

Table 1. Examples of task scenarios

Task components	Canadian Art Exhibition (Gerri)	Natural Disaster (Joan)	Disadvantaged Children (Lynn)
Topic	A special Canadian Art exhibition will take place at the famous Istanbul Museum of Modern Art.	There has been a nuclear accident at the power reactor on the mainland.	Twenty 12-year-old disadvantaged children who had difficult lives (some were sick, others abandoned) are learning how to hope for a better life.
Location	One of the paintings from the collection located in this building should be selected for display in the Istanbul Museum of Modern Art.	People are being evacuated to Tipontia island for safety.	They are coming to Tipontia island for a holiday.
Roles	You are curators selected by a Canadian culture committee to choose art for the collection.	You are an evacuation team.	You are a team that plans activities for these children.
Exploration	As a group, explore the paintings included in this collection and choose one that you would recommend for the Istanbul Exhibition.	As a team, explore the island and make observations of the island and its resources.	As a team, explore the environment and think about how it can be used for the children's vacation.
Goal	Your goal is to choose one painting and convince the committee that it should be included in the exhibition.	Your goal is to determine how the island resources can be used to help people survive on the island.	Your goal is to come up with a plan of how to use the island to help children become healthy, learn to trust others, and gain self-confidence.
Collaboration	Use collaboration boards to prepare a plan of how to convince the committee to select the painting of your choice.	Use collaboration boards to come up with a plan.	Use collaboration boards to come up with your plan.
Outcome	Reasons for the selection of the painting. Speech to convince the committee.	Plan of how to use the island resources. Presentation of the plan.	Plan of the activities. Giving an individual tour of an island to a teacher and explain your plan.

In this task sequence, brainstorming corresponds to the preparatory stage during which learners engage with the topic of the task and activate the vocabulary, whereas the next three stages are parts of the target task as described in Willis and Willis (2007).

Stage 2. Providing Input

In the task, learners interact with linguistic input; they also process information required to solve the task problem or fill in the information gap. In Stage 2, designers decide how the information learners need to achieve the task is presented to learners. For example, in the Canadian Art Exhibition task by Gerri, learners had to collect interesting facts about the selected painting using the Internet. In the Natural Disaster task by Joan, learners were required to interact with the oral input. AvayaLive™ Engage, the environment used for the teacher training project, did not have non-player avatars or sticky notes that could be posted in the environment. So, Joan used player avatars, by recruiting her colleagues to play the role of park workers, to supply learners with the information about the waterfall, lake, treehouses, etc., upon learners' request.

Lynn, who developed the Disadvantaged Children task, chose learner-generated input. She hoped that learners would generate input for other learners as they came up with creative ideas while exploring the environment. Since some environments, like VirBELA, offer many possibilities for presenting the input, e.g., non-player avatars, collaboration boards, sticky notes, objects, or other player avatars, it could be very difficult to decide which sources of input to choose. Therefore, the designer's choice should be the input source that realistically matches the topic of the task as well as the task goal.

Stage 3. Environment Exploration

3D worlds provide learners with visual and "culturally authentic experience … (e.g., a garden centrally located in a home)" (Collentine, 2011, p. 63). Immersive environments also offer learners the opportunity to experience the environment and engage in "experiential problem solving and complex and spatially distributed forms of collaboration" (Cornille et al., 2012, p. 245). Experiential problem-solving is coming up with solutions using cues from the environment, the same way people do in the real world. For example, in the Natural Disasters task, learners had to find sources of fresh water and food on the island, decide where the evacuees would sleep, and talk about how to use landmarks such as the lighthouse or campfire. When designing the environment exploration component of the task, it is important to understand what exactly students need to observe, how their observations can contribute to the task outcome, what learners could talk about, and what language they will use.

Another decision that task designers make at this stage is how learners will participate in this activity. For example, learners can walk together as a group and discuss what they immediately see, or they can each explore a specific place and share their observations with their group members. Planning this stage outside the environment is practically impossible because designers first need to explore the environment themselves and decide which features of the environment are most relevant to the task.

Stage 4: Collaboration

This stage focuses on how learners will work together, in groups or pairs, and on what communication and collaboration tools learners will use for collaboration. Leaners can use audio- or text-based chat, or both, to interact with their group members depending on which skills (speaking, listening, reading, or writing) are the focus of the task. Some decisions that designers make at this stage include which real-time editor to use, e.g., Google Docs, and which of the collaboration boards to use. Since the territories of some environments are quite vast, it is more practical to choose boards located close to the location where the task is implemented, which reduces travel time and allows students to quickly go back to double-check the environment or make additional observations. Other factors to consider are whether learners know how to use collaboration boards, what collaboration involves, and whether they have prior experience with such an activity. If students are not familiar with this type of activity, then they need to be taught how to collaborate; otherwise, they will not be able to complete the task (see Kozlova, 2018b).

Stage 5: Autonomy

Although this stage had not emerged in the design process of the six teacher trainees, learner autonomy emerged later in the process of task implementation (see Kozlova, 2018a). After adding most of the components of the 3D task, Stage 5 is the time to double-check if the task design inspires learners to take control of their learning. Kozlova (2018a) argues that "[l]earner autonomy can take various shapes depending on the affordances available in a 3D environment" (p. 69). Therefore, it is important to identify what kind of learner actions would be considered as autonomous, e.g., searching for additional information on the Internet or paying attention to various details in the environment.

Some learners require training on how to become autonomous (Nunan, 1997), so it would be helpful to have the expectations explicitly stated. If learners are to explore the environment, then they need to know what exactly to pay attention to; if they are expected to learn new vocabulary, then they need to be instructed to negotiate the meaning of the new vocabulary and to include it in their final report. Most importantly, "reaching the task outcome (e.g., solving a problem) and students taking control of their learning as operationalized in the task (e.g., generating and controlling topics) should be considered as a successful task outcome" (Kozlova, 2018a, p. 69).

Stage 6: Teacher Role

Deciding on the teacher's role is another important decision to make. When learners work toward the completion of the task in a 3D world, most of the time they do not remain in the same location as other learners or the teacher. Even when they collaborate on the collaboration boards, groups may be located in different virtual rooms or places. Because the teacher cannot be at all of the locations at the same time, it is important to think ahead of time about how to stay connected with students, e.g., sending them text-messages to check how they are doing or teleporting to their location. Another challenge for the teacher is providing feedback to students. Since 3D worlds simulate real-life experiences, learners communicate like they do in real life. To maintain the authenticity of learners' real-life experiences, teachers need to consider feedback techniques that occur naturally in real life and do not interrupt the flow of interaction, such as clarification requests or recasting.

Stage 7. Preparing Instructions

Giving instructions for tasks in 3D worlds is almost an art. Because tasks consist of mini-tasks or activities sequenced in a way that helps learners achieve the task outcome, they involve a series of instructions telling learners what to do at each of the stages. If a task requires learners to process L2 input and task requirements simultaneously, remembering all of the information may be cognitively demanding no matter whether the instructions are provided orally or posted on a collaboration board (Kozlova & Priven, 2015). Even if students can revisit the posted instructions at their leisure, it would be impractical and time consuming for students to travel long distances or constantly back and forth within the 3D environment to do so. Some environments may not have enough boards to keep the instructions posted throughout the task.

Often, instructions are taken down so boards can be repurposed after the instructor introduces the task to learners. To help learners remember instructions and avoid information overload, teachers can provide instructions in chunks, before each part of the task. To illustrate, when teacher trainees from Kozlova and Priven's (2015) study divided instructions into several chunks and gave instructions before each part of the task, students remembered the instructions better. Kozlova and Priven (2015) also show that it is equally difficult for teachers to give instructions as it is for students to remember them. To make the practice of giving instructions easier and keep the instructions concise, teacher trainees wrote scripts for their instructions because "it was very difficult for teacher trainees to control avatars, explain the task, give directions in the environment, and manage the classroom" (p. 94).

Stage 8: Testing the Task

Testing the task is critical to the task design process. Because 3D tasks are very complex, it is easy to overlook details. Also, according to Breen (2009), those who engage in the tasks can interpret them in their own ways. Asking colleagues to test the task as if they were learners is very helpful as task-testing may reveal if the task will be interpreted the way it is expected. Testing the task can also generate a lot of helpful suggestions for improvement, but the most important feedback is related to the task functionality because it will be difficult for learners to complete the task if components are not well-coordinated, instructions are not clear, or the task is too complicated.

Stage 9: Teaching Stage

The teaching stage may bring some unexpected challenges that the testing stage may not reveal, so teachers need to be ready to solve problems that may emerge during the task (see Kozlova, 2018a, 2018b; Kozlova & Priven, 2015). Students may not understand instructions or what they are expected to do, or they may have problems with technology, e.g., the real-time editor will not open. Since task design is an ongoing process, the problems students encounter should be documented to be addressed later.

Stage 10: Reflection and Changes

Reflection on and analysis of the task that learners have just completed is very important. This helps teachers review learners' experiences with the task and make all necessary changes to it or to other tasks of similar structure so that the task can be implemented more smoothly in the future. As shown in Kozlova and Priven (2015), teacher trainees reflected on their teaching experience and the challenges they faced during the task. Since their tasks had similar structures, they made changes to the tasks that they taught in the following weeks, which improved not only the design of their tasks but also task functionality and students' participation in the task.

Issues, Controversies, Problems

The immersive framework of 3D task design presented in this chapter draws on the experiences of novice teachers learning how to develop 3D tasks and teach in 3D worlds. While this framework takes into consideration the fact that both learners and teachers may re-interpret the task in the process of its completion or implementation (Breen, 2009; Mori, 2002; Samuda, 2015), this framework does not address the issue of when and how to pre-teach the target structure and vocabulary that learners are expected to use in the task, or the issue of post-task activities used to improve accuracy (Skehan, 2018). The reason for that is that the teacher trainees, whose task development experiences were used for this framework, did not develop the curriculum themselves but were instead provided with the topics as well as with the grammar and vocabulary associated with each of the topics that were included in the course syllabus.

Another issue that needs to be addressed is that the teacher trainees were new to both 3D technology and TBLT, and it is possible that teachers more experienced with TBLT or 3D teaching could approach

3D task design differently. At the same time, even teachers who have experience using technology spend some time to explore, understand, and experiment with a new environment "in the situated contexts" (Haines, 2015, p. 176). This suggests that even though the framework was created using data from the experiences of novice teachers, it could still be a valuable resource for anyone new to working with 3D environments.

The immersive approach to task design brings some controversy over the practicality of the non-immersive approach to the design of computer-mediated tasks. Although the non-immersive frameworks developed by Chapelle (2003), González-Lloret and Ortega (2014), and Hampel (2010) incorporate key components of task design such as the focus on meaning, goal orientation, task outcome, and learner-centeredness, without careful consideration of the affordances of the environment, these frameworks do not guarantee the functionality of a computer-mediated task. As reported in the study of Kozlova and Priven (2015), one of the participants Jack developed a task outside of the 3D environment. Instead of exploring the space and its tools, he took a task originally developed for a f2f context and chose to slightly adjust it for an online context. Although his task was meaning-oriented and learner-centered, and had a goal and task outcome, Jack's colleagues found his task undoable. The tools and the space were not used effectively, and the scenario could not be realistically implemented in the geographical location he had chosen. To be more specific, Jack missed out on an important step of the proposed framework—teacher collaboration and task-testing at the pre-teaching stage of the designing process. This step is extremely important as it reveals task functionality.

However, testing the task in some teaching contexts could be problematic if no one is familiar with the environment. Although online teaching has become mainstream due to global pandemic, not all online environments are equally explored or used. While it would not be difficult to find someone to test tasks developed for the web-conferencing platform Zoom because of its popularity among educators, there are not many educators who use 3D worlds on an everyday basis.

Lessons Learned

The most valuable lesson learned from the teacher training in 3D virtual worlds (Kozlova & Priven, 2015) is that 3D task design is an immersive experience. Because 3D worlds resemble geographical locations and their landmarks feature many details, it is impossible to design a task without exploring the environment, e.g., visiting a room in a building, checking the availability of computers in the rooms, or food in the fridge. Being in the environment while designing a task and exploring the function of available tools is also critical because learner participation fully depends on the functionality of communication and collaboration tools. If a link to a document or an Internet resource does not work, learners will not be able to complete the task. Since 3D task design so heavily relies on the environment and its various features, for 3D designers, an immersive experience seems to be imperative.

SOLUTIONS AND RECOMMENDATIONS

Although 3D pedagogy attracts attention from many scholars and practitioners, our knowledge about how to use these environments for language instruction and, specifically for task-based learning and teaching, remains rather limited. To continue building the knowledge base for 3D task-based instruction including 3D task design, further exploration of these spaces is urgently needed.

One of the areas that is missing from 3D literature is how to use 3D worlds to pre-teach new vocabulary or grammatical structures that students would use in the task. Creating vocabulary games such as a scavenger hunt or problem-solving activities would help learners associate the new word with the objects or activities in the environment. If associations are created during the pre-task stage, it would be easier for learners to retrieve the words during the task when they see these objects or talk about the activities. Teaching and practicing grammar in the environment are also possible. When learning verb tenses, learners can talk about their experiences and observations using the simple past, e.g., I visited a coffee shop downtown and talked to a nurse in the hospital. Since language is learned for communication in the real world, using the simulated world for teaching vocabulary and grammar will help learners practice the target language in authentic contexts.

FUTURE TRENDS

The 3D task design framework presented in this chapter is informed by the research on teaching and learning languages in 3D worlds. Task-based teaching and learning, however, is not exclusive to language pedagogy; other disciplines may benefit from this framework as well. The stages of this task design framework encompass general practices, such as how to frame the task, how to organize learner collaboration, and how to address learner autonomy in the task design. Collaborative learning, which is at the center of the theoretical approach to the immersive 3D task design, is also used in other disciplines and is part of the social constructivist theory of learning. Therefore, this framework is highly applicable to other educational fields. The framework is also viable for use in other virtual environments. Technology-mediated tasks are highly reliant on the features of the specific environments; therefore, designing tasks while being in the environment is important and sometimes almost necessary. This chapter opens the discussion about how the task design can be approached and what path it can take, but more insights from researchers and practitioners are needed to continue this discussion.

CONCLUSION

To conclude, this chapter proposes a framework for 3D task design and shows that the process of designing tasks for immersive environments should also be immersive. 3D environments are sophisticated systems with various communication and collaboration tools for the participants to use in the environment as they travel through the virtual space and work together on a task. With so many technological features and tools available to users, it is easy to overlook important details, which will make the task difficult to complete.

The ten-step framework clearly shows that the affordances of specific environments should be integrated in the task design to ensure task functionality. The steps of the immersive task design are chronologically organized and guide task developers through the entire design process consisting of pre-teaching, teaching, and post-teaching stages. Starting with creating a general frame for the task and setting a tentative task scenario at the pre-teaching stage, designers make decisions on how learners will interact with the linguistic input and with virtual space, how they will collaborate and exercise learner autonomy, and how they will receive instructions and instructor feedback. The teacher role is also to be defined and explained. Testing the task at the end of the pre-teaching stage gives the opportunity to see what needs to be revised. Since learners bring their perspectives to the task design, the teaching stage can illuminate new problems, which can be addressed retrospectively.

Unlike other frameworks for task design, this immersive model takes into account the collaborative nature of task design and shows that task designers, who are typically the teachers implementing the task, and learners contribute to task design by re-interpreting and re-shaping the task both in the process of the task implementation and retrospectively. This framework is developed based on the research on teaching second/foreign languages in 3D immersive environments, but it can be applied in other virtual environments and inform other disciplines interested in task-based pedagogy.

REFERENCES

Blake, C. (2009). Potential of text-based Internet chats for improving oral fluency in a second language. *Modern Language Journal*, *93*(2), 227–240. doi:10.1111/j.1540-4781.2009.00858.x

Breen, M. P. (2009). Learner contributions to the task design. In K. Van den Branden, M. Bygate, & J. M. Norris (Eds.), *Task-based language teaching: A reader* (pp. 333–356). John Benjamins.

Chapelle, C. A. (2003). *English language learning and technology: Lectures on applied linguistics in the age of information and communication technology*. John Benjamins. doi:10.1075/lllt.7

Collentine, K. (2011). Learner autonomy in a task-based 3D world and production. *Language Learning & Technology*, *15*(3), 50–67.

Cooke-Plagwitz, J. (2008). New directions in CALL: An objective introduction to Second Life. *CALICO Journal*, *25*(3), 547–557. doi:10.1558/cj.v25i3.547-557

Cornille, F., Thorne, S. L., & Desmet, P. (2012). Digital games for language learning: From hype to insight? *ReCALL Journal*, *24*(3), 243–356. doi:10.1017/S0958344012000134

Dalton, G., & Devitt, A. (2016). Irish in a 3D world: Engaging primary school children. *Language Learning & Technology*, *20*(1), 21–33.

Deutschmann, M., Panichi, L., & Molka-Danielsen, J. (2009). Designing oral participation in Second Life: A comparative study of two language proficiency courses. *ReCALL Journal*, *21*(2), 206–226. doi:10.1017/S0958344009000196

Donato, R. (2004). Aspects of collaboration in pedagogical discourse. *Annual Review of Applied Linguistics*, *24*, 284–302. doi:10.1017/S026719050400011X

Ellis, R. (2003). *Task-based Language Learning and Teaching*. Oxford University Press.

Ellis, R. (2009). Task-based research and language pedagogy. In K. Van den Branden, M. Bygate, & J. M. Norris (Eds.), *Task-based language teaching: A reader* (pp. 109–129). John Benjamins.

Ellis, R., Skehan, P., Li, S., Shintani, N., & Lambert, C. (2020). *Task-based language teaching: Theory and practice*. Cambridge University Press.

Gánem-Gutiérrez, G. A. (2014). The third dimension: A sociocultural theory approach to the design and evaluation of 3D virtual worlds tasks. In M. Gonzalez-Lloret & L. Ortega (Eds.), *Technology-mediated TBLT: Researching technology and tasks* (pp. 213–237). John Benjamins. doi:10.1075/tblt.6.08gan

Gánem-Gutiérrez, G. A. (2018). Collaborative activity in the digital world. In J. P. Lantolf, M. E. Poehner, & M. Swain (Eds.), *The Routledge handbook of sociocultural theory and second language development* (pp. 391–408). Routledge. doi:10.4324/9781315624747-25

Gerhard, M., Moore, D., & Hobbs, D. (2004). Embodiment and copresence in collaborative interfaces. *Human-Computer Studies*, *61*(4), 453–480. doi:10.1016/j.ijhcs.2003.12.014

Gonzalez-Lloret, M., & Ortega, L. (2014). *Towards technology-mediated TBLT: An introduction. Technology-mediated TBLT: Researching technology and tasks.* John Benjamins. doi:10.1075/tblt.6

Haines, K. J. (2015). Learning to identify and actualize affordances in a new tool. *Language Learning & Technology*, *19*(1), 165–180.

Hampel, R. (2006). Rethinking task design for the digital age: A framework for language teaching and learning in a synchronous online environment. *ReCALL Journal*, *18*(1), 101–121. doi:10.1017/S0958344006000711

Hampel, R. (2010). Task design for a virtual learning environment in a distance language course. In M. Thomas & H. Reinders (Eds.), *Task-Based language learning and teaching with technology* (pp. 131–153). Continuum.

Hartwick, P., & Savaskan Nowlan, N. (2018). Integrating virtual spaces: Connecting affordances of 3D virtual learning environments to design for twenty-first century learning. In Y. Qian (Ed.), *Integrating multi-user virtual environments in modern classrooms* (pp. 111–136). IGI Global. doi:10.4018/978-1-5225-3719-9.ch006

Johnson, K. (2003). *Designing Language Teaching Tasks.* Palgrave Macmillian. doi:10.1057/9780230596672

Kozlova, I. (2018a). Factors affecting learner collaboration in 3D virtual worlds. In M. Kruk (Ed.), *Assessing the effectiveness of virtual technologies in foreign and second language instruction* (pp. 26–60). IGI Global.

Kozlova, I. (2018b). Task-based language learning and learner autonomy in 3D virtual worlds. In Y. Qian (Ed.), *Integrating multi-user virtual environments in modern classrooms* (pp. 50–73). IGI Global. doi:10.4018/978-1-5225-3719-9.ch003

Kozlova, I., & Priven, D. (2015). ESL teacher training in 3D virtual worlds. *Language Learning & Technology*, *19*(1), 83–101.

Lan, Y. J., Kan, Y. H., Sung, Y. T., & Chung, K. E. (2016). Oral performance language tasks for CSL beginners in Second Life. *Language Learning & Technology*, *20*(3), 60–79.

Lantolf, J. P. (2000). Introducing sociocultural theory. In J. P. Lantolf (Ed.), *Sociocultural theory and second language learning* (pp. 1–26). Oxford University Press.

Lin, T., Wang, S., Grant, S., Chien, C., & Lan, Y. (2014). Task-based teaching approaches of Chinese as a foreign language in Second Life through teachers' perspectives. *Procedia Technology*, *13*, 16–22. doi:10.1016/j.protcy.2014.02.004

Merriam-Webster. (n.d.). Design. In *Merriam-Webster.com dictionary*. Retrieved September 28, 2020 from https://www.merriam-webster.com/dictionary/design

Mori, J. (2002). Task design, plan, and development of talk-in-interaction: An analysis of a small group activity in a Japanese language classroom. *Applied Linguistics*, *23*(3), 323–347. doi:10.1093/applin/23.3.323

Nunan, D. (1997). Designing and adapting materials to encourage learner autonomy. In P. Benson & P. Voller (Eds.), *Autonomy and independence in language learning* (pp. 192–203). Longman.

Nunan, D. (2004). *Task-based language teaching*. Cambridge University Press. doi:10.1017/CBO9780511667336

Oxford, R. (2006). Task-based language teaching and learning: An overview. *Asian EFL Journal*, *8*(3), 94–121.

Panichi, L., & Deutschmann, M. (2012). Language learning in virtual worlds: Research issues and methods. In M. Dooly & R. O'Dowd (Eds.), *Researching online foreign language interaction and exchange: Theories, methods and challenges* (pp. 205–231). Peter Lang.

Peterson, M. (2006). Learner interaction management in an avatar and chat-based virtual world. *Computer Assisted Language Learning*, *19*(1), 79–103. doi:10.1080/09588220600804087

Peterson, M. (2011). Towards a research agenda for the use of three-dimensional virtual worlds in language learning. *CALICO Journal*, *29*(1), 67–80. doi:10.11139/cj.29.1.67-80

Pica, T., Kanagy, R., & Falodun, J. (1993). Choosing and using communication tasks for second language instruction and research. In C. G. Crookes & S. M. Gass (Eds.), *Tasks and language learning: Integrating theory and practice* (pp. 9–34). Multilingual Matters.

Robinson, P. (2009). Task complexity, cognitive resources, and syllabus design: A triadic framework for examining task influences on SLA. In K. Van den Branden, M. Bygate, & J. M. Norris (Eds.), *Task-based language teaching: A reader* (pp. 193–226). John Benjamins.

Rosell-Aguilar, F. (2005). Task design for audiographic conferencing: Promoting beginner oral interaction in distance language learning. *Computer Assisted Language Learning*, *18*(5), 417–442. doi:10.1080/09588220500442772

Samuda, V. (2005). Expertise in second language pedagogic task design. In K. Johnson (Ed.), *Expertise in language teaching* (pp. 230–254). Palgrave Macmillian. doi:10.1057/9780230523470_12

Samuda, V. (2015). Tasks, design, and architecture of pedagogical spaces. In M. Bygate (Ed.), *Domains and directions in the development of TBLT: A decade of plenaries from the international conference* (pp. 271–301). John Benjamins. doi:10.1075/tblt.8.10sam

Samuda, V., Bygate, M., & Van den Branden, K. (2018). Introduction. In V. Samuda, M. Bygate, & K. Van den Branden (Eds.), *TBLT as a researched pedagogy* (pp. 1–22). John Benjamins. doi:10.1075/tblt.12.01sam

Schwienhorst, K. (1998). The "third place": Virtual reality applications for second language learning. *ReCALL Journal*, *10*(1), 118–126. doi:10.1017/S095834400000433X

Skehan, P. (1996). A framework for implementation of task-based instruction. *Applied Linguistics*, *17*(1), 38–62. doi:10.1093/applin/17.1.38

Skehan, P. (2018). *Second language task-based performance: Theory, research assessment*. Routledge. doi:10.4324/9781315629766

Skehan, P., & Foster, P. (2001). Cognition and tasks. In P. Robinson (Ed.), *Cognition and second language instruction* (pp. 3–32). Cambridge University Press. doi:10.1017/CBO9781139524780.009

Van den Branden, K. (2016). The role of teachers in task-based language education. *Annual Review of Applied Linguistics*, *36*, 164–181. doi:10.1017/S0267190515000070

Willis, D., & Willis, J. (2007). *Doing task-based teaching*. Oxford University Press.

KEY TERMS AND DEFINITIONS

3D Task: A task designed to be used in a 3D immersive virtual environment.

Immersive Task Design Process: Planning and developing a task while immersed in a 3D world.

Non-Player Avatar: A digital image of a character that cannot be controlled by a player.

Player Avatar: A digital image of a character controlled by a player, or a user of a 3D environment.

Task Design: A plan explicating how various components of a task are combined to function in a particular (virtual) environment. It is both a process and a result of a multilevel collaboration of task designers/teachers and learners.

Technology-Mediated Task: A task that integrates technology in the task design.

This research was previously published in Implementing Augmented Reality Into Immersive Virtual Learning Environments; pages 34-55, copyright year 2021 by Information Science Reference (an imprint of IGI Global).

Chapter 29
POV in XR:
How We Experience, Discuss, and Create the Virtual World

Eve Weston

ⓘ https://orcid.org/0000-0002-8841-5491

Exelauno, USA

ABSTRACT

This chapter will introduce and explain the applications of a taxonomy for discussing point of view (POV) in XR. The simple designations of first, second, and third person that are used to categorize books, movies, and video games don't cover all the options and combinations available in immersive media. Accordingly, XR requires a new taxonomy that will allow for clear communication about content and experiences. This chapter will do three things: (1) present the four main POV tiers: narrative, visual, effectual, and experiential; (2) address less common tiers and how they might be incorporated and acknowledged in future XR experiences; and (3) show the taxonomy in action by using it to describe contemporary XR content.

INTRODUCTION

Literary point of view and its complications have been analyzed in detail by French literary theorist Gerard Genette (1983), and Dutch cultural theorist Mieke Bal (1997), each of whom has contributed significantly to the study and discussion of narrative. In film studies, many of their terms were taken up and expanded to include the complexity of image and sound. With virtual reality, new complexities, opportunities, and fields present themselves. The world of storytelling has expanded. With the development of immersive media---collectively known as extended reality (XR)---comes a need to extend the vocabulary we use to define and discuss point of view concepts. The simple designations of first, second, and third person used to categorize books, movies, and video games don't cover all the options

DOI: 10.4018/978-1-6684-7597-3.ch029

and combinations available in XR. Accordingly, the immersive medium of virtual reality requires a new taxonomy for discussing point-of-view. Having a taxonomy that specifically addresses what is possible in virtual reality will facilitate better and clearer discussion, analysis, and communication about this medium.

This chapter first reviews the existing terms for Point of View (POV) from traditional media. Next, it explores how these terms do and don't apply to virtual reality. Then, to help facilitate clearer communication about the options available in XR, this chapter presents and explains applications of the taxonomy as used within virtual reality. This proposed taxonomy, represented in Figure 1, is a marriage of old and new ideas and includes four POV tiers: 1) narrative, 2) visual, 3) effectual and 4) experiential. The shared vocabulary that this taxonomy provides is both descriptive and prescriptive, serving as a way to describe existing work and also as a menu of options for what's possible.

Figure 1. Tiers of immersive POV
Source: Exelauno, 2019

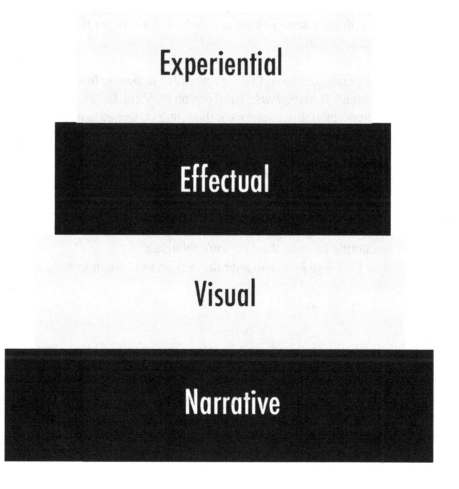

NARRATIVE POV

POV is most commonly thought of in terms of narrative point-of-view: first, second or third person, which is the point of view from which the story is being told. Before examining how narrative point-of-view intersects with the other tiers in virtual reality, it serves to have a brief review of narrative point of view.

In a first-person narrative, the narrator is telling you his or her own story. *Moby Dick*'s famous opening line, "Call me Ishmael," is a classic example. First person narrative POV is also exemplified by Ernest Cline's *Ready Player One* (2012).

My mom once told me that my dad had given me an alliterative name, Wade Watts, because he thought it sounded like the secret identity of a superhero.

The words "my" and "me" in the passage above, along with the word "I" in general are excellent first-person indicators. From them, we can determine that Wade, the narrator, is telling us his own story, in the first person.

Second person narrative POV can be found in the Choose Your Own Adventure books. As exemplified by the following passage from R.A. Montgomery's *The Trail of Lost Time* (2011), the narrator is telling not his or her, but your, experience.

You stare at the envelope with your name written in faded ink. The lawyer handed it to you an hour ago after he read your grandfather's will.

And examples of third-person narrative POV are plentiful in books, from Jane Austen's *Pride and Prejudice* to Michael Crichton's *Jurassic Park*. Third person POV can be limited in scope or omniscient, knowing only one characters' thoughts, everyone's thoughts, or somewhere in between. An example follows below from J.K. Rowling's *Harry Potter & the Deathly Hallows* (2007).

Harry's mind wandered a long way from the marquee, back to afternoons spent alone with Ginny in lonely parts of the school grounds.

The key is that a third person narrator is neither telling his or her own thoughts or experiences, nor yours, and, rather, is recounting another, third person's thoughts.

This recap of narrative POV will be useful after the next section, when looking at how narrative and visual POV work together in immersive experiences.

VISUAL POV

In addition to narrative point-of-view, in film and other visual media such as television and video games, there is also visual point-of-view, the POV from which the story is being *seen*. Visual point-of-view can be similarly broken down into the three categories of person: Third Person Objective, First Person, and Second Person, which are next discussed in this order.

Third Person Objective point-of-view is the most common visual point-of-view utilized in film. Movies that use this POV include *Casablanca, Indiana Jones, Star Wars, Wonder Woman*, and most others. When a movie uses third person objective POV, it means that the moviegoer is not a character in the film, no matter how good their Captain America costume or how many lines of *Endgame*'s dialog they're reciting from that second-row aisle seat.

First person visual point-of-view means that the viewer is a character in the film, namely the protagonist in the visual experience. First person POV is incredibly common in video games. Most people are familiar with the concept of "first person shooter" where the player is the one holding the gun and shooting it at the enemies within the game. Even in a 2D world, this engages the player as a character in the story. In film, however, first-person visual point-of-view is rare, though it has been done. The 1947 American film noir *Lady in the Lake* is an adaptation of the 1943 Raymond Chandler first person murder mystery novel by the same name. First-time director Robert Montgomery's ambition was to create a cinematic version of Chandler's Philip Marlowe novels, known for their first-person narrative style. As a result, the entire film is shot from the viewpoint of the central character, with the exception of a couple of moments when the central character addresses the audience directly. Because of this POV, the film was promoted by MGM with the claim that it was the first of its kind. Another example of first person visual POV is when a wedding videographer entreats a guest to, "Say something to the happy couple!" The videographer anticipates that the couple will be watching the video and the intention is for the couple to feel like they're experiencing their wedding day all over again. As a side note, the happy couple watching that wedding video moment was the closest thing to first person visual POV plus first person narrative POV... until virtual reality.

So, if in third person visual point-of-view the viewer *isn't* in the story and in first person visual point-of-view the viewer *is* in the story, what is second person visual point-of-view? It splits the difference: the viewer is straddling the worlds. "You," the viewer, have one foot in the story and one foot outside of it; second person point-of-view acknowledges the medium. In books, second person acknowledges there's a reader: you. In film, it acknowledges there's a viewer: you. Sometimes this is done fantastically, by the character breaking the fourth wall and talking to the audience, sometimes it's done logically with the conceit of a documentary film crew: as is the case in the television show *The Office* and even in the video game *Mario 64,* where the player sees action from the POV of Latiku, a monster and cameraman, while still controlling Mario.

To recap, with third person visual POV, the viewer is outside the story, in first person visual POV, the viewer is inside the story, and with second personal visual POV, the viewer is very aware it is a story.

NARRATIVE AND VISUAL POV TOGETHER IN VIRTUAL REALITY

So, how do narrative and visual point-of-view work in virtual reality? In virtual reality the viewer *becomes* the camera or the player. Figure 2 is representative of that, showing the image from each of two 180 lenses, fashioned as eyes. As a result of the viewer "being" the camera, it is easy to think that POV in VR is as simple as saying that virtual reality is always first person. In the purely visual sense, it is. The virtual reality participant is always having a first person visual experience of the 360 degree space around them in which they are immersed. However, POV is not simply about the viewer's relationship to the space; it is also about the viewer's relationship to the story. Since, at this point in the VR industry most experiences do provide a first person visual perspective (1PPV) on the story, this section will begin with a focus on first person visual perspective and then address some other (at the time of this writing) less common options.

1PPV is employed in VR experiences as diverse as *Beat Saber*, *Notes on Blindness*, *The BizNest* and *The Dinner Party,* all of which will be examined more closely later in this chapter.

One might think that by defining a VR work as 1PPV, most of the heavy lifting regarding POV is done. However, there is more to be resolved. Certainly, the viewer is seeing a story from the first-person perspective, but whose story is it? And, is the viewer (you) learning the narrative from that person or someone else? In other words, what is the narrative point of view? In visual media, there is more than one way to convey narrative. To illustrate the difference between narrative and visual point of view and the importance of being able to distinguish between them, it will be instructive to examine VR experiences with voiceover narration.

Figure 2. A modified, unstitched 360 production image from the set of the world's first immersive sitcom, The BizNest, showing Associate Producer and Stage Manager Rachel Shanblatt, right, hard at work
Source: Exelauno, 2019

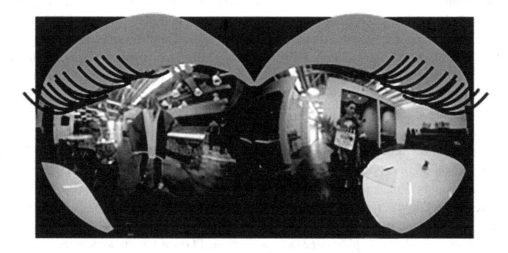

Take for example the above-mentioned immersive virtual reality project *Notes on Blindness*. This VR project premiered at Sundance in 2016, complementing the story world of its eponymous, coordinate feature film (Puschmann, 2016). It is based on author John Hull's sensory and psychological experience of blindness.[1] The voiceover narration that provides the backbone for the *Notes on Blindness* VR experience is Hull's actual audio diary; he is narrating, in the first person, his experience of going blind. He is describing what he is seeing in real time. This gives the experience a first person narrative POV. At the same time, in the VR experience, the viewer is seeing the filmmakers' approximation of what John Hull would have been seeing, recreated with real-time 3D animations. This gives the experience a first-person visual point of view. And, because the visuals match the narration—the viewer is witnessing firsthand what is being described in the first person—the viewer can conclude that the viewer is meant to be John Hull. Such an experience, in which there is first person narrative and first person visuals that "match," is an example of embodied first-person narrative (e1N).

Another immersive experience worth looking at is *52 Places to Go: Iceland*, a 360° travel experience produced by the New York Times.[2] In *52 Places to Go: Iceland*, the viewer is traveling with Jada Yuan, a 52 Places Traveler, and Lucas Peterson, Frugal Traveler. The main narration for the 360 piece is Jada's first-person narration. This gives the experience a first person narrative POV, much like *Notes on Blindness*. However, in contrast to *Notes on Blindness*, in *52 Places to Go: Iceland* the viewer sees the narrator Jada, and not her visual point of view. Because the viewer is seeing Jada, the viewer can conclude that the viewer is not meant to be Jada. While both *52 Places to Go: Iceland* and *Notes on Blindness* have first-person narrative plus first-person visuals, they clearly provide different types of experiences; in one, you are the "main character," in another, you are not. *52 Places to Go: Iceland*, an immersive experience in which the first person narrative and first-person visuals do not match, is a disembodied first-person narrative (d1N).

It is an important point to note that an embodied experience will immerse the viewer in the narrative and a disembodied experience will detach the audience from the moment at hand. An embodied experience will encourage empathy and a disembodied experience will shut down the participant's emotional response and ignite their intellectual response, prompting them to think and question. An embodied experience helps the viewer believe they are living the virtual experience. By contrast, a disembodied experience is Brechtian in its nature. The theatrical practice of Bertolt Brecht—German theatre practitioner, playwright, and poet—embodied his belief that a play should not cause the spectator to identify emotionally with the characters or action but should instead provoke rational self-reflection and a critical view of the action on the stage (Squiers, 2015). He wanted his audiences to adopt a critical perspective and employed techniques that reminded the spectator that the play was a representation of reality and not reality itself, a philosophy that is certainly relevant to VR. This discussion should serve as a reminder that there is no right or wrong way to construct an immersive experience, but rather, there are ways to succeed or fail at achieving one's ultimate objective. Creators should be mindful not only of what decisions they make, but also of why they make them.

As mentioned previously, experiences providing first person visual perspective (1PPV) on the story are quite prevalent. However, there are other options, and it is worth taking a moment to acknowledge some of these and how they might be created. Narrative POV is about the viewer's narrative relationship to the story. And visual POV is about the viewer's visual relationship to the story. As such, it is possible to give the viewer a third-person visual perspective on the story while still having them see the 360 space "first-hand" in VR. As has already been alluded, if the viewer is the protagonist in the VR experience and is controlling their avatar with their real body, the viewer is engaged in a first person narrative experience. If the viewer has first person perspective (1PPV), they would experience an embodied first person narrative; in the virtual world, they might see their hands and arms in front of them, but they could not see their back or the top of their head, etc. However, if there were a virtual camera mounted behind their avatar or body, as in Figure 3, they could then see their back or the top of their head. The viewer could, in such an instance, control their body in the virtual world while at the same time viewing it as an outside observer. These two different experiences are exactly what were created by a team of European researchers. Geoffrey Gorisse, Olivier Christmann, Etienne Armand Amato, and Simon Richir set out to compare the impact and potentialities enabled by first person perspective (1PPV) versus third person perspective (3PPV) in immersive virtual environments. However, virtual environments are not the only place that this sort of out-of-body experience is possible. The following still images from a video by the team at Mepi.pl shows how it's possible to use XR to give someone a third person perspective in the real world (Gorisse, 2017).

Figure 3. This camera mounted in the viewer's backpack with the visual feed going directly into his headset allows the viewer to have a third-person visual perspective on his own real-world first-person experience
Source: Mei.pi. Real World Third Person Perspective VR / AR Experiment, 2014

Thanks to the VR headset being worn by the gentleman in the photo on the left, which is receiving a visual feed from the cameras mounted from his backpack, he is able to view himself in the real world from a third-person visual perspective (3PPV). Accordingly, it is possible to give the viewer a third-person visual perspective on the story while still having them see the 360 space "first-hand" in VR. While it was not necessarily intuitive that this might be done in 360, third person visual POV was clearly a possibility for game-engine built VR games and has indeed been adopted by VR games. Even so, *Lucky's Tale* and *Edge of Nowhere* made waves by opting for third person over first person POV. When *Lucky's Tale* was released by Playful Corp back at Electronic Entertainment Expo (E3) in Los Angeles in 2014 it was a heated topic of discussion on account of its then-uncommon third person POV. The game tells the story of a young fox, Lucky, who sets out to save his friend Pig, when Pig gets taken by a purple tentacle beast with large eyes and an appetite for pork. The player can lean in to see the fox they control, or they sit back to take in the whole level at a distance—in "god mode"—but at no time does the player take Lucky's POV. In *Edge of Nowhere,* Victor Howard is searching for his fiancé, Ava Thorne, who is part of a lost expedition in Antarctica. However, the player controls Victor while seeing Victor, not seeing as Victor. The idea of third person POV VR games has proven to have some staying power. More recently the industry has welcomed *Chronos,* an atmospheric hero's quest Role Playing Game, or RPG, among others.

As for what a second person visual perspective (2PPV) might be in VR, there is still much room for exploration. Since visual POV is about the viewer's visual relationship to the story, one way to achieve second person visual perspective in a fully immersive virtual world is to have the viewer take the visual perspective of a character in the game or story, but not the character they are controlling. To use *Mario 64* as an example, if the level with Latiku the cameraman was turned into a VR game, the player would be seeing the story world as Latiku, from his visual point of view, while controlling Mario.

The narrative and visual points-of-view discussed thus far describe the viewer's narrative and visual relationship to an immersive story. But are those the only types of relationships that a viewer can have with an immersive story? In *Notes on Blindness*, the viewer is a character, John Hull. But that's not the case in *52 Places to Go: Iceland.* What are the options for how the viewer can "be" in the space? That's the next topic of discussion.

EFFECTUAL POINT OF VIEW

The Effectual POV describes the effect the viewer's presence itself has on the scene. In the simplest terms, can the person experiencing an immersive work impact it? If so, to what extent? There are three effectual points of view: non-entity, entity and participant. This section gives a description of each, followed by examples.

As a non-entity, the viewer is an invisible observer. The viewer is present in the scene, but no one and nothing in the scene can tell. The viewer has no impact on the scene and it's as if the viewer is not even there. One example of this is Baobab Studios' *Crow: The Legend,* which takes place in a world where, when Winter comes for the very first time, much-admired Crow is cajoled by his friends into flying to the Heavens to bring back Spring. In this story, the viewer is not Crow. Rather, the viewer is sometimes standing on the ground, sometimes floating in the air, but never looked at. The viewer is not a character; moreover, the viewer is not acknowledged, addressed or given any indication that they exist. Another example of non-entity effectual POV is Felix & Paul's *Traveling While Black,* a 360 video exploring the complicated legacy of the Jim Crow-era travel guide for African-Americans, The Green Book (Freedom du Lac, 2010). Multiple times during this piece, the viewer is seated in a restaurant booth with people, but none of these people ever talks to the viewer or looks at the viewer.

Table 1. A breakdown of the different types of effectual POV and their determining factors

Effectual POV	Detectable in scene?	Has agency?
Non-Entity	No	No
Entity	Yes	No
Participant	Yes	Yes

By contrast, with an entity effectual POV, the viewer is acknowledged and interacted with but has no agency. Characters in the story or scene are aware of the viewer's presence—they see the viewer and they may interact with the viewer. In this way, the viewer has an impact on the scene even though they can't actively make choices that affect it. One example of entity POV is Exelauno's *Human/Art/Object*, in which the viewer gets to experience what it is like to be a work of art in an art gallery. This experience, fimed at bG Gallery in Los Angeles, has been shown at numerous galleries and art shows in the US and, at time of publication, is available free on Exelauno's website www.exelauno.co. In this 360 experience, the viewer, tagged with a gallery label (shown in Figure 4, top), is examined by gallery visitors and clearly feels present in the space as something—in this case a work of art. The viewer-as-art is impacting the scene in the sense that his or her presence influences the behavior of the other people in the scene. Another example of entity is Felix and Paul's *Miyubi*. The viewer in *Miyubi* is cast as a robot that can engage with people. The conceit of the piece is that Miyubi was given as a birthday gift in 1982 to a young boy, Dennis. Early in the piece, the viewer sees the birthday boy looking at him or her. And when Dennis requests that Miyubi say his name, Miyubi does. But the viewer doesn't control if or when he or she speaks or what he or she says as Miyubi; that's all pre-programmed. The viewer doesn't have agency but does have a place within the story world.

The next and highest level of effectual POV is participant. As a participant, the viewer has agency. He or she feels like—and is—somebody or something that can do things. The viewer is no longer just a viewer: he or she can do things that are perceived by or affect the scene. A great example of this is the popular VR game *Beat Saber,* a rhythm game in which the player slashes the beats of adrenaline-pumping music, visually represented as boxes that fly toward the player. The player can use their saber to hit the boxes and, when he or she does, the box goes away, the player's score goes up and, ultimately, the player can win or lose. Other examples include VR games where the player is moving themselves around, opening a door or employing a tool (i.e. paintbrush, weapon, laser pointer). *Tilt Brush,* Google's 3D-painting experience, is another good example of participant effectual POV. The viewer-as-participant isn't affecting a narrative or game but is affecting the space around them and how it is going forward.

Figure 4. Top: The gallery label associated with the viewer in Human/Art/Object. Bottom: Still image from Human/Art/Object of a woman examining the viewer as a work of art
Source: Exelauno, 2019

Anonymous
Human, 2017
Energy, Emotion, Thought, Spirit, Consciousness
167.5 x 119.2 cm

Some interactive VR experiences fall under participant, depending on what the interactivity allows the viewer to affect. If the interactivity affects the scene or story, it would be participant. Hulu's *Door No. 1*, a live-action multiple choice comedy adventure, is an example of an interactive experience with participant effectual POV. In it, the viewer is "Alex", attending his ten-year high school reunion. At various junctures, the viewer gets to choose whether to follow one high-school classmate or another. By contrast, when an XR experience's interactivity allows the viewer to affect things beyond the scene or story, such as the way the viewer experiences the scene, it falls under a different POV tier, which will be explored in the next section.

It is the impact the viewer has on the scene (as summarized in Table 1) that determines an experience's effectual POV, not the mechanism by which they impact the scene. To elaborate on this concept a bit, in addition to the aforementioned tools, as the XR industry advances there will be an increasing number of ways that the viewer-as-participant can have agency. There are currently VR games that respond to the player's heart rate. In *Bring to Light*, a horror title from Red Meat Games, the player's level of fear affects the virtual world. On the more calming side of the spectrum, StoryUP Studios' *Healium* offers data-driven virtual escapes powered by the user's brain and proven to decrease stress and anxiety. Thanks to an electrical-activity-sensing headband and smart watch, the participant can use their brain's positive vibes to hatch butterflies from a chrysalis and their heart rate to illuminate the planets. Hopefully these examples help to illustrate that it is not the way that the player impacts the scene (e.g. using buttons, triggers, brainwaves, heart rate, etc.) but simply the fact that the viewer/player/user is able to impact the story and/or scene that makes an immersive experience participant effectual POV. Because of this, the taxonomy for XR will still hold as the industry evolves and as additional means of influencing XR experiences come to market.

EXPERIENTIAL POINT OF VIEW

Experiential POV describes the impact that the viewer has on how they experience the scene or story. There are three types of experiential POV: robot, mortal and deity. This section gives a description of each, followed by examples.

Table 2. A breakdown of the different types of experiential POV and their determining factors.

Experiential POV	Control Over Degrees of Freedom (DOF)
Robot	Has no control over at least 1 DOF
Mortal	Has control over 1-6 DOF
Deity	Has control over more than 6 DOF

As robot, the viewer's experience is programmed. The viewer can't control it. Included in this designation is any experience where the viewer experiences the sensation of moving but is not actually walking or in or on a vehicle. One example of this experiential POV is Breaking Fourth's *BroBots*, a four-part series available on SamsungVR in which two British robots, Otis and Roberto, arrive in New York and join the NYPD. Another is Secret Location's *The Great C*, in which the viewer follows Clare, a young woman who finds her life upended when her fiancé is summoned for this year's pilgrimage to the all-powerful supercomputer, The Great C. Of the latter, Mike of Virtual Reality Oasis says, "The camera movement itself may be a bit intense for some as you have no control over it" (Virtual Reality Oasis, 2018); that is robot experiential POV, case in point. In both the aforementioned titles, the viewer has an experience much like that of riding on the crane of a crane-shot from traditional cinema: their effectual POV is non-entity and they move through the space seeing the action from the vantage point desired by the director. Many "cinematic" VR experiences fall into the category of robot experiential POV, however, one should be wary of jumping to such conclusions as "cinematic," much like "interactive," can be more broadly descriptive and is not a taxonomic term. Robot experiential POV also includes experiences that exercise control over the viewer's field of view at any given moment in the narrative or experience. A much-talked about concern when it comes to VR filmmaking is that the director doesn't have control over what the viewer is looking at in any given moment. To combat this, Sean Liu, Stanford PhD student and recipient of the Brown Institute for Media Innovation's Magic Grant, is creating *NeverEnding 360*. Her team built a 360-degree video editor that allows authors to specify "visual triggers" which deploy when an important event is approaching in the video and the viewer is looking elsewhere (The Brown Institute for Media Innovation, 2018). *NeverEnding 360* will allow the creator of a project to freeze the VR experience so that it won't continue until the viewer looks where the director wants them to be looking.[3] Any experience that employs *NeverEnding 360* will then have robot experiential POV. To recap, Robot covers any experience with forced perspective or movement. Some Positron chair VR experiences will likely also fall under this experiential POV.[4] As discussed above with regard to effectual POV, an experience's experiential POV is determined by what impact the viewer has on how they experience the scene, not the mechanism by which they are able or unable to control their experience.

With mortal experiential POV, the viewer can control their experience much as they would in real life. An example of an experience with mortal experiential POV is the 2019 Auggie Award Finalist and the world's first 360VR immersive sitcom, *The BizNest* (also described in a dedicated chapter in this book.). Imagine if instead of watching the TV show *The Office* from the couch in their apartment, a viewer could watch it from the desk next to Jim, a fellow employee. That's the experience of *The BizNest*, a workplace comedy that takes place in a co-working space where the viewer is one of the members. The viewer sits at their desk or stands in the hallway, and the other characters in the show engage with them: giving them a sidelong glance, reminding them of an assignment, telling them they have food in their teeth, as pictured in Figure 5. In the mortal experiential POV, the viewer has control over all of the experience's provided Degrees of Freedom (DOF), which may include anywhere from 1-6 DOF.

For those readers who may not be familiar with Degrees of Freedom, each degree is an independently variable factor affecting any of the directions in which independent motion can occur in three-dimensional space. The first three degrees include rotational movement: rolling (head pivots side-to-side), pitching (head tilts along a vertical axis), and yawing (head swivels along a horizontal axis). The next three degrees include rotational and translational movement: elevating (moving up or down), strafing (moving left or right), and surging (moving forwards or backwards). In robot experiential POV, the experience itself may provide some degrees of freedom—the aforementioned examples allow rolling, pitching and yawing—but at least one of them is being controlled by the experience. In mortal experiential POV, the viewer/player has control over all degrees of freedom in the 1-6 DOF range available within the immersive experience. And, as Table 2 summarizes, in deity experiential POV, the viewer/player has control of degrees of freedom beyond the 1-6 DOF range.

Figure 5. Sadie, the viewer's co-worker in Exelauno's immersive sitcom, The BizNest, tells the viewer that they have food in their teeth
Source: Exelauno, 2019

With this knowledge, one can see how a whole range of XR experiences might fall under the mortal experiential POV. To give an example from the world of Augmented Reality, the game *Pokémon Go* (one of the most used and most profitable apps of 2016) uses mortal experiential POV. In it, the player uses their smartphone to reveal the game world overlaid on the real world and then has to locate, capture, battle, and train virtual creatures, called Pokémon. Because the player is navigating through the real world as they navigate the virtual world, they logically have the ability to exercise control over 6 degrees of freedom. Alejandro González Iñárritu's location-based art experience, *Carne y Arena*, also gives the viewer mortal experiential POV, placing them among a group of immigrants who are led by a coyote across the Mexican border into the U.S. until they are stopped by the border patrol.

The viewer having control over any more than six degrees of freedom makes the immersive experience a deity experiential POV. Since the six degrees of freedom cover all the possible independent motions in three-dimensional space, to get more than six degrees of freedom, one needs to be able to move in or through more dimensions. For example, the fourth dimension is time. So, if a VR experience allows the viewer to travel through time, then it is giving the viewer more than six degrees of freedom. Superstring Theory posits that the universe exists in ten dimensions (Williams, 2014). This leaves many future possibilities for what might fall under deity experiential POV. To focus on what might be most relevant, without getting too deep into Superstring Theory, a simple way to think about it is that, as deity, the viewer can experience the world as various people or things, teleport or time travel. It is helpful to provide a few examples of deity experiential POV. *U Turn,* a 360 narrative about what happens when a young female coder joins a male-dominated floundering startup, provides an excellent example of how the viewer can experience the world as various people or things. This award-winning piece, produced by Nathalie Mathe, gives the viewer a choice: in any given moment, simply by turning their head, the viewer can experience the story as a dedicated female coder or as a male tech entrepreneur. This choice won't affect the narrative path or outcome of the story—that's predetermined; it only affects how the viewer experiences the story. Jessica Kantor's *The Dinner Party* provides a useful example of teleportation as a means of providing experiential options. Hers is a gaze-based experience. This means that where the viewer is looking determines the vantage point from which they'll experience the next scene. For example, if the viewer is focused on the hostess of the dinner party, they might be near her in the kitchen for the next scene. If they're focused on her ex-boyfriend, they might be situated near him, in the foyer, for the next scene. Either way, wherever the viewer is situated, the story of that next scene plays out the same. And finally, Flyover Zone Productions' *Rome Reborn* series, particularly *Rome Reborn: The Roman Forum* is a great example of how a viewer can have the experiential option of time travel. In the VR experience, which offers a guided tour of the Roman Forum, the viewer can toggle back and forth between the Roman Forum in ruins, as it is today, and the Roman Forum in its prime, as it was in Ancient Rome.

Figure 6. A menu of immersive POV options
Source: Exelauno, 2019

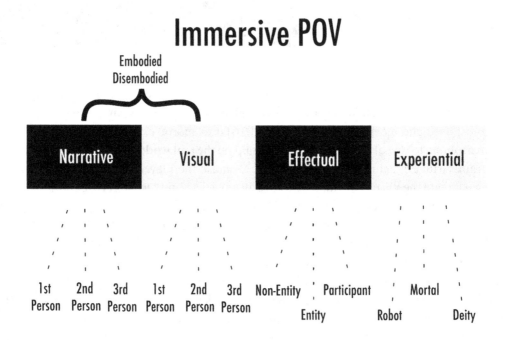

THE FOUR (OR MORE?) POV TIERS

This proposed taxonomy summarized in Figure 6 is a successful marriage of old and new concepts and terms. While there will be an initial learning curve, ultimately, it will greatly simplify and streamline conversations about existing and forthcoming 360 and/or VR content.

This taxonomy should allow for description of any possible XR experience. It also raises some questions. The first two tiers—narrative and visual—as used in relationship to VR seem to correlate to two of the five senses: hearing and sight. That is not entirely accurate. While examples of narrative that utilized voiceover were particularly helpful for showing the contrast between narrative and visual point of view, and while dialog is also a way in which people aurally consume narrative, auditory narrative is by no means the only method to achieve this VR POV. Narrative can be expressed in many other ways, such as by written text, or by physical action, and the list goes on. That leaves visual POV as the only purely sensory POV tier. However, it begs an important question: if there is a POV specifically for what one experiences visually, shouldn't there be a POV specific to each of the five senses? Yes, there should be.

The reason those were not laid out earlier is because use of them is incredibly uncommon and, in some cases, still technically impossible. But this doesn't mean that innovative storytelling using all five senses in a wide variety of ways won't happen in the future. The question, really, is not if, but why. For the right story, the various sensory POVs could prove to be valuable storytelling tools. And the era of XR storytelling has just begun; people are about to be able to tell stories that they could never tell before.

The other potential sensory POVs would include olfactory POV, tactile POV, gustatory POV and auditory POV. Olfactory POV is possible thanks to the innovations being done by folks like Jacquelyn Ford Morie and Simon Niedenthal, who have created scent devices that can pair with VR. First-person olfactory POV would involve a faithful scent map of the virtual scene so that the viewer would experience any smells present in the scene from the appropriate distance and at the appropriate strength. Third-person olfactory POV would be if the viewer smelled something completely unrelated to the scene at hand, like smelling the pungent bird guano of the seaside while inside a kitchen in the mountains where a chef is baking banana bread. And second person olfactory POV would be if the viewer smelled what another character in the scene were smelling; for example, in a scene that takes place in a bedroom, the viewer is looking through the closet—which may have the scent of mothballs—but the viewer doesn't smell mothballs and instead smells the rose that his or her companion in the scene is smelling, from where they're sitting next to the planter in the window box. This pattern of first, second and third person experience can be applied to all of the sensory POVs. In this way, the taxonomy presented here covers a wide range of possible XR experiences, experiences that transcend even what is possible in the real world.

USING THE TAXONOMY TO DESCRIBE 360 AND VR EXPERIENCES

It is certainly instructive to have all four or more POV tiers defined and explained. But how does one use them in practice to describe immersive experiences? This section will put theory into practice, applying the taxonomy for XR to specific pieces of immersive content.

The following abbreviations will allow for concise denotation:

Abbreviations
    1PP = 1st person perspective*
    2PP = 2nd person perspective
    3PP = 3rd person perspective
    e = embodied
    d = disembodied
    1N = 1st person narrative

2N = 2nd person narrative
3N = 3rd person narrative
N = Non-Entity
E = Entity
P = Participant
R = Robot
M = Mortal
D = Deity

If multiple sensory POVs are being used, it will be helpful to follow PP with the first letter of the relevant sensation: V (visual), O (olfactory), T (tactile), G (gustatory), A (auditory)

Examples

U Turn: *U Turn*, as discussed, is a live-action VR series set at a floundering tech startup. The first person visuals are complemented by first person narrative. This narrative is provided not by narration but by characters in the scene. The viewer's character does speak and because the first person narrative matches the first-person visuals, it is clear that *U Turn* is an embodied 1st person narrative. The viewer's character—either the female coder or the male tech entrepreneur—is acknowledged and interacted with, but has no agency, so the effectual POV is entity. However, the viewer does have agency when it comes to how they experience the scene, either as the female coder or the male tech entrepreneur. This is more than any human could do in real life; it is deity experiential POV.

e+1N+E+D = embodied 1st person narrative entity deity

The BizNest: *The BizNest* is a comedy that takes place in a co-working space where you are one of the members, so like *U Turn*, *The BizNest* is also embodied first person narrative entity. However, where *U Turn* allows the viewer to affect how they experience the scene, as a male or female, *The BizNest* aims to ground the viewer more completely in reality, using one scene to fill all 360 degrees and having the viewer's ability to affect how they experience the scene be in keeping with a person's ability to affect how they experience any given moment in life.

e+1N+E+M = embodied 1st person narrative entity mortal

Henry: *Henry* is an Emmy award-winning VR experience by Oculus Story Studio. It's the animated tale of a lonely Hedgehog celebrating his birthday and wishing for more. In this experience, there is voiceover narration, but it is not first person, it's third person. As such, it doesn't match the first person visuals, so the experience is disembodied third person narrative. As the viewer looks around in this experience, it becomes clear that they are not a character of any sort; they are not acknowledged or a part of the story, and they do not affect the scene in any way. The viewer is a non-entity. And, as far as how the viewer can affect their experience of the scene… well, their experience is not programmed—the viewer has the freedom to use one to six degrees of freedom—but they don't have the ability to teleport, travel through time or see the story unfold from the perspective of another character. The viewer's experiential POV is mortal.

d+3N+NE+M = disembodied 3rd person narrative non-entity mortal

Beat Saber: In *Beat Saber*, while there is no voiceover narration or dialog, there is a narrative: the player's progression in the game. How the player fares in the game is connected to their actions; the player's score matches up with what they are seeing and doing. Accordingly, the game experience is embodied first person narrative. Because the player can affect the scene and has agency, their effectual POV is participant. And because they can affect their experience of the scene using only 1-6 Degrees of Freedom, their experiential POV is mortal.

e+1N+P+M = embodied 1st person narrative participant mortal

The Dinner Party: In this 360 dramatic comedy short about a young woman throwing a dinner party to raise funds for her new company, the viewer is not a character. As such, *The Dinner Party* presents a third person narrative that the viewer witnesses first-hand—1PP visual, the default option—offering a third person disembodied narrative experience. Not only is the viewer not a character, their presence is never acknowledged, and they are unable to be seen by the characters in the story, so the effectual point of view is non-entity. However, the viewer does have some control over how they experience the story. Thanks to gaze-based technology built with game-engine based VR creator tools, where the viewer looks determines what vantage point they will view the next scene from. As a result, the viewer's effectual POV is deity.

d+3N+N+D = disembodied 3rd person narrative non-entity deity

Pokémon Go: In this popular AR experience, the viewer/player has a first person visual perspective and is experiencing the story world first-hand. They also have agency; the player can throw Poke Balls, catch Pokémon, battle other Trainers and more. In keeping with the fact that, as this game is actually Augmented Reality, or AR, it is played with the visuals overlaid on the physical world, the player cannot affect how they experience the game; they have a mortal experiential POV.

e+1N+P+M = embodied 1st person narrative participant mortal

Chronos: Gunfire Games' VR action roleplaying game has the player exist outside of the character he or she is controlling. As a result, it is a disembodied third person narrative experience. Because the player has agency, it is participant effectual POV. One interesting twist that *Chronos* has is that every time the player dies, they come back a year older. This aging actually shows up on the player's character as graying hairs and a wrinkling face. Because the player seemingly defies the rules of the real world by coming back from death and suddenly being and looking a year older when less than a year has passed, it is tempting to wonder if the experiential POV is deity. However, it is worth remembering that experiential POV is determined by the degree to which the player can control how they experience the scene. The player isn't controlling their aging. They are forcibly moved forward in time and they cannot move backward in time. Because the player has no agency as to how they experience time, the experiential POV is not deity. Rather, because they can affect their experience of the scene, but only using 1-6 degrees of freedom, the experiential POV is mortal.

d+3N+P+M = disembodied 3rd person narrative participant mortal

The Blu (Dreamscape Immersive): *The Blu* is one of the three social, location-based "adventures" with which Dreamscape, a VR experience company, launched. In *The Blu*, the viewer is one of several divers that plunges into the depths of the ocean on a mission to help reunite a family of whales. Wearing a virtual diver's suit and an actual haptic backpack, the viewer has an AquaScooter at his or her disposal to maneuver through the depths of the sea. Because the viewer is a character in the space and what they see is—and matches—their story, it is an embodied first person narrative experience. As hinted at by the mention that you have an AquaScooter, the viewer's character has agency. Another example of the viewer's agency that won't end up being a story spoiler is that if the viewer chooses to poke at any of the sea anemones in the underwater scene, the anemones will react to that touch and close up. The viewer does not, however, have the ability to affect their own experience of the story or scene by more than 6 degrees of freedom.

e+1N+P+M = embodied 1st person narrative participant mortal

Door No. 1: In Hulu's interactive comedy, the viewer is "Alex," who has returned to his high school for a reunion. As such, the 1st person narrative experience matches the visuals, making this an embodied first person narrative. The viewer is a character and, on top of that, has the agency to decide which of two paths he wants to take at various moments throughout the experience, making the viewer a participant. These decisions affect the story, but not the way the viewer experiences the story; the viewer experiences the story as a human would, in keeping with the laws of physics. As such, the experiential POV is mortal.

e+1N+P+M = embodied 1st person narrative participant mortal

Healium: Butterflies: Using a brain-wave-sensing headband, StoryUP Studios' VR experience and AR app encourages the viewer to think happy thoughts and rewards them by hatching virtual butterflies when the viewer successfully recalls a time when they felt love, joy or appreciation. The viewer is having a first-hand experience of the butterflies hatching and their visual experience matches the narrative of their brain-wave activity. The viewer's brain waves have an impact on the narrative of the scene—butterflies hatching or not hatching—so the viewer has agency. And the viewer can only affect how they experience the scene using 1-3 degrees of freedom, so the experiential POV is mortal.

e+1N+P+M = embodied 1st person narrative participant mortal

CONCLUSION

This taxonomy of immersive POV and story experience doesn't change what can be possible in VR. There's nothing that people can talk about by using this taxonomy that they couldn't talk about without it. However, using it provides several advantages. Without the taxonomy, it might take up to ten minutes or more to describe the functionality and POV of a VR experience; with this taxonomy, as seen in the above examples, that description shrinks down to five words and takes less than one minute. The advantages of this are multiple: it saves time, it gets everyone on the same page, and it promotes clarity of vision and of comprehension, making it easier for developers to move forward and for buyers to make decisions. It also gives VR creators a clear framework in which to think about what's possible in VR, as it provides a menu of options, a visible toolkit. Having these tools visible enables a creator to better make informed decisions, choosing a certain POV for the desired effect that it has on the viewer or player, rather than because it's the option that came to mind first or one of the few options that occurred to them. The common language provided by this taxonomy also facilitates critical literature and community, increasing transparency of ideas and the ability to communicate widely about the medium.

VR doesn't just allow us to look at the world in a new way, it allows us to look at the world in many new ways. And, in order to explore, discuss, recount, critique, develop and promote virtual reality successfully, we need to be able to communicate clearly about the various points of view that virtual reality gives us. This taxonomy facilitates that collective conversation.

REFERENCES

Bal, M. (1997). *Narratology: Introduction to the Theory of Narrative*. Toronto, Canada: University of Toronto Press.

Brown Institute for Media Innovation. (2018). *NeverEnding 360*. Retrieved from https://brown.columbia.edu/portfolio/neverending-360/

Cline, E. (2012). *Ready Player One: A Novel*. New York: Broadway Books.

Freedom du Lac, J. (2010). Guidebook that aided black travelers during segregation reveals vastly different D.C. *Washington Post*. Retrieved from http://www.washingtonpost.com/wp-dyn/content/article/2010/09/11/AR2010091105358.html

Genette, G. (1983). *Narrative Discourse: An Essay in Method*. Ithaca, NY: Cornell University Press.

Gorisse, G., Christmann, O., Amato, E., & Richir, S. (2017). First-and third-person perspectives in immersive virtual environments: Presence and performance analysis of embodied users. *Frontiers in Robotics and AI, 4*(33).

Guarino, B. (2016). Edge of Nowhere, Lucky's Tale, and the case for third person VR. *Inverse*. Retrieved from https://www.inverse.com/article/9996-edge-of-nowhere-lucky-s-tale-and-the-case-for-third-person-vr

Hayden, S. (2016). 'Sequenced' creates truly reactive storytelling in VR. *Road to VR*. Retrieved from https://www.roadtovr.com/vr-animated-series-sequenced-creates-truly-reactive-storytelling-vr/

Joyce, K. (2017). Review: Lucky's Tale: Playful Corp.'s Lucky's Tale defines what it means to be a platform videogame in VR. *VR Focus*. Retrieved from https://www.vrfocus.com/2016/03/review-luckys-tale/

mei.pi [Username]. (2014, June 25). *Real World Third Person Perspective VR/AR Experiment* [Video file]. Retrieved from https://www.youtube.com/watch?v=RgBeRP4dUGo

Miller, L. (2018). Hulu tests whether VR can be funny with new interactive 360 experience 'Door No. 1.' *IndieWire*. Retrieved from https://www.indiewire.com/2018/05/hulu-door-no-1-interactive-video-nora-kirkpatrick-1201968459/

Montgomery, R. A. (2011). *The Trail of Lost Time*. Chooseco, LLC.

Puschmann, M. (2016). Notes on Blindness, a virtual reality journey into the world of blindness. *The Drum*. Retrieved from https://www.thedrum.com/news/2016/10/21/notes-blindness-virtual-reality-journey-the-world-blindness

Rowling, J. K. (2007). *Harry Potter and the Deathly Hallows*. Bloomsbury.

Squiers, A. (2015). A Critical Response to Heidi M. Silcox's 'What's Wrong with Alienation?'. *Philosophy and Literature*, *39*(1), 243–247. doi:10.1353/phl.2015.0016

Sundance Institute. (2016). Notes on Blindness. *Sundance Institute Projects*. Retrieved from https://www.sundance.org/projects/notes-on-blindness

Tarrant, J., Viczko, J., & Cope, C. (2018). Virtual reality for anxiety reduction demonstrated by quantitative EEG: A pilot study. *Frontiers in Psychology*, *9*(1280). PMID:30087642

Turner, N. K. (2017). Virtual Reality + Digitizing Scent with Simon Niedenthal and Jacki Morie. *Art and Cake*. Retrieved from https://artandcakela.com/2017/07/18/virtual-reality-digitizing-scent-with-simon-niedenthal-and-jacki-morie/

Virtual Reality Oasis [Username]. (2018, October 11). *The Great C: The first 5 minutes of this cinematic virtual reality movie* [Video File]. Retrieved from https://youtu.be/lwL9FpnSlrk

Williams, M. (2014). A Universe of 10 Dimensions. *Universe Today*. Retrieved from https://phys.org/news/2014-12-universe-dimensions.html

ENDNOTES

[1] As of the date of publication of this book, according to the film's website, http://www.notesonblindness.co.uk, the *Notes on Blindness* VR experience is available for free on Samsung Gear.

[2] As of the date of publication of this book, *52 Places to Go: Iceland* is available for free on the TimesVideo website and also on the NYTimes 360 app.

[3] Author's discussion with Sean Liu on May 17, 2019.

[4] Positron is a company that makes chairs designed specifically for fully immersive cinematic VR that move in tandem with the VR content.

This research was previously published in the Handbook of Research on the Global Impacts and Roles of Immersive Media; pages 264-283, copyright year 2020 by Information Science Reference (an imprint of IGI Global).

Chapter 30
INSIDE:
Using a Cubic Multisensory Controller for Interaction With a Mixed Reality Environment

Ioannis Giannios
Hellenic Open University, Greece

Dimitrios G. Margounakis
https://orcid.org/0000-0002-7598-0934
Hellenic Open University, Greece

ABSTRACT

The field of electronic games is a great experimental area that contributes to the implementation of new technologies in a variety of applications. This article explores the field of mixed reality through the use of physical computing for the development of the electronic game Inside. In such an interactive environment, the physical and the virtual worlds coexist and interact with each other. A user can alter the virtual world's characteristics through a special controller designed for the game that contains electronic components that can sense real-world properties. The attention of the user is not focused only on the screen but also on the controller through which a two-way interaction is achieved. A virtual environment created by a game engine can receive messages from the controller and vice versa. Changes on the properties of the virtual world can be communicated to the controller aiming at the alteration of the characteristics of the physical world. As a result, the user experiences an immersion in an environment in which real and virtual objects coexist.

INTRODUCTION

Technology increasingly assists the creation of new environments by achieving distortion, strengthening or replacement of reality. The real or physical world which we live in consists of physical objects that we can feel with all our senses. Through technology, our senses can be augmented offering the oppor-

DOI: 10.4018/978-1-6684-7597-3.ch030

tunities to experience new environments. In a different reality, it is not mandatory for all our senses to participate. However, the more of them participate the easier it becomes for the user to experience the illusion of immersion, that is, the feeling of experiencing something real rather than something unreal (O' Sullivan & Igoe, 2004). Human sight is the sense that can mostly be augmented since what we can perceive is what we define as real (Welch, 1978).

The term of virtual reality is often mistaken for environments not fully generated by a computer so the boundaries between different categories of such environments are somewhat blurred. Mixed reality combines knowledge from a wide variety of disciplines, like computer vision, signal processing, graphics, user interfaces and sensors (Costanza et al., 2009). Experiences that do not fully fit into the real or virtual world transform existing technologies, relationships and locations into a game platform, by expanding their structure mixing it with daily experiences (Bonsignore et al., 2012).

The aim of the game *Inside* is to familiarize the user with a mixed reality environment through a tangible interface where the input devices play the central role and the screen is a window to the virtual world. Unlike most mixed reality applications, the human sight is the one that we try to displace in an attempt to give users an illusion that blends the real and the virtual without the need to augment their sight. Gestures and physical world actions are mixed and affect the progress of the game and vice versa. That is, conditions and actions in the virtual world can affect the physical world. A special cubic multisensory controller is designed, and its purpose is to make the user immerse between the physical and the synthetic world exceeding ordinary gameplay.

BACKGROUND

Mixed Reality

Milgram and Kishino (1994) presented the *Virtuality Continuum*, an attempt to categorize the multiple reality genres. On the one end of the continuum there is the real environment and on the other there is the virtual environment. *Mixed Reality* consists of all the reality categories between the opposites of this continuum. *Augmented Reality* is closer to the end of the real environment and *Augmented Virtuality* is closer to that of the virtual environment. This concept is illustrated in Figure 1.

Figure 1. The Virtuality Continuum (Milgram & Kishino, 1994)

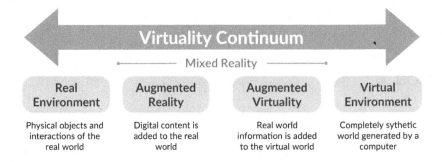

Although this notion, which stems from the beginning of the 90s, is the most popular on how to define a mixed reality environment, it is not widely accepted because it is mostly focused on visual displays. Other aspects of reality can be simulated in a virtual environment like audio, motion, haptics, taste/flavor and smell (Speicher et al., 2019). Mixed reality experiences can extend beyond visual domain (Hughes et al., 2005) but the central idea remains the blend and alignment of digital and physical objects. Therefore, a mixed reality environment can be defined as an experience that is not fully contained by virtual or physical worlds (Bonsignore et al., 2012).

A mixed reality environment is a mixture of the real and the virtual in which the two worlds coexist. Augmented reality and augmented virtuality are subcategories of mixed reality, which include all these environments in which both the virtual and the real world more or less participate. Thus, the user is not fully cut off from the real world, and sounds, video, graphics, haptics and spatial data are put together serving the ultimate goal of altering the real world into a new and enhanced experience (Glover, 2018).

In this kind of environments, the characteristics of the user's reality interfaces are usually fully exploited by including types of interaction that we encounter in the real world, such as movements, gestures and speech that do not require any kind of instruction to the user (Coulton et al., 2006). The main means of interaction with the graphic elements of a system's interface are the user's hands through which the appropriate physical actions are translated by the device as commands. The user gives these commands to the system through an interface, such as a keyboard, a mouse, a touch screen or a trackpad. Touch screens are considered to be a significant leap when it comes to humans and computers interacting since a user's actions bear more physical importance as they touch the object of interest instead of pointing at it. If we add haptics when the user operates a system, then there is no significant difference with operating a real mechanical device. Interfaces in which physical objects play a central role as both physical representations and controls for digital information are called *tangible interfaces* (Ullmer & Ishii, 2000).

The screen plays a dominant role in human-computer interaction whether is placed on a desk, held in one's hand, worn on one's head or embedded in the physical environment. Many researchers define the augmented - and therefore also the mixed reality systems - in a way that requires the use of a head-mounted display (HMD) to achieve the full immersion of the user. In an attempt to define these systems in a way that is not limited to particular technologies, like HMDs, Azuma (1997) proposed the three following characteristics.

A mixed reality system should:

- Combine the real with the virtual
- Be interactive in real time
- Take place in three dimensions

Mixed Reality Applications

A variety of applications, which are compatible with mixed reality platforms, keep on launching. Such mixed reality systems are more affordable than ever, and everyone can enjoy them in the comfort of their own home. The majority of contemporary smartphones and tablets, as well as devices like Microsoft Kinect, Nintendo Wii, Google Daydream View, Microsoft HoloLens and Oculus Rift are only a small sample of those which support mixed reality games. Most devices are mainly HMDs (optical see-through or video see-through) or systems which connect to a monitor (usually a television set) and take advantage of data like user gestures, spatial data, posture, and speech. The games of these devices make extensive use of various techniques, like computer vision, depth information, and video detection and thus the alignment of real and virtual objects is of major importance (Gimeno et al., 2011). Real-time requirements of these systems are the cause of the gravest errors, such as the complete misalignment of different objects or misalignment between the user and their environment after a signal delay (Wursthorn et al., 2018).

An example of a mixed reality game demonstrating a tangible interface is *Scorpiodrome*. In this game, physical objects like remote controlled toy vehicles, control interactive virtual entities on a projected on a surface terrain. The vehicles go on a quest of virtual diamonds and synthetic creatures can affect the way they operate. (Metaxas et al., 2005)

Another example is the *Virtual Chemistry Lab* which suggests a method for improving teaching and implementing chemical experiments the safest way. Students can simulate a chemical experiment in a virtual lab, interacting with virtual objects, which they can see using HMDs and handle with the aid of hand controllers. (Duan et al., 2020)

In 2005, Sandor et al., presented an immersive mixed reality configuration that allows a user to reconfigure a running hybrid user interface, where information can be distributed over a variety of different, but complementary, displays. The user interacts with physical input devices and 3D objects drawn on several desktop displays. Then, a manual input device can be associated with a 3D object and the user can transform the object through it. Using an HMD the user can see the link between the displayed on the desktop monitors 3D objects and the input device, by a line that connects the two parts.

CETA is a mixed reality system with tangible interaction for school-aged children that was designed to enhance mathematical learning. The game is composed by a tablet, a mirror, a holder and a set of wooden blocks and the aim is to help a robot collect some screws. Using the blocks on the table, a child must compose a number that matches the distance between the screw and the robot, as displayed on the screen of the tablet. The system detects through the mirror and the tablet's camera the actions of the child, and once they succeed, the virtual robot collects the screw. (Marichal et al., 2017)

Nevertheless, the majority of relevant projects recommend the use of a head unit or that the screen be put in a central point. Our approach differentiates from the rest of the similar games by including a specially designed controller to support the developed game. Both the controller and the game create a mixed reality environment that interacts with the user bidirectionally.

Physical Computing

Physical computing describes the discussion between the physical and the virtual world, the conversion of one source of energy to another in the form of devices that interact with their environment through sensors (O'Sullivan & Igoe, 2004). Physical computing platforms, like *Arduino*, aim at facilitating the creation of electronic circuits and programming without requiring any prior knowledge or experience by the user (Booth et al., 2016).

These projects are usually divided into three parts: input, processing and output. Activities (input and output) can be either digital or analog. The digital ones are those that can be in two conditions (e.g. on/off) but the analog ones can bear a range of values (e.g. temperature).

Physical computing platforms consist of a microcontroller and various energy transformers. The microcontroller, which is a very simple computer, is an expert on receiving information from the sensors, manipulating basic machines and sending information to other devices. Its main use is to operate a device by using a predefined code, stored in its ROM memory that cannot be modified during its operation. (Ayala, 2005).

The energy transformers are connected to the microcontroller and can be sensors of various types that can help us detect or create changes in the characteristics of the physical world. For example, IR sensors and ultrasonic sensors can be used to sense location, while potentiometers, accelerometers and gyroscopes can be used to sense rotation, and DC motors and solenoids can be used to create motion. Haptic techniques can be implemented by force-sensitive resistors or flex sensors. A thermistor can sense temperature changes and a photoresistor can sense a change on the levels of brightness. Hybrid systems can take advantage of multiple sensors combining detection techniques in order to avoid errors or get more accurate data.

Arduino was chosen among other physical computing platforms, such as *Parallax Basic Stamp*, *MIT's Handyboard* or *Raspberry Pi*, due to its popularity in creating interactive applications that target novice users. Additionally, Arduino is highly acknowledged in the development of *internet of things* devices and is one of the most successful educational tools in S.T.E.M. (Science, Technology, Engineering and Mathematics).

A user can develop code or *sketches* and upload it to the Arduino board. Each sketch is divided into two key parts: the *setup* section, which is the initialization of the project and runs once when the device starts, and the *loop* section, which provides all the information about the project functionality and it is constantly repeated.

GAME CONCEPT DESIGN

Inside is a puzzle game in which the user must lead a white sphere to a specific location of the virtual world. This finishing point is of a different color on each level. In order to have a successful outcome, the user must guide and color the sphere to signal the completion of the level. Each level is of escalating difficulty and complexity which is signified with the combination of colors and the path the sphere must follow to reach the finish line. Figure 2 shows the 1ˢᵗ level's white finishing point and the sphere heading to it, as pointed by arrows. The sphere can get or change its color on specific points of the virtual world at which it undergoes a super-exposure to a light of the tint in which it will be painted. The users are called on to explore these points themselves, while shedding light on holes at the exterior of the controller. The location and the color of the finishing point will not be provided at the beginning of each level, meaning that the user needs to experiment with different colors until they successfully color the sphere with the finish point color of each level. Once this happens, the finish point indicated by a bright colored spotlight in the virtual world, becomes visible. The possible colors are the primary ones: red, green and blue, while combinations of these can produce even more colors at levels of greater difficulty.

While most mixed reality games focus the user's attention on the screen, whether it is an HMD or a mobile device, the presented approach stands on a different basis. The computer screen located nearby is just the window to the virtual world and not the focal point in the evolution of the game. Through the screen, the user can observe what is happening on the virtual world, without interacting with it. The whole interaction between the user and the virtual environment is implemented through a controller/ box, especially designed for this game. The virtual world is shaped to give the user the impression that it is enclosed in the box object that they examine with their hands. The cubic controller functions using natural gestures by the user that provoke expected virtual world reactions. At the same time, the user can observe the result of their actions taking place inside the box through the screen.

Figure 2. Screenshot of the Inside's 1ˢᵗ level

The total control of the game is achieved exclusively through the controller so that the user can experience the illusion that the game is unfolding in the box, the inside of which can be monitored through the screen.

In order to achieve the desired functionality and user experience, the requirements we have taken into account regarding the design of the game and the controller were the following:

- The virtual world should be of a similar environment to the interior of the controller. A cubic shape was chosen.
- The complete control of the game should be done exclusively by the controller. The user must not be distracted by using keyboards or other peripherals.
- The controller must support user gestures corresponding to the functionality of the game.
- The material of the controller must be hard and sturdy.
- The user must interact with the virtual world in a bidirectional way in order for the feeling of immersion between the two worlds to be enhanced.

IMPLEMENTATION

Arduino (Assembly and Programming)

The elements that were used for the physical part of the game were: an Arduino UNO (rev.3) edition board and basic electronic components. More specifically:

- 4 Photoresistors that can sense the amount and brightness of light on their surface.
- A tilt sensor that can tell whether its position is in normal or upside-down state.
- A piezoelectric sensor that can catch a vibration, like a user's knock.
- A thermistor that can measure temperature on its body.
- A solenoid that can produce a movement of a metal bar.

Cables, resistors, diodes and more electronic parts were used to connect the elements together and create the circuit. In addition, two touch sensors were implemented, using Paul Badger's *CapacitiveSensor* library available for use in Arduino (Badger, 2020). To keep things tidy, a breadboard was used, that is a board that allows the connection of separate parts and cables and helps avoid an overcrowding of cables. The microcontroller and the rest of the electronic parts that were combined are presented in Figure 3.

Figure 3. Arduino board, breadboard and electronic parts combined

The code developed and uploaded to Arduino includes declarations of the variables and the constants, the inputs and the outputs of the board as well as their respective methods, the readings of the sensors connected to the digital or analog pins of the board, and finally the serial communication commands to send and receive messages, between the Arduino and a computer.

The four photoresistors are initialized in the setup section of the Arduino code, in which for each sensor a total amount of 10 values are collected and their average is calculated and considered to be the ambient light value. Based on this value, a threshold is calculated and indicates when a photoresistor receives light from the user or not. When a read value exceeds the threshold, a respective message is sent to the computer to alert of the existence of light.

The value of the tilt sensor is read repeatedly on the loop section of the code to determine if the box is placed in a normal or an upside-down position. Any change in the status of the tilt sensor triggers a message through the serial to update the system of the new condition.

The piezo records the values of vibrations and when the system detects a value over the piezo threshold, the corresponding message is sent to inform the system.

The thermistor calculates the ambient temperature and a threshold is set on the setup section of the code uploaded to the board. This threshold indicates if the user affects the temperature sensor through their actions (rubbing or breathing on it). In case of a rise in temperature above the threshold, a message is sent to the computer to alert for special functionality on the game.

The touch sensor can detect the change of the electrical load and thus the human touch, since the human body carries electricity. After the implementation of these sensors, a human touch can be detected when someone touches the bare wire of the circuit. This wire can be hidden behind solid surfaces, even of non-conductive materials, like plastic or wood, while its sensitivity can be increased using conductive materials, e.g. aluminium foil (Fitzgerald & Shiloh, 2012). The values of the touch sensors are read during the execution of the program (loop section) to check if a value exceeds the threshold, meaning that the user is touching it.

Finally, the program reads the messages that the computer may have sent through the serial to Arduino, in order to perform suitable actions, such as the electrification of the solenoid in order to perform a knock on the wooden box whenever the virtual sphere hits with a floor.

Unity (Game Development)

Unity is a game engine platform for Mac and Windows that was created in 2005. The program is responsible for collecting all the pieces of the game's scenes, graphics and algorithms.

The initial design on Unity included a basic and simple form of a game level. In other words, a pilot was used to check the connectivity between the Arduino and a computer and achieve the functionality of the game objects. Thus, a virtual 3D environment that resembles the interior of the box/controller was designed, as shown in Figure 4. Afterwards, the necessary game objects were created and filled the interior of this virtual box, such as walls, floors, the player's character and spotlights. Each of these objects has its own properties and extra functionality can be given through scripts that are attached on them. These scripts can control the objects via code and have a similar structure with the Arduino sketches, including a Start() section that plays the part of the initialization of the object, and an Update() section that repeatedly executes the included code and controls the functions of the object.

Figure 4. Creating a game level on Unity

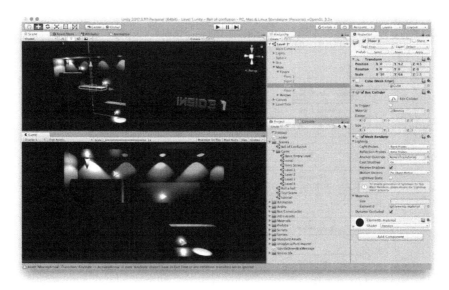

Through the scripts and properties of each object, a virtual world was created with a sphere as the player's main character. This object obeys the laws of physics.

In this way, an autonomous electronic game was created that can be controlled through the keyboard. The ultimate goal is that the interaction between the user and the game takes place exclusively through the cubic controller that will send the respective commands for every action to Unity. Thus, each message sent from Arduino to Unity will be assigned to a particular key on the keyboard and the game will get full functionality via the designed controller.

The framework of the system is illustrated in Figure 5, which explains the interaction between the controller and the game.

Additional 3d objects were designed to serve as guiding support to the user. Objects like blinking arrows can appear in certain locations of the virtual environment. They provide the user with useful information in order to solve the puzzle. These hints may relate to the control of the sphere and the possible actions the users should perform, such as moving the sphere, flipping the box or illuminating a hole with the flashlight.

The finishing point consists of a bright spot on the floor, generated by a spotlight, at a different location at each level. Figure 6 shows a screenshot in which the color of the sphere gets red and an arrow indicates where the sphere should go next.

Animations were created for the game objects to fulfil aesthetic demands. More specifically, guiding arrows flicker as they move towards the pointed direction, while light gradually floods the inside of the box when a user sheds light through a hole and the sphere gets a new hue through an animation that gradually changes its color. Other than offering aesthetic value, animations also may link to events that trigger specific actions, such as a script execution or a change in an object's properties. For instance, after the successful completion of a level, an animation is activated, at the end of which an event will trigger the next level to load.

Figure 5. Block diagram of the proposed framework that shows the interaction between the real and the virtual environment

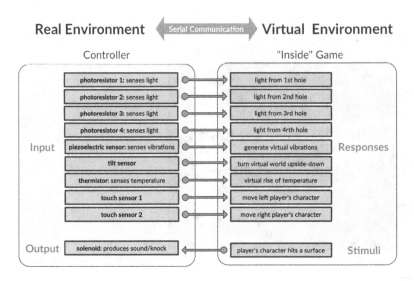

Figure 6. Screenshot of a game level where the main character is painted red and the finish point is prevalent

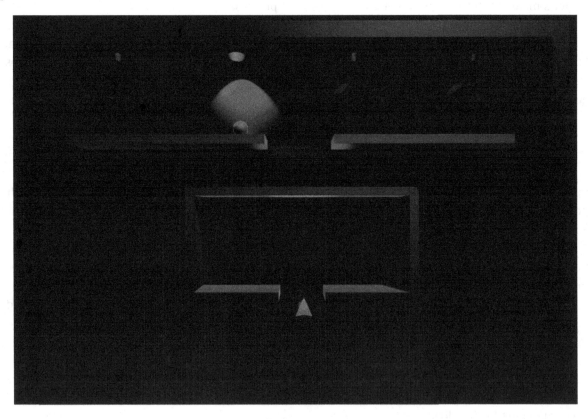

A menu consisting of three-dimensional words and lighting elements has been designed. The aforementioned objects were placed on a scene to create a central display via which the users can choose the desirable action, as shown in Figure 7. Messages that appear on screen instruct the user how to control the menu. So, as soon as the user touches the controller on the left (or right), they can choose an action (play game or exit), while using both hands they can execute the desirable action (enter).

Figure 7. Main menu of the game

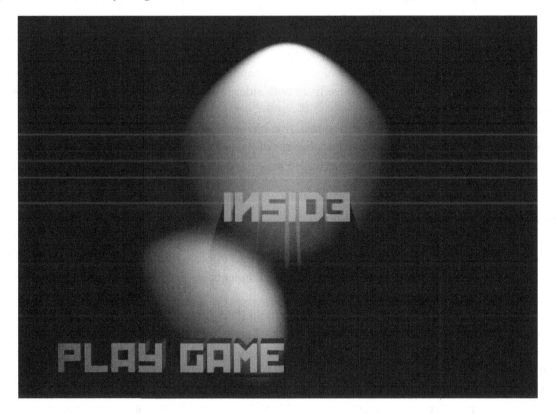

Through the gameplay, the user is gradually instructed on how to use the possible gestures as the game progresses. For example, the first level involves as few gestures as possible and then more are added on the next levels. The fact that the physical box/controller has characteristics of the virtual box (like the material, the shape or the position of the holes), makes the instruction of the gestures even easier for the user. The ultimate goal is to give the user the opportunity to act intuitively, while being guided by virtual messages, hints and indications.

Arduino – Unity Interface

Arduino and Unity are connected via a USB cable and the exchange of messages is possible through serial communication. One side sends a message and the other side recognizes it, reads it and performs the respective actions, depending on the content of the message. Scripts that were written for both Arduino and Unity contain all the relevant commands that make this serial communication possible.

On the Arduino, commands on the board's uploaded code open the serial communication and every message sent to Unity is executed via this serial. Similarly, if a message is received through serial, it will be read by Arduino. At every loop section cycle, there is a reading of the values of all sensors. To ensure proper functionality and avoid overflooding, the system was designed in such a way to send as many messages as necessary. Thus, duplicate messages that repeat the same values or the same piece of information are avoided. Instead, only when the system detects a change on the values of a sensor that can affect the virtual world, will it send a message that bears this information. For example, if a user touches a capacity surface, the values of the touch sensor will be above threshold, which means that a corresponding message will be sent towards Unity to inform that the user is touching the specific sensor. During this touch and while the sensor's values are above threshold, no more messages will be sent. Only when the user removes their hand and the value drops below threshold, will a corresponding message be sent. This way, the exchange of messages happens only when there is a change in the conditions thus achieving immediate response from both sides, avoiding delays due to serial overflooding because of multiple messages.

Respectively, in Unity the serial communication channel opens through a script which is responsible for sending any message regarding the changes of the game in the virtual world. Messages sent by Arduino and received by Unity through serial are processed and read so as to respond and modify the progress of the game.

Prototype (Controller Assembly)

The controller box was constructed by wooden surfaces for convenience reasons. These surfaces were joined together, creating a cube, in which all electronic elements were placed, such as the Arduino board, the breadboard, sensors, and wiring.

Four holes, which are the points where the user should shed light to illuminate the inner virtual world, were created on the top side of the box. Photoresistors were placed inside and within close proximity to the holes trying to avoid the direct exposure of ambient light but also to be able to measure any change in the brightness in case the user sheds light into the hole. In order to avoid noise on the values due to the proximity of the photoresistors with each other, each of them was isolated from the rest using plastic caps.

Two holes were created on opposite sides of the box through which the cables from the touch sensors found passage to the exterior of the box. Additional wooden pieces were coated with *velostat* - a conductive material similar to plastic - and were placed over the holes. The conductive material was properly placed in such a way to be in contact with the bare wires of the touch sensors and its aim is to increase the touch surface available to the user. As a result, when the user touches any of the two sides of the box, the Arduino board can sense this touch and send a message to the computer bearing this information.

The rest of the electronic elements were placed and secured inside the box so as to remain stable. The solenoid was placed in such a way that each time it receives electrical charge it causes a knock in the inner body of the box. As the virtual sphere hits the virtual floor this knock creates a vibration and a sound, which is perceived by the user and consequently creates an opposite interaction from the controller to the user. The placement of the electronics inside the box is shown in Figure 8.

Figure 8. The electronics inside the box-controller

The implementation of the circuit and the construction of the controller allows the following possible user gestures:

- **Touch gestures:** Touching the left or the right side of the box causes the movement of the virtual sphere to the left or to the right respectively. Simultaneous touch of both sides (left and right) can cause specific function (enter).
- **Flipping of the box:** This move enables the user to turn the virtual world upside down.
- **Lighting:** With a flashlight at their disposal, the user can illuminate specific holes on the box. Shedding light at each hole creates a different virtual glimmer of light inside the box. Each hole represents a different color of light, for example the first hole produces white light, the second one red, the third one blue and the fourth one green. These holes on the physical box are at the same spot as the ones of the box in the virtual world in order to avoid confusion.
- **Vibrations / knocks:** The user can produce virtual vibrations by knocking on the exterior of the box, affecting the virtual environment. For example, when the user knocks on the box, the sphere jumps.
- **Temperature change:** The user can blow air or rub their fingers on a specific spot on the box to bring about change to the temperature. When the thermistor inside the box senses a rise on the temperature, specific actions can take place in the virtual environment, like the melting of ice.

All the above suggest actions that can enable the user to interact with the virtual environment. But interaction is also bidirectional, i.e. from the virtual world towards the user and the real world, though the controller.

Possible feedback on the system by the user is:

- **Solenoid's knock:** A solenoid located inside of the box creates a sound and a vibration when the virtual sphere hits a surface.

The implementation of the above reverse interaction was of great importance and pushes the user to greater immersion in the mix of the two worlds since a player gets used to interacting with a virtual world but not getting feedback from it.

The final form of the controller is presented in Figure 9.

Figure 9. The controller of the game

EVALUATION

A primary evaluation to review the usability and the user experience of the proposed game and prototype has been executed in order to obtain useful data and initial feedback.

For the purpose of this user study, the System Usability Scale (SUS) questionnaire has been used and distributed to the participants. This questionnaire is considered to be one of the most effective questionnaires in terms of validity and reliability of the results produced (Brooke, 1996). The main reasons of the growing popularity of the SUS questionnaire in recent years are:

- The cost of it, since it is free of charge.
- Its validity that has been established in a series of studies in both conventional software and websites, as well as other devices such as mobile phones etc.
- It produces the same or more reliable results compared to other questionnaires even with a small number of participants (Tullis & Stetson, 2004).

SUS questionnaire contains ten simple questions and the participants were asked to reflect to their answers their user experience and kind of immersion between the real and the virtual. The complete list of the questions and the structure of the SUS questionnaire can be referred to the relevant literature (Brooke, 1996). Additionally, after filling the questionnaire, each participant was interviewed in order for qualitative feedback on the prototype, as well as further impressions and suggestions, to be gained.

The sample of this primary study included 17 participants aged 22-39. No prior knowledge was required but a mere experience on video games and different kind of controllers, a characteristic that all participants satisfied.

After receiving a brief explanation on the game's hypothesis, each participant was instructed to experiment handling the controller after the start of the game. No further instructions were given on how to use the flashlight or which the full capabilities of the controller are. Each user had to discover how to navigate and progress through each of the 7 levels that were developed.

Results

The participants of the evaluation process found it easy to use the controller and showed fluency on navigating through the game. The instructions at the beginning of the game inform the players how to navigate through the main menu, by touching right, left, or using both hands to select a command. This plain instruction proved to be enough to get the users started and to continue experimenting on the next levels.

It took around 15 minutes for each participant to successfully finish all 7 levels of the game. During the interview and after the use of the prototype, all participants showed excitement and they were willing to play again. The average score that was achieved on the SUS scale through the questionnaires was 80.25, which by conventional standards is considered to be above average and may be described as a good experience (Bangor et al., 2009). The gathered users' suggestions regarding improvements and different approaches on the prototype are listed in the next section.

DISCUSSION AND FUTURE WORK

The evolution of technology can lead to new paths. Weaknesses and defects can be limited or even eliminated while new features can expand the utility and usability of the device.

The cubic controller is the main user's interface and the interaction between the two worlds exists. This is a *real interface* since a user's actions cause expected results in the game. Thus, shedding light to a hole can indeed produce light to the corresponding virtual hole in the virtual world and the flipping of the box can turn the virtual world upside down. This intuitive behavior makes the user's acquaintance with the controller easier and simpler. The only differentiation is the touch pad interface in which the user's touch produces an action on the virtual world which is not linked to a respective one in the natural world. This interaction, which has to do with the movement of the player's character to the left or to the right, is quite familiar even to a rookie player, and is linked to the common practice of a game in which a user presses left or right buttons to move the virtual character to the left or to the right. Therefore, even this arbitrary correlation suggests an interaction that the user can sense intuitively from the first moments playing the game without causing any confusion. What contributes to this usefulness is also the fact that the movement of the sphere keeps its consistency even when the world is upside down, meaning that touching left remains linked to the movement to the left and touching right to the right movement, as the user sees it on the screen.

One of the advantages of the controller is the elimination of a keyboard, a mouse or any other kind of controlling device. The only device the user needs to fully operate the game is the cubic controller. Indeed, all users during the evaluation process commented that they enjoyed the fact that they only had to experiment with the box in front of them without any distractions. This enhances the user's immersion feeling in the mixed reality environment with no need of interrupting the interaction to turn to the keyboard or to any other device for additional manipulations.

One of the limitations of the device in its current form is its weight and size, as noted by user comments during the evaluation of the system. Although it gives the illusion of real-size objects existing and moving inside the box (the box size is analogous to typical laptop screen sizes), the need to use both hands to place the box upside down, lifting a load of approximately 1,5 kg might delay the game as it is proven it is not a simple task. Moreover, during the flipping of the box, the user's hands might get in contact with one of the touch sensors and result in unintentional movement of the virtual sphere. On the contrary, these are the characteristics which force the user to place the controller on a flat surface in front of them instead of holding it, something that might render the device difficult to use and might also tamper with noise readings for the inclination of the box. Figure 10 presents the proportions of the controller and a user controlling the game using the device.

Figure 10. User playing the game using the controller

The size of the controller is also a subject of review for usability reasons. In the present form, the size is not proportional to its contents and almost 80% of the interior is empty. The main reason why this is implemented that way, is simply to facilitate the fitting of all the electronic parts inside the box as well as the fact that a prototype is not a subject of scrutiny, in terms of physical dimensions and usability. Of course, we must bear in mind that the four holes on the top of the box require enough space so that when the user tries to point the flashlight at one of them, it will not shed light on its neighbors. Anyhow, replacing the material of the box and downsizing the box would change the way a user interacts with it since the controller would constantly be held in their hands without the need of placing it on a flat surface.

A key point that could be developed is the ability of the controller to detect its inclination. In the present form, a tilt sensor can make the position of box perceived through two distinct situations, normal or upside down. The use of a gyroscope and/or an accelerometer can provide us with additional data regarding three dimensions, and thus, it would be possible to detect the inclination of the box in three dimensions so that the projection of the virtual world is not based on only two states. Additionally, the virtual sphere inside the box could move into three dimensions by eliminating the two-dimensional movement that applies to the present implementation. By doing so, extra complexity to the game levels can be added and additional increase of the feeling of immersion to the user can be achieved since the slightest inclination of the controller can also be transferred to the virtual world.

In a different approach, motors could be used inside the box to enable a real sphere to be inserted. This sphere will pop up in the virtual world and this could signify the beginning of another level. The target of this level might also be to lead the sphere to an exit that is related with a real exit on the box. When the user successfully moves the sphere out of the box in the virtual world, the actual sphere could jump out of the box in the real world as well. Obviously, consistency of the position of the entrance and exit points between real and virtual box is of utmost importance if we want to avoid confusion. On the other hand, this approach would pose more limitations on the level of creativity for the game.

Finally, to achieve portability, the controller can wirelessly connect to a computer (e.g. through Bluetooth, or WiFi) and operate on batteries. This implementation demands a microcontroller with wireless connectivity. This way, we could eliminate the limitation of keeping the controller near a computer or a monitor as well as get rid of the cables, something that would also offer greater functionality to the device.

CONCLUSION

After the implementation of the game in its physical form (controller) as well as in software level (code development), a mixed reality environment was created, the interaction between real and virtual world being of great importance. The characteristics of the natural or reality interfaces are fully utilized, and the user interacts through gestures and actions in a real environment. Unlike most similar projects, the user's attention is not focused entirely on a screen but also in the accompanying controller through which the alignment of the physical and the virtual world is achieved. The touch of the controller causes motion in the virtual world, the use of light can affect the properties of virtual objects and the position of the box (normal or upside down) can flip the virtual world around. Additionally, the interaction between the two worlds works both ways, as events in the virtual world can change the characteristics of the real world, like the collapse of the sphere to the floor that causes a knock inside the box.

The game mainly focuses on creating the illusion/immersion that the user experiences an environment in which the virtual and the real objects coexist meaning that the virtual world unfolds within a physical object in front of them. A user's actions on this object suggest the interaction with the virtual world and vice versa. Changes that take place in the virtual environment, like sounds and vibrations, can result in changes in the physical world. The combination of all the above stimuli is what creates a sense of immersion in a mixed reality world, rendering the boundaries between the real and the virtual loose and encouraging the user to instinctually operate the game. Finally, a mixed reality system's standards are fully met by making the game a successful example of mixed reality use in which the real and the virtual coexist, the interaction occurs in real time and in all three dimensions.

ACKNOWLEDGMENT

The publisher has waived the Open Access Processing fee for this article.

REFERENCES

Ayala, K. J. (2005). *The 8051 microcontroller*. Cengage Learning.

Azuma, R. T. (1997). A Survey of Augmented Reality. Presence: Teleoperatores and Virtual Environments, 6(4), 355-385. doi:10.1162/pres.1997.6.4.355

Badger, P. (2016). *Arduino*. Retrieved from Arduino Playground – CapacitiveSensor: https://playground.arduino.cc/Main/CapacitiveSensor/

Bangor, A., Kortum, P., & Miller, J. (2009). Determining what individual SUS scores mean: Adding an adjective rating scale. *Journal of Usability Studies*, *4*(3), 114–123.

Bonsignore, E., Hansen, D. L., Toups, Z. O., Nacke, L. E., Salter, A., & Lutters, W. (2012). Mixed Reality Games. In *2012 ACM Conference on Computer Supported Cooperative Work (CSCW 2012)*, 11-15 February 2012 (pp. 7-8). 10.1145/2141512.2141517

Booth, T., Stumpf, S., Bird, J., & Jones, S. (2016, May). Crossed wires: Investigating the problems of end-user developers in a physical computing task. In *Proceedings of the 2016 CHI Conference on Human Factors in Computing Systems* (pp. 3485-3497). ACM. 10.1145/2858036.2858533

Brooke, J. (1996). SUS-A quick and dirty usability scale. *Usability Evaluation in Industry, 189*(194), 4-7.

Costanza, E., Kunz, A., & Fjeld, M. (2009). *Mixed Reality: A Survey*. In D. Lalanne & J. Kohlas (Eds.), Lecture Notes in Computer Science (Vol. 5440, pp. 47–68). Springer-Verlag. doi:10.1007/978-3-642-00437-7_3

Coulton, P., Rashid, O., & Bamford, W. (2006). Experiencing Touch in Mobile Mixed Reality Games. *4th International Conference in Computer Game Design and Technology*.

Duan, X., Kang, S. J., Choi, J. I., & Kim, S. K. (2020). Mixed Reality System for Virtual Chemistry Lab. *Transactions on Internet and Information Systems (Seoul)*, *14*(4), 1673–1688.

Fitzgerald, S., & Shiloh, M. (Eds.). (2012). *Arduino projects book*. Arduino LLC.

Gimeno, J., Olanda, R., Martinez, B., & Sanchez, F. M. (2011, September). Multiuser augmented reality system for indoor exhibitions. In *IFIP Conference on Human-Computer Interaction* (pp. 576-579). Springer. 10.1007/978-3-642-23768-3_86

Glover, J. (2018). *Unity 2018 Augmented Reality Projects: Build four immersive and fun AR applications using ARKit, ARCore, and Vuforia*. Packt Publishing Ltd.

Hughes, C. E., Stapleton, C. B., Hughes, D. E., & Smith, E. M. (2005). Mixed reality in education, entertainment, and training. *IEEE Computer Graphics and Applications*, 25(6), 24–30. doi:10.1109/MCG.2005.139 PMID:16315474

Marichal, S., Rosales, A., Perilli, F. G., Pires, A. C., Bakala, E., Sansone, G., & Blat, J. (2017, September). Ceta: designing mixed-reality tangible interaction to enhance mathematical learning. In *Proceedings of the 19th International Conference on Human-Computer Interaction with Mobile Devices and Services* (pp. 1-13). 10.1145/3098279.3098536

Metaxas, G., Metin, B., Schneider, J., Shapiro, G., Zhou, W., & Markopoulos, P. (2005, June). SCORPIODROME: an exploration in mixed reality social gaming for children. In *Proceedings of the 2005 ACM SIGCHI International Conference on Advances in computer entertainment technology* (pp. 229-232). 10.1145/1178477.1178514

Milgram, P., & Kishino, F. (1994). A Taxonomy of Mixed Reality Visual Displays. *IEICE Transactions on Information and Systems*, E77-D(12), 1321–1329.

O'Sullivan, D., & Igoe, T. (2004). *Physical Computing: Sensing and controlling the physical world with computers*. Thomson Course Technology PTR.

Sandor, C., Olwal, A., Bell, B., & Feiner, S. (2005, October). Immersive mixed-reality configuration of hybrid user interfaces. In *Fourth IEEE and ACM International Symposium on Mixed and Augmented Reality (ISMAR'05)* (pp. 110-113). IEEE. 10.1109/ISMAR.2005.37

Speicher, M., Hall, B. D., & Nebeling, M. (2019, May). What is mixed reality? In *Proceedings of the 2019 CHI Conference on Human Factors in Computing Systems* (pp. 1-15). ACM.

Tullis, T. S., & Stetson, J. N. (2004, June). A comparison of questionnaires for assessing website usability. In Usability professional association conference (Vol. 1, pp. 1-12). Academic Press.

Ullmer, B., & Ishii, H. (2000). Emerging frameworks for tangible user interfaces. *IBM Systems Journal*, 39(3.4), 915-931.

Welch, R. B. (1978). *Perceptual Modification: Adapting to Altered Sensory Environments*. Academic Press Inc.

Wursthorn, S., Coelho, A.H. & Staub, G. (2018). *Applications for Mixed Reality*. Academic Press.

This research was previously published in the International Journal of Virtual and Augmented Reality (IJVAR), 5(2); pages 40-56, copyright year 2021 by IGI Publishing (an imprint of IGI Global).

Chapter 31
The Effects of Using On-Screen and Paper Maps on Navigation Efficiency in 3D Multi-User Virtual Environments

Hakan Tüzün
 https://orcid.org/0000-0003-1153-5556
Hacettepe University, Turkey

Dilek Doğan
 https://orcid.org/0000-0001-6988-9547
Ankara University, Turkey

ABSTRACT

This study aims to analyze the effects of using on-screen and paper maps on navigation efficiency in 3D MUVEs. There were 48 participants in the study, which has a randomized true experimental design. The researchers administered a demographics questionnaire and the spatial visualization test to the participants and formed three groups by checking a variety of independent variables, the On-Screen Map (OSM) group, the Paper Map (PM) group, and the Coordinate System (CS) group, which did not use any kind of map. The participants completed three tasks with increasing difficulty levels. There was a statistically significant difference between the methods for the completion times of the first task and aggregate tasks. This difference was between CS and PM as well as between CS and OSM. Participants got confused and lost the most in the CS group and the least in the OSM group. The CS group took longer to complete the tasks and got lost more frequently. Navigational aids that included visual tips about the environment increased the navigation efficiency of the participants using the MUVE.

DOI: 10.4018/978-1-6684-7597-3.ch031

INTRODUCTION

With the widespread use of the Internet, social networks, and three-dimensional multi-user virtual environments (3D MUVEs) in every field, interest in 2D and 3D graphics has increased. The transfer of our living environment to the Internet by use of rich and realistic graphics has resulted in the emergence of new concepts such as simulations, virtual reality, and virtual worlds. Since the world we live in is three-dimensional, it is more intuitive to use three-dimensional features when creating virtual realities in the computer environment. Since the designs created with the use of three-dimensional artifacts are closer to reality, they attract more attention than web sites including two-dimensional images and animations made of texts, pictures, and vector graphics. Designers can present visualizations that are closer to reality thanks to three-dimensional technology. These visualizations are used in many different fields such as business, education, art, and design (Uğur, 2002).

A MUVE can provide exploration, interaction, and immersion affordances when users navigate and do activities in a virtual environment and communicate among themselves at the same time (Tüzün & Özdinç, 2016). MUVEs, in particular, can be used to reveal the effect of navigation on spatial perception. In these environments, individuals can navigate like they do in real life with the help of the avatars that represent them. These three-dimensional environments include many contexts or places where users can navigate and communicate with each other. However, it becomes more difficult for users to navigate as the environment becomes more complicated and the number of contexts increases (Ballegooij & Eliens, 2001). Besides, it may become more difficult for users to recognize the context and the people around them if they see a context in the virtual environment for the first time without seeing it in reality beforehand. To address these difficulties, the influence of navigational aids on navigation efficiency in 3D MUVEs is worth studying.

RELEVANT LITERATURE AND THEORETICAL FRAMEWORK

3D MUVEs combine textual and audio transfer technologies and enable navigation in realistic three-dimensional virtual worlds. The origin of this kind of environment is the text-based and multi-user games such as Space War, which was a popular game in the UNIX operating system (Tüzün, 2010). For many years, virtual environments have been assigned many names such as Multi-User Dungeon (MUD), Object-Oriented MUD (MOO), Massively Multiplayer Online Role-Playing Game (MMORPG) and Multi-User Virtual Environment (Mayrath, Traphagan, Jarmon, Trivedi, & Resta, 2010).

MUVEs have real-time and open world features. These features make them closer to reality (Fırat, 2008). Although many multi-user games also have real-time feature, players need to perform certain operations and tasks to make progress in these environments. However, MUVEs usually do not include planned tasks. When users enter the environment, their experiences are random. Another aspect of MUVEs is that they are available for creating environments with different levels of complexity, making measurements during interactive navigation and checking the spatial learning parameters (Peruch, Belingard, & Thinus-Blanc, 2000). Navigation in MUVEs refers to reaching a desired object or location by moving in these environments (Raees, Ullah & Rahman, 2019). Virtual environment navigation allows users to control their position and orientation of the virtual camera which they see the virtual world (Galyean, 1995) and to move around, manipulate and interact with virtual objects possible (Geszten et al., 2018).

When navigating in a new environment, a mental image of the place is created in the subconscious. This image is called a cognitive map, and it is stored in the hippocampus of the brain. However, the image in the hippocampus is not the same in every person's brain. Some people very rapidly create spatial knowledge about places they see for the first time and create maps of these places in their minds without any difficulties. Others find it difficult to do so (Çubukçu & Çubukçu, 2006; Green & Bavelier, 2003). Lynch (1960) and Golledge (1999) describe wayfinding as creating a mental image of the physical world in the process of following a road or path and making decisions based on this image. In the process of wayfinding, people create cognitive maps using three different types of spatial knowledge, which are: 1) landmarks, 2) procedural knowledge, and 3) survey knowledge (Bowman et al., 2004). These cognitive maps help people during their navigation.

According to the wayfinding model by Chen, Chang, and Chang (2009), people need to collect spatial knowledge with the help of their senses, combine it with their existing knowledge, and create cognitive maps to understand the environment of their navigation task. The decision-making process depends on the creation of cognitive maps of individual movements and structures for the entire wayfinding plan. Movement to a specific destination is the result of a plan that includes a predetermined path and accurate information about the movements. The plan provides feedback to the memory as spatial knowledge. During navigation, the decisions are transformed into physical movements. Physical movements require the implementation of the decision or movement in the decided path, that is, the navigation. During their movements, users proceed in the planned direction with the help of the stimuli in the environment. In the wayfinding process, users make new wayfinding decisions while creating cognitive maps to reach a goal when they make a decision, the plan is completed, or the plan or the decision goes wrong. Then, they re-create the decision-making process. In these processes, the most important factors that influence wayfinding efficiency are experience, searching methods, differences in abilities, motivation, navigational aids, environmental arrangement, and structure. Without these factors, any person can be disoriented at one time or another. Disorientation is an uncomfortable and unsettling feeling to be unfamiliar with a person's proximal context and unable to determine how to compensate the situation. The goal of navigation research in virtual environments is to create a situation where everyone is oriented properly all the time and knows where they are and how to get there (Darken & Peterson, 2015).

3D MUVEs allow the use of either first-person perspective (egocentric frame of reference) or third-person perspective (allocentric frame of reference) for navigation (Tüzün & Özdinç, 2016; Chen & Chen, 2019). Considering 3D MUVEs, the design of efficient navigation is a problem because users' viewpoint cannot encompass the entire environment. This problem causes disorientation and bad user perception of the virtual worlds' usability. If users cannot find their way to a destination called losing way, they cannot use the virtual world for its desired purpose (Minocha & Hardy, 2016). In the relevant literature, there are many different terms used to describe losing way, such as being lost, getting lost, lostness and disorientation. Karadeniz (2006) uses the term "lostness" to describe users' state of being lost, and the term "disorientation" to describe a general situation including users' failure to orient themselves in the environment. According to Dudchenko (2010), getting lost or disorientation means a person's failure to find their way. Lynch (1960) stated that getting lost was very unlikely when an environment includes maps, street numbers, and path symbols and people are supported by special devices. Karadeniz (2006) describes getting lost in a multimedia environment as users' not knowing where they are, how they have come to a place, and how to go to another place. In other words, users are unable to answer the questions: "Where am I?" "How did I get here?" and "Where will I go?" Dudchenko (2010) reported that users get lost: 1) when they have no familiar users around them, 2) when there are no symbols to help them decide which way to go, and 3) when they cannot reorient themselves by reconstructing their previous experiences. In this study, the researchers define the term "getting lost" as straying from the ideal path.

Altan (2011) and Riis (2016) determined that getting lost in MUVEs is an important issue. Users navigating in MUVEs, particularly for the first time, fail to follow the ideal paths and get lost. Preventing users from getting lost and supporting them with different navigational aids is important for users (Akçapınar, Altun, & Menteş, 2012). These environments use a variety of navigational aids to facilitate their users' navigation. Navigational aids such as flying, spatial audio, breadcrumb markers, coordinate feedback, districting, landmarks, grid navigation, and map view (Darken & Sibert, 1993) help prevent users from getting lost and provide visual hints to users about the ideal path to follow. Maps are one of the most familiar mediators and powerful tools for navigation because they provide wealthy environmental information to users (Darken & Peterson, 2015). They offer intuitive ways to extend the capacities of the human cognitive systems as external representations of the environment with landmarks (McKenzie & Klippel, 2016).

Task completion times in virtual environments are also an important aspect of MUVEs' usability. Individual differences between users along with the design and usability of the aids used in virtual environments influence the accomplishment of tasks and task completion times. Many studies of MUVEs have found that males completed tasks more quickly than females (Astur, Ortiz, & Sutherland, 1998; Lövden et al., 2007; Chen, Chang, & Chang, 2009). A few studies reported no differences between users' task completion times by gender. Studies of the influence of gender on route-learning report that males are capable of meeting the required criteria with fewer errors and difficulties than females, while females are able to remember the landmarks better than males (Galea & Kimura, 1993; Saucier et al., 2002; Tlauka et al., 2007). Cutmore et al. (2000) conducted a study of the influence of the factors of cognition and gender on the navigation in virtual environments and found that males managed to find the exit with less effort. These findings are consistent with the findings of the studies by Moffat, Hampson, and Hatzipantelis (1998) and Sandstrom, Kaufman, and Huettel (1998). The results of the study by Vila, Beccue, and Anandikar (2003) contrast with these studies and indicate that there was no difference between navigation durations by gender. Ross, Skelton, and Mueller (2006) reported that the difference between genders in virtual environments was correlated with the characteristics of the task assigned.

In the light of such information, this study examines the effect of maps, a navigational aid used in 3D MUVEs, on navigation efficiency. Therefore, research questions of this study are: 1) Is there any differences among the use of the Coordinate System (CS) which does not use any maps, Paper Map (PM) and On-Screen Map (OSM) in 3D MUVEs in terms of task completion times?, and 2) Is there any differences among the use of CS, PM and OSM in 3D MUVEs in terms of users getting lost? There are commercial games such as Anarchy Online, which includes in its distribution package paper maps of its worlds; therefore, it is worthwhile to study the effect of paper maps along with on-screen maps.

METHODOLOGY

Research Design

This study has a mixed design. The researchers used a true experimental design, a quantitative research method. The study utilized true experimental matched random design to be able to make the experimental and control groups similar. Moreover, the researchers used observation, a qualitative data collection tool, to analyze the participants' progress with the three methods.

3D Multi-User Virtual Environment

This study used an educational game called Quest Atlantis (QA). This game is based on the Active Worlds (AW) MUVE infrastructure. AW offers real-time and three-dimensional content with interaction (ActiveWorlds, 2015). Furthermore, AW has different pre-designed and used environments for educational purposes. Researchers think that designing a new environment could cause different usability problems that would affect the research results. Therefore, an existing virtual world design in QA on AW has been used in the study. Another reason for selecting QA is that it can be edited by researchers to determine tasks' coordinates. All objects in AW are stored in a grid of 10 by 10-meter cells. Locations correspond to the longitude and latitude coordinates that are encountered within the AW. For example, a location located at 11S 3E would be located 11 cells south and 3 cells east of the "ground zero" cell (i.e., the cell located at 0N 0W). By default, the current location of a user's avatar is displayed on the AW browser title bar, and this is the only navigational aid users can use while navigating within the virtual environment (Figure 1). In Quest Atlantis, an OSM navigational aid is located in the upper right corner of the environment. It allows users to see both their location and a bird's eye view of the virtual environment in real-time (Figure 1). This OSM can be turned off by users.

Figure 1. View of the virtual environment

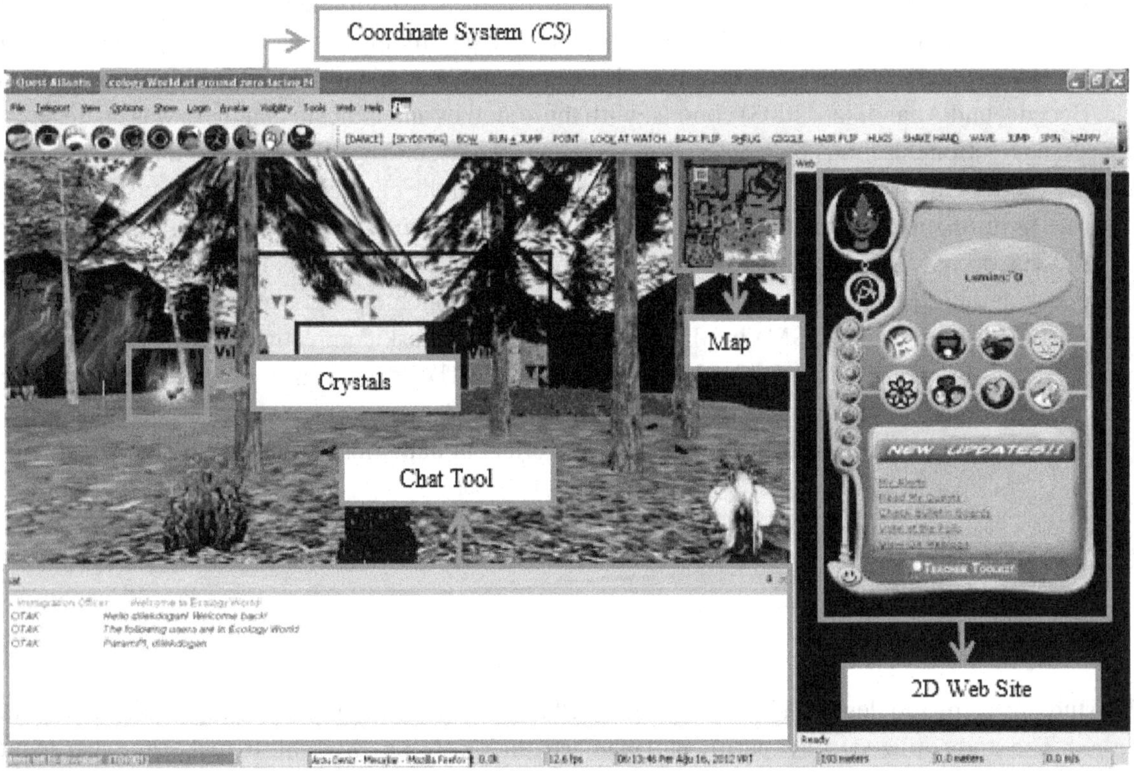

Data Sources

Demographics Questionnaire

The questionnaire has three sections: one about the participant's gender, year of birth and Grade Point Average (GPA), one about their computer and Internet use and one about their use of MUVEs and computer games.

Spatial Visualization Test

This test was created by Winter et al. (1989) and translated into Turkish by Yıldız (2009). The test includes 15 multiple-choice questions, and each question has five options. Five questions concern aerial views of isometric images of the structures made with cubes. The other questions are about views of cubes from the right, left, front, and behind. The highest possible score on the test is 15, and Yıldız (2009) found its reliability coefficient to be 0.971.

Observation

The researchers observed the routes taken by the participants and their difficulties when they got lost.

Participants

The participants of this study included 125 Instructional Technology students at a large-scale public university in the Eastern Turkey. The researchers conducted this study in this context because the students were familiar with these kinds of environments since their curriculum included the use of OpenSim, a 3D MUVE, for design purposes. Based on data collected from the participants, 16 of them were assigned to the pilot test, and 48 of them were assigned to the implementation.

Three participants with the same year of birth and gender were matched by similar GPAs, spatial visualization scores, years of playing games, weekly hours of playing games, and years of using the computer and the Internet. As the computer skill of the participants and their age-related reaction times would affect the results across groups, it was aimed that participants with similar computer skills and ages existed in all 3 groups. For this purpose, the researchers planned to include 16 participants in each group (48 participants in 3 groups) due to logistic limitations. Overall, two groups of three males and two groups of three females from each year of birth were matched. The demographic data for the participants in these matched pairs are presented in Table 1. It was not possible to match participants with perfectly identical features for all independent variables. Thus, the researchers embraced the independent variables with the closest values. Participants in each of the trios were randomly assigned to one of the three methods (CS, PM, and OSM). One-fourth of the participants were born in 1990, one-fourth were born in 1991, one-fourth were born in 1992, and one-fourth were born in 1993. Half of the participants were females, and the other half were males.

Table 1. The distribution of groups according to the independent variables

Trios	Participant	Year of birth	Gender	Grade	Spatial visualization score	Years of playing games	Weekly hours of playing games	Years of computer use	Years of Internet use	Method Assigned
1	P32 P35 P58	1993	M	2.21 2.39 2.47	11 13 12	4 3 3	6 6 4	4 2 4	3 2 2	CS PM OSM
2	P40 P61 P52	1993	M	3.50 3.26 3.53	6 4 6	4 1 0	1 2 0	4 3 2	3 2 2	CS PM OSM
3	P47 P31 P62	1993	F	2.76 3.00 2.83	11 8 11	0 0 0	0 0 0	2 2 4	1 2 4	CS PM OSM
4	P63 P54 P38	1993	F	3.10 3.26 3.35	4 2 4	3 0 2	5 0 1	2 2 2	1 2 1	CS PM OSM
5	P51 P93 P122	1992	M	2.25 2.35 2.36	3 5 4	3 2 2	2 4 6	3 1 1	3 2 1	CS PM OSM
6	P79 P65 P72	1992	M	2.92 2.62 2.98	8 7 7	1 2 4	6 1 3	2 2 4	2 1 3	CS PM OSM
7	P34 P76 P80	1992	F	2.88 2.90 2.79	3 4 4	3 2 2	6 1 2	3 2 2	2 2 2	CS PM OSM
8	P87 P45 P69	1992	F	3.09 3.29 3.27	10 10 12	0 6 0	0 2 0	1 2 2	1 1 2	CS PM OSM
9	P53 P29 P121	1991	M	2.38 2.62 2.70	6 4 4	0 4 0	0 2 0	3 4 1	3 4 1	CS PM OSM
10	P118 P100 P108	1991	M	3.11 3.44 3.51	6 5 4	0 3 1	0 1 2	2 3 2	2 3 2	CS PM OSM
11	P105 P109 P92	1991	F	2.80 2.96 2.75	10 8 10	0 0 0	0 0 0	3 2 1	2 2 1	CS PM OSM
12	P64 P71 P124	1991	F	3.53 3.28 3.40	12 11 11	4 2 0	5 6 0	2 2 2	1 2 1	CS PM OSM
13	P88 P25 P125	1990	M	2.53 2.60 2.43	6 5 4	0 2 3	0 4 5	3 3 2	2 3 3	CS PM OSM
14	P18 P82 P9	1990	M	3.04 3.10 3.11	11 11 9	0 2 2	0 1 1	3 2 2	3 2 2	CS PM OSM
15	P112 P23 P101	1990	F	2.70 2.98 3.00	8 9 7	0 0 0	0 0 0	2 2 4	2 2 2	CS PM OSM
16	P24 P4 P116	1990	F	3.67 3.79 3.81	6 10 6	0 0 0	0 0 0	2 3 3	2 2 2	CS PM OSM

Procedures

For the pilot test and the implementation, the researchers used one control group (CS) and two experimental groups (PM and OSM). The control group did not use any maps, and the participants were asked to use the default coordinate system (CS) to perform the tasks (Figure 1). One of the experimental groups was asked to use the on-screen map (OSM) (Figure 1) to perform the tasks. The other experimental group was asked to use the paper map (PM) with an aerial view of the environment, while the OSM was turned off. Both maps are 2D top-down view maps and were used as navigational aid to facilitate users' navigation. Furthermore, they provided visual cues about the environment. PM was presented to users as a static map, while OSM showed where they were. The researchers gave an orientation text to the participants. The text included information about the methods, tasks, locations, and destinations. In the Turkish cultural context, cardinal directions such as north, south, east, and west are rarely used in daily life by ordinary citizens, and relative directions are used for reference. For this reason, the orientation text also included a compass rose to remind the participants of the cardinal and inter-cardinal directions.

The participants were assigned three tasks for each of which they were required to find crystal artifacts placed in different locations in the virtual environment: "Your current coordinates are 0, 0. Your first task is to find the crystal artifact at 9N, 5E," "Your current coordinates are 9N, 5E. Your second task is to find the crystal artifact at 9N, 10W," "Your current coordinates are 9N, 10W. Your third task is to find the crystal artifact at 11S, 3E." The participants were required to go from O to 1 for the first task, from 1 to 2 for the second task, and from 2 to 3 for the third task (Figure 2). The tasks progressively became more complicated and longer to complete as the participants accomplished the tasks.

Sixteen participants took part in the pilot test. Afterwards, the researchers held interviews with the participants, identified the problems with the tasks, the orientation text, and the environment, and fixed them. The researchers did not use the data from the pilot test for the analyses.

After the pilot test, the implementation took 12 days to complete. Each implementation was completed with a single participant. Before the implementation, the researchers gave the orientation text to a participant and task completion times were recorded with a chronometer. The researchers also observed and took notes about the routes taken by a participant. All participants completed all the tasks in the implementation.

Certain technical arrangements were made to ensure that the groups performed the tasks in the AW environment under the same conditions. Only the arrow keys could be used for movement. Key combinations such as running with Ctrl key and walking through the objects with Shift key were turned off. The chat window and web browser window were closed, and the three-dimensional virtual environment was used in the full-screen mode. The participants were provided with a first-person perspective of the virtual environment.

Data Analysis

The researchers conducted one-way ANOVA to determine any differences between the groups by their GPAs, spatial visualization scores, weekly hours of playing games, and hours of using MUVEs. In addition, the researchers conducted the chi-square test for independence to identify any differences between the group's experience with games, computers, and the Internet. To compare the task completion times of the groups, the researchers used descriptive statistics, two-way ANCOVA, Fisher's exact test, Levene's Test, and Fisher's LSD Test. Fisher's exact test was also used to determine whether the groups got lost. The significance threshold for this study's statistical analyses was 0.05. The observation data were analyzed using content analysis.

Figure 2. Display of participants' tasks in the virtual environment

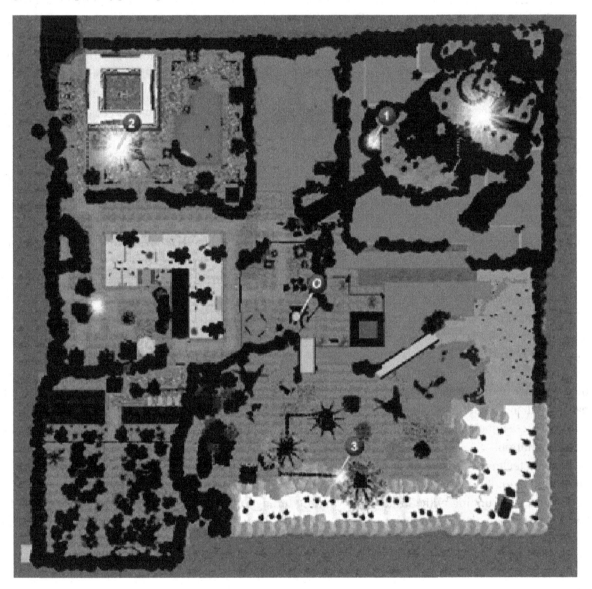

RESULTS

A Comparison of the Groups by the Independent Variables

The descriptive statistics regarding the groups' GPAs, spatial visualization scores, weekly hours of playing games, and the duration of their MUVE uses were shown in Table 2.

Table 2. Descriptive statistics of the groups according to the independent variables

	Group	N	Mean	SD
Grade point average	CS	16	2.90	0.43
	PM	16	2.99	0.39
	OSM	16	3.01	0.43
Spatial visualization score	CS	16	7.56	2.99
	PM	16	7.25	3.22
	OSM	16	7.19	3.17
Weekly hours of playing games	CS	16	1.94	2.62
	PM	16	2.13	2.30
	OSM	16	1.50	2.00
Weekly hours of using MUVEs	CS	16	2.63	2.80
	PM	16	2.69	2.60
	OSM	16	3.63	2.42

According to ANOVA results, there was no significant difference among the groups' GPAs (F (2, 45) = 0.31, p = 0.73), spatial visualization scores (F (2, 45) = 0.07, p = 0.94), weekly hours of playing games (F (2, 45) = 0.31, p = 0.74), and weekly durations of using MUVEs (F (2, 45) = 0.74, p = 0.49). The chi-square test for independence was conducted to see any differences among the groups' experiences in playing games, computers, and the Internet. Fisher's exact test was administered when the number of cells smaller than 5 was above 20% of the total number of cells. According to the test results, there was no significant difference among the groups' experience with playing games (X^2 (8, N = 48) = 10.83, p = 0.16), experiences in using computer (X^2 (6, N = 48) = 7.25, p = 0.29), and experiences in using the Internet (X^2(6, N = 48) = 7.14, p = 0.24). These results suggested that the groups of 16 participants were similar in terms of the independent variables.

A Comparison of the Groups' Task Completion Times

The data should have a normal distribution to conduct parametric tests, and the variances of the different groups should be equal. The normality of the dependent variable was observed using histograms for each group (CS, PM, and OSM), and Levene's test was conducted to determine the homogeneity of the variances. Although the researchers tried to match the groups by considering their characteristics, and their age and gender distributions were equal, other characteristics differed. The variables that differed were taken as covariates, and the covariates assumed to be associated with the tasks were checked while comparing the task completion times. All participants completed all the tasks reaching the determined goals. Table 3 presents the completion times of the tasks by both methods and genders. A visualization of these data is presented in Figure 3.

Table 3. A comparison of the completion times of tasks 1, 2, 3, and all the tasks by method and gender

	Method	Gender	Mean	SD
Task 1	CS	Female	347.38	219.05
		Male	266.88	225.46
		Total	307.13	218.73
		Corrected Total	313.15	38.06
	PM	Female	151.63	89.76
		Male	172.88	173.83
		Total	162.25	134.10
		Corrected Total	173.17	37.96
	OSM	Female	193.50	117.53
		Male	73.63	24.69
		Total	133.56	102.77
		Corrected Total	116.62	38.28
Task 2	CS	Female	286.00	135.36
		Male	200.38	75.30
		Total	243.19	114.68
		Corrected Total	244.89	22.08
	PM	Female	207.87	85.91
		Male	157.63	66.31
		Total	182.75	78.55
		Corrected Total	180.08	22.03
	OSM	Female	212.88	78.23
		Male	180.50	57.33
		Total	196.69	68.33
		Corrected Total	197.66	22.21
Task 3	CS	Female	300.62	179.97
		Male	226.63	112.99
		Total	263.63	150.11
		Corrected Total	262.14	33.44
	PM	Female	250.75	92.77
		Male	178.88	58.12
		Total	214.81	83.49
		Corrected Total	221.28	33.36
	OSM	Female	277.00	204.06
		Male	206.00	93.60
		Total	241.50	157.69
		Corrected Total	236.52	33.64

continues on following page

Table 3. Continued

		Method	Gender	Mean	SD
Total	CS		Female	934.00	289.93
			Male	693.88	306.42
			Total	813.944	313.72
			Corrected Total	820.18	61.16
	PM		Female	610.25	213.20
			Male	509.38	207.28
			Total	559.81	209.70
			Corrected Total	574.52	61.00
	OSM		Female	683.38	308.54
			Male	460.13	117.20
			Total	571.75	253.23
			Corrected Total	550.80	61.52

Figure 3 shows that the male participants completed the first task faster using the OSM, while the female participants completed the same task faster using the PM. The participants completed the second and third tasks faster when they used the PM, while they completed the same tasks more slowly when they used the CS. The male participants completed the tasks faster when they used the OSM, while the female participants completed the tasks faster when they used the PM. Participants completed the tasks more slowly when they used the CS method. Analysis of the participants' task completion times indicated that males completed the tasks more quickly.

The researchers also tested the equality of the variance among the groups for the first, second, third tasks, and all the tasks. It was found that the variance among the groups was equal for the first task (Levene's test $F = 2.83$, $p > 0.05$), the second task (Levene's test $F = 1.46$, $p > 0.05$), the third task (Levene's test $F = 2.15$, $p > 0.05$), and for all the tasks (Levene's test $F = 1.27$, $p > 0.05$). Table 4 shows the results of the covariance analysis. This analysis was conducted to consider the gender variable, which might affect the methods used in the tasks. The researchers also checked the GPAs, spatial visualization scores, weekly durations of playing games and using MUVES, which were taken as covariates. The results indicated a statistically significant difference between the methods for the first task's completion times ($p < 0.05$). For the other tasks, the difference in methods was not statistically significant ($p > 0.05$). The difference between the methods for the completion times of all three tasks was statistically significant ($p < 0.05$). The influence of the interaction between the method and gender on the completion time of the first task, the second task, the third task, and all the tasks was not statistically significant ($p > 0.05$).

The researchers conducted Fisher's LSD test to find out which groups differed from each other by method for the first task (Table 5). The results showed that the differences between the CS and PM methods, as well as the CS and OSM methods, were statistically significant ($p < 0.05$). The difference between the PM and OSM methods was not statistically significant ($p > 0.05$).

The researchers conducted Fisher's LSD test also to determine which groups differed by aggregate task completion times and method (Table 6). The results showed that the differences between the CS and PM methods, as well as the CS and OSM methods, were statistically significant ($p < 0.05$). The difference between the PM and OSM methods was not statistically significant ($p > 0.05$).

Figure 3. Distribution of participants' tasks completion by gender

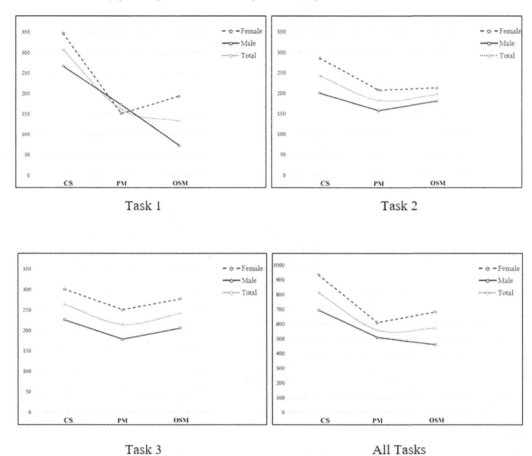

Table 4. The results of the ANCOVA analysis of the average completion times of the tasks

	Source	Sum of Squares	df	Mean Square	F	p	Partial eta Squared
	Corrected Model	556841.03	9	61871.23	2.72	.02	.39
	Intercept	50352.36	1	50352.36	2.21	.15	.06
	Spatial information score	378.79	1	378.79	.02	.90	.00
	Grade point average	6833.48	1	6833.48	.30	.59	.01
	Weekly hours of playing games	68924.16	1	68924.16	3.03	.09	.07
Task 1	Weekly hours of using MUVEs	94489.84	1	94489.84	4.15	.05	.10
	Method	316799.71	2	158399.85	6.95	.00	.27
	Gender	22304.95	1	22304.95	.98	.33	.03
	Method * Gender	53166.14	2	26583.07	1.17	.32	.06
	Error	865925.95	38	22787.53			
	Corrected Total	1422766.98	47				

continues on following page

Table 3. Continued

	Source	Sum of Squares	df	Mean Square	F	p	Partial eta Squared
Task 2	Corrected Model	100416.19	9	11157.35	1.45	.20	.26
	Intercept	310.00	1	310.00	.04	.84	.00
	Spatial information score	4637.90	1	4637.90	.61	.44	.02
	Grade point average	16819.14	1	16819.14	2.19	.15	.06
	Weekly hours of playing games	6301.80	1	6301.80	.82	.37	.02
	Weekly hours of using MUVEs	615.92	1	615.92	.08	.78	.00
	Method	35289.75	2	17644.87	2.30	.11	.11
	Gender	16130.04	1	16130.04	2.10	.16	.05
	Method * Gender	3437.64	2	1718.82	.22	.80	.01
	Error	291501.73	38	7671.10			
	Corrected Total	391917.92	47				
Task 3	Corrected Model	100416.19	9	11157.35	1.45	.20	.26
	Intercept	310.00	1	309.99	.04	.84	.00
	Spatial information score	4637.90	1	4637.90	.61	.44	.02
	Grade point average	16819.14	1	16819.14	2.19	.15	.06
	Weekly hours of playing games	6301.80	1	6301.80	.82	.37	.02
	Weekly hours of using MUVEs	615.92	1	615.92	.08	.78	.00
	Method	35289.75	2	17644.87	2.30	.11	.11
	Gender	16130.04	1	16130.04	2.10	.16	.05
	Method * Gender	3437.64	2	1718.82	.22	.80	.01
	Error	291501.73	38	7671.10			
	Corrected Total	391917.92	47				
Total	Corrected Model	1.520E6	9	168877.36	2.87	.01	.41
	Intercept	217639.19	1	217639.19	3.70	.06	.09
	Spatial information score	47623.25	1	47623.25	.81	.37	.02
	Grade point average	651.16	1	651.160	.01	.92	.00
	Weekly hours of playing games	169146.27	1	169146.27	2.88	.10	.07
	Weekly hours of using MUVEs	109380.14	1	109380.14	1.86	.18	.05
	Method	692584.75	2	346292.38	5.89	.01	.24
	Gender	195686.41	1	195686.41	3.33	.08	.08
	Method * Gender	74996.89	2	37498.44	.64	.53	.03
	Error	2235961.76	38	58841.10			
	Corrected Total	3755858.00	47				

Table 5. The LSD test results of the completion times of the first task by method

Method (I)	Method (J)	Mean Difference (I-J)	Std. Error	p
CS	PM	139.99	53.76	0.01
	OSM	196.53	54.43	0
PM	CS	-139.99	53.76	0.01
	OSM	56.54	54.23	0.3
OSM	CS	-196.53	54.43	0
	PM	-56.54	54.23	0.3

Table 6. The LSD test results of the total task completion times by method

Method (I)	Method (J)	Mean Difference (I-J)	Std. Error	p
CS	PM	245.66	86.38	0.01
	OSM	269.38	87.47	0
PM	CS	-245.66	86.38	0.01
	OSM	23.72	87.14	0.79
OSM	CS	-269.38	87.47	0
	PM	-23.72	87.14	0.79

A Comparison of the Groups' Getting Lost

This study defined getting lost as straying from the ideal route. Table 7 shows the data about participants' getting lost by method, gender, and task.

The researchers conducted a two-way chi-square test (Fisher's exact test) to compare the groups' getting lost by method. The results of the test showed that there was a significant difference between their getting lost in the first task ($X^2(2, N = 48) = 8.18, p = 0.02$), the second task ($X^2(2, N = 48) = 8.54, p = 0.01$), and the third task ($X^2(2, N = 48) = 7.81, p = 0.02$). Using the CS caused the participants to get lost the most frequently, while the OSM caused the fewest participants to get lost. With all three methods, participants got lost more often as they proceeded performing the tasks.

The researchers used a two-way chi-square test to compare the participants' getting lost by gender. For the CS method, there was no difference between males and females' getting lost in the first task ($X^2 (1, N = 16) = 1.33, p = 0.57$), in the second task ($X^2 (1, N = 16) = 0.00, p = 1.00$), and in the third task ($X^2 (1, N = 16) = 1.07, p = 1.00$). There was no difference between genders for the PM method in the first task ($X^2 (1, N = 16) = 0.25, p = 1.00$), in the second task ($X^2 (1, N = 16) = 2.29, p = 0.32$), and in the third task ($X^2 (1, N = 16) = 1.33, p = 0.57$). For the OSM method, there was no difference between the genders in the first task ($X^2 (1, N = 16) = 5.33, p = 0.08$), in the second task ($X2 (1, N = 16) = 0.00, p = 1.00$), and in the third task ($X^2 (1, N = 16) = 1.00, p = 0.62$). The researchers used a two-way chi-square test to compare the groups' getting lost by gender. The test results showed that there was a difference by gender in the first task ($X^2 (1, N = 48) = 4.09, p = 0.04$), while there was no difference by gender in the second ($X^2 (1, N = 48) = 0.78, p = 0.38$), and third tasks ($X^2 (1, N = 48) = 0.11, p = 0.75$).

Table 7. Numbers of participants who got lost by gender and task

Method	Lost	Gender	Task 1	Task 2	Task 3	Total
CS	Lost	Male	5	7	8	41 (85%)
		Female	7	7	7	
	Not Lost	Male	3	1	0	7 (15%)
		Female	1	1	1	
		Total	16	16	16	48 (100%)
PM	Lost	Male	3	3	5	28 (58%)
		Female	4	6	7	
	Not Lost	Male	5	5	3	20 (42%)
		Female	4	2	1	
		Total	16	16	16	48 (100%)
OSM	Lost	Male	0	3	5	18 (38%)
		Female	4	3	3	
	Not Lost	Male	8	5	3	30 (62%)
		Female	4	5	5	
		Total	16	16	16	48 (100%)

Observations Related to Getting Lost Using the CS

The researchers observed that the participants failed to follow the ideal route using the CS method on their first attempt and got lost. When using this method, the participants focused on the coordinates on the title bar and did not pay much attention to their surroundings. Some participants used roads they already walked many times. They passed by the goal while changing direction. However, they did not recognize the goal since they were concentrating on the coordinates. Some discovered the goals of the second and third tasks while attempting to perform the first task.

Observations Related to Getting Lost Using the PM

The participants who got lost using the PM method while performing the first task said they did not understand how to use the paper map at the beginning and did not find the bridges. In second and third tasks, they used the PM to get close to the goal, then stopped using the PM and began to use the CS, which caused them to lose their way. Their use of the coordinate system increased as they got closer to the goals. The participants focused on the coordinate system when they were very close to the goal and failed to recognize their location using this method, too. Since there were no indicators on the PM showing their location, the participants had difficulty telling where they were.

Observations Related to Getting Lost Using the OSM

Using this method, the participants noticed that they were going in the wrong direction thanks to the location indicator, and they switched to the correct direction. This indicator made it easy for the participants to find the bridges they were supposed to use particularly in the first and third tasks, but participants could not see them using the other methods. The reason for the OSM task completion times being longer than the PM times was that the participants followed the routes first on the OSM, and then they searched for the crystal artifact without checking the coordinate system. For a majority of the participants using the OSM, it took longer to find the crystal artifact than it took them to get to its location. The participants used fewer routes when they used this method. The participants who used both the OSM and the CS together completed the task faster.

DISCUSSION

This study analyzed the effects of on-screen and paper maps as navigational aids in 3D MUVEs on navigation efficiency. It was found that the method used in the first task and all the tasks influenced the task completion times, and there was a difference between the CS and PM methods, as well as between the CS and OSM methods. The group that did not use any maps completed the tasks more slowly and got lost more frequently. The differences between the CS and PM methods and the CS and OSM methods resulted from the fact that the CS method did not include a navigational aid giving participants visual cues about the environment. For instance, the CS method did not include any visual cues about the bridge they were supposed to cross, which lengthened participants' task completion times. A review of the relevant literature also showed that Tlauka et al. (2005) found that the types of maps used for tasks influenced task completion times. Yokosawa, Wada, and Mitsumatsu (2005) found that participants were more successful in MUVEs when they used methods, which gave them visual cues about the environment.

Although the participants in this study had experience in using three-dimensional multi-user virtual environments (3D MUVEs), they did not have any cognitive maps of the environment since they completed tasks in a virtual world they had not seen before. In MUVEs, one of the most important influences on participants' wayfinding performance is their experience in the environment (Sadeghian et al., 2006). This explains why the method used in the first task influenced the task completion time while those used in the second and third tasks did not. In a majority of the studies in the relevant literature, participants were provided with training in the same implementation environment beforehand. This improves participants' cognitive maps of the environment. Thus, the researchers suggest that user orientations should be conducted in an environment that is not used for the implementation.

CS was the method that caused the most participants to lose their way, and the OSM caused them to get lost the least. With the CS method, the participants could not obtain the general information about the environment since they only followed the coordinates on the title bar, and thus, they got lost more often. If the users do not know about the environment spatially and the location of their destination is known, navigational aids such as teleportation tools and GPS can be used to reach the goal accurately and rapidly. In this situation, users' performances will be better since they do not need to explore the environment (Li et al., 2013). When users do not know about the environment and do not have navigation tools to help them reach the goal, they need to explore the environment to find the goal. When users do not have navigational aids providing direct access to the goal in unfamiliar environments, they tend to concentrate on visual information about the environment provided by navigational aids. Users' orientation in the environment depends on analyzing their location and spatial relationships in the environment and requires landmarks, links, and directions to be able to determine their location and intentionally reach their destinations (Özen, 2006). According to Gramopadhye et al. (2014), if maps and directions are placed in the environment for wayfinding purposes, it will both increase the usability of the environment and reduce workloads. Although the same map was used for both the OSM and PM methods, participants easily reached their goals with the OSM thanks to the affordance indicating their real-time location. However, comparing task completion times showed that the PM method was faster than the OSM method and that the OSM method was faster than the CS method. Although the OSM method enabled participants to move towards their goals more rapidly and get lost less frequently, most participants took more time to get there than they did with PM since they did not use it with CS. With the PM method, the participants got lost more frequently than they did with the OSM method since they made navigation errors and incorrectly estimated distances.

With all these methods, males completed the tasks in shorter times than females (except for the first task performed with PM) but this difference was not statistically significant. Males and females got lost at the same rate. This study is one of the few studies that found no difference in rates of getting lost and task completion times by gender (for another example, see Vila, Beccue, & Anandikar, 2003; Török & Török, 2018). Presumably, there was no difference between participants by gender because they were all students in an instructional technology department. In this respect, users' experience plays an important role in their task completion by gender in MUVEs. In particular, task completion times of users may be long in environments that the users experience for the first time. As participants get more familiar with the environment, their task completion times also get shorter. Female participants got lost more frequently than male participants only while performing the first task, which may be explained by this fact. In this study, the researchers did not match male and female participants according to their characteristics, and they suggest that future studies match the characteristics between genders after an analysis of the differences between males and females.

A review of the relevant literature reveals that the characteristics of users influence their navigation efficiency in MUVEs. Darken and Peterson (2015) stressed that users' spatial visualization skills should be known by researchers and that the spatial skills of users who play games will be higher than those who do not. Darken and Cevik (1999) studied the use of maps in virtual environments and found that individuals with strong spatial skills use maps better than those with weak spatial skills in any given environment. Other studies are reporting that spatial ability influences navigation efficiency and is one of the essential parts of navigation (Bowman et al., 2004; Chen & Stanney, 1999; Downs & Stea, 1973; Sjolinder, 1998; Wu, Zhang, & Zhang, 2009). Çubukçu, Çubukçu, and Nasar (2006) claim that playing computer games played a major role in perceiving the space and transforming it into spatial knowledge. Another study found that users who played computer games were more successful at using maps in MUVEs than those who did not play games (Darken & Cevik, 1999). To mitigate the influence of the participants' characteristics on the implementation results, the researchers created groups considering their spatial visualization scores, weekly durations of playing games and using MUVEs and their experiences with games, computers, and the Internet. Then the researchers checked the groups and confirmed that there was no significant difference between the groups by these independent variables. The researchers also suggest that future empirical studies of this phenomenon similarly check this kind of independent variables.

The participants who used the OSM and the CS together completed the tasks the fastest. Thus, the most important implication of this study's findings is that different navigational aids should be located close to each other for optimum navigation efficiency. This means that the coordinate system should be located closer to the OSM or should be integrated with it. It is a common problem that maps cannot be scaled properly for really large virtual environments (Darken & Peterson, 2015). Therefore, users should be allowed to personalize their navigational aids so that they can be resized and the colors on the map can be changed for people with visual disorders such as color blindness. If it is not possible to use another window for the navigational aid when the size of the window is restricted, then the zoom technique should be used.

CONCLUSION AND FUTURE WORK

In this study, there were differences between the methods by the completion times in the first task, while there was no difference between the methods in the second and third tasks. Had the research been carried out on a single task, the result differences between the different tasks would not have been achieved. Therefore, the researchers suggest that future studies in this field include multiple tasks. The use of objective data collection tools for the implementation will make it possible to analyze the navigation in a micro-dimensional way. To do so, future studies could follow and record users' eye movements during navigation using eye-tracking devices. This will yield objective data about the operations conducted by users during their navigation such as their completion times, their routes, and the number of turns. These data can be used to compare different navigational aids. In this study, the spatial experience involved only two dimensions. However, MUVEs can contain information on the Z-axis. Future studies could examine users' navigation efficiency in spaces containing multiple dimensions and the influence of maps on their spatial experiences.

ACKNOWLEDGMENT

QA is based upon work supported by the National Science Foundation under Grant Nos. 9980081 and 0092831, and by the MacArthur Foundation.

REFERENCES

ActiveWorlds. (2015). *ActiveWorlds: Home of the 3D Internet since 1995*. Retrieved from http://www. activeworlds.com

Akçapınar, G., Altun, A., & Menteş, T. (2012). Hipermetinsel ortamlarda ön bilgi düzeylerinin gezinim profilleri üzerine etkisi [The effect of prior knowledge on navigational profiles in hypertext environments]. *Journal of Education and Science, 37*(163), 143–156.

Altan, T. (2011). *Teknoloji-zengin eğitsel bir yenilik olarak quest atlantis'in örgün eğitime entegrasyonu: Fen ve teknoloji dersi örneği* [Integration of quest atlantis as a technology-rich educational innovation to formal education: A science course case]. Unpublished master's thesis, Hacettepe University, Ankara, Turkey.

Astur, R. S., Ortiz, M. L., & Sutherland, R. J. (1998). A characterization of performance by men and women in a virtual Morris water task: A large and reliable sex difference. *Behavioural Brain Research, 93*(1-2), 185–190. doi:10.1016/S0166-4328(98)00019-9 PMID:9659999

Ballegooij, A. V., & Eliens, A. (2001). Navigation by query in virtual worlds. In *Proceedings of the Web 3D 2001 Conference* (pp. 19-22). Academic Press. 10.1145/363361.363380

Bowman, D. A., Kruijff, E., LaViola, J. J., & Poupyrev, I. (2004). *3D user interfaces: Theory and practice*. Boston, MA: Addison-Wesley.

Chen, C.-H., Chang, W.-C., & Chang, W.-T. (2009). Gender differences in relation to wayfinding strategies, navigational support design, and wayfinding task difficulty. *Journal of Environmental Psychology*, 2(29), 220–226. doi:10.1016/j.jenvp.2008.07.003

Chen, J. L., & Stanney, K. M. (1999). A theoretical model of wayfinding in virtual environments: Proposed strategies for navigational aiding. *Presence*, 8(6), 671–685. doi:10.1162/105474699566558

Chen, M. X., & Chen, C. H. (2019, July). User experience and map design for wayfinding in a virtual environment. In *Proceedings of the International Conference on Human-Computer Interaction* (pp. 117-126). Springer. 10.1007/978-3-030-22649-7_10

Çubukçu, E., Çubukçu, K. M., & Nasar, J. L. (2006). Mekansal bilgi ve bilgisayar oyunu oynama alışkanlığı [Spatial Knowledge and the Computer Game Playing]. *Yapı Mimarlık Kültür ve Sanat Dergisi, 293*, 85–87.

Cutmore, T. R. H., Hine, T. J., Maberly, K. J., Langford, N. M., & Hawgood, G. (2000). Cognitive and gender factors influencing navigation in a virtual environment. *International Journal of Human-Computer Studies*, 53(2), 223–249. doi:10.1006/ijhc.2000.0389

Darken, R. P., & Cevik, H. (1999). Map usage in virtual environments: Orientation Issues. *In Proceedings of IEEE Virtual Reality 99* (pp. 133-140). IEEE Press. 10.1109/VR.1999.756944

Darken, R. P., & Peterson, B. (2015). Spatial orientation, wayfinding and representation. In K. S. Hale & K. M. Stanney (Eds.), *Handbook of Virtual Environments: Design, Implementation, and Applications* (2nd ed., pp. 467–492). New York, NY: CRC Press.

Darken, R. P., & Sibert, J. L. (1993). A toolset for navigation in virtual environments. *In Proceedings of ACM User Interface Software & Technology* (pp. 157-165). ACM. 10.1145/168642.168658

Downs, R. N., & Stea, D. (1973). Cognitive maps and spatial behavior: Process and products. In R. N. Downs & D. Stea (Eds.), *Image and environment: Cognitive mapping and spatial behavior* (pp. 8–26). Chicago: Aldine.

Dudchenko, P. A. (2010). *Why people get lost: The psychology and neuroscience and spatial cognition*. New York, NY: Oxford University Press. doi:10.1093/acprof:oso/9780199210862.001.0001

Fırat, M. (2008). Second life ve sanal ortamda otantik öğrenme deneyimleri. In *Proceeding of 25th National Informatics Congress* (pp. 22-25). Academic Press.

Galea, L. A., & Kimura, D. (1993). Sex differences in route learning. *Personality and Individual Differences*, 14(1), 53–65. doi:10.1016/0191-8869(93)90174-2

Galyean, T. A. (1995). Guided navigation of virtual environments. In *Proceedings of the 1995 Symposium on Interactive 3D Graphics* (pp. 103-104). Academic Press. doi:10.1145/199404.199421

Geszten, D., Komlódi, A., Hercegfi, K., Hámornik, B., Young, A., Köles, M., & Lutters, W. G. (2018). A content-analysis approach for exploring usability problems in a collaborative virtual environment. *Acta Polytechnica Hungarica, 15*(5), 67–88.

Golledge, R. G. (1999). Human wayfinding and cognitive maps. In R. G. Golledge (Ed.), *Wayfinding behavior: Cognitive mapping and other spatial processes* (pp. 5–45). Baltimore: Johns Hopkins University Press.

Gramopadhye, N., Madathil, K. C., Bertrand, J., & Blair, C. S. (2014). An investigation of the effectiveness of navigational aids in a virtual environment. In *Proceedings of the Human Factors and Ergonomics Society 58th Annual Meeting (Vol. 58*, pp. 1949-1953). Academic Press. 10.1177/1541931214581407

Green, C. S., & Bavelier, D. (2003). Action video game modifies visual selective attention. *Nature, 423*(6939), 534–537. doi:10.1038/nature01647 PMID:12774121

Karadeniz, Ş. (2006). Kaybolma açısından kullanışlı çoklu ortamların tasarlanması [Designing usable multimedia in terms of disorientation]. *Journal of Yüzüncü Yıl University Faculty of Education, 3*(2), 79–97.

Li, B., Zhu, K., Zhang, W., Wu, A., & Zhang, X. (2013). A comparative study of two wayfinding aids with simulated driving tasks-GPS and a dual-scale exploration aid. *International Journal of Human-Computer Interaction, 29*(3), 169–177. doi:10.1080/10447318.2012.702634

Lövdén, M., Herlitz, A., Schellenbach, M., Grossman-Hutter, B., Krüger, A., & Lindenberger, U. (2007). Quantitative and qualitative sex differences in spatial navigation. *Scandinavian Journal of Psychology, 48*(5), 353–358. doi:10.1111/j.1467-9450.2007.00582.x PMID:17877549

Lynch, K. (1960). *The image of the city.* Cambridge, MA: MIT Press.

Mayrath, M. C., Traphagan, T., Jarmon, L., Trivedi, A., & Resta, P. (2010). Teaching with virtual worlds: Factors to consider for instructional use of Second Life®. *Journal of Educational Computing Research, 43*(4), 403–444. doi:10.2190/EC.43.4.a

McKenzie, G., & Klippel, A. (2016). The interaction of landmarks and map alignment in you-are-here maps. *The Cartographic Journal, 53*(1), 43–54. doi:10.1179/1743277414Y.0000000101

Minocha, S., & Hardy, C. (2016). Navigation and wayfinding in learning spaces in 3D virtual worlds. In S. Gregory, M. J. W. Lee, B. Dalgarno, & B. Tynan (Eds.), *Learning in Virtual Worlds: Research and Application* (pp. 3–41). AU Press.

Moffat, S. D., Hampson, E., & Hatzipantelis, M. (1998). Navigation in a virtual maze: Sex differences and correlation with psychometric measures of spatial ability in humans. *Evolution and Human Behavior, 19*(2), 73–87. doi:10.1016/S1090-5138(97)00104-9

Özen, A. (2006). *Mimari sanal gerçeklik ortamlarında algı psikolojisi.* Denizli: Bilgi Teknolojileri Kongresi IV, Akademik Bilişim.

Pazzaglia, F., & Taylor, H. A. (2007). Perspective, instruction, and cognitive style in spatial representation of a virtual environment. *Spatial Cognition and Computation, 7*(4), 349–364. doi:10.1080/13875860701663223

Peruch, P., Belingard, L., & Thinus-Blanc, C. (2000). Transfer of spatial knowledge from virtual to real environments. In C. Freksa, W. Brauer, C. Habel, & K. F. Wender (Eds.), *Spatial cognition II. Lecture notes in artificial intelligence* (pp. 253–264). Berlin: Springer. doi:10.1007/3-540-45460-8_19

Raees, M., Ullah, S., & Rahman, S. U. (2019). VEN-3DVE: Vision based egocentric navigation for 3D virtual environments. *International Journal on Interactive Design and Manufacturing, 13*(1), 35–45. doi:10.100712008-018-0481-9

Riis, M. (2016). *Avatar, mediation and transformation of practice in a 3d virtual world: Meaning, identity, and learning.* Unpublished doctoral dissertation, Aalborg University, Denmark.

Ross, S. P., Skelton, R. W., & Mueller, S. C. (2006). Gender differences in spatial navigation in virtual space: Implications when using virtual environments in instruction and assessment. *Virtual Reality (Waltham Cross), 10*(3-4), 175–184. doi:10.100710055-006-0041-7

Sadeghian, P., Kantardzic, M., Lozitskiy, O., & Sheta, W. (2006). The frequent wayfinding- sequence (FWS) methodology: Finding preferred routes in complex virtual environments. *International Journal of Human-Computer Studies, 64*(4), 356–374. doi:10.1016/j.ijhcs.2005.08.014

Sandstrom, N. J., Kaufman, J., & Huettel, S. A. (1998). Males and females use different distal cues in a virtual environment navigation task. *Brain Research. Cognitive Brain Research, 6*, 351–360. doi:10.1016/S0926-6410(98)00002-0 PMID:9593991

Saucier, D. M., Green, S. M., Leason, J., MacFadden, A., Bell, S., & Elias, L. J. (2002). Are sex differences in navigation caused by sexually dimorphic strategies or by differences in the ability to use the strategies? *Behavioral Neuroscience, 116*(3), 403–410. doi:10.1037/0735-7044.116.3.403 PMID:12049321

Sjolinder, M. (1998). Spatial cognition and environmental descriptions. In N. Dahlnack (Ed.), *Exploring navigation: Towards a framework for design and evaluation of navigation in electronic spaces* (pp. 61–72). Stockholm: Swedish Institute of Computer Science.

Tlauka, M., Brolese, A., Pomeroy, D., & Hobbs, W. (2005). Gender differences in spatial knowledge acquired through simulated exploration of a virtual shopping centre. *Journal of Environmental Psychology, 25*(1), 111–118. doi:10.1016/j.jenvp.2004.12.002

Török, Z. G., & Török, Á. (2018, August). Looking at the map-or navigating in a virtual city: Interaction of visuospatial display and spatial strategies in VR. In *Proceedings of the 2018 9th IEEE International Conference on Cognitive Infocommunications (CogInfoCom)* (pp. 327-332). IEEE.

Tüzün, H. (2010). Dünya üzerine yayılmış çok-kullanıcılı çevrim-içi eğitsel bir bilgisayar oyununun teknik yapısı ve türkiye'de yaklaşımlar. In G. Telli-Yamamoto, U. Demiray, & M. Kesim (Eds.), *Türkiye'de e-öğrenme: Gelişmeler ve uygulamalar* (pp. 261–281). Ankara, Turkey: Cem Web Ofset.

Tüzün, H., & Özdinç, F. (2016). The effects of 3D multi-user virtual environments on freshmen university students' conceptual and spatial learning and presence in departmental orientation. *Computers & Education, 94*, 228–240. doi:10.1016/j.compedu.2015.12.005

Uğur, A. (2002). İnternet üzerinde üç boyut ve Web3D teknolojileri. In Proceedings of the VIII. Türkiye'de İnternet Konferansı (INET-TR 2002). Academic Press.

Vila, J., Beccue, B., & Anandikar, S. (2003). The gender factor in virtual reality navigation and way-finding. In *Proceedings of the 36th Hawaii International Conference on System Sciences*. IEEE Press. 10.1109/HICSS.2003.1174239

Winter, J. W., Lappan, G., Fitzgerald, W., & Shroyer, J. (1989). *Middle grades mathematics project: Spatial visualization*. NY: Addison-Wesley.

Wu, A., Zhang, W., & Zhang, X. (2009). Evaluation of wayfinding aids in virtual environment. *International Journal of Human-Computer Interaction*, 25(1), 1–21. doi:10.1080/10447310802537582

Yıldız, B. (2009). *Üç-boyutlu sanal ortam ve somut materyal kullanımının uzamsal görselleştirme ve zihinsel döndürme becerilerine etkileri [The effects of using three-dimensional virtual environments and concrete manipulatives on spatial visualisation and mental rotation abilities]*. Unpublished master's thesis, Hacettepe University, Ankara, Turkey.

Yokosawa, K., Wada, E., & Mitsumatsu, H. (2005). Coding and transformation of cognitive maps in a virtual environment. *Electronics and Communications*, 88(4), 43–50. doi:10.1002/ecjc.20096

This research was previously published in the International Journal of Gaming and Computer-Mediated Simulations (IJGCMS), 11(4); pages 21-41, copyright year 2019 by IGI Publishing (an imprint of IGI Global).

Chapter 32
The Effect of List–Liner–Based Interaction Technique in a 3D Interactive Virtual Biological Learning Environment

Numan Ali
University of Malakand, Pakistan

Sehat Ullah
University of Malakand, Pakistan

Zuhra Musa
University of Malakand, Pakistan

ABSTRACT

Various interaction techniques (such as direct, menu-based, etc.) are provided to allow users to interact with virtual learning environments. These interaction techniques improve their performance and learning but in a complex way. In this chapter, we investigated a simple list-liner based interface for gaining access to different modules within a 3D interactive Virtual Learning Environment (VLE). We have implemented a 3D interactive biological VLE for secondary school level students by using virtual mustard plant (VMP), where students interact by using 3D interactive device with the help of list-liner based interface. The aim of this work is to provide an easy interaction interface to use list-liner interaction technique by using 3D interactive device in an information-rich and complex 3D virtual environment. We compared list-liner interface with direct interface and evaluations reveal that the list-liner interface is very suitable and efficient for student learning enhancement and that the students can easily understand and use the system.

DOI: 10.4018/978-1-6684-7597-3.ch032

1. INTRODUCTION

The use of advance technology for teaching and training purposes is increasing day-by-day and many fields such as surgery, aeronautic assembly, architecture, businesses and education etc, are using digital technology applications to achieve efficiency in their work processes (Fung, 2002; Johansson & Wickman, 2018). These technologies are very helpful for the improvement of skill and independent learning (de Oliveira & Galembeck, 2016; Emvalotis & Koutsianou, 2018). As technological development are rapidly growing in science education, to develop new strategies and to enable teachers to develop pedagogical content knowledge around novel topics (Williams, Eames, Hume, & Lockley, 2012). According to Dalgarno and Lee, "technologies themselves do not directly cause learning to occur but can afford certain tasks that themselves may result in learning" (Dalgarno, Hedberg, & Harper, 2002). One of the advance technologies is the use of Virtual Reality (VR) technology that provides an efficient solution for problems where the physical alternative is not available, the cost of doing the actual work is high or the procedure of the task is very dangerous to perform, particularly in education because of their unique technological characteristics that differentiate them from the other Information and Communication Technologies (ICT) applications (Baggott la Velle, Wishart, McFarlane, Brawn, & John, 2007).

1.1 Virtual Reality (VR)

The recent advances in computer hardware and software have made VR technology capable to be used in many fields such as medical, military and education. According to Howard Rheingold VR is a three-dimensional computer-generated environment where user feels his/her presence. In the virtual environment user is able to navigate freely from one point to another, observe it from different sides, to get in touch with it, to seize it and manipulate it (Rheingold, 1991). VR can be described as a montage of technologies that support the creation of synthetic, highly interactive Three Dimensional (3D) spatial environments that represent real or non-real situations (Mikropoulos & Natsis, 2011). VR allows user to change the flow of occurrences in a virtual environment and hence to interact with virtual things. It uses many hardware components and software techniques for each application area. Virtual environment presents the 3D representation of the real or imaginary facts and provides to users a real time interaction (Hachet, 2010). Virtual reality can be classified into three basic schemes that are interaction, immersion and involvement (Pausch, Proffitt, & Williams, 1997). Interaction can be performed by pointing and gesturing, and by picking objects to manipulate them or examine them. The 3D interaction interfaces provide to users more realism and immersion in a virtual environment where users feel their presence. In virtual reality the 3D interaction is considered as a coercing component which allows the user to navigate, select, control and manipulate objects in a virtual environment (Ullah, 2011). Involvement is the user participation in a virtual world where he/she can navigate in a passive or active way (Pausch et al., 1997). Therefore, we must design the virtual environments in a way that is based on 3D interaction techniques where user feels more realism and immersion in it.

1.2 Virtual Reality in Education

In the teaching-learning process innovative approaches have been developed by using new technologies, in which VR is considered the essential one (Richard, Tijou, Richard, & Ferrier, 2006). VR is one of the most imperative contrivance that support students learning in different fields. Therefore, there are a lot of special virtual learning environments developed for different purposes in education such as Virtual Reality Physics Simulation (VRPS) (Kim, Park, Lee, Yuk, & Lee, 2001), Construct 3D for Mathematics Education (Sheridan, 2000), Virtual ChemLab Projects (Woodfield et al., 2004a) and biological education (Shim et al., 2003a) etc.

Virtual Learning Environment (VLE) is one of the most powerful tools that supports the learning process as ICT (Rajaei & Aldhalaan, 2011; Reis & Escudeiro, 2014). It is findings from the previous research that virtual learning environments are often more effective than traditional teaching tools (Clase et al., 2009). With the help of VR technology immersive and interactive virtual environments are created to facilitate or aid learning (Nonis, 2005; Richards & Kelaiah, 2012). These activities enable students to experience phenomena through their own eyes, ears and hands rather than through the eyes of a teacher or textbook writer (Ling & Rui, 2016; Totkov, 2003). Winn et al. suggested that interaction is more important facilitator for learning than immersion for some kinds of task (Winn et al., 1997). Therefore, the use of VR has become familiar technology in education for students learning improvement particularly in practical education.

Designing of virtual learning environment needs display hardware, tracking system, input device, environment model(s), rendering / display software and interaction software (Bowman et al., 2008; Wickens, 1992).

1.3 Virtual Reality in Biology Education

One of the solutions of the above problems and limitations is the use of VR technologies in biology education. Biology experiments are among the difficult tasks to be performed by students in laboratories (Mikropoulos, Katsikis, Nikolou, & Tsakalis, 2003a). Virtual biology laboratory curricula have been used efficiently as alternative or preliminary activities for hands-on experiments in high school and college level bi- ology courses, respectively. Virtual biology laboratories provide momentous benefits especially for the distance education, because it can be used anywhere and anytime for virtual experiments (Shim et al., 2003b). Virtual biology laboratories facilitate the students to perform the experiments many times without any costs and accidents. VR also enables students to explore very small (microscopic information), big or hazardous objects that cannot be accessed in normal situation in the real world (Bonser et al., 2013). The students' performance and learning capabilities can be enhanced by using visual, audio and haptic feedback in a virtual environment. Therefore, the use of VR has become familiar technology in biology education for students learning enhancement.

In this paper, we introduce a framework called virtual mustard plant (VMP), which uses a novel list-liner interaction technique, with a haptic interactive device. We invited, secondary school students for the evaluation of list-liner interaction technique in VMP. The students performed different tasks using list-liner as well as a direct interface. The experimental results reveal that the list-liner technique is efficient, more user friendly, easy in searching and exploration and has a higher user-satisfaction as compare to direct interface.

The rest of the paper is organized as follows. Section 2 elaborates some related studies in the field of virtual system for learning. Section 3 presents our proposed system. Section 4 is about the experiment and evaluation results of our proposed system. Finally, section 5 is related with conclusion and future work.

2. BACKGROUND

This section presents existing work in VR on biological education both in two-dimensional (2D) and Three Dimensional (3D) environments.

2.1 Virtual Biological Learning Environments

This subsection presents Virtual Biology Laboratories (VBLs) both in 2D and 3D environments.

Different Virtual Learning Environments (VLEs) have been developed for learning purposes by researchers that improve the learning capabilities of learners in biology education. Some of these learning environments are the following:

In 2005, Dede et al. developed an online graphical Multi-User Virtual Environments (MUVEs) in biology education to enhance middle school student motivation and learning about science and society (Dede, Clarke, Ketelhut, Nelson, & Bowman, 2005). Virtual environments for the structure of the plant cell and the process of photosynthesis were developed by Mikropoulos et al. In this VE exploration and interaction inside the virtual plant cell starts by navigation through the external plant tissue of the virtual cell. The internal cell structure is visible and the user can freely navigate, observe and study. The student can study about the organization of organelles in the 3D space inside the cell and the way they work together in order for the cell to function (Mikropoulos, Katsikis, Nikolou, & Tsakalis, 2003b). A typical cell environment was constructed at NDSU (North Dakota State University) by While et al. This VE contains 3D representations of all the components and organelles of a cell such as the nucleus, mitochondria, and chloroplasts. Students learn the structure and functions of a cell by interactively performing goal-oriented tasks in the 3D virtual cell (McClean, Slator, & White, 1999). Virtual environments for the structure of the plant cell and the process of photosynthesis were developed by Mikropoulos and Natsis (2011). Where the internal cell structure is visible and the user can freely navigate, observe and manipulate different objects. Here students can study about the organization of organelles in the 3D space inside the cell and the way they work together in order for the cell to function. This virtual environment is useful for teachers, but the user can lose orientation and navigation in this environment. Slator developed a Virtual Cell that provides an authentic problem-solving experience, engaging students in actively learning structures and functions of eukaryotic cells. The Virtual Cell simulation implements a series of cellular environments with a variety of assays, molecules, proteins, and tools providing an experimental context for the student. A virtual avatar acts as a guide and gives out assignments, and intelligent software tutor agents provide content and problem-solving advice. The Virtual Cell supports multi-user collaborations, where both students and teachers from remote sites can communicate with each other and work together on shared goals (Slator, 1999). VRBS (virtual Rety Biology Simulation) was developed to study the structure and function of human eye. Here the iris and pupil of the human eye have been visualized. While changing the viewpoint by repositioning some objects in the environment, the change in the iris and pupil have been visualized for understanding how these objects are seemed. In this system the interaction was based on number keys pressing in keyboard and it is difficult for students to memorize the functionality of each key to interact with different shapes (Shim et al., 2003c). Another approach was designed and implemented that is prototype web-based virtual 3D environment for teaching vertebrate biology for high school and middle school students. This 3D learning environment called Frog Island contains a Virtual Frog along with a rich array of related resources (images, sounds, data, and simulations) that students and teachers can use to study about information of frogs (Dev et al.,

1998). In 2012, Cheng and Annetta evaluated students' learning outcomes and their learning experiences through playing a Serious Educational Games (SEGs). They used different game based virtual learning environments (i.e. SEGs) to evaluate students learning interest. They found that students take more interest in learning by using actively immersing and enjoying the game worlds (Cheng & Annetta, 2012). In 2013, Bonser et al. developed a virtual microscopy for botany teaching. Virtual microscopy uses high-resolution digital 'virtual slides' that facilitate students to know about the using of actual microscope and glass slides. The framework is an effective tool for increasing student satisfaction in introductory botany courses (Bonser et al., 2013).

In a VLE it is necessary to provide some guidance where students take interest and perform their task more easily. However, most of the previously discussed techniques are providing a direct navigation to each individual part/object in the system. In addition, these techniques are complex and mostly useful for only expert users.

3. METHODS AND MATERIALS

The objective of this research work is to study the effect of list-liner and direct based interface in a complex 3D interactive VLE. We have developed a 3D interactive Virtual Mustard Plant (VMP) environment with simple list-liner and direct based interface. Our proposed system provides some advantages over previous:

- It provides 3D interaction interface with list-liner based technique for information rich and complex 3D virtual environment.
- It attracts the naive users by providing a direct simple 2D visual interface with each part of the plant in the virtual environment.
- It enhances students learning interest by hiding the irrelevant information and guessing the students learning.
- It provides detailed visual information about different parts of the plant.
- It provides two types of interaction techniques i.e. direct interaction and list-liner based interaction.

The proposed system is a 3D virtual environment like a real garden which contains a Virtual Mustard Plant (VMP) as shown in Figure 1. When the student selects any part of the plant then they get textual information about the selected part of the plant. This information is very useful for student learning enhancement where he/she comes to know about the properties of the plant.

3.1 Software Architecture

In this section we are going to discuss the principle components of the software architecture as shown in Figure 2, on which the VMP is based.

Figure 1. The inside scenario of VMP

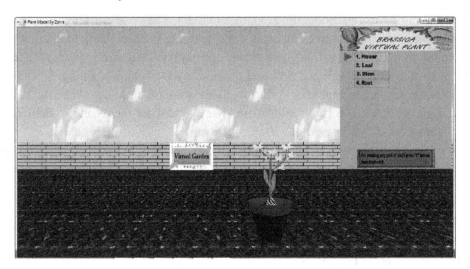

Figure 2. Software architecture of VMP

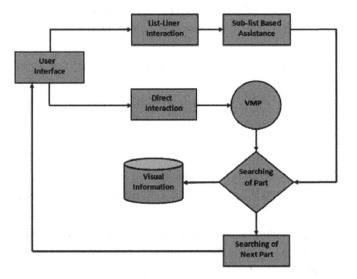

3.1.1 User Interaction

The first module of this architecture is the user interaction module. This provides an interface between the user and VMP enabling the user to navigate/move and select/manipulate virtual objects. User interacts with VMP through both direct based and list-liner based interaction. We use Nintendo Wiimote as an input device. This subsection contains the following categories.

a. Nintendo Wiimote's Interface: There are many devices for 3D interaction like Microsoft Kinect (Microsoft Kinect, 2018), leap motion (Leap Motion Company, 2018), Nintendo Wiimote (Nintendo Wiimote, 2018), phantom (Phantom Company, 2018), joystick brand Joystick ("Joystick," 2018), etc. In VMP we have used Nintendo Wiimote for 3D interaction because it is a cost-effective device than other 3D interaction interfaces, it can also provide haptic sensation in the form of vibration. Wiimote is a 3D video game controller device which allows the user to interact with the virtual environment as shown in Figure 3.

It senses every action of user and makes user feels less like a player and represents user's existence in the virtual environment Nintendo Wiimote (Wiimote, 2018). It contains 3- axis accelerometers, multiple buttons, a small speaker and a vibrator which support in game sound effects and user feedback. For connection with the system it uses Bluetooth technology. Its workspace is quite large and allows the interaction from a distance of 18 meters. The user in VMP is represented by a pointer which is controlled via Wiimote. Through Wiimote user can freely navigate and rotate any plant's object according to their hand's position and rotation and can feel them more immersion where he/she feels realism inside the virtual learning environment.

Figure 3. Wiimote's buttons and coordinates

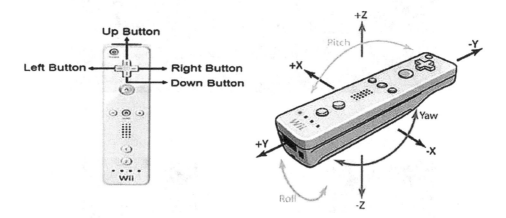

3.1.2 Direct Based Interaction

In this type of interaction, there is direct access to the plant by using Wiimote. The user can select different parts of the plant directly. When the student selects any part of the VMP textual information directly appears on the screen. The direct based interaction interface as shown in Figure 4.

a. Navigation in Direct based Interaction: The pointer representing the user can move (navigate) freely in all directions in the VMP. The navigation of pointer along X-axis is achieved through the rotation of Wiimote along its Y-axis as shown in part (b) of Figure 5. Similarly, the movement of pointer along Y-axis is controlled through the rotation of Wiimote along its X-axis as shown in part (a) of Figure 5. The Z-axis movement of pointer is controlled through the up and down buttons of Wiimote.

b. Selection and Manipulation in Direct based Interaction: Selection and manipulation are the important activities in any virtual environment. For the manipulation of a plant's object it needs to be selected first. In VMP an object becomes selectable when the pointer collides with it. After collision if the user presses the button "A" of the Wiimote, the object is selected the corresponding part of plant gets zoom- in on the screen. After selection the user is able to manipulate it i.e. to change its position or orientation and other attributes. For example he/she can zoom-in the selected plant's object and can explore it in depth and release it by just pressing the Wiimote "A" button again.

Figure 4. Direct based interaction interface

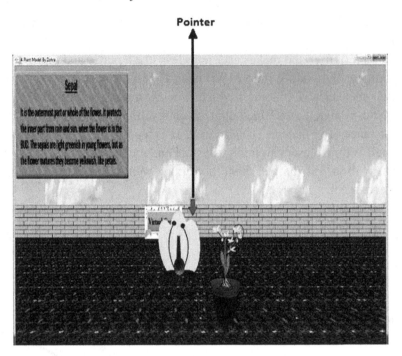

Figure 5. Wiimote's rotations

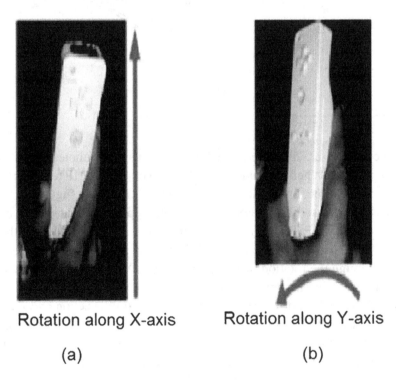

Rotation along X-axis   Rotation along Y-axis

(a)   (b)

3.1.3 List-Liner Based Interaction

In this type of interaction there is given a list, in which information about the parts of the plant is displayed. When a student selects a list item by using Wiimote, the corresponding part of plant point-out clearly by liner and can be zoom-in on the screen. Similarly, textual information is also displayed for the corresponding part of the plant.

a. Sub-List based Assistance: This is a very important module; it contains a list of all parts of the plant. First of all users select the name of a part of the plant from the list as shown in Figure 6 and then study its information. Navigate the pointer is representing the user can move from top to down freely in the list. The movement of a pointer from top to down or down to top is achieved by pressing buttons "plus (+)" and "minus (-)". Similarly for sub-list the movement of a pointer from left to right or from right to left is controlled by pressing buttons "left" and "right."

Figure 6. List-Liner based interaction interface

b. Selection and Manipulation in List-Liner based Interaction: For the manipulation of a plant's object it needs to be selected first from the list through a pointer. If the user presses the button "A" of the Wiimote, the object is selected the corresponding part of plant gets zoom-in on the screen. After selection the user is able to manipulate it i.e. to change its position or orientation and other attributes. For example he/she can zoom-in the selected plant's object and can explore it in depth by pressing button "down" of the Wiimote.

3.1.4 Textual Information in VMP

Whenever a student selects any part of the plant, information about its name, proper ties and other details are provided in textual form which is shown in Figure 7, here student selects flower from the list and the sub-part i.e sepal of the flower zoom in and also its detailed information in textual form displayed. This information is very useful for students learning enhancement and improving their exam score.

Figure 7. Textual information about plant's part in VMP.

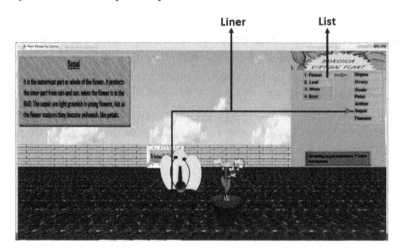

4. METHODS

This section describes the experiment and evaluation of the 3D interactive VMP. We have implemented the 3D interactive VMP in MS Visual Studio 2012 using OpenGL on HP Corei3 Laptop having specication 2.4GHz processor, 2GB RAM and Intel(R) HD Graphics card. The Nintendo Wiimote was used as interfacing device. Similarly, an LED screen of 40 inches was used for display during experimentation.

4.1 Participants and Context

In order to evaluate the VMP, forty-five students participated in the evaluation. They were from secondary school level. They were from different institutes and had ages from 14 to 16 years. These students were divided into two groups (i.e. G1, G2) containing equal numbers of students. There were eight females in G1 and nine in G2. As all the participants had no prior experience of VR systems or games, therefore, they were briefed with the help of a 25-minute demonstration about the use of the Nintendo Wiimote and VMP. For example, they were taught how they will navigate in the environment. Similarly, they were also guided about the selection and manipulation of different parts of the plant. Then each participant was asked to search different parts of the plant. The students in G1 tested the environment by using direct interaction with different parts of the plant. The students in G2 tested the same environment by using list-liner interaction with different parts of the plant. The students perform their tasks in VMP as shown in Figure 8. Here we recorded the search completion (plant's parts searching time) along with errors for each student. Each participant filled a questionnaire after getting experience in VMP. The subjective response of students was collected through a questionnaire.

The subjective responses of students regarding the easiness of the list-liner based interaction and its effect on the students' performance in VMP. The students answered each question on a scale of three to five options.

Figure 8. Task performing by participant in 3D interactive VMP

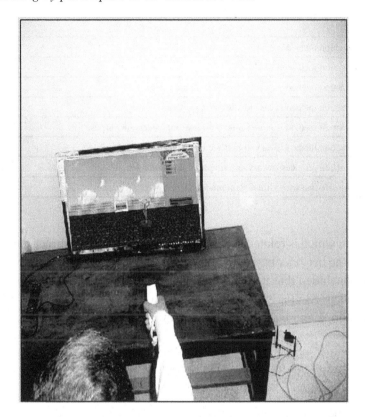

4.2 Data Sources and Data Analysis

This section describes analysis of the data accumulated during evaluation of the interaction techniques. Data was collected from the students of G1 (Group 1) and G2 (Group 2) through questionnaire, after evaluating both interaction techniques in VMP. The following aspects of the VMP were analyzed.

4.2.1 Questionnaire Interview

In first part of the analysis, data were gathered from the students of G1 and G2 using a questionnaire interview when they evaluated both interaction techniques in VMP with the help of direct and list-liner based interaction techniques. The questionnaire interview contained the following questions as shown in Table 1. During questionnaire interview the students answered each question on a scale of three to five options.

5. RESULTS

In this section we present the responses to the questions and also the analysis of the data recorded/ collected during the experiments. We used a statistical method Analysis of Variance (ANOVA) to find statistically significant difference between two groups.

Table 1. Questionnaire interview from students

S. No.	Questions
1	Which interaction method is easy?
2	Which interaction method is intuitive?
3	Which interaction method puts cognitive load on the user?
4	Which interaction method is easy to search/find a part(s) of the plant?
5	Which interaction method is more suitable for learning/education purpose?
6	Which interaction method is easy to find/search a known part of the plant?
7	Which interaction provides an easy and simple exploration method?
8	Overall, I am satisfied with virtual plant model.

For the first question, which is related to the easiness of list-liner and direct-based interaction, 65.7% of the students selected the list-liner based interaction and 34.3% of the students selected the direct-based interaction. It can be concluded that it is very easy to use the list-liner based interaction to evaluate the different parts of the plant. Similarly to answer Q2 regarding the intuitiveness, 59.2% chose list-liner based interaction and 40.8% chose direct based interaction as shown in Figure 9.

Figure 9. Users' responses about the easiness and intuitiveness of interaction

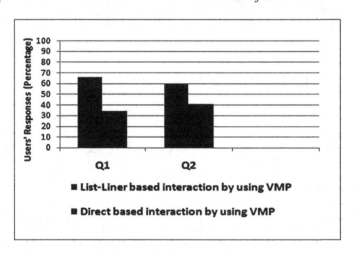

The third question, which was related to the cognitive load about both interaction interfaces, 66.5% of the students selected the list-liner based interaction method that it does not put more cognitive load on users' performance and 33.5% of the students selected the direct based interaction method. Similarly to answer Q4, regarding the searching of plant's parts, 70.3% choose list-liner interaction method and 29.7% choose direct interaction method as shown in Figure 10. The next question related to learning/education, for which 69.8% of the students selected that list-liner interaction method is more suitable for learning/education purposes and 30.2% of the students selected the based interaction method. Similarly to answer Q6, regarding the searching of already known parts of plant, 51.4% selected list-liner interaction method and 49.6% selected direct interaction method as shown in Figure 11.

Figure 10. Cognitive load and ease of searching of plant's parts

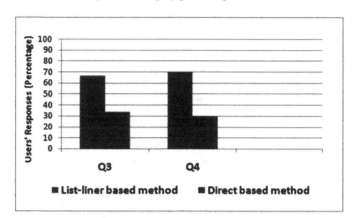

Figure 11. Learning and already known searching of plant's parts

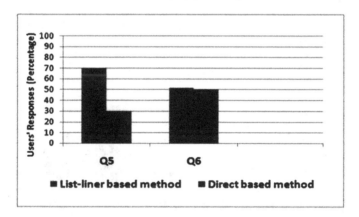

The next question, which was related to the exploration that which interaction method is simple for exploration of the plant's part, 51.4% selected list-liner interaction method and 49.6% selected direct interaction method as shown in Figure 12. The last question, which was related to satisfaction about VMP, 54.3% students selected the higher level and 35.2% selected the highest level of satisfaction after using VMP as shown in Figure 13.

5.1 Performance Measure of Direct and List-Liner Interactions in VMP

The second part of the analysis was to check the performance of both groups (G1 and G2) in searching the same part of the plant in VMP using their respective interactional conditions. The conditions were the following for the groups:

G1: searched the plant's parts in VMP by using direct interaction.
G2: searched the plant's parts in VMP by using list-liner interaction.

Figure 12. Exploration of plant's parts

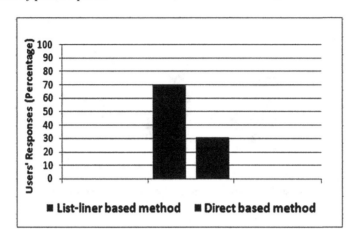

Figure 13. Satisfaction about VMP

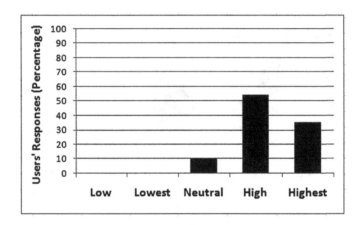

5.2 Task Assigning and Completion

For task assigning and completion we selected different main parts of the plant (i.e flower, leaf, stem and roots) to find their sub-parts and to read their textual information in detail. During searching of targeted plant's part and sub-part we counted students' searching time and errors of both groups i.e G1 and G2. After searching and reading of different sub-parts' textual information we asked different questions from both groups are given in Table 2. As stated earlier, textual information regarding each plant's part was equally avail- able to both groups (i.e. G1 and G2). The data recorded in this section consist of their search of parts completion times and the mean of errors that occurred during parts' searching.

5.3 Task Completion Time

The Analysis of Variance (ANOVA) for task completion time is significant ($F(1, 47) = 22.24$, $P < 0.05$). The average task completion time and standard deviation for each group are given in Table 3 and Figure 14. Comparing the task completion time of G1 with that of G2, we obtained a considerable difference, which means that students who used list-liner interaction method for searching of targeted plant's part in VMP were far better compared with those who used direct interaction method for searching of targeted plant's part in VMP.

Table 2. Questionnaires from students about different parts of plant

S. No	Questions
1	What is a pollen grain in flower?
2	What is a filament?
3	What is a calyx and how many sepals it contains?
4	What is a sepal and role of sepal in flower?
5	What is a stele and how many types of stele?
6	What is the role of veins in leaf?
7	What is a midrib and the role of midrib in leaf?
8	What is a vascular bundle?
9	What is the role of pericycle in stele?
10	What is the role of pericycle in stele?

Table 3. Average task completion time and standard deviation for G1 and G2

Groups	Mean (Mints)	Standard Deviation (Mints)
G1	1.80	0.68
G2	0.67	0.40

Figure 14. Average task completion time of G1 and G2

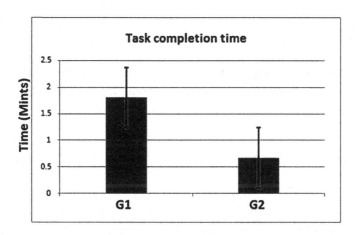

5.4 Number of Errors during Searching of Plant's Parts

In this portion, we present a comprehensive analysis of errors occurred during searching of targeted plant's part which is shown in Table 4 and Figure 15. We counted the number of errors that has been done by a student during searching of targeted plant's part. These errors are the invalid/incorrect selection of plant's part.

Table 4. Average number of errors with standard deviation for G1 and G2

Groups	Mean (Errors)	Standard Deviation (Errors)
G1	3.91	1.05
G2	1.95	0.87

Figure 15. Average number of errors with standard deviation for G1 and G2

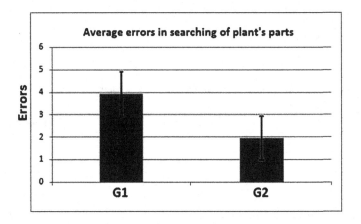

5.5 Measuring Students' Learning in VMP

In order to find the individual learning of students, we asked different questions from the two groups such as identifying various parts of plant, information about parts and their functions in the plant. We used the following equation (1) for students' success rate.

$$SuccessRate = \frac{CorrectAnswer}{TotalQuestionsAsked} * 100 \tag{1}$$

Here the mean success rate of G1 (Group 1) and G2 (Group 2) were 78.3% (SD= 10.2) and 82.7% (SD= 12.5) as shown in Figure 16. It was found that the learning capabilities of G2 to be slightly better than that of the G1, because both G1 and G2 guided by VMP by different interaction interfaces. However, on the bases of time and errors we observed a significant difference between the performance of G2 (students who used list-liner based interaction) and G1 (students who used direct-based interaction). We can say that students were overall satisfied with various aspects of the VMP such as textual information, direct and list-liner based interactions interfaces.

Figure 16. Mean success rate of G1 and G2 with standard deviations

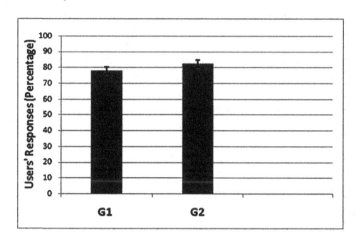

6. CONCLUSION

In this paper, we presented a 3D interactive VMP that we have developed for secondary school level students. Through evaluations of both groups (G1 and G2), we found that our proposed framework is very helpful for education institutions where students can simulate their biological tasks about plant like in a real world. Our proposed framework provides to students an advanced 3D interaction interface, visual information and list- liner interaction with different parts of the plant. We have combined the 3D interaction interface, visual information and list-liner interaction in VMP which show that it improves students' learning skills and they took more interest in biology learning. The visual information is very helpful for students' learning enhancement and also in improving their exam score.

The proposed framework is also suitable in the upgrading of education system. The introduction of this novel based interaction interface and 3D interactive advance technology explore and disclose new ways in the educational institutes for the upcoming students and also provide them with a sort of stimulus which are very useful for the encouragement of students and provoke them for further exploration and innovation in the field of education. Through this way the dignity and honor of the educational institutions can also be enhanced.

REFERENCES

Alam, A., Ullah, S., & Ali, N. (2016). A student-friendly framework for adaptive 3d-virtual learning environments. *Proceeding of Pakistan Academy of Sciences*, *53*(3), 255–266.

Alam, A., Ullah, S., & Ali, N. (2018). The effect of learning-based adaptivity on students performance in 3d-virtual learning environments. *IEEE Access*, *6*, 3400–3407. doi:10.1109/ACCESS.2017.2783951

Baggott la Velle, L., Wishart, J., McFarlane, A., Brawn, R., & John, P. (2007). Teaching and learning with ict within the subject culture of secondary school science. *Research in Science & Technological Education, 25*(3), 339–349. doi:10.1080/02635140701535158

Bonser, S. P., de Permentier, P., Green, J., Velan, G. M., Adam, P., & Kumar, R. K. (2013). Engaging students by emphasising botanical concepts over techniques: Innovative practical exercises using virtual microscopy. *Journal of Biological Education, 47*(2), 123–127. doi:10.1080/00219266.2013.764344

Bowman, D. A., Coquillart, S., Froehlich, B., Hirose, M., Kitamura, Y., Kiyokawa, K., & Stuerzlinger, W. (2008). 3d user interfaces: New directions and perspectives. *IEEE Computer Graphics and Applications, 28*(6), 20–36. doi:10.1109/MCG.2008.109 PMID:19004682

Cheng, M.-T., & Annetta, L. (2012). Students' learning outcomes and learning experiences through playing a serious educational game. *Journal of Biological Education, 46*(4), 203–213. doi:10.1080/00219266.2012.688848

Clase, K. L., Adamo-Villani, N., Gooding, S. L., Yadav, A., Karpicke, J. D., & Gentry, M. (2009). Enhancing creativity in synthetic biology with interactive virtual environments. In Proceedings of the 39th IEEE Frontiers in education conference FIE '09 (pp. 1–6). doi:10.1109/FIE.2009.5350646

de Oliveira, M. L., & Galembeck, E. (2016). Mobile applications in cell biology present new approaches for cell modelling. *Journal of Biological Education, 50*(3), 290–303. doi:10.1080/00219266.2015.1085428

Dede, C., Clarke, J., Ketelhut, D. J., Nelson, B., & Bowman, C. (2005). Students motivation and learning of science in a multi-user virtual environment. In *Proceedings of the American educational research association conference* (pp. 1–8). Academic Press.

Dev, P., Pichumani, R., Walker, D., Heinrichs, W., Karadi, C., & Lorie, W. (1998). Formative design of a virtual learning environment. *Studies in Health Technology and Informatics, 50*, 392–398. PMID:10180582

Emvalotis, A., & Koutsianou, A. (2018). Greek primary school students images of scientists and their work: Has anything changed? *Research in Science & Technological Education, 36*(1), 69–85. doi:10.1080/02635143.2017.1366899

Fung, Y. Y. H. (2002). A comparative study of primary and secondary school students' images of scientists. *Research in Science & Technological Education, 20*(2), 199–213. doi:10.1080/0263514022000030453

Hachet, M. (2010). *3D User Interfaces, from Mobile Devices to Immersive Virtual Environments* [Habilitation `a diriger des recherches]. Universit'e Sciences et Technologies - Bordeaux I. Retrieved from https://tel.archives-ouvertes.fr/tel-00576663

Johansson, A.-M., & Wickman, P.-O. (2018). The use of organising purposes in science instruction as a scaffolding mechanism to support progressions: A study of talk in two primary science classrooms. *Research in Science & Technological Education, 36*(1), 1–16. doi:10.1080/02635143.2017.1318272

Joysticks. (2018). Newegg. Retrieved From http://www.newegg.com/pc-game-controllers/subcategory/id-123

Kesner, M., Frailich, M., & Hofstein, A. (2013). Implementing the inter- net learning environment into the chemistry curriculum in high schools in Israel. In *Technology-rich learning environments* (p. 209-234). Retrieved from https://www.worldscientific.com/doi/abs/10.1142/97898125644120010

Kim, J.-H., Park, S., Lee, H., Yuk, K.-C., & Lee, H. (2001). Virtual reality simulations in physics education. *Interactive Multimedia Electronic* Additional Reading. *Journal of Computer-Enhanced Learning*, *3*(2).

Leap Motion Company. (n.d.). Retrieved from https://www.leapmotion.com/company

Ling, H., & Rui, L. (2016, Aug). Vr glasses and leap motion trends in education. In *Proceedings of the 2016 11th international conference on computer science education (ICCSE)* (p. 917-920). 10.1109/ICCSE.2016.7581705

McClean, P. E., Slator, B. M., & White, A. R. (1999). The virtual cell: An interactive, virtual environment for cell biology. In *Edmedia: World conference on educational media and technology* (pp. 1442–1443). Academic Press.

Mikropoulos, T. A., Katsikis, A., Nikolou, E., & Tsakalis, P. (2003a). Virtual environments in biology teaching. *Journal of Biological Education*, *37*(4), 176–181. doi:10.1080/00219266.2003.9655879

Mikropoulos, T. A., & Natsis, A. (2011). Educational virtual environments: A ten-year review of empirical research (1999–2009). *Computers & Education*, *56*(3), 769–780. doi:10.1016/j.compedu.2010.10.020

Nintendo Wiimote. (2018). Retrieved from https://store.nintendo.com

Nonis, D. (2005). *3d virtual learning environments (3d VLE)*. Singapore: Ministry of Education.

Pausch, R., Proffitt, D., & Williams, G. (1997). Quantifying immersion in virtual reality. In *Proceedings of the 24th annual conference on computer graphics and interactive techniques* (pp. 13–18). New York: ACM Press/Addison-Wesley Publishing Co. doi:10.1145/258734.258744

PCGamer. (2018). Microsoft Kinect. Retrieved from http://www.pcgamer.com/microsoft-ceases-production-of-kinect-for-windows

Phantom Company. P. C. (2018). Retrieved from http://www.immersion.fr/en/phantom-touch-x/

Rajaei, H., & Aldhalaan, A. (2011). Advances in virtual learning environments and class- rooms. In *Proceedings of the 14th communications and networking symposium* (pp. 133–142). San Diego, CA, USA: Society for Computer Simulation International. Retrieved From; http://dl.acm.org/citation.cfm?id=2048416.2048434

Reis, R., & Escudeiro, P. (2014). A model for implementing learning games on virtual world platforms. In *Proceedings of the XV international conference on human computer interaction* (pp. 98:1–98:2). New York: ACM. doi:10.1145/2662253.2662351

Rheingold, H. (1991). *Virtual reality*. New York: Simon & Schuster, Inc.

Richard, E., Tijou, A., Richard, P., & Ferrier, J.-L. (2006). Multi-modal virtual environments for education with haptic and olfactory feedback. *Virtual Reality (Waltham Cross)*, *10*(3), 207–225. doi:10.100710055-006-0040-8

Richards, D., & Kelaiah, I. (2012). Usability attributes in virtual learning environments. In *Proceedings of the 8th Australasian conference on interactive entertainment: Playing the system* (pp. 9:1–9:10). New York, NY, USA: ACM. doi:10.1145/2336727.2336736

Schofield, D., & Lester, E. (2010). Virtual chemical engineering: Guidelines for e-learning in engineering education.

Sheridan, T. B. (2000). Interaction, imagination and immersion some research needs. In *Proceedings of the ACM symposium on virtual reality software and technology* (pp. 1–7). ACM. 10.1145/502390.502392

Shim, K.-C., Park, J.-S., Kim, H.-S., Kim, J.-H., Park, Y.-C., & Ryu, H.-I. (2003a). Application of virtual reality technology in biology education. *Journal of Biological Education*, *37*(2), 71–74. doi:10.1080/0 0219266.2003.9655854

Slator, B. M. (1999). Intelligent tutors in virtual worlds. In *Proceedings of the 8th international conference on intelligent systems (ICIS-99)* (pp. 24–26). Academic Press.

Totkov, G. (2003). Virtual learning environments: Towards new generation. In *Proceedings of the 4th international conference on computer systems and technologies: E-learning* (pp. 8–16). New York: ACM. doi:10.1145/973620.973622

Ullah, S. (2011). *Multi-modal Interaction in Collaborative Virtual Environments: Study and analysis of performance in collaborative work* [Theses]. Universit'e d'Evry-Val d'Essonne. Retrieved From https://tel.archives-ouvertes.fr/tel-00562081

Wickens, C. D. (1992, October). Virtual reality and education. In *Proceedings of IEEE international conference on systems, man, and cybernetics* (Vol. 1, pp. 842-847). IEEE Press.

Williams, J., Eames, C., Hume, A., & Lockley, J. (2012). Promoting pedagogical content knowledge development for early career secondary teachers in science and technology using content representations. *Research in Science & Technological Education*, *30*(3), 327–343.

Winn, W., Hoffman, H., Hollander, A., Osberg, K., Rose, H., & Char, P. (1997). The effect of student construction of virtual environments on the performance of high-and low-ability students. In *Proceedings of the Annual meeting of the American educational research association. Academic Press.*

Woodfield, B. F., Catlin, H. R., Waddoups, G. L., Moore, M. S., Swan, R., Allen, R., & Bodily, G. (2004a). The virtual chemlab project: A realistic and sophisticated simulation of inorganic qualitative analysis. *Journal of Chemical Education*, *81*(11), 1672. doi:10.1021/ed081p1672

Yoon, S. A., Anderson, E., Park, M., Elinich, K., & Lin, J. (2018). How augmented reality, textual, and collaborative scaffolds work synergistically to improve learning in a science museum. *Research in Science & Technological Education*, 1–21.

ADDITIONAL READING

Alam, A., Ullah, S., & Ali, N. (2018). The Effect of Learning-Based Adaptivity on Students' Performance in 3D-Virtual Learning Environments. *IEEE*, *6*(1), 3400–3407. doi:10.1109/ACCESS.2017.2783951

Eman, S., Florica, M., & Alin, M. (2012). A 3d virtual learning environment for teaching chemistry in high school. *Annals of DAAAM for 2012 & Proceedings of the 23rd International DAAAM Symposium*, *23*, 2304–1382.

Katrina, B. S., Selcen, S. G., Richard, L., Michael, M., Christopher, D., Hazel, S. S., ... Janet, M. D. (2018). Learning neuroscience with technology: A scaffolded, active learning approach. *Journal of Science Education and Technology, Springer*, *27*(6), 566–580. doi:10.100710956-018-9748-y PMID:31105416

Kihyun, R., Kristin, B., & Amanda, S. (2018). Promoting linguistically diverse students short-term and long-term understanding of chemical phenomena using visualizations. *Journal of Science Education and Technology, Springer*, *27*(6), 508–522. doi:10.100710956-018-9739-z

Mehta, S., Bajaj, M., & Banati, H. (2019). An Intelligent Approach for Virtual Chemistry Laboratory. In Virtual Reality in Education: Breakthroughs in Research and Practice (pp 454-488). Academic Press. doi:10.4018/978-1-5225-8179-6.ch023

Tory, W., Jonathan, S., Jacqueline, K., Christopher, R., & Julia, R. (2019). Measuring Pedagogy and the Integration of Engineering Design in STEM Classrooms. *Journal of Science Education and Technology*, *28*(3), 179–194. doi:10.100710956-018-9756-y

Ullah, S., Ali, N., & Rahman, S. (2016). The effect of procedural guidance on students' skill enhancement in a virtual chemistry laboratory. *Journal of Chemical Education*, *93*(12), 2018–2025. doi:10.1021/acs.jchemed.5b00969

Winkelmann, K., Keeney-Kennicutt, W. L., Fowler, D., & Macik, M. (2017). Development, Implementation, and Assessment of General Chemistry Lab Experiments Performed in the Virtual World of Second Life. *Journal of Chemical Education*, *94*(7), 849–858. doi:10.1021/acs.jchemed.6b00733

Wu, B., Wong, K., & Li, T. (2019). Virtual titration laboratory experiment with differentiated instruction. *Computer Animation and Virtual Worlds*, *30*(3-4), e1882. doi:10.1002/cav.1882

KEY TERMS AND DEFINITIONS

3D Interaction: 3D interaction is a form of human-machine interaction where users are able to move and perform interaction in 3D space.

3D Interactive Virtual Environment: A virtual learning environment which is based on 3D interaction.

Biological Education: the study of structure, function, heredity, and evolution of all living organisms.

Cognitive Load: the used amount of working memory resources.

Computational Biology: is the science of using biological data to develop algorithms or models to understand biological systems and relationships.

Computer Animations: It is the process used for digitally generating animated images.

Computer-Based Learning: Computer-based learning (CBL) is the term used for any kind of learning with the help of computers.

Computer-Generated Environment: The application of computer graphics to create or contribute to images in art, printed media, video games, films, television programs, shorts, commercials, videos, and simulators.

Human Computer Interaction: It is a multidisciplinary field of study focusing on the design of computer technology and, in particular, the interaction between humans (the users) and computers.

Interactive Interface: It is the field of human–computer interaction, is the space where interactions between humans and machines occur.

Interactive Tutorials: media to allow students to interact with the content that they are learning.

Learning Technology: Technologies that can be used to support learning, teaching and assessment.

Virtual Learning Environment: a system for delivering learning materials to students via the web.

Virtual Reality: an artificial environment that is created with software and presented to the user in such a way that the user suspends belief and accepts it as a real environment.

Virtual Reality in Biology: using computer generated environment regarding structure, function, heredity, and evolution of all living organisms.

This research was previously published in Mobile Devices and Smart Gadgets in Medical Sciences; pages 297-317, copyright year 2020 by Medical Information Science Reference (an imprint of IGI Global).

Chapter 33
3D Virtual Learning Environment for Acquisition of Cultural Competence:
Experiences of Instructional Designers

Stephen Petrina
University of British Columbia, Canada

Jennifer Jing Zhao
University of British Columbia, Canada

ABSTRACT

As educational systems emphasize and experiment with forms of online and remote learning, it is increasingly important to investigate the cultural competence of instructional designers. This chapter addresses the experiences of instructional designers in a 3D virtual learning environment designed for development of cultural competence. Design-based research (DBR) and user experience (UX) methodologies were employed to explore experience of six instructional designers in 3D virtual environment. A taxonomy of experience (ToE) established by Coxon guided qualitative data collection and analysis. Through examples and data, the chapter emphasizes the necessity for instructional designers to keep in mind the challenge of cultural diversity in the backgrounds of students and their own, and bring guidelines and principles into culturally sensitive and responsive instructional design processes. The authors recommend four future research directions, including cross-cultural instructional designer competencies along with research into cultural personas, avatars, and guest-host relations.

DOI: 10.4018/978-1-6684-7597-3.ch033

INTRODUCTION

Research in face-to-face and online classrooms suggests that students who have diverse cultural backgrounds present learning challenges if instructional designers fail to design culturally sensitive learning environments (Au & Kawakami,1994; Gay, 2000; Capell, Veenstra, & Dean, 2007). With the pervasive use of educational technologies, more and more online learning platforms have become easily accessible to global learners, often with diverse cultural backgrounds. How educational and instructional designers design curriculum and courses in VLEs to best facilitate learning is a popular focus of research (Allen & Seaman, 2013; Chen, & Oakley, 2020; Mohamed, Schroeder, & Wosnitza, 2014). With advanced learning technologies (ALTs) integrated into games, online platforms, and virtual reality (VR) systems, questions of cultural competence are intensified.

New technologies provide new affordances and options for instructional designers, and the complexity of design to accommodate learners' cultural differences increases. Research suggests the need for instructional designers to be more aware of and responsive to cultural complexity during the design process, and to prevent developing culturally blind systems or unintentionally exclude cultural nuances, which results in culturally homogeneous educational resources or VLEs (Chen, Mashhadi, Ang, & Harkrider, 1999; Kawachi, 2000; Bentley, Tinney, & Chia, 2005; Young, 2008). Shortcomings of affordances are made abundantly clear as instructors transform traditional material and resources into digital formats for remote learning during Covid-19. Naïve assumptions that remote learning merely necessitates conversion of material from analog to digital prevail as students counter with expectations and demands for cultural competence and empathy. Out of convenience, most instructional designers and educators prioritized limited VLEs (e.g., learning management system) or video conferencing systems (e.g., Zoom). For more complex remote learning, 3D virtual worlds nonetheless have great potential.

To contribute to research in this area, this chapter reviews research on the acquisition of cultural competence in education and explores six instructional designers' experiences in virtual world design. To elicit responses and insights, we used OpenSimulator, an open-source platform for hosting 3D virtual worlds and the metaverse. The design of the virtual world went through multiple design-based research (DBR) iterations and was used to develop healthcare students' cultural competence (Zhao, 2019). We recommend four future research directions, including cross-cultural instructional designer competencies along with research into cultural personas, avatars, and guest-host relations. Although since the late 1960s, "instructional design" (ID) has often been used interchangeably with "curriculum design," "educational design" and "educational technology," in this chapter ID refers to the design and construction of learning objects on a micro level and learning systems on a macro level (Geis & Klaassen, 1972; Laverde, Cifuentes, & Rodríguez, 2007; Nelson, 2013; Petrina, 2004).

BACKGROUND

This section presents a review of the literature regarding cultural considerations for instructional designers in VLEs. Culture shapes not only how people feel, value, think, and behave, but also how people learn. "Multiculturalism," "cultural diversity," and "cultural pluralism" have been researched for decades. Cultural differences in increasingly global learning environments are also a well recognized fact (Au & Kawakami, 1994; Biggs, 1990; Edwards, 2000; Mahbubani, 2002; Young, 2008). The premise of instructional design for student or user variation is that "different continents, nations, regions, and communities hold different cultural, mental and cognitive models—customs, manners and behaviours—that provide kaleidoscopic perspectives in the way people see, feel, understand, and connect with the world" (Cabrero, 2014, p. 247).

Addressing the needs of learners with culturally diverse backgrounds, instructional design processes have been comprehensively researched. Research indicates that the more emphasis instructional designers place on cultural needs of students, the more significant are improvements in motivation, self-regulated skills, and academic achievement (Au & Kawakami, 1994; Gay, 2000; Hollins, 1996; Hood, Littlejohn, & Milligan, 2015; Kleinfeld, 1975; Ladson-Billings, 1994, 1995). However, aspects of culturally diverse learners in VLEs have not been as fully explored as those in face-to-face classrooms (Edmundson, 2003, 2004; Catterick, 2007). With the development of new technologies, students' multicultural backgrounds that influence learning and the relevant pedagogical designs used in the development of VLEs have begun to be more widely researched (Chen & Oakley, 2020; Phan, 2018; Wang & Reeves, 2007).

For example, with the significant growth of global educational exchange, the population of international student and adult trainees worldwide have become more culturally diverse. There is a growing body of literature exploring the cultural aspects of developing and teaching cross-cultural online courses in North American and Asia. North American cities such as Vancouver are major destinations for international students and trainees. Chinese immigrants represent a bit more than 25% of all immigrants to metro Vancouver. Chinese students represent about 38% of all international students in British Columbia's postsecondary institutions (Heslop, 2018). Asian learners exhibit different learning styles and academic approaches compared to their western counterparts in VLEs (Biggs 1990, Watkins & Regmi 1990, Kember & Gow 1991; Chen & Oakley, 2020; Friesner & Hart, 2004; McCarty, 2005; Robinson, 1999). Zhang and Zhou (2010) investigated the experience of Chinese students in Canadian educational systems. Among a range a communication and social networking challenges, Chinese students are challenged to adjust to demands of group work for activities and projects. There are cultural differences in the experiences that students have in group work: instructional designers should have a level of cultural competence in recognizing the need to scaffold group work expectations and procedures. Culturally relevant learning objects and systems to respond to and accommodate students with various backgrounds make education more accessible and effective in VLEs (Edwards & Usher, 2000; Foster, 1995; Gay, 2000; Ladson-Billings,1995; Nieto, 1999; Allen & Seaman, 2013; Chen & Oakley, 2020).

Instructional designers' cultural backgrounds implicitly and explicitly affect the design of VLEs. Spronk (2004) states that culture, in learning contexts, is more profound and dynamic than surface features suggest. Instructional designers are not immune from the influence of their own cultural biases. A range of challenges and concerns are presented to instructional designers in cross-cultural contexts. Even though instructional designers are trained in professional settings, who they are and what they bring makes a difference in how design is approached (Rogers, Graham, & Mayes, 2007). Instructional design approaches can be selected without the instructional designers being fully aware of the cultural roots and philosophies that underpin them. Most design techniques are presented at face value rather than in a deeper cultural and philosophical context. Pedagogical choices made by instructional designers in online education are one of the most important focuses for researchers and practitioners alike (Van den Branden & Lambert, 1999; Pan et al., 2003; Chen & Oakley, 2020).

Therefore, it is imperative to raise the awareness of instructional designers to be more culturally competent and responsive in designing educational environments and scaffolding learning activities among students with diverse cultural backgrounds. It is also imperative to recognize cultural assumptions of instructional designers themselves, which is perhaps more fundamental. It is somewhat idealistic, as

McLoughlin (1999) proclaims, to ensure that instructional designers need to cover every culture prior to adopting an instructional design model. But as an instructional designer, we can probably consciously trace significant educational origins to our cultural roots, further examine and reconcile our design practice to have a deeper understanding, and achieve possible pedagogical symbiosis (Henderson, 2007). For example, Pan et al. (2003) have tried in a longitudinal study to reveal the elements embedded in Confucian pedagogy and Western pedagogy, and determine whether there is symbiosis or asymbiosis for these different pedagogies.

In VLEs, interactions between instructors and students, and among student peers, are different compared to those characterizing traditional classrooms. The presence of nonverbal communication cues is generally missing, which presents a very different situation for instructional designers (Phan, 2018). Also, practices and approaches usually applied in virtual learning often include different ways of thinking and acting by learners of diverse cultural backgrounds, which cause major barriers for designing VLEs and e-Learning resources (Ke, Chávez, & Herrera 2013; Dillon, Wang, & Tearle, 2007; Phan, 2018). Further, instructional designers' own cultural backgrounds manifest dynamically, which is different than in a traditional classroom as well.

Conceptualization and development of cultural competence are significant challenges as physical and virtual experience become noticeably blended and reality noticeably augmented and mixed. New media and technology are enabling more and more multisensory interactions including high-fidelity VR, artificial intelligence (AI), and other ALTs (Li, Daugherty, & Biocca, 2002, 2003; Soukup, 2000). Virtual experiences in 3D virtual worlds are multi-dimensional (e.g., affective, cognitive, haptic). In addition, they reduce temporal and psychological distance. According to Heeter's (2000) categorization, virtual experiences and indirect experiences are consistently mediated, and for the purposes of this chapter, mediated by a range of phenomena including cultural competence and sensitivity.

Cultural Competence

Cultural competence "emphasizes the ability to function effectively with members of different groups through cultural awareness and sensitivity" (Friedman & Hoffman-Goetz, 2006, p. 427). The "inter" prefix of intercultural competence indicates a two-way exchange of development and the give and take nature of two cultures in interaction. Bennett's (1986, 1993, 2004) "Developmental Model of Intercultural Sensitivity" (DMIS) gives a sense of cultural competence acquisition and promotes a movement from Denial to Defense to Minimization to Acceptance to Adaptation to Integration. Hammer, Bennett, and Wiseman (2003) describe this as a movement from "ethnocentrism" to "ethnorelativism" and developed an effective inventory for measuring intercultural competence acquisition (p. 424). The development of cultural competence is central to education and healthcare, among a range of other professions. This chapter limits the focus to instructional design.

Within an intercultural competence framework, the challenge is for both students and designers to change in ways that reflect awareness and sensitivity in exchange. While striving to meet academic and professional development milestones. A lack of intercultural competence in students and designers is a cause of the ineffectiveness of learning. Enhancing intercultural competence for students and designers has been a significant challenge for educational organizations across various disciplines (Sit, Mak, & Neill, 2017). Cross-cultural sensitivity training dates back to the late 1950s and continues to generate contradictory results and debates over its effectiveness (Bezrukova, Spell, Perry, & Jehn, 2016). Generally, cultural competence acquisition suggests a more comprehensive experience.

With intercultural competence training increasingly multi-method, researchers are interested in how variation in delivery methods and program formats could be delivered to improve the desired outcome. According to results from evaluation studies for cultural competence acquisition, with the same content coverage, whether delivered continuously in one session or in multiple sessions over a period of short time up to four weeks, the variation in the delivery methods, such as online or face to face in physical classrooms, did not differ significantly in training outcome (Goldstein & Smith, 1999; Caligiuri & Tarique, 2012).

To be more effective in cultural integration, training has been recommended for international students and trainees to increase their intercultural competence (Bhawuk & Brislin, 2000; Sit, Mak, & Neill, 2017). A variety of learning resources, courses, and curricula have been developed to foster and nurture the cultural competence of students and trainees, and a variety of methods were designed to help them understand different customs, beliefs, and communication strategies (Bhawuk & Brislin, 2000). Research suggests that cultural competence acquisition is more effective when distributed over longer periods of time, usually for several years as cultural competence goes beyond diversity awareness and sensitivity. It requires the development of an ability of individuals to effectively interact among others with different cultural backgrounds. However much we can rely on these findings for students, research on instructional designers' cultural competence acquisition is inadequate.

To facilitate cultural competence acquisition, there are two major aspects: culture-general and culture-specific (Capell, Veenstra, & Dean, 2007). Culture-general aspects are designed to apply to different groups of clients, while the culture-specific ones are usually limited to specific ethnic groups of clients. Ideally, instructional designers would be culturally responsive in a general sense and culturally sensitive in a specific sense. Here, general sense refers to the environments and procedures through which cultural competence can be gained, it is independent of any specific cultural context. Cultural-specific aspects refer to the cultural context the instructional design is situated in, which can be east African, east Indian, etc. These contexts are still dynamic and constructive instead of static, essentialist stereotypes. Cultural competence is dynamic and fluid but there are characteristics experts agree on (Campinha-Bacote, 1995, 1999; Hammer, Bennett, & Wiseman, 2003).

In summary, researchers have sought to embed cultural considerations so cultural pluralism can be accommodated in instructional design practice (Branch, 1997). It seems realistic to adopt functional instructional design models with cultural components already embedded into the model structures and design workflows. Various design models have been developed with cultural responsiveness in mind. Early on, Henderson (1996) emphasized that instructional design was a product of culture— instructional designers need to take culture into consideration. In turn, Henderson (1996, 2007) developed a Multiple Cultural Pedagogical Model for interactive multimedia instructional design. Edmundson (2007) introduced the cultural adaptation process (CAP) model for designing e-Learning for another culture. The CAP model includes guidelines for evaluating e-learning courses and matching them to the cultural profiles of targeted learners. Universal Design for Learning (UDL) is a framework proposed by Eberie and Childress (2007) for culturally diverse online learning design, to ensure that learning environments are universally consistent. For various reasons, no single ID model is sufficient for ensuring cultural sensitivity.

MAIN FOCUS: 3D VIRTUAL LEARNING ENVIRONMENT DESIGN

The research focuses on instructional designers' cultural experiences in a 3D virtual world initially designed for healthcare students. More specially, it focuses on the experiences of instructional designers in addressing the needs of culturally diverse learners, and how they provide pedagogically positive designs based on affordances of 3D virtual worlds. Most importantly, it also focuses on how instructional designers reflect on their own cultural roots and values during the design process in the interactive and dynamic 3D virtual world to avoid bias and further develop more culturally competent instructional design practices.

As indicated, the research product is a 3D virtual world designed in OpenSimulator, which is also the field site. Simulation, embodiment, and interactivity were key affordances utilized to facilitate the acquisition of cultural competence (Anderson & Shattuck, 2012; Corder & U-Mackey, 2018; McKenney & Reeves, 2012; Reeves, Herrington, & Oliver, 2005; Squire, 2006; Zhao, 2019). The final 3D virtual world includes four main rooms: classroom, conference room, clinic, and café, which are elaborated below with screen shots (Figures 1-5).

Figure 1. Classroom in the 3D virtual world

Figure 2. Conference room in the 3D virtual world

Figure 3. Clinic in the 3D virtual world

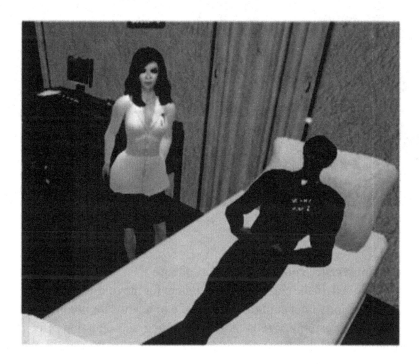

Figure 4. Café in the 3D virtual world

Figure 5. The roles of the doctor, the nurse, and the patient in the 3D virtual world

1. **Classroom and Conference room:** Participants choose their session themes and character roles instead of being assigned. In the classroom, the content for the role-play scenarios is given through training packages for cultivating cultural competence in healthcare in multiple formats, including text, PowerPoint, and streaming videos. After discussing and planning effective and interesting scenarios for role-play, and then choosing roles and adopting appropriate clothes to symbolize the avatars, users enter the conference room. Doctor, nurse, and patient clothes help users imagine themselves in respective roles for expressing various questions or concerns about cultural compe-

tence in a healthcare scenario they create. Virtual clothes for cultural variety were created and are stored in an inventory.

2. **Clinic:** Experiential learning in the virtual world begins in the virtual clinic. In the clinic, users play roles of doctor, nurse, and patient in open-ended scenarios. Scenarios adopted by users varied. A few scenarios challenged the English-speaking nurse and doctor to respond appropriately to patients that spoke English as a second language. This is a common communication scenario in healthcare professions. In another example scenario, users adopted different ethnic and cultural identities that then challenged the nurse and doctor to competently and appropriately give a positive diagnosis. These could be debriefed or informed in the conference room or users could enter the café to relax and debrief.

3. **Café:** The café room provides a casual setting for users to debrief content and scenarios, socialize, or plan ahead for another scenario.

In different sessions, participants can choose different themes or exchange roles with other players when in the virtual world, signaled in part by the avatar wearing clothes from the inventory. "Repeating a scenario with the same or different characters can sometimes afford a more in-depth examination and add to the experience" (Lowenstein, 2011, p. 194). Users in this research were able to repeat the scenarios and play the same or different roles in the virtual environment.

Participant Recruitment and Setting

Data were collected by gathering the responses and attending to instructional designer experiences in 3D virtual world in related healthcare education fields in postsecondary institutions. Participants were recruited on voluntary basis. Consent was obtained before participation.

Initial participants included two instructional designers, who have more than ten years experience in curriculum design in VLEs in health disciplines in Canadian universities. A subsequent iteration was added with four instructional designers from Canadian universities and Chinese universities. The ethnic backgrounds of instructional designers include Asian Canadian, Caucasian Canadian, and Chinese. Participants represent eastern and western backgrounds. The designers had wide-ranging experiences of cross-cultural design working in a variety of subjects (Table 1).

Table 1. Participant List

DBR Iteration	Date	Participants	Pseudonyms
3	January – March 2018	2 instructional designers	2 instructional designers: Yuliana, Yvette
5	March – July 2018	2 instructional designers	2 instructional designers: Yuliana, Yvette
8	March – July 2020	4 instructional designers	4 instructional designers: Hua, Olivia, Daisy, Leo

Methods: Design-Based Research (DBR) and User Experience (UX)

The primary methodology was design-based research (DBR) while the secondary methodology was user experience (UX). The two were used in complementary ways to explore instructional designers' experience in a 3D virtual learning environment. The taxonomy of experience (ToE) established by Coxon (2007) guided data collection and qualitative data analysis (QDA). McKenney and Reeves's (2012) DBR model was adopted, in which the iterative process does not prescribe fixed, set pathways for iterations. Rather, many potential routes can be designed according to this model.

A secondary methodology in this study is User Experience (UX). Touloum, Idoughi, and Seffah (2012) define UX as "something felt by the user, or by a group of users, following the use of a product (or service), or during its interaction with the product (usability and aesthetics), or even a possible use (or purchase) of a product". "We use the word 'something,'" they continue, "to refer to the broad meaning that covers the term experience (emotions, perceptions, reactions)" (pp. 2994-2995).

Design-Based Research (DBR) Iterations

This initial study followed a DBR process through early work and testing pilots, building prototypes, and developing design products over seven iterations between January 2017-December 2018 (Table 2).

Table 2. DBR iterations, participants and focuses

DBR Iteration	Participants	Data Source	Focus
First Micro-cycle: Analysis and Exploration	The researcher	No formal data collection	Problem identification and diagnosis.
Second Micro-cycle: Design and Construction	The researcher, 1 digital arts builder.	No formal data collection	Instructional design, 3D virtual world, and tentative product production.
Third Micro-cycle: Evaluation and Reflection	2 instructors, 2 instructional designers, 2 digital arts builders.	Audio recordings and notes from interviews with instructors, instructional designers, and digital arts builders.	Evaluation of the skeleton design through in-world observation and individual interview methods. Data collection and qualitative, inductive analysis conducted.
The Fourth Micro-cycle: Re-design and Construction	The researcher, 1 digital arts builder.	No formal data collection	Based on the previous evaluation and reflection, improvements including managing user cognitive load, broader roles in role plays, and creating more objects for the learning environment.
Fifth Micro-cycle: Re-Evaluation and Reflection	10 students, 5 instructors, 2 instructional designers, 2 digital arts builders.	Nurse Cultural Competence Scale instrument (NCCS) Audio recordings and notes from interviews with students. In-world images captured during the process of student learning activities.	Survey using the NCCS instrument provides an initial perspective on students' prior learning. In-depth interviews with the participants using the framework of Taxonomy of Experience.
Sixth Micro-cycle: Re-design and Construction	The researcher, 1 digital arts builder.	In-world images captured during the process of student learning activities.	Three more clinics created, more patient beds, medical equipment and supplies added, more clothes for different professions created to provide greater flexibility for participants to do role plays and other activities. A student café room created.
Seventh Micro-cycle: Implementation and Spread	The researcher	In-world images captured during the process of student learning activities.	Two main outputs, maturing interventions, and theoretical understanding summarized.
Eighth Micro-cycle: Re-design and Construction	6 instructional designers	Audio recordings and notes from interviews with instructional designers.	Interviews with four added instructional designers. Data collection and qualitative, inductive analysis conducted.

A new iteration, the eighth micro-cycle was added in March-July 2020, with a focus on exploring instructional designer experiences. To produce a more culturally sensitive and responsive VLE, in the newly added iteration more avatars were designed representing different ethnic backgrounds. Also, four additional instructional designers, Hua, Olivia, Daisy, and Leo, were recruited and interviewed.

Data Coding and Analysis

We developed a usable system to support learning in a 3D virtual world as well as to facilitate exploration of instructional designer experiences. The data analysis is organized through iterative reviews of interview scripts, screen shots, and notes taken in the virtual world. Interview participants were recruited on a voluntary basis. Potential participants were presented with a cover letter, consent form, and interview questionnaire. Users were encouraged to express their experiences during the semi-structured interview. Experiential and existential elements of the ToE helped shape the questions for instructional designers. Interview data were entered into Microsoft Office 365 Excel spreadsheets and analyzed using the SEEing technique created by Coxon (2007), which is a structural interpretation of the experiential phenomena. Details of this analysis are provided in the next section.

Taxonomy of Experience (TOE)

The ToE established by Coxon (2007) guided data collection and qualitative data analysis. This ToE offers a multi-layered way to understand user experience and is responsive to researching virtual experience and user experience. Figure 6 depicts Coxon's (2007) taxonomy, which contains sensorial, affective, cognitive, and contextual experiential elements within an existential framework of temporality, spatiality, relationality, and corporeality. These existentials derive from van Manen's (1990, pp. 101-106) distillation of Merleau-Ponty's (1962) units of experience.

Figure 6. Taxonomy of experience. Adapted from Coxon (2007)

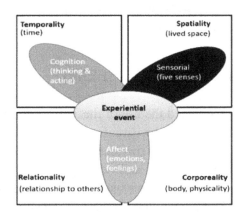

Coxon (2007) described three types of experience. Sensorial experience includes five senses. It involves a "sense of" things, such as sight, smell, touch, and sound, and contributes to aesthetic and ergonomic appreciation within experiences. Affective experience contains emotions, feelings, and moods, which significantly influence the nature of an experience. Cognitive experience includes conation, which is reflective thought of external doing, and cognition, which is reflexive thought of internal thinking, such as personal identity (Petrina, 2010). Cognition and conation are interwoven constructs in which experiential information is processed and considered in terms of possible future interactions.

The contextual components are the existential parameters within which any experience takes place, with many layers of complexity. They are usually understood in relation to a specific experiential event. This contextual space has layers of complexity and can be partially understood by being broken down into existential component parts in relation to a specific experiential event (Coxon, 2007). In order to understand the nature of experience, inputs from sensorial, affective, cognitive, and contextual factors all need to be thoroughly considered. The nature of experience requires understanding within a context, which includes "four dimensions" of existence (space, time, the physical body, and its relationships to other people). These existential factors are differentiated from contextual factors (Table 3).

Table 3. Meta-themes and sub-themes of ToE

	Meta-themes	Sub-themes
Experiential elements	body- somatic experience/ sensorial experiences (five senses)	sight, touch, sound, comfort-ergonomics, and appearance aesthetics
	heart- affective experience (emotions, feelings)	Positive-negative emotions
	head-cognitive experience (thinking and acting)	conation- reflective experience, reflective thought of external doing; cognition- reflexive experience, reflexive thought of internal thinking
Existential factors	spatiality (space)	
	temporality (time)	
	corporeality (body, physicality)	motion, standing, moving, sitting, body movements
	relationality (Relation to others)	
Contextual factors	environmental factors, regulatory factors, social factors	

Data Coding and Analysis Through TOE-SEEing

The analytic approach of SEEing facilitated the use of the ToE for data analysis, which includes nine steps to categorize and analyze users' interview data. User experience is analyzed through a series of progressive steps to extract the essences of the experience and allow them to be "seen", which provides a way to make abstract concepts comprehensible and visible. This method offers an opportunity to look deeper into the data collected while extracting conclusions (Coxon, 2007). The nine-step process of the ToE-SEEing process is described in the following paragraphs. The nine steps are:

Step 1 Submersion and Data Gathering
Step 2 Descriptive Narratives
Step 3 Sorting Fragments into ToE Themes

Step 4 Developing Meaning(s)
Step 5 Essential Elements
Step 6 Super-Ordinary Elements
Step 7 Weight
Step 8 Superordinary Summary Words
Step 9 Summary Word Descriptions

It begins by transforming the users' interview fragments and ends by synthesizing them into superordinary themes. Overall, the first three steps of the ToE-SEEing included gathering and transcribing data, establishing structure, and storing information about an experience. Steps four to five are the analysis phases to allow deeper meaning to be "seen". Finally, this analytical process results in seven overall category elements. Microsoft Office 365 Excel worksheet was customized and adopted for this analysis.

FINDINGS AND DISCUSSION

In step 7 of the SEEing process, with the rating from 1 to 7 in relation to how important the superordinary elements are to instructional designers' cultural competence acquisition experience (7 is the most important), we set the weight based on the knowledge gained during the immersion in step 1, our extensive literature review, and comprehensive working experience: Epistemology -7, Simulation - 6, Embodiment - 5, Language and Translation - 4, Management support - 3, Training - 2, Technical Aspects - 1.

Moreover, the number of times the experience was mentioned by instructional designers during interviews was also counted in the study. In the end, superordinary elements with the weight of higher values and appearing more times have higher importance levels. The final outcomes are listed in the following paragraphs in an order of decreased importance from the highest to lowest. Relevant literature and participant comments are summarized in each element category to inform deeper layers of understanding of instructional designers' experiences.

Epistemology Supportive of Multiple Perspectives and Embedded Values - 7

Based on the extensive research in online learning, a culturally responsive instructional design built upon eclectic pedagogical paradigms and shared epistemological systems are recommended (Bentley, Tinney, & Chia, 2005; Henderson, 1996; Henderson, 2007; McLoughlin, 1999; Rogers, Graham & Mayes, 2007). Research recommends adopting an epistemology that is supportive of multiple perspectives, so as to create learning environments in which instructors and students from different cultural backgrounds feel comfortable enough to share their opinions (McLoughlin, 1999; McLoughlin & Oliver, 2000, Wang & Reeves, 2007), and to discuss embedded values honestly, explicitly, and upfront with students in class (Bentley, Tinney, & Chia, 2005; Chen, Mashhadi, Ang, & Harkrider, 1999). During the interviews in this study, one instructional designer commented:

Look[s] like western instructional design models and protocols have become global standards. A westernized pattern of thinking has been dominated during [the] instructional design process for virtual learning. Hopefully there are some Asian, African, and other pedagogical orientations [that] will be introduced to construct and implement culturally-sensitive online education. (Iteration 8/Hua)

Another clarified: "For instructional design in 3D virtual worlds, the inclusion of the culture components should be educationally meaningful from pedagogical perspectives to improve learning rather than superficial cosmetic design, such as modifications to the skin coloring, hair, or eyes of avatars. We need to focus on cognitive functions" (Iteration 8/ Olivia).

Therefore, instructional designers recommend understanding how different pedagogies are perceived in different cultures, and seek ways to incorporate various pedagogies into the 3D virtual learning environment design. This includes setting goals, tasks, and assessment so that learners from different cultural backgrounds can have options and choose those that best match their educational needs.

Language and Translation - 6

During the process of instructional design in VLEs, cultural issues may arise not only from pedagogical assumptions, but also from language problems. Language barriers are a major concern in globalized e-Learning, including in 3D virtual learning environments. We probably have all learned through experience that language cannot solely rely on online automatic translations of English into the targeted language or vice versa as they can be too literal and therefore inaccurate. If used this way, students have to guess what the instructor really means, which prevents effective communication and sharing ideas (Hutchinson et al., 2005; Tractinsky, 2000). An instructional designer commented on her own experiences during the study:

We had one course which needed to translate traditional Chinese content to simplified Chinese. It can be performed automatically by auto translation software. But the actual terms and idioms have different underlying meanings in mainland of China compared to Hong Kong, Macau, and Taiwan where traditional Chinese is used. It is recommended that local professionals have proofreading for the courses. (Iteration 8/Hua)

Therefore, cultural differences should be addressed during local processes of curricular and course design so differences in context can be handled thoroughly and cultural values embedded in the contexts can be fully acknowledged instead of simply literally translated. Another instructional designer commented "We as instructional designers consider educational context including stories, etiquette, and images, and make sure they are familiar to the targeted culture. We should avoid taboos and etc. to make curriculum and courses compatible to another culture" (Iteration 8/Daisy).

Researchers recommend the use of simplified writing structures, and standardized language as much as possible to avoid local expressions, idioms, slang and colloquialisms, which would possibly enhance communication for all (Bentley, Tinney, & Chia, 2005). "Translation processes can also be to practise standard language," one participant agreed, "such as rewriting the content without idioms or dialects, and changing spelling and phrases to more standard ones" (Iteration 8/Leo).

Management Support - 5

The designers reflected and expressed the urgent need to address culture components in instructional design processes in virtual learning environments, but noted that they were bound by organizational expectations and policies: the extra time and resources needed to understand, evaluate, and design cultural contexts during design are not supported.

Instructional Designers in this study commented on the organizational challenges they faced. "I would say it is probably mostly organizational because peer instructional designers usually understand the value of culture components during design, but their academic levels usually are not decision makers in university, so we need to get buy-in" (Iteration 8/Hua). "Our management just ignored it as they don't think understanding and supporting cultural design is feasible and important" (Iteration 8/Olivia). "The management thinks there are a lot of constraints of budget and resources" (Iteration 8/Daisy). A fourth instructional designer added:

It is difficult to get buy-in from key stakeholders to access necessary resources and on-going support. The proposed solutions can be an ongoing process of informing and educating the management.... One possible solution to address this issue can be through disseminating relevant educational research during seminars and workshops, and inviting management to attend and get informed about the significance of cultural design in facilitating effective learning of global learners. (Iteration 8/Leo)

Training Through Workshops and Seminars - 4

In this study instructional designers expressed the needs for training through workshops to build cultural competence among themselves. Currently there are no defined standards and levels for cultural competence requirements. Instructional designers need to acquire more knowledge and skills to address a variety of cultures during design processes.

Two participants commented: "I as an instructional designer do have a strong desire to learn more about the cultural needs of learners. Currently we do not have a clear approach and focus for cultural analysis during the needs assessment process" (Iteration 8/Leo). "There must be some personal bias. We lack knowledge on how to approach the instructional design process with cultural components embedded; not sure what exactly to look for in culture related design" (Iteration 8/Hua).

Standards and common knowledge pools for the workshops and seminars are recommended by instructional designers. "It is difficult to access cultural resources. defined training and information resources may help build instructional designers' cross-cultural design skills and increase their level of cultural expertise" (Iteration 8/Hua). "Making information on cultural profiles easily accessible for designers during needs assessment and other design process are helpful" (Iteration 8/Olivia).

Complexity of the Technical Aspects - 3

Comments regarding the technical interface of the 3D virtual world were generally mixed. For example, one instructional designer acknowledged: "It's easy to use. It can create blended learning scenarios to provide the flexibility of learning. Students can be either in a classroom, or at home through distributed learning" (Iteration 5/Yuliana).

However, the findings in this study also revealed that participants needed technical support at the beginning in order to learn effectively. The participants' previous experience with online games, even with 3D virtual worlds directly, does not automatically transfer to the mastery of essential controls in the OpenSimulator 3D virtual world. "A training package should be provided as an option from my instructional design perspective, which can reduce the learning curve and anxiety. A short instructional video can help users to get many features quickly" (Iteration 5/Yuliana).

Therefore, orientation sessions for the navigation control, view control, and other basics are recommended to increase users' confidence early in the course. After a short orientation, ample time should be arranged to let participants explore and learn how to control their avatars, such as moving and changing clothes, and how to click on various objects to easily participate in the activities in the virtual world. Also, various and flexible communication methods are advocated as well. "It is really helpful students and instructors can have private discussions, as well as group discussions. Various communication channels allow students to send private messages to someone and to the whole class publicly" (Iteration 8/Olivia).

Supporting users requires more than just explaining how the technical pieces work and helping them get familiar with tools and controls in the virtual world. Social skills and cultural awareness are essential in the orientation session (Jones, Ramanau, Cross, & Healing, 2010). An instructional designer commented: "For the group work, instructional designers should provide multiple options. Students with different cultural backgrounds may have different learning preferences. In addition to addressing pedagogical objectives in online education, we need to take students' learning preferences based on their cultural backgrounds into consideration as well" (Iteration 8/Daisy).

Experiences in Simulation in 3D Learning Environments - 2

As media rich platforms, 3D virtual worlds offer the possibility of learner experiences that enhance deep learning through realistic simulation (Corder & U-Mackey, 2018; Davies et al., 2015; Delwiche, 2006; de Freitas & Neumann, 2009). Virtual worlds allow the development of simulation activities that otherwise would be difficult due to its high cost. Most instructional designers' experiences regarding simulation were positive. "There is no risk. It's always safe for students to try. No concerns as those when they have when deal with real patients, feeling a much safer environment. No ethical concern" (Iteration 5/Yuliana). "The simulated environment is pretty realistic. Some cultural aspects of learning can definitely transfer more effectively through this contextual layer" (Iteration 8/Leo).

To create educative experience for students, it is essential to design in the 3D virtual world with concrete association with real world learning spaces. To best facilitate learning transfer, the virtual space should often replicate real world scenarios and simulations, scaffolds, and virtual learning activities. Lectures presented with PowerPoint, professional seminars, the virtual clinic and hospital visits, role plays, and video streams in this research are drawn from the real-world experiences of health subject-related scenarios.

Synchronous role plays decrease interpersonal boundaries and facilitate group dynamics to conduct learning tasks. Complex decisions can be taken in real time to apply theory to practice in complex situations (Hew & Cheung, 2010). "You don't know the reaction the patient [avatar] will present. It is dynamic in real time. It is two-way interaction" (Iteration 5/Yuliana).

Experiences in Embodiment in 3D Learning Environments - 1

Virtual worlds shape the embodiment of learners in the form of avatars, among other features (Thomas & Brown, 2009). With identities acted out or expressed through avatars, learners can immerse in 3D content through interacting with other users' avatars. Through role play scenarios in the 3D virtual world in this study, instructional designers understand more about their own powers and limitations. "I like the play scenarios to practice cultural competency. Things are so dynamic. Decisions are made in real time. This really helped me realize the cultural context [in which I was] originally situated" (Iteration

5/Yuliana). Enhancements were suggested as well. "The avatar is a bit simplified, hope to have more facial expressions" (Iteration 5/Yuliana). The more control one has over an avatar the more one experiences a sense of embodiment, immersion, and presence. In our research with students, a participant independently reiterated what Yuliana, an instructional designer, indicated: "I like the clothes and my appearance in the [virtual] world. If the facial mapping is more like me, it will make me feel more like the avatar is me" (Iteration 5/Ethan).

The success level with which avatars engage learners is highly dependent on the level participants can project themselves into or identify with the avatar. Designers can adopt a variety of design methods through which learning activities develop within the learning space, encourage learners to characterize themselves as avatars to enhance the experience of virtual worlds and promote engagement. An instructional designer commented: "Embodiment depends on how much control you have over the avatar. Also, the time, you won't get the embodiment feeling if you just play 15 minutes. But if you have played for days, more embodiment will be built" (Iteration 5/Yuliana). She continued: "Interestingly, if you watch the video games kids play, the avatars are not polished at all, no real face, actually just boxes. But they are so attached to them. I think because they have the full control over it. I think more control brings more embodiment feeling" (Iteration 5/Yuliana). "Students can learn from peers. When students switch to different roles (different embodiments), they all bring their own prior knowledge and experiences. Multiple perspectives and approaches contribute to the cultural learning scenarios" (Iteration 5/Yuliana).

FUTURE RESEARCH DIRECTIONS

Despite the development of competencies and standards for instructional designers, cultural competence is nearly systematically overlooked or taken for granted (Rogers, Graham, & Mayes, 2007). Two of the International Board of Standards for Training, Performance and Instruction's (IBSTPI) (2012) *Instructional Designer Standards* allude to cultural sensitivity but are overly general:

7(b) Determine characteristics of the physical, social, political, and cultural environment that may influence learning, attitudes, and performance.

12(e) Accommodate social, cultural, political, and other individual factors that may influence learning. (pp. 4, 5)

Similarly, the International Society for Technology in Education's (ISTE) (2017) *Standards for Educators* includes cultural competence as a collaborator item rather than a design item:

4(d) Demonstrate cultural competency when communicating with students, parents and colleagues and interact with them as co-collaborators in student learning. (p. 2)

One future research direction is identifying, detailing, and evaluating or measuring cultural competencies for instructional designers. Bezrukova, Spell, Perry, and Jehn's (2016) review of research in cultural sensitivity training is poignant: "A key finding from our analysis is that integrated training worked well along with training that focused on both skill-building and awareness. From these conclusions a question arises: what exactly needs to be integrated" (p. 1245)? Future research into instructional designers' cultural competence should attend to scales, such as Hammer, Bennett, and Wiseman's (2003), along with characteristics identified by cross-cultural communication experts (Lynch, 2011):

- Respects individuals from other cultures
- Makes continued and sincere attempts to understand the world from others' points of view
- Is open to new learning
- Is flexible
- Has a sense of humor
- Tolerates ambiguity well
- Approaches others with a desire to learn (p. 104)

The Association for Talent Development (ATD) (2015) builds on these for their global designer and trainer competencies. Identifying and measuring competencies of instructional designers assumes an acknowledgement of their cultural biases and stereotypes. Documenting what designers know (i.e., cognition) and what they may express in addition (i.e., implicit cognition) require creative, comprehensive measures.

A second research direction is testing virtual worlds and other related objects and systems for access, equity, and inclusion, or cultural pluralism and variation, through diverse personas and UX methods (Cabrero, 2014; Cabrero, Winschiers-Theophilus, & Abdelnour-Nocera, 2016). In design, a persona is a fictitious user that shares commonalties with a target audience or small group when interacting with the process or product. More specifically, a persona is a "communicational evocation of a set of users with shared aims on technological needs and requests, and it is mostly built by designers based on users' real data" (Cabrero, Winschiers-Theophilus, & Abdelnour-Nocera, 2016, p. 149). Research should focus on the challenges of developing diverse personas in instructional design and the procedures designers use to make learning objects and systems inclusive. As Cabrero, Winschiers-Theophilus, and Abdelnour-Nocera (2016) caution, "a lack of cross-cultural validity, local relevancy, and designerly liability make personas prone to false or oversimplified representations in depicting local populaces" (p. 149). Personas are underutilized in instructional design and it is important that researchers document how and when designers collect "users' real data" to depict target student groups. Research into development and uses of personas is increasingly imperative as AI tutors, pedagogical agents, VR systems, and related ALTs are included in products for interactive learning (Aleven, Beal, & Graesser, 2013; Baylor, 2007; Gutica & Petrina, 2020; Wang & Petrina, 2013; Wang, Petrina, & Feng, 2017).

In short, instructional designers should keep in mind the challenge of diversity in their products. Although not stressed by participants, avatars and associated features, such as skin tone and clothing, should reflect cultural diversity. Closely related to research into personas, this is a third recommended direction for research within 3D virtual worlds, ALTs, and VR platforms as user content and vendor content often limit avatars and clothing to western skin features and styles. An avatar is "the graphical representation of a user of a digital media product functioning as a focus for the user's agency within a virtual world" (Liboriussen, 2014, p. 38). Nowak and Fox's (2018) extensive review found that users "select avatars they believe will help them meet interaction goals, which could include revealing or concealing elements of their identity to other users" (p. 40). Granted, as instructional designers in our research reported, users split attention between avatar representation and virtual world content and rules. Hence, it is important for researchers to explore whether and how designers provide a range of choices of avatars with visible cultural or racial characteristics and roles. Harrell and Lim (2017) stress that rather than considering avatars as "mere technically constructed visual artifacts," "a more expansive view holds that virtual identities serve as important ways through which people represent or express themselves" (p. 53). Along with Harrell and Harrell (2012), they prove insightful findings and methods for researching diverse avatars within an empirical "computational identity systems" framework (p. 57).

Fourth, we recommend future research into guest-host relations as analogous to interdependencies among students or users, instructional designers, and their objects or systems (Zhao, 2019, pp. 137-142). Eames (1972) describes the guest and host relationship that he and his wife emphasized in their design work: "One of the things we hit upon was the quality of a host.... a very good, thoughtful host, all of whose energy goes into trying to anticipate the needs of his [or her] guests— those who enter the building and use the objects in it" (p. 16). Williams (2018) elaborates, arguing that the "designer as host" "is catalyst for a series of actions and encounters to take place, which may involve a specific piece or shape, or may include the transformation of that piece through learning experiences. The host facilitates learning, exploration, adaptation and interaction" (p. 287). Host-guest relations are conceptually dimensions of hospitality (Hawthorne, 1932). This could be a productive analogy for conceptualizing cultural competence in instructional design in that not all hosts and guests act the same (e.g., some hosts are frustrating or uncomfortable while some guests are rude). Aitken's (1991) commentary on the *Wu-Men Kuan* is insightful: "Host and guest... we switch roles and have fun" (p. 99). Instructional design may require role switching and code switching in ways that can be informed by other forms of design, such as architectural and fashion design. The host does not always have full authority and the guest is not always being controlled. The dynamic interactions between the host and guest build the fundamental relationship among them. And further, the host and guest cooperate with each other. This demands reconceptualizing the traditional hierarchical structure of design into one of a networked heterarchy (Williams & Fletcher, 2010).

CONCLUSION

This chapter addressed the challenges and problems of the cultural competence of instructional designers. We stressed the importance of empirical research with instructional designers. We found that using a tangible instructional product as a sounding board, such as the 3D virtual world designed in OpenSimulator, keeps the participants grounded and concrete. That said, we analyzed interview data collected from six instructional designers' experiences and found seven themes related to the cultural aspects of the virtual world design. These themes can potentially contribute to building culturally effective virtual worlds and sensitive learning environments. An effective instructional designer needs to consider not only the students' cultural background, but also their own cultural background and biases. In turn researchers need to explore the cultural competence of instructional designers. We recommended four future research directions, including cross-cultural instructional designer competencies along with research into cultural personas, avatars, and guest-host relations. As educational systems across the world are emphasizing and experimenting with forms of online and remote learning, it is increasingly important to enhance and improve the cultural competence of instructional designers.

REFERENCES

Adamo-Villani, N., Richardson. J., Carpenter, & Moore, G. (2006). A photorealistic 3d virtual laboratory for undergraduate instruction in microcontroller technology. In *SIGGRAPH '06: ACM SIGGRAPH 2006 Educators program* (pp. 21-25). ACM Digital Library.

Aitken, R. (1991). *The gateless barrier: Translation and commentary on the Wu-Men Kuan*. North Point.

Aldrich, C. (2009). *Learning online with games, simulations, and virtual worlds*. Jossey-Bass.

Aleven, V., Beal, C. R., & Graesser, A. C. (2013). Introduction to the special issue on advanced learning technologies. *Journal of Educational Psychology*, *105*(4), 929–931. doi:10.1037/a0034155

Allen, I. E., & Seaman, J. (2013). *Changing course: Ten years of tracking online education in the United States*. Sloan Consortium.

Anderson, T., & Shattuck, J. (2012). Design-based research: A decade of progress in education research? *Educational Researcher*, *41*(1), 16–25. doi:10.3102/0013189X11428813

Association for Talent Development. (2015). 10 Cultural competencies of the successful global trainer. *Culture Ready*. http://www.cultureready.org/blog/10-cultural-competencies-successful-global-trainer

Au, K. H., & Kawakami, A. J. (1994). Cultural congruence in instruction. In E. R. Hollins, J. King, & W. C. Hayman (Eds.), *Teaching diverse populations: Formulating a knowledge base* (pp. 5–23). State University of New York Press.

Baylor, A. L. (2007). Pedagogical agents as a social interface. *Educational Technology*, *47*(1), 11–14.

Bell, M. W. (2008). Toward a definition of "virtual worlds.". *Journal of Virtual Worlds Research*, *1*(1), 1–5.

Bennett, M. J. (1986). A developmental approach to training intercultural sensitivity. *International Journal of Intercultural Relations*, *2*(2), 179–186. doi:10.1016/0147-1767(86)90005-2

Bennett, M. J. (1993). Towards ethnorelativism: A developmental model of intercultural sensitivity (revised). In R. M. Paige (Ed.), *Education for the intercultural experience* (pp. 21–41). Intercultural Press.

Bennett, M. J. (2004). Becoming interculturally competent. In J. S. Wurzel (Ed.), *Toward multiculturalism: A reader in multicultural education*. Intercultural Resource Corporation.

Bentley, J., Tinney, M. V., & Chia, B. (2005). Intercultural internet-based learning: Know your audience and what they value. *Educational Technology Research and Development*, *53*(2), 117–126. doi:10.1007/BF02504870

Betancourt, J. R., Green, A. R., & Carillo, J. E. (2002). *Cultural competence in health care: Emerging frameworks and practical approaches*. The Commonwealth Fund.

Bezrukova, K., Spell, C. S., Perry, J., & Jehn, K. (2016). A meta-analytical integration of over 40 years of research on diversity training evaluation. *Psychological Bulletin*, *142*(11), 1227–1274. doi:10.1037/bul0000067 PMID:27618543

Bhawuk, D. P. S., & Brislin, R. W. (2000). Cross-cultural training: A review. *Applied Psychology*, *49*(1), 162–191. doi:10.1111/1464-0597.00009

Biggs, J. (1990) *Asian students' approaches to learning: Implications for teaching overseas students.* Paper presented at the Eighth Australasian Learning and Language Conference, Brisbane, QLD: Australia.

Cabrero, D. G. (2014). Participatory design of persona artefacts for user eXperience in non-WEIRD cultures. *Proceedings of PDC '14 Companion*, 247-250. 10.1145/2662155.2662246

Cabrero, D. G., Winschiers-Theophilus, H., & Abdelnour-Nocera, J. (2016). A critique of personas as representations of "the other" in cross-cultural technology design. *Proceedings of AfriCHI '16*, 149-154. 10.1145/2998581.2998595

Caligiuri, P., & Tarique, I. (2012). Dynamic cross-cultural competencies and global leadership effectiveness. *Journal of World Business*, *47*(4), 612–622. doi:10.1016/j.jwb.2012.01.014

Campinha-Bacote, J. (1999). A model and instrument for addressing cultural competence in health care. *The Journal of Nursing Education*, *38*(5), 203–206. doi:10.3928/0148-4834-19990501-06 PMID:10438093

Campinha-Bacote, J., & Padgett, J. (1995). Cultural competence: A critical factor in nursing research. *Journal of Cultural Diversity*, *2*(1), 31–34. PMID:7663899

Capell, J., Veenstra, G., & Dean, E. (2007). Cultural competence in healthcare: Critical analysis of the construct: Its assessment and implications. *Journal of Theory Construction & Testing*, *11*, 30–37.

Catterick, D. (2007). Do the philosophical foundations of online learning disadvantage non-western students? In A. Edmundson (Ed.), *Globalized e-learning cultural challenges* (pp. 116–129). IGI Global. doi:10.4018/978-1-59904-301-2.ch007

Chen, A., Mashhadi, A., Ang, D., & Harkrider, N. (1999). Cultural issues in the design of technology-enhanced learning systems. *British Journal of Educational Technology*, *30*(3), 217–230. doi:10.1111/1467-8535.00111

Chen, K., & Oakley, B. (2020). Redeveloping a global MOOC to be more locally relevant: Design-based research. *International Journal of Educational Technology in Higher Education*, *17*(1), 9. doi:10.118641239-020-0178-6

Collis, B. (1999). Designing for differences: Cultural issues in the design of WWW-based course-support sites. *British Journal of Educational Technology*, *30*(3), 201–215. doi:10.1111/1467-8535.00110

Corder, D. & U-Mackey, A. (2018). Intercultural competence and virtual worlds. In S. Gregory & D. Wood (Eds), *Authentic virtual world education: Facilitating cultural engagement and creativity* (pp. 25-44). New York, NY: Springer.

Coxon, I. (2007). *Designing (researching) lived experience* (Unpublished Ph.D. Dissertation). University of Western Sydney, QLD.

Davies, D., Arciaga, P., Dev, P., & Heinrichs, W. L. (2015). Interactive virtual patients in immersive clinical environments: The potential for learning. In I. Roterman-Konieczna (Ed.), Simulations in medicine: Pre-clinical and clinical applications (pp. 139-178). Berlin: Walter de Gruyter GmbH & Co KG.

de Freitas, S., & Neumann, T. (2009). The use of 'exploratory learning' for supporting immersive learning in virtual environments. *Computers & Education, 52*(2), 343–352. doi:10.1016/j.compedu.2008.09.010

de Freitas, S., Rebolledo-Mendez, G., Liarokapis, F., Magoulas, G., & Poulovassilis, A. (2010). Learning as immersive experiences: Using the four-dimensional framework for designing and evaluating immersive learning experiences in a virtual world. *British Journal of Educational Technology, 41*(1), 69–85. doi:10.1111/j.1467-8535.2009.01024.x

Delwiche, A. (2006). Massively multiplayer online games (MMOs) in the new media classroom. *Journal of Educational Technology & Society, 9*(3), 160–172.

Eames, C. (1972). Digby Diehl's interview with Charles Eames. *Los Angeles Times*. Retrieved from https://www.eamesoffice.com/the-work/the-guest-host-relationship/

Eberie, J. H., & Childress, M. D. (2007). Universal design for culturally diverse online learning. In A. Edmundson (Ed.), *Globalized e-learning cultural challenges* (pp. 239–254). Information Science. doi:10.4018/978-1-59904-301-2.ch014

Edmundson, A. (2003). Decreasing cultural disparity in educational ICTs: Tools and recommendations. *Turkish Online Journal of Distance Education, 4*(3).

Edmundson, A. (2007). The cultural adaptation process (CAP) model. In A. Edmundson (Ed.), *Globalized e-learning cultural challenges* (pp. 267–290). Information Science. doi:10.4018/978-1-59904-301-2.ch016

Edwards, R., & Usher, R. (2000). *Globalisation and pedagogy: Space, place and identity*. Routledge.

Foster, M. (1995). African American teachers and culturally relevant pedagogy. In J. A. Banks & C. A. M. Banks (Eds.), *Handbook of research on multicultural education* (pp. 570–581). Macmillan.

Friedman, D. B., & Hoffman-Goetz, L. (2006). A systematic review of readability and comprehension instruments used for print and web-based cancer information. *Health Education & Behavior, 33*(3), 352–373. doi:10.1177/1090198105277329 PMID:16699125

Friesner, T., & Hart, M. (2004). A cultural analysis of e-learning for China. *Electronic Journal on E-Learning, 2*(1), 81–88.

Gay, G. (2000). *Culturally responsive teaching: Theory, research, and practice*. Teachers College Press.

Geis, G. & Klaassen. (1972). It's a word, it's a name, It's ... an educational technologist. *Educational Technology, 12*(12), 20–22.

Goldstein, D. L., & Smith, D. H. (1999). The analysis of the effects of experiential training on sojourners' cross-cultural adaptability. *International Journal of Intercultural Relations, 25*(1), 157–173. doi:10.1016/S0147-1767(98)00030-3

Hammer, M. R., Bennett, M. J., & Wiseman, R. (2003). Measuring intercultural sensitivity: The intercultural development inventory. *International Journal of Intercultural Relations, 27*, 421–443.

Harrell, D. F., & Harrell, S. V. (2012). Imagination, computation, and self-expression: Situated character and avatar mediated identity. *Leonardo Electronic Almanac, 17*(2), 74–91.

Harrell, D. F., & Lim, C.-U. (2017). Reimagining the avatar dream: Modeling social identity in digital media. *Communications of the ACM, 60*(7), 50–61.

Hawthorne, C. O. (1932). Hospital provision as a social service. *British Medical Journal, 2*(3736), 117–121.

Heeter, C. (2000). Interactivity in the context of designed experience. *Journal of Interactive Advertising, 1*(1), 3–14.

Henderson, L. (1996). Instructional design of interactive multimedia: A cultural critique. *Educational Technology Research and Development, 44*(4), 85–104.

Henderson, L. (2007). Theorizing a multiple cultures instructional design model for e-learning and e-teaching. In A. Edmundson (Ed.), *Globalized e-learning cultural challenges* (pp. 130–153). Information Science.

Heslop, J. (2018). *International students in BC's education systems— Summary of research from the Student Transitions Project.* https://www2.gov.bc.ca/assets/gov/education/post-secondary-education/data-research/stp/stp-international-research-results.pdf

Hew, K. F., & Cheung, W. S. (2010). Use of three-dimensional (3-D) immersive virtual worlds in K-12 and higher education settings: A review of the research. *British Journal of Educational Technology, 41*(1), 33–55.

Hollins, E. R. (1996). *Culture in school learning: Revealing the deep meaning.* Erlbaum.

Hutchinson, H. B., Rose, A., Bederson, B. B., Weeks, A. C., & Druin, A. (2005). The international children's digital library: A case study in designing for a multilingual, multicultural, multigenerational audience. *Information Technology and Libraries, 24*(1), 4–9.

International Board of Standards for Training. Performance and Instruction. (2012). *Instructional designer standards.* https://ibstpi.org/download-center-free/

International Society for Technology in Education. (2017). *Standards for educators.* https://www.iste.org/standards/for-educators

International Standards Organisation. (2019). *Ergonomics of human-system interaction— Part 210: Human-centred design for interactive systems* (ISO 9241-210:2019) https://www.iso.org/obp/ui/#iso:std:iso:9241:-210:ed-2:v1:en

Jones, C., Ramanau, R., Cross, S., & Healing, G. (2010). Net generation or digital natives: Is there a distinct new generation entering university? *Computers & Education, 54*(3), 722–732.

Kawachi, P. (2000). To understand the interactions between personality and cultural differences among learners in global distance education: A study of Japanese learning in higher education. *Indian Journal of Open Learning, 9*(1), 41–62.

Kember, D., & Gow, L. (1990). Cultural specificity of approaches to study. *The British Journal of Educational Psychology, 60*, 356–363.

Kennedy, P. (2002). Learning cultures and learning styles: Myth-understandings about adult (Hong Kong) Chinese learners. *International Journal of Lifelong Education, 21*(5), 430–445.

Kleinfeld, J. (1975). Effective teachers of Eskimo and Indian students. *The School Review, 83*(2), 301–344.

Komiyama, Y. (2007). Japanese learning styles in the online learning environment. In J.B. Son (Ed.), Internet-based language instruction: Pedagogies and technologies. Toowoomba, AU: Asia-Pacific Association for Computer-Assisted Language Learning.

Ladson-Billings, G. (1995). Toward a theory of culturally relevant pedagogy. *American Educational Research Journal, 32*(3), 465–491.

Laverde, A. C., Cifuentes, Y. S., & Rodríguez, H. Y. R. (2007). Toward an instructional design model based on learning objects. *Educational Technology Research and Development, 55*(6), 671–681.

Li, H., Daugherty, T., & Biocca, F. (2001). Characteristics of virtual experience in electronic commerce: A protocol analysis. *Journal of Interactive Marketing, 15*(3), 13–30.

Li, H., Daugherty, T., & Biocca, F. (2002). Impact of 3-D advertising on product knowledge, brand attitude, and purchase intention: The mediating role of presence. *Journal of Advertising, 31*(3), 43–57.

Liboriussen, B. (2014). Avatars. In M.-L. Ryan, L. Emerson, & B. J. Robertson (Eds.), *The Johns Hopkins guide to digital media* (pp. 37–40). Johns Hopkins University Press.

Lynch, E. W. (2011). Developing cross-cultural competence. In E. W. Lynch & M. J. Hanson (Eds.), *Developing cross-cultural competence: A guide for working with children and their families* (pp. 71–118). Brookes.

Mahbubani, K. (2002). *Can Asians think: Understanding the divide between East and West*. Steerforth Press.

McCarty, S. (2005). Cultural, disciplinary and temporal contexts of e-learning and English as a foreign language. *eLearn, 4*. Retrieved May 12, 2006, from http://www.elearningmag.org/subpage.cfm?section=research&article=4-1

McGreal, R. (2004). Learning objects: A practical definition. *International Journal of Instructional Technology & Distance Learning, 1*(9).

McKenney, S. E., & Reeves, T. C. (2012). *Conducting educational design research*. Routledge.

McLoughlin, C. (1999). Culturally responsive technology use: Developing an on-line community of learners. *British Journal of Educational Technology, 30*(3), 231–243.

McLoughlin, C., & Oliver, R. (2000). Designing learning environments for cultural inclusivity: A case study of indigenous online learning at tertiary level. *Australian Journal of Educational Technology, 16*(1), 58–72.

Mohamed, A. M. F. Y., Schroeder, A. C. U., & Wosnitza, M. (2014). What drives a successful MOOC? An empirical examination of criteria to assure design quality of MOOCs. In *The proceedings of 2014 IEEE 14th international conference on advanced learning technologies*. Athens, GR: IEEE.

Nelson, W. A. (2013). Design, research, and design research: Synergies and contradictions. *Educational Technology, 53*(1), 3–11.

Nieto, S. (1999). *The light in their eyes: Creating multicultural learning communities.* Teachers College Press.

Nisbett, R. (2004). *The geography of thought.* Simon & Schuster.

Nowak, K. L., & Fox, J. (2018). Avatars and computer-mediated communication: A review of the definitions, uses, and effects of digital representations. *Review of Communication Research, 6,* 30–53.

Pan, C.-C., Tsai, M.-H., Tsai, P.-Y., Tao, Y., & Cornell, R. (2003). Technology's impact: Symbiotic or asymbiotic impact on differing cultures? *Educational Media International, 40*(3-4), 319–330.

Petrina, S. (2004). The politics of curriculum and instructional design/theory/form. *Interchange, 35*(1), 81–126.

Petrina, S. (2010). Cognitive science. [Design and engineering cognition] In P. Reed & J. E. LaPorte (Eds.), *Research in technology education* (pp. 136–151). Glencoe-McGraw Hill.

Phan, T. (2018). Instructional strategies that respond to global learners' needs in massive open online courses. *Online Learning, 22*(2), 95–118.

Reeves, T. C., Herrington, J., & Oliver, R. (2005). Design research: A socially responsible approach to instructional technology research in higher education. *Journal of Computing in Higher Education, 16*(2), 97–116.

Robinson, B. (1999). Asian learners, western models: Some discontinuities and issues for distance educators. In R. Carr, O. Jegede, W. Tat-meg, & Y. Kin-sun, (Eds.), The Asian distance learner (pp. 33-48). Hong Kong, ROC: Open University of Hong Kong.

Rogers, P., Graham, C. R., & Mayes, C. T. (2007). Cultural competence and instructional design: Exploration research into the delivery of online instruction cross-culturally. *Educational Technology Research and Development, 55*(2), 197–217.

Sit, L., Mak, A. S., & Neill, J. T. (2017). Does cross-cultural training in tertiary education enhance cross-cultural adjustment? A systematic review. *International Journal of Intercultural Relations, 57,* 1–18.

Soukup, C. (2000). Building a theory of multi-media CMC. *New Media & Society, 2,* 407–425.

Spronk, B. (2004). Addressing cultural diversity through learner support. In B. J. Walti & C. O. Zawacki-Richter (Eds.), *Learner support in open, distance and online learning environments* (pp. 169–178). Bibliothecksund Informationssystem der Universitat Oldenburg.

Squire, K. (2006). From content to context: Videogames as designed experience. *Educational Researcher, 35*(8), 19–29.

Stork, M. G., Zhang, J., & Wang, C. X. (2018). Building multicultural awareness in university students using synchronous technology. *TechTrends, 62*(1), 11–14.

Thomas, D., & Brown, J. S. (2009). Why virtual worlds can matter. *International Journal of Learning and Media, 1*(1), 37–49.

Touloum, K., Idoughi, D., & Seffah, A. (2012). User eXperience in service design: defining a common ground from different fields. In J. C. Spohrer & L. E. Freund (Eds.), *Advances in the human side of service engineering* (pp. 257–269). Springer.

Tractinsky, N. (2000). A theoretical framework and empirical examination of the effects of foreign and translated interface language. *Behaviour & Information Technology, 19*(1), 1–13.

Tu, C. H. (2001). How Chinese perceive social presence: An examination of interaction in online learning environment. *Educational Media International, 38*(1), 45–60.

Wang, C., & Reeves, T. C. (2007). The meaning of culture in online education: implications for teaching, learning and design. In A. Edmundson (Ed.), *Globalized e-learning cultural challenges* (pp. 1–17). IGI Global.

Wang, F., & Hannafin, M. J. (2005). Design-based research and technology-enhanced learning environments. *Educational Technology Research and Development, 53*(4), 5–23.

Wang, Y., & Petrina, S. (2013). Using learning analytics to understand the design of an intelligent language tutor– Chatbot Lucy. *International Journal of Advanced Computer Science and Applications, 4*(11), 124–131.

Wang, Y., Petrina, S., & Feng, F. (2017). Designing VILLAGE (Virtual Immersive Language Learning Environment): Immersion and presence. *British Journal of Educational Technology, 48*(2), 431–450.

Watkins, D., & Regmi, M. (1990). An investigation of the approach to learning of Nepalese tertiary students. *Higher Education, 20*, 459–469.

Williams, D. (2018). Fashion design. In K. Fletcher & M. Tham (Eds.), *Routledge handbook of sustainability and fashion* (pp. 234–242). Routledge.

Williams, D., & Fletcher, K. (2010). Shared talent: An exploration of the potential of the "shared talent" collaborative and hands on educational experience for enhanced learning around sustainability in fashion practice. In *Sustainability in design: Now! challenges and opportunities for design research, education and practice in the XXI century* (pp. 1096–1004). Greenleaf Publishing Ltd.

Working Party on the Information Economy. (2011). *Virtual worlds- Immersive online platforms for collaboration, creativity and learning*. OECD.

Young, P. A. (2008). Integrating culture in the design of ICTs. *British Journal of Educational Technology, 39*(1), 6–17.

Zhang, Z., & Zhou, G. (2010). Understanding Chinese international students at a Canadian university: Perspectives, expectations, and experiences. *Canadian and International Education. Education Canadienne et Internationale, 39*(3), 43–58.

Zhao, J. J. (2019). Design of a 3D virtual learning environment for acquisition of cultural competence in nurse education: Experiences of nursing and other health care students, instructors, and instructional designers (Unpublished Ph.D. Dissertation). University of British Columbia, Vancouver, BC.

KEY TERMS AND DEFINITIONS

Cultural Competence: Ability to design and respond for "diverse values, beliefs and behaviors, including tailoring delivery to meet [students'] social, cultural, and linguistic needs" (Betancourt, Green, & Carillo, 2002, p. 5).

Instructional Design: Analysis and development or design of learning objects, products, and systems.

Intercultural Competence: The "inter" prefix added to "cultural competence" indicates a two-way exchange of development and the give and take nature of individuals from two different cultures in interaction.

User Experience: Methodology to account for "perceptions and responses that result from the use and/or anticipated use of a product, system or service" (International Standards Organisation, 2019).

This research was previously published in the Handbook of Research on Teaching With Virtual Environments and AI; pages 17-42, copyright year 2021 by Information Science Reference (an imprint of IGI Global).

Chapter 34
Instructional Design Applied to TCN5 Virtual World

Andressa Falcade
Federal University of Santa Maria, Brazil

Aliane Loureiro Krassmann
Federal Institute Farroupilha, Brazil & Federal University of Rio Grande do Sul, Brazil

Roseclea Duarte Medina
Federal University of Santa Maria, Brazil

Vania Cristina Bordin Freitas
Federal University of Santa Maria, Brazil

ABSTRACT

This chapter presents the development and implementation of an instructional design (ID) for computer networks learning within a three-dimensional (3D) virtual world (VW) that considers characteristics of cognitive style and level of expertise of the student, titled TCN5. For this purpose, a hybrid model of ID was created based on ADDIE and Dick and Carey models. To facilitate the inclusion and management of didactic materials, an educational resources manager called GRECx was developed, which was allocated to the VW through web pages inserted in 3D media objects. The approach was submitted to the evaluation of a sample of students, who pointed out that it allows greater use of didactic materials within the immersive environment, and that GRECx can actually help teachers in the inclusion of resources, avoiding the need to deal with VW settings.

INTRODUCTION

The use of virtual environments aimed at education, which offer the generation of knowledge in an innovative and appropriate way to the current computerized society, is becoming increasingly popular. However, only the existence of technology in the school environment is not enough for the success in the learning process (NASCIMENTO, 2006).

DOI: 10.4018/978-1-6684-7597-3.ch034

In this sense, there is an advance in the need of virtual environments customized for each student's specifications. According to Bates and Wiest (2004), a personalization of contents and of the environment according to their characteristics increase the motivation to learn. Cakir and Simsek (2010) also argue that this customization affects positively student performance.

In order to deal with this demand, differentiated ways to plan courses that fit these needs are being considered. One utilized method with this objective is the Instructional Design (ID), which according to Filatro (2008) aims to organize the learning script.

In this perspective, this study approaches the structuring of a ID for the learning of Computer Networks within a three-dimensional (3D) Virtual World (VW) called TCN5 (Teaching Computer Networks in a Free Immersive Virtual Environment) (VOSS, 2014), which has attributes of ubiquitous computing, as the adaptation to the student level of knowledge (expertise) in Computer Networks (POSSOBOM, 2014), and organization of pedagogical paths according to the preferences of the student Cognitive Styles (CS), being Holistic, Serialist, Divergent or Reflective (MOZZAQUATRO, 2010).

In order to expand the possibilities of this ID proposition, the educational resources manager aware of expertise (which we named GRECx) was developed. In this manager, the teacher can include files such as slide show, text, online text, image, video, task, and quiz, through a simple web interface. These features are sent directly to the VW and displayed on web pages allocated to 3D objects.

In the next sections we explain the concepts that embody this research, the development of the ID and the GRECx system, as well as the results achieved from their applications.

Virtual Worlds

A Virtual World (VW) can be considered a faithful simulation of a real environment, or the formulation of an imaginary, fictitious environment, created for coexistence and communication among people represented by avatars who perform actions and interact with one another (BACKES, 2012). These simulated environments have no concrete existence (DEMETERCO; ALCÂNTARA, 2004).

According to Freire et al. (2010), VW are interactive environments that allow the simulation of some real-world characteristics, such as topography, real-time actions, gravity, locomotion and interpersonal communication. Nelson and Erlanderson (2012) define VW as environments with coordinates in three dimensions. In this space the user is represented by an avatar and will move in order to explore the environment, being accompanied by other avatars or alone.

For Bainbridge (2010), VW are online environments that continue to exist even after users leave, keeping changes made by them within the scenario, and allowing people to interact as if they were in the real world. Mueller et al. (2011) highlight that a VW must allow synchronous interaction among many users, even if they are not in the same physical space. So, there must be several forms of communication, such as texts, voice and body language. Also, the VW must be persistent, that is, it must continue to function, even if it is not being used, remember the location of the people and the possession of the objects.

Some functionalities of Virtual Worlds are presented by Freire et al. (2010) and Greis and Reategui (2010), which are:

1. **Graphic Modeling of Three-Dimensional Objects:** Used for creating and editing 3D objects that make up the environment;
2. **Communication Between Residents:** Communication among users happens through textual conversations (chats and instant messages) or audio conferences;

3. **Interaction With the Environment:** Possibility of assigning behavior to objects;
4. **Screen Capture:** Lets the user take "photos" of the virtual environment, saving it for later use;
5. **Importing Multimedia Files:** Allows the user to import image, audio and animation files;
6. **Tele Transport:** It allows users to tele transport to various locations inside the Virtual World.

Boulos et al. (2007) present some features offered by Virtual Worlds, such as: browse multimedia content; search for information spaces and documents in 3D libraries; visit new places and experiencing different cultures; play multi-player games, including serious games; trade in three-dimensional stores; develop social skills, or training (e.g. medical skills); interact with other people or with specific situations; participate and attend live events (e.g. lectures and conferences); build communities.

Holden et al. (2010) suggest that Virtual Worlds can be used to build communities and games, for business collaboration and for educational purposes, and in the latter, the environment facilitates student-centered approaches. For the authors, the use of the VW in an educational environment can provide the student's familiarity with the content through practices, procedures, demonstrations and decision-making activities. In addition, it allows the conduction of self-assessments and tests of knowledge, generating learning through social interaction.

For the creation of a VW, initially it is necessary to choose a development platform. Among the most popular options are Second Life, OpenSimulator and Open Wonderland, the last two being open source platforms. The VW TCN5 (VOSS, 2014), chosen as the target tool for the implementation of this research, was built on the OpenSimulator platform.

The TCN5 is divided into five regions: a central one, called "networks" and other four regions representative of each one of the Cognitive Styles used as a parameter (Mozzaquatro, 2010): Serialist, Holistic, Divergent and Reflective. This organization aims to provide an environment adapted for the student, according to this characteristic. In each of these four regions, it was added two more rooms by Herpich (2015) (having three rooms in each CS), designed to direct the student to one of the three levels of knowledge (expertise) on Computers Networks defined by Possobom (2014): basic, intermediate and advanced.

In this study it is proposed to structure a course for the teaching of Computer Networks immersed in a VW, taking into account ubiquitous learning characteristics implemented in the TCN5, using Instructional Design as a method.

Ubiquitous Learning

Ubiquitous learning emerge as the possibility of learning anything, anywhere, anytime, using technology (OGATA; YANO, 2004, SAKAMURA; KOSHIZUKA, 2005). According to Sung (2009), learning does not only occur in the classroom, but anywhere. Curtis et al. (2002) and Hwang (2006) point out some characteristics that define ubiquitous learning, among them:

1. **Permanence:** Students' work remains accessible, in addition to daily records of all learning processes;
2. **Accessibility:** Access to resources happens anywhere, through any device;
3. **Immediacy:** Information can be obtained immediately, wherever the student is.
4. **Interactivity:** Interaction with other participants can happen synchronously (in real time) or asynchronous (offline, at any time).

Bellavista et al. (2012) define some context properties that can be taken into account in ubiquitous learning settings:

1. Computational context, which concerns the network, cost of communication, connectivity and resources, such as stations and printers;
2. Physical context, which refers to lighting, noise level, humidity and temperature;
3. User context, which refers to the location, network speed, Cognitive Style, level of knowledge, close people and mood;
4. Context of time, which refers to the date and time of year.

Graf and Kinshuk (2010) argue that students' learning outcomes and progress improve when their personal differences, such as Cognitive Styles, levels of expertise, motivation, and interests are considered. Based on these assumptions, this study takes into account the level of expertise and the CS of the student when designing and implementing the ID within the VW TCN5. Thus, in the following subsections are presented some concepts and applications of these characteristics.

LEVEL OF EXPERTISE

Research on expertise is one of the fastest growing areas within psychology and cognitive science (ER-ICSSON; SMITH, 1991). According to French and Sternberg (1989), expertise is the ability, acquired through practice, to qualitatively exercise a specific task of a domain. So that the student acquire a certain aptitude. Gagné (1985) identifies three phases that need to be covered:

1. **Initial Cognitive Stage:** Where initial behaviors and concepts of a subject are learned;
2. **Intermediate Cognitive Stage:** Where procedures and rules that define sequences are organized;
3. **Final Cognitive Stage:** Where the student has access to more advanced knowledge in order to obtain a complete mastery of the subject.

After the study of these phases, Possobom (2014) developed a system called SistEx, which, aiming to release adapted contents in a virtual learning environment, identifying the level of knowledge or expertise of students on the discipline of Computer Networks, of courses of the Computing area. Through a questionnaire composed of objective questions, it classifies each student in one of these levels: basic, intermediate or advanced. In this study SistEx was used to guide students to their most suitable environment in TCN5.

Cognitive Styles

According to Allinson and Hayes (p.119, 1996) Cognitive Styles (CS) are the "consistent individual differences of preferred forms of organization and processing of information and experiences". Dunn (1989) defines CS as the way that the individual focus, internalize, process, and retain information.

Mozzaquatro (2010) suggests that CS can be used to indicate the most effective instructional strategies for learning. The author conducted a study in order to detect the predominant dimensions of CS in a sample of undergraduate students, avoiding the need to contemplate a very large number of dimensions, arriving at the conclusion that the most recurrent were: Divergent, Serialist, Holistic and Reflective. In this study, these four Cognitive Styles are considered, as well as the questionnaire used to diagnose them, as a reference for the adequacy of the ID to the students' individual preferences.

The main characteristics of each one of these CS, based mainly on the researches of Bariani (1998), Ph.D. in Educational Psychology, Cassidy (2004) Ph.D. in Applied Psychology and Pedagogical Theory and Geller (2004) Ph.D. in Informatics in Education, are presented as follows.

Holistic

In the Holistic-style dimension, individuals prefer a more global context, examining large amounts of data and looking for relationships and patterns among them. They use more complex hypotheses, combining different data (BARIANI, 1998).

Cassidy (2004) complements, saying that Holistic begins by using significant amounts of information, to have a more global perspective, which results in a tendency of precipitation on decision-making, based on insufficient analysis and information.

Geller (2004) presents in her study that in adaptations of didactic resources to Holistic CS can be used: texts in the form of links; search engines; articles and books; images in the form of diagrams; and communication tools such as e-mail and chat. For the author, the student of this dimension has intrinsic motivation and, therefore, the teacher must propose studies in the internet, where the results can be shared with the group.

Serialist

For Bariani (1998), Serialists prefer separate topics that have a logical sequence of information, for later analysis and search of patterns in order to confirm their hypotheses. They work on a logical and linear approach, studying simpler hypotheses.

Cassidy (2004) argues that a Serialist individuals perceive the learning task as a series of independent topics and issues, focusing on developing the links among them. The author also notes that this style has a step-by-step progression, narrow focus, it is cautious and critical, operating with small amounts of information and material.

Geller (2004) says that the didactic resources for individuals of this dimension learning can be: texts in format of booklets, tutorials and topics; images, such as sequential drawings and graphics; and communication tools like forums and chat. The student is also motivated by activities composed of questionnaires.

Divergent

Bariani (1998) states that the Divergent being is creative, has original, fluent and imaginative responses, and opts for less structured issues, being skilled at working with problems that admit several acceptable responses.

The Divergent student is characterized by creativity and the ability to combine ideas and examine varied possibilities of doing things, arriving at several results (BARIANI, 1998).

According to Geller (2004), the most appropriate didactic resources for the Divergent style are: text, presented in links, topics and search sites; diagrams and graphs; and communication tools from e-mail, mailing lists and forums. According to the author, in this dimension the teacher needs to promote constant challenges for the student to be motivated.

Reflective

For Bariani (1998), Reflective individuals have more organized, sequential thoughts and previously evaluate the answers. Cassidy (2004) complements, saying that individuals of this dimension examine each alternative before making a decision.

Geller (2004) states that the most appropriate didactic resources for the Reflective CS are: texts in the form of tutorials, books, chapters of books and articles; pictures with diagrams and graphics; and communication tools such as mailing lists, forums and e-mail. Activities such as questionnaires and critical reviews should be proposed.

Instructional Design

In order to better determine the proper arrangement of a course, there are some methods that allow a detailed planning, with preprogrammed steps, such as the so-called Instructional Design (ID), which according to Filatro (p. 3, 2008) are an "intentional and systematic action of teaching that involves the planning, development and application of methods and techniques in order to promote, from known principles of learning and instruction, the human learning".

According to Behar et al. (2008), the term design is the development of a project that visually composes an intentional planning that, as affirms Filatro (2008), should contain techniques and methods applied in specific educational situations, with the purpose of promoting learning.

The use of technology in educational environments has been increasingly studied in order to improve and upgrade the ways of learning. Studies that expose digital educational tools, such as Shih and Yang (2008) and Wang and Hsu (2009), are already presenting ways to ensure the best ID for knowledge generation. Essalmi et al. (2011) point out that learning can occur more easily when the organization of an environment is in according to the characteristics and preferences of the student.

To develop an instructional project there are some methodologies that describe the organization, partitioning and conduction of learning (VAHLDICK; KNAUL, 2010). Among these methodologies, we highlight ADDIE, ASSURE, Gerlach and Ely, PIE, AIM-CID, DEI, 4C / ID, ILDF Online and Dick and Carey. For this study we used a hybrid model proposed by Falcade et al. (2016), presented in Table 1, adapted from ADDIE and Dick and Carey models.

Research Method

The nature of this research is applied, since it aims to generate knowledge in a practical way, directed to the resolution of specific problems. The approach to the problem is qualitative, because it aims to build a relationship between the world and the subject, objectively and subjectively (GIL, 2010).

This study deals with the implementation of an ID, using the hybrid model adapted from ADDIE and Dick and Carey models (Falcade et al., 2016). This ID was built for the dynamic learning of Computer Networks, within the TCN5 VW (VOSS, 2014; HERPICH, 2015), which has regions for each of the four CS (Holistic, Serialist, Divergent and Reflective) and rooms for each of the three levels of expertise considered (basic, intermediate and advanced) in those regions.

Table 1. Hybrid model for ID construction

Steps of ADDIE	Steps of Dick and Carey	Steps of the Adapted ID
Analyze: expertise, cognitive style, Internet bandwidth, online experience, resources and data	Identify instructional aims	Adaptation to the cognitive style and expertise of the student and choice of the content
	Write goals of performance	
	Identify input behavior	
Design: types of resources and evaluation methods	Perform analysis of instruction	Definition of the level of expertise of each resource, and choice of the evaluation forms
	Develop referenced criterion tests	
	Develop and select instructional material	
	Develop an continuous and informative evaluation	
Development: software conception and material adaptation	Project execution plan	Structuring of the didactic materials within the TCN5 Virtual World according to the Cognitive Styles
Implementation: course is used by students		Use of the environment by students
Evaluation of the course and the ID	Conduct the continuous informative evaluation	Direction of the path evaluation, analysis of learning results and revision of the ID.
	Review instruction	

(© 2016, Falcade et al.)

In order to allow a better analysis, it was determined the topic of Computer Networks Security, because it presents a great variety of materials available on the Internet, as well as being a topic of interest to the target audience even outside the classroom.

In this sense, we selected contents and didactic materials corresponding to the levels of expertise, and defined the forms of evaluation and organization of the environment for each CS. The materials were exposed within the VW TCN5, following a pedagogical route built on the basis of the preferences of each CS (BARIANI, 1998; GELLER, 2004; CASSIDY, 2004).

In order to provide a dynamic learning in a contextualized ID (FILATRO, 2008), an educational resource manager was created, called GRECx - Educational Resources Manager Aware of Expertise, which allowed the organization of teaching materials outside the VW, in a simpler way, according to theme and associated level of knowledge. The connection between GRECx and the VW takes place via web pages connected with the system database, which have transparent filters according to the room in which they were allocated. A theme filter has also been implemented, which allows the students to choose the subject they want to view.

The evaluation of the ID happened through an execution test denominated acceptance test (RIOS; MOREIRA, 2013), with individuals that had profile similar to the future users of the VW, whom would be students of courses related to the Computer Science area with basic knowledge in Computer Networks Security. This test happened in two moments, described below.

First, the evaluators answered a questionnaire that defined their individual Cognitive Styles. After this moment, they were exposed to the four learning routes (regardless of CS). In the end, the participants indicated the route they most self-identified. The result of this analysis shows if the profile defined by the questionnaire corresponds to the preference of use within the VW.

In the second evaluation, the appraiser were exposed to the two versions of TCN5: the version without the adaptations made (before the ID) and the version with the adaptations implemented (after the ID). The route for each version consisted of going through all the spaces of the environment, using each one of the didactic materials and objects available.

In addition, it was sought to determine if the evaluator felt difficulty in assimilating the contents exposed in the VW due to the level of expertise, as well as to investigate a possible mass use of the VW with the ID adaptations, checking if it was easy to use the objects within the adapted VW and investigating the possibility of learning improvements in the topic of Computer Networks Security.

From the two stages and the goals described above, some questions were explored in order to operate the evaluation (BARBOSA; SILVA, 2010). These questions were adapted from Savi et al. (2010) and Wangenhein (2012), composing a questionnaire of 12 closed questions and three open questions. They were:

1. Which environment (among the four CS) is according to your study organization preference? Why?
2. Among the Virtual Worlds visualized, did you like better the environment 1 (VW in its first version) or environment 2 (VW with ID)? Why?
3. Did the possibility of choosing the subject of study within the objects motivate you to continue exploring the environment?
4. Did you feel stimulated to learn within the VW with the ID?
5. Is the VW organization with ID appropriate to your way of learning?
6. Were the contents at a level of difficulty appropriate to your knowledge?
7. Were you able to understand a good portion of the content?
8. Would you like to use the VW with ID again?
9. Would you recommend this VW to others?
10. Is the object interface attractive?
11. Were the objects easy to use?
12. Did you need help to understand how to use objects in the VW with ID?
13. Do you believe that the VW with ID can be efficient for learning if used for a longer period of time?
14. Extra question: If you could modify the organization or the interface of objects, how would you do it?

In order to analyze the results more precisely, the Likert scale (LIKERT, 1932; CUNHA, 2007) of five alternatives was used as response options of the closed questions. The scale allows the structuring of levels of the evaluator manifestation, being determined the measures: "totally agree", "partially agree", "indifferent", "partially disagree" and "totally disagree".

Modeling and Development of the Instructional Design

Based on the assumption that the application of a planning technique, such as ID, for the organization of a course within a technological environment aims to allow greater learning, the ID presented in this work is dynamic, as the didactic materials and educational activities are adapted to the individual preferences.

Among the contents implemented in the ID, which involve the topic of Computer Networks Security, there are encryption, attack, and firewall. The teaching materials were selected by the professor advisor of the discipline of Computer Networks at the Federal University of Santa Maria, located in Brazil, and adapted from the works of Thibes (2011) and Rodrigues (2013).

In Figure 3 it is possible to observe the types of didactic materials available in the VW, ordered according to the preferences by Cognitive Style identified in the work of Mozzaquatro (2010).

Figure 1. Order of the types of didactic materials by CS made available within the VW.

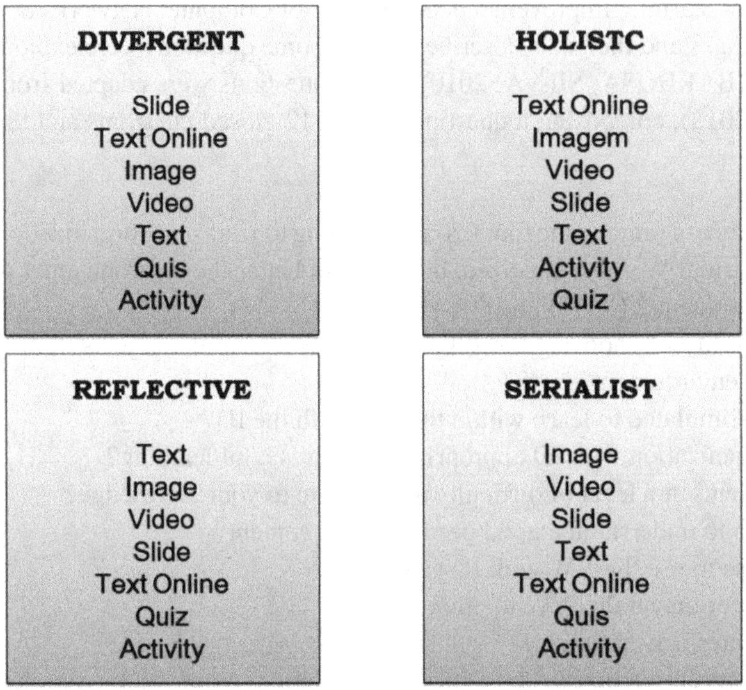

DIVERGENT	HOLISTC
Slide	Text Online
Text Online	Imagem
Image	Video
Video	Slide
Text	Text
Quis	Activity
Activity	Quiz

REFLECTIVE	SERIALIST
Text	Image
Image	Video
Video	Slide
Slide	Text
Text Online	Text Online
Quiz	Quis
Activity	Activity

According to the specifications of Bariani (1998), Geller (2004), Cassidy (2004) and Mozzaquatro (2010), CS preferences can be summarized in some formats. The authors do not present an exact sequence of presentation, only suggestions of didactic resources considered more relevant by group of CS. Thus, for this study a pedagogical route was structured based on these preferences.

In Figure 1, the text resource represents materials such as apostilles, tutorials, books and articles, which in GRECx are included in the PDF format. The image resource represents any image, be it in graph, diagram or map format, being attached to the system in the formats JPEG or PNG.

Online video and text resources can be attached as links that redirect to web addresses. The slides resource represents any type of content presentation, however it should be saved in PDF format before being attached to GRECx. The activity resource is shelved as text in PDF format, and can present any description of activity that the student can do to achieve the goals of the course, and the questionnaire resource is attached to the GRECx system in stages, by filling fields in its interface.

In view of the contents, the selected didactic materials and the specifications on the preferences of each CS addressed in the theoretical framework, the pedagogic paths for the students according to the CS were organized and implemented in the VW TCN5. Figures 2, 3, 4 and 5 present the visualization order of the resources in Serialist, Holistic, Divergent and Reflective CS environments, offering a clear view of the route to be followed by the student within the VW, followed by a brief explanation of the characteristics taken into account. It is worth mentioning that each room in TCN5 regions has its own architecture, which was not altered in the implementation of the ID, focusing only on the disposition of didactic materials.

Figure 2. Organization of didactic materials in the environment of the Serialist CS

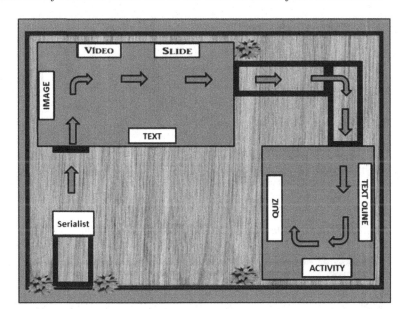

As already mentioned, the Serialist CS prefers images, texts in topics and videos; so the features that the user of this style will see are in this order: 1 - image, 2 - video and 3 - slide. In addition, this individual prefers to view all content before performing the activities; therefore, activities are allocated in the second room.

The Holistic CS, shown in Figure 3, shows that the online text resource is the first to be presented, because this style prefers a more global and dynamic context, examining large amounts of data and looking for relationships and patterns among them.

Were allocated after the resource *online text* the materials: 2 - image, 3 - video, 4 - slide and 5 - text. The activity resource is presented before the questionnaire because it is preferential of this profile of student, which seeks to analyze the information in a broader way, sharing with the group its considerations.

The path presented in Figure 4 shows the exposure of the resources within TCN5 according to the preferences of Divergent CS. Since the scenario of this region consists of two rooms, it was decided to present an activity in each room, assuming that this individual is motivated by constant challenges.

As this style has preference for texts presented in topics and links, the first two didactic materials displayed in the room are slides and online text. The other resources were exposed in a further room.

In TCN5, the region referring to the Reflective CS is subdivided in two separate rooms, with distinct entrance to each of them. In this sense it was decided to keep the didactic materials in one room and the activities in another, as can be observed in Figure 5.

Figure 3. Organization of didactic materials in the Holistic CS environment

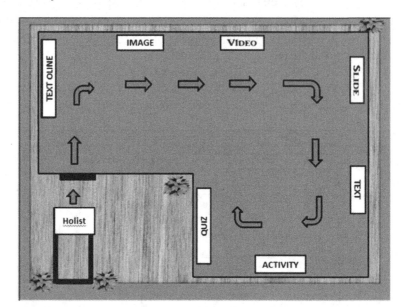

Figure 4. Organization of didactic materials in the Divergent CS environment

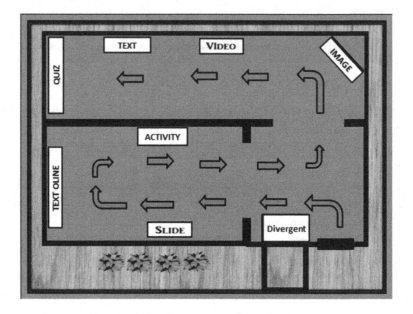

GRECx Development

GRECx (an acronym from the Portuguese Educational Resources Manager Aware of Expertise) aims to facilitate the work of the teacher, regarding the organization and storage of didactic materials according to the theme and level of expertise required for their understanding, and can be accessed by any device with internet access. The system interface offers two main features: add feature and manage feature, as can be seen in the activity diagram (Figure 6).

Figure 5. Organization of didactic materials in the environment of the Reflective CS

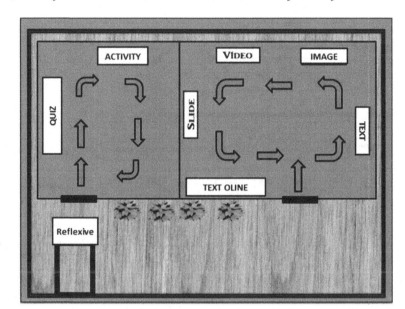

Figure 6. Activity diagram of the GRECx system

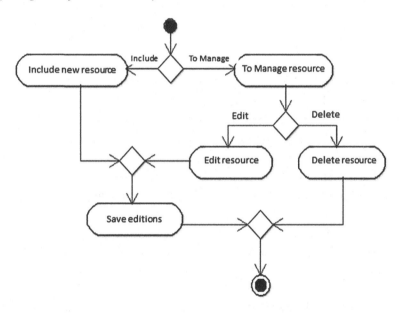

Due to the complexity of the functions, we opted to separate the presentation of each one (adding and managing). In this sense, it can be observed in Figure 7 the activity diagram of the add function, and in Figure 8 the activity diagram of the manage function.

By including a new educational resource, the teacher will have to determine the level of expertise, the theme and the type of category which it belongs (Figure 7).

Figure 7. Activity diagram: add function of the GRECx system

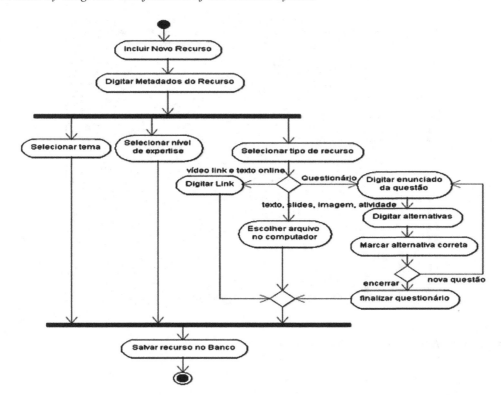

The manage function is subdivided into two main parts, delete and edit feature. As can be seen in Figure 8, there are two branches in the manage function, where the user can choose to either modify metadata, file / link, questions, change expertise level, download files or delete a resource.

The home page of the manage function (Figure 9) lists the features contained in the system database, where you can select the feature you want to change. The edit and delete options are represented by the "pencil" and "X" buttons, respectively, as can be seen in Figure 9.

In the webpage allocated to the a VW object, which automatically links the material inserted in GRECx to the VW, the theme filter can be seen in the upper right (Figure 10), allowing the student to choose which theme to visualize within the same object

The organization of objects within the Virtual World occurred with the support of the GRECx tool, according to the order for each Cognitive Style (Figures 2, 3, 4). The link for the preferred order by CS was allocated in each object using the media texture feature (Figure 11). The difference of each web page is perceived in its address, which presents indications of type of didactic material and level of expertise.

It was decided to configure the objects with zoom elements and the automatic execution feature, which is triggered (started or presented) by the students avatars approximation to the object.

Figure 8. Manage function of GRECx system

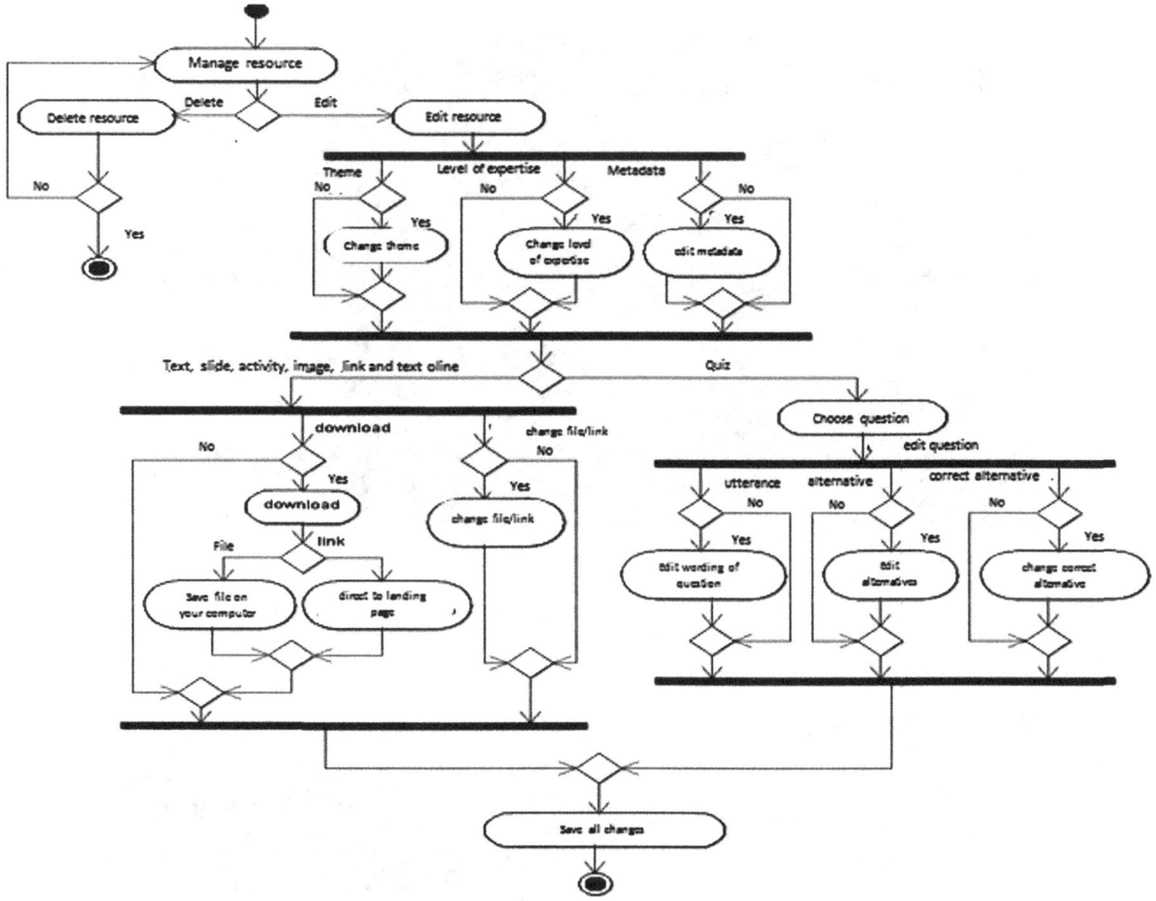

Figure 9. GRECx system manage interface

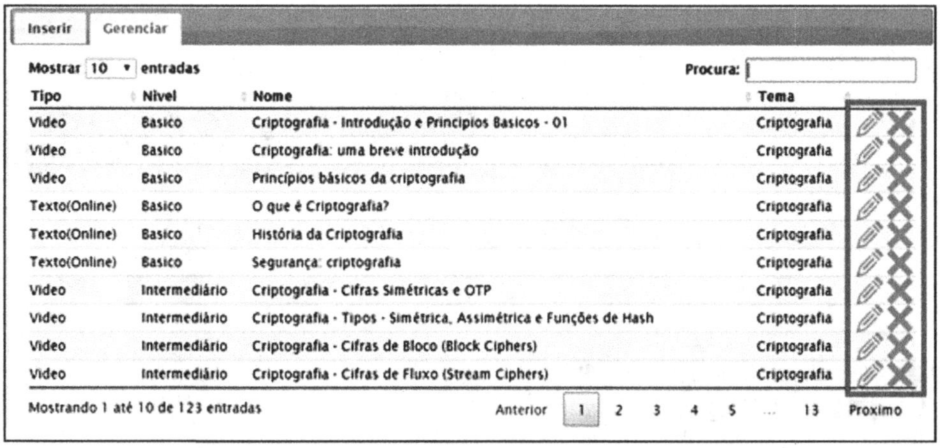

Tipo	Nivel	Nome	Tema
Video	Basico	Criptografia - Introdução e Principios Basicos - 01	Criptografia
Video	Basico	Criptografia: uma breve introdução	Criptografia
Video	Basico	Princípios básicos da criptografia	Criptografia
Texto(Online)	Basico	O que é Criptografia?	Criptografia
Texto(Online)	Basico	História da Criptografia	Criptografia
Texto(Online)	Basico	Segurança: criptografia	Criptografia
Video	Intermediário	Criptografia - Cifras Simétricas e OTP	Criptografia
Video	Intermediário	Criptografia - Tipos - Simétrica, Assimétrica e Funções de Hash	Criptografia
Video	Intermediário	Criptografia - Cifras de Bloco (Block Ciphers)	Criptografia
Video	Intermediário	Criptografia - Cifras de Fluxo (Stream Ciphers)	Criptografia

Figure 10. Web page of the video resource viewed in an object within the VW

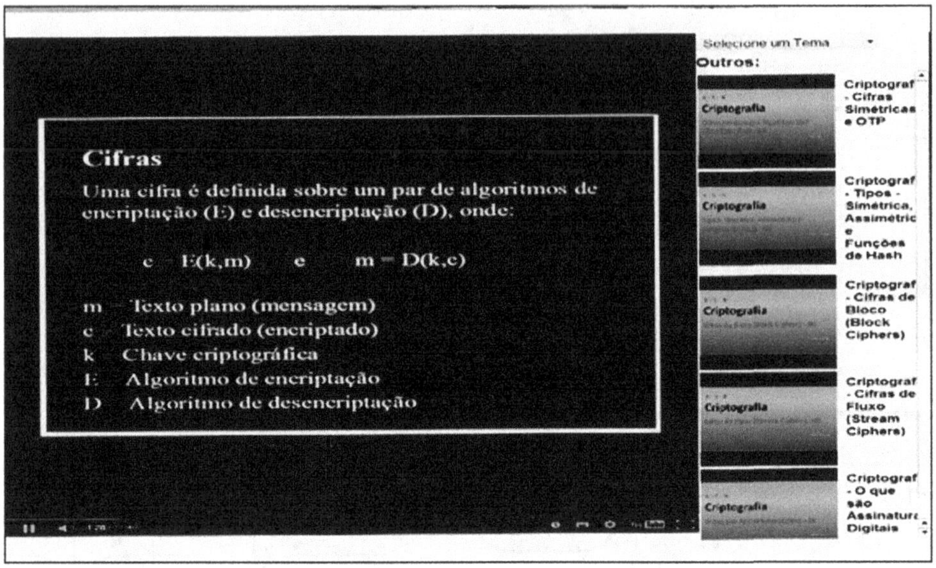

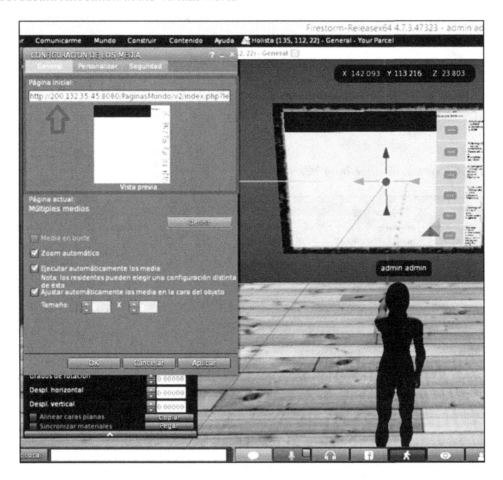

Figure 11. Media Allocation in the Virtual World

Analysis of Results

For the evaluation of the ID in the VW TCN5, 18 students with the profile of the ultimate users were recruited, that is, that they had the same characteristics of the target audience of this study, following the two steps defined in section 6 for the use of the 3D environment.

In the first stage, the evaluators answered a questionnaire for the definition of the individual CS, being in the sequence exposed to the four pedagogic routes (regardless of CS), needing at the end to indicate the one they liked the most. The result of this analysis shows if the profile diagnosed by the questionnaire corresponds to the preference of use within the VW. In this evaluation, it was identified an inconsistency between the preference for CS defined by the questionnaire and the preferential environment (region). Seven users chose environments equal to the result obtained in the test, but ten chose different environments from the test result, and one student was indifferent to the contents organization.

It was noticed in the evaluators' speech that, eventually, the architecture of the rooms may have influenced their choice. One of the students who chose the environment with a different style from the one inferred by the questionnaire commented that he felt more free in the other environment, because it was bigger, wider and more spacious. The student who was indifferent to the organization of resources said that he did not notice a great difference between the organizations of the resources, finding all equally good.

In the second stage of the evaluation the students were exposed to the two versions of the TCN5: the version without the adaptations made (before the ID) and the version with the implemented adaptations (after the ID). The route foreseen for each of the versions consisted of going through all the spaces of the environment, using each of the available didactic materials. The purpose of this stage was to determine if the student would have a higher preference for the VW in its initial version or the VW after the ID adaptations.

In this aspect, three individuals chose the VW in its first version and 15 chose the VW with ID. The first ones pointed out as important features of the VW in its first version the intuitive organization of objects and the more colorful visual presentation, drawing more attention to the content. The comments on the color of the objects may have occurred due to the greater amount of didactic resources displayed on the walls of the VW rooms in the first version. In the VW with ID, since it allows the visualization of more than one resource within the same object, the quantity of elements (objects with didactic materials) was reduced. The second group highlighted the organization of resources in a more pleasant, dynamic and intuitive layout, presenting the contents in a more condensed way, making the environment clearer and with the possibility of visualizing more than one theme within the same object.

On the questionnaire that received the feedback about the experience of the users in the VW, the first question referred to the possibility of choosing the subject: if this motivated the evaluator to continue interacting with the object. Ten people reported that yes and seven said that this motivation was partial. It is possible to affirm that a limitation in the answers occurred because some users did not perceive in the interface, in their first visualization, the option to change the theme, and therefore did not interact with this function. In this sense, it may be interesting a change in the interface to improve the visualization of the theme filter.

The second question asked if the user felt stimulated to learn within the VW with ID. Among the responses, nine of the students commented that yes, six said they were partially stimulated and three were indifferent. This shows that the use of a VW with the possibilities of the implementation of the Instructional Design can be relevant with respect to the stimulus to learning, helping in the generation of knowledge.

The third question sought to verify if the evaluator felt that the organization of the didactic materials was adequate to his way of learning. Twelve participants said yes, five commented that this appropriateness was partial and one was indifferent to the organization, showing that most participants enjoyed the different organizations proposed. However, it should be noted that these responses may have been influenced by the architecture of the rooms visited, which were not homogeneous.

Two questions were elaborated in order to ascertain if the student had difficulties in assimilating the knowledge due to the level of expertise of the content to which he was exposed. The first one asked if the users felt that the contents were in agreement with their level of expertise and the second asked if the students were able to understand much of the content presented. In the first question, twelve users said that the contents were adequate to their knowledge and six said that this adequacy was partial. In the second question, eleven users said they were able to understand much of the content and seven said that this understanding was partial. The result obtained allows to affirm that the diagnostic tool (POSSOBOM, 2014) and the adaptation of the contents to the three levels of expertise in Computer Networks was somehow adequate, since none of the participants stated that did not understand the contents.

Thinking about evaluating a possible use of VW with ID adaptations in real classroom environment, two questions were answered. The first asked if the user would like to use the VW with ID again. Thirteen students fully agreed and five partially agreed. The second question investigated whether the participant would recommend the VW to other people. Of the eighteen evaluators, twelve said they would definitely recommend it, five said they could recommend, and one person remained indifferent. This result shows that the experiencing of the VW with the adaptations of Instructional Design was considered relevant in the educational field by the students, opening space to be explored in the classroom in a massive way.

Aiming to verify if there was ease of use of the objects within the VW adapted with ID, three questions were explored. The first question asked whether the user found the object interface attractive. Five people said totally agreed, eleven found the interface to be partially attractive, one evaluator was indifferent to this issue and another said he did not find the interface very attractive. This low acceptance of users may have occurred due to the variable room size and the small amount of didactic materials posted on the walls and with a neutral color, to do not divert the attention from the resource presented in it. One of the evaluators explained his opinion about the possibilities of using more vivid colors in the interface of the objects, to catch the attention of the users. The second question asked whether the objects were easy to use, where twelve participants fully agreed and four partially agreed, but two individuals disagreed partially. It is believed that this difference in responses was due to the experience of each student regarding the use of Virtual Worlds: of the eighteen evaluators, six had some experience with VW and eight with 3D games. This allows us to relate the ease of interaction to the users with some experience in simulations or immersive 3D environments.

Still referring to the objects ease of use, the third question sought to verify if the users needed help to understand how to use the didactic materials inserted in objects in the VW with ID. Six participants said no, two said they needed some help and two were indifferent to the issue. However, eight evaluators said they needed help in understanding this use. It was evidenced that the users who did not need help refer to those who were already familiar with VW, which allows to infer that the ease of interaction is due to this experience, and that the others found difficulties due to their first contact with the 3D environment in this evaluation.

Finally, we tried to question the student about the possibility of using the VW, adapted with the ID, in the improvement of learning about the topic of Computer Networks Security. In this aspect, a question asked if the user believed that this environment could be efficient for learning if used by students in the classroom and for a longer time. Of the 18 individuals, 13 agreed totally and five partially agreed. As the experiment (VW experimentation and questionnaire response) lasted on average between 40 and 60 minutes, the evaluators may not have had enough time in the environment to check for some learning progress. In this sense, a question was asked to verify if the participants consider the possibility of learning if the time of VW use was longer. According to the answers, all the evaluators concluded that somehow the environment can be efficient in its purpose of assisting in the generation of knowledge if used for a longer time.

After the questions that aimed to answer the main aspects of the evaluation, an extra open question was stipulated in order to identify improvements in the ID built for the TCN5 VW through comments from the participants. As the main positive point identified by the evaluators is the concentration of several didactic materials within the same object, which, according to them, can improve students' attention to the content being studied. In addition, this variety of resources was pointed out as a learning benefit. It was also highlighted the need to have a visual distinction among the objects, in order to allow a clearer representation of the type of didactic material that is being exposed by it. In agreement with this modification it was suggested the allocation of an identifier icon on each object.

According to the evaluators, a feature that can also be improved in the VW is the standardization of rooms' architecture, in order to prevent a negative influence of the environment appearance on learning. In addition, it has been suggested that the resources may be arranged in a smaller environment, so that the student does not need to move his avatar for very long distances to visualize different didactic materials. One of the evaluators stressed again the importance of presenting more colors in the environment, seeking to capture the user's attention with a more attractive setting. Regarding the web pages allocated to objects within the VW, some modifications related to interface improvement were suggested. First, the letters from the theme choice function need to be larger, since some of the students did not identify it at first.

Concerning the didactic materials, one of the students commented about the questionnaire feedback. According to him, next to the message warning a result of error could come suggestions of ways to solve the question. One way to enable this possibility would be to indicate in the error message some of the didactic resources available in the environment for a better understanding of the subject. Another evaluator exposed the need to increase the letter size of the activity resource and standardize the size of the images within the objects.

After conducting the evaluation, the authors identified some limitations that may have influenced the answers given to the questionnaire. Firstly, it should be noted that at the time of the experiments occurred an oscillation in the internet speed, causing impairment in the visualization of the resources, which require a good streaming speed, especially when hosted directly on the internet (links).

Another aspect that was highlighted is that, although it was informed to the evaluators that the 3D environment to be tested had no game characteristics, but that it was a three-dimensional learning environment, some of the users requested improvements related to games, such as medals when the avatar did something right and interface with more playable features, giving as examples war games.

From these results, it can be seen many valid considerations regarding the implementation of Instructional Design and the developed resource manager (GRECx), allowing the identification of several improvements to be implemented in similar cases.

FUTURE RESEARCH DIRECTIONS

The use of Virtual Worlds in education allows new pedagogical possibilities. However, it is being realized the need of a personalization of these environments according to the specificities of each student. To do this, the method applied in this study was the Instructional Design.

This chapter deals with the structuring of an Instructional Design for the learning of Computer Networks within the Virtual World TCN5. This ID has attributes of ubiquitous computing, with the adaptation of educational resources to the level of knowledge of the student, as well as the organization of pedagogical routes according to the preferences of four Cognitive Styles (Holistic, Serialist, Divergent and Reflective).

Following the ID approach constructed by Falcade et al. (2016), adapted from ADDIE and Dick and Carey methods, the course was designed for Computer Networks learning, being deployed within the VW TCN5 (VOSS, 2014; HERPICH, 2015). This three-dimensional environment was chosen because it possesses a classroom architecture prepared to receive a course adapted to the three levels of expertise and the four Cognitive Styles contemplated in the research, automatically allocating its users in one of its regions and rooms according to the profile identified in the questionnaire (POSSOBOM, 2014; MOZZAQUATRO, 2010).

Some assumptions were made about the preferences of each CS addressed in TCN5, based on the studies of Bariani (1998), Geller (2004) and Cassidy (2004). With this, an organization of presentation was generated to attend to the four predominant CS according to the work of Mozzaquatro (2010): Holistic, Serialist, Divergent and Reflective. In total, seven different didactic materials, ordered according to the preference by CS identified in the work of Mozzaquatro (2010), were included: slide presentation, text, online text, image, video, activity and questionnaire.

The inclusion of didactic materials in the VW TCN5 was done manually, directly editing the objects of the environment, requiring the teachers to have a basic knowledge about VW platforms so that they could be used in class. From this limitation an Educational Resources Manager Aware of Expertise (GRECx) was created, which feeds web pages allocated to objects in the Virtual World. In this manager there is the possibility of including the seven types of didactic resources mentioned, separating them by theme and level of knowledge (basic, intermediate or advanced).

The web pages created, which are linked to each of the resources inserted in the GRECx, were allocated in the VW following the preferred organization by CS, and are visualized by the students according to the level of expertise they have. Another feature is the opportunity to choose the theme to be visualized, that can be made by the student directly on the object, allowing a content filtering from his need.

The development of this research has encountered some limitations, such as in the development of the GRECx system. Some commands configured on web pages were not recognized within the VW (e.g., use of two linked pages per link). The solution found was the use of *iframes*, which makes reference to another HTML page without leaving the main page. In addition, the oscillation of internet speed at the time of the experiment may have directly influenced the evaluation, making it difficult for the participants to properly view some of the resources.

As contributions of this research stands out:

1. The contextualized and ubiquitous Instructional Design, formed by the organization of the didactic materials in the environment from the preferences of Cognitive Style, as well as the availability of the contents according to the level of knowledge of the user;

2.   The expanded use of the VW TCN5, by the possibility of viewing multiple content themes within the same object, with transparent to the user filters of level of expertise;

3.   The possibility of implementing this ID in other Virtual Worlds or learning environments that approach the Holistic, Serialist, Divergent and Reflective CS, and use the same (or similar) types of didactic materials;

4.   The development of Resources Manager Aware of Expertise (GRECx) that allows:

   a.   The organization of didactic materials according to the theme (subject), level of knowledge and type of resource, through a friendly web interface, which does not require training or specific notions of VW by teachers, due to its similarity with other web softwares used by them, such as Moodle;

   b.   The consequent facilitation in the inclusion and management of resources within the VW TCN5, without the need of knowledge on the 3D environment programming, because it happens from an external interface linked to its objects; and

   c.   The possibility of sharing didactic materials among teachers, because the GRECx system admits collaborative work in downloading and uploading the materials inserted in its database.

As future works, it is proposed the optimization of some GRECx system characteristics, such as the automatic resizing of images when included in the system by the teacher. This modification will make the visualization of images within VW objects more standardized and accessible, reducing the size of the files. Another function to be improved is the way to include the activity resource, which could be implemented directly on the system interface instead of requiring the loading of files with the description of it.

As for web pages, a possibility of customization is to allow the modification of the font size, to improve the visualization of the text, and the change of the page background. In addition, the location of the graphical presentation of the option "change theme" needs to change, seeking a greater visibility of the function.

The modifications related to the VW TCN5 are the standardization of the rooms' architecture, making the environment more homogeneous and allowing greater salience of the ID; the modeling of objects that incorporate didactic materials with the inclusion of labels, making them more distinguishable, in order to allow the immediate identification of the type of resource presented in each of them; and the use of more vivid and harmonic colors in the textures of the environment.

Through this research, it is possible to conclude that the development and implementation of Instructional Design for the VW TCN5 allowed a more adequate follow-up of the preferences of Cognitive Style and level of student's expertise, personalizing the arrangement of didactic materials for each user profile. For the evaluators, the application of the ID allowed a more organized and clean scenario, maximizing the offer of didactic resources within the same object. In addition, to the teacher it was offered a facilitating tool that allows the management of didactic materials outside the VW, and the presentation of contents in an organized way within the VW, without the need of skills in programming objects in the 3D environment.

REFERENCES

Allinson, C. W., & Hayes, J. (1996). The Cognitive Style Index: A Measure of Intuition-Analysis For Organizational Research. *Journal of Management Studies, 33*(1), 119–135. doi:10.1111/j.1467-6486.1996.tb00801.x

Backes, L. (2012). The manifestations of authorship in the formation of the educator in virtual digital spaces. Journal of Education. *Science and Culture, 2*(17).

Bainbridge, W. S. (Ed.). (2010). *Online Worlds: the convergence of the real and the virtual*. London, UK: Springer.

Barbosa, S.D. & Silva, B.S. (2010). *Human-Computer Interaction*. Elsevier.

Bariani, I. C. (1998). *Cognitive Styles of University Students and Scientific Initiation* (PhD thesis). Campinas: UNICAMP.

Bates, E. T., & Wiest, L. R. (2004). Impact of personalization of Mathematical Word Problems on Student Performance. *The Mathematical Educator, 14*(2), 17–26.

Behar, P.A., Torrezan, C.A.W., & Rückert, A.B. (2008). PEDESIGN: the construction of a learning object based on pedagogical design. *New technologies in education, RENOTE, 2*(6).

Cakir, O., & Simsek, N. (2010). A comparative analysis of the effects of computer and paper customization on student performance. *Computers & Education, 55,* 1524–1531. doi:10.1016/j.compedu.2010.06.018

Cassidy, S. (2004). Learning Styles: An overview of theories, models, and measures. Educational Psychology: An International Journal of Experimental Educational Psychology, 4(24), 419-444.

Cunha, L. M. A. (2007). *Rasch models and Likert and Thurstone scales in measuring attitudes* (Master's Dissertation in Probability and Statistics). University of Lisbon, Faculty of Sciences, Department of Statistics and Operational Research.

Dallacosta, A., Cazetta, G., & Souza, S. G. (2010). New technologies applied in the elaboration of instructional material online. In *3rd Symposium Hypertext and Technologies in Education (social networks and learning)*. Recife PE.

Dunn, R., Beaudry, J. S., & Kiavas, A. (1989). Survey of research on learning styles. *Educational Leadership, USA, 6*(46), 50–58.

Ericsson, K. A., & Smith, J. (1991). *Toward a General Theory of Expertise: Prospects and Limits*. New York: Published by the Press Syndicate of the University of Cambridge.

Essalmi, F., Ben Ayed, L. J., Jemni, M., Kinshuk, & Graf, S. (2011). Evaluation of Personalization Strategies Based on Fuzzy Logic. *Advanced Learning Technologies (ICALT), 2011 11th IEEE International Conference on*, 6-8.

Falcade, A., Krassmann, A. L., Freitas, V., Kautzmann, T., Bernardi, G., & Medina, R. D. (2016). Instructional Design: a comparison of methodologies for definition of virtual world approach. *XXVII Brazilian Symposium on Informatics in Education*.

Filatro, A. (2008). *Instructional Design in Practice*. Sao Paulo: Person Education of Brazil.

Flatschart, F. (2011). *HTML5: Immediate shipment*. Rio de Janeiro: Brasport.

Franciscato, F. T. (2010). *ROAD: Semantic Repository of learning objects for mobile devices* (Masters dissertation). Federal University of Santa Maria - UFSM.

French, P. A., & Sternberg, R. J. (1989). Expertise and intelligent thinking: when is it worse to know better? In Advances in the psychology of human intelligence. Lawrence Erlbaum Associates.

Gagné, R. (1985). *The conditions of learning*. New York: Holt, Rinehart and Winston.

Geller, M. (2004). *Educação a Distância e Estilos Cognitivos: construindo um novo olhar sobre os ambientes virtuais*. Porto Alegre: UFRGS. Tese (Doutorado em Informática na Educação), Programa de Pós-Graduação em Informática na Educação, Universidade Federal do Rio Grande do Sul.

Graf, S., & Kinshuk, C. (2010). A Flexible Mechanism for Providing Adaptivity Based on Learning Styles in Learning Management Systems. In *IEEE International Conference on Advanced Learning Technologies* (pp. 30-34). IEEE. 10.1109/ICALT.2010.16

Herpich, F. (2015). *ELAI: intelligent agent adaptive to the level of expertise of students* (Masters dissertation). Federal University of Santa Maria, Santa Maria, RS.

Holden, J. T., Westfall, P. J. L., & Emeriti, C. (2010). An Instructional Media Selection guide for distance learning - implications for learning with an introduction to virtual worlds. In *USDLA* (2nd ed.). United States Distance Learning Association.

Likert, R. (1932). A technique for Measurement of Attitudes. Archives of Psychology.

Moreira, M. A., & Masini, E. F. S. (2001). *Significant Learning: The theory of David Ausubel*. São Paulo: Centauro.

Mozzaquatro, P. M. (2010). *Adaptation of Mobile Learning Engine Moodle (MLE MOODLE) to different cognitive styles using Adaptive Hypermedia* (Masters dissertation). Federal University of Santa Maria, Santa Maria, RS.

Nascimento, A.C.A.A. (2006). The design of the online course favoring the construction of a learning community of future teachers. *New Technologies Magazine in Education – RENOTE, 1*(4).

Nunes, I. D., & Schiel, U. (2011). Instructional Design and its follow-up at runtime using Activity Network. *XXII Brazilian Symposium on Informatics in Education - XVII Workshop on Informatics in Education*.

Ogata, H., & Yano, Y. (2004). Context-aware support for computer-supported ubiquitous learning. In: Wireless and Mobile Technologies in Education. *The 2nd IEEE International Workshop on. Opensimulator. Project History*. Retrieved May 07, 2014, from http://goo.gl/CnuWGy

Possobom, C. C. (2014). *SistEX - a dynamic system to detect the student's experience* (Master's thesis). Federal University of Santa Maria, Santa Maria, RS.

Rios, E., & Moreira Filho, T. (2013). *Software Testing* (3rd ed.). Rio de Janeiro: Books.

Rodrigues, R. (2013). *Teaching Plan - Systems Security and Audit*. Federal Institute of Education, Science and Technology Farroupilha.

Savi, R., von Wangenhein, C. G., Ulbrict, V., & Vanzin, T. (2010). Proposal for an Evaluation Model of Educational Games. *RENOTE - Magazine New Technologies in Education, 3*(8).

Shih, Y.-C., & Yang, M.-T. (2008). A Collaborative Virtual Environment for Situated Language Learning Using VEC3D. *Journal of Educational Technology & Society, 11*(1), 56–68.

Sung, J.-S. (2009). U-Learning Model Design Based on Ubiquitous Environment. International Journal of Advanced Science and Technology, 13.

Thibes, R. F. (2011). *Teaching Plan - Security and Audit of Information Systems*. University Alto Vale do Rio do Peixe.

Vahldick, A., & Knaul, J. C. (2010). Web Tool for Managing the Production of Learning Objects. *The Brazilian Symposium on Informatics in Education*.

von Wangenhein, C. G., & von Wangenhein, A. (2012). *Teaching Computing with Games*. Florianópolis: Bookess Editora.

Voss, G. B. (2014). *TCN5 - Teaching Computer Networks in a Free Immersive Virtual Environment* (Master's thesis). Federal University of Santa Maria, Santa Maria, RS.

Wang, S.-K., & Hsu, H.-Y. (2009). Using the ADDIE Model to Design Second Life Activities for Online Learners. *TechTrends, 6*(56).

This research was previously published in Optimizing Instructional Design Methods in Higher Education; pages 147-175, copyright year 2019 by Information Science Reference (an imprint of IGI Global).

Chapter 35

Comparing Two Teacher Training Courses for 3D Game-Based Learning:
Feedback From Trainee Teachers

Michael Thomas
https://orcid.org/0000-0001-6451-4439
Liverpool John Moores University, UK

Letizia Cinganotto
INDIRE, Università Telematica degli Studi, Italy

ABSTRACT

This chapter explores data form two online language teacher training courses aimed at providing participants with the skills to create and use games in 3D immersive environments. Arising from a two-year project which explored how game-based learning and virtual learning environments can be used as digital tools to develop collaborative and creative learning environments, two training courses were developed to support teachers to use two immersive environments (Minecraft and OpenSim). The first course was self-directed and the second was moderated by facilitators. Both courses provided a variety of games and resources for students and teachers in different languages (English, German, Italian, and Turkish). This chapter explores feedback from the teacher participants on both courses arising from a questionnaire and interviews with teachers and provides recommendations about the technical and pedagogical support required to develop immersive worlds and games for language learning.

INTRODUCTION

As computer-assisted language learning (CALL) has often been driven by technological innovation rather than pedagogy, a constantly recurring finding has been the need for more research on the effectiveness of CALL teacher training that aims to integrate technological and pedagogical literacies (Torsani, 2015).

DOI: 10.4018/978-1-6684-7597-3.ch035

This chapter contributes to this gap in the research by investigating two online language teacher training courses, and is significant in that it examines the teacher feedback on the potential of digital game-based learning in two 3D immersive environments (Minecraft and OpenSim). In particular the chapter contributes to the knowledge base in this area by critically exploring the potential of immersive training for teachers who use the CLIL (Content and Integrated Language Learning) approach in two different formats: a self-study course and a teacher-led training course. The main difference between the courses was that the self-study course provided a theoretical framework for games design without the need for participants to develop technical skills to build games themselves. In the teacher-led course the participants' goal was to design and create a language learning game in a virtual world. The two courses were designed as part of a two-year research project exploring game-based language learning funded by the European Commission, and included participating teachers from Italy, the UK, Germany and Turkey.

The chapter first briefly summarizes relevant research literature before describing the rationale, aims and scenarios that informed the planning and implementation of the two courses as examples of continuing professional development (CPD) for teachers in immersive worlds. The research was guided by the following two research questions which led to a mixed methods research design involving interviews, an online questionnaire and participants' self-reflections:

1. How beneficial and effective is CPD on game-based learning and immersive worlds for foreign language teachers?
2. What are foreign language teachers' perceptions of being trained in a community of practice (CoP) in an immersive world?

Background

The use of digital games in different contexts has become increasingly popular over the last decade. Industry and educational professionals are regularly using digital games to foster users' motivation and engagement, as confirmed by Johnson et al. (2013), who argued that "game play has traversed the realm of recreation and has infiltrated the worlds of commerce, productivity, and education, proving to be a useful training and motivation tool" (p. 21). Research has shown that games play a crucial role when it comes to education but it is important to reiterate that several categories and concepts have overlapping boundaries and they are not always clearly defined. Several authors, for example, use the terms gamification and game-based learning to describe the same concept (Callaghan, McCusker, Losada, Harkin & Wilson 2013). In order to bring more clarity to this fast changing landscape, in this chapter we define gamification in terms of a style of competitive learning related to the integration of 'game mechanics' such as badges, points, levels and leaderboards to non-game situations (Hamari, Koivisto & Sarsa 2014; Seaborn & Fels 2015) and game-based learning as the use of specifically designed games that have pedagogical or training content added to them along with defined learning outcomes (Van Eck, 2006). Game-based learning and gamification have become particularly popular in primary and secondary school contexts, thus the need for more effective and flexible modes of pre- and in-service teacher training to develop and sustain teacher competences in this rapidly moving area (Wiggins, 2016).

THEORETICAL FRAMEWORK

The use of game mechanics is often linked with the attempt to enhance student engagement and motivation (Hanus & Fox, 2015). Efforts have also been made to integrate gamification techniques more overtly into curricula, which aided by the use of dashboards, can help to visualise a student's progress against a series of tasks (Kapp, 2012). While there are promising signs of some improvement in these areas, as is inevitable with technology-enhanced learning, several challenges have also been identified. These include the lack of resources and support for teaching staff, and opportunities to integrate game-based approaches into formal and often tightly controlled, examination focused contexts. Moreover, gamification is at odds with more traditional approaches to learning which do not specify the need for external rewards to incentivise student achievement. Given the obstacles, an understanding of effective games design in the context of educational goals and learning outcomes is required by teaching staff (Lee & Hammer, 2011). So, while there has been an increasing use of games in education, particularly in the primary and secondary school sectors, as these learners use games most extensively and seamlessly in their out of school social life (Wiggins, 2016), teachers' approaches have often been ad hoc rather than based on sound pedagogy or training.

Teacher training courses and continuing professional development (CPD) opportunities for teachers are often hosted by a variety of elearning platforms. Moodle is one of the most popular and user-friendly open source platforms which has been increasingly used in all sectors of public and private education in recent decades, particularly as a result of its alignment with the principles of social and collaborative modes of learning. Moodle is based on a Learning Content Management System (LCMS), which includes:

- an 'author' tool that allows teachers to create and re-use learning objects;
- a dynamic interface;
- an administrative interface that allows teachers to manage and track the activities of users.

The virtual environment created by Moodle is inspired by the following pedagogical principles and frameworks (Huang & Liang, 2018):

- *constructivism*, according to which students actively build new knowledge by interacting with the environment in which it is integrated;
- *constructionism*, which is aimed at highlighting how learning is particularly effective when engaged in building knowledge and skills intended for use by other users (Kafai & Resnick, 1996);
- *social constructivism*, which aims to extend the ideas previously illustrated within a social group engaged in constructing educational materials in a collaborative way for each other, thus creating a cooperative culture of shared products with shared meanings;
- *connected behaviour* or *related behaviour*, as opposed to *dissociated behaviour*, refers to a more empathetic approach that promotes a variety of perspectives in a constant attempt to listen, ask questions and try to understand as far as possible the point of view of others (Boon, 2007).

Based on these affiliations, Moodle has strong theoretical links with *cooperative learning* (Kaye, 1994), which aims to foster group work for educational purposes, so that students can collaborate with each other to maximize their learning potential. Specific research has shown that cooperation, compared to competitive and individualistic efforts, generates the following results in most cases:

- greater productivity and effectiveness in the development of the training path;
- greater self-esteem, social competence and satisfactory results from a psychological point of view;
- more committed, attentive and collaborative interpersonal relationships.

In fact, teachers can be considered as special lifelong learners as they have to be able to innovate and adapt to different students and contexts throughout their careers. Constant learning is therefore a priority for them, because they are reflective practitioners, whose practice involves a willingness to participate actively in a continuous process of growth, requiring ongoing critical reflection on both classroom practices and core beliefs (Larrivee, 2008). If, on the one hand, learning is a never-ending process, there are some phases that are more critical and strategic than others. In this context, it is worth mentioning Mezirow's (1991) research on how adults learn by giving meaning to their experiences through perspective transformation and the work of Schön (1983) on the teacher as a reflective practitioner, which is a key dimension of personal and professional growth. Reflecting 'on' and 'in' action is an essential aspect of learning, as it helps teachers understand the strengths and weaknesses in their teaching styles, in order to improve them constantly. Indeed, this aim was among the rationale of both training courses. As a transversal task in both courses, the digital portfolio was specifically designed to fulfill this aim. Moreover, forum interaction was encouraged as a tool for self-reflection and mutual enrichment.

Online learning for teachers needs an effective and "scientifically well-grounded" learning environment, complying not only with the principles of andragogy (Knowles, 1975) which at the same time leave sufficient space for self-determination and the adoption of a heutagogical approach. Heutagogy is considered as the study of self-determined learning. It applies a holistic approach to developing learner capabilities, with learning perceived as an active and proactive process, in which learners serve as "the major agent in their own learning, which occurs as a result of personal experiences" (Hase & Kenyon, 2007, p.112). Heutagogy can be seen as a theory of distance education which extends the andragogical approach.

In developing the training courses, the designers took advantage of their previous experience in the field of online adult learning through different initiatives aimed at meeting the apparently conflicting needs of socialisation and autonomy of an adult audience by offering an andragogical and heutagogical approach (Benedetti, 2018).

In 2000 Garrison, Anderson and Archer defined the model of the "community of enquiry" (CoE) as consisting of three key elements which should be included in every online learning environment, according to the constructivist and constructionist models: the cognitive element, the social element and the teaching element. The three dimensions were developed in the training courses as follows:

- *the cognitive element* was represented by the learning material provided in the platform as a starting point for reflection and via the shared forum spaces; in particular, it was a key part of the self-study course;
- the *social element* referred to the interaction among the participants both in the synchronous mode through webinars and live meetings in Minecraft and OpenSim and in asynchronous mode through the forums, where they were asked to post their reflections on the learning materials provided in the platform;
- the *teaching element* referred to the coaching and moderating role of the forum moderators and the teaching activities during the live online meetings.

The development of the training courses was led by the idea that knowledge is generated by the ability to build connections within a network. Knowing how to choose what to select and understand the meaning of information is in itself a learning process. The ability to identify connections between fields, ideas and concepts is a central skill to be acquired. The learner approaches the study in the way s/he prefers, individualizing his or her approach to the content through autonomous selection leading to the personalization of the learning pathway.

In distance learning, participants are encouraged to prepare projects linked to objectives in relation to the specific subject and context (Alan & Stoller, 2005). The project requires constant negotiation between the interior and the exterior. Each learner develops his or her own project by collecting the ideas received from the teacher and subject tutor, transforming cultural learning into an instrument of experience and personal appropriation. The project implies 'double thinking', in the sense of foreseeing and imagining a possible world, while working at the same time to achieve it. The project assigned the participants opportunities for forum interaction in the self-study course, while in the teacher-led course, the project was represented by the game they had to build in-world (Beckett, 2002, 2006; Beckett & Miller, 2006).

Self-knowledge includes the possibility of making the student rediscover his/her design skills, so that the individual can not only make his choices but also return and change them if a choice is no longer suitable. In distance learning, each training course is aimed at strengthening the spirit of a scientific community based on individual and collective collaboration, sharing and creativity (Beckett & Slater, 2005, 2018, 2019).

Technology can support this cooperative approach offering tools and virtual environments for sharing different participants' experiences. By creating a Personal Learning Environment (PLE) (Chatti et al., 2010) centred on the student's individual needs and learning styles, trying to plan and implement tailored learning pathways, the potential of webtools and media may be exploited in order to make the learning experience effective and powerful. To this end, it is important to foster as many formal and informal learning environments as possible within training pathways and to build a Community of Practice (Wenger et al. 2002), consisting of teachers and practitioners.

COURSE CONTEXT AND PLANNING

Both of the teacher training courses were planned and delivered with the aim of enabling individual and cooperative learning. Individual learning was fostered especially through the delivery of learning materials and video-tutorials, which were meant to elicit content-based learning and at the same time reflection and meta-cognition. Cooperative learning was mainly fostered through discussion forums and during live events in the teacher-led course, in particular via the weekly webinars and synchronous meetings with experts in the two immersive environments, Minecraft or OpenSim. Minecraft was chosen because it is widely used by children internationally, while OpenSim is an open access immersive environment, supported by a community of educators and technicians. Both platforms have been used extensively in education with a particular focus on constructivist approaches to problem-solving and project-based learning (Kuhn & Stevens, 2017; Ryoo, Techatassanasoontorn, Lee & Lothian, 2011). This combination of autonomous learning and cooperative learning was meant to be the most effective formula to enhance life-long learning.

The training courses' teaching model was based on Scardamalia and Bereiter's (2006) theoretical model of knowledge building, which emphasized collaborative work and research rather than individual inquiry. This means that distance learning does not lead to 'studying alone' as it is organized to ensure collaboration and the sharing of ideas for all involved.

The knowledge building perspective adopted was also supported by UNESCO (Meek & Davies, 2009) and the training courses addressed language and CLIL teachers' continuous professional development from a life-long learning perspective. Both the self-study course and teacher-led course were delivered through a Moodle platform and involved 5 modules, each containing several tasks, reading lists, videos, resources and instructions. The core learning material was provided by reports and resources arising from the teachers. Universal Design Principles led its development as per the following four areas.

Course Information

Moodle was relatively intuitive to use and provided the complete course syllabus in one long page view. Following the design principles, an image of the relevant virtual world prefaced the course followed by an introduction chapter, a brief course description, an introduction video, a syllabus and recommendations for study time. Clear instructions for students followed about where to begin and how to navigate current content, thus meeting the 'less than three clicks' design principle. Each module provided tasks, communication instructions for the forum and guidelines. Students were made aware of participation expectations, technology requirements, access instructions to the various virtual environments, reading lists and course materials.

Course Content

Care was taken not to infringe any copyright laws when presenting course material. There was a "Welcome" and "Let's get acquainted" discussion. Each module began with an image or video and a clear title as well as a coloured text title marker which included the number of the module. In the self-study course personalized learning was evident. All of the modules were open from the beginning and no prerequisites were imposed on the students. All of the tasks were designed for self-study and none of the assignments had due dates or grading deadlines. Modules included three forms of interaction:

1. student-student interaction (e.g. discussion forums);
2. student-teacher interaction (feedback provided by the tutors in the discussion forums, students' portfolios were open and accessible to peers);
3. student-content interaction (engaging and varied content such as reading, watching videos and playing games in-world was provided).

Assessment

Multiple methods of assessment were used, such as forum discussions, tasks, portfolios, written essays and detailed instructions and guidelines for completing assignments and discussions were provided at the outset.

Course Accessibility

Instructions on how to login to the virtual spaces were provided. Consistent module and text styles were used and hyperlink text incorporated the destination, words and phrases to provide context for screen-readers.

METHODOLOGY

Two questionnaires were delivered to the participants in both courses: one at the beginning and one at the end. Interviews were also conducted at the end of both courses in June 2019. Relevant data from the questionnaires, together with data from the interviews and the final student reflections posted in the forums on the elearning platform were used to answer the following research questions:

1. How beneficial and effective is CPD on game-based learning and immersive worlds for foreign language teachers?
2. What are foreign language teachers' perceptions of being trained in a community of practice (CoP) in an immersive world?

The Self-Study Course

The self-study course was attended by 24 participants, the vast majority of whom were upper secondary school teachers of English from Italy and Turkey. As already mentioned, the self-study course was planned to foster autonomous and independent learning through the learning materials in the platform. Forum discussion was elicited to foster reflections and opinions about the study materials. The initial questionnaire was aimed at understanding the participants' background, learning styles and needs in order to plan and deliver the course accordingly. The final questionnaire was aimed at investigating the impact of the course on the participants in terms of learning outcomes, professional development, knowledge acquired and skills developed.

In the initial questionnaire the majority of the participants self-evaluated their digital competences as 'good', and indicated that they often used learning technologies in their work (Beetham & Sharpe, 2019). Active and interactive methodologies such as work group and project work emerged as the most frequently applied. The majority of teachers affirmed that they used games to motivate and reward their students, to foster collaboration and develop creativity, socialization and peer learning. Regarding their knowledge and use of immersive 3D worlds, the majority of respondents reported that they had never used these platforms, but they felt that game based-learning in school curricula would be beneficial for students, especially in terms of increased motivation and the development of 21st century skills.

The Teacher-led Training Course

The teacher-led course represented the second iteration of the online course although with a different format. Live sessions in-world in OpenSim and Minecraft and weekly webinars to conclude each week's work were regularly scheduled as an integral part of the course, requiring more active and engaging participation from the teachers in the immersive worlds. Like the self-study course, it was developed as a five-week format and provided the participants with the opportunity to choose between two immersive environments to explore for language learning and teaching (OpenSim and Minecraft). 16 participants joined the course and the majority were Italian teachers of English at the upper secondary level. Their previous experience in the topics addressed by the project were self-evaluated as 'quite highly' skilled in ICTs. The majority also declared that they used learning technologies 'quite often' in class. The course was designed for two groups to work in parallel in different environments and with different learning materials. In the forum, the participants were encouraged to interact and share their ideas and comments about the learning materials. At the end of each week, a weekly webinar was organised and involved all of the participants in a lecture related to the main content of the week. The digital portfolio was the transversal task of the course, as it was positioned in the self-study course to encourage participants to collect memories from their learning experience and to have a positive impact on their professional development.

FINDINGS AND DISCUSSION

The Teachers' Voice from the Self-Study Course

The discussion fora worked very effectively throughout the self-study course in particular where they represented a core element of the course and were appreciated by the teachers, who used them to share their opinions and reflections on game-based learning in immersive worlds and on the learning material provided in the platform. These discussions were aimed at encouraging peer learning, so that the participants could feel like integral members of a community of practice. Several comments from the discussion fora clearly identified how the CoP supported their training. In particular, two detailed comments from one of the participants are reported below:

What are the advantages of learning through the making of a game? What about the development of cooperation skills in the creation of a game? The constructionist gaming combines, in a metacognitive approach, game-based learning with project-based learning, developing team working skills or cooperation skills or role-play based learning.

The four freedoms of play (fail, experiment, assume different identity and effort) lead students to a new idea of learning, more enjoyable and motivating. It's the immersive dimension of the 3D world which helps students experience a 'real' situation they can be involved in. Moreover, the chance of synchronous activities in a setting where the foreign language is the only way of communication urges [them] to act according to the rules of 'real life' situations, finding out linguistic solutions immediately, so playing games in a virtual environment definitely enhances language learning. (Participant 5)

The comments show how powerful the learning experience in a 3D world was for the trainee teachers, enhancing their motivation, enthusiasm and engaging them in very challenging and rewarding activities. Such activities included role-plays and production tasks involving ICTs as participant 5 continues:

Role-Play activities are fit for the purpose of learning a foreign language in 3D worlds; the constructivist paradigm (to be active creators of one's own knowledge) is the natural infrastructure to implement such activities: the more the students are the makers of their own scenarios, the more they will be motivated and engaged. Once the scenarios are ready, the playing of the roles can be enriched by the element of improvisation and the methodology of problem-solving.

3D worlds are, in some way, closed worlds, because you make use of elements from its immediate environment, even if you can import elements from outside, and it's not easy to show other people the activities and the final results, unless you shoot pictures or videos to publish on a website or blog or social network on the Internet. There is still much to do in the technology area of usability and accessibility (user-friendly tools, easy-to-use software for hearing and speech impaired students) and in the field of evaluation and assessment (creation of rubrics with criteria planned for 3D world didactical activities). (Participant 5)

Based on these comments it is worth underlining how conscious the trainees were of the potential of game-based learning in immersive worlds, as a practical implementation of the constructionist approach. They also pointed out the social dimension of the games, particularly beneficial for students who used the target language in a meaningful context, thereby reducing their affective filter (Krashen, 1985).

After downloading the theoretical material on game-based learning in immersive worlds and exploring the potential of 3D immersive worlds from a 'passive' perspective, mainly through videos and other resources, in the final questionnaire the participants stated that they were quite satisfied with the introduction to virtual worlds, as not much active engagement was required. This was done on purpose, as the ultimate goal of the initial training course was to guide the participants through an introductory learning experience in a virtual and immersive world, following a tailored pathway designed to be adjusted to individual participants' learning needs and free time.

This more 'passive' approach was appreciated by the participants as it was perceived as a 'teaser' to activate their curiosity to learn more about language learning in immersive worlds through a more practical 'hands on' approach in the second teacher-led course. The fact that there were no time constraints on the activities in the first course was also appreciated by the participants who did not have scheduled meetings to attend.

One of the participants in the self-study course decided to continue the learning experience and enrolled in the teacher-led course as well. It would be interesting to offer such learning pathways within the continuous professional development courses attended online and face-to-face by teachers in Italy and Europe more broadly. As the participants indicated, language learning with technologies and in particular language learning in virtual and immersive worlds is still an unexplored teaching field that could be encouraged more among teachers. This is partly due to the fact that specific technical skills are required. Training on technical and digital literacy and language learning and teaching in immersive worlds could have a significant impact on school curricula and contribute to improve students' level of competence in foreign languages. According to the teachers, the self-study course helped them to develop the following competences:

Building games in virtual worlds. (Participant 3)

It consolidated or deepened the use of different strategies to gamify teaching activities and base them more on learning by doing and situated learning approach. (Participant 1)

Building some gaming activities for children. (Participant 6)

I developed a further understanding of new virtual worlds and their possible uses in education.

Relations. (Participant 2)

Instructional design competencies, from analyzing learner needs to developing training assets. (Participant 8)

Innovative approaches to learning about game-based learning additional ways of involving students, new ways to build educational games and other ways to develop creativity. (Participant 4)

One of the questions on the final questionnaire was related to the possible use of the different immersive worlds for their future teaching: "How likely are you to use the following in your teaching in future?". Answers suggested that Minecraft and OpenSim were popular because of the lack of privacy constraints on the students.

The Teachers' Voice from the Teacher-Led Course

In the teacher-led course the forum was a valuable learning space as it enabled the trainee teachers to share ideas, comments and experiences. As a moderated forum it provided several opportunities for the participants to learn from their colleagues. Every week a specific forum was created to collect the participants' ideas and comments on the various learning materials and readings. As a result, the forum collected a wide range of meaningful insights and reflections, as shown in the selection of three extracts (1-3), where examples of comments from each of the five weeks have been quoted. The quotes can be considered learning materials in themselves as they are dense with reflections and relevant literature references chosen by the trainees.

Extract 1
Re: Does it make sense to build a boardgame in an immersive environment?
Saturday 22 June 2019, 22:33

"In a virtual world, board games should use some of the features offered by that unique environment, like leader boards and feedback for players. There is also the opportunity to build in multimedia and have students respond to sound, pictures, and/or video.

Another reason to play board games in a virtual world even if no extra features are added would be if the players were physically distant, and playing in the virtual world gave them an opportunity to hang out and play in a common virtual space. This is true of most MMORPGs [Massive Multiplayer Online Role-Playing Games], but smaller more traditional card and board games are often played by geographically distant players in Second Life and Open Sims.

P7, what you did with that map of the British Isles is AMAZING. I love the way it is physically and audibly interactive in the Open Sim, and then also has the online quiz element, with the two complementing one another and facilitating learning from more than one direction. Brilliant!" (Participant 6)

Extract 2

Re: Week 4 Suggested Readings

Saturday 1 June 2019, 19:15

[the review of research provided] "is such extensive and interesting reading that one does not know what to tackle first! My comments will not be very systematic as the material would need several readings and much thought to be processed decently.

A. I am familiar with MOOCs [Massive Open Online Courses] and 3DVLEs as I have tried several examples of the former (for example three courses by the European Schoolnet Academy and a number by EVO) and am a regular attendant of WVBPE [Virtual World Best Practices in Education] conferences and the like. Conversely, I have no experience in PBL [Project-based Learning], even though I attempt, from time to time, to create classroom experiences that may 'feel authentic'.

Among the three, I feel that MOOCs are least relevant to me as a teacher, being MOOCs a modality that works very well with adults but not with under-age students. 3DVLEs are at the core of our interests - we would not be here otherwise, while PBL makes sense just as a possible component of a teaching activity in a virtual environment. On the other hand, these three modalities might be combined. For example, in an eTwinning (telecommunication) project taking place in a virtual world, learning to build a specific object could be an example of PBL.

B. While academic works need to distinguish between and categorize different teaching approaches, the real teacher often has to combine different methods finding a unique way to satisfy

- administration requirements: timing, syllabus, organizational demands...
- class requirements: size, diversity of students, special needs, social background....
- community (fellow teachers) requirements: sharing of spaces and devices, consistency of methods with the same groups of students, interpersonal challenges (innovators are often perceived as challenging by their peers and are often met with irritation or jealousy).

Finally, I wonder which school would be willing to pay me for the needed skills ... In Italy teachers do not have a 'career': either they are teachers, or they are not. Consequently, the professional who takes the pain to acquire digital, pedagogical and organizational skills is paid as much as the teacher who totally relies on pre-packaged materials that s/he delivers frontally to a class, year after year. Innovators here have a totally intrinsic motivation!" (Participant 7)

Extract 3

Re: Week 4 Suggested Readings

Sunday 2 June 2019, 19:00

"The readings and both of your comments are fascinating. I used to teach more PBL, TBL [Task-based Learning] or communicative approaches when I was working as a corporate trainer. Now I'm teaching more English for Academic Purposes, writing development, speaking objectives and so on. I'm also involved in CLIL courses too, such as Economics, Psychology & Sociology. When I was reading about the authentic contexts, I think it's relative. Is EAP an authentic purpose, or is English for Specific Purposes, more authentic? Or does it mean realistic compared to the real world, but they not have to ever do that task in the real world, like flying an airplane. I love the intercultural interaction possibilities of telecollaboration, and often do contrastive cultural role playing.

It's a steep learning curve to use 3DVLE's [3D virtual learning environments] with the main barrier, getting all the students online. At the same time, being able to design motivating tasks for the students is always the challenge, and I think a 3DVLE would help that. A first step for me, may be for one student to interact with a Bot/task to develop and demonstrate the functionality. I hope I'll be able to do this". (Participant 8)

From the comments reported in extracts 1-3, it is worth underlining that the participants in the teacher training course had the opportunity to reflect on and discover new ways of teaching, to reshape their teaching strategies, and consider new game-based scenarios for language learning and CLIL. A clear result of the course was the level of synergy and cooperation among the participants, which opened the way to further possible cooperation and joint projects in future, as stated by participant 6 in the following comment:

I really appreciated the effort to apply the gamification theory to designing and then creating an educational game within a virtual world. I also found exchanging ideas with the other participants greatly helpful. I am already planning some further collaboration with P3 (on a different course). (Participant 6)

Based on questionnaire data, the trainee teachers indicated that they developed several inter-related competences as a result of their participation (see Figure 1): language competence (10%), digital competence (14%), teaching competence (14%), knowledge of immersive methodology (21%), ability to design games (14%), and their ability to create games (17%).

Figure 1. Teacher competences developed during the course

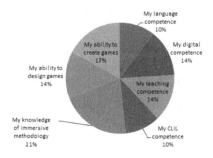

The trainee teachers' comments provided several insights into the competences they developed during the course:

The course has shown me a new way to teach in the CLIL approach using games. (Participant 2)

Again, as someone already quite informed on the theory behind all the competencies listed, the course really only helped me improve in regard to the practical implementation of said theory, namely, how exactly to build what I already knew I should be building. (Participant 1)

I really appreciated the effort to apply the gamification theory to designing and then creating an educational game within a virtual world. I also found exchanging ideas with the other participants greatly helpful. I am already planning some further collaboration with P3 (on a different course). Furthermore, there were many opportunities to reflect about teaching methodology and I loved that. After all, I am taking these kinds of courses to become a better teacher! (Participant 3)

I feel I've learnt a lot of new skills. (Participant 4)

All the course was really interesting and I hope to put in practice what I learnt during my next school year. (Participant 5)

It was a new world of teaching for me, and really inspired me to present about my experiences at an ESP conference, and consider for many months, how I can develop this as a teaching weapon. As yet, it is still a feasibility study, but I want to use it with my university students next semester. (Participant 6)

The Final 'Show and Tell'

The main goal of the teacher-led course was for the participants to learn more about immersive worlds for language learning and to help them create games in-world with specific learning objectives, considering their specific target students. Therefore, a final 'Show & Tell' exhibition was held at the end of the course, so that the participants could describe and comment on their creations. For the majority of the participants the use of game-based learning in school curricula was perceived as beneficial, as the following comment shows:

Games make students interested in the lessons. The students are already familiar with the games and they do not want to work on papers, write long paragraphs. They do not realize that they learn while playing games, but implicitly, they learn and it stays in their brain for longer. (Participant 8)

They mostly rated their students' reactions to game-based learning and digital games as 'quite positive', as shown in Figure 2 (positive 25%, quite positive 50%, very positive 25%).

Figure 2. Students' reactions to game-based learning and digital games in the school curriculum

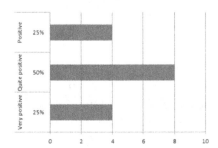

They also thought game-based learning would result in improvements in the students' learning outcomes, with particular reference to increased motivation, as illustrated in Figure 3 (related to language competence, increased motivation, subject knowledge, and 21st Century skills).

Figure 3. Improvements in the students' learning outcomes

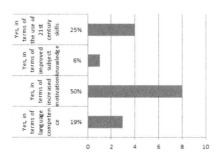

The attitude of the parents to game-based learning was considered neutral (38%) and positive (31%) as shown in Figure 4.

Figure 4. Reactions of the students' parents to game-based learning?

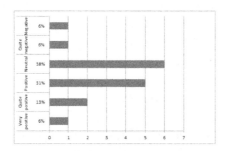

In the teacher-led course the final live exhibition presented an opportunity for the participants to share and discuss with their peers the games they had created and the rationale behind them: it represented the core of the course. Several types of game were created as described below.

Academic Research Game

The Academic Research Game (Figure 5) was designed by two participants to be played by teams of players and to provide hands-on practice of picking a topic and beginning a literature review with library based tools and databases. Each square prompted the students with a task in the text chat. By the end, students had developed a research document in their race to the top.

Figure 5. Academic Research Game

Topographical Map Utilizing Sound Script

The topographical map (Figure 6) was created in an application called Blender and imported into Open-Sim. The game was dynamic and physical as bumping into the cylinders triggered a script that named a city. Interacting with the map helped student to complete this web-based exercise successfully.

Figure 6. Topographical Map Utilizing Sound Script

Alice in Wonderland Hunt and Image Sort

This Cheshire cat based hunt and image sorting exercise (Figure 7) tested students' understanding of the story line by asking them to put the images from the original illustrations in order.

Figure 7. Alice in Wonderland Hunt and Image Sort

The Board Game

This hand drawn game (Figure 8) included a variety of elements and was noteworthy both for the hand-drawn board and the variety of different types of activities used to engage students in language practice. The variety of well-designed tasks (including listening comprehension that used embedded video and audio clips) was created to sustain high degrees of class engagement.

Mysterious Forest Maze

The mysterious forest maze game (Figure 9) was an example of how important preparation is to designing activities in virtual worlds. The students created an inviting woodland landscape peppered with clues and puzzles to be discovered and solved by participants. While the use of the puzzles may have attracted some students' interest, the landscape was especially designed to stimulate learner engagement.

Memory Game

This memory game (Figure 10) is an example of what can be done with a traditional game in a virtual world that could not be done in the classroom. As soon as the student matched the correct image to what was being said in the picture, the game told the player in the text chat, "That is correct." If incorrect, the cards quickly reverted to face down to indicate the students' need to try again.

Figure 8. Board Game

Figure 9. Mysterious Forest Maze

Bank of Japan (Simulation)

This role-playing game (Figure 11) allows players to interact with bot tellers in the bank to ask for help and the correct forms, and to interact with the ATM machines to practise recognizing which buttons need to be pressed to initiate different transactions.

Figure 10. Memory Game

Figure 11. Bank of Japan (Simulation)

Quest in Minecraft

The Secret Lab of Dr Moreau (Figure 12) was designed as a quest in Minecraft, located in the basement of a house, where a mysterious portal leading to another world appeared.

The gallery of immersive games represented a very powerful repository which could also be used for future teacher training initiatives.

Figure 12. Minecraft Quest The secret lab of Dr. Moreau

SOLUTIONS AND RECOMMENDATIONS

At the end of the two teacher training courses it was deemed crucial to collect feedback from the participants to investigate the strengths and weaknesses of the two courses, especially considering a possible future reiteration of both training pathways. Several solutions and recommendations arose from the teachers' interviews.

Two online sessions aimed at interviewing the participants were organized using the Zoom virtual conferencing platform. During the first meeting a series of relevant issues were discussed, with a view to further development and continuation of the project aims. The informal agenda of the meeting was focused on a post-intervention evaluation, starting from a general overview and leading to the more specific analysis of a small subset of aspects: level of interaction, adequacy of resources and organizational timing.

In general, all of the trainee teachers agreed that the courses were both very interesting and well-structured. The duration was judged as coherent in terms of the courses' purpose and, in one case, was even deemed too short. Other participants pointed out that the courses had been very useful, as they helped attendees "to discover" new skills. Furthermore, all of the trainees agreed that game-based learning is strongly inclusive: it encouraged collaboration and developed creativity while engaging students. A very interesting insight came from one of the participants who pointed out how game-based learning could also be beneficial for special needs students in terms of improving their self-esteem.

Collaboration was identified as one possible weak aspect of both courses. Several participants agreed that collaborating with other teachers should be improved; more opportunities for collaboration would be better in future, for example, to enable trainees to perform tasks collaboratively, such as designing and making games together. The topic of collaboration arose directly from discussions about the opportunity to transform the participants' group into a community of practice. The possibility of building a sustainable community of practice involving the trainee teachers was proposed by participants who were already members of other CoPs (for example in Edmondo world) and therefore had experienced the support and the benefits it can provide.

As far as the learning contents of the courses were concerned, the participants agreed that the theoretical oversight provided, as well as the reading materials, were adequate to the courses' purposes and the participants' characteristics. The Moodle-based course structure received very good evaluations because it was able to provide information in a step-by-step process. No problems were reported regarding self-study, motivation or the course length. On the other hand, practical sessions were not sufficiently developed: as one trainee pointed out, "we built things but did not test them". Linked to this aspect, a participant observed that a possible limitation stemmed from the lack of scripting-related competences needed to make artefacts that were able to react to interaction and suggested that scripting could be included in future course planning.

One remark about the time needed to perform reading tasks was that due to time constraints for many participants, as it was difficult to complete some tasks. On the other hand, the reading list was only a suggestion and the task was not compulsory; indeed, the possibility of incorporating brief descriptions of the core content of the readings at the very beginning of the sessions was welcomed. The readings were unanimously judged positively and highly relevant to what was going on and not difficult to understand or filled with technical jargon. Finally, the relationship between synchronous and asynchronous events was evaluated as positive and balanced.

At the end of the two training courses, all of the participants were asked in Moodle to express their final reflections in order to better understand the added value of their learning experience and its impact on their professional profile. Their comments and insights underline the teachers' belief in the potential of immersive worlds for redesigning language learning and CLIL teaching pathways.

Some of the answers from the participants can help us to understand how teacher training initiatives can improve teaching skills and techniques and lead to innovative learning environments and methodologies in future, such as video creation (Barwell, Moore & Walker, 2011; Thomas & Schneider, 2018):

I believe a virtual world is the world where most of the modern teaching/ learning should happen. This kind of vision is strictly connected with the new tech world of education, where teachers are tutors and students work and learn together (peer-to-peer) to create new didactical material to be shared on the Internet: when students make and share games, they learn not only about course content but also about their own thinking. (Participant 1)

On the other hand, gamification and Digital Pedagogy can help create a system that enables learners to rehearse real-life scenarios and challenges in a safe environment. There are many benefits a learner can get from a game-based learning experience, in the friendly environment the students can easily progress through the content and it can help higher recall and retention of the acquired knowledge. Additionally, an immediate feedback and the guidelines suggesting behavioural change motivate action or give a sense of achievement. Also, the new approach praises games and stresses their additional therapeutic or cathartic load. Indeed, the VR can provide constant electronic stimulation which surely can facilitate language learning. (Participant 3)

I definitely feel immersion in a virtual world could contribute to language learning classes in loads of different ways, not very easy to sum up. Just to mention the main ones: boosting students' motivation for learning, drawing on their 'natural' drive for technologies and videogames; creating new, different and engaging areas to socialize their language and communication skills; providing catching and challenging game-like learning environments, open to a never ending range of variations; feeding their crave for 'making' things, manipulating and moving while learning. (Participant 2)

Avatars can speak in-world and listen but can also text in the target language in a variety of ways (Instant messages, local chat, notecards), so listening, speaking, reading and writing will all be thoroughly practised. Virtual worlds a+ can be powerful storytelling tools as well: by creating short in-world movies (machinimas) students will be able to narrate simple or complex stories and act their roles as in a real movie and be filmed using an infinite variety of outfits and clothes and settings/environments. (Participant 4)

When you teach through immersive teaching, your class becomes a players community, opened to anyone. In Immersive teaching everyone looks out for others, because they work peer to peer. Pupils with more experience learn to help their schoolmates who are still beginners. Pupils learn to respect everyone's needs, planning and organizing their activity to solve the immersive game. In order to allow everyone to participate to the learning path actively, usefully and independently.(Participant 5)

You can plan an interesting CLIL lesson according to Coyle et al's (2010) model: language of learning (content) essential vocabulary and grammar associated with the topic for a communicative approach. The language is used in authentic interactive settings in order to develop communicative skills, rather than focusing exclusively on grammar; language for learning (meta-cognition and grammar system) the kind of language needed to operate in a foreign language environment. Learners need skills for pair work, cooperative group work, asking questions, debating, enquiring, thinking, memorizing... language through learning (cognition) new meanings would require new language. It needs to be captured while during the learning process, then recycled and developed later.(Participant 6)

Minecraft can offer students a virtual canvas for creating nearly anything they like using pixelated building blocks. Their creativity has almost no boundaries. At the same time, and for this reason, it is a recognized learning tool, used by teachers around the world to teach Math, History, Art, Physics, or nearly any other subject. Apart from that, it is, of course, an excellent tool to generate interest in your students. (Participant 7)

Some disadvantages were also pointed out in terms of lack of flexibility, technical infrastructure, collaboration at school, as shown in the following comments:

3D worlds are, in some way, closed worlds, because you make use only of elements from its immediate environment, even if you can import elements from outside, and it's not easy to show other people the activities and the final results, unless you shot pictures or videos to publish on a website or blog or social network on the Internet. (Participant 2)

There is still much to do in the technology area of usability and accessibility (user-friendly tools, easy-to-use software for hearing and speech impaired students) and in the field of evaluation and assessment (creation of rubrics with criteria planned for 3D world didactical activities). (Participant 1)

FUTURE RESEARCH DIRECTIONS

As a general recommendation to policymakers, stakeholders and practitioners, the two training pathways represented a significant example of innovation in the field of language learning and CLIL (Coyle et al., 2010; Cinganotto, 2016), using technologies which are recommended by the European Commission in the 2014 report "Improving the effectiveness of CLIL and language learning: Computer Assisted Language Learning".

Working in immersive worlds and playing games with the students can represent an effective way to bridge 'role-play' and 'real-play', which is the common paradox in foreign language classes. On the contrary, it is quite evident both to students and to learners that this is a fictional situation, in which real life is actually far from what happens in class. Therefore, it is significant how immersive worlds can reproduce real life situations and interactions, reducing Krashen's affective filter; through their avatar in-world, the learners can speak and text chat without anxiety, thereby disguising his/her identity or face and promoting uninhibited interaction.

Benefits in terms of language competences can be significant, as well as in terms of CLIL, as also stated by some of the trainee participants who mentioned the possibility of building games or objects in-world related to History, Science, Art or other subjects. Participants can therefore participate in 'hands on' and concrete activities about subject content, an essential ingredient of CLIL. Moreover the 'learning by doing' and 'learning by playing' principles are borrowed from language teaching and can represent an important added value of this approach.

The courses' use of 3D immersive gameworlds like Minecraft and in Open Sim represented an effective way to stimulate language awareness in teachers, as recommended by the latest European Council Recommendation (2019) on the need for a comprehensive approach to the teaching and learning of languages, which states that the language dimension should be a transversal element of the school curriculum, in any subject, not only in foreign languages. Moreover, the topics of plurilingualism, pluriculture and language diversity can be addressed through an online course similar to those we have seen in this project. Considering the nature of many language classes, which are more and more multi-ethnic and plurilingual, temporarily hiding one's own identity, origin and home language through an avatar, can push learners to express themselves freely and independently, embracing language and cultural diversity, equity and social justice.

As a final consideration, attending online courses similar to the ones created as part of this project may help enhance visual literacy: images, video, graphics, infographics can play an important part in learning a language, as mentioned in the European Commission's Key Competences Framework (Council of Europe, 2018), where visual literacy is listed in the descriptor of the first Key Competence, named 'literacy'. A foreign language should be taught through visual, multi-modal and immersive inputs, as happens in-world. That is why both training courses may lead to new training initiatives in the field of immersive language teaching and learning: making teachers aware of the importance of game-based and immersive learning may help innovate their teaching strategies and techniques, contributing to general school innovation, from a holistic point of view.

CONCLUSION

This chapter has compared two online teacher training initiatives, a self-study course and a teacher-led course, as part of a two-year European Commission funded project focusing on the potential of game-based learning and immersive worlds for language learning and CLIL. The two courses were delivered through the online Moodle platform and structured with learning materials for each week which required participants to read and comment on specific forum threads. The participants were guided through the exploration of the different learning environments with the help of digital content, tutorials and videos.

The self-study course was designed as an introduction to the topic, mainly through suggested readings, videos and forum discussions. The teacher-led course was developed as a blended course with learning materials in an approach combining forums with synchronous meetings in OpenSim and Minecraft. The weekly webinars in the Zoom video conferencing platform were designed to enable the participants to reflect on different topics related to game-based learning and gamification, with reference to the learning materials available in the platform (Marino, 2004).

The teacher-led course was aimed at helping teachers actively work in-world and create games for language learning and teaching: some of the games produced in-world have been described in the chapter. The course was quite demanding, especially because of the fixed appointments in OpenSim and Minecraft and the weekly webinars. Despite that, the teachers found the workload rewarding and stimulating.

The teachers' voice, collected from the forums, the interviews and the final reflections, provide several insights for teachers and teacher trainers working in the field. Virtual and immersive worlds are still a field yet to be fully investigated, particularly as some teachers believe that they require specific and very demanding digital skills, which are often not easy to develop (Middleton & Mather, 2008; Mawer, 2016). However, as the lessons learnt from a comparison of the two courses show, a relatively small amount of commitment, passion and willpower is often enough to start navigating in-world learning environments. An increasing number of online courses on language learning in Minecraft and OpenSim can help to guide teachers to innovate their teaching style and techniques, moving beyond the traditional lecture approach to classroom instruction. As a consequence, more communities of practice could help teachers grow and learn together with their colleagues, interweaving formal and informal training at the same time. Moreover, this could be a good way to introduce gamification and workshop activities with students and to persuade their parents that playing games in class is not a waste of time, but on the contrary, a potentially powerful way of improving their level of communicative competence in a foreign language. As a general suggestion, disseminating the results of the course, especially the games created by the participants in-world, is one way which we have found to encourage teachers to experiment and understand the added value of immersive worlds for language learning. The games created by the participants have also been made available as open educational resources for teachers to play and learn with their students in a virtual and immersive library.

ACKNOWLEDGMENT

The authors acknowledge the contribution to this project by INDIRE and Università Telematica degli Studi IUL Directorate and Presidency and the GUINEVERE Consortium partners. This research arose from a project funded with support from the European Commission (Project number: 2017-1-UK01-

KA201-036783). The information in this publication reflects the views only of the authors, and the Commission cannot be held responsible for any use which may be made of the information contained therein.

REFERENCES

Alan, B., & Stoller, F. L. (2005). Maximizing the benefits of project work in foreign language classrooms. *English Teaching Forum, 43*(4), 10-21.

Barwell, G., Moore, C., & Walker, R. (2011). Marking machinima: A case study in assessing student use of a web 2.0 technology. *Australasian Journal of Educational Technology, 27,* 765–780.

Beckett, G. (2002). Teacher and student evaluations of project-based instruction. *TESL Canada Journal, 19*(2), 52–66.

Beckett, G. (2006). Project-based second and foreign language education: Theory, research and practice. In G. Beckett & P. Miller (Eds.), *Project-based second and foreign language education* (pp. 3–18). Information Age Publishing.

Beckett, G., & Miller, P. (Eds.). (2006). *Project-based second and foreign language education.* Information Age Publishing.

Beckett, G., & Slater, T. (2005). The project framework: A tool for language, content, and skills integration. *ELT Journal, 59*(2), 108–116.

Beckett, G. H., & Slater, T. (2018). Technology-integrated project-based language learning. In C. Chapelle (Ed.), *The encyclopedia of applied linguistics* (pp. 1–8). Wiley-Blackwell.

Beckett, G. H., & Slater, T. (2019). *Global perspectives on project-cased language learning, teaching, and assessment: Key approaches, technology tools, and frameworks.* Routledge.

Beetham, H., & Sharpe, R. (Eds.). (2019). *Rethinking pedagogy for a digital age: Principle and practices of design.* Routledge.

Benedetti, F. (2018). Designing an effective and scientifically grounded e-learning environment for Initial Teacher Education: The Italian University Line Model. *Journal of e-Learning and Knowledge Society, 14*(2), 97-109.

Boon, A. (2007). Building bridges: Instant messenger cooperative development. *Language Teaching, 31*(12), 9–13.

Callaghan, M. J., McCusker, K., Losada, J. L., Harkin, J., & Wilson, S. (2013). Using game-based learning in virtual worlds to teach electronic and electrical engineering. *IEEE Transactions on Industrial Informatics, 9*(1), 575–584.

Chatti, M. A., Agustiawan, M. R., Jarke, M., & Specht, M. (2010). Toward a personal learning environment framework. *International Journal of Virtual and Personal Learning Environments, 1*(4), 71–82.

Cinganotto, L. (2016). CLIL in Italy. A general overview. *Latin American Journal of Content and Language Integrated Learning, 9*(2), 374–400.

Council of Europe. (2018). *Council recommendation of 22 May 2018 on key competences for lifelong learning.* Retrieved from https://eur-lex.europa.eu/legal-content/EN/TXT/PDF/?uri=CELEX:32018H0604(01)

Council of Europe. (2019). *Council recommendation on a comprehensive approach to the teaching and learning of languages.* Retrieved https://ec.europa.eu/education/education-in-the-eu/council-recommendation-improving-teaching-and-learning-languages_en

Coyle, D., Hood, P., & Marsh, D. (2010). *Content and language integrated learning.* Cambridge.

European Commission. (2014). *Improving the effectiveness of language learning: CLIL and computer assisted language learning.* Retrieved from https://ec.europa.eu/education/content/improving-effectiveness-language-learning-clil-and-computer-assisted-language-learning_it

Garrison, D. R., Anderson, T., & Archer, W. (2000). Critical inquiry in a text-based environment: Computer conferencing in higher education. *The Internet and Higher Education, 2*(2–3), 87–105.

Hamari, J., Koivisto, J., & Sarsa, H. (2014). Does gamification work? A literature review of empirical studies on gamification. In *System Sciences (HICSS), 2014 47th Hawaii International Conference* (pp. 3025-3034). London: IEEE.

Hanus, M. D., & Fox, J. (2015). Assessing the effects of gamification in the classroom: A longitudinal study on intrinsic motivation, social comparison, satisfaction, effort, and academic performance. *Computers & Education, 80,* 152–161.

Hase, S., & Kenyon, C. (2007). Heutagogy: A child of complexity theory. *Complicity: An International Journal of Complexity and Education, 4*(1), 111–119.

Huang, H.-M., & Liang, S.-S. (2018). An analysis of learners' intentions toward virtual reality learning based on constructivist and technology acceptance approaches. *International Review of Research in Open and Distributed Learning, 19*(1), 91–115.

Johnson, L., Adams Becker, S., Cummins, M., Estrada, V., Freeman, A., & Ludgate, H. (2013). *NMC Horizon Report: 2013 Higher Education Edition.* The New Media Consortium.

Kafai, Y., & Resnick, M. (1996). *Constructionism in practice: Designing, thinking, and learning in a digital world.* Lawrence Erlbaum Associates.

Kapp, K. (2012). Gaming elements for effective learning. *Training Industry Quarterly,* 31-33.

Kaye, A. (1994). Apprendimento collaborativo basato sul computer. *Tecnologie Didattiche, 4.*

Knowles, M. (1975). *Self-directed learning: A guide for learners and teachers.* Cambridge Adult Education.

Krashen, S. (1985). *The input hypothesis: Issues and implications.* Longman.

Kuhn, J., & Stevens, V. (2017). Participatory culture as professional development: Preparing teachers to use Minecraft in the classroom. *TESOL Journal, 8*(4), 753–767.

Larrivee, B. (2008). *Authentic classroom management: Creating a learning community and building reflective practice.* Pearson.

Lee, J., & Hammer, J. (2011). Gamification in education: What, how, why bother?'. *Academic Exchange Quarterly*, *15*(2), 146.

Marino, P. (2004). *3D game-based filmmaking: The art of machinima*. Paraglyph Press.

Mawer, M. (2016). Observational practice in virtual worlds: Revisiting and expanding the methodological discussion. *International Journal of Social Research Methodology*, *19*(2). http://www.tandfonline.com/doi/abs/10.1080/13645579.2014.936738#.VKu_9yuG_To

Meek, V. L., & Davies, D. (2009). *Policy dynamic in higher education and research: concepts and observations*. In L. V. Meek, U. Teichler & M. L. Kearney (Eds.), *Higher education, research and innovation: Changing dynamics, Report on the UNESCO Forum on Higher Education, Research and Knowledge, 2001-2009* (pp. 41-84). Kassel: International Centre for Higher Education Research.

Mezirow, J. (1991). *Transformative dimensions of adult learning*. Jossey-Bass.

Middleton, A. J., & Mather, R. (2008). Machinima interventions: Innovative approaches to immersive virtual world curriculum integration. *ALT-J. Research in Learning Technology*, *16*(3), 207–220.

Ryoo, J., Techatassanasoontorn, A., Lee, D., & Lothian, J. (2011). Game-based infosec education using OpenSim. *Proceedings of the 15th Colloquium for Information Systems Security Education*.

Scardamalia, M., & Bereiter, C. (2006). Knowledge building: Theory, pedagogy and technology. In K. Sawyer (Ed.), *Cambridge handbook of the learning sciences* (pp. 97–118). Cambridge University Press.

Schön, D. A. (1983). *The reflective practitioner: How professionals think in action*. Basic Books, Inc.

Seaborn, K., & Fels, D. I. (2015). Gamification in theory and action: A Survey. *International Journal of Human-Computer Studies*, *74*, 14–31.

Torsani, S. (2015). *CALL teacher education: Language teachers and technology integration*. Springer.

Van Eck, R. (2006). Digital game-based learning: It's not just the digital natives who are restless. *Educause*, *41*(2), 16–30.

Wenger, E., McDermott, R., & Snyder, W. M. (2002). *Cultivating community of practice*. Harvard Business School Press.

Wiggins, B. E. (2016). An overview and study on the use of games, simulations, and gamification in higher education. *International Journal of Game-Based Learning*, *6*(1), 18–29.

ADDITIONAL READING

Cornillie, F., & Desmet, P. (2016). Mini-games for language learning. In F. Farr & L. Murray (Eds.), *The Routledge handbook of language learning and technology* (pp. 431–446). Routledge Handbooks.

De Freitas, S. (2006). *Learning in immersive worlds: a review of game-based learning*. Joint Information Systems Committee.

Peterson, M. (2016). Virtual worlds and language learning: an analysis of research. In F. Farr & L. Murray (Eds.), *The Routledge handbook of language learning and technology* (pp. 308–320). Routledge Handbooks.

Rushkoff, D. (2006). *Screenagers: Lessons in chaos from digital kids*. Hampton Press.

Sadler, R., & Dooly, M. (2014). Language learning in virtual worlds: Research and practice. In M. Thomas, H. Reinders, & M. Warschauer (Eds.), *Contemporary computer-assisted language learning* (pp. 159–182). Bloomsbury.

Thomas, M., Benini, S., Schneider, C., Rainbow, C. A., Can, T., Simsek, T., Biber, S. K. & Cinganotto, L. (2018). Digital Game-Based Language Learning in 3D Immersive Environments: The Guinevere Project. *Conference Proceedings: Innovation in Language Learning*, Florence, Italy.

Thomas, M., & Schneider, C. (2018). Language learning with machinima: Video production in 3D immersive environments. In P. Hubbard & S. Ioannou-Georgiou (Eds.), *Teaching English reflectively with technology*. IATEFL.

Whitton, N. (2014). *Games and learning: Research and theory*. Routledge.

KEY TERMS AND DEFINITIONS

CLIL: Content and Language Integrated Learning or CLIL is an approach to foreign language teaching in which a content-based subject (e.g. business studies) is taught in the target language rather than in the first language or L1 of the learners.

Community of Practice: or CoP is a group of people who interact to share a mutual interest or passion in order to improve their understanding and learning.

Game-Based Learning: Or GBL is a type of teaching in which the principles of games are used, often to improve learner motivation, engagement and/or performance. These principles may include points or leaderboards for example.

Immersive Worlds: These are online environments that aim to mirror the physical and/or fantasy world, in which users can build and create objects and interact, often in spoken and written language.

Minecraft: A 3D immersive video game in which users build structures and buildings from resources that they discover and mine. Depending on the mode (either game or survival mode) users can cooperate or compete against other users to achieve their objectives.

Moodle: A virtual learning environment (VLE) or course management system (CMS), Moodle is an open-source learning platform that enables teachers to store learning materials and activities to organise courses.

OpenSim: Or OpenSimulator is a multi-user open-source 3D immersive environment which enables users to create and customize content and can be used for education and learning via voice and/or text chat.

This research was previously published in the Handbook of Research on Teaching With Virtual Environments and AI; pages 267-292, copyright year 2021 by Information Science Reference (an imprint of IGI Global).

Chapter 36
Design Process of Three-Dimensional Multi-User Virtual Environments (3D MUVEs) for Teaching Tree Species

Gamze Mercan
iD https://orcid.org/0000-0001-5515-999X
Hacettepe University, Turkey

Pınar Köseoğlu
iD https://orcid.org/0000-0002-6222-7978
Hacettepe University, Turkey

Dilek Doğan
iD https://orcid.org/0000-0001-6988-9547
Ankara University, Turkey

Hakan Tüzün
iD https://orcid.org/0000-0003-1153-5556
Hacettepe University, Turkey

ABSTRACT

This study aims to realize the concept of biodiversity, which is one of the subjects covered by environmental education, with 3D virtual worlds platform and to realize the biological richness of users in their environment and to provide awareness of the species they see in their immediate surroundings. It is aimed to design 3D MUVE to teach tree species to pre-service teachers within framework of Instructional design process in 3D MUVEs based on problem-based learning approach. Four different design groups are third year undergraduate students (N=21) from the Department of Computer Education and Instructional Technology in the Faculty of Education at a large state university. For design process, participants with collaborative work designed 3D environments with a problem-based learning approach. The design process of 3D MUVEs was realized with the participation of researchers as trainers, guides, technical support personnel, and observers during the 16 weeks within the scope of the course. Also, participants were involved in the role of both learner and instructional designer.

DOI: 10.4018/978-1-6684-7597-3.ch036

INTRODUCTION

The environment can be defined as the space units of living beings that are connected and influenced by vital bonds, as the habitat of the living creatures/creature's community, and in short, it can be defined as all of the external factors that affect the living creatures (Atasoy, 2006). Based on this context; air, water, soil, vegetation, animals and everything else on or off the Earth is included in the concept of environment (Atik, Öztekin, & Erkoç, 2010).

Individuals in society interfere with their environment to survive and influence their environment through various activities. The following can be given as examples of today's environmental problems: rapid population growth, uncontrolled urbanization, industrialization, air pollution in cities and pollution in water, global warming and a decrease in biological diversity (Kocataş, 2006). The existence of human beings depends on both acting by the ecosystem they live in as well as helping to protect the balance and biodiversity (Atasoy, 2006). The destruction of biological diversity, a strategic asset that humanity has but cannot fully realize its importance, will be the major cause of worldwide poverty. For this reason, biodiversity constitutes one of the most important parts of the world heritage (Çepni, 2005).

The aim of the biodiversity training in environmental education aims to raise awareness of individuals about the importance of biological diversity and to provide them with the responsibility and competence to protect biological diversity. However, since environmental education in Turkey is made up of biology courses that students take until they graduate from high school, these courses are insufficient for effective environmental education. Since students study by memorizing the information given in the courses for the exam, this information cannot provide the desired behavioral change in the individual (Özcan, 2003). For this reason, it is possible for the students to know about the local species by observing the plants and animals directly through the education of biodiversity, i.e. through an effective training process (Lindemann-Matthies, 2002; Şahin, 2018). At this point, pre-service teachers have great responsibilities as future teachers. In this context, it is very important to determine the perceptions of pre-service teachers in the preparation of the course content that meets the expectations of environmental education (Özmen & Özdemir, 2016).

The convention on biological diversity, which is a vital issue, and the protection of this diversity is under human responsibility, but the future generation is not sufficiently level of direct interaction with nature and its concerns about the future include the reduction of biodiversity (Bergseng & Vatn, 2009; Şenel, 2015). Therefore, biodiversity education, which is a subject of environmental education, is one of the most important issues within the conceptual framework of biology education (Mercan & Köseoğlu, 2019).

Integrating technology into the field of education has increased the use of technological resources in learning environments. One of them is three-dimensional (3D) virtual applications. In the 21st century, 3d technology, which is popular all over the world, affects educational technologies to a great extent. Three-dimensional virtual worlds with a convenient interface are accessible environments where online users log on with the help of a virtual character (avatars). In these environments, users can communicate with each other through audio or instant messaging tools and with authentic content. 3d virtual worlds also provide users with socialization, research and learning environments (Güler, 2014). In particular, three-dimensional multi-user virtual environments (3d Muves) can be used to reveal the effect of spatial perception. In these environments, individuals can move around with avatars that represent themselves in the authentic world. Besides, these environments consist of many places or sub-worlds where users can walk and communicate with each other in 3d Muves (Campbell, Wang, Hsu, Duffy, & Wolf, 2010).

Student-centered teaching approaches are important in these environments where students are not only active but also play a role (Dillenbourg, Schneider & Synteta, 2002). In these environments, teaching and environment designs should be conducted according to these approaches. Scenario-based, event-driven, and problem-based approaches offer learners many advantages in 3d Muves. One of these approaches is problem-based learning and student-centered activities within the framework of an authentic problem, the interaction of small groups and also the teacher is a guide in this process (Barrows, 1986). This approach enables effective use of 3d Muves. However, in the study of Duncan, Miller and Jiang (2012), in which they examined the use of virtual worlds in education, it is stated that these environments are mostly used for cooperative learning. Studies conducted on problem-based learning (PBL), didactic learning, and interactive learning are relatively rare. Also, it is observed that it is not sufficiently focused on how to design 3d Muves based on the problem in the field (Işık et al., 2008; Tokel & Cevizci-Karataş, 2013). Based on this information, it is aimed to develop a learning environment using 3d Muves to enable pre-service teachers to recognize the trees around them and to create awareness of tree species.

The Aim and Importance of the Study

3d virtual worlds, which have become widespread in recent years, provide both educators and students with opportunities such as navigating in a virtual environment, representing themselves with avatars, communicating by voice or text while in different places and interacting with 3d objects present in the environment. In these environments, educators can design interactive environments related to the subject and content they want, and students can access these virtual content simultaneously and get miscellaneous feedback. Thanks to their flexible structure, virtual worlds become attractive as an educational environment and can be used for many different disciplines and subject areas. New 3d technologies emerge every day, offering a variety of opportunities for traditional and distance education. With these opportunities, it is predicted that 3d virtual worlds will have an immense impact on education in the future and will be used more widely (Dillenbourg et al., 2002; Tokel & Cevizci-Karataş, 2013).

3d Muves can create effective learning environments for all disciplines. This study, which integrates environmental education and technology, has an interdisciplinary approach. In this study, it is aimed to bring users together with nature and provide them a positive learning environment in a 3d virtual context to teach tree species. Three-dimensional applications increase the motivation of users, providing the opportunity to learn by living and facilitate the establishment of effective communication. In this respect, 3d applications are distinguished from other learning environments. Therefore, the study aims to provide pre-service teachers with the opportunity to learn the tree species. For this purpose, 3d Muves were designed by participants who are students at the Department of Computer Education and Instructional Technology in the Faculty of Education at a large state university in Ankara, Turkey. Target audience of designs is pre-service teachers. Also, this research aims to design a problem-based learning environment that addresses the familiarization of the nearby trees using the OpenSimulator (OpenSim) application platform from 3d virtual environments. OpenSim is among the most important 3d open-source application that supports virtual learning and provides learning environments. OpenSim ensures a 3d interface that allows users to access and design these environments from anywhere via 3rd party viewers such as FireStorm. It also enables customization of virtual worlds created by users and provides server services under the control of researchers and users with open source code support. OpenSim was preferred in the research because of these features. Depending on the purpose of the scenario, designs were implemented to provide users an immersive environment. To realize the purpose of the research, photographs of trees that users can see most in their surroundings were taken by experts through their field trips. Selected tree species were limited to 24 trees.

Another aim of the implementation is to emphasize the concept of biodiversity and lake and forest ecosystems have been added to the platform in this direction. Human beings must continue to exist and act by the ecosystem they live in to help protect the balance and biodiversity (Külköylüoğlu, 2009). The destruction of Biological Diversity, a strategic asset that humanity has but cannot fully reach its significance, will be the major cause of worldwide poverty. For this reason, biodiversity constitutes one of the most important parts of the World Heritage (Çepni, 2005). Furthermore, it is thought that tree awareness will provide a more effective learning for users. In a 3d muve where technology and education are integrated, it might provide permanent learning for users.

BACKGROUND

The focus of this part of the chapter is the literature review about biodiversity and environmental awareness and three-dimensional multi-user virtual environments (3D MUVEs). Moreover, 3D MUVEs design process and problem-based learning are the other important foci of this chapter.

Biodiversity and Environmental Awareness

Biodiversity is the differentiation between land, sea and other water ecosystems and living organisms in all sources, including ecological structures that are part of these ecosystems. In other words, it is a living nature. Biodiversity is the foundation of living resources, which has an indispensable place for meeting the basic needs of people, especially food, and has vital importance for people like the chemical structure of the atmosphere and the climate of the world. In addition, it provides services that can only be provided by the continuity of healthy and complex ecosystems. Half of the drugs used in medicine are derived from living creatures and relatives of wild animals. Today, wild species are used to obtain new varieties of agricultural products or to improve existing ones according to the needs of people. Ecosystems also gained importance as a result of the interaction of living and non-living creatures with each other and within themselves to maintain the existence of wild species, evolve, diversify and gain new genetic features. Furthermore, it is complex depending on the environmental conditions and has acquired different structures and functions, each of which is different from the other. The integrity and diversity of ecosystems are important in maintaining natural balances, such as climate, rainfall regime, and species sociology (Ekim, 2005; Elçin, Erkoç, Öztekin, Atik, Sarıkaya, & Selvi, 2010).

Today, living resources, which are important for food and agriculture and are increasingly decreasing, are among the most important advantages a country can have. Agricultural areas and water resources of the world can be quickly polluted and destroyed. Scientists believe that people will face serious food and water problems soon. In light of these developments, the biological diversity of countries is becoming a major challenge, especially in terms of genetic resources, because wild living resources are used for the development of varieties that are resistant to environmental pressures (Erten, 2004).

Turkey is a rich country in terms of biodiversity due to its geographical location in Asia and Europe, topographic structure and climate effects in the regions. Also, the number of endemic species is quite high in Turkey. As a result of the studies, over 3.000 plant species from about 12.000 plant species in Turkey flora are endemic. It is also estimated that there are about 80.000 animal species in the Turkish flora and three of the 34 global high diversity points (Mediterranean, Caucasus & Iran-Anatolia) in Turkey. Despite the history of Turkey's intense natural resource exploitation and human land use over 10.000 years, it has rich biodiversity heritage as a center of genetic diversity. Since biodiversity has an important cultural and commercial value for approximately 20 million rural people in Turkey, conservation of this heritage also requires a great responsibility (Şekercioğlu et al., 2011; Şenel, 2015).

According to the 2050 Organization for Economic Co-operation and Development (OECD) environment prediction report, forests rich in biodiversity in Turkey will be reduced as a result of the expansion of commercial forestry activities and human interventions (OECD Environmental Outlook to 2050, 2012). It is a matter of vital importance that Biological Diversity and conservation of this diversity are under human responsibility, but the lack of direct interaction with nature of the future generations is likely to diminish biodiversity (Bergseng & Vatn, 2009; Şenel, 2015).

It has great importance to cooperate with the people of the region to ensure the effective implementation of the management and conservation of a field in terms of biodiversity. Teachers working in the region play a major role in protecting the existing resources of the people of the region and ensuring that the students have environmental awareness. For this reason, the teachers working in rural areas are informed about biodiversity recognition and protection. Teachers are important keys in achieving the objectives set out in the development plans that are targeted to provide information about biodiversity with well-planned environmental education (Erten, 2004; Şenel, 2015).

The biodiversity training in environmental education aims to raise awareness of individuals about the importance of biological diversity and to provide them with the responsibility and competence to protect biological diversity. However, since environmental education in Turkey consists of biology courses that students take until they graduate high school, these courses are insufficient for effective environmental education. Since the information provided in the lessons are based on memorization of the test, this information does not provide the desired change in behavior in the individual (Özcan, 2003). For this reason, the students can know about the local species by observing the plants and animals directly through the education of biodiversity, i.e. through an effective training process. This can be achieved through educational environments in which students can examine the interactions between nature and living creatures and their interactions (Lindemann-Matthies, 2002; Özmen & Özdemir, 2016).

Three-Dimensional Multi-User Virtual Environments (3D MUVEs) and Design Process

In recent years, the rapidly expanding three-dimensional (3D) virtual worlds offer both educators and students the opportunity to navigate in virtual environments, communicate with sound or instant messaging tools with other users in different locations, represent themselves with avatars, and interact with 3d objects in these environments (Doğan & Tüzün, 2017). There are many different 3d virtual world platform examples used and the number of users is increasing exponentially since the 2000s. Today, there are some popular applications such as SecondLife, OpenSimulator (OpenSim), Active Worlds and Instant Messaging Virtual Universe (IMVU). These 3d virtual platforms provide users content creation tools (3d object libraries and modeling tools, etc.), communication tools (instant messaging, audio, video conference), customization tools (avatar library and object movements, etc.) and resource tools (Web page integration) (Dickey, 2005). Users have access to these 3d virtual platforms easily although some platforms are accessible to only specific users. However, it is seen that the SecondLife platform is preferred in studies because technical infrastructure is provided. However, due to the increase in the use of open-source software in recent years, it is striking that different virtual world platforms are being developed (Kapp & O'Driscoll, 2010).

The most prominent features of these environments include the advanced user representation of avatars; 3d interface, permanent design, imaginative/immersive media, multichannel communication and socialization, rich interaction, presence perception and user engagement (Dalgarno & Lee, 2010; Warburton, 2009). It is stated that effective learning environments can be created in spite of the features it carries, although it used to create fantastic environments based on the power of games, entertainment, and imagination. Thus, it is emphasized that it has the potential to increase user engagement and facilitate learning through more visual and realistic experiences. For this reason, it has attracted the attention of educational researchers by separating from other environments and in recent years it has become widespread in education environments for various purposes (Dalgarno & Lee, 2010; Dickey, 2005; Warburton, 2009).

By combining educational needs and user experience, learning content can be made more interesting by incorporating entertainment factor into 3d virtual worlds offering alternative learning platforms that users can be actively involved. In this respect, it not only provides users with a real representation but also invites them to participate actively in role-playing activities by inviting them as a player to the variable learning activities that require effort. This allows users to perceive activities as a game and enjoy them, and helps to make learning easier (Minocha & Reeves, 2010; Xu, Park & Baek, 2011).

3d virtual worlds provide a high interactive framework for appropriate behavior and learning, enabling effective environments in social interaction with individuals in remote locations and various branches. It enables users in different locations to communicate. These users communicate and express their feelings and movements through the help of a voice and instant messaging, thus enabling them to perceive the environment as authentic world and engage in this experience (Masters & Gregory, 2010; Bouta, Retalis, & Paraskeva, 2012). Therefore, due to cost, time and physical distance/geographical limitation, it also helps to eliminate problems in collaborative work. Also, scenario-based 3d environments can contribute positively to their motivation and occupation to encourage individuals to learn life-long and can increase their ability to transfer academic knowledge to the authentic world (Nelson, 2007).

Studies have shown promising results that are used to support learning in these environments, and 3d Muves that is known as a new learning platform has emerged. The 3d Muves have the potential to provide individuals gain with more meaningful and long-lasting information than traditional interactive multimedia environments (Tüzün & Özdinç, 2016). There are a large number of studies in these environments in the literature and the potential and possible contributions of 3D virtual environments to education are emphasized (Dalgarno & Lee, 2010; Gregory et al., 2015; Helmer & Light, 2007; Perera, Allison, & Miller, 2012; Warburton, 2009). Educational contributions of 3d virtual worlds are listed below (Doğan, Çınar & Tüzün, 2018):

It provides social interactions and collaborations via text, VOIP (voice over IP), or some animation movements.

It provides open-source environments.

It offers active participation or learning by doing via authentic learning activities.

It influences learner engagement, motivation, collaboration, and communication.

It offers new opportunities for creativity in learning such as roleplaying mentoring.

It offers the opportunity to do things that cannot be done easily in the authentic world by embedding simulations

It provides customized environments.

It ensures broader capabilities for learner-centered activity as well as problem-based and exploratory learning.

It provides remote access.

It allows the creation of a parallel world without limits to creativity and possibilities.

In addition to the educational potential of 3d virtual worlds, there are some problems and limitations encountered in these environments. New technology must be adopted by users. However, factors such as users' perspective on technology, social norms, and cultural differences can affect the technology acceptance process. Also, the design and implementation of such environments involves a long and comprehensive process (Gregory et al., 2015; Warburton, 2009).

3d virtual world platforms are used for different purposes in various subjects in many branches of the world. These include military, health, engineering, science, space sciences, history, geography, sociology, psychology, fine arts, advertising, marketing and education (Hew & Cheung, 2010). There are a large number of examples of educational studies and usage, where different variables are examined in the field of literature, taking into account the strengths and weaknesses of these environments as stated in educational terms. For example, one of the largest projects with OpenSim is completed by The National Aeronautics and Space Administration (NASA) between 2014 and 2017. The project is called Virtual Missions and Exoplanets (vMAX). This projects' target audience was middle school students and educators. Its' aim was to create a wide NASA resource to engage students, educators, and the public in the search for worlds beyond Earth (Doğan et al., 2018).

Thanks to the ability to bring together users from different locations of 3d virtual worlds, many universities around the world have developed virtual campuses and started to support educational processes with these environments through distance education (Bulu & İşler, 2011; Minocha & Reeves, 2010). As an example of virtual campuses established in 3d virtual worlds; Stanford, University of Texas and in Turkey, Middle East Technical University's virtual campus.

Considering the learning environments based on problems and scenarios established in 3d virtual worlds, the followings can be given as an example; the field of education (Cheryan, Meltzoff & Kim, 2011; Rappa, Yip, & Baey, 2009; Verhagen, Feldberg, van den Hooff, Meents & Merikivi, 2012), and health (Loke, Blyth, & Swan, 2012; Puterbaugh, Shannon & Gorton, 2010). Moreover, there are also environments in which real-life spaces are simulated and presented in 3d virtual worlds called spatial simulations. 3d virtual worlds are also effectively used to promote different tourist destinations. In these environments, users can navigate and experience real-life locations in 3d simulated ways (Lindgren, 2012).

Lots of 3d virtual worlds support social interaction. The following can be given as an example of the social impact in 3d virtual worlds, health (Puterbaugh et al., 2010), library (Cote, Kraemer, Nahl, & Ashford, 2012) and tourism (Denizci-Guillet & Penfold, 2013). It is observed that these practice examples are used to increase communication between individuals in professional groups. The technological and educational features of 3d virtual worlds always provide a learning environment that teachers do not need to be present. Thus, users are allowed to discover and learn (Ibáñez et al., 2011).

To use 3d virtual worlds in the field of education, these platforms must be ready for use without any design and usability problems. In particular, the visualization of 3d objects and the graphics card features used in the process of loading and Internet bandwidth plays an active role. In some applications where these environments are used, students often encounter problems with the Internet connection, graphics card, sound problems and the inability to load objects in a 3d environment (Bulu & İşler, 2011;

Warburton, 2009). Besides, such environments are 3d platforms based on a client-server connection. For example, users' access rights on the server belonging to the SecondLife virtual world platform are restricted by system administrators. In other words, although users can connect to the system server, they cannot make any changes to the server. However, on platforms with open-source code structure, such as OpenSim, users can create their servers. Moreover, they can create as many design areas as they want without paying a fee and control the design elements they create in these areas anyway they want (Doğan, 2019). In this context, like OpenSim with open-source code structure, the server infrastructure to be used in 3d virtual world platforms must be carefully selected. Besides, given the technical details mentioned on the OpenSim web site, the operating system feature of the platform must be taken into consideration for the user to have access to the virtual world platform and server. Also, it is emphasized that additional adjustments should be made, such as firewall and port configuration (OpenSim, 2015).

Problem-Based Learning (PBL) in 3D MUVEs

Problem-based learning (PBL) refers to different learning approaches in the normal context. However, in the literature, projects related to 3d Muves are characterized by both problem-based and questioning approaches. The reason is, virtual worlds are suitable for the presentation of problems from real life due to their structure. Besides, it is a structure that requires the student to perform a self-inquiry to attract the attention of the student with mysterious elements. Students can access hidden information through interactive objects in the virtual world. With the teleportation feature, they can switch to different areas, communicate their solutions to the teacher with communication tools or share them with their friends. Therefore, virtual worlds contribute positively to high-level thinking skills such as questioning, problem-solving and metacognition (Ketelhut, 2007; Pellas, 2014).

Pbl approaches are frequently used to give virtual worlds a sense of play. Interrogative learning is a type of skill that a person can gain in time and cannot learn directly, such as asking questions and setting up a hypothesis (Ketelhut, Nelson, Clarke, & Dede, 2010). Implementation of this learning approach can be quite easy in virtual worlds.

One of the best examples of the problem-based learning approach is the Quest Atlantis project, where life-based learning and portfolio evaluation approaches are used together. This project aims to develop children's awareness of social situations such as soil, air and water pollution, environmental events, racism, and personal rights to improve social responsibility awareness (Barab, Thomas, Dodge, Carteaux, & Tüzün, 2005). The virtual part allows students to navigate through avatars, interact with various objects and avatars. Students can ask questions in the message section for ready guides (avatars) and other students. The information that the student should collect in the web browser is given in textual form. The most important task of the web browser is to provide information about the student's performance and to allow the environment to return to a real playground. This field also serves as a task to show all the information of the students, i.e. the things they have collected, messages, friends, etc., all together. In the webspace, there is also a star symbol consisting of 8 quadrangular slices and student aims to illuminate all slices. When all the island tasks are finished, 8 slices are illuminated. Thus, the environment has been given a game feature. Students are expected to solve some ill-structured problems in islands developed for each theme (each social situation). Every event that needs to be resolved is realistically at the entrance of the island. Students gather clues on the island and write their own opinions on the solution of the problem and send them to their teachers. So, this process is not automatically controlled by the teacher. Thus, the environment provides the opportunity to evaluate a portfolio. On the other hand, both the web environment and some elements in the authentic world have been utilized to enable the environment to play feature, which is an important feature for the students to be motivated to use the environment.

Another example of the virtual world that applies an interrogator and problem-based approach is River City, which is built on the Active Worlds platform (Ketelhut, 2007). In this project, students are asked to solve epidemic diseases in a city called River City. Thus, it is aimed to increase the scientific inquiry skills in students. In this environment, students solve the problems by navigating and communicating with other students by collecting digital materials. Children gain an investigative learning experience through guides that provide little clues when they need help. Students can observe authentic simulations and interactive objects on River City Island. In addition, they can ask questions to guides who do not represent real people in the environment, examine books and other sources of information in the environment, use tools to collect and analyze data, conduct experiments, plan a research process with a scientific approach, report their answers to research, and present them orally in their classrooms. Studies have shown that students have positive developments in terms of scientific inquiry skills, learning of concepts related to biology and scientific thinking skills (Keteulhut, 2007; Ketelhut et al., 2010). Also, in the affective sense, more participation was observed in students.

Quest Atlantis and river city projects were successful in creating an appealing environment in a 3d virtual environment. On the other hand, an authentic environment is needed for students to evaluate their performance and get feedback. This indicates that the virtual world and the authentic world should be designed together for all other learning approaches.

INSTRUCTIONAL DESIGN PROCESS IN THREE-DIMENSIONAL MULTI-USER VIRTUAL ENVIRONMENTS (3D MUVEs) BASED ON PROBLEM-BASED LEARNING APPROACH TO TEACH TREE SPECIES

In this study, it is aimed to design a three-dimensional multi-user virtual environments (3D MUVEs) to teach tree species to pre-service teachers within the framework of Instructional design process in three-dimensional multi-user virtual environments based on problem-based learning approach developed by Doğan (2019) to pursue an appropriate strategy for 3d Muves development process. According to this model, there are 6 stages. These stages include determination of the problem situation, scenario design, instructional and technical analysis, instructional and technical design, evaluation and updating (Figure 1).

Design Groups

The design groups are 3rd grade undergraduate students (N=21), who were taking the course Innovative Technologies and Applications and who took the Instructional Design course in previous years, from the Department of Computer Education and Instructional Technology, Faculty of Education at a large state university in Ankara, Turkey in the 2018-2019 academic year. A total of 21 students participated in the study and 11 of them were female (52%) and 10 of them were male (48%). The students participated in the study voluntarily and signed the research volunteer participation form. A total of 4 design groups were created. Two of them had 5 group members. Others had 6 group members. When determining the design groups, participants' programming, instructional design knowledge, and gender were taken into consideration.

Figure 1. Instructional design model in three-dimensional multi-user virtual environments based on problem-based learning approach (Doğan, 2019)

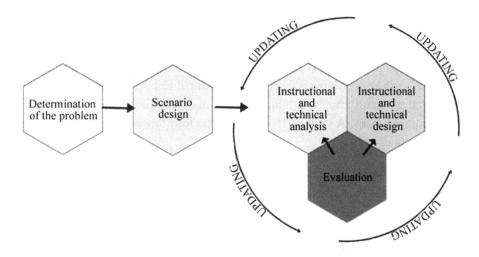

Design Environment of the Three-Dimensional Multi-User Virtual Environments (3D MUVEs)

OpenSimulator (OpenSim) was chosen among three-dimensional multi-user virtual environments (3D MUVEs) platforms during the design process of the research. The reason why this application is chosen is that the application supports individual and multi-user. Besides, it provides opportunities for all kinds of interventions and arrangements. To encourage the collaborative work of the participants who took the course for the application environment of the research, necessary technical adjustments were made to access the server by installing the OpenSim application on a server that can be accessed 24/7 by the researchers. Also, participants used FireStorm as a 3d viewer.

Design Process

The design process of the study was carried out in the computer laboratory of the department where there are 40 computers with 21 participants who took the Innovative Technologies and Applications course voluntarily. 3d Muves were designed for 8 weeks within the scope of the Innovative Technologies and Applications course. The design process of the study was realized with the participation of researchers as trainer, guide, technical support and observer during the 16 weeks within the scope of the course. During the design process, the participants were involved in the role of both learner and instructional designer. Furthermore, the participants also played different roles in design groups such as animation and visual design experts, software experts, assessment and evaluation experts, etc. Before starting the 3D MUVEs design process on the server, the design groups were given an 8-week training on 3D environment design by the researcher. According to training, 3D viewer interface was introduced and preparation of interaction via programming, animation, using media tools (web-pages, audio, video, etc.), Non-Player Characters (NPC), HUD (Heads-Up Display) menu were taught.

In the first week of the design process, the participants were asked to produce problem-based learning scenarios to be created in 3D MUVEs for the protection of tree species within the concept of biodiversity, which is a vital subject of the research. In this context, the participants were presented with sample scenarios created with 3D MUVEs. Design groups presented their scenarios. Also, each design group has found their group name according to their scenario. Researchers made brainstorming by giving feedback to the groups. One of the scenario sample is given in Figure 2. According to this scenario, there is a character called Maple. Maple is a senior at Yggdrasil Ent Academy. There is a thing he needs to do to become a tree protector after he graduates. He must recognize a forest. During the mission, he must perform the required tasks. A total of 15 quests in the forest await him. If he completed all of the quests, he will desire his Ent diploma.

Figure 2. Sample of scenario

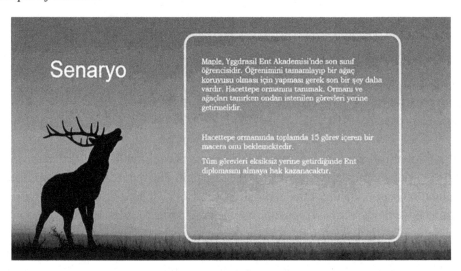

After the scenarios were created in detail, the design groups drew out the draft views of the 3d environment (Figure 3). The drawings on paper or computer help the designers to know what to do and where to start the design before starting the design of the environment. Also, it facilitates group works and collaboration process.

A total of 24 photographs of trees (remote view, leaf, trunk, and fruit, if any) that are covered within the scope of the study were given to the students to be designed. The types of trees covered in the research are; Cupressus, Willow, Chestnut, Sweetgum, Juniper, Northern Hackberry, Ladin, Lime, Hornbeam, Poplar, Larch, Calabrian Pine, Elaeagnus, Yew, Birch, Oak, Scotch Fir, Ash Tree, Deodar, Fir, Mountain alder. Trees were divided into 4 groups and each group was given 6 trees. In this way, it helped the participants to decrease the workload and progress the process faster. Photographs of trees that users can see most in their surroundings were taken by experts who take photographs from the land trips of Necati Güvenç Mamikoğlu. Trees model sample in the authentic world and 3d virtual world is shown in Figure 4.

Figure 3. Example of participants' drafting work on computer

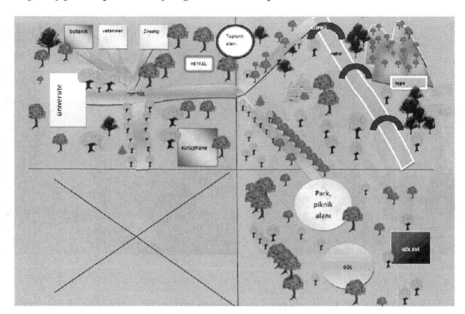

Figure 4. Sample of 3d trees designed by groups

The participants came together face-to-face with the group members and developed their designs weekly. They also work with group members on the server during 7/24. To facilitate the work of the design groups, ready-to-use object libraries were added to the environment. Within the scope of the course, the students brainstormed each week with the researchers and the necessary feedback was given during the whole design process (Figure 5).

Figure 5. Participants and field experts in the design development process of the research

During the design process, participants prepared 3d environments with learning activities and quests according to their scenarios on 3d multi-user virtual environment (Figure 6). They modeled 3d objects (house, tree, etc.) and loaded these models to OpenSim via 3d viewer. They created animation, HUD Menu and Non-Player Characters for interaction with 3d objects. Also, they create educational content (audio, video, web page, text, photos, etc.). In addition, they used environment-specific programming language LSL (Linden Script Language) to increase interactions with objects. The designers produced different content according to the quests.

Figure 6. Sample of 3d Muves design during design process

CONCLUSION AND RECOMMENDATIONS

Use of three-dimensional (3D) virtual worlds for educational purposes and research is increasing day by day. In virtual worlds where physical boundaries have been removed, new opportunities for global cooperation and distance education can be offered to provide equal opportunities in education. In this way, 3d virtual environments can be created in various branches where authentic and virtual environments combine. Although 3d virtual worlds have powerful features and opportunities, such as every new emerging technology, these environments have some weaknesses and obstacles that can be encountered. For example; users who have an account on a virtual world platform cannot be found in another virtual world with the avatar they have created because they need to create a different identity for each virtual world. For this reason, communication between the rapidly growing platforms becomes difficult. Besides, since the development and implementation stages of these environments are long and comprehensive, they should be designed in a meaningful way according to their educational purposes. So, it is important to research different application areas. The features of 3d virtual environments allow the user to discover places of interest for self-learning and to interact with objects. However, there may be problems in applications in these environments where control is left to the user. In addition, due to negative elements such as entering inappropriate dialogs with instant messaging tools, the user's problems of not being able to fulfill the task of learning, distraction, and abandonment of learning environment can be experienced. At this point, it is stated that guidance to the user is important. Furthermore, in 3d virtual learning environments, it is possible to see the different applications of guidance. However, it was determined that the teacher who has an important role in the learning process has a lack of guide role in a 3d virtual environment with the representative avatar. Therefore, new studies are needed in this field (Eschenbrenner, Nah & Siau, 2008; Kapp & O'Driscoll, 2010).

In the study, participants in the role of instructor designer in 3d Muves of the participants have assumed different roles as signs of progress in the design process. These roles determined as instructional designer, field specialist, animation and visual design expert, software expert, measurement assessment expert, media producer, etc. (Doğan, 2019). Moreover, designers have undertaken different tasks by preparing content, designing 3d models, preparing scenarios, and conducting research in the process. The designers who had to deal with technical problems in individual studies received help from the researchers as technical support when they started to work in groups.

The participants were given necessary information about the design of the environment during the 16-weeks with implementation and design. The detailed presentation of all the steps in the process of developing a learning environment is important in terms of identifying the mistakes made in the process, identifying the failures and sharing the experiences gained. Thus, more effective learning environments can be developed by preventing this failure and repetition of errors. Technology such as 3d virtual worlds can be carefully designed by taking into account the various dimensions of the interface. In the analysis phase, which is the first step in developing a 3d virtual learning environment, a simple, easy-to-use 3d virtual learning environment can be created by analyzing the needs of the target audience (Akgün, Nuhoğlu, Tüzün, Kaya & Çınar, 2011; Warburton, 2009).

In the design phase, learning approaches should be based on considering that technological tools can meet the need if it is used by integrating pedagogical approaches in the size of teaching design. Also, to make the environment visually more interesting, the principles of multimedia design should be taken into consideration to select the materials suitable for the content type and to ensure interaction in the environment (Doğan, 2019). In the implementation process, the ability to determine the computer skills for the user or the students who will be trained in 3d environments and provide the necessary gains can help the students in pedagogical terms. Besides, pre-information about the 3d platform, preliminary studies in these environments, and identification of possible problems that may arise as a result of these studies can help students from a pedagogical perspective as well. In this context, before performing learning activities in 3d environments, the activities should be structured very well and students' responsibilities and roles should be clearly stated.

In the design of 3d virtual worlds, media, 3d materials, programming languages, user interface, access to 3d environment, design tools in 3d environments are import to develop a 3d virtual world. Therefore, researching these issues before starting 3d environment design will contribute positively to the design and development process. It is important to determine and eliminate the disruptions that can be encountered at all stages of the process of creating a 3d virtual learning environment in order not to have any disruptions at all other stages. Thus, the evaluation must continue throughout the process (Doğan, 2019). In this way, interesting and interactive 3d virtual learning environments can be developed, where pedagogical elements are taken into consideration, which can respond to user needs by giving the environment its final shape.

If such pedagogical obstacles continue in front of 3d virtual environments, it is seen that these environments will not have any educational appeal. Besides, many researchers believe that the positive impact of 3d virtual worlds on learning and teaching is expected to be global; however, because of these problems, the use of 3d virtual environments in education is still limited (Jarmon, Traphagan, Mayrath, & Trivedi, 2009).

Cognitive involvement of individuals with learning environment is related to internal psychological characteristics, so it is difficult to determine the individual's involvement in this direction when dealing with the task. Since there is a similar situation in 3d virtual environments, it is a very difficult process to practice and measure cognitive gains. Therefore, in academic studies, it is thought that determining strategies for the development of 3d virtual environments that meet the minimum requirements for the target acquisition in this direction will be an important step for the future of these environments.

The research, in which environmental education and technology are integrated, has an interdisciplinary approach. Three-dimensional multi-user virtual environments can create effective learning environments for all disciplines. In this study, it is aimed to provide a positive learning environment by bringing users together with nature in a 3d Muves to teach tree species. Three-dimensional applications are separated from other learning environments by increasing the motivation of users because they are prone to learning by living and providing effective communication.

FUTURE RESEARCH DIRECTIONS

This section provides design and research process recommendations for researchers planning to design in three-dimensional multi-user virtual environments (3D MUVEs):

First of all, to achieve the learning outcomes as fast as possible, the 3d virtual learning environment should be designed in such a way that it can attract the attention of the users, optimize their cognitive load, and allow the users to move around and interact without being bored and lost. Therefore, various features of 3d virtual environments should be used and the design should be user-oriented, motion-based and consistent with pedagogical principles.

It is important to create a work schedule to ensure the environment developing process proceeds smoothly, to follow up on the completed phases and to facilitate the determination of the next step. Also, the work schedule allows the detection of points and failures that do not comply with the planning and taking the necessary measures in advance to overcome these difficulties. It is important to get the opinions of the team members in determining the work schedule as this will minimize the disruptions in the process.

The basic information to be taught on the subject to be designed should be determined in consultation with the subject area experts. It should also be determined in which order users can learn content more easily. The 5E rule (Engage, Explore, Explain, Elaborate, Evaluate) should be considered in this process and detailed information about the content should be acquired. In this context, effective planning of the learning environment can eliminate all the problems that may occur in the learning process. Thus, the learning process can be made more effective and meaningful learning can be provided for the students.

REFERENCES

Akgün, E., Nuhoğlu, P., Tüzün, H., Kaya, G., & Çınar, M. (2011). Bir eğitsel oyun tasarımı modelinin geliştirilmesi (Development of an educational game design model). *Educational Technology Theory and Practice*, *1*(1), 41–61.

Atasoy, E. (2006). *Çevre için eğitim, çocuk doğa etkileşimi (Education for the environment, the interaction of nature in children)*. Bursa: Ezgi Publication.

Atik, A. D., Öztekin, M., & Erkoç, F. (2010). Biyoçeşitlilik ve Türkiye'deki endemik bitkilere örnekler (Biodiversity and examples of endemic plants in Türkiye). *Gazi University Journal of Gazi Educational Faculty*, *30*(1), 219–240.

Barab, S., Thomas, M., Dodge, T., Carteaux, R., & Tüzün, H. (2005). Making learning fun: Quest Atlantis, a game without guns. *Educational Technology Research and Development*, *53*(1), 86–107. doi:10.1007/BF02504859

Barrows, H. S. (1986). A taxonomy of problem-based learning methods. *Medical Education*, *20*(6), 481–486. doi:10.1111/j.1365-2923.1986.tb01386.x PMID:3796328

Bergseng, E., & Vatn, A. (2009). Why protection of biodiversity creates conflict–Some evidence from the Nordic countries. *Journal of Forest Economics*, *15*(3), 147–165. doi:10.1016/j.jfe.2008.04.002

Bouta, H., Retalis, S., & Paraskeva, F. (2012). Utilising a collaborative macroscript to enhance student engagement: A mixed method study in a 3D virtual environment. *Computers & Education*, *58*(1), 501–517. doi:10.1016/j.compedu.2011.08.031

Bulu, S. T., & İşler, V. (2011). ODTÜ Second Life Kampüsü(METU Second life Campus). İnönü Üniversitesi Akademik Bilişim Kongresi (Academic Informatics Congress, Inonu University), Malatya.

Campbell, T., Wang, S. K., Hsu, H. Y., Duffy, A. M., & Wolf, P. G. (2010). Learning with web tools, simulations, and other technologies in science classrooms. *Journal of Science Education and Technology*, *19*(5), 505–511. doi:10.100710956-010-9217-8

Çepni, S. (2005). *Kuramdan uygulamaya fen ve teknoloji öğretimi (Science and technology teaching from theory to practice)*. Ankara: Pegem Academy.

Cheryan, S., Meltzoff, A. N., & Kim, S. (2011). Classrooms matter: The design of virtual classrooms influences gender disparities in computer science classes. *Computers & Education, 57*(2), 1825–1835. doi:10.1016/j.compedu.2011.02.004

Cote, D., Kraemer, B., Nahl, D., & Ashford, R. (2012). Academic librarians in Second Life. *Journal of Library Innovation, 3*(1), 20–46.

Dalgarno, B., & Lee, M. J. W. (2010). What are the learning aff ordances of 3-D virtual environments? *British Journal of Educational Technology, 41*(1), 10–32. doi:10.1111/j.1467-8535.2009.01038.x

Denizci-Guillet, B., & Penfold, P. (2013). Conducting immersive research in Second Life: A hotel co-branding case study. *International Journal of Hospitality & Tourism Administration, 14*(1), 23–49. doi:10.1080/15256480.2013.753803

Dickey, M. D. (2005). Brave new (interactive) worlds: A review of the design aff ordances and constraints of two 3D virtual worlds as interactive learning environments. *Interactive Learning Environments, 13*(1-2), 121–137. doi:10.1080/10494820500173714

Dillenbourg, P., Schneider, D., & Synteta, P. (2002). Virtual learning environments. *Communication, 8*(6), 3–18.

Doğan, D. (2019). *Üç-boyutlu çok-kullanıcılı sanal ortamlarda probleme dayalı öğrenme yaklaşımına göre öğretim tasarımı süreci (Instructional design process in three-dimensional multi-user virtual environments based on problem-based learning approach)* (Unpublished Ph.D.Thesis). Hacettepe University Graduate School of Educational Sciences, Ankara.

Doğan, D., Çınar, M., & Tüzün, H. (2018). Multi-user Virtual Environments for Education. In N. Lee (Ed.), *Encyclopedia of Computer Graphics and Games*. Cham: Springer; doi:10.1007/978-3-319-08234-9_172-1

Doğan, D., & Tüzün, H. (2017). *Üç-boyutlu çok-kullanıcılı sanal ortamların tasarım aracı olarak kullanımı: Opensim örneği (Three-dimensional multi-user virtual environments as a design tool the use: Opensim example)*. 5th International Instructional Technologies & Teacher Education Symposium (ITTES'17), İzmir, Türkiye.

Duncan, I., Miller, A., & Jiang, S. (2012). A taxonomy of virtual worlds usage in education. *British Journal of Educational Technology, 43*(6), 949–964. doi:10.1111/j.1467-8535.2011.01263.x

Ekim, T. (2005). *Türkiye'nin biyolojik zenginlikleri (Turkey's biological riches)*. Ankara: Türkiye Çevre Vakfı Publications.

Elçin, A. S., Erkoç, F., Öztekin, M., Atik, A. D., Sarıkaya, R., & Selvi, M. (2010). *Biyoloji laboratuvarı ve arazi uygulamaları: canlılar, ekoloji, doğayı koruma (Laboratory and field applications of biology: organisms, ecology, nature protection)*. Ankara: Palme Yayınevi.

Erten, S. (2004). Uluslararası düzeyde yükselen bir değer olarak biyolojik çeşitlilik (Biological diversity as international rising value). *Hacettepe University Journal of Education, 27*(27), 98–105.

Eschenbrenner, B., Nah, F., & Siau, K. (2008). 3-D virtual worlds in education: Applications, benefits, issues, and opportunities. *Journal of Database Management, 19*(4), 91–110. doi:10.4018/jdm.2008100106

Gregory, S., Scutter, S., Jacka, L., McDonald, M., Farley, H., & Newman, C. (2015). Barriers and enablers to the use of virtual worlds in higher education: An exploration of educator perceptions, attitudes and experiences. *Journal of Educational Technology & Society, 18*(1), 3–12.

Güler, O. (2014). *Eğitimde etkileşimli 3 boyutlu teknolojilerin kullanımı ve bilişim teknolojileri derslerine uygulanması (Using interactive 3 dimensional technologies in education and application of the information technology lessons)* (Unpublished Ph.D. Thesis). Gazi University Graduate School of Educational Sciences, Ankara.

Helmer, J., & Light, L. (2007). *Second Life and virtual worlds.* Learning Light Limited.

Hew, K. F., & Cheung, W. S. (2010). Use of three-dimensional (3-D) immersive virtual worlds in K-12 and higher education settings: A review of the research. *British Journal of Educational Technology, 41*(1), 33–55. doi:10.1111/j.1467-8535.2008.00900.x

Ibáñez, M. B., García, J. J., Galán, S., Maroto, D., Morillo, D., & Kloos, C. D. (2011). Design and Implementation of a 3D multi-user virtual world for language learning. *Journal of Educational Technology & Society, 14*(4), 2–10.

Işık, İ., & Işık, A. H., & Güler, İ. (2008). Uzaktan eğitimde 3 boyutlu web teknolojilerinin kullanılması (Using the 3D web technologies in distance education). *Gazi University International Journal of Informatics Technologies, 1*(2), 75–78.

Jarmon, L., Traphagan, T., Mayrath, M., & Trivedi, A. (2009). Virtual world teaching, experiential learning, and assessment: An interdisciplinary communication course in Second Life. *Computers & Education, 53*(1), 169–182. doi:10.1016/j.compedu.2009.01.010

Kapp, K. M., & O'Driscoll, T. (2010). *Learning in 3D: Adding a new dimension to enterprise learning and collaboration.* San Francisco, CA: Pfeiffer.

Ketelhut, D. J. (2007). The impact of student self-efficacy on scientific inquiry skills: An exploratory investigation in River City, a multi-user virtual environment. *Journal of Science Education and Technology, 16*(1), 99–111. doi:10.100710956-006-9038-y

Ketelhut, D. J., Nelson, B. C., Clarke, J., & Dede, C. (2010). A multi-user virtual environment for building and assessing higher order inquiry skills in science. *British Journal of Educational Technology, 41*(1), 56–68. doi:10.1111/j.1467-8535.2009.01036.x

Kocataş, A. (2006). *Ekoloji ve çevre biyolojisi (Ecology and environmental biology).* İzmir: Ege University Publication.

Külköylüoğlu, O. (2009). *Çevre ve çevre: İnsan-doğa ilişkisi (The environment and the environment: human-nature relationship).* Bolu: Abant Izzet Baysal University Revolving Fund Publication.

Lindemann-Matthies, P. (2002). The influence of an educational program on children's perception of biodiversity. *The Journal of Environmental Education, 33*(2), 22–31. doi:10.1080/00958960209600805

Lindgren, R. (2012). Generating a learning stance through perspective-taking in a virtual environment. *Computers in Human Behavior*, *28*(4), 1130–1139. doi:10.1016/j.chb.2012.01.021

Loke, S. K., Blyth, P., & Swan, J. (2012). In search of a method to assess dispositional behaviours: The case of Otago Virtual Hospital. *Australasian Journal of Educational Technology*, *28*(3), 441–458. doi:10.14742/ajet.844

Masters, Y., & Gregory, S. (2010). Second Life: Harnessing virtual world technology to enhance student engagement and learning. In R. Muldoon (Ed.), *Rethinking learning in your discipline. Proceedings of the University Learning and Teaching Futures Colloquium*. Armidale, Australia: Teaching and Learning Centre, University of New England.

Mercan, G., & Köseoğlu, P. (2019). Biyoloji öğretmen adaylarının yakın çevrelerindeki ağaçları tanıma düzeyleri: Ankara ili örneği (Biology teacher candidates' identification levels of trees in their immediate surrroundings: Ankara example). *YYU Journal of Education Faculty*, *16*(1), 538–560.

Minocha, S., & Reeves, A. J. (2010). Design of learning spaces in 3D virtual worlds: An empirical investigation of Second Life. *Learning, Media and Technology*, *35*(2), 111–137. doi:10.1080/1743988 4.2010.494419

Nelson, B. C. (2007). Exploring the use of individualized, reflective guidance in an educational multi-user virtual environment. *Journal of Science Education and Technology*, *16*(1), 83–97. doi:10.100710956-006-9039-x

OpenSim. (2015). *Build Instructions*. Retrieved from http://opensimulator.org/wiki/Build_Instr uctions

Özcan, N. (2003). *A group of students' and teachers' perceptions with respect to biology education at high school level* (Unpublished Ph.D. Thesis). Middle East Technical Universty Instute of Education Science, Ankara.

Özmen, H., & Özdemir, S. (2016). Fen ve teknoloji öğretmen adaylarının çevre eğitimine yönelik düşüncelerinin tespiti (Determination of pre-service science and technology teachers' views on environmetal education). *Kastamonu Education Journal*, *24*(4), 1691–1712.

Pellas, N. (2014). The influence of computer self-efficacy, metacognitive self-regulation and self-esteem on student engagement in online learning programs: Evidence from the virtual world of Second Life. *Computers in Human Behavior*, *35*, 157–170. doi:10.1016/j.chb.2014.02.048

Perera, I., Allison, C., & Miller, A. (2012). *3D multi user learning environment management an exploratory study on student engagement with the learning environment*. INTECH Open Access Publisher. doi:10.5772/36254

Puterbaugh, M. D., Shannon, M., & Gorton, H. (2010). A survey of nurses' attitudes toward distance education and the educational use of 3-D virtual environments. *Journal of Electronic Resources in Medical Libraries*, *7*(4), 292–307. doi:10.1080/15424065.2010.527243

Rappa, N. A., Yip, D. K. H., & Baey, S. C. (2009). The role of teacher, student and ICT in enhancing student engagement in multiuser virtual environments. *British Journal of Educational Technology*, *40*(1), 61–69. doi:10.1111/j.1467-8535.2007.00798.x

Şahin, Ü. G. (2018). *Ortaokul öğrencilerinin biyoçeşitlilik konusunda farkındalıklarının çeşitli değişkenlere göre incelenmesi (Investigation of the awarness of the secondary students on biodiversity)* (Unpublished Ph.D. Thesis). Akdeniz University Graduate School of Educational Sciences, Antalya.

Şekercioğlu, Ç., Anderson, S., Akçay, E., Bilgin, R., Can, Ö. E., Semiz, G., ... Nüzhet Dalfes, H. (2011). Turkey's globally important biodiversity in crisis. *Biological Conservation, 144*(12), 2752–2769. doi:10.1016/j.biocon.2011.06.025

Şenel, T. (2015). *Analysis of university students' perception of and attitudes towards biodiversity* (Unpublished Master Thesis). Istanbul Technical University Eurasia Institute Of Earth Sciences, İstanbul.

Tokel, S. T., & Cevizci-Karataş, E. (2013). *Üç Boyutlu Sanal Dünyalar: Eğitimciler İçin Yol Haritası.* Paper presented at the Akademik Bilişim 1013, Akdeniz Üniversitesi Hukuk Fakültesi, Antalya.

Tüzün, H., & Özdinç, F. (2016). The effects of 3D multi-user virtual environments on freshmen university students' conceptual and spatial learning and presence in departmental orientation. *Computers & Education, 94*, 228–240. doi:10.1016/j.compedu.2015.12.005

Verhagen, T., Feldberg, F., van den Hooff, B., Meents, S., & Merikivi, J. (2012). Understanding users' motivations to engage in virtual worlds: A multipurpose model and empirical testing. *Computers in Human Behavior, 28*(2), 484–495. doi:10.1016/j.chb.2011.10.020

Warburton, S. (2009). Second Life in higher education: Assessing the potential for and the barriers to deploying virtual worlds in learning and teaching. *British Journal of Educational Technology, 40*(3), 414–426. doi:10.1111/j.1467-8535.2009.00952.x

Xu, Y., Park, H., & Baek, Y. (2011). A new approach toward digital storytelling: An activity focused on writing self-efficacy in a virtual learning environment. *Journal of Educational Technology & Society, 14*(4), 181–191.

ADDITIONAL READING

Hodge, E., Collins, S., & Giordano, T. (2011). *The virtual worldshandbook: How to use Second Life and other 3D virtual worlds. LLC.* Jones and Bartlett.

Luo, L., & Kemp, J. (2008). Second Life: Exploring the immersive instructional venue for library and information science education. *Journal of Education for Library and Information Science, 49*(3), 147–166.

McMahan, R. P., Kopper, R., & Bowman, D. A. (2014). Principles for Designing Effective 3D Interaction Techniques. In K. S. Hale & K. M. Stanney (Eds.), *Handbook of virtual environments: design, implementation, and applications* (2nd ed.). Boca Raton, FL: CRC Press. doi:10.1201/b17360-16

Omale, N., Hung, W. C., Luetkehans, L., & Cooke-Plagwitz, J. (2009). Learning in 3-D multiuser virtual environments: Exploring the use of unique 3-D attributes for online problem-based learning. *British Journal of Educational Technology, 40*(3), 480–495. doi:10.1111/j.1467-8535.2009.00941.x

Peterson, M. (2005). Learning interaction in an avatar-based virtual environment: A preliminary study. *PacCALL Journal, 1*(1), 29–40.

Thackray, L., Good, J., & Howland, K. (2010). Learning and Teaching in Virtual Worlds: Boundaries, Challenges and Opportunities. In A. Peachey, J. Gillen, D. Livingstone, & S. Smith-Robbins (Eds.), *Researching Learning in Virtual Worlds* (pp. 139–158). London: Springer London. doi:10.1007/978-1-84996-047-2_8

Tüzün, H. (2006). Educational computer games and a case: Quest Atlantis. *Hacettepe University Journal of Education, 30*, 220–229.

Yıldız, B., & Tüzün, H. (2011). Effects of using three-dimensional virtual environments and concrete manipulatives on spatial ability. *Hacettepe University Journal of Education, 41*, 498–508.

KEY TERMS AND DEFINITIONS

Biodiversity: It is the differentiation between land, sea and other water ecosystems and living organisms in all sources, including ecological structures that are part of these ecosystems.

Biodiversity Training: It raises awareness of individuals about the importance of biological diversity and provides them with the responsibility and competence to protect biological diversity.

Environment: All of the external factors that affect living creatures.

OpenSimulator (OpenSim): It is a platform with a 3D interface that allows users to access and design these environments from anywhere.

Problem-Based Learning: It is student-centered activities within the framework of an authentic problem, the interaction of small groups, and also the teacher is a guide in this process.

Three-Dimensional (3D) Virtual Worlds: It is a highly interactive framework for appropriate behavior and learning, enabling effective environments in social interaction with individuals in remote locations and various branches.

This research was previously published in Enriching Teaching and Learning Environments With Contemporary Technologies; pages 117-137, copyright year 2020 by Information Science Reference (an imprint of IGI Global).

Index

W

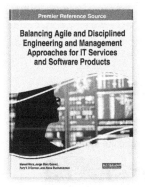

Ensure Quality Research is Introduced to the Academic Community

Become an Evaluator for IGI Global Authored Book Projects

Premier Reference Source

Stabilizing Currency and Preserving Economic Sovereignty Using the Grondona System

Patrick Collins

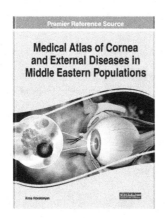

Premier Reference Source

Medical Atlas of Cornea and External Diseases in Middle Eastern Populations

Anna Hovakimyan

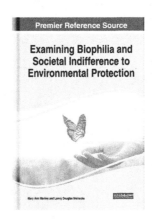

Premier Reference Source

Examining Biophilia and Societal Indifference to Environmental Protection

Gary Ann Markey and Lenny Douglas Meinecke

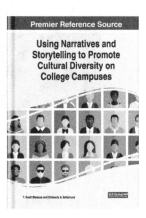

Premier Reference Source

Using Narratives and Storytelling to Promote Cultural Diversity on College Campuses

T. Scott Bledsoe and Kimberly A. Setterlund

The overall success of an authored book project is dependent on quality and timely manuscript evaluations.

Applications and Inquiries may be sent to:
development@igi-global.com

Applicants must have a doctorate (or equivalent degree) as well as publishing, research, and reviewing experience. Authored Book Evaluators are appointed for one-year terms and are expected to complete at least three evaluations per term. Upon successful completion of this term, evaluators can be considered for an additional term.

If you have a colleague that may be interested in this opportunity, we encourage you to share this information with them.

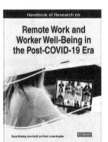